SECOND SUPPLEMENT

TO THE

CATALOGUE OF BOOKS

IN THE

MERCANTILE LIBRARY

OF THE

CITY OF NEW YORK.

(ACCESSIONS, OCTOBER, 1869, TO APRIL, 1872.)

PUBLISHED BY THE MERCANTILE LIBRARY ASSOCIATION.

New-York:

JAMES SUTTON & CO., PRINTERS, 23 LIBERTY STR

1872.

PREFACE.

The Directors herewith offer to the members of the Mercantile Library Association a second Supplement to the Catalogue. This, it is hoped, will materially facilitate the searcher, who will now have but three alphabetical lists to examine (not including novels), instead of about twenty as heretofore.

No changes of consequence have been made in the plan of cataloguing for this Supplement. The French novels and the German novels have been placed in separate lists in the classified part, for the convenience of our increasing constituency of readers in those languages. The novels have been catalogued in one alphabet instead of two, but each book is catalogued exactly as before, viz.: 1st. Under its author's name, and 2d, by its title; so that the whole of both the two lists heretofore used are retained. It is believed that this use of one alphabet instead of two will be a convenience.

These alterations, as far as they go, point towards a modification of our system of cataloguing which will probably be thought worthy of adoption whenever a complete new catalogue shall be made. The need of such a complete new catalogue grows daily more obvious. Our cataloguing system has been so shaped during the past few years as to admit of the modification referred to, without any great changes or great expense. It is probable that the best model for such a catalogue would be that recently published by the Philadelphia Mercantile Library. On this plan, at least as it ought to be developed for our own purposes, each book would be entered in three places, viz: 1st, under the author's name; 2d, by the title of the book; 3d, under the name of the subject of the book; and all these entries would be arranged in a single alphabetical list. This would satisfy a need which is incessantly felt by our subscribers, and by our staff; for, in the great majority of cases, it is the title of a book which the applicant remembers, or else it is a subject about which he wants some book, without knowing what book. Our present alphabetical catalogue is a respectable list of authors' names. Most of the titles would serve their purpose for the second proposed method as they stand; and the section heads of our present classification form a good basis for the third method. It is with a view to their ultimate use in this manner that these sections have, from time to time, been sub-divided and increased in number, to be ready, as far as possible, for a transfer bodily to a place in one single alphabeted catalogue.

The collection of books catalogued in this second Supplement well upholds, it is believed, the reputation of our Library. It includes not only a full representation of both the solid and lighter literature of our own country, but an extensive array of the most useful and interesting English publications of all kinds, and a considerable number of valuable French and German works, both in belles lettres and in more weighty departments of knowledge. We are confident that no library in or near this city approaches this in the opportunities it affords its patrons for keeping up with the intellectual activity of the world.

It is due to Mr. A. I. Cotheal that a word should be said here in acknowledgment of the large number of books presented by him, whose titles appear in this Supplement, and which constitute, it is believed, the largest single donation of books ever given to the Library. While many of them have become obsolete, they form collectively a curious and valuable record of the history of business, and of the progress of instruction in modern languages; and they also include many books of interest and value which could not easily be replaced.

On behalf of the Board of Direction.

GEORGE C. CLARKE,
CHARLES H. WILSON,
JAMES BRUCE, Jr., } Catalogue Committee.

MERCANTILE LIBRARY, N. Y.,
April, 1872.

Officers and Members of the Board of Direction,

AND

OFFICERS OF THE ASSOCIATION FOR 1871-72.

President,
ARTHUR W. SHERMAN.

Vice-President,
SAMUEL PUTNAM.

Corresponding Secretary,
WILLIAM A. SHERMAN.

Recording Secretary,
JOHN O. EGBERT.

Treasurer,
GEORGE B. MILLS.

Class for One Year,

GEORGE B. MILLS,
JOHN O. EGBERT,
WILLIAM T. PEOPLES,
CHARLES H. WILSON.

Class for Two Years,

CHARLES F. ALLEN,
WILLIAM A. SHERMAN,
ARTHUR W. SHERMAN,
SAMUEL PUTNAM.

Class for Three Years,

WILLIAM H. GUION, Jr.,
GEORGE C. CLARKE,
WILLIAM H. LEWIS,
JAMES BRUCE, Jr.

Librarian,
ALBERT M. PALMER.

Assistant Librarian,
GEORGE COOPE.

Counsel to the Association,
WILLIAM HENRY ARNOUX.

SECOND

SUPPLEMENT TO THE CATALOGUE

OF THE

MERCANTILE LIBRARY

AA., C. van der. Geschiedenis van den Jongst-geëindigden Oorlog. 8 v. 8°. Amst. 1802–8.

ABBADIE, J. Chemical Change in the Eucharist. Trans. by Hamersley. Sm. 4°. Lond. n.d.

ABBOT, E. H. Review of Humphrey and Abbot's Report upon the Physics and Hydraulics of the Mississippi River. (Reprint from N. A. Review, April, 1862.) 8°. Bost. 1862.

ABBOTT, B. V. and A. Digest of N.Y. Statutes and Reports. 3d Supplement. L. 8°. N.Y. 1870.

ABBOTT, E. The Baby's Things. 12°. N.Y. n.d.

ABBOTT, E. A. Bible Lessons. 12°. Lond. 1871.

—— Shakspearean Grammar. 16°. Lond. 1869.

—— and Seeley, J. R. English Lessons for English People. 12°. Lond. 1871.

—— Same. 12°. Bost. 1872.

ABBOTT, Jacob. Alexander the Great. 16°. N.Y. 1869.

—— Cleopatra 16°. N.Y. 1869.

—— Cyrus the Great. 16°. N.Y. 1868.

—— Darius the Great. 16°. N.Y. 1868.

—— Gentle Measures in the Management of the Young. 12°. N.Y. 1871.

—— Heat. 12°. N.Y. 1871.

—— Inquiries concerning the Intellectual Powers. 16°. N.Y. 1866.

—— Light. 12°. N.Y. 1871.

—— Water and Land. 12°. N.Y. 1872.

—— Xerxes. 16°. N.Y. 1868.

ABBOTT, John S. C. History of Frederick the Great. 8°. N.Y. 1871.

—— History of Queen Hortense. 16°. N.Y. 1870.

—— Joseph Bonaparte. 16°. N.Y. 1869.

—— History of Louis XIV. 16°. N.Y. 1871.

—— History of Louis Philippe. 16°. N.Y. 1871.

—— Romance of Spanish History. 12°. N.Y. 1869.

ABBOTT, L. Old Testament Shadows of New Testament Truths. Sm. 4°. N.Y. 1870.

ABBOTT, O. A Peep into Sacred Tradition. 2d ed. 12°. Chicago. 1867.

A B C BUCH; Erstes Buch. 18°. N.Y. 1837.

ABÉCÉDAIRE Religieux, etc. 16°. Halifax. 1817.

ABEILLE, A. C. Latin Grammar. 2 v. 16°. Lond. 1836.

ABERT, S. T. Is a Ship Canal practicable? (Notes upon an Interoceanic Canal between the Atlantic and Pacific.) 8°. Cinc. 1872.

ABOUT, E. Causeries. 2 v. 12°. Paris. 1865–6.

—— La Grèce Contemporaine. 12°. Paris. 1863.

—— Le Fellah. 2d ed. 12°. Paris. 1870.

—— L'Infame. 8°. Paris. 1869.

—— Maitre Pierre. 16°. Paris. 1862.

—— Les Mariages de Paris. 12°. Paris. 1868.

ABRANTES, Duchesse d'. Memoirs of Celebrated Women. 8°. Lond. 1834.

ABRÉGÉ du Grand Dictionnaire de Technologie. 3 v. 8°. Brussels. 1837–8.

ABRÉGÉ de l'Histoire Naturelle, après Buffon. 4 v. 8°. Paris. 1800.

ABSTRACT of Infantry Tactics for Militia of U. S. 12°. Bost. 1830.
ACADEMY. v. 1–2. 4°. Lond. 1870–1.
ACCOMPANIMENT to Mitchell's Map of the World. 8°. Phil. 1834.
—— Same. 8°. Phil. 1826.
ACCOUNT of Abimelech Coody, etc. 8°. N.Y. 1815.
ACCOUNT of the Growth of Deism in England. 8°. Lond. 1709.
ACCOUNT of Mississippi Repudiation. (PC. 23.) 8°. Bost. 1842.
ACCOUNT of the Prot. Epis. Clerical Asso. of N.Y. City. 8°. N.Y. 1829.
ACHARD, A. Marcelle. 12°. Paris. 1870.
—— Maxence Humbert. 12°. Paris. 1867.
—— Récits d'un Soldat. 12°. Paris. 1871.
—— Olympe de Mezières; Le Mari de Delphine. 16°. Paris. 1870.
ACHILLI *vs.* Newman. Trial. (PC. 17.) 8°. N.Y. n.d.
ACROSTICS from across the Atlantic. Sq. 16°. Lond. 1869.
ACTON, W. Treatise on Venereal. 8°. N.Y. 1848.
ACTORS' Protective Union. (PC. 23.) 8°. n.p. n.d.
ADAMS and Dixon. Abstract and Argument in Mississippi *vs.* Johnson. 16°. Jackson. 1853.
ADAMS, Amos. Sermon, Ordination of Rev. S. Kingsbury. 8°. Bost. 1762.
—— Sermon, Ordination of Rev. J. Moore. 8°. Bost. 1768.
—— Sermon, Ordination of Rev. J. Wyeth. 8°. Bost. 1766.
(The above three bound together.)
ADAMS, Andrew L. Notes in the Nile Valley and Malta. 12°. Edin. 1870.
ADAMS, Andrew N. History of Fair Haven, Vt. 8°. Fair Haven. 1870.
ADAMS, Arthur. Travels in Japan and Manchuria. 8°. Lond. 1870.
ADAMS, Charles, D.D. Memoir of Washington Irving. 16°. N.Y. n.d.
ADAMS, C. B. Catalogue of Shells. (PC. 11.) 16°. Middlebury. 1847.
—— Monograph on Vitrinella. (PC. 18.) Sm. 4°. Amherst. 1850.
—— Monograph on Stoastoma. (PC. 21.) Sm. 4°. Amherst. 1849.
ADAMS, C. F. Struggle for Neutrality in America. 8°. N.Y. 1871.
ADAMS, C. F. Jr. A Chapter of Erie. 16°. Bost. 1869.
ADAMS, C. F. and H. Chapter of Erie and other Essays. 12°. Bost. 1871.
ADAMS, F. A. Arithmetic. 12°. Lowell. 1846.
ADAMS, H. G. Favorite Song Birds. 3d ed. 12°. Lond. n.d.
—— Beautiful Shells. 12°. Lond. 1871.
ADAMS, John Jay. Charter Oak and other Poems. 16°. N.Y. 1839.
ADAMS, John Q. Jubilee of the Constitution. 8°. N.Y. 1848.
ADAMS, John Q. and C. F. Life of John Adams. 2 v. 16°. Phil. 1871.
ADAMS, N. A Voyage Round the World. 16°. Bost. n.d.
—— Sermon on Death of D. Webster. 2d ed. (PC. 11.) 8°. Bost. 1852.
ADAMS, Rev. W. Address before N. E. Soc. (PC. 1.) 8°. N.Y. 1853.
—— Discourse on Life of Rev. J. C. Brigham. (PC. 1.) 8°. N.Y. 1863.
—— Discourse on Prof. M. Stuart. 8°. N.Y. 1852.
ADAMS, W. H. D. Before the Conquest. 12°. Edin. 1870.
—— Circle of the Year. 12°. N.Y. n.d.
—— Lighthouses and Light-Ships. 16°. N.Y. 1870.
—— Men at the Helm. 16°. n.d.
—— Queen of the Adriatic; or Venice Past and Present. 12°. Lond. 1870.
ADAMSON, H. T. Gospel of Matthew Expounded. 8°. Lond. 1871.
ADDRESS to Christians, etc., by the Clergy of the Confederate States. 8°. Lond. 1863.
ADDRESS of the Ohio Soldiers in the Army of the Cumberland. 8°. Toledo. 1863.
ADDRESS on Removal of Marine Hospital, Staten Island. (PC. 11.) 18°. Stapleton. 1847.
ADDRESSES, etc., of Bar of New York, on Death of Wm. Kent. 8°. N.Y. n.d.
ADLARD, George. Amye Robsart and the Earl of Leycester; containing a History of Kenilworth Castle. 8°. Lond. 1870.
ADLER, G. J. Letters of a Lunatic. 8°. N.Y. 1854.
ADMIRALTY Manual of Scientific Inquiry. *See* MANUAL, etc.
ADVICE from a Lady of Quality to her children. *See* PARENTAL Legacies.
ÆSCHYLUS. Tragedies (Greek.) Ed. by Paley. 18°. N.Y. 1860.

—— Tragedies; transl., Bohn's ed. 12°. Lond. 1863.

ÆSOP's Fables, Romanized by Phaedrus, with Interlinear transl. 4th ed. 16°. Lond. 1833.

AFRICA, History of. 18°. Lond. 1830.

AFRICAN Repository. v. 41–47. 8°. Wash. 1865–71.

AFRICANS at Home. (PC. 1.) 8°. n.p. n.d.

AGASSIZ, L. Contributions to the Natural History of the U. S. n.p. n.d.

—— Methods of Study in Natural History. 12°. Bost. 1871.

AGNEW, C. A. Protestant Exiles from France under Louis XIV. 2d ed. v. 1. 4°. Lond. 1871.

AGONIE (L'), de la Commune: Paris en Feu. 8°. Bruss. n.d.

AHN, F. Method of Learning the German Language. 2d Course. 8°. N.Y. 1862.

AIDS to Faith. 3d ed. 8°. Lond. 1870.

AIKEN, J. Labor and Wages. (PC. 1.) 8°. Lowell. 1849.

AIKEN, South Carolina. A Description of, etc. 8° N.Y. 1870.

AIKIN, Lucy. Court of Elizabeth. 12°. Lond. 1869.

—— Same. 12°. N.Y. 1870.

AIKMAN, W. Future of the Colored Race in America. 8°. Phil. 1862.

—— Government and Administration; a Sermon. (PC. 11.) 18°. Wilmington. 1863.

—— Life at Home. 12°. N.Y. 1870.

AILENROC. Musings of a Middle-Aged Woman. Essays. 16°. Phil. 1872.

AIMARD, G., and Crisafulli, H. Le Comte de Warrens. 12°. Paris. 1867.

AINSLEY, T. L. Engineers' Manual of Marine Examinations. 4th ed. 8°. South Shields. 1871.

AINSWORTH, R. Dictionary, abridged by Dymock and Anthon. 12°. Phil. 1838.

AINSWORTH, W. F. The Earth Delineated. 4°. Lond. n.d.

—— Wanderings in Every Clime. 4°. Lond. n.d.

AIRY, G. B. Magnetism. 12°. Lond. 1870.

ALABASTER, H. The Wheel of the Law. (Buddhism.) 8°. Lond. 1870.

ALAGIYAVANNA. Mohottala Kusa Jotakaya. Transl. by T. Steele. 12°. Lond. 1871.

ALBANY Directory, 1870–71. 2 v. 8°. Alb. 1870–1.

ALBANY Institute. Transactions. v. 5, 6. 8°. Alb. 1870.

ALBERGER, J. Monks, Popes and their Political Intrigues. 12°. Balt. 1871.

ALBERT, Mary. Freddie's Latin Lessons 18°. Lond. 1871.

ALBERT Hill Mining Co. Reports on Coal., etc. (PC. 8.) 8°. N.Y. 1870.

ALBRECHTSBERGER, J. G. Méthodes d' Harmonie. French of Choron. v. 2. Musique. 8°. Paris. 1830.

ALDINE PRESS. v. 3–4. f°. N.Y. 1870–1.

ALEMBERT, J. L. d'. Élémens de Musique. 8°. Lyons. 1772.

ALEXANDER, H. C. Life of Rev. J. A. Alexander. 2 v. 12°. N.Y. 1870.

ALEXANDER, J. The Jews; A History. 16°. Lond. 1870.

ALEXANDER, J. H. The Mountains of Palestine. 18°. Richmond. n.d.

ALEXANDRIA Directory. *See* WASHINGTON.

ALEXIS, W. *See* HÄRING.

ALFORD, H. How to Study the New Testament: (Epistles and Revelations.) 2 v. 12°. Lond. 1868–9.

—— The Riviera. f°. Lond. 1870.

ALISON, Rev. A. Essays on Taste. *See* JEFFREY; Essay on Beauty.

—— Life of Marlborough. 3d ed. 2 v. 8°. Edin. 1855.

ALL about California. 8°. San Fr. 1870.

ALL the Year Round. v. 12 to New Ser., v. 6. L. 8°. Lond. 1865–71.

ALLBUTT, T. C. Ophthalmoscope in Diseases of Nervous System and Kidneys. 8°. Lond. 1871.

ALLEMANDS (Les) en France. Huit Jours dans Seine-et-Oise. 12°. Paris. 1871.

ALLEN, Lewis F. American Cattle. 12°. N.Y. n.d.

ALLEN, P. Aural Catarrh. 12°. Lond. 1871.

ALLEN, R. W. World in Miniature. 16°. N. Lond. 1842.

ALLEN, Z. Memorial of R. Williams. (PC. 11.) 24°. Prov. 1860.

ALLERTON, R. G. Brook Trout Fishing. 16°. N.Y. 1869.

ALLIBONE, S. A. Dictionary of Authors. 3 v. R. 8°. Phil. 1859–71.

ALLINGHAM, W. Fistula and other Diseases of the Rectum. 8°. Lond. 1871.

ALLNUTT, H. Diary of the War of 1870–1. 16°. Lond. n.d.

ALLYN, A. Ritual of Freemasonry. 12°. N.Y. n.d.

ALMANACH Français des États-Unis, 1852. 16°. N.Y. 1852.

ALMANACH de Gotha, for 1870–72. 3 v. 32°. Gotha. n.d.

ALMANACH du Marin pour 1840. Sq. 16°. Paris. 1840.

ALMANACS for 1871, bound together. 8°. v.p. 1871.

ALMANACS for 1871. (Illustrated Almanacs bound together.) 4°. v.p. 1871.

ALMEIRA. Ein Drama in Californien. 16°. Berlin. n.d.

ALPHABET of Physical Geography. 18°. Lond. 1836.

ALPINE Journal. v. 1–4. 8°. Lond. 1864–70.

ALSTON, J. W. Hints on Landscape painting. 3d ed. 8°. Lond. n.d.

ALTHAUS, F. Englische Charakterbilder. 2 v. 8°. Berlin. 1869.

ALTHAUS, J. Medical Electricity. 2d ed. 12°. Lond. 1870.

ALVORD, J. W. Historical Address, Stamford, Conn. 8°. N.Y. 1842.

AMATEUR Mechanic's Workshop. 8°. Lond. 1870.

AMÉLIE Mansfield. 4 v. 18°. Paris. 1802.

AMERICAN Agriculturist. v. 28–30. 4°. N.Y. 1869–71.

AMERICAN Annual Cyclopedia. v. 9–10, for 1869–70. R. 8°. N.Y. 1870–1.

AMERICAN Antiquarian Society. Proceedings, 1867 to 1871. 8°. Wor. 1870–71.

AMERICAN Artificial Stone Co. Prospectus. (PC. 20.) 8°. N.Y. 1855.

AMERICAN Artizan. New Ser., v. 9–11. 4°. N.Y. 1869–70.

AMERICAN Boys' Book of Sports and Games. 12°. N.Y. n.d.

AMERICAN Catalogue of Books for 1869. 8°. N.Y. 1870.

AMERICAN Chess-Player's Hand-Book.

AMERICAN Eclectic Magazine. v. 2. 8°. N.Y. 1841.

AMERICAN Eclectic Medical Review. v. 1, 3–5. 8°. N.Y. 1867–70.

AMERICAN Educational Monthly. v. 5, 6, 7, 8. 8°. N.Y. 1869–71.

AMERICAN Exchange and Review. v. 17. 8°. n.p. 1870.

AMERICAN Gas-Light Journal. v. 12. Imp. 4°. N.Y. 1870.

AMERICAN Geographical and Statistical Society. Journal. v. 2. 8°. N.Y. 1860.

—— Journal. v. 2, part 2. 8°. N.Y. 1870.

—— Report, etc., on Syrian Exploration. (PC. 3.) 8°. N.Y. 1857.

AMERICAN Horological Journal. v. 2. 8°. N.Y. 1871.

AMERICAN Industrial Association. 1st An. Report. (PC. 11.) 16°. N.Y. 1857.

AMERICAN Institute of Architects. Proceedings of the 1st, 2d, 3d, and 4th Annual Conventions. 2 v. 4°. N.Y. 1867–71.

AMERICAN and Italian Cantatrici. By Lucius. 12°. Lond. 1867.

AMERICAN Journal of Education. 1867–68–71. 8°. Hartf. 1867–71.

AMERICAN Journal of Phonography. v. 1. 1871. 16°. N.Y. 1871.

AMERICAN Journal of the Medical Sciences. New Ser. v. 57–67. 2 v. 8°. Phil. 1869–71.

AMERICAN Journal of Numismatics. v. 1–4. R. 8°. N.Y. 1866–70.

AMERICAN Journal of Pharmacy. 3d Ser., v. 17, 18; 4th Ser., v. 1. 8°. Phil. 1869–71.

AMERICAN Journal of Science and Arts. 2d Ser., v. 47–50; 3d series, v. 1. 7 v. 8°. New Haven 1868–71.

AMERICAN Law Review. v. 3–5. 8°. Bost. 1868–71.

AMERICAN Naturalist. v. 2–5. 8°. Salem. 1869–71.

AMERICAN Odd Fellow. v. 10. 8°. N.Y. 1870.

AMERICAN Pharmaceutical Association. Proceedings, 1869–70. 8°. Phil. 1870.

AMERICAN Philological Association. Proceedings, 1st, 2d and 3d Annual Sessions. 8°. N.Y. 1870–2.

AMERICAN Philosophical Society. Paper by R. P. Smith, on County Maps. (PC. 11.) 12°. Phil. 1864.

AMERICAN Presb. Review. New ser. v. 1–2. 8°. N.Y. 1869–70.

AMERICAN Quarterly Church Review. v. 18–22. 8°. Phil. 1867–71.

AMERICAN Republican Party of N.Y. City. Address. (PC. 6.) 8°. N.Y. 1845.

AMERICAN Social Science Association. Hand-Book for Immigrants. 12°. N.Y. 1871.

—— Journal of Social Science. No. 3. 8°. N.Y. 1871.

AMERICAN Tour of Messrs. Brown, Jones and Robinson. L. 4°. N.Y. 1872.

AMERICAN Tract Society. Tracts for Young Men, viz:

Defaulters, by Rev. H. S. Brown.

Independence of Mind, by Rev. T. Dwight.

Mother's Sorrow, by Rev. C. Wadsworth.

The Imagination, its Use and Abuse, by Rev. T. Welsh.

A Sound Mind, by Rev. J. Hamilton.

The Law of Labor a Law of Love, by Rev. H. Stowell.

Man and his Masters, by J. B. Gough.

Young Man beginning Life, by Rev. J. A. James.

Life a Race, by Rev. T. Dwight.

Dignity of Labor, by Rev. N. Hall.

Young Man Succeeding r Failing in Business.

Young Man Undecided in Religion, by Rev. J. A. James.

Bound in 1 v. 18°. N.Y. n.d.

AMERICAN (The) Union, the New Heaven and Earth. 8°. N.Y. 1865.

AMERICAN Unitarian Association. Tracts. Army Series. 8°. Bost. 1865.

AMERICAN Vegetarian Society. 11th Annual Meeting. (PC. 11.) 16°. N.Y. 1860.

AMERICAN Year Book. 12. Hartf. 1869.

AMES, C. G. Discourse on Morals in America. (PC. 11.) 8°. Alb. 1864.

AMMIANUS Marcellinus. Roman History; transl. 12°. Lond. 1862.

AMORY, R. Physiological Action of Nitrous Oxide. 8°. Bost. 1870.

AMPELIUS, L. Liber Memorialis. *See* FLORUS, L. A.

AMUNDESHAM, J. de. Annales Monasterii S. Albani. (Rolls Chronicles.) 2 v. R. 8°. Lond. 1870–71.

ANACREON. Odes. Tr. by T. J. Arnold. 18°. Lond. 1869.

ANAYA, A. Discours sur la Manière d'apprendre les Langues. 16°. Lond. 1818.

ANCELOT, Mme. Marguerite L. V. Un Nœud de Ruban. 4°. Paris. n.d.

ANCIENT Edom. 18°. Phil. n.d.

ANCIENT Laws of Ireland. Senchus Mor. (Rolls Chronicles.) 2 v. R. 8°. Dublin. 1865–69.

ANDERSEN, H. C. Der Glücks Peter. 12°. Leip. 1871.

—— In Spain and Portugal. 12°. N.Y. 1871.

—— Pictures of Travels in Sweden, etc. 12°. N.Y. 1871.

—— A Poet's Bazaar. 12°. N.Y. 1871.

—— The Story of My Life. 12°. N.Y. 1871.

ANDERSON, B. Journey to Musardu. 12°. N.Y. 1870.

—— Appendix to Journey to Musadu. 16°. N.Y. 1870.

ANDERSON, J. The Crime of Drunkenness; a Discourse. (PC. 22.) 8°. Waterbury. 1867.

ANDERSON, R. Foreign Missions. 12°. N.Y. 1869.

—— Letter to Dr. Candlish. 8°. Bost. 1862.

ANDERSON, W. Model Women. 16°. Lond. 1870.

ANDERSON, W. J. Life of the Duke of Kent. 12°. Ottawa. 1870.

ANDRÉOLI, É. Le Gouvernement du 4 Sept., et la Commune de Paris. 12°. Paris. 1871.

ANDREW, J. A. Address to Legislature, Jan. 3, 1862. 8°. Bost. 1862.

—— Address to N. E. Historic-Genealogical Society. (PC. 11.) 8°. Bost. 1867.

ANDREWS, E. A. First Lesson in Latin. 18°. Bost. 1837.

ANDREWS, I. W. Why is Allegiance Due? and Where is it Due? An Address. 8°. Cinc. 1863.

ANDREWS, J. Choice Garden Flowers. 18°. Lond. 1860.

ANDREWS, J. R. Life of Cromwell. 8°. Lond. 1870.

ANDREWS, Solomon. The Art of Flying. 8°. N.Y. 1865.

ANDREWS, Stephen P. Basic Outline of Universology. R. 8°. N.Y. 1872.

—— and Batchelor, G. Pronouncer and Key (French). 12°. N.Y. 1856.

—— and Boyle, A. F. Phonographic Class Book. 12°. Bost. 1846.

—— Same. 12°. N.Y. 1848.

—— Phonographic Reader. 12°. Bost. 1846.

—— Same. 12°. N.Y. 1848.

ANDROS Tracts, v. 2. Sm. 4°. Bost. 1869.

ANDY'S Trip to the West, together with a Life of its Hero. 16°. N.Y. 1866.

ANECDOTES of Alamayu. Sq. 18°. Lond. n.d.

ANGELL, J. K., and Ames, S. Law of Private Corporations Aggregate. 9th ed., by Lathrop. 8°. Bost. 1871.

ANGELL, O. Select Reader. 12°. Phil. 1834.

ANGELS of Heaven. Sm. 4°. Lond. 1870.

ANGOT, A. Nos Ruines. 16°. Paris. 1871. *See* HANS et Blanc.

ANNALS of Europe. 8°. Lond. 1779.

ANNENKOV, —. La Guerre de 1870, et le Siége de Paris. 12°. Paris. 1872.

ANNUAL Register for 1869–70. 8°. Lond. 1870–71.

ANNUAL Review and History of Literature. v. 4, for 1805. R. 8°. Lond. 1806.

ANNUAL of Scientific Discovery for 1870–71. 2 v. 12°. Bost. 1871.

ANQUETIL et Norvins. Histoire de France. 5 v. R. 8°. Paris. 1852.

ANSELL, C. Friendly Societies. 8°. Lond. 1835.

ANSELL, G. F. The Royal Mint. Imp. 8°. Lond. 1870.

—— Same. 1871.

ANTE-NICENE Christian Library; v. 13–22. 8°. Edin. 1869–71.

v. 13. Cyprian, etc.
14. Methodius, etc.
15. Tertullian, v. 1–2.
16. Apocryphal Gospels.
17. Clementine Homilies; Apostolical Constitutions.
18. Tertullian, v. 3.; Victorianus; Commodianus.
19. Arnobius adversus Gentes.
20. Gregory Thaumaturgus; Dionysius of Alexandria; Archelaus.
21. Lactantius, v. 1.
22. Lactantius, v. 2. Testaments of the Twelve Patriarchs; Fragments of 2d and 3d Centuries.

ANTHON, C. Classical Dictionary. R. 8°. N.Y. 1869. Same, 1870.

ANTHON, G. C. Narrative of Displacement. 8°. N.Y. 1852.

ANTHON, J. Law Student. 8°. N.Y. 1850.

ANTHROPOLOGICAL Review. v. 7. 8°. Lond. 1869.

ANTHROPOLOGICAL Society of London. Memoirs. v. 3. 8°. Lond. 1870.

ANTIDOTE to "The Gates Ajar." By J. S. W. 8°. N.Y. 1871.

ANTIETAM. McClellan and Fremont. (PC. 3.) 8°. N.Y. 1862.

ANTISELL, T. Address on Physical Geography and Agriculture. (PC. 3.) 8°. n.p. n.d.

ANTONINUS. Thoughts; transl. by Long. 2d ed. 16°. Lond. 1869.

APOCRYPHAL Acts of the Apostles. Ed. by W. Wright. v. 1. Syriac Texts. 8°. Lond. 1871.

APOSTOLIC Constitutions. *See* ANTE-NICENE Christian Library, v. 17.

APPEAL (An) to the People of the North. (PC. 3.) 2d ed. 8°. Louisville. 1861.

APPERLEY, C. J. Chace, Turf, and Road. 16°. Lond. 1870.

APPLETON, N. Power Loom, and Origin of Lowell, 8°. Lowell. 1858.

APPLETON'S Cyclopædia of Drawing. R. 8°. N.Y. 1869.

APPLETON'S Dictionary of Machines, Mechanics, Engine Work and Engineering. 2 v. R. 8°. N.Y. 1869.

APPLETON'S European Guide book. Illustrated. 12°. Lond. 1871.

APPLETON'S Hand-Book; Northern and Eastern Tour. 12°. N.Y. 1870.

APPLETON'S Journal. v. 1–6. 4°. N.Y. 1869–71.

APULEIUS. Works; transl. With Tighe's Psyche. (Bohn's Ed.) 12°. Lond. 1853.

ARABIAN Nights' Entertainments. 16°. Bost. 1870.

ARAGO, E. Les Aristocraties. 16°. Lond. 1868.

ARAGO, F. Popular Astronomy. Tr. and Ed. by Smyth and Grant. 2 v. 8°. Lond. 1855–8.

ARBER'S English Reprints. 13 v. 18°. Lond. 1868–71.

v. 1. Milton's Areopagitica; Latimer's Sermon on the Ploughers; Gosson's Schoole of Abuse; Gosson's Apologie of the Schoole of Abuse.
2. Sidney's Apologie for Poetrie; Webbe's Travailes; Selden's Table Talk.
3. Ascham's Toxophilus; Addison's Criticisms of Paradise Lost.
4. Lyly's Euphues, the Anatomy of Wit; Lyly's Euphues and his England.
5. Gascoigne's Steel Glass; Gascoigne's Complaynt of Phylomene; Earl's Micro-Cosmographie.
6. Latimer's Seven Sermons; More's Utopia.
7. Puttenham's Art of English Poetrie.
8. Howell's Instructions for Foreign Travel; Udall's Roister Doister; Revelation to the

Monk of Evesham; James VI., Essays in Poesie; James VI., Counter Blaste to Tobacco.
9. Naunton's Fragmenta Regalia; Watson's Passionate Centurie of Love, etc.
10. Habington's Castara; Ascham's Scholemaster.
11. Tottel's Miscellany (Surrey's Songs and Sonettes).
12. Lever's Sermons; Webbe's Discourse of English Poetrie.
13. Harmony of Bacon's Essays.

ARCANA Lodge, N.Y. Obsequies of C. L. Peters. 8°. N.Y. 1853.

ARCHELAUS. *See* ANTE-NICENE Library, v. 20.

ARCHER, T. Terrible Sights of London. 12°. Lond. n.d.

ARCHER, T. C. Economic Botany. Sq. 12°. Lond. 1853.

ARCHITECTURAL Magazine. v. 1–2. 8°. Lond. 1834–5.

ARCHITECTURAL Review. v. 2. R. 8°. Phil. 1870.

ARCHIVES Curieuses de l'Histoire de France depuis Louis XI jusqu'â Louis XVIII. 27 v. 12°. Paris. 1834.

ARE there Romanizing Germs in the Prayer-Book? (PC. 4.) 8°. N.Y. 1868.

ARGENTINE Republic. Código Civil. 8°. N.Y. 1870.

ARGOSY. v. 7–12. 8°. Lond. 1869–71.

ARGUMENT of Domesticus on Marrying Deceased Wife's Sister, Considered. By Clericus. (PC. 23.) 8°. N.Y. 1827.

ARGUMENT on Tolls on Coal on Erie Canal. (PC. 1.) 8°. N.Y. 1862.

ARGYLL, Duke of. Iona. 16°. Lond. 1870.

—— Reign of Law. 12°. N.Y. n.d.

ARIOSTO, Orlando Furioso. 4 v. 18°. Leghorn. 1797.

—— Orlando Furioso. Tr. by Hoole. 24°. Lond. 1819.

ARISTOPHANES. Comedies; transl. (Bohn's ed.) 2 v. 12°. Lond. 1869.

ARISTOTLE. Ethics; Books 1–4. Ed. by Rev. E. Moore. 12°. Lond. 1871.

—— Works; transl. (Bohn's ed.) 7 v. 12°. Lond. 1853–67.

ARIZONA Historical Society. Charter. Constitution and By-Laws. 8°. Prescott. 1864.

—— Resources of Arizona Territory. 8°. San Francisco. 1871.

ARKANSAS, Natural Resources of. (PC. 4.) 8°. Little Rock. 1869.

ARLOT, M. A Complete Guide for Coach Painters. 12°. Lond. 1871.

ARMAILLÉ, Comtesse d'. Marie Thérèse et Marie Antoinette. 16°. Paris. 1870.

ARMAND. Der Krösus von Philadelphia. 2 v. 16°. Hanover. 1870.

ARMATAGE, G. Horseowner and Stableman's Companion. 16°. Lond. n.d.

ARM-CHAIR (An) in the Smoking-Room. 12°. Lond. n.d.

ARMFIELD, H. T. Legend of Christian Art. 12°. Salisbury. (Eng.) 1869.

ARMIT, R. H. The Wind in his Circuits. 12°. Lond. 1870.

ARMITAGE, T. Past, Present and Future of the U.S.; a Sermon. 8°. N.Y. 1862.

ARMOUR, J. Iron and Heat. 16°. Lond. 1871.

—— Power in Motion. 16°. Lond. 1871.

ARMSTER, Sophie. Neues Kochbuch. 9th ed. 12°. Stade. 1865.

ARMSTRONG, J. Art of Preserving Health. 16°. Lond. 1796.

ARMY and Navy Gazette. v. 2, 3, 5, 11. f°. Lond. 1861–70.

ARNDT, J. True Christianity. 2 v. 8°. Lond. 1815.

ARNOBIUS. Adversus Gentes. *See* ANTE-NICENE Christian Library, v. 19.

ARNOLD, F. Path on Earth to the Gate of Heaven. 16°. N.Y. n.d.

ARNOLD, M. Essays in Criticism. 12°. Bost. 1869.

—— Same. 12°. Lond. 1869.

—— Friendship's Garland (Thunder-ten-tronckh Letters). 16°. Lond. 1871.

—— St. Paul and Protestantism. 12°. Lond. 1870.

ARNOLD, T. K. English Grammar. 3d ed. 16°. Lond. 1843.

—— First Greek Lessons. 12°. N.Y. 1846.

—— First and Second Latin Book. 12°. N.Y. 1846.

—— Greek Prose Composition. 12°. N.Y. 1847.

—— Latin Prose Composition. 12°. N.Y. 1847.

—— Spelling turned Etymology. Part 1. 16°. Lond. 1844.

ARNOLD, W. The Life and Death of the Sublime Society of Beef Steaks. Sq. 12°. Lond. 1871.

ARNOT, W. Life of J. Hamilton, D.D. 2d ed. 12°. N.Y. 1870.
AROSEMENA, D. Sensaciones en Oriente. 12°. N.Y. 1859.
ARSAC, J. d'. Mémorial du Siége de Paris. 5th ed. 12°. Paris. 1871.
—— La Guerre Civile et la Commune de Paris. 12°. Paris. 1871.
ART JOURNAL. New Ser., v. 9. 4°. Lond. 1870.
ARTHUR, T. S. Wreaths of Friendship. 12°. N.Y. 1870.
ARTIZAN. v. 27-28. 4°. Lond. 1869-70.
ARVINE, K. Cyclopædia of Anecdotes. 8°. Bost. 1870.
—— Our Duty to the Fugitive Slave; a Sermon. 8°. Bost. 1850.
ASGRIMSSON, E. Lilja; an Icelandic Poem. 12°. Lond. 1870.
ASHBURNER, J. Animal Magnetism and Spiritualism. 8°. Lond. 1867.
ASHER and Adams. Map of New York. L. 4°. N.Y. n.d.
—— New Commercial and Statistical Atlas and Gazetteer of the U.S. v. 1. f°. N.Y. 1872.
ASHLEY, J. M. (Ed'r.) A Year with Great Preachers; 52 Sermons. v. 1. 16°. Lond. 1871.
ASHMUN, J. Memoir of Rev. S. Bacon. 8°. Wash. 1822.
ASHTABULA and Lisbon R. R. Report on Economic Geology. (PC. 19.) 8.° Clevel. 1857.
ASHURST, W. H. Law of Railways and Insolvency. (P. 77.) 8°. Lond. 1838.
ASSOCIATION Belge pour la Réforme Douanière. 1st publication. (P.C. 11.) 16°. Brussels. 1856.
ASSOCIATION Monthly. v. 1. 4°. N.Y. 1870.
ASSURANCE Magazine. v. 13-14. 8°. Lond. 1867-9.
ASTLE, T. Origin and Progress of Writing. 4°. Lond. 1784.
AT Home and Abroad. 16°. N.Y. n.d.
ATHENÆUM. 1863, and Jan.-July, 1870. 3 v. 4°. Lond. 1863-70.
ATHENÆUS. Deipnosophists; tr. by Yonge. (Bohn's ed.) 3 v. 12°. Lond. 1854.
ATKINSON, E. Report to Boston Board of Trade on Cotton Manufacture. (P.C. 22.) 8°. Bost. 1863.
ATKINSON, J. J. Gases in Coal Mines. 16°. Newcastle. 1871.
ATKINSON, W. P. Classical and Scientific Studies and the Great Schools of England. 8°. Camb. (Eng.) 1865.
ATLANTIC Monthly. v. 24-28. 8°. Bost. 1869-71.
ATTFIELD, J. Chemistry. 12°. Lond. 1869.
ATTHILL, L. Clinical Lectures on Diseases Peculiar to Women. 12°. Dubl. 1871.
ATTIC Wit, from the pens of Tom Taylor, and others. 12°. N.Y. 1864.
ATWOOD, D. T. Country and Suburban Houses. 12°. N.Y. n.d.
AUB, T. Real Estate Transactions. 8°. N.Y. 1871.
AUCHINCLOSS, W. S. The Practical Application of the Side Valve and Link Motion. 8°. N.Y. 1871.
AUBIGNÉ, J. H. M. d'. Reformation in the 16th Century. 4°. Glasg. n.d.
—— Reformation in Time of Calvin. 5 v. 12°. N.Y. 1870.
AUCHER, P. Armenian and English Grammar. 12°. Venice. 1832.
AUDEBRAND, P. Histoire Intime de la Révolution du 18 Mars. 12°. Paris. 1871.
AUDOUARD, Mme. O. A travers l'Amérique. Le "Far West." 12°. Paris. 1869.
AUDUBON, Mrs. Life of J. J. Audubon. 12°. N.Y. 1869.
AUERBACH, B. Das Landhaus am Rhein. 16°. Stuttgart. 1869.
—— Schwarzwälder Dorfgeschichten. 4 v. 12°. Stuttgart. 1871.
—— Spinoza. 4th ed. 2 v. 12°. Stuttgart. 1860.
—— Wieder Unser. 12°. Stuttgart. 1871.
AUERSPERG, Count. The Last Knight. 8°. N.Y. 1871.
AUGIER, É. Lions et Renards. 16°. Paris. '70.
—— Le Post Scriptum. 16°. Paris. 1870.
AUGSBURG Confession. Transl. by Krauth. 12°. Phil. 1868.
AUGUSTINE, Saint. City of God. 2 v. 8°. Edin. 1871.
—— The Origin of the Two Cities, Heavenly and Earthly. Books 11-14, Transl. by Walker. 12°. Lond. 1871.
AULD, A. Ministers and Men in the Far North. 12°. Wick. 1868.
AUNT RACHEL'S Letter about Water and Air. 18°. Lond. 1871.
AURELLE de Paladines (Le Général d'). La Première Armée de la Loire. 8°. Paris. 1872.

AUSTIN, A. Poetry of the Period. 12°. Lond. 1870.
— Vindication of Lord Byron. 2d ed. 8°. Lond. 1869.
AUSTIN, J. Gospel Doctrine Vindicated. 8°. New Bedford. 1818.
AUSTIN, J. L. Lectures on Jurisprudence. 3d ed., by R. Campbell. 2 v. 8°. Lond. 1869.
AUSTRALIAN Hand-Book and Almanac for 1872. 8°. Lond. n.d.
AUSTRO-Hungarian Empire, and Policy of Count Beust. 8°. Lond. 1870.
AVÉ-LALLEMANT, F. C. B. Der Erb-und Gerichtsherr. 16°. Hanover. 1870.
AVIANUS. Fabulæ. *See* PHÆDRUS; Fabulæ. Deuxponts. 1784.
AVIS, R. The Canary. 18°. Lond. 1870.

BACHE, A. D. Experiments on Radiation, etc., of Heat. (PC. 3.) 8°. Phil. 1835.
— Safety Apparatus for Steam Boilers. (PC. 3.) 12°. Phil. 1832.
BACHER, J. Auf dem Wiener Congress. 4 v. in 2. 16°. Liep. 1869.
BACHI, P. Spanish and Portuguese Languages. 12°. Camb. 1831.
BACHMAIR, J. J. German Grammar. 3d ed. 12°. Phil. 1811.
BACLER D'Albe, A. L. Carte de la Théâtre de la Guerre en Italie. 50 maps, folded. 4°. Paris. 1802.
BACON, F. Lord. Conference of Pleasure. 8°. Lond. 1870.
— Letters and Life. Ed. by Spedding. v. 5. 8°. Lond. 1869.
— Poems. *See* FULLER Worthies' Library; Miscellanies.
BACON, G. B. Sabbath Question. 16°. N.Y. 1868.
BACON, L. Conciliation; a Discourse. 8°. New Haven. 1862.
— Discourse on the Traffic in Spirituous Liquors. 8°. New Haven. 1838.
BACON, L. W. Historical Discourse, 200th Anniversary Hopkins Grammar School. 8°. New Haven. 1860.
BADGER, G. P. State of the Dead. 2d ed. 16°. Lond. 1871.
BAEDEKER, K. Hand-Books for Travellers:
1. Belgium and Holland. 16°. Coblenz. 1871.
2. Paris. 16°. Coblenz. 1867.
3. Italy. 3 v. 16°. Coblenz. 1870.
4. Rhine and Northern Germany. 16°. Coblenz. 1870.
5. Southern Germany. 16°. Coblenz. 1871.
— Travellers' Manual of Conversation. 16°. Coblenz. 1870.
BAILLON, H. Natural History of Plants. Transl. by Hartog. v. 1. Imp. 8°. Lond. 1871.
BAILY, F. Annuities and Assurance. 2 v. 8°. Lond. 1864–6.
BAIN, A. Composition and Rhetoric. 12°. N.Y. 1870.
— Logic. 2 v. 12°. Lond. 1870.
— Senses and Intellect. 3d ed. 8°. N.Y. 1872.
BAINES, E. History of the County Palatine and Duchy of Lancaster. 2 v. 4°. Lond. 1868–70.
BAIRD, C. W. History of Rye, N. Y. 8°. N.Y. 1871.
BAIRD, R. Transplanted Flowers. (Memoirs of Mrs. Rumpf and Duchess de Broglie.) 18°. N.Y. 1839.
BAKER, B. Strength of Beams, Columns and Arches. 12°. Lond. 1870.
BAKER, G. M. The Mimic Stage. 12°. Bost. 1869.
— The Social Stage. 12°. Bost. 1870.
— Same. 1871.
BAKER, J. M. Commerce of the U. S. and Mediterranean. 8°. Phil. 1847.
BAKER, J. W. Grammar of Moral Philosophy. 24°. N.Y. 1817.
BAKER, T. History of St. John's College. Ed. by Mayor. 2 v. 8°. Camb. (Eng.) 1869.
BAKER, W. Harmonic Maxims of Science and Religion. 12°. Lond. 1864.
BALDWIN, B. A. Nathaniel Baldwin and Descendants. 8°. Bost. 1871.
BALDWIN, D. Evils of Tobacco. (PC. 6.) 12°. N.Y. 1854.
BALDWIN, G. C. The Model Prayer. 12°. Bost. 1871.
BALDWIN, J. D. Ancient America in Notes on American Archæolgy. 12°. N.Y. 1872.
BALDWIN, J. G. Flush Times of Alabama and Mississippi. 12°. N.Y. 1870.
BALE, John (Bishop). Temptacyion of Jesus. *See* FULLER Worthies' Library; Miscellanies.
BALFOUR, Clara L. Working Women of this Century. 3d ed. 16°. Lond. n.d.

BALL, J. Guide to Eastern Alps. 12°. Lond. 1868.

—— Guide to Western Alps. 12°. Lond. 1870.

BALL, R. S. Experimental Mechanics. 8°. Lond. 1871.

BALLAD Minstrelsy of Scotland. 12°. Lond. 1871.

BALLOU'S Monthly Magazine. v. 34. July to Dec. 1871. 8°. Bost. n.d.

BALMASEDA, F. J. Confinados á Fernando Po. 16°. N.Y. 1869.

—— Fabulas Morales. 3d ed. 18°. Havana. 1863.

BALME, J. R. Synopsis of the American War. 16°. Lond. 1865.

BALTIMORE Directory, 1870, '71. 2 v. 8°. Balt. 1870–71.

BALZAC, H. de. La Cousine Bette; le Cousin Pons. f°. Paris. n.d.

—— Un Début dans la Vie; Maître Cornelius. f°. Paris. 1855.

—— Le Père Goriot. f°. Paris. 1858.

—— Oeuvres Complètes. 20 v. 8°. Paris. 1855.

—— Ursule de Mirouët. 12°. Paris. 1868.

BANCROFT, G. and his Boston Critics. (PC. 3.) 8°. N.Y. 1862.

—— Letter on Exchange of Prisoners in Revolutionary War. (PC. 3.) 8°. N.Y. 1862.

BANGOR and Brewer Directory for 1871–2. 8°. Bangor. 1871.

BANK (The) Torpedo. 16°. N.Y. 1810.

BANK of the U. S. (Reprinted from N. A. Review.) 8°. Bost. 1831.

BANKER'S Magazine and Statistical Register. v. 25. 8°. N.Y. 1870–1.

BANKING Almanac for 1870. 8°. Lond. n.d.

BANNERMAN, H. Essays on Christian Unity. 12°. Lond. 1871.

BANTING, W. Letter on Corpulence. 6th ed. 16°. Phil. 1868.

BAPTIST Quarterly. v. 3–5. R. 8°. Phil. 1869–71.

BAR Association of N. Y. City. Proceedings. (PC. 6.) 8°. N.Y. 1870.

BARBER, E. C. Crack Shot, or Young Rifleman's Guide. 12°. N.Y. 1868.

BARBER, J. Treatise on Gesture. 12°. Cambr. 1831.

BARBOUR, J. The Bruce. Ed. by Jamieson. 16°. Glasgow. 1860.

BARCLAY, A. Wilde's Summer Rose. 12°. Savannah. 1871.

BARETTI, G. Introduction to Italian. 8°. Lond. 1751.

—— Italian and English Dictionary. 6th ed. 2 v. 8°. Lond. 1820.

BARHAM, R. D. Life of R. H. Barham. 2 v. 12°. Lond. 1870.

BARING, E. Staff College Essays. 8°. Lond. 1870.

BARKER, Lady. Station Life in New Zealand. 12°. Lond. 1871.

BARKER, T. C. Aryan Civilization. 12°. Lond. 1871.

BARNARD, C. Simple Flower Garden. 8°. Bost. 1870.

—— Strawberry Garden. 12°. Bost. 1870.

BARNARD, F. A. P. Analytic Grammar. 12°. N.Y. 1836.

—— Metric System of Weights and Measures. 8°. N.Y. 1872.

—— Report on Machinery, etc. *See* U. S. Report of Paris Exposition, etc.

—— Report on Plan of Instruction. 8°. N.Y. 1855.

BARNARD, H. Military Schools and Special Instruction in the Art of War in different Countries. 8°. N.Y. 1872.

—— National Education. Systems, Institutions and Statistics of Public Instruction in different Countries. Part I. Europe.—German States. Part II. Europe.—France, Switzerland, etc. 2 v. 8°. N.Y. 1872.

—— Practical Illustrations of School Architecture. 8°. Hartford. 1851.

—— Systems, Institutions and Statistics of Scientific Instruction in different Countries. v. 1. 8°. N.Y. 1872.

BARNARD, J. G. Dangers and Defences of New York. 8°. N.Y. 1859.

—— The Peninsular Campaign. 16°. N.Y. 1864.

BARNES, A. Notes on Acts. 12°. N.Y. 1869.

BARNES, J. S. Submarine Warfare. 8°. N.Y. 1869.

BARNES, R. Lectures on Obstetrics. 2d. ed. 8°. Lond. 1871.

BARNES, W. Poems in the Dorset Dialect. 16°. Lond. 1870.

BARNES, W. H. The Fortieth Congress. 2 v. 8°. N.Y. 1870.

BARNI, J. Manuel Republicain. 12°. Paris. 1872.

BARNUM, P. T. Struggles and Triumphs. 8°. Hartford. 1869.

BARNUM, S. W. Romanism As It Is. 8°. Hartford. 1872.
BARRATT, A. Physical Ethics. 8°. Lond. 1869.
BARRE, W. L. Lives of Illustrious Men of America. 8°. N.Y. 1858.
BARRETT, B. F. The New View of Hell. 12°. Phil. 1872.
BARRETT, T. S. Examination of Gillespie's Argument for a First Cause. 2d ed. 12°. Lond. 1871.
BARRETT, W. *See* SCOVILLE.
BARRY, A. Life of Sir C. Barry. 2d ed. 8°. Lond. 1870.
BARRY, C. A. How to Draw. 16°. Bost. 1871.
BARRY, H. Russia in 1870. 12°. Lond. 1871.
BARRY, P. Wealth and Poverty. 16°. Lond. 1870.
BARRY, W. Moorland and Stream. 12°. Lond. 1871.
BARTHELEMY, P. Rev. A. Verren Judged by his Works. 12°. N.Y. 1820.
BARTHOLOMEW, J. Student's Atlas. Imp. 8°. Phil. 1871.
BARTHOLOW, R. Manual of Hypodermic Medication. 12°. Phil. 1869.
BARTLE, G. Doctrine of Hades. 12°. Lond. 1869.
BARTLETT, E. Discourse on Hippocrates. 8°. N.Y. 1852.
BARTLETT, J. Familiar Quotations. 5th ed. 12°. Bost. 1869.
BARTLETT, J. R. Dictionary of Americanisms. 3d ed. 8°. Bost. 1860.
—— Literature of the Rebellion. 4°. Bost. 1866.
BARTLETT, W., and Chapman, H. Handy Book for Investors. 12°. Lond. 1869.
BARTLETT, W. A. Memorial for Restoration. (PC. 3.) 8°. Wash. 1856.
—— Reply to Testimony, etc. 8°. Wash. 1856.
BARTLETT, W. H. Walks About Jerusalem. R. 8°. Lond. 1870.
—— Pictures from Sicily. 12°. Lond. 1869.
BARTLEY, G. C. T. Schools for the People. 8°. Lond. 1871.
BARTOL, C. A. Immediate Vision of God; a S rmon (PC. 11.) 8°. Bost. 1860.
—— Radical Problems. 12°. Bost. 1872.
—— Sermon on D. Webster. (PC. 6.) 8°. Bost. 1852.
—— Tribute to Gen. Lowell. (PC. 6.) 8°. Bost. 1861.
BARTON, J. Comic Recitations. 16°. N.Y. n.d.
BARWELL, R. Lateral Curvature of the Spine. 2d ed. 12°. Lond. 1870.
BASCOM, J. Æsthetics. 12°. N.Y. 1872.
—— Psychology. 12°. N.Y. 1869.
—— Science, Philosophy and Religion. 12°. N.Y. 1871.
BASTIAN, A. Reisen in China. 8°. Jena. 1871.
BASTIAN, H. C. Modes of Origin of Lowest Organisms. 12°. Lond. 1871.
BASTIAT, F. Political Economy. 16°. Lond. n.d.
—— Sophisms of the Protectionists. 16°. N.Y. 1870.
BASTILLE in America. (PC. 6.) 8°. Lond. 1861.
BATCHELOR, G. History of Teachers' Associations in New York City. 16°. N.Y. 1861.
BATEMAN, F. Aphasia, or Loss of Speech. 8°. Lond. 1870.
BATES, D. Poetical Works. 16°. Phil. 1870.
BATES, Mrs. D. B. Incidents on Land and Water. 12°. Bost. 1860.
BATES, H. W. Illustrated Travels. Imp. 4°. Lond. n.d.
BATES, S. P. Teachers' Institutes. 12°. N.Y. 1862.
BATH, Brunswick and Richmond Directory for 1871–2. 8°. Bath. 1870.
BAUDISSIN, U. Marotte. 2 v. 12°. Stuttgart. 1871.
—— Stiefkinder. 3 v. 12°. Stuttgart. 1870.
BAUERMAN, H. Metallurgy of Iron. 12°. Lond. 1868.
BAUR, W. Religious Life in Germany. 2 v. 12°. Lond. 1870.
BAXTER, R. God's Purpose in Judgment. Sq. 18°. Lond. 1869.
—— What Must we Do to be Saved? Ed. by Grosart. 16°. n.p. 1868.
BAXTER, R. D. National Debts. 8°. Lond. 1871.
—— Taxation of the United Kingdom. 8°. Lond. 1869.
BAYER, C. R. Nomaden. 2 v. 12°. Leip. 1871.
—— Sphinx. 3 v. 12°. Berlin. 1870.
—— Zwischen zwei Nationen. 3 v. 12°. Berlin. 1871.
BAYES, W. Applied Homœopathy. 8°. Lond. 1871.

BAYLDON, G. Icelandic Grammar. 12°. Lond. 1870.

BAYLEE, J. Blessed Dead. 2d ed. Sm. 18°. Lond. n.d.

BAYLEY, R. J. Catholic Church in New York. 2d ed. 16°. N.Y. 1870.

BAYNE, P. Life and Letters of Hugh Miller. 2 v. 8°. Lond. 1871.

—— Same. 2 v. 12°. Bost. 1871.

BAYNES, H. S. Horæ Lucanæ. 12°. Lond. 1870.

BAZAINE, F. A. Rapport Sommaire sur les Opérations de l'Armée du Rhin. 8°. Berlin. 1871.

BAZAR Book of Decorum. 16°. N.Y. 1870.

BEACH and Hickey. Discussion on the Trinity. 12°. Dayton. 1867.

BEACH, A. E. Science Record for 1872. 12°. N.Y. 1872.

BEACH, W. B. Duke of Edinburgh's Visit to Hong-Kong. 4°. Hong-Kong. 1869.

BEADLE, J. H. Life in Utah. 8°. Phil. n.d.

BEAL, S. Catena of Buddhist Scriptures, from the Chinese. 8°. Lond. 1871.

BEALE, Lionel S. Disease Germs. 12°. Lond. 1870.

—— Life Theories and Religious Thoughts. 12°. Lond. 1871.

—— The Mystery of Life. 12°. Lond. 1871.

—— Protoplasm. 12°. Lond. 1870.

BEALE, S. T. Trial and Conviction. (PC. 17.) 8°. Phil. 1855.

BEAMAN, C. C., Jr. Alabama Claims. 8°. Wash. 1871.

BEARD, G. M. Eating and Drinking. 12°. N.Y. 1871.

—— Stimulants and Narcotics. 12°. N.Y. 1871.

BEAUCHESNE, A. de. Vie de Mme. Elisabeth. 2 v. 8°. Paris. 1869.

BEAUMONT, Sir J. Poems. *See* FULLER Worthies' Library, v. 10.

BEAUMONT-Vassy, E. de. Le Prince Max à Paris. 16°. Paris. 1870.

BEAUSSIRE, E. La Guerre Etrangère et la Guerre Civile. 12°. Paris. 1871.

BEAUTY is Power. 12°. N.Y. 1871.

BEAUVOIR, Marquis de. Voyage round the World. 2 v. 12°. Lond. 1870.

BEAVER Mining Co. Prospectus. (PC. 9.) 8°. Bost. 1864.

BECHSTEIN, J. M. Natural History of Cage Birds. 16°. Lond. n.d.

BECHSTEIN, L. Der Dunkelgraf. 12°. Frankf. 1854.

BECHTINGER, J. Ost Afrika. 8°. Vienna. 1870.

BECK, J. B. New Medical School in Columbia College. (PC. 6.) 8°. N.Y. 1832.

BECKER, A. Der Karfunkel. 12°. Berlin. 1870.

—— Der Nixenfischer. 12°. Berlin. 1870.

—— Des Rabbi Vermächtniss; I. Der Maler. II. Der Kabbalist. III. Der Erbgraf. 3 v. 12°. Berlin. 1866–67.

—— Das Thurmkätherlein. 2 v. 12°. Leip. 1871.

BECKER, K. F. Weltgeschichte. 8th ed. Ed. by Schmidt; continued by Arnd. 20 v. in 10. 8°. Leip. 1869–71.

BECKER, W. A. Charicles; trans. by Metcalfe. 3d ed. 12°. Lond. 1866.

—— Gallus; transl. by Metcalfe. 3d ed. 12°. Lond. 1866.

BECKETT, G. A. á. A Comic History of England. 8°. Lond. n.d.

BECKSTEIN, Dr. Wasserkatechismus. 16°. Berlin. 1836.

BEDE. Historia Ecclesiastica Gentis Anglorum. Ed. by Moberly. 12°. Oxford. 1869.

—— Ecclesiastical History; transl. by Gidley. 12°. Oxford. 1870.

BEDELL, G. T. Present Profit of Godliness; a Sermon. (PC. 11.) 8°. N.Y. 1852.

BEDFORD, H. Life of St. Vincent de Paul. 12°. N.Y. n.d.

BEECHER, Miss C. E. Receipt Book. 3d ed. 12°. N.Y. 1858.

—— Woman's Profession as Mother and Educator. 12°. Phil. 1871.

—— and Stowe, H. B. American Woman's Home. 12°. N.Y. 1870.

BEECHER, E. and C. Review of Proceedings of Council. (PC. 3.) 8°. Bost. 1863.

BEECHER, H. W. Address at Manchester, Eng. (PC. 2.) 8°. N.Y. 1863.

—— Lecture Room Talks. 12°. N.Y. 1870.

—— Life of Jesus, the Christ. v. 1. 8°. N.Y. 1871.

—— Morning and Evening Exercises. 8°. N.Y. 1870.

—— Overture of Angels. 12°. N.Y. 1870.

BEECHER, H. W. Sermons. 1st.–4th Series. 8°. N.Y. 1868–71.
BEECHER, T. K. Our Seven Churches. 16°. N.Y. 1870.
BEECHER's Magazine. v. 1–4. 8°. Trenton. 1871.
BEEKMAN, J. W. Centenary Address, N.Y. Hospital. 8°. n.p. 1871.
—— Founders of New York; an Address before the St. Nicholas Society. L. 8°. N.Y. 1870.
BEETON's Boy's Annual for 1870. 8°. Lond. 1870.
BEETON's Dictionary of Practical Recipes and Every-Day Information. 12°. Lond. n.d.
BEETON's Dictionary of Universal Biography. 2d ed. 12°. Lond. n.d.
BEETON's Great Book of Poetry. R. 8°. Lond. n.d.
BEETON, S. O. Fact, Fiction, History and Adventure. 8°. Lond. n.d.
BEEVER, W. H. The Daily Life of our Farm. 12°. Lond. 1871.
—— Notes on Fields and Cattle. 12°. Lond. 1870.
—— Successful Farming. 12°. Lond. 1870.
BEGGYNHOF, (The,) or the City of the Single. 16°. Lond. 1869.
BEHAGHEL, A. L'Algérie. 12°. Paris. 1870.
BEHIND the Bars. 12°. Bost. 1871.
BEIGEL, H. The Human Hair. 16°. Lond. 1869.
BEKE, C. T. The Idol in Horeb. 12°. Lond. 1871.
BELAIR, A. P. Élémens de Fortification. 2d ed. 12°. Paris. 1793.
BELCHER, Lady. Mutineers of the Bounty. 12°. Lond. 1870.
—— Same. 12°. N.Y. 1871.
BELGRAVIA. v. 7–15. 8°. Lond. 1869–71.
BELIEF: What is it? 8°. Lond. 1869.
BELL, A. History of Canada. 2d ed. 2 v. 8°. Montreal. 1862.
BELL, Sir C. Letters. 12°. Lond. 1870.
BELL, Mrs. Emma M. Poems. 16°. Phil. 1872.
BELL, J. System of Geography. 8°. Lond. 1845–48.
BELL, R. Early Ballads. 16°. Lond. 1856.
BELL, W. A. New Tracks in North America. 2 v. 8°. Lond. 1869.
BELLEFONTAINE and Indiana R. R. Co. Exhibit, 1851. (PC. 10.) 8°. N.Y. 1851.
BELLENGER. Nouvelles Conversations, Françaises, Anglaises et Allemandes. Sq. 16°. Brussels. 1837.
BELLENGER and Witcomb. Guide to French Conversation. 16°. N.Y. 1870.
BELLOWS, H. W. Address at Funeral of Mrs. M. Bellows. 8°. Cambridge. 1870.
BELOT, A. L'Article 47. 16°. Paris. 1870.
—— Le Drame de la Rue de Paix. 16°. Paris. 1867.
—— L'Habitude et le Souvenir. 12°. Paris. 1865.
—— et Daudet; La Vénus de Gordes. 16°. Paris. 1867.
BENEDICT. Memorial of L. and S. Benedict. L. 8°. N.Y. 1870.
BENEDICT, E. C. Discourse to Philomathean, etc., Societies. (PC. 7.) 8°. N.Y. 1841.
BENEDICT, H. M. Benedict Genealogy. 8°. Alb. 1870.
—— Stafford Genealogy. 8°. Alb. 1870.
BENEDIX, R. Eigensinn. *See* WILHELMI, A. Einer muss heirathen.
—— Der Weiberfeind. *See* ELZ, A. Er ist nicht eifersüchtig.
BENET, S. V. Electro-Ballistic Machines. 4°. N.Y. 1871.
BENGER, Miss E. O. Memoirs of Anne Boleyn. 2d ed. 2 v. 12°. Lond. 1821.
BENJAMIN, S. G. W. Choice of Paris. 16°. N.Y. 1870.
BENNET, J. H. Winter and Spring on the Mediterranean. 12°. N.Y. 1870.
BENNETT, J. R. Cancerous and other Intra-Thoracic Growths. 12°. Lond. 1872.
BENSON, L. (Ed'r.) Remarkable Trials and Notorious Characters. 12°. Lond. n.d.
BENTHAM, J. Theory of Legislation. From the French of Dumont, by Hildreth. 2d ed. 12°. Lond. 1871.
BENTLEY, RICHARD. Works. 3 v. 8°. Lond. 1836.
BENTLEY, ROBERT. Manual of Botany. 2d ed. 16°. Lond. n.d.
BENTLEY's Miscellany. v. 62–64. 8°. Lond. 1867–8.
BERBRUGGER, A. Curso de Temas Franceses. 16°. Paris. 1825.
BERENDT, C. H. Analytical Alphabet for the Mexican and Central American Languages. 8°. N.Y. 1869

BERG, J. F. The Great Apostasy Identical with Papal Rome. 16°. Phil. 1847.
—— The Inquisition; A Sketch. (PC. 23.) 8°. Phil. 1851.
BERGERET, L. F. E. The Preventive Obstacle. 12°. N.Y. 1870.
BERKELEY, G. Works. Ed., with Memoir, by Fraser. 4 v. 8°. Oxford. 1871.
BERNARD, C. de. La Peau du Lion; la Chasse aux Amants. 12°. Paris. 1868.
BERNARD, F. Wonderful Escapes. 12°. N.Y. 1871.
BERNARD, J. Retrospections of the Stage. 2 v. in 1. 12°. Bost. 1832.
BERNARD, M. Neutrality of Great Britain during the American Civil War. 8°. Lond. 1870.
BERNARD, T. D. Progress of Doctrine in the New Testament. 12°. Bost. 1870.
BERNAYS' German Grammar. Ed. by Bokum. 16°. Phil. 1832.
BERNI, F. Orlando Innamorato. In Prose by Rose. 12°. Edin. 1823.
BERRI, D. G. Monograms, Historical and Practical. 8°. Lond. 1869.
BERRIAN, H. Catechism of the Ancient Schools. 18°. N.Y. 1867.
BERSIER, E. The Oneness of the Race. 12°. Lond. 1872.
BERTHET, E. Les Houilleurs de Polignies. 12°. Paris. n.d.
BERWICK, G. Forces of the Universe. 12°. Lond. 1870.
BESANT, W. and Palmer, E. H. Jerusalem, the City of Herod and Saladin. 12°. Lond. 1871.
BESANT, W. H. Notes on Roulettes and Glissettes. 8°. Cambr. (Eng.) 1870.
BESCHERELLE, N. ainé. Applications de la Géographie à l'Histoire. 2 v. 12°. Paris. 1845.
BESSON. Life of a Dominican Artist (Father Besson). 12°. Lond. 1870.
BEST of Everything. 12°. Phil. 1869.
BEST Reading; Hints on Selection of Books, with Classified Bibliography. 16°. N.Y. 1872.
BESWICK, S. Swedenborg Rite and Masonic Leaders. 12°. N.Y. 1870.
BEUGNOT, Count. Life. Ed. by Miss Yonge. 2 v. 8°. Lond. 1871.
BEULÉ, E. Le Drame du Vésuve. 8°. Paris. 1872.
—— Causeries sur l'Art. 2d ed. 12°. Paris. 1867.
BEVAN, E. The Honey Bee; its Natural History and Management. 12°. Lond. 1870.
BEWICK, T. Memoir by Himself. 8°. Lond. 1862.
BEWICK, W. Life and Letters. Ed. by Landseer. 2 v. 12°. Lond. 1871.
BÉZOUT, É. Differential and Integral Calculus. 8°. Cambr. 1824.
BHAVABUTI. Mahá-Virá-Charitá. Tr. by Pickford. 16°. Lond. 1871.
BIAGIOLI, G. Grammatica Francese. 8°. Paris. 1814.
—— Grammaire Italienne. 16°. Paris. 1822.
BIART, L. Adventures of a Young Naturalist in Mexico. 12°. N.Y. 1871.
—— Aventures d'un jeune Naturaliste. 12°. Paris. n.d.
—— Pile et Face. 16°. Paris. n.d.
—— La Terre Chaude. 12°. Paris. n.d.
—— La Terre Temperée. 12°. Paris. 1866.
BIBLE. Rheims and Douay Version. 12°. Dubl. 1852.
—— Vol. 1. Pts. 1–2; Gen.–Deut. With Commentary. Ed. by Cook. (*i.e.* "The Speaker's Commentary.") 2 v. 8°. Lond. 1871.
—— Psalms; Conant's Version. 8°. N.Y. 1870.
—— Psalms; New Translation. *See* DIDHAM.
—— Psalms: Transl. by W. Kay, D.D. 12°. Lond. 1871.
—— Hebrew Prophets. Tr. by R. Williams. 2 v. 8°. Lond. 1871.
—— Prophets during the Assyrian Empire; Version by R. Williams. 8°. Lond. 1866.
—— Daniel and the Minor Prophets; Ed. by Wordsworth. Sm. f°. Lond. 1871.
—— Greek Testament, with Vulgate. Ed. by Tregelles. 4°. Lond. n.d.
—— First Printed English New Testament. By Tyndale. Photo-lithographed Fac-simile. (Ed. by Arber). Sm. 4°. Lond. 1871.
—— Critical English New Testament. 8°. Lond. 1870.
—— New Testament; Noyes' Transl. 12°. Bost. 1870.
—— New Testament, in Spanish. 12°. N.Y. 1823.

BIBLE. Nuovo Testamento. (Version of Diodati, Revised by Rolandi.) 8°. Lond. 1819.
—— New Testament, in Danish. 16°. Lond. 1814.
——New Testament (Gospels and Acts); Notes by Warren. 8°. Bost. 1871.
——Galatians. New Transl. with Notes by J. H. Godwin. 12°. Lond. 1871.
—— Revelation, with Notes. *See* COWLES, H.
—— Apocrypha. Greek and English. Sm. 4°. Lond. 1871.
—— New Testament. The Suppressed Gospels and Epistles. 8°. Lond. 1863.
BIBLE Difficulties. 8°. Lond. 1869.
BIBLE (The) in Public Schools. *See* LIBRARY of Education, v. 5.
BIBLE (The) in the Public Schools. 8°. Cinc. 1870
BIBLE (The) Student. 16°. Lond. 1870.
—— Same. 1871.
BIBLE, G. W. Great European Conflict. (Franco-Prussian War.) 12°. N.Y. 1872.
BIBLICAL Repertory and Princeton Review. v. 41–3. 8°. N.Y. 1869–71.
BIBLIOTHECA Sacra. v. 26–8. 8°. Andover. 1869–70.
BIBRA, E. Von. Abenteuer eines Jungen Peruaners in Deutschland. 3 v. 8°. Jena. 1870.
—— El Paso de las Animas. 12°. Leip. 1870.
BICKERSTETH, E. Comforting Thoughts for the Weak and Weary. 12°. Lond. 1870.
—— Same. 12°. Lond. 1871.
—— Hades and Heaven; or Blessed Dead and Risen Saints. 16°. N.Y. 1869.
—— Two Brothers, and other Poems. 12°. N.Y. 1871.
—— Yesterday, To-day and Forever. 12°. N.Y. 1871.
—— Same. Sm. 4°. N.Y. 1871.
BICKNELL'S Village Builder. 4°. Troy. 1870.
—— Supplement. 4°. N.Y. n.d.
BICKMORE, A. S. Sketch of a Journey through the Interior of China. (Bound pamphlet.) 12°. Shanghai. 1867.
BIDDLE, D. The Spirit Controversy. 16°. Lond. 1869.
BIERBOWER, A. System of Philosophy. 16°. N. Y. 1870.
BIGELOW, J. Useful Arts. 2 v. 12°. N.Y. 1871.
BIGELOW, John. France and Hereditary Monarchy. 8°. Lond. 1871.
BIGELOW, L. J. Bench and Bar. 8°. N.Y. 1871.
BIGELOW, M. M. Life and Accident Insurance Cases. 8°. N.Y. 1871.
BIGELOW, T. Address, Opening of Williams' Hall. (PC. 7.) 8°. Bost. 1853.
BIGLAND, J. Study and Use of History. 12°. Phil. 1814.
BIGNANI, E. La Percée des Alpes. 12°. Paris. 1872.
BILL, L. History of the Bill Family. 8°. N.Y. 1867.
—— Minnesota; Climates for Invalids. 12°. N.Y. 1871.
—— Winter in Florida. 2d ed. 12°. N.Y. 1869.
BILLROTH, T. Surgical Pathology. Tr. by Hackley. 8°. N.Y. 1871.
BINGHAM, Capt. Journal of the Siege of Paris. 12°. Lond. 1871.
BINKERD, A. D. The Mammoth Cave. 8°. Cinc. 1869.
BINNEY, A. Helices of the U. S. 8°. Bost. 1837.
BINNS, W. Orthographic Projection; First and Second Courses. 2 v. 8°. Lond. 1868–9.
BIOGRAPHICAL Sketches and Anecdotes of Friends. 12°. Phil. 1871.
BIRCH, S. B. Constipated Bowels. 12°. Phil. 1868.
BIRCHALL, J. England under the Tudors. 12°. Lond. 1870.
BIRD, R. Physiological Essays. 8°. Lond. 1870.
BISHOP, J. P. First Book of the Law. 8°. Bost. 1868.
—— Law of Married Women. v. 1. 8°. Phil. 1871.
—— Thoughts for the Times. 8°. Bost. 1863.
BISHOP, N. Human Power in the Divine Life. 12°. Lond. 1871.
BISMARCK, Otto (Fürst von). Reden. 1ste Sammlung, 1862–6. 2d ed. 8°. Berlin. 1870.
—— Reden. 2te und 3te Sammlung. 1869–70. 8°. Berlin. 1869–70.
BISSET, A. Essays on Historical Truth. 8°. Lond. 1871.
—— Memoirs and Papers of Sir A. Mitchell. 2 v. 8°. Lond. 1850.

BITER (The) Bit; or Dana's Sun. 8°. Wash. 1870.

BITTER, A. Grüne Sträucher aus dem Schweizerland. 12°. Zurich. 1870.

BIZARRE. v. 1-6. R. 8°. Phil. 1852-5.

BIZET, P. Affaire Rossel. 8°. Paris. 1871.

BLACKBURN, H. Art in the Mountains. (Passion Play). Sm. 4°. Lond. 1870.

—— Normandy Picturesque. Sm. 4°. Lond. 1869.

BLACKBURN, W. M. Coligny and the Rise of the Huguenots. 2 v. 12°. Phil. 1869.

BLACKIE, J. S. Four Phases of Morals. 16°. Edin. 1871.

—— Musa Burschicosa. 18°. Edin. 1869.

—— War Songs of the Germans. 16°. Edin. 1870.

BLACKMORE, W. Colorado; its Resources, etc. 4°. Lond. 1869.

BLACKSTONE, W. Commentaries on the Laws of England. 4 v. 8°. Lond. 1829.

BLACKWOOD'S Edinburgh Magazine. v. 106-110. Lond. 1869-71.

BLADES, W. How to Tell a Caxton. 18°. Lond. 1870.

BLAIKIE, J. Among the Goths and Vandals. 8°. Lond. 1870.

BLAIR, D. Child's Book of Reading. 16°. Lond. 1806.

—— Grammar of Chemistry. 4th ed. 24°. Lond. 1810.

—— Grammar of Natural Philosophy. 15th ed. 24°. Lond. 1823.

—— Grammar of Philosophy. 15th ed. 18°. Lond. 1823.

BLAIR, H. Rhetoric, etc. 8°. Phil. n.d.

—— Rhetoric and Belles-Lettres. Ed. by Mills. 12°. N.Y. 1832.

BLAKE, Mrs. L. D. Woman Suffrage. (PC. 23.) 4°. n.p. 1871.

BLAKE, W. O. Slavery and the Slave Trade, Ancient and Modern. R. 8°. Columbus. 1860.

BLAKE, W. P. California Fossils and Shells. (PC. 11.) 8°. Wash. 1855.

BLAKEY, R. History of Political Literature. 2 v. 8°. Lond. 1855.

BLANDEAU, H. R. La Dictature de Gambetta. 12°. Paris. 1871.

BLANDFORD, G. F. Insanity and its Treatment. 12°. Edin. 1871.

—— Same. 12°. Phil. 1871.

BLANDIN, P. F. Anatomie du Corps Humain. 2d ed. 8°. Brussels. 1837.

BLANFORD, W. T. Geology and Zoology of Abyssinia. 8°. Lond. 1870.

BLANKENBURG, H. Der Deutsche Krieg von 1866. 8°. Leip. 1868.

BLEEK, J. F. Introduction to the New Testament. v. 1. 8°. Edin. 1869.

BLENKINSOP, E. L. Development in Bible and Church. 12°. Lond. 1869.

BLIND Harry. *See* HENRY the Minstrel.

BLISMON. *See* BLOCQUEL, S.

BLITZ, Signor. Fifty years in the Magic Circle. 12°. Hartford. 1871.

BLOCQUEL, S. Les Mille et Un Amusements. 18°. Paris. n.d.

BLOOD, Caleb. Thanksgiving Discourse, Aug. 6, 1863. 8°. Indianapolis. 1863.

BLOOR, A. J. Architectural and other Art Societies of Europe. 4°. N.Y. 1869.

BLOT, P. Hand-book of Practical Cookery. 12°. N.Y. 1871.

BLOXAM C. L. Chemistry, Inorganic and Organic. 12°. Lond. 1867.

—— Metals. 12°. Lond. 1870.

BLUMENBACH, J. F. Physiology. Transl. by Elliotson. 2d ed. 8°. Phil. 1817.

BLUNT, I. J. Reformation in England. 26th ed. 18°. Lond. n.d.

BLUNT, J. Discourse to N.Y. Hist. Society. 8°. N.Y. 1828.

BLUNT, J. H. Dictionary of Theology. R. 8°. Lond. 1870.

—— Household Theology. 16°. Lond. 1869.

—— Key to Christian Doctrine and Practice. 16°. Lond. 1871.

—— Plain Account of the English Bible. Sq. 12°. N.Y. 1870.

BOARDMAN, G. D. Addresses, Apr. 14, 16, 19, 1865. 8°. Phil. 1865.

BOARDMAN, H. A. Prelatical Doctrine of the Apostolical Succession Examined. 12°. Phil. 1844.

—— Discourse on D. Webster. 8°. Phil. 1852.

—— The Federal Judiciary; a Discourse. 8°. Phil. 1862.

BOARDMAN, W. E. Higher Christian Life. Am. Revised Ed. 12°. Bost. n.d.

BOBTAIL Gold Mining Co. Prospectus. (PC. 9.) 8°. N.Y. 1864.

BOCCACCIO, G. Decameron. French of Barbier. L. 8°. Paris. 1846.

BÖCKH, R. Der Deutschen Volkszahl und Sprachgebiet. 8°. Berlin. 1870.

BODENSTEDT, T. Aus deutschen Gauen. 12°. Jena. 1871.

BODENSTEDT, T. Vom Hofe Elisabeths und Jacobs. 12°. Jena. 1871.
BOETHIUS. *See* EARLY English Text Soc., Extra Series, No. V.
BOEUF, J. F. A. French Reader. 12°. N.Y. 1831.
—— Same; 3d ed. by de Billier. 16°. N.Y. 1836.
BOGART, W. H. Daniel Boone and the Hunters of Kentucky. 12°. Bost. 1869.
BOHN'S Hand-Book of Proverbs. 12°. Lond. 1867.
BOHN'S Hand-Book of Washington. 4th ed. 18°. Wash. n.d.
BOHN, H. G. Polyglot of Foreign Proverbs. 12°. Lond. 1867.
BOHURS, D. Life of St. Francis Xavier. 12°. Belfast. 1837.
BOILEAU, D. Nature and Genius of the German Language. 16°. Lond. 1843.
BOILEAU, N. Œuvres. 16°. Paris. 1862.
BOITARD, P. Le Jardin des Plantes. 4°. Paris. 1842.
BOKER, G. H. Konigsmark. 16°. Phil. 1869.
BOKUM, H. The Stranger's Gift. 12°. Bost. 1833.
BOLLAERT, W. Wars of Succession of Portugal and Spain. 2 v. 8°. Lond. 1870.
BOLLES, J. A. Essay on True Catholic Liberty. 8°. Bost. 1867.
—— Holy Matrimony. 16°. N.Y. 1870.
BOLMAR, A. Colloquial Phrases. 16°. N.Y. n.d.
—— Fables, with Key. 12°. Phil. 1829.
BÖLTE, A. Ein Thron und kein Geld. 2 v. 16°. Leip. 1869.
BOLTON, F. Telegraph Code. Ob. f°. Lond. 1871.
BOLUS, F. Synoptical Account of European Battles, 1800-69. 12°. Lond. 1870.
BONAR, A. A., and McCheyne, R. M. Mission to the Jews. 12°. Edin. 1845.
BONAR, H. Life of Rev. J. Milne. 12°. N.Y. 1870.
—— Light and Truth; or Bible Thoughts and Themes. 4 v. 12°. N.Y. 1870.
—— Light and Truth. Old Testament. 12°. Edin. 1868.
—— Life of Dr. Judson. 16°. Lond. 1871.
BONER, C. Memoirs and Letters. 2 v. 8°. Lond. 1871.
BONIE, T. La Cavalerie Française. 12°. Paris. 1871.
BONIFACE, A. Corrigé des Exercices Grammaticaux. 12°. Paris. 1833.
—— Dessin Linéaire. 4th ed. 2 v. Ob. 4°. Brussels. 1826.
—— Grammaire Française. 4th ed. 16°. Paris. 1834.
BONIFACE, Pope. Decretalia. Fo. Spire. 1481.
BONNEAU, H. Life of Mme. de Miramion. 12°. Lond. 1870.
BONNECHOSE, E. de. Bertrand du Guesclin. Tr. by Jeune. 16°. Lond. 1869.
BONNEFOUX, L. Extracts from Treatise on the Constitution. (PC. 2.) 8°. N.Y. 1863.
BONNER, J. Child's History of the U.S. 3 v. 16°. N.Y. 1868.
BONWICK, J. Curious Facts of Old Colonial Days. 12°. Lond. 1870.
—— Daily Life of the Tasmanians. 8°. Lond. 1870.
—— Last of the Tasmanians. 8°. Lond. 1870.
BONWICKE, J. Life of A. Bonwicke. 16°. Camb. (Eng.) 1870.
BOOK of Blunders. 16°. Phil. 1871.
BOOK of Table Talk. 18°. Lond. 1847.
BOOKWORM. Fourth Year. R. 8°. Lond. 1869.
BOONE, Anna B. Increase of Crime and its Cause. 12°. Bost. 1871.
BOOTH, A. Reign of Grace. 12°. N.Y. 1854.
BOOTH. A. J. Saint Simon and Saint Simonism. 8°. Lond. 1871.
—— Robert Owen, the Founder of Socialism in England. 12°. Lond. 1869.
BOOTH, (Edwin) in Twelve Dramatic Characters. f°. Bost. 1872.
BOOTH, J. The Lord's Supper. 12°. Lond. 1870.
BOOTH, R. R. Personal Forgiveness; a Sermon. 8°. N.Y. 1869.
BORCHARDT, A. Littérature Française pendant la Guerre 1870–1. 12°. Berlin. 1871.
BORDONE, (Le Général.) Garibaldi et l'Armée des Vosges. 8°. Paris. 1871.
BOREL d'Hauterive, A. F. J. Les Siéges de Paris. 12°. Paris 1871.

BORMANN, Gen. Shrapnell Shell. 8°. Brussels. 1859.

BÖRNE, L. Lichtstrahlen. 18°. Leip. 1870.

BORRAS, J. Lengua Castellana. 16°. Belfast. 1827.

BORREGO, A. Le Général Trochu devant l'Histoire. 12°. Paris. n.d.

BOSANQUET, C. Consoler and Sufferer: Sermons. 12°. Lond. 1870.

BOSANQUET, J. W. Messiah the Prince. 2d ed. 8°. Lond 1869.

BOSSANGE, H. Livres Grecs, Latins, etc. 8°. Paris. 1846.

BOSSUET, J. B. Unité de l'Église. 4°. Tours. 1862.

—— Discours sur l'Histoire Universelle. 2 v. 12°. Paris. 1811.

BOSSUT, l'Abbé. French Word-Book. 4th ed. Sq. 16°. Bost. 1836.

BOSTON. Report on Schools of N. Y., Phila., Balt. and Wash'n. 8°. Bost. 1867.

BOSTON Directory, 1870. 8°. Bost. 1870.

BOSTON Lectures, 1870; Christianity and Scepticism. 12°. Bost. 1870.

BOSTON Public Library. 17th, 18th and 19th Annual Reports. 8°. Bost. n.d.

BOSTON and Maine R. R.. Report of Investigating Committee. 8°. Bost. 1855.

BOSTON Miscellany of Literature and Fashion. Ed. by Nathan Hale. v. 1-2, Jan.-Dec. 1842. R. 8°. Bost. 1842.

BOSTON Submarine and Wrecking Circular. (PC. 13.) 8°. Bost. 1854.

BOSTWICK, H. Family Dentist. 18°. N.Y. 1835.

BOTTRELL, W. Traditions of West Cornwall. 8°. Penzance. 1870.

BOTTS, J. M. Speech on Washington's Birthday. (PC. 12.) 8°. N.Y. 1859.

BOUBÉE, N. Géologie Populaire. 24°. Paris. 1833.

BOUBÉE, P. I. Nouvelles Napolitaines. 12°. Naples. 1871.

BOUCHER, A. Histoire des Jésuites. 2 v. L. 8°. Paris. 1846.

BOULAINVILLIERS, H. de. La Vie de Mahomed. 2d ed. 16°. Amst. 1731.

BOULARD, A. M. H. Essai de Traductions de cinq Langues. 8°. Paris. 1802.

BOULIGNY, Mrs. M. E. P. Bubbles and Ballast. 12°. Balt. 1871.

BOULTBEE, T. P. Exposition of the 39 Articles. 12°. Lond. 1871.

BOURNE, G. Picture of Slavery in the United States. 18°. Middletown. 1834.

BOURNE, H. R. F. English Seamen under the Tudors. 2 v. 8°. Lond. 1868.

—— Famous London Merchants. 16°. Lond. 1869.

BOURNE, J. Improvements in the Steam Engine. 12°. Lond. 1869.

BOURNE, W. O. History of the Public School Society. 8°. N.Y. 1870.

BOUTELL, C. Bible Dictionary. 4°. Lond. 1871.

BOUTERWEK, F. History of Spanish Literature. 12°. Lond. 1847.

BOUTMY, E. Philosophie de l'Architecture en Grèce. 16°. Paris. 1870.

BOUTMY, E. et Ponelle. Encyclopédie Classique. 18°. Paris. 1830.

BOUTWELL, G. S. Address to Hillsborough Agr. and Mech. Society. (PC. 7.) 8°. Bost. 1859.

BOVEE, M. H. Christ and the Gallows. 12°. N.Y. 1870.

BOVET, F. Voyage en Terre Sainte. 12°. Paris. 1867.

BOWDEN, J. Letters to Dr. Miller. 2d Series. 12°. N.Y. 1831.

BOWDEN, J. E. Life and Letters of F. W. Faber. 8°. Balt. 1869.

BOWDISH, J. Poem before Montgomery Co. Agr. Soc. (PC. 2.) 8°. Alb. 1862.

BOWDITCH, H. I. Young Stethoscopist. 12°. N.Y. 1846.

BOWDITCH, H. L. Brief Plan for an Ambulance System. 8°. Bost. 1863.

BOWEN, E. Pictorial Sketch-Book of Pennsylvania. 8th ed. 8°. Phil. 1854.

BOWEN, F. Political Economy. 12°. N.Y. 1870.

BOWLES, T. G. The Defence of Paris. 8°. Lond. 1871.

BOWMAN, F. C., and Dana, C. A. Household Book of Songs. 4°. N.Y. 1871.

BOWMAN, J. E. Medical Chemistry. 12°. Phil. 1850.

BOWRING, L. Eastern Experiences. 8°. Lond. 1871.

BOX, T. Heat. 16°. Phil. 1869.

—— Practical Hydraulics. 2d ed. 12°. Lond. 1870.

BOYD, A. Lincoln Bibliography. R. 8°. Albany. 1870.

BOYD, A. K. H. Present Day Thoughts. 12°. Lond. 1871.
BOYD, J. R. Elements of Rhetoric and Criticism. 18°. N.Y. 1844.
BOYD, M. Reminiscences of Fifty Years. 12°. Lond. 1871.
BOYER, A. Complete French Master. 12°. Lond. 1794.
—— Dictionnaire Français-Anglais. Abrégé par Salmon. 8°. Paris. 1831.
BOYLE, E. Thistle Down; Poems. 12°. Phil. 1871.
BOYNTON, C. B. God's Hand in the War; a Sermon. 8°. Cinc. 1862.
BOYNTON, E. C. Register of Cadets, West Point. 16°. Wash. 1870.
BRACE, C. L. Best Method for Pauper and Vagrant Children. (PC. 1.) 8°. N.Y. 1859.
—— Manual of Ethnology. (Same as "Races of Men.") 12°. Lond. 1869.
BRACHVOGEL, A. E. Aus drei Jahrhunderten. 16°. Schwerin. 1870.
—— Beaumarchais. 2 v. 16°. Jena. 1865.
—— Benoni. 2 v. 16°. Leip. 1864.
—— Der Fliegende Holländer. 2 v. 12°. Berlin. 1871.
—— Glancarty. 2 v. 12°. Hanover. 1871.
—— Ludwig XIV. 2 v. 16°. Berlin. 1870.
—— Das Räthsel von Hildburghausen. 2 v. 12°. Hanover. 1871.
—— Schubart und Seine Zeitgenossen. 2 v. 12°. Leip. 1864.
—— Der Trödler. 16°. Leip. 1862.
BRADLEY, E. Rook's Garden. 12°. Lond. 1865.
BRADSTREET, Anne. Works. Ed. by Ellis. Imp. 8°. Charlestown. 1867.
BRADY, W. N. The Kedge Anchor. 18th ed. 8°. N.Y. 1872.
BRAINERD, D. S. Sermon. 25th Anniv. of Pastorate. 8°. N. Hav. 1867.
BRAINERD, M. Life of Rev. T. Brainerd. 12°. Phil. 1870.
BRAINERD, T. Patriotism aiding Piety; a Fast Sermon. 8°. Phil. 1863.
BRAITHWAITE'S Retrospect. v. 57-62. 12°. Lond. 1868-71.
—— Same. v. 57-62. 8°. N.Y. 1868-71.
BRAND, J. Popular Antiquities. 3 v. 12°. Lond. 1853.
BRASBRIDGE, J. Memoirs. 2d ed. 8°. Lond. 1824.
BRAUN, K. Bilder aus der Deutschen Kleinstaaterei. 2 v. 8°. Berlin. 1870.
BRAUN, K. Während des Kriegs. 8°. Leip. 1871.
BRAY, Mrs. Revolt of the Protestants of the Cevennes. 12°. Lond. 1870.
BRAYBROOK, E. W. Law of Industrial and Provident Societies. 16°. Lond. 1869.
BREBAN, J. Interest Tables. 12°. Phil. 1870.
BREESE, S. Origin and History of the Pacific Railroad. (1st Report in Congress in 1846.) 8°. Chicago. 1870.
BRÉHAT, A. de. Les Amours du Beau Gustave. 12°. Paris. 1867.
—— Le Bal de l'Opéra. 16°. Paris. 1870.
—— Les Chasseurs d'Hommes. 12°. Paris. 1867.
—— Les Chauffeurs Indiens. 12°. Paris. n.d.
—— Le Cousin aux Millions. 12°. Paris. 1870.
—— Deux Amis. 12°. Paris. 1870.
—— Un Drame á Trouville. 12°. Paris. 1869.
—— Les Maitresses du Diable. 16°. Paris. 1870.
—— Petits Romans. 12°. Paris. 1861.
—— Scènes de la Vie Contemporaine. 12°. Paris. 1858.
—— Le Testament de la Comtesse. 16°. Paris. 1868.
—— La Vengeance d'un Mulâtre. 12°. Paris. 1867.
BREMEN Lectures on Religious Questions. 12°. Bost. 1871.
BREMER, Frederika. Life, Letters and Posthumous Works. 12°. N.Y. 1869.
—— Life in the Old World. 2 v. 12°. Phil. n.d.
BRENNAN, E. Ambrosia Amoris. 16°. Lond. 1869.
BRENNECKE, W. Länder an der Untern Donau. 8°. Hanover. 1870.
BRENT, J. C. Life of Archbishop Carroll. 12°. Balt. 1843.
BRENTANO, L. History of Gilds and Trade-Unions. 8°. Lond. 1870.
BRENTS, J. A. Patriots and Guerrillas. 12°. N.Y. 1863.
BRESSE, M. Hydraulic Motors. Tr. by Mahan. 8°. N.Y. 1869.
BRETT, E. Notes on Yachts. 12°. Lond. 1869.

BRETT, E. Notes on Yachts. 16°. Lond. 1870.

BREUILLAC, G. Campagnes de la Loire et de la Sarthe. 12°. Niort. 1871.

BREWER, E. C. Dictionary of Phrase and Fable. 12°. Lond. n.d.

—— Poetical Chronology. 12°. Lond. n.d.

BREWER, T. Memoir of John Carpenter. 8°. Lond. 1856.

BREWER Directory. *See* BANGOR.

BRIDGEMAN, T. Fruit Cultivator's Manual. 12°. N.Y. 1847.

BRIDGMAN, C. D. W. Address, Obsequies of Col. Benedict. 8°. Alb. 1866.

BRIEF Comments on the Revised Speech of Mr. Lowe, Feb. 13, 1862. 8°. Lond. 1862.

BRIEF Review of "Considerations on Annexation of Boston and Charleston." (PC. 5.) 8°. Bost. 1854.

BRIGGS, J. P. Heathen and Holy Lands. 12°. Lond. 1859.

BRIGHTWELL, D. B. Concordance to Tennyson's Works. 8°. Lond. 1869.

BRILLAT-SAVARIN, A. Physiologie du Gout. 16°. Paris. 1869.

BRINCKLÉ, J. G. Poems. 16°. Phil. 1872.

BRINTON, D. G. Floridian Peninsula. 12°. Phil. 1859.

—— and Napheys, G. H. Personal Beauty. 12°. Springfield. 1870.

BRINTON, W. Food and Digestion. 12°. Lond. 1861.

BRISBANE, T. Early years of Alexander Smith. 16°. Lond. 1869.

BRISBANE, W. D. Ready Reckoner. 18°. N.Y. n.d.

BRISBIN, J. F. Belden, the White Chief. 12°. Cinc. 1870.

BRISSON, M. de. Ombres et Perspective. 8°. Brussels. 1827.

BRISTED, C. A. A Few Words of Warning on a Railroad in 5th Avenue. 8°. N.Y. 1863.

BRISTED, John. Oration on the Utility of Literary Establishments. 8°. N.Y. 1814.

BRITISH Almanac and Companion, 1870–2. 3 v. 16°. Lond. 1870–2.

BRITISH Association for the Advancement of Science. Reports, 38th, 39th, 40th and 41st Meetings. 4 v. 8°. Lond. 1869–72.

BRITISH Chess Association. Transactions, 1868 and 1869. 8°. Lond. 1870.

BRITISH Controversialist. v. 1–4. 16°. Lond. 1850–2.

BRITISH and Foreign Medico-Chirurgical Review. v. 43–48. 8°. Lond. 1869–71.

BRITISH Heroes and Worthies. Sm. 4°. Lond. n.d.

BRITISH Quarterly Review. v. 49–52. 8°. Lond. 1869–70.

BRITISH Statesmen. 16°. Lond. 1854.

BROADDUS, J. A. Preparation and Delivery of Sermons. 12°. Phil. 1871.

BROADSIDE for the Times. By E. Pluribus Unum. (PC. 20.) 16°. N.Y. 1861.

BROADWAY, 1869–71. 7 v. 8°. Lond. 1869–71.

BROADWAY Annual. 8°. Lond. n.d.

BROCK, Miss Sallie A. Richmond during the War. 12°. N.Y. 1867.

—— The Southern Amaranth. 8°. N.Y. 1869.

BROCK, Wm. Life of Sir H. Havelock. 16°. N.Y. 1869.

BROCKETT, L. P. The Year of Battles; Franco-German War of 1870–71. 8°. N.Y. 1871.

—— Paris under the Commune. 8°. N.Y. 1871.

BROCKLESBY, J. Amateur Microscopist. 12°. N.Y. 1871.

BROCKWAY, J., Sr. Lecture on Dentistry. 8°. Albany. 1869.

BRODHEAD, J. R. History of the State of New York. v. 2. 8°. N.Y. 1871.

BRODHURST, B. E. Deformities of the Human Body. 8°. Lond. 1871.

BROMBY, C. H. Letter to Mr. Lowe on the Education Code. 8°. Lond. 1861.

—— Revised Education Code. Letter to Earl Granville. 8°. Lond. 1861.

BRONSON Library. Catalogue. 8°. Waterbury. 1870.

BROOKE, Lord. Works. v. 1–2. *See* FULLER Worthies' Library, v. 11–12.

BROOKE, S. A. Christ in Modern Life. 12°. N. Y. 1872.

BROOKLINE, Jamaica Plain and West Roxbury Directory for 1871. 8°. Bost. 1871.

BROOKLYN Directory, 1870–71, 1871–2. 2 v. 8°. Brookl. 1870–71.

BROOKS, C. Statement on Ministers' Salaries. 8°. Bost. 1854.

BROOKS, C. T. Homage of the Arts. 16°. N.Y. n.d.

BROOKS, J. G. Poem, before the Phi Beta Kappa. (PC. 1.) 8°. N.Y. 1826.

BROOM, H., and Hadley, E. A. Commentaries on the Laws of England. 4v. 8°. Lond. 1869.

BROOM, W. W. Great and Grave Questions for American Politicians. 8°. N.Y. 1865.

BROTHERSON, J. Executor's and Administrator's Instructor. 16°. N.Y. 1829.

BROUGHAM, Henry (Lord). Life and Times by Himself. 3 v. 8°. Lond. 1871.

—— Same. 3 v. 12°. N.Y. 1871.

BROUGHAM, J. Po-ca-hon-tas. 16°. N.Y. n.d.

BROUGHTON, (Lord). Plates to Journey through Albania. 4°. Phil. 1817.

BROUSSAIS, F. J. V. Annales de la Médecine Physiologique. v. 1–12. 8°. Paris. 1822–7.

BROWN, D. P. Reply to Binney on Habeas Corpus. 2d ed. 8°. Phil. 1862.

BROWN, F. T. Sermon on Union Victories. 8°. Wash. 1863.

BROWN, Goold. English Grammar. 12°. N.Y. 1823.

—— Same. Ed. by Kiddle. 12°. N.Y. 1866.

BROWN, H. Shakspeare's Sonnets Solved. 8°. Lond. 1870.

BROWN, H. S. Defaulters. *See* AM. TRACT Soc. Tracts for Young Men.

BROWN, H. T. Mechanical Movements. Sm. 4°. N.Y. 1869.

BROWN, James. American Grammar. 2d ed. 18°. N.Y. 1823.

BROWN, James. The Forester. 3d ed. R. 8°. Edin. 1861.

BROWN, J. B. Christian Policy of Life. 12°. Lond. 1870.

—— First Principles of Ecclesiastical Truth. 8°. Lond. 1871.

—— Misread Passages of Scripture. 12°. Lond. 1871.

—— Sunday Afternoon. 12°. Lond. 1871.

BROWN, R. History of Cape Breton. 8°. Lond. 1869.

BROWN, Samuel G. Life of Choate. 2d ed. 12°. Bost. 1870.

BROWN, Solyman. Essay on American Poetry, with Poems. 12°. New Haven. 1818.

BROWN, T. A. History of the American Stage. 12°. N.Y. n.d.

BROWN, Wm. Wells. The Black Man. 12°. N.Y. 1863.

BROWNE, C. F. Artemus Ward's Panorama. 12°. N.Y. 1869.

—— Complete Works. 12°. Lond. n.d.

BROWNE, D. J. Elements of Geology. 18°. Bost. 1832.

BROWNE, J. Balfour. Medical Jurisprudence of Insanity. 8°. Lond. 1871.

BROWNE, J. R. Crusoe's Island. 12°. N.Y. 1867.

—— Whaling Cruise. 8°. N.Y. 1846.

BROWNE, W. Works. v. 2. Sm. 4°. Lond. n.d.

BROWNELL, H. H. Lyrics of a Day. 16°. N.Y. 1864.

BROWNELL, T. Documents in Case of. (PC. 7.) 8°. n.p. n.d.

BROWNING, R. Balaustion's Adventure. 16°. Bost. 1871.

—— Prince Hohenstiel Schwangau. 16°. Lond. 1871.

BROWNSON, O. A. Liberalism and the Church. 16°. N.Y. 1870.

BRUCE, A. B. The Training of the Twelve. 8°. Edin. 1871.

BRUNEL, I. Life of I. K. Brunel. 8°. Lond. 1870.

BRÜNNOW, F. Spherical Astronomy. 8°. N.Y. 1865.

BRUNSWICK Directory. *See* BATH.

BRUNTON, R. Compendium of Mechanics. 16°. Bost. 1830.

BRYANT and Stratton's Commercial Bookkeeping. 8°. N.Y. n.d.

BRYANT, A. Forest Trees for Shelter, Ornament and Profit. 12°. N.Y. 1871.

BRYANT, W. C. Letters from the East. 12°. N.Y. 1869.

—— (Ed'r.) Library of Poetry and Song. R. 8°. N.Y. 1871.

—— Poems. 2 v. 16°. N.Y. 1871.

—— Poems. Sm. 4°. N.Y. 1871.

—— The Song of the Sower. Sm. 4°. N.Y. 1870.

—— The Story of the Fountain. Sm. 4°. N.Y. 1872.

—— Thirty Poems. 16°. N.Y. 1871.

BRYDGES, E. Character of Byron. Sm. 8°. Lond. n.d.

—— Imaginative Biography. 2 v. 12°. Lond. 1834.

BUCHAN, A. Handy Book of Meteorology. 2d ed. 12°. Edin. 1868.

—— Introductory Text-Books of Meteorology. 12°. Edin. 1871.

BUCHANAN, G. History of Scotland. 3 v. 8°. Edin. 1821.

BUCHANAN, R Book of Orm. 12°. Lond. 1870.

—— Land of Lorne. 2 v. 12°. Lond. 1871.

—— Same. 12°. N.Y. 1871.

—— Napoleon Fallen: A Lyrical Drama. 12°. Lond. 1871.

BÜCHNER, L. Aus Natur und Wissenschaft. 8°. Leip. 1869.

——Die Stellung des Menschen. 16°. Leip. 1869–70.

BUCKINGHAM, Duke of. Rehearsal. *See* ARBER'S Reprints.

BUCKLAND, A. S. Diary of Nannette Dampier. 12°. Edin. 1870.

BUCKLAND, F. T. Curiosities of Natural History. 2d ser., 6th ed.; 3d ser., 2d ed. 2 v. 16°. Lond. 1867–8

BUCKLAND, W. Geology and Mineralogy. 4th ed. 2 v. 12°. and long 8°. Lond. 1869–70.

BUDDHAGHOSHA'S Parables. Trans. by Rogers. 8°. Lond. 1870.

BUDINGER, Dr. M. Abridged Bible. 8°. Lond. n.d.

BUFFALO Board of Trade. Constitution, etc. (PC. 11.) 12. Buff. 1845.

—— Trade and Commerce of Buffalo, 1869. 8°. Buff. 1870.

—— Same, for 1870. 8°. Buff. 1871.

BUFFALO Directory, 1870, 71. 2 v. 8°. Buff. 1870–1.

BUFFALO and N. Y. City Railroad Co. First Mortgage Bonds. (PC. 10.) 8°. N.Y. 1851.

BUFFUM, E. G. France, Germany and Switzerland. 12°. N.Y. 1869.

BUILDER (The). v. 27. Sm. f°. Lond. 1869.

BUILDING News and Engineering Journal. v. 16–20. Sm. f°. Lond. 1869–71.

BUISSONET, E. De Pékin à Shanghai. 12°. Paris. 1871.

BUIST, R. American Flower Garden Directory. 12°. N.Y. 1865.

BULFINCH, S. G. Evidences of Christianity. 12°. Bost. 1869.

BULKLEY, H. D. Address to N. Y. Co. Medical Societies. (PC. 12.) 8°. N.Y. 1861.

BULL, M. Answer to Reply to Defence of Experiments on Fuel. (PC. 2.) 8°. Phil. 1828.

BULLEN, G. The Story of Count Bismarck's Life. 12°. Lond. n.d.

BULLETIN de l'Ami des Arts. v. 1, 2. R. 8°. Paris. 1843–4.

BULLETIN des Lois de la Commune de Paris. 16°. Paris. 1871.

BULLIONS, A. Trial before Presbytery and Synod. 8°. N.Y. 1831.

BULLIONS, P. English Grammar. 12°. N.Y. 1843.

—— Same. 12°. N.Y. 1845.

—— Same. 12°. N.Y. 1849.

BULLOCK'S Quartz Crusher Co. Incorporation, etc. (PC. 9.) 8°. N.Y. 1856.

BULOS, A. Perspective, Dessin, Peinture et Gravure. 18°. Paris. 1825.

BULWER, H. L. Historical Characters. 12°. Lond. 1870.

—— Life of Palmerston. 2 v. 12°. Phil. 1871.

—— Same. 2 v. 8°. Lond. 1870.

BUND, L. Puck's Nightly Pranks. Tr. by Brooks. Sm. 4°. Bost. 1871.

BUNDY, J. M. Are we a Nation? 8°. N.Y. 1870.

BUNGAY, G. W. Temperance Anecdotes. 16°. N.Y. 1870.

BUNGENER, F. Rome and the Council. 12°. Edin. 1870.

—— Pape et Concile. 16°. Paris. 1870.

BUNKER Hill Monument Association. Annual Meeting, June 11, 1871. 8°. Bost. 1871.

BUNSEN, C. C. J. God in History. 3 v. 8°. Lond. 1870.

—— Hippolytus and His Age. 2d ed. 2 v. 8°. Lond. 1854.

—— Philosophy of Universal History. 2 v. 8°. Lond. 1854.

—— Prayers. Selected and transl. by Miss Winkworth. 16°. Lond. 1871.

BUNSEN, Baroness Frances. Freiherr C. C. J. von Bunsen. 3 v. 8°. Leip. 1868–71.

BUNYAN, J. Holy War. 8°. Lond. n.d.

—— Pilgrim's Progress (in Malay). 12°. n.p. 1854.

BURDETT, C. Life of Kit Carson. 12°. Phil. 1866.

BURGESS, G. The Swedenbergian Delusion; a Sermon. 16°. Hartf. 1870.

BURGESS, W. R. Relations of Language to Thought. 12°. Lond. 1869.
BURGH, A. Anecdotes of Music. 3 v. 12°. Lond. 1814.
BURGH, N. P. Modern Screw Propellers. 4°. Lond. 1869.
—— Link Motion and Expansion Gear. 4°. Lond. 1870.
—— Practical Treatise on the Condensation of Steam. Sm. 4°. Lond. 1871.
BURGON, J. W. The Last Twelve Verses of Mark, Vindicated against Critical Objections. 8°. Oxford. 1871.
—— Letters from Rome. 12°. Lond. 1862.
BURKE, B. Dormant and Extinct Peerages. R. 8°. Lond. 1866.
—— Peerage and Baronetage. 32d ed. R. 8°. Lond. 1870.
—— Same. 33d ed. R. 8°. Lond. 1871.
—— Royal Descents and Pedigrees of Founders' Kin. R. 8°. Lond. 1864.
BURKE. E. Speech on American Taxation, Apr. 19. 1774. 3d ed. 8°. N.Y. 1775.
BURLEIGH, W. H. Poems. 12°. N.Y. 1871.
BURLINGTON (Vt.) Directory for 1871–2. 16°. Burlington. 1871.
BURN, R. Rome and the Campagna. 4°. Cambr. (Eng.) 1871.
—— Stagnation of Trade. 8°. Manch. (Eng.) 1869.
BURNAND, F. C. More Happy Thoughts. 16°. Bost. 1871.
—— Out of Town. Sq. 16°. Lond. 1868.
BURNES, A. Journey to and Residence in Cabool. 2d ed. 8°. Lond. 1843.
BURNHAM, R. H. Burnham Family. 8°. Hartf. 1869.
BURNOUF, J. L. Méthode pour la Langue Grecque. 8°. Paris. 1830.
BURNS, Mrs. Eliza B. Self Instructor in Steno-Phonography. 12°. N.Y. 1870. Same. 1871.
—— Steno-Phonography, 12°. N.Y. 1870.
BURNS Anniversary. N. Y. Jan'y 25, 1870. (PC. 17.) 8°. N.Y. 1870.
BURNS, I. Life of Rev. W. C. Burns. 12°. N.Y. 1870.
BURR, C. C. History of the Union and the Constitution. 12°. N.Y. 1863.
—— Same. 12°. Hackensack. 1862.
BURR, E. F. Ad Fidem. 12°. Bost. 1871.
—— Ecce Cœlum. 12°. Bost. 1870.
—— Pater Mundi. v. 1. 12°. Bost. 1870.
BURRELL, A. B. Reminiscences of G. LaBar. 8°. Phil. 1870.
BURRITT, E. Prayers and Devotional Meditations from the Psalms. 12°. Lond. 1870.
—— Essays. 16°. Lond. 1869.
BURROUGHS, John. Wake-Robin. 16°. N.Y. 1871.
BURROWS, M. Constitutional Progress. 2d ed. 12°. Lond. 1872.
BURT, N. C. The Far East. 12°. Cinc. 1869.
BURTON, A. W. A Key to the Solar Compass. 16°. N.Y. 1871.
BURTON, J. H. History of Scotland. v. 5–7. 8°. Edin. 1870.
BURTON, R. Anatomy of Melancholy. 8°. Phil. 1868.
—— Anatomy of Melancholy. 3 v. 12°. N.Y. 1870.
BURTON, R. F. Battle-Fields of Paraguay. 8°. Lond. 1870.
—— Zanzibar. 2 v. 8°. Lond. 1872.
BURY, Lady C. Diary at Court of Geo. IV. 8°. Lond. 1839.
BUSCH, M. Geschichte des Mormonen. 12°. Leip. n.d.
BUSEY, S. C. Immigration, its Evils and Consequences. 12°. N.Y. n.d.
BUSH, R. J. Reindeers, Dogs, and Snow Shoes. 8°. N.Y. 1871.
BUSHNELL, H. Nature and the Supernatural. 12°. N.Y. 1870.
—— Women's Suffrage. 12°. N.Y. 1869.
BUSK, H. Steam Life Ships. Sm. 4°. Lond. 1870.
BUTLER, A. Lives of the Saints. v. 4. 8°. N.Y. 1862.
BUTLER, B. C. Lake George and Lake Champlain. 2d ed. 16°. N.Y. 1869.
BUTLER, B. F. Defence of Commodore Levy. 8°. N.Y. 1868.
BUTLER, C. M. Modern Necromancy; a Sermon. (PC. 7.) 8°. Wash. 1854.
BUTLER, D. P. The Lifting Cure. 8°. Bost. 1869.
BUTLER, F. Breeding, Training, Management, Diseases, etc., of Dogs. 12°. N.Y. 1865.
BUTLER, Jas. D. Address to Vermont Historical Society. 16°. Montpelier. 1846.
BUTLER, Josephine. Woman's Work and Woman's Culture. 8°. Lond. 1869.
BUTLER, T. B. Atmospheric System. 12°. Norwalk. 1870.

BUTLER, W. Land of the Veda (India). R. 8°. N.Y. 1872.
BUTLER, Wm. Allen. Lawyer and Client. 16°. N.Y. 1871.
—— Nothing to Wear. 16°. N.Y. 1866.
—— Poems. 16°. Bost. 1871.
BUTTS, I. R. Rights of Seamen. 12°. Bost. 1848.
BYFORD, W. H. Chronic Inflammation of Uterus. 8°. Phil. 1871.
—— Obstetrics. 8°. N.Y. 1870.
BYR, Robert. (pseudo.) *See* BAYER, C. R.
BYRON, Lord. Works. 8°. N.Y. 1872.
BYRON. True Story of Lord and Lady Byron. 16°. Lond. n.d.
BYRON. Vindication of Lady Byron. 8°. Lond. 1871.

CABEÇA DE VACA, A. N. Relation; trans. by Buckingham Smith. 4°. N.Y. 1871.
CABELL, Mrs. M. A. Sketches and Recollections of Lynchburg. 12°. Richm. 1858.
CABINET Maker's and Upholsterer's Companion. 16°. Phil. 1850.
CÆSAR, C. J. Commentaries; transl. (Bohn's ed.) 12°. Lond. 1868.
—— Commentaries; (Latin, ed. by Moberly.) 16°. Oxf. 1871.
—— Opera. Latin. Notes by Godwin and Clark. 8°. Phil. 1813.
CAHILL, Dr. Holy Eucharist; a Lecture. (PC. 7.) 8°. Alb. 1860.
CALDERON de la Barca, P. Three Dramas, with Transl. by MacCarthy. Sm. 4°. Dubl. 1870.
CALDWELL, G. C. Agricultural Chemical Analysis. 12°. N.Y. n.d.
CALDWELL, S. L. Discourse, Completion 1st Century of Warren Association. 8°. Prov. 1867.
CALIFORNIA. Geological Survey; Ornithology, v. 1, and Palæontology, v. 2. 2 v. 4°. n.p. 1870.
—— Catalogue of State Library. 2 v. 8°. Sacram. 1870–1.
—— State Normal School. Rules and Course of Study. (PC. 12.) 8°. Sacram. 1863.
—— Surveyor General's Report, 1867–9. 8°. Sacram. 1869.
CALIFORNIA Mail Bag, June 1871. 8° San Fr. 1871.
CALKINS, A. Opium and the Opium Appetite. 12°. Phil. 1870. Same, 1871.
CALCOTT, J. W. Musical Grammar. 16°. Bost. n.d.
CALLIÈRES, F. de. Art of Negotiating with Princes. 18°. Lond. 1716.
CALLINGHAM, J. Sign Writing and Glass Embossing. 12°. Lond. 1871.
—— Same 12°. Phil. 1871.
CALLIOPEAN Society. Constitution, etc. (PC. 20.) 12°. N.Y. 1829.
CAMBRIDGE Directory for 1871. 8°. Cambridge. 1871.
CAMERON, P. Directions for Reading the Hygrometer. 8°. Lond. 1868.
CAMOENS, L. de. Lusiad. Books 1–5. Transl. by Quillinan. 12°. Lond. 1853.
CAMPAGNE de 1870. Traduit du Times, par R. Allou. 12°. Paris. 1871.
CAMPAIGN (The) of 1870. Reprinted from the *Times*. 12°. Lond. 1871.
CAMPBELL, G. The Irish Land. 12°. Lond. 1869.
CAMPBELL, John, (Lord). Lives of Lyndhurst and Brougham. (v. 8 of the Lives of the Chancellors.) 8°. Lond. 1869.
CAMPBELL, J. R. How to See Norway. 12°. Lond. 1871.
CAMPBELL, R. The Law of Negligence. 8°. Lond. 1871.
CAMPBELL, T. H. Poetical Works, ed. by Rossetti. 12°. Lond. n.d.
CAMPIN, F. Principles and Construction of Machinery. 16°. Lond. n.d.
—— Construction of Iron Roofs. Sm. 4°. N. Y. 1868.
CANADIAN Illustrated News, v. 1–2. f°. Montreal. 1870.
CANONS of Good Breeding. 24°. Phil. 1839.
CANSICK, F. T. Epitaphs from the Church and Burial Grounds of St. Pancras, Middlesex. 12°. Lond. 1869.
CAPE of Good Hope Association. (PC. 20.) 12°. Cape Town. 1833.
CAPENDU, E. Comte de Saint Germain. 12°. Paris. 1865.
CAPOUE en Crimée. 2v. 16°. Paris. 1869.
CAPPER, J. The Duke of Edinburgh in Ceylon. Sm. 4°. Lond. 1871.
CAPPER, S. J. Wanderings in War Time. Journeys in France and Germany, 1870–1. 12°. Lond. 1871.
CARACCIOLO, Enrichetta. Mysteries of Neapolitan Conventa. 12°. Hartf. 1869.

CARDELL, W. S. Essay on Language. 12°. N.Y. 1825.

CAREW, T. Poems. Ed. by W. C. Hazlitt. Sm. 4°. n.p. 1870.

CAREY, H. C. Principles of Social Science. 3 v. 8°. Phil. 1868.

CAREY, M. Signs of the Times. (PC. 12.) 8°. n.p. 1831.

CARION, Franz. König August und sein Goldschmid. 12°. Leip. 1870.

CARL Pretzel's Vedder Brognostdikador, Almineck Kalinder, 1871. 8°. Chicago. 1871.

CARLETON, Wm. Traits and Stories of the Irish Peasantry. 12°. Lond. n.d.

CARLYLE, T. Choice of Books. 2d ed. 16°. Lond. n.d.

—— Cromwell's Letters and Speeches. 8°. Lond. 1870.

—— Essays. 6 v. 8°. Lond. 1869.

—— French Revolution. 3 v. 8°. Lond. 1869.

—— Heroes and Hero Worship. 8°. Lond. 1870.

—— Same. 16°. N.Y. 1872.

—— History of Friedrich II. 10 v. 8°. Lond. 1871.

—— Same. 3 v. 12°. N.Y. 1870.

—— Life of John Sterling. 8°. Lond. 1870.

—— Past and Present. 8°. Lond. 1870.

—— Sartor Resartus. 12°. N.Y. 1871.

CARNOTA, Conde da. The Marquis of Pombal. 2d ed. 8°. Lond. 1871.

CARPENTER, J. E. Public School Speaker and Reader. 12° Lond. 1869.

CARPENTER, W. B. Mechanical Philosophy. 12°. Lond. 1857.

CARPENTER, W. H. History of Massachusetts. 16°. Phil. 1865.

—— History of Tennessee. 16°. Phil. 1868.

CARPENTER, W. H. and Arthur, T. S. History of Connecticut. 16° Phil. 1865.

——History of Georgia. " " 1869.

—— " Illinois. " " 1869.

—— " Kentucky. " " 1860.

—— " New Jersey. " " 1865.

—— " New York. " " 1860.

—— " Ohio. " " 1865.

—— " Pennsylvania. " " 1869.

—— " Vermont. " " 1865.

—— " Virginia. " " 1865.

CARR, F. C. Hand-book of the Administrations of Great Britain, 1801–69. 16°. Lond. 1869.

CARRINGTON, H. B. The Hour, the Peril, etc.; an Address. (PC. 12.) 8°. Columbus, O. 1861.

CARTER, T. T. Devout Christian's Help. 2 v. 18°. Lond. 1870.

CARTWRIGHT, W. C. Gustave Bergenroth. 12°. Edin. 1870.

CARVER Centenary. (PC. 7.) 8°. St. Paul. 1867.

CARY, Alice. Lover's Diary. 16°. Bost. 1868.

CAS, Abbé. Nouveau Manuel Épistolaire. 16°. Paris. 1828.

CASES and Queries. (PC. 12.) 8°. N.Y. 1809.

CASEY, W. Gramatica Inglesa. 2d. ed. 8°. Lond. 1827.

CASPERS, A. The Footsteps of Christ. Trans. by Rodham. 12°. Edin. 1871.

CASSELL'S Illustrated History of England. 8 v. R. 8°. Lond. n.d.

CASSELL'S Illustrated Readings. 2 v. 4°. Lond. n.d.

CASSELL'S Magazine, v. 4, and new ser., v. 1–3. R. 8°. Lond. n.d.

CASSELL'S Popular Natural History. 2 v. Imp. 8°. Lond. n.d.

CASTELLANI, A. Gems. Trans. by Mrs. Brogden. 12°. Lond. 1871.

CASTLE, E. J. Law of Commerce in Time of War. 8°. Lond. 1870.

CASTLIN, Mrs. E. B. Autumn Dreams. 12°. N.Y. 1870.

CATALOGUE of MSS. and Relics in Washington's Headquarters. 8°. Newburgh. 1858.

CATECHISM of the Christian Faith. 12°. N.Y. 1811.

CATHCART, G. R. Youth's Speaker. 16°. N.Y. 1872.

CATHELINEAU (le Général). Le Corps Cathelineau pendant la Guerre. 2 v. 12°. Paris. 1871.

CATHOLIC World. v. 8.–13. 8°. N.Y. 1868–71.

CATLIN, G. Breath of Life. 8°. N.Y. 1869.

—— Lifted and Subsided Rocks of America. 12°. Lond. 1870.

——North American Indians. 2 v. 8°. Lond. 1857.

CATNACH (The) Press. A collection of the Books and Wood-cuts of James Catnach. 12°. Lond. n.d.

CATULLUS, Tibullus, etc.; trans. by Kelly. (Bohn's ed.) 12°. Lond. 1854.

—— Poems and Fragments; transl by Ellis. 16°. Lond. 1871.

CAUSES (Des) qui ont Amené la Capitulation de Sedan. 8°. Bruss. n.d.

CAUSES (Des) qui ont Amené les Désastres de l'Armée Française. 8°. Bruss. 1870.

CAUSTEN, J. H. Review of Pierce's French Spoliation Veto. 8°. n.p. n.d.

CAUVIN, J. Treasury of English and German. 12°. Edin. 1870.

CAVÉ, Mme. Color. 12°. N.Y. 1869.

—— Drawing. 12°. N.Y. 1868.

CAVERT, P. *Study of English.* 8°. Alb. 1866.

CELLARIUS. La Danse des Salons. 8°. Paris. 1847.

—— Drawing-Room Dances. 12°. Lond. 1847.

CELNART, Mme. E. F. Book of Politeness. 18°. Bost. 1833.

—— Jeux de Société. 3d ed. 24°. Paris. 1836.

CEMETERY of the Cypress Hills. (PC. 20.) 8°. N.Y. 1849.

CENTURY Association. Proceedings in honor of the Memory of G. C. Verplanck. 8°. N.Y. 1870.

CENTRAL PARK under Ring Leader Rule. (Reprint from Nat. Quar. Review.) 8°. N.Y. 1870.

CHABOT, C. and Twistleton, E. The Handwriting of Junius Professionally Investigated. R. 4°. Lond. 1871.

CHAFFERS, Wm. The Keramic Gallery. 2 v. 8°. Lond. 1872.

CHALLAMEL, A. Histoire Musée de la République Française. 3d ed. 2 v. R. 8°. Paris. 1857.

CHALLEN, H. Publisher's Uniform Trade List Directory, 1868; same, 1869. 2 v. R. 8°. Phil. 1868–9.

CHALLICE, A. E. Memories of French Palaces. 12°. Lond. 1871.

CHALUMEAU de Verneuil, F. T. A. Grammaire Espagnole. 2 v. 8°. Paris. 1821.

CHAMBAUD, L. Exercises in French. 19th ed. 12°. Lond. n.d.

—— Themes. François et Anglois. 8°. Lond. 1776.

CHAMBERLIN, F. American Commercial Law. 8°. Hartf. 1869.

CHAMBERS, W. France, its History and Revolutions. 12° Edin. 1871.

—— Memoir of Robert Chambers. 12°. N.Y. 1872.

—— Readings in English Literature. 12°. Phil. 1871.

—— Wintering at Mentone. 12°. Lond. 1852.

CHAMBERS' Journal for 1864–70. 7 v. R. 8°. Lond. 1864–70.

CHAMIER, F. France and the French. 2 v. 8°. Lond. 1852.

CHAMPFLEURY, J. F. Les Demoiselles Tourangeau. 16°. Paris. 1864.

CHAMPLIN, J. T. English Grammar. 16°. N.Y. 1850.

CHANDLER, P. W. Trial of Col. Henley. 16. Bost. n.d.

CHANGE for American Notes. 8°. N.Y. 1843.

CHANNING, W. E. Sermon. Ordination of Rev. F. A. Farley. 2d ed. 12°. Bost. 1828.

CHANNING, W. E. The Wanderer. 16°. Bost. 1871.

CHANZY, (Le Général). La Deuxième Armée de la Loire. 3d ed. Avec Atlas. 8°. and f°. Paris. 1871.

CHANUTE, O. and Morrison, G. The Kansas City Bridge. 4°. N.Y. 1870.

CHAPIN, E. H. The Crown of Thorns. 12°. Bost. n.d.

CHAPLIN, J. Life of Henry Dunster. 16°. Bost. 1872.

CHARETON, V. Projet Motivé de Réorganisation de l'État Militaire. 12°. Paris. 1871.

CHARLESTON Directory, 1869–70. 8°. Charleston. 1869.

CHARLESTON, S. C., Sketch of. *See* SOUTH CAROLINA Inst. Premium List.

CHARLESTOWN (The) Convent; its Destruction by a Mob. 8°. Bost. 1855.

CHARLESTOWN Directory, 1872. 8°. Charlestown. n.d.

CHARLESTOWN Public Library. Reports and Catalogues, 1862–70. 8°. Charlestown. 1863–70.

CHARLEVOIX, P. F. X. de. New France. Transl. by Shea. v. 4. L. 8°. N.Y. 1870.

CHARNOCK, R. S. Patronymica Cornu-Britannica. 12°. Lond. 1870.

CHARRIAUT, F. Lois et Décrets du Gouvernement Français. v. 1. 8°. Paris. 1871.

CHARTON, E. Voyageurs Anciens et Modernes. 3 v. Imp. 8°. Paris. 1854–6.
CHARZEAU, A. Methodical Syntax of French. 12°. N.Y. 1836.
CHASE, A. W. Dr. Chase's Recipes; or Information for Everybody. 12°. Ann Arbor. 1867.
CHASE, B. History of Old Chester. (New Hampshire). 8°. Auburn. N.H. 1869.
CHASE, E. Tables of Discount on British Sterling. Ob. 8°. Bost. 1830.
CHASE, S. P. Speeches in Ohio, Indianapolis and Baltimore, October, 1863. 8°. Wash. 1863.
CHASE, W. The American Crisis. 12°. Bost. 1862.
CHATEAUBRIAND, F. A. de. Œuvres. v. 4–20. 16°. Paris. 1833.
—— Œuvres Illustrées. 4°. Paris and N.Y. 1852.
—— Genius of Christianity. 8°. Balt. 1870.
CHATTERBOX (The). R. 4°. Lond. 1869–70–71.
CHATTERTON, T. Poetical Works. Essay by Skeat and Memoir by Bell. 2 v. 12°. Lond. 1871.
CHAUCER, G. On the Astrolabe. Ed. by Brae. 8°. Lond. 1870.
—— Canterbury Tales, *See* CHAUCER Society.
—— Prologue, Knight's Tale, etc. Ed. by Morris. 18°. Oxf. 1867.
—— Treatise on the Chylindre. *See* CHAUCER Society.
CHAUCER Society. Publications. [Unbound; not circulated.] 10 v. Ob. 4°. and 8°. Lond. 1868.

1st. Series:

I. Six-Text Print of Canterbury Tales, ed. by Furnivall, Pt. 1; Prologue and Knight's Tale.
II. Ellesmere MS of same.
III. Hengwrt " "
IV. Cambridge " "
V. Corpus " "
VI. Petworth " "
VII. Lansdowne " "

2nd. Series:

I. A. S. Ellis on Early English Pronunciation, Part 1.
II. Essays on Chaucer, Pt. 1; Ebert's Review of Sandras; Treatise on the Chylindre.
III. Temporary Preface to the Six-Text Canterbury Tales, by Furnivall.

CHAVASSE, P. H. Advice to a Mother. 12°. Phil. 1871.
—— Advice to a Wife. 16°. Phil. 1871.
—— Physical Training of Children. 8°. Phil. 1871.
—— Woman as a Wife and Mother. 12°. Phil. n.d.
CHECKLEY, J. Speech on his Tryal. 2d (*See* LESLIE, C. Short and Easie Method, 1723). 8°. Lond. 1738.
CHEEVER, G. B. Bible in Common Schools. 16°. N.Y. 1859.
—— Capital Punishment. 18°. N.Y. 1843.
—— Poets of America. 16°. N.Y. n.d.
—— Sermon to Foreign Missionary Society. 8°. N.Y. 1854.
CHEEVER, H. T. Fellowship with Churches or Individuals that Tolerate or Practice Slavery. 8°. N.Y. 1859.
CHENEY, Mrs. E. B. Nat the Navigator. (Life of Bowditch.) 16°. Bost. 1870.
CHENEY, Mrs. O. A. Sunday School Speaker. 12°. Bost. 1869.
CHENIER, L. S. Histoire de Maroc. 3 v. 8°. Paris. 1787.
CHERBULIEZ, V. Paul Meré. 12°. Paris. 1865.
—— Le Roman d'une Honnête Femme. 16°. Paris. 1870.
CHESEBROUGH, A. S. Christian Polities; a Fast Day Sermon. 8°. Hartf. 1863.
CHESNEY, F. R., and Reeve, H. Military Resources of Prussia and France. 12°. Lond. 1870.
CHESS Hand-book. By an Amateur. 16°. Phil. 1859.
CHESS Player. 16°. Bost. 1840.
CHESTER, G. J. Transatlantic Sketches. 12°. Lond. 1869.
CHESTERFIELD, Philip Stanhope (Lord). Letters to his Son. ed. with Memoir by Carey. 2 v. 12°. Lond. 1872.
CHEVALLIER, J. G. A. Le Conservateur de la Vue. 4th ed. 8°. Paris. 1820.
CHEVIGNI, M. de., and others. Science des Personnes du Cour. (lacks v. 6.) 17 v. 12°. Amst. 1752–7.
CHEVREUL, M. E. Laws of Contrast of Color. 16°. Lond. 1857.
—— Harmony and Contrast of Colors. 12°. Lond. 1860.

CHICAGO Board of Trade, 2d Annual Statement, for 1859. 8°. Chic. 1870.
CHICAGO Convention. Memorial for River and Harbor Improvements. L. 8°. N.Y. 1848.
CHICAGO Directory. 1870. 8°. Chic. 1870.
CHICAGO Relief and Aid Society. 1st Special Report. 8°. Chic. 1870.
CHICKERING, J. Population of Massachusetts. 8°. Bost. 1846.
CHILD, A. B. Plea for Farming and Farming Corporations. 12°. Bost. 1862.
CHILD, G. W. Essays on Physiological Subjects. 12°. Lond. 1869.
CHILD, Lydia M. Married Women. 16°. N.Y. 1871.
CHILD'S Hospital in New York, Remarks on. (PC. 12.) 8°. N.Y. 1852.
CHOUQUET, G. Conversations in French. 18°. N.Y. 1851.
—— Conversation and Dialogues. 16°. N.Y. 1870.
CHRIST the Consoler. 16°. Lond. 1872.
CHRISTIAN, G. J. Mécanique Industrielle. 4 vols. 4°. Paris. 1822–25.
CHRISTIAN Convention, Aurora, Ill., Oct., and Nov. 1867. Minutes. 12°. Chic. 1867.
CHRISTIAN Examiner, v. 86–7. 8°. N.Y. 1869.
CHRISTIAN Mother. 16°. Hartf. 1871.
CHRISTIAN Observer, 1868–70. 3 v. 8°. Lond. 1868–70.
CHRISTIAN Work. New ser., v. 3, 4. 8°. Lond. 1869–70.
CHRISTIAN Work on the Battle Field. 12°. Lond. 1870.
CHRISTIAN World. v. 22. 8°. N.Y. 1871.
CHRISTMAS Magazine Annuals, Broadway Belgravia, &c. 8°. v.p. 1870–71.
CHRISTIE, W. D. Life of Earl of Shaftesbury. 2 v. 12°. Lond. 1871.
CHURCH, G. E. Mexico; its Revolutions. 8°. N.Y. 1866.
CHURCH, P. Seed Truths. 12°. N.Y. 1871.
CHURCH, R. W. St. Anselm. 12°. Lond. 1871.
CHURCH of England, its Apostolical Foundations. By a Presbyter of Tennessee. 2d ed. 18°. Hartf. 1870.
CHURCHILL, F. and F. Jr. Diseases of Children. 3d ed. 12°. Lond. 1870.
CICERO, M. T. Opera. (Latin, variorum notes.) 22 v. 8°. Amsterdam. 1683–1761.
CICERO M. T. Cato Major, Lælius. Latin, Notes by Barker. 16°. Lond. 1818.
—— De Claris Oratoribus; vel Brutus. 8°. Oxf. 1716.
—— De Officiis. Latin, with French Version and Notes by DuBois. 16°. Paris. 1729.
—— Select Letters (Latin) with Notes, etc., by Watson. 8°. Oxf. 1870.
—— Orationes Selectæ. Ed. by Klotz. 16°. Leip. 1860.
—— Orations against Catiline. Tr. by Wilkins; Ed. by Halm. 16°. Lond. 1871.
—— De Oratore. Tr. by Calvert. 12°. Edin. 1870.
—— Select Orations (Latin). Notes by Anthon. 12°. N.Y. n.d.
—— Works; trans. (Bohn's ed.) 7 v. 12°. Lond. 1867.
CICERONE, (Le) de Versailles. 24°. Versailles. 1815.
CIMAROSA. Il Matrimonio Segreto. 16°. N.Y. 1834.
CINCINNATI Directory, 1870. 8°. Cinc. 1870.
CITY Library of Lowell. Catalogue. 8°. Lowell. 1861.
CIVIL Rights; the Hibernian Riot and Insurrection of the Capitalists. 8°. N.Y. 1871.
CIVIL Service of the U. S. [Reprint from N. A. Review of Oct. 1867.] 8°. Bost. 1867.
CLAIMS (The) of Labor. 16°. Lond. 1844.
CLAIRBOIS, E. de. Elements of Naval Architecture. 8°. Lond. 1846.
CLARETIE, J. La Débâcle. 12°. Paris. 1871.
—— L'Empire, les Bonaparte et la Cour. 12°. Paris. 1871.
—— La France Envahie. 12°. Paris. 1871.
—— Paris Assiégé. 12°. Paris. 1871.
CLARK, Alex'r. Christian Courage; a Sermon. 18°. Phil. 1862.
CLARK, B. F. Mirthfulness. 12°. Bost. 1870.
CLARK, David. The Way Rev. M. L. Scudder Secured a Cottage at Martha's Vineyard. 8°. Hartf. 1870.
CLARK, D. W. Anecdotes of Birds and Fishes. 16°. Cinc. 1856.
CLARK, E. History of 2d Company, 7th Regt. v. 1. 8°. N.Y. 1864.
CLARK, F. G. Our National Restoration; a Sermon. 8°. N.Y. 1862.

CLARK, F. L. G. Surgical Diagnosis. 8°. Lond. 1870.

CLARK, H. H. Address on Battle of Hubbardton. (PC. 1.) 8°. Rutland. 1859.

CLARK, J. Memoir of John Conolly, M. D. 12°. Lond. 1869.

CLARK, John. Second Book of Drawing. 16°. Edin. 1840.

—— Same. 16°. Edin. 1845.

CLARK, Joseph. History and Theory of Revolutions. (Reprint from Princeton Review.) 8°. Phil. 1862.

CLARK, L. and Sabine, R. Electrical Tables and Formulæ. 12°. Lond. 1871.

CLARK, R. W. Discourse, Obituary of H. Townsend, M. D. 8°. Albany. 1867.

CLARK, S. W. Grammar. 12°. N.Y. 1848.

CLARKE, A. Commentary on the Bible. 6 v. L. 8°. Lond. n.d.

CLARKE, E. D. Greece, Egypt, and Holy Land. 3 v. 16°. N.Y. 1814.

CLARKE, F. G. American Shipmaster's Guide. R. 8°. Bost. 1837.

CLARKE, G. R Campaign in Illinois in 1778–9. 8°. Cinc. 1869.

CLARKE, I. E. Oration, July 4, 1867. 8°. Bost. 1867.

CLARKE, J. F. Discourse: Aspects of the War. 8°. Bost. 1863.

—— Sermons; The Hour which Cometh, and now Is. 12°. Bost. 1868.

—— Steps of Belief. 16°. Bost. 1870.

—— Ten Great Religions. 12°. Bost. 1871.

CLARKE, L. L. Objects for the Microscope. 2d ed. 16°. Lond. 1863.

CLARKE, Mary R. Clytie and Zenobia; a Poem. 12°. N.Y. 1871.

CLARKE, R. W. Question of the Hour. 18°. Bost. 1870.

CLARKE, S. C. Clarke Descendants. 8°. Bost. 1869.

—— Curtis Descendants. 8°. Bost. 1869.

—— Fuller Descendants. 8°. Bost. 1869.

CLARKE, T. C. Account of the Iron Railway Bridge at Quincy, Illinois. 4°. N.Y. 1869.

CLARKSON, T. Portraiture of Quakerism. 8°. Indianapolis. 1870.

CLATER, F. Every man his own Cattle-doctor. 16°. Phil. 1844.

CLATER'S Cattle Doctor; rewritten by Armatage. 8°. Lond. 1870.

CLAY, C. M. Speech before the Law Department of the University of Albany, Feb. 3, 1863. 8°. N.Y. 1863.

CLAY, H. Private Correspondence. Ed. by Colton. 8°. Bost. 1856.

CLAYTON, J. M. Speech on Polk's Veto of the French Spoliation Bill. (PC. 12.) 8°. Phil. 1846.

CLAYTON, J. W. Scenes and Studies. 12°. Lond. 1870.

CLEASBY, R., and others. Icelandic-English Dictionary. Parts 1 & 2 (A to Rid) temporarily bound. 4°. Oxf. 1869–71.

CLEAVELAND, E. L. Discourse on Morals in New Haven. (PC. 22.) 8°. New Haven. 1850.

CLEF (La); Journal Politique. No. 1. 8°. Bruss. 1870.

CLEF de la Correspondance Commerciale, Anglaise et Française. 16°. Paris. 1825.

CLEMENS, S. L. Innocents Abroad. 8°. Hartf. 1869.

—— Mark Twain's Autobiography. 12°. N.Y. 1871.

—— Roughing It. 8°. Hartf. 1872.

CLEMENT, Clara E. Handbook of Legendary and Mythologic Art. 12°. N.Y. 1871.

CLEMENTINE Homilies. *See* ANTE-NICENE Christian Library, v. 17.

CLERC, L. Address before Governor and Legislature of Conn. (PC. 22.) 8°. Hart. 1818.

CLÈRE, J. Les Hommes de la Commune. 3d ed. 12°. Paris. 1871.

CLERGYMAN'S (The) Assistant in Reading the Liturgy. 12°. Phil. 1847.

CLERK'S Assistant. 8°. Poughk. 1805.

CLERVAL, G. de. Les Ballons pendant le Siége de Paris. 12°. Paris. 1871.

CLEVELAND, A. B. Studies in Poetry and Prose. 12°. Balt. 1832.

CLEVELAND, C. D. American Literature. 12°. Phil. n.d.

—— Classical Literature. 12°. Phil. 1869.

—— Compendium of Grecian Antiquities. 12°. Bost. 1831.

—— English Literature of 19th Century. 12°. Phil. 1869.

CLEVELAND Directory, 1870, 1871. 2 v. 8°. Clevel. 1870–1.

CLIFFE, J. H. Notes and Recollections of an Angler. 12°. Lond. n.d.

CLIFFORD, E. Fractional Arithmetic. 16°. Lond. 1842.

CLIFT, W. Tim Bunker Papers. 12°. N.Y. n.d.

CLIFTON and Dufriche-Desgenettes. Manual of Conversation. 16°. Paris. n.d.
CLIFTON Mining Co. Report, etc. (PC. 9.) 8°. N.Y. 1864.
CLINICAL Society of London. Transactions. v. 1-3. 8°. Lond. 1868-70.
CLINTON, H. L. Argument against the Excise Law of April 14, 1866. 8°. N.Y. 1866.
CLINTON Directory. *See* UTICA.
CLINTON, Walter. Sword and Pen; or English Worthies in the Reign of Elizabeth. 12°. N.Y. n.d.
CLISSOLD, A. Present State of Christendom. 8°. Lond. 1871.
—— The Prophetic Spirit. 8°. Lond. 1870.
CLODE, C. M. Military Forces of the Crown. 2 v. 8°. Lond. 1869.
CLOISTER Legends; or Convents and Monasteries in the Olden Time. 2d ed. 12°. Lon. 1871.
CLOUGH, A. H. Poems and Prose Remains. 2 v. 12°. Lond. 1869.
CLUTE Lead Mining Co. Organization, etc. (PC. 9.) 8°. N.Y. n.d.
CLYMER, M. Notes on the Nervous System. 8°. N.Y. 1870.
COAST Survey. Introduction, Explanatory, etc. (PC. 12.) n.p. 1858.
—— Reply to Official Defence. (PC. 3.) 8°. n.p. n.d.
COBBE, T. History of the Norman Kings of England. 8°. Lond. 1869.
COBBETT, W. Trial of, in King's Bench. (PC. 17.) 8°. N.Y. 1831.
—— and Perrin, J. Grammaire Anglaise. 12°. Paris. 1841.
COBBOLD, T. S. Entozoa. Imp. 8°. Lond. 1869.
COBDEN, R. Speeches. Ed. by Bright and Rogers. 2 v. 8°. Lond. 1870.
COCHRANE, A. B. Francis I. 2 v. 12°. Lond. 1870.
COCHRANE, J. Resurrection of the Dead. 12°. Edin. 1869.
COCKBURN, A. Nationality; or the Law relating to Subjects and Aliens considered with a View to Future Legislation. 8°. Lond. 1869.
COCKER, B. F. Christianity and Greek Philosophy. 12°. N.Y. 1870.
CODE of Health of School of Salernum. Ed. and trans. by Ordronaux. 12°. Phil. 1871.
COE, D. B. Family Record. 8°. N.Y. 1856.
COFFIN, C. C. Seat of Empire. 16°. Bost. 1870.
—— Four Years of Fighting. 8°. Lond. 1866.
COFFIN, J. Account of Slave Insurrections. 8°. N.Y. 1860.
COFFIN, J. H. Psychrometrical Table for Aqueous Vapor. (PC. 12.) 8°. Wash. 1856.
COFFIN, R. B. Castles in the Air. 12°. N.Y. 1871.
COGGESHALL, W. T. Protective Policy in Literature; a Discourse. 12°. Columb. 1859.
COHN, A. Shakspeare in Germany. Sm. 4°. Lond. 1865.
COHOES Directory. *See* TROY.
COILA's Whispers, by the Knight of Morar. Poems. Sq. 12°. Edin. 1869.
COIT, T. W. Lecture on Ecumenical Councils. 18°. Hartford. 1870.
COLBURN, J. Bibliography of Local History of Massachusetts. R. 8°. Bost. 1871.
COLBURN, Z. Locomotive Engineering and the Mechanism of Railways. 2 v. At. f°. Lond. 1871.
COLBURN's United Service Magazine, for 1869-70. 5 v. 8°. Lond. 1870.
COLEMAN, Mrs. C. Life of John Crittenden. 2 v. 8°. N.Y. 1871.
COLEMAN, J. Penn Pedigree. 8°. Lond. 1871.
COLEMAN, J. M. Job. Tr., with Notes. 4°. Lond. 1869.
COLEMAN, L. The Unpossessed Land; a Sermon. 8°. Bost. 1867.
COLENSO, J. W. New Bible Commentary Critically Examined. Part 1. 8°. Lond. 1871.
—— The Pentateuch and Joshua Critically Examined. Part VI. 8°. Lond. 1871.
—— The Pentateuch and Joshua Examined. 12°. N.Y. 1863.
COLERIDGE, D. Education of the People; a Letter. 3d ed. 8°. Lond. 1861.
COLERIDGE, H. Dictionary of Oldest Words in the English Language. 8°. Lond. 1862.
COLERIDGE, Sir J. T. Memoir of J. Keble. 3d ed. 12°. Oxf. 1870.
COLERIDGE, S. T. Biographia Literaria. 2 v. 12°. N.Y. 1848.

—— Same. 8°. N.Y. 1852.

COLERIDGE and his Writings. 8°. N.Y. 1844.

COLES, J. O. Deformities of the Mouth. 2d ed. 8°. Phil. 1870.

COLLECTION of Italian Colloquial Phrases. 24°. Phil. 1832.

COLLECTION of Old Ballads. 3 v. 8°. Lond. n.d.

COLLEGIAD (The): or Scraps from Sawney's Wallet. 16°. Lond. 1837.

COLLETTE, C. H. Reply to Cobbett's History of the Reformation in England and Ireland. 8°. Lond. 1869.

COLLIER, W. F. History of English Literature. 12°. Lond. 1863.

COLLINGWOOD, C. Rambles of a Naturalist in the China Sea. 8°. Lond. 1868.

COLLINS, C. W. Sophocles. 16°. Edin. 1871.

COLLINS, J. E. Private Book of Useful Alloys and Memoranda for Goldsmiths, etc. 16°. Lond. n.d.

COLLINS, Miss Jennie. Nature's Aristocracy. 12°. Bost. 1870.

COLLINS, M. The Secret of Long Life. 8°. Lond. 1871.

COLLINS, W. L. The Education Question. Revision a Necessity. 8°. Edin. 1862.

—— Homer; the Iliad. 18°. Edin. 1870.

—— Same. 16°. Phil. 1871.

—— Homer; the Odyssey. 16°. Edin. 1871.

—— Virgil. 16°. Phil. 1871.

COLLYER, Robert. Life That Now Is. 16°. Bost. 1871.

COLMAN, George. (The Younger.) Broad Grins, and other Humorous Works. With Life. 12°. Lond. n.d.

COLONIAL Adventures and Experiences. 12°. Lond. 1871.

COLTON, C. Junius Tracts. 12°. N.Y. 1844.

COLTON, W. Visit to Constantinople and Athens. 12°. N.Y. 1836.

COLUMBIA College. Inauguration of President Barnard, Oct. 3, 1864. 8°. N.Y. 1865.

COLUMBUS Directory, 1870. 8°. Columb. 1870.

COLVILE, F. L. Worthies of Warwickshire. Sm. 4°. Warwick. n.d.

COLVIN, V. A Bear Hunt in the Adirondacks. (Paper read before the Albany Inst.) 8°. Albany. 1870.

COLYER, V. Services by the Freed People to the U. S. Army. 8°. N.Y. 1864.

COMBE, A. Management of Infancy. 12°. N.Y. 1871.

COMFORT, G. F. German Course. 12°. N.Y. 1870.

—— German Reader. 12°. N.Y. 1871.

COMIC Almanack. By Cruikshank and others. 2d Series, 1844-53. 12°. Lond. n.d.

COMIC English Grammar. 12°. Lond. 1840.

COMMENTS of the Medical Press on Walsh vs. Sayre. 8°. N.Y. 1871.

COMMERCIAL and Financial Chronicle. v. 10. f°. N.Y. 1870.

COMMERCIAL and Financial Register. 8°. N.Y. 1870.

COMMERCIAL Laws of the States. 8°. N.Y. 1870.

COMMERCIAL Resources, etc., of British India. 8°. Lond. 1837.

COMMODIANUS. Writings. *See* ANTE-NICENE Christian Library, v. 18.

COMMON Prayer Book of Edward VI. Ed. by Walton & Goldsmith. 16°. Lond. 1869.

COMMON Sense. 8°. Phil. n.d.

COMPLETE (The) Governess. 8°. Lond. 1826.

COMPLETE Triumph of Moral Good over Evil. 12°. Lond. 1870.

COMPLICITY of Democracy with Treason in Ohio. (PC. 4.) 8°. Columbus. n.d.

COMTE, A. Positive Philosophy. 8°. N.Y. 1868.

COMTESSE (La.) de Monte Cristo. 8°. N.Y. 1868.

COMSTOCK, A. System of Elocution. 8th ed. 12°. Phil. 1846.

CONCORDANCE to Keble's Christian Year. 16°. Oxf. 1871.

CONDE, J. Historia de los Arabes en España. 3 v. 8°. Madrid. 1820–21.

CONDILLAC, E. B. de. Logic; transl. by Neef. 18°. Phil. 1809.

CONE, A., and Johns, W. R. Petrolia. 12°. N.Y. 1869.

CONE, S. W. Revenue Digest and Custom House Guide. 8°. N.Y. 1853.

CONFEDERATE States vs. J. H. Gilmer. Argument and Opinion. 8°. Richmond. 1862.

CONGDON, C. T. The Warning of War; a Poem. 8°. N.Y. 1862.

CONGREGATIONAL Church in Columbia, Ct. 150th Anniversary. 8° Hartf. 1867.

CONGREGATIONAL Quarterly. v. 9–13. 8°. Bost. 1867–71.

CONGREGATIONAL Review. 2d Ser. v.1–2, 1870–1. 8°. Chic. n.d.

CONGRESSIONAL Globe, 38th to 41st Congress inclusive, 1863 to 1871. 60 v. 4°. Wash. 1864–71.

—— Same, 42d Congress, 1st Sess. Parts 1 and 2. 2 v. 4°. Wash. 1871.

CONGRESSIONAL Directories. *See* U. S.

CONKLING, C. Slavery Abolished. 8°. Oberlin. 1862.

CONKLING, F. A. Remarks on the Promotion of Medical Science. (PC. 7; PC. 12.) 8°. Alb. 1854.

CONNAISSANCE des Tems, An. X (1802); 1834; additions for 1830. 3 v. R. 8°. Paris. 1799.

CONNECTICUT. Annual Report of the Board of Education. 8°. Hartf. 1866.

—— Colonial Records. 1706–16. Ed. by Hoadly. 8°. Hartf. 1870.

—— Gov. Buckingham's Message, with number of Drafted Men. 8°. N. Hav. 1862.

—— Reports of Superintendents of Common Schools, 1846–52; 1855–61; 1863–64. 16 v. 8°. N.H. & Hartf. v.d.

CONNECTICUT Common School Journal. 4 v. in 2. 4°. Hartf. 1838–42.

CONNECTICUT and Schuylkill Coal and Iron Co. Act of Incorporation. (PC. 21.) 8°. N. Lond. 1858.

CONNER, J. & Son. Specimens of Printing Types and Ornaments. 8°. N.Y. 1841.

—— Same. 8°. N.Y. 1850.

CONSCIENCE, Henri. Le Chemin de la Fortune. 16°. Paris. 1869.

CONSTITUTIONAL Law. Decisions on Taxation of Bank stock, etc. 8°. N.Y. 1863.

CONTRABANDS' Relief Commission of Cincinnati. Report on Vacated Territories. 8°. Cinc. 1863.

CONTEMPORARY Annals of Rome, 1st Ser. 12°. Lond. 1870.

CONTEMPORARY Review. v. 10–16. 8°. Lond. 1869–71.

CONVENTION (La) Boîteuse. 12°. Bruss. 1871.

CONVENTION of Loyal Leagues, Utica, May 26, 1863. Proceedings. 8°. N.Y. 1863.

CONVERSATIONS on Nature and Art. 12°. Phil. 1839.

CONWAY, E. H. Le Maître de Danse, 2d ed. 8°. N.Y. 1827.

CONWAY, M. D. The Earthward Pilgrimage. 12°. Lond. 1870.

—— East and West; Inaugural Discourse. (PC. 22.) 8°. Cinc. 1859.

CONWELL, R. H. Why and How; Chinese Emigration. 12°. Bost. 1870. Same. 1871.

CONYBEARE, W. T. Life of St. Paul. 8°. N.Y. 1870.

COOK, D. Art in England. 12°. Lond. 1869.

COOK, Eliza. Poetical Works. 12°. Phil. 1869.

COOK, J. T. Sermon on the Origin of the War. 8°. Geneseo, Ill. 1862.

COOKE, M. Hand-book of British Fungi. 2 v. 12°. Lond. 1871.

COOKE, S. Morals of Bethesda; a Sermon. (PC. 7.) 8°. N.Y. 1858.

COOPER, H. C. Thoughts in Verse. 8°. N.Y. 1870.

COOPER, J. W. Game Fowls. 8°. West Chester. n.d.

COOPER, S. Instructions for Militia. 16°. Phil. 1836.

COOPER, T. The Bridge of History over the Gulf of Time. 16°. Lond. 1871.

COOPER, T. T. Travels of a Pioneer of Commerce. 8°. Lond. 1871.

COOPER, W. M. History of the Rod in all Countries. 12°. Lond. n.d.

COOPER's Dictionary of Practical Surgery. v. 1. ed. by Lane. 8°. Lond. 1861.

COPINGER, W. A. Law of Copyright. 8°. Lond. 1870.

COPLESTON, R. S. Æschylus. 16°. Phil. 1871.

COPLEY, F. S. A Set of Alphabets, for Draughtsmen, etc. Obl. 8°. N.Y. 1870.

COPPERHEAD (The) Catechism. 16°. N.Y. 1864.

COQUEREL, A., fils. Libres Paroles d'un Assiégé. 12°. Paris. 1871.

CORD, W. H. Rights of Married Women. 8°. Phil. 1861.

COREAL, F. Voyages aux Indes Orientals; avec le Guiane de Raleigh, et le Voyage de Narbrough. 3 v. (v. 2 missing). 16°. Amst. 1722.

CORFIELD, W. H. Treatment and Utilisation of Sewage. 8°. Lond. n.d.

CORNHILL Magazine. v. 20–24. 8°. Lond. 1869–71.
CORNISH, G. J. Come to the Woods, and other Poems. 16°. Lond. 1869.
CORNISH, S. W. Waverley Manual; or Hand-Book of the Waverley Novels. 16°. Edin. 1871.
CORRESPONDENCE (On the) between the Governor (Andrew) and General Butler. (PC. 12.) 8°. Bost. 1862.
CORRESPONDENCE of Bishop of Conn. and Dr. Ewer, on the Sacraments. 8°. N.Y. 1870.
CORVIN, J. von. Life of Adventure; An Autobiography. 3 v. 12°. Lond. 1871.
—— Der Dräumling. 12°. Berlin. 1872.
—— Ein Frühling. 2d ed. 12°. Berlin. 1871.
—— Der Regenbogen. 2 v. in 1. 12°. Stuttgart. 1869.
CORWIN, E. T. Manual of the Reformed Church. 2d ed. 8°. N.Y. 1869.
COSSON, A. Trozos Selectos de Literatura. v. 1. 16°. N.Y. 1870.
COSMOS. v. 19. 8°. Paris.
COTHEAL, W. New Method of Keeping Accounts. (PC. 3.) 8°. N.Y. 1860.
COTTA, B. von. Ore Deposits. 8°. N.Y. 1870.
COTTER, J. R. Mass and Rubrics of Roman Catholic Clergy. 12°. Dublin. 1845.
COTTERILL, C. C., and Little, E. D. Ships and Sailors. 12°. Lond. 1868.
COTTON, Mrs. Memoir of Bishop Cotton. 8°. Lond. 1871.
COTTON, R. P. Phthisis and the Stethoscope. 4th ed. 18°. Lond. 1869.
COURSE des Sciences et des Arts. v. 2–13. 8°. Paris. 1808.
COURSE of Calisthenics. 18°. Hartf. 1831.
COURTENAY, E. H. Mechanics. 8°. N.Y. 1833.
COURTHOPE, W. J. Ludibria Lunæ; or, The Wars of the Women and the Gods. 12°. Lond. 1869.
COURTISANES du Second Empire. 8°. Bruss. 1871.
COUSIN, V. Mme. de Hautefort. 12°. Paris. 1868.
—— Psychology. 12°. N.Y. 1838.
—— Secret History of French Court. Tr. by Booth. 12°. N.Y. 1871.
COVELL, L. T. English Grammar. 12°. N.Y. 1852.
COWAN, J. The Science of a New Life. 8°. N.Y. 1871.
—— Use of Tobacco. Sq. 18°. N.Y. 1870.
COWAN, T. Sermons, Notes, etc. 16°. Lond. 1871.
COWDIN, E. C. Agriculture; an Address. (PC. 1.) 8°. N.Y. 1866.
—— France in 1870–1; an Address. 8°. N.Y. 1872.
—— Report on Silk and Silk Manufactures. Paris Exposition of 1867. 8°. Wash. 1868.
—— Tribute to Mr. Burlingame. 8°. N.Y. 1870.
COWIE, B. M. The Voice of God. 12°. Lond. n.d.
COWLES, H. Proverbs, Ecclesiastes, etc., with Notes. 12°. N.Y. 1870.
—— Revelation of John, with Notes. 12°. N.Y. n.d
COWLES, S. Conflict of Races; a Sermon. 8°. n.p. n.d.
COWPER, B. H. Syriac Miscellanies. 8°. Lond. 1861.
COWTAN, R. Memories of the British Museum. 8°. Lond. 1872.
COX, E. W. Spiritualism Answered by Science. 12°. N.Y. 1872.
COX, G. W. Mythology of the Aryan Nations. 2 v. 8°. Lond. 1870.
—— and Jones, E. H. Popular Romances of the Middle Ages. 12°. Lond. 1871.
COX, J. E. (Ed'r.) The Old Constitutions of the Freemasons. 8°. Lond. 1871.
COX, S. S. Eulogy on S. A. Douglas. (PC. 1.) 8°. Wash. 1862.
—— Search for Winter Sunbeams. 8°. N.Y. 1870.
CRABB, G. Synonyms. 8°. N.Y. 1820.
CRABBE, G. Tales. 2 v. 16°. Lond. 1820.
CRAFTS, J. M. Qualitative Analysis. 12°. N.Y. 1869.
CRAIK, D. Practical American Miller and Millwright. 8°. Phil. 1870.
CRAIK, Mrs. D. M. Fair France. 8°. Lond. 1871.
—— Same. 12°. N.Y. 1871.
CRAIK, J. The Church and the World. 16°. Louisville. 1871.
CRAMP, J. M. Baptist History. 12°. Lond. 1871.
CRAVEN, Mme. Augustus. Anne Severin. 12°. Paris. 1869.
—— Fleurange. 2d ed. 2 v. 12°. Paris. 1872.

CRAWFORD, T. J. Doctrine of Scripture on the Atonement. 8°. Edin. 1871.
CRAWFORD, W. Remarks on Chesterfield's Letters. 16°. Dubl. 1776.
CREAK, A. Dictionary to Cæsar's Gallic War. 12°. Lond. 1870.
CREAM of Tartar; a Lay of Alexis. Sm. 4°. N.Y. 1871.
CREAMER, D. Methodist Hymnology. 16°. N.Y. 1848.
CREASY, E. S. History of England. v. 2. 8°. Lond. 1870.
CREECY, J. R. Scenes in the South. 12°. Phil. 1860.
CRESSWELL, S. Secular Diary for Ascertaining any day of the week or month from 1601-1900. 18°. n.p. 1849.
CRISIS (The). 8°. N.Y. 1863.
CRITIC. v. 19. f°. Lond. 1859.
CRITIQUES Militaires. Par un Officier Inférieur. 12°. Paris. 1871.
CROFF, B. G. Model Suburban Architecture. f°. Saratoga. n.d.
CROKER, T. C. Fairy Legends. 12°. Lond. n.d.
CROOKES, W. Beet-Root Sugar. 12°. Lond. 1870.
—— Select Methods in Chemical Analysis. 12°. Lond. 1871.
CROSBY, D. Trial of, for Malpractice. 8°. Woodstock. (Vt.) 1854.
CROSBY, H. Jesus, his Life and Work. 8°. N.Y. 1871.
CROSS, L. True Masonic Chart. 16°. New Haven. 1824.
CROSSLÉ, C. Constitutional History of the Church, Briefly Examined. 12°. Lond. 1871.
CROZIER, O. R. L. The Fortress of the Rebellion. 2d ed. 16°. Grand Rapids. 1864.
CROWE, J. A. and Cavalcaselle, G. B. History of Painting in North Italy. 2 v. 8°. Lond. 1871.
CROWELL, M. The Counsellor. 16°. Ithaca. 1844.
CRUDEN, A. Concordance. Ed. by Youngman. Imp. 8°. Lond. 1868.
CRUIKSHANK, G. Table Book. Imp. 8°. Lond. 1869.
CRUISE Round the World of the Flying Squadron, 1869-70, under Admiral Hornby. 8°. Lond. 1871.
CRUTTENDEN, D. H. Systematic Arithmetic. 16°. Schenect. 1845.
CUBI I SOLER, M. English Translator (from Spanish). 12°. Cambr. 1828.
—— Latin Translator. 12°. Bost. 1829.
—— Le Traducteur François. 2d ed. 12°. Bost. 1828.
—— El Traductor Español. 12°. Balt. 1826.
CUBITT, J. Church Design for Congregations. 8°. Lond. 1870.
CULLEY, R. S. Hand-Book of Practical Telegraphy. 5th ed. 8°. Lond. 1871.
CULLUM, G. W. Graduates, etc., of West Point. 2 v. 8°. N.Y. 1868.
CULTIVATOR. v. 35. f°. Albany. 1870.
CUMMING, Gordon. Wild Men and Wild Beasts. 8°. Edin. 1871.
—— Same. 12°. N. Y. 1872.
CUMMING, J. The Cities of the Nations Fell. 12°. Lond. 1871.
—— Fall of Babylon Foreshadowed. 12°. Lond. 1870.
—— Lectures on the Parables. 12°. Lond. n.d.
—— Seventh Vial. 12°. Lond. 1870.
—— Same. 12°. N.Y. 1872.
CUMMING, R. G. Lion Hunter of South Africa. 6th ed. 12°. Lond. 1870.
CUNNINGHAM, A. Ancient Geography of India. Part 1st. Buddhist Period. 8°. Lond. 1871.
CUNNINGHAM, R. O. Natural History of the Strait of Magellan. 12°. Edin. 1871.
CUPS and their Customs. 2d ed. 12°. Lond. 1869.
CURIOSITIES of Entomology. 8°. Lond. n.d.
CURIOSITIES of Ornithology. 8°. Lond. n.d.
CURRIE, R. O. Sermon Commemorative of Rev. G. A. Shelton. 8°. N.Y. 1865.
CURTIS, G. T. Life of Daniel Webster. v. 1, 2. 8°. N.Y. 1870.
CURTIUS, E. Elucidation of the Student's Greek Grammar. 12°. Lond. 1870.
—— History of Greece. v. 3. 8°. Lond. 1870.
—— Same. v. 1-3. 12°. N.Y. 1871-2.
CURWEN, H. Echoes from the French Poets. 18°. Lond. 1870.
CUSACK, M. F. History of the Kingdom of Kerry. 8°. Lond. 1871.
—— Student's Manual of Irish History. 12°. Lond. 1870.

CUSHING, L. Parliamentary Manual. 18°. Bost. 1870.
CUST, E. Lives of the Warriors, 1648–1704. 2 v. 12°. Lond. 1869.
CUSTOMS and Manners of the Bedouins. 18°. n.p. n.d.
CUTLER, J. Laws of Naturalization. 16°. Lond. 1871.
CUTTER, C. Analytic Anatomy, Physiology and Hygiene. 12°. Phil. 1871.
CUVILLIER-Fleury, A. A. Nouvelles Études Historiques et Littéraires. 12°. Paris. 1855.
CUYLER, T. L. Discourse for City Missions. (PC. 7; PC. 12.) 8°. N.Y. 1854.
—— The Empty Crib. 16°. N.Y. 1869.
DABNEY, R. L. Sacred Rhetoric. 12°. Richm. 1870.
DADMUN, J. W. Revival Melodies. 8°. Bost. 1858.
DAHEIM. v. 7. 4°. Leip. 1871.
DAHLGREN, J. A. Memoir of Ulric Dahlgren. 12. Phil. 1871.
DAILY News, 1869–70. 4 v. At. f°. Lond. 1869–70.
DAKE, O. C. Nebraska Legends and Poems. 12. N.Y. 1871.
DALE, R. W. Jewish Temple and Christian Church. 12°. Lond. 1871.
—— Ten Commandments. 12°. Lond. 1871.
DALE, T. P. A Life's Motto. 16°. N.Y. n.d.
DALL, W. H. Alaska and its Resources. R. 8°. Bost. 1870.
DALLAS, G. M. Letters from London. 8°. Phil. 1869.
—— Life and Writings of A. J. Dallas. 8°. Phil. 1871.
DALSÈME, A. J. Paris pendant le Siége et les 65 Jours de la Commune. 12°. Paris. 1871.
DALTON, H. Jr. Address, Coll. of Phys. and Surgeons, 1855. (PC. 13.) 8°. N.Y. 1855.
—— Same, 1860. (PC. 13.) 8°. N.Y. 1860.
DALTON, H. Reisebilder aus dem Orient. Sm. 4°. St. Petersb. 1871.
DALTON, J. C. Human Physiology. 8°. Phil. 1867.
DALY, C. P. G. C. Verplanck; an Address. 8°. N.Y. 1870.
DANA, C. A. Household Book of Poetry. 11th ed. R. 8°. N.Y. 1872.
DANA, James. Sermon preached at his Installation. 12°. New Haven. 1789.
DANA, R. H. Jr. Enemy's Territory and Alien Enemies. 8°. Bost. 1864.
—— Two Years before the Mast. New ed. 16°. Bost. 1869.
DANA. Reminiscences of S. H. Dana. 12°. Bost. 1856.
DANN, T. J. and GONZALEZ, G. Spanish Commercial Correspondent. 8°. Lond. 1871.
DANTE Alighieri. Divina Commedia. Tr. by Ford. 12°. Lond. 1870.
—— Divine Comedy. Tr. by Longfellow. 12°. Bost. 1871.
DA PONTE, L. Dramme, con Memorie. 18°. N.Y. 1826.
—— History of Florence. 2 v. 12°. N. Y. 1833.
DARBY, John. Odd Hours of a Physician. 12°. Phil. 1871.
DARK Blue. v. 1. 1871. 8°. Lond. n.d.
DARLING, J. Encyclopædia Bibliographica. Subjects: Holy Scriptures. R. 8°. Lond. 1859.
DARLING, W. A. New York Tax Book. 8°. N.Y. 1851.
DARWIN, C. Descent of Man. 2 v. 12°. Lond. 1871.
—— Same. 2 v. 12°. N.Y. 1871.
—— Journal of Researches into Natural History and Geology during Voyage of the Beagle. New ed. 12°. N.Y. 1871.
—— Origin of Species. 12°. N.Y. 1870.
—— Entstehung der Arten. 8°. Stuttg. 1870.
DASHWOOD, R. L. Chiploquorgan; or, Life by the Camp Fire in Canada and Newfoundland. Sq. 12°. Dubl. 1871.
DAUDET, A. Lettres de mon Moulin. 12°. Paris. n.d.
DAUDET, E. L'Agonie de la Commune. 12°. Paris. 1871.
—— Duperies de l'Amour. 16.° Paris. 1865.
—— Roman d'une jeune Fille. 12°. Paris. 1869.
DAVANZATI, B. Scisma d'Inghilterra, etc. 8°. Milan. 1807.
DAVENANT, S. What Shall My Son be? 12°. Lond. n.d.
DAVENPORT Directory, 1870–1. 8°. Davenport. 1871.

DAVIDSON, I. Introduction to the Old Testament. 3 v. 8°. Lond. 1862–3.
DAVIDSON, J. W. Living Writers of the South. 12°. N.Y. 1869.
DAVIDSON, Lucretia M. Poems. 12°. N.Y. 1871.
DAVIES, A. M. Meteoric Theory of Saturn's Rings. 8°. Lond. 1871.
DAVIES, C. Descriptive Geometry. 8°. N.Y. 1832.
—— Elements of Surveying and Leveling. 12°. N.Y. 1871.
—— Legendre's Geometry and Trigonometry. 8°. N.Y. 1869.
—— Logic of Mathematics. 12°. N.Y. 1869.
—— The Metric System. 12°. N.Y. 1871.
DAVIES, G. C. Songs of the Church. 12°. N.Y. 1859.
DAVIES, J. History and Literature of the Stuart Period. 16°. Lond. 1871.
DAVIES, Sir J. Poems. *See* FULLER Worthies' Library, v. 4.
DAVIES, T. A. How to Make Money. 12°. N.Y. 1870.
DAVIS, A. Antiquities of Central America and Discovery of America by the Northmen. 8°. Buffalo. 1842.
DAVIS, A. J. Death and the After Life. 16°. N.Y. 1866.
—— The Fountain, with Jets of New Meaning. 16°. Bost. 1870.
—— Great Harmonia. 5 v. 12°. Bost. 1868.
—— Mental Disorders. 12°. N.Y. 1871.
DAVIS, C. H. S. History of Wallingford and Meriden. 8°. Meriden. 1870.
DAVIS, E. A. Collection Laws of Indiana. 2d ed. 8°. Indianapolis. 1868.
DAVIS, J. G. Historical Discourse to Hollis Association. 8°. Concord. 1862.
DAVIS, R. B. Poems, with Life. 12°. N.Y. 1807.
DAVIS, T. T. Eulogy on Edward Everett. 8°. Syracuse. 1865.
DAVISON, G. M. Traveler's Guide. 18°. Saratoga. 1837.
DAVY, H. Salmonia. 5th ed. 16°. Lond. 1869.
DAVYS, G. Short History of England. 16°. Lond. 1870.
DAWES, Mrs. S. E. Light from The Star of Bethlehem. 12°. Bost. 1870.
DAWSON, C. Musical Composition. 16°. Lond. 1845.
DAWSON. H. B. Current Fictions, etc. (Jay and Dawson Correspondence). 8°. N.Y. 1864.
DAY, B. H. American Ready Reckoner. 12°. N.Y. n.d.
DAY, St. J. V. Great Pyramid. 8°. Edin. 1870.
DAYTON, W. L. Address to Am. Whig and Cliosophic Societies. (PC. 13.) 8°. Princeton. 1843.
DEAN, A. History of Civilization. 6 v. 8°. Alb. 1868–9.
DEAN, G. A. Fallacies and Tendencies of the Age. 12°. Lond. 1871.
DEAN, J. W. History of N. E. Hist.-Genealogical Register. (PC. 13.) 8°. Bost. 1863.
—— Memoir of Rev. M. Wigglesworth. 2d ed. 8°. Albany. 1871.
DEAN, N. Proceedings of Croton Department at death of Mr. Dean. 8°. N.Y. 1856.
DEAN, S. The War, etc.; a Sermon. 8°. Prov. 1862.
DEANE, J. B. Life of Richard Deane. 8°. Lond. 1870.
DEBOW'S Review, 1868–9. 3 v. 8°. N.Orl. 1868–9.
DEBRETT'S Illustrated Baronetage for 1870. 12°. Lond. 1871.
—— Illustrated Peerage for 1870. 12°. Lond. 1871.
DEBRIT, M. La Guerre de 1870. 12°. Geneva. 1871.
DEBURTON, A. Ten Months' Tour in the East. 12°. Lond. 1870.
DECOSTA, B. F. Northmen in Maine. 8°. Albany. 1870.
—— Rambles in Mt. Desert. 16°. N.Y. 1871.
—— Sailing Directions of Henry Hudson. 8°. Alb. 1869.
DECREMPS, M. La Magie Blanche Devoilée, etc. 5 v. 8°. Paris. 1788.
DEDENROTH, E. H. von. Die Geliebte des Prinzen. 16°. Berlin. n.d.
DEEDES, H. South and West. 16°. Edin 1869.
DEEMS, C. F. Jesus. 8°. N.Y. 1872.
—— Sermons. R. 8°. N.Y. 1872.
—— What Now? 16°. N.Y. 1869.
—— (and Carey, Phœbe. Hymns for all Christians. 18°. N.Y. 1869.
DEERFIELD Directory. *See* UTICA.
DEERING, T. W. Temperance. Sq. 18°. N.Y. 1870.

DÉGRANGE, E. La Tenue des Livres. 8°. Paris. 1802.

DEGRANGE, E. Teneduria de Libros. 8°. Bourdeaux. 1826.

DEKAY, J. E. Address on Natural Sciences. 8°. N.Y. 1826.

DELAFIELD, R. Foundations in Compressible Soils. 8°. Wash. 1868.

DELAITRE. Manuel de l' Architecte et de l'Ingénieur. 24°. Paris. 1825.

DELAMOTTE, P. St. Sketching from Nature. 4°. Lond. 1871.

DE LA SALLE Monthly. v. 1-4. 8°. N.Y. 1869-71.

DELAUNAY, F. Histoire de la Campagne de France, 1870-1. 8°. Paris. 1871.

DELAVOYE, J. G. Catechism of French Grammar. 24°. Lond. 1825.

DELEVANTE, E. R. Orthoepy and Orthography of English. 12°. Lond. 1869.

DELIGNY, E. L'Héritage d'un Banquier. 12°. Paris. 1867.

—— Secret de M. Boisonnange. 12°. Paris. 1870.

—— Le Talisman de Robert Nels. 12°. Paris. 1871.

DELITZSCH, F. Commentaries on Hebrews. v. 2. 8°. Edin. 1870.

—— Commentary on Psalms. v. 1-2. v. 2. 8°. Edin. 1871.

DELLEY de Blancmesnil, Comte de. M. le Comte de Bismarck. 8°. Brussels. 1871.

DELMAR, A. The National Banks. (PC. 3.) 8°. N.Y. 1865.

DEL MAR, E. Spanish Grammar. 16°. N.Y. 1826.

DELMAS, É. De Froeschwiller à Paris. 12°. Paris. 1871.

DE MAN, E. F. The Beet Root Sugar Question. 8°. Lond. 1871.

DEMAUS, R. Hugh Latimer. 12°. Lond. n.d.

DEMERSON, J. L. Les Mille Récréations de Société. 18°. Bruss. 1830.

DEMMIN, A. Weapons of War. Transl. by Black. 12°. Lond. 1870.

DEMOCRATIC National Convention, Baltimore, June 1852. Proceedings. 8°. Wash. 1852.

DEMONFERRAND, J. F. Manuel d'Electricité. 8°. Paris. 1823.

DEMOREST'S Monthly. v. 6-7. 4°. N.Y. 1869-70.

DEMOREST'S Young America. v. 4-5. 12°. N.Y. 1869-70.

DEMOSTHENES. Orations. Transl. by Kennedy. (Bohn's ed.) 5 v. 12°. Lond. 1866-69.

—— Oration on the Crown. Transl. by Brandt. 12°. Lond. 1870.

DEMPSEY, J. M. Our Ocean Highways. 12°. Lond. 1870.

—— and Hughes, W. Same. 12°. Lond. 1871.

DENIS, J. Théories et Idées Morales dans l'Antiquité. 2 v. 8°. Paris. 1856.

DENISON, E. Letters and other Writings. 8°. Lond. 1872.

DENISON, E. B. Astronomy without Mathematics. 12°. N.Y. 1869.

DENISON, W. Varieties of Vice-Regal Life. 2 v. 8°. Lond. 1870.

DENSLOW, V. B. Fremont and McClellan, their Political and Military Careers Reviewed. 2d ed. 8°. Yonkers. 1862.

DENT, E. J. The Dipleidoscope. 5th ed. 8°. Lond. 1850.

DENTON, W. Commentary on Epistles for Sundays, etc. 2 v. 8°. Lond. 1869-71.

DENTON, W. Radical Rhymes. 12°. Bost. 1871.

DE PEYSTER, J. W. History of General Kearney. 8°. N.Y. 1869.

DEPPING, G. Wonders of Bodily Strength and Skill. 16°. N.Y. 1870.

DE QUETTEVILLE, P. W. Pardon of Guingamp. 12°. Lond. 1870.

DE QUINCEY, T. Logic of Political Economy. 8°. Edin. 1844.

DE ROOS, F. F. Travels in U. S. and Canada. 3d ed. 8°. Lond. 1827.

DESCARTES, R. Opera Philosophica. 2d ed. Sm. 4°. Amst. 1650.

DESCHANEL, A. P. Natural Philosophy; Pt. 1. 8°. Lond. 1870.

DESPRETZ, C. Traité Élémentaire de Physique. R. 8°. Bruss. 1837.

DESPREZ, P. S. John; or, The Apocalypse. 12°. Lond. 1870.

DESTRUCTION of Troy. *See* EARLY Eng. Text Society, No. 39.

DETROIT. Board of Education. 28th An. Rep. for 1870. 8°. Detr. 1871.

DETROIT. Directory, 1870, 1871-2. 2 v. 8°. Detroit. 1870-1.

DETROIT Young Men's Society. Catalogue of Library. 8°. Detroit. 1859.

DEUS Semper. 12°. Phil. 1869.
DEUTSCHE Ausstellungs-Zeitung. Nos. 1–73. f°. Paris. 1869.
DEUTSCHER Novellenschatz. Herausgegeben von Heyse und Kurz. 6 v. 12°. Munich. n.d.
DE VERE, Mary A. Love Songs, etc. sq. 16°. N.Y. 1870.
DE VERE, M. S. Americanisms. 12°. N.Y. 1871.
—— The Great Empress. 12°. Phil. 1870.
—— Leaves from the Book of Nature. 12°. N.Y. 1872.
—— Spanish Grammar. 12°. N.Y. 1854.
—— Studies in English. 12°. N.Y. 1869.
—— Wonders of the Deep. 12°. N.Y. 1869.
DE VINNÉ, D. The Methodist Episc. Church and Slavery. 8°. N.Y. 1857.
DE VOE, T. F. Market Assistant. 12°. N.Y. 1867.
DEVOTION, J. Sermon: Obituary of Madam Ursula Griswold. 8°. N. Haven. 1788.
DEWALDEN, E. Ball-room Companion. 16°. N.Y. n.d.
DEWEES, W. P. Treatment of Children. 8°. Phil. 1825.
DEWEY, Mary E. Life and Letters of Catherine M. Sedgwick. 12°. N.Y. 1871.
DEWEY, O. Laws of Human Progress; a Lecture. (PC. 5.) 8°. N.Y. 1852.
DEWITT, Mme. Charlotte de la Trémouille, Comtesse de Derby. 12°. Paris. 1870.
—— Citadins et Campagnards. 12°. Paris. 1870.
—— Riches et Pauvres. 12°. Paris. 1870.
—— Scènes d'Histoire et de Famille. 12°. Paris. 1869.
—— The Lady of Latham. (Countess of Derby). 8°. Lond. 1869.
DEWITT, S Elements of Perspective. 8°. Alb. 1813.
DEWITT, T. Discourse, Opening of Reformed Dutch Church, 5th Ave. and 29th St. 8°. N.Y. 1854.
DHOMBRES, E. Foi et Patrie. 12°. Paris. 1871.
DIABLE (Le) à Paris. 16°. Paris. 1862.
DIALOGHI Francesi, Italiani, Tedeschi ed Inglesi. 11th ed. 16°. Milan. 1818.
DIALOGUE on the Atonement. (PC. 18.) 16°. Bost. 1833.
DIALOGUE aux Enfers entre Charles X et Louis Philippe Ier. 4th ed. 12°. Paris. 1871.
DIALOGUES Françaises et Allemands. 12°. Paris. 1811.
DIALOGUES on the Writings of Swedenborg. 12°. N.Y. 1821.
DIARIO de Lisboa, Jan.–June 1866. 2 v. f°. Lisbon. 1866.
DICEY, E. The Morning Land. 2 v. 12°. Lond. 1870.
DICK, T. Philosophy of a Future State. 12°. N.Y. 1831.
DICK, W. Veterinary Papers. 8°. Edin. 1869.
DICKENS, C. Child's History of England. 12°. Bost. 1871.
—— Speeches, Letters and Sayings. 8°. N.Y. 1870.
DICKENS. Charles Dickens; the Story of his Life. 12°. Lond. 1870.
—— Same. 8°. N.Y. 1870.
DICKERSON, O. C. Revel of the Rum Fiend. (PC. 12.) 18°. Brookl. 1859.
DICKSON, J. H. Fibre Plants. 8°. Lond. n.d.
DICKSON, W. Japan. 8°. Edin. 1869.
DICKSON, W. B. Poultry. 12°. Lond. 1853.
DICTIONARY of Correspondences. 16°. Bost. 1847.
DICTIONARY of Machines, Mechanics and Engineering. 2 v. R. 8°. N.Y. 1850–1.
DICTIONNAIRE de Géographie ancienne et moderne. 8°. Paris. 1870.
DICTIONNAIRE des Hérésies. 8°. Lyons. 1847.
DIDEROT, D. Œuvres Choisies. 2 v. 16°. Paris. 1856.
DIDHAM, R. C. New Translations of the Psalms. Part 2. 8°. Lond. 1870.
DIEDRICHS, J. The Theory of Strains. 8°. Balt. 1871.
DIEZ, Kathrina. Heinrich Heine's Erste Liebe. 12°. Berlin. 1870.
DIFINICIONES de la Orden de Calatrava. f°. Madrid. 1748.
DIGEON, J. M. Nouveaux Contes turcs et arabes. 2 v. 16°. Paris. 1781.
DIGESTION made Easy. 24°. Glasg. 1838.
DINCKLAGE, E. von. Durch die Zeitung. 2 v. 12°. Leip. 1871.
—— Sara. 12°. Leip. 1871.
DINGLER's Polytechnisches Journal, v. 199. 8°. Augsburg. 1871.

DINGMAN, J. H. Booksellers' Directory, 1869–70. 2 v. 8°. 1869–70.

DIOGENES Laertius. Lives of the Philosophers; transl. by Yonge. (Bohn's ed.) 12°. Lond. 1853.

DIONYSIUS of Alexandria. *See* ANTE-NICENE Library. v. 20.

DISRAELI, B. Lord G. Bentinck; a Political Biography. 8°. Lond. 1852.

DIRCKS, H. Perpetuum Mobile. 2 v. 12°. Lond. 1861–70.

DISTRICT of Columbia Merchants' and Farmers' Directory. *See* MARYLAND.

DISTURNELL, J. List of Post Offices, etc., to Nov. 1869. 4°. N.Y. 1870.

—— New York Business Manual for 1870. 8°. N.Y. 1860.

—— New York State Register, 1858. 12°. N.Y. 1858.

DIVINE (The) Kingdom on Earth as it is in Heaven. 8°. Lond. 1871.

DIX, J. Lions, Living and Dead. 16°. Lond. n.d.

DIX, M. Inspiration of the Scriptures; a Sermon. (PC. 18.) 16°. N.Y. 1862.

DIXON, E. Tables of Gold, by Act of March, 1843. 8°. N.Y. n.d.

DIXON, E. H. The Kidney. 16°. N.Y. 1871.

—— Organic Law of the Sexes. 8°. N.Y. n.d.

—— Sexual and Pelvic Organs. 8°. N.Y. 1870.

—— Some Abnormal Conditions of Sexual and Pelvic Organs. 8°. N.Y. n.d.

DIXON, F. B. Hand-Book of Marine Insurance. 2d ed. 8°. N.Y. 1866.

—— Law of Shipping. 8°. N.Y. 1859.

DIXON, W. H. Free Russia. 2 v. 12°. Lond. 1870.

—— Same. 12°. N.Y. 1870.

—— Her Majesty's Tower. 4 v. 8°. Lond. 1868–71.

—— Same. 2 v. 8°. Phil. 1871.

—— The Switzers. 8°. Lond. 1872.

DOANE, G. H. To and from the Passion Play in 1871. 16°. Bost. 1871.

DOBELL, H. Reports on the Progress of Medicine. 2 v. 8°. Lond. 1870–1.

DOBSON, E., and Tarn, E. W. Measuring and Valuing Artificers' Works. 8°. Lond. 1871.

DOD's Peerage, Baronetage, and Knightage for 1871. 16°. Lond. 1871.

—— Same for 1872. 16°. Lond. 1872.

DODD, G. Dictionary of Manufactures, etc. 16°. N.Y. 1869.

DODD, H. P. The Epigrammatists. 8°. Lond. 1870.

DODDRIDGE, P. Life of Col. Gardiner. 16°. Bost. 1785.

DODDS, J. Thomas Chalmers; a Biographical Study. 16°. N.Y. n.d.

DODGE, Miss Mary Abigail. Battle of the Books. 12°. Cambr. 1870.

—— Woman's Worth and Worthlessness. 12°. N.Y. 1872.

DODSLEY, R. L'Économie de la Vie Humaine. Sm. 4°. Frankfort. 1752.

—— L'Économia della Vita Umana. Tr. by Aloisi. 24°. N.Y. 1824.

DOGGETT's Map of the U. S. *See* SMITH, J. Calvin.

DOGMA, (The); or What is our Faith? By Ezion. 12°. Lond. 1871.

DOLBEAR's Penmanship. 3d ed. 18°. N.Y. 1837.

DOLBY, Anastasia. Church Vestments. Sm. 4°. Lond. 1868.

DÖLLINGER, J. J. I. Von. Fables respecting the Popes of the Middle Ages. Tr. by Plummer. 8°. Lond. 1871.

DOMESDAY Book (Lincolnshire and Rutlandshire). Transl. by Chas. G. Smith. 8°. Lond. n.d.

DOMINIC. Life of St. Dominic. With Sketch of the Dominican Order. 12°. Lond. 1857.

DONALDSON, T. L. Hand-Book of Specifications. 2 v. 8°. Lond. n.d.

DONKIN, A. S. The Skim-Milk Treatment of Diabetes and Bright's Disease. 12°. Lond. 1871.

DONNE, W. B. Essays on the Drama. 12°. Lond. 1858.

DONOVAN, C. Hand-Book of Phrenology. 8°. Lond. 1870.

DORCHESTER in 1630, 1776, and 1855. 8°. Bost. 1855.

DORN, H. Aus Meinem Leben. 8°. Berl. n.d.

DORNER, J. A. History of Protestant Theology. 2 v. 8°. Edin. 1871.

DORNROSEN. Erstlingsblüthen deutscher Lyrik in America. 18°. N.Y. 1871.

DORR, Mrs. J. C. R. Poems. 16°. Phil. 1871.

DORSEY, C. Testamentary Law of Maryland. 8°. Balt. 1838.

DOTEN, Lizzie. Poems of Progress. 16°. N.Y. 1871

DOUAI, A. The Kindergarten. 12°. N.Y. 1871.

DOUBLEDAY, E., and Westwood, J. O. Diurnal Lepidoptera. 2 vols. f°. Lond. 1846-52.

DOUBLEDAY, T. Matter for Materialists. 8°. Lond. 1870.

DOUGLAS, J. Reply to an Anonymous Letter. (PC. 18.) 16°. N.Y. 1824.

DOUGLAS, S. A. Life and Speeches. 12°. N.Y. 1860.

DOUGLAS, T. Review of Autobiography of. (PC. 12.) 8°. n.p. 1857.

DOUGLASS, Wm. Annals of First African Church. 12°. Phil. 1862.

DOVER Marble Co. Prospectus, etc. (PC. 9.) 8°. N.Y. 1864.

DOWLER, B. Tableaux of New Orleans. (PC. 12.) 8°. N.Orl. [1851 ?]

DOWNING, A. J. Fruit and Fruit-Trees. Ed. by C. Downing. R. 8°. N.Y. 1869.

DRAKE, D. Pioneer Life in Kentucky. 8°. Cinc. 1870.

DRAKE, F. S. Dictionary of American Biography, including Men of the Time. R. 8°. Bost. 1872.

DRAKE, S. G. French and Indian Wars. Sm. 4°. Alb. 1870.

DRAKE, W. Notes on Amos, with Transl. 16°. Lond. 1869.

DRAPER. Silver Wedding of Mr. and Mrs. F. P. Draper, including Essays on the Draper and Preston Families. 8°. Alb. 1871.

DRAPER, J. W. Address to Alumni of University of N. Y. City. (PC. 12.) 8°. N.Y. 1853.

—— Civil War in America. Vol. 3. 8°. N.Y. 1870.

DRAPER, J. W. Human Physiology. 7th ed. 8°. N. Y. 1868.

DRAPER, L. C., and Croffut, W. A. Helping Hand for Town and Country. 8°. Cinc. 1870.

DRAWING-Room Portrait Gallery of Eminent Personages. 2 v. At. f°. Lond. n.d.

DRÉOLLE, E. La Journée du 4 Sept. au Corps Legislatif. 12°. Paris. 1871.

DRESS and Care of the Feet 12°. N.Y. 1871.

DRESSER, H. E. Internal Revenue and Tariff Laws. 8°. N.Y. 1870.

DREUILLETTES, G. Epistola ad J. Wintrop. 16°. N.Y. 1869.

DROUÉT, H. Sur Terre et Sur Mer. 16°. Paris. 1870.

DROWNE, T. S. Commemorative Discourse, Church of Holy Trinity, Brooklyn. 8°. N.Y. 1870.

DROZ, Gustave. Autour d'une Source. 2d ed. 16°. Paris. n.d.

—— Monsieur, Madame, et Bébé. 16°. Paris. 1869.

—— Un Paquet de Lettres. 16°. Paris. n.d.

DRUMMOND, A. J. The Carbon Process. 16°. N.Y. 1868.

DRURY, D. Exotic Entomology. Ed. by Westwood. 3 v. 4°. Lond. 1837.

DRYDEN, J. Poetical Works. 8°. N.Y. n.d.

DUANE, W. American Military Library. 2 v. 8°. Phil. 1809.

DUBLIN Review. v. 11-14. 8°. Lond. 1869-70.

DUBLIN University Magazine. v. 74-76. 8°. Dubl. 1869-71.

DUBOC, E. Vermächtniss des Millionärin. 12°. Leip. 1870.

—— Eusebius Hützlers einfältige Selbstbekenntnisse. 18°. Hamb. 1871.

—— Gehrt Hansen. 4 v. 16°. Berlin. 1862.

DUBOIS, U. Cosmopolitan Cooking. Imp. 8°. Lond. 1870.

DU BOIS, W. G. Revised Weights and Silver Currency. 8°. N.Y. 1869.

DU BREUIL, A. Fruit Trees. Tr. by Wardle. 12°. Lond. n.d.

DU CAMP, M. Les Buveurs de Cendres. 12°. Paris. 1866.

DU CASSE (Baron). Journal Authentique du Siége de Strasbourg, 1870. 8°. Paris. 1871.

DU CHAILLU, P. B. Country of the Dwarfs. 12°. N.Y. 1871.

—— Equatorial Africa. 8°. N.Y. 1870.

—— Lost in the Jungle. 16°. N.Y. 1870.

—— My Apingi Kingdom. 12°. N.Y. 1870.

—— Stories of the Gorilla Country. 12°. N.Y. 1869.

—— Wild Life under the Equator. 12°. N.Y. 1869.

DUCHESNE, E. Géométrie Descriptive. 16°. Paris. 1828.

DUCRAY-Duminil, F. G. Les Contes de Famille. 3d ed. 24°. Paris. 1805.

—— Contes des Fées. 4th ed. 4 v. 24°. Paris. 1822.

DUCROT (le Général). La Journée de Sedan. Nouvelle ed. 8°. Paris. 1871.
DUDEVANT, Mme. André. 12°. Paris. 1868.
—— Césarine Dietrich. 12°. Paris. 1871.
—— Constance Verrier. 12°. Paris. 1863.
—— La Famille de Germandre. 12°. Paris. 1862.
—— Journal d'un Voyageur Pendant la Guerre. 12°. Paris. 1871.
—— Les Maitres Sonneurs. 12°. Paris. 1865.
—— Narcisse. 16°. Paris. 1860.
—— Tamaris. 12°. Paris. 1863.
—— Théatre de Nohant. 12°. Paris. 1865.
—— Voyages et Impressions. 12°. Paris. 1865.
DUER, J. Party Divisions; a Lecture. (PC. 5.) 8°. N.Y. 1841.
DUFF, M. E. G. Elgin Speeches. 8°. Edin. 1871.
DUFFIELD, G. Humiliation and Hope; a Discourse, Nov. 14, 1862. 8°. Detroit. 1862.
DUFFIELD, S. W. Warp and Woof. 12°. N.Y. 1870.
DUFRÉNOY, Mme. Le Tour du Monde. 6 v. in 3. 24°. Paris. 1814.
DUGANNE, A. J. H. History of Governments. 12°. N.Y. n.d.
DULCKEN, H. W. (Ed.) The Book of German Songs. 12°. Lond. 1871.
DUMAS, A. Acté. 12°. Paris. 1865.
—— Aventure d'Amour. 16°. Paris. 1867.
—— Isabel de Bavière. 16°. Paris. 1862.
—— Louis XV. et sa Cour. 16. Paris. 1866.
—— Louis XVI. et la Révolution. 16. Paris. 1866.
—— Le Maître d' Armes. 16°. Paris. 1866.
—— Les Mille et Un Fantomes. 12°. Paris. 1869.
—— La Princesse de Monaco. 12°. Paris. 1865.
—— La Régence. 16°. Paris. 1866.
—— La San Felice. 16. Paris. 1865.
DUMAS, A. fils. Antonine. 12°. Paris. 1870.
—— Une Lettre sur les Choses du Jour. 12°. Paris. 1871.
—— La Princesse Georges. 8°. Paris. 1872.
—— Sophie Printems. 16°. Paris. 1869.
—— Le Regent Mustel. 12°. Paris. 1869.
—— Théâtre Complet. 4v. 16°. Paris. 1870.
DUMÉRIL, A. M. C. Mineralogie et Botanique. 3d ed. 8°. Paris. 1825.
DUMONT, A. L'Administration et la Propagande Prussiennes en Alsace. 12°. Paris. 1871.
DU MOULIN, M. French Tutor. 2d ed. 16°. Phil. 1811.
DUNCAN, G. Mind and Brain. 12°. Lond. 1869.
DUNCAN, G. B. Argument in Relf *et al.* *vs.* Gaines. 8°. n.p. 1851.
DUNCAN, J. Colloquia Peripatetica. 16°. Edin. 1870.
DUNCAN, J. M. Mortality of Childbed and Maternity Hospitals. 8°. Edin. 1870.
DUNCAN, P. M. Transformation of Insects. 8°. Lond. 1871.
—— Same. 8°. Phil. n.d.
DUNCAN, W. Mortuary Record of Savannah. (PC. 17.) 8°. Savannah. 1870.
DUNGLISON, R. Human Health. 8°. Phil. 1844.
DUNHAM, C. Homœopathy the Science of Therapeutics (Reprint from Am. Homœpathic Review). 8°. N.Y. 1863.
DUNHAM, T. Hebrew Grammar. 16°. Lond. n.d.
DUNKIN, E. Midnight Sky. 4°. Lond. n.d.
DUNLAP, W. History of the American Theatre. 8°. N.Y. 1832.
DUNN, H. Study of the Bible. 12°. N.Y. 1871.
DUNN, J. B. The Good Samaritan; a Sermon. 12°. N.Y. 1871.
DUNPHY, T. and CUMMINS, T. J. Remarkable Trials. 8°. N.Y. 1870.
DUPLAIS, ainé, et jeune. Manufacture and Distillation of Alcoholic Liquors. 8°. Phil. 1871.
DUPLESSIS, G. Merveilles de la Gravure. 16°. Paris. 1869.
—— Wonders of Engraving. Sq. 12°. Lond. 1871.
—— Same. 16°. N.Y. 1871.
DU PONCEAU, P. S. View of the Constitution. 16°. Phil. 1834.
DUPREZ, G. Un Barde au XIXme Siècle. 8°. Bruss. 1871.
DUQUET, A. Irlande et France. 12°. Paris. 1872.
DURANT, G. Hygiene of the Voice. 8°. N.Y. 1870.
DURFEE, C. Williams' Biographical Annals. 8°. Bost. 1871.

DUSSAUCE, H. Fabrication of Matches, etc. 12°. Phil. 1864.

—— Manufacture of Vinegar. 8°. Phil. 1871.

DUVAL, J. C. Big Foot Wallace (Life of Wm. A. Wallace). 12°. Phil. 1870.

DUVERGER, W. Comparison of French and English. 3d ed. 12°. Lond. 1820.

DWIGHT, B. W. Descendants of Elder John Strong. 2 v. 8°. Albany. 1871.

DWIGHT, T. Discourse, Fast Day, July 23, 1812. 8°. N. Hav. 1812.

—— Independence of Mind. *See* AM. TRACT SOC. Tracts for Young Men.

—— Life a Race. *See* AM. TRACT SOC. Tracts for Young Men.

DWINELL, I. E. Hope for our Country; a Sermon. 8°. Salem. 1862.

DWYER, F. Seats and Saddles. 12°. Phil. 1869.

DYER, Mrs. C. C. J. Old World seen with Young Eyes. 16°. N.Y. n.d.

DYER, H. T. History of Modern Europe. 4 v. 8°. Lond. 1861–4.

DYER and Color Maker's Companion. 16°. Phil. 1850.

EAGAR, J. H. Doctrine of the Trinity Defended. 16°. Bost. 1864.

EAGLE Gold Co. Prospectus. (PC. 9.) 8°. N.Y. 1864.

EARLE, J. C. English Premiers, Walpole to Peel. 2 v. 12°. Lond. 1871.

EARLE. Micro-Cosmographie. *See* FULLER Worthies' Library.

EARLY English Text Society Publications, viz., Percy Folio MS. v. 2. 8°. Lond. 1868.

No. 38. Langland's Vision of Piers Plowman. Part 2. 8°. Lond. 1869.

No. 39. Destruction of Troy. 8°. Lond. 1869.

Extra series, No. V. Boethius de Consolatione. Transl. by Chaucer. 3 v. 8°. Lond. 1868–9.

EASTLAKE, C. L. Contributions to Literature of Fine Arts. 2d series. 8°. Lond. 1870.

—— History of the Gothic Revival. 4°. Lond. 1872.

EASTLAKE, Lady. Life of J. Gibson. 8°. Lond. 1870.

EASTMAN, S. Topographical Drawing. 8°. N.Y. 1837.

EASTMAN, Z. Slavery a Falling Tower; a Lecture. 12°. Chicago. n.d.

EASTWICK, E. B. Venezuela. 2d ed. 8°. Lond. 1868.

EASY Lessons for Beginners in Landscape. Obl. 8°. Lond. n.d.

EATON, A. Mensuration, Surveying and Engineering. 2d ed. 8°. Alb. 1830.

EBEL, J. G. Atlas to Guide to Switzerland. 18°. Lond. 1819.

EBERS, G. Eine Aegyptische Königstochter. 3 v. 12°. Stuttg. 1869.

EBELING, A. Sketches of Modern Paris. 12°. Lond. 1870

ECCLESIA. Church Problems Considered 8°. Lond. 1870.

—— A Second Series of Essays on Theological and Ecclesiastical Questions. Ed. by Reynolds. 8°. Lond. 1871.

ECHOES from the South. 12°. N.Y. n.d.

ECKARDT, J. Modern Russia. 8°. Lond. 1870.

ECKFELDT, J. R., and Du Bois, W. E. Gold and Silver Coins. 8°. N.Y. 1851.

ECLECTIC Magazine. v. 6–17. New ser. 8°. N.Y. 1867–71.

ECONOMIST. v. 10 in 2; parts 1 of v. 12, 13, 16; v. 18; pt. 1 of v. 19; v. 21, in 2; v. 22, pt. 2; v. 28. Together. 11 v. f°. Lond. 1852–71.

EDDY, D. C. Europa; or, Scenes in England, etc. 12°. Bost. 1860.

EDDY, T. M. Illinois in the War for the Union. 2 v. 8°. Chic. 1865–6.

EDELMANN, G. W. Guide to Value of Cal. Gold (PC. 1.) 8°. Phil. 1850.

EDEN, F. The Nile Without a Dragoman. 12°. Lond. 1871.

EDEN, Lizzie S. Fairy Fancies. 12°. Lond. 1870.

EDES, R. T. Physiology and Pathology of the Nervous System. 8°. N.Y. 1869.

EDGAR, C. H. The Curse of Canaan Rightly Interpreted. Three Lectures. 8°. N.Y. 1862.

EDGELL, A. W. Soldiers' Songs. S. 4°. Lond. n.d.

EDGERTON, J. K. Relations of the Federal Government and Slavery: a Speech. 8°. Ft. Wayne. 1861.

EDGEWORTH, Maria. Comic Dramas. *See* PATRONAGE, with novels.

—— On Bores. *See* HARRINGTON, with novels.

—— Essay on Irish Bulls. *See* CASTLE RACKRENT, with novels.

EDINBURGH Review. v. 129–134. 8°. Lond. 1869–71.

EDKINS, J. China's Place in Philology. 12°. Lond. 1871.

EDMONDS, C. R. John Milton. 16°. Lond. 1851.

EDMONDS, Geo. Philosophic Alphabet. 8°. Lond. 1832.

EDMUNDS, F. Names of Places. 12°. Lond. 1869.

EDUCATIONAL Association of Virginia. Reports and Papers, July 1867. 8°. n.p. 1867.

EDUCATIONAL Congress, Manchester, Nov. 1869. Report. 8°. Lond. 1869.

EDWARD I. Life and Reign of Edward I. 12°. Lond. 1872.

EDWARDS, E. Free Town Libraries. 8°. N.Y. 1869.

—— Lives of the Founders of the British Museum. 8°. Lond. 1870.

EDWARDS, F., Jr. Our Domestic Fireplaces. R. 8°. Lond. 1870.

EDWARDS, H. S. Life of Rossini. 16°. Bost. n.d.

EDWARDS, J. Essay on Brokers and Factors, or Commission Merchants. 16°. Alb. 1870.

EDWARDS J. English Composition. 3d ed. 16°. Lond. 1841.

—— Same. 5th ed. 16°. Lond. 1847.

EDWARDS, J. Sabbath Manual; Nos. 1, 2, 3. 18°. N.Y. n.d.

EDWARDS, Jonathan. Selections from Unpublished Writings. Ed. by Grosart. 8°. n.p. 1865.

EDWARDS, J. E. The Confederate Solider; Sketch of G. M. and B. W. Harris. 12°. N.Y. 1868.

EHLERT, L. Letters on Music. Transl. by Fanny R. Ritter. 16°. Bost. n.d.

EIGHTEENTH Ward Republican Festival. Speeches. 8°. N.Y. 1860.

EIKON Basilike. The Portraiture of His Majesty King Charles 1st. 16°. Oxford. 1869.

EITEL, E. J. Hand-Book for the Student of Chinese Buddhism. 8°. Lond. 1870.

—— Three Lectures on Buddhism. 8°. Hongkong. 1871.

ELAM, C. Medicine, Disease and Death. 8°. Lond. 1870.

—— Physician's Problems. 12°. Lond. 1869.

—— Same. 16°. Bost. 1869.

ELDER, W. Questions of the Day, Economic and Social. 8°. Phil. 1871.

ELDRIDGE, R. B. Scriptural Discourses. 2d ed. 12°. New Bedford 1870.

ELEMENTARY Treatise on Mathematical Instruments. 16°. Bost. 1830.

ELEMENTS of Drawing. 4°. N.Y. 1804.

ELFORD, J. M. 2d ed. of Longitude Tables. 8°. Charleston. 1818.

ELLET, Mrs. E. T. Court Circles of the Republic. 8°. Hartf. 1869.

ELLICOTT, C. J. Life of our Lord. 8°. Lond. 1869.

—— Revision of the Eng. Version of the New Testament. 12°. Lond. 1870.

ELLIOT, H. M. Races of Northwestern India. 2 vols. 8°. Lond. 1869.

ELLIOT, R. H. Planter in the Jungles of Mysore. 2 v. 8°. Lond. 1871.

ELLIOTT, Charlotte. Thoughts in Verse. 12°. Lond. 1869.

ELLIOTT, J. D. Address to his Early Companions. Delivered Nov. 24, 1843. 8°. Phil. 1844.

ELLIOTT, S. Address, Opening of Medical College. (PC. 6.) 8°. Charleston. 1826.

ELLIS, A. J. Charlie's House (in Phonetics). 18°. Lond. 1848.

—— Early English Pronunciation. *See* CHAUCER Society.

—— Phonetic Primer. 4th ed. 18° Lond. '49.

—— Phonography in Foreign Languages. 18°. Lond. 1848.

—— Plea for Phonetic Spelling. 8°. Lond. 1848.

ELLIS, E. Diseases of Children. 12°. Lond. 1869.

ELLIS, G. E. Memoir of Sir B. Thompson, Count Rumford. 8°. Phil. n.d.

ELLIS, R. Asiatic Affinities of the Old Italians. 12°. Lond. 1870.

ELLIS, Mrs. Sarah S. Daughters of England. 16°. N.Y. 1843.

—— Education of the Heart. 16°. Lond. 1869.

ELLIS, W. Progressive Lessons in Social Science. 2d ed. 18°. Lond. 1862.

ELLIS, W. Martyr Church of Madagascar. 12. Lond. 1870.

ELLIS, W. S. Antiquities of Heraldry.

ELLISON, Andrew. Art of Cutting. Sm. 4°. Bost. 1827.

ELTON, Sir A. H. Below the Surface. 16°. Lond. 1864.

ELWELL, J. J. Malpractice and Medical Evidence. 3d ed. 8°. N.Y. n.d.

ELZ, A. Er ist nicht eifersüchtig. *Also* Benedix, R. Der Weiberfeind; and Müller, H., Im Wartesalon erster Klasse. 16°. Bost. 1870.

ELZE, K. Lord Byron. 8°. Berlin. 1870.

—— Lord Byron; A Biography. 8°. Lond. 1872.

EMANUEL, H. Diamonds and Precious Stones. 12°. Lond. 1867.

EMBURY, Mrs. Emma C. Poems. 12°. N.Y. 1869.

EMERSON, F. Arithmetic, First Part. 16°. Phil. n.d.

—— Arithmetic, Part 2. 16°. Phil. n.d.

—— Arithmetic, 3d Part. 12°. Bost. 1851.

EMERSON, J. Our Nation; an Address. 8°. Beloit. 1862.

EMERSON, R. W. Prose Works. 2 v. 12°. Bost. 1870.

—— Society and Solitude. 12°. Bost. 1870.

EMMONS, E. Introductory Discourse, Albany Med. Coll. (PC. 1.) 8°. Alb. 1845.

EMPIRE (L') et l' Opposition devant la France. 8°. Bruss. 1870.

ÉNAULT, L. Les Perles Noires. 12°. Paris. 1870.

END of Life. 12°. Lond. 1871.

ENFIELD, W. Compendium of the Laws of England. 24°. Lond. 1809.

ENGEL, C. Music of the Ancient Nations. 2d ed. 8°. Lond. 1870.

ENGINEER. v. 31. f°. Lond. 1871.

ENGINEERS', etc., Pocket Book for 1870. 16°. Lond. 1870.

ENGLISH Catalogue of Books for 1869–70. 2 v. 8°. Lond. 1870.

ENGLISH Artists of the Present Time. 4°. Lond. 1872.

ENGLISH Drama under Tudors and Stuarts. Sm. 4°. Printed for the Roxburghe Library. 1869.

ENGLISH Painters of the Present Day; Essays. f°. Lond. 1871.

ENGLISHWOMAN'S Domestic Magazine. v. 10. New Series. 4°. Lond. n.d.

ENTICK, J. Latin-English Dictionary. Sq. 12°. Lond. 1837.

ENTOMOLOGICAL Society. Transactions, series 1, v. 1–5; series 2, v. 5, series 3, v. 1, 4, and 5. 9 v. 8°. Lond. 1836–67.

EPISODES of Fiction, or Choice Stories from the Great Novelists. With Biographical Introductions. Sm. 4°. N.Y. n.d.

ERA Almanack and Annual. 8°. Lond. 1871.

ERAS, W. Volkswirthschaftliche Aufsätze. 12° Leip. 1871.

ERCKMANN, E. and Chatrian, A. Histoire d'un Sous-maître. 12°. Paris. n.d.

—— Madame Thérèse. 16°. Paris. n.d.

—— Neue Erzählungen. Ed. by K. Braun. 12°. Berlin. 1872.

ERNESTI, J. A. Clavis Ciceroniana. 8°. Lond. 1819.

ERSKINE, Rev. T. The Spiritual Order, etc. 12°. Edin. 1871.

ERSKINE, T. (Lord). Speeches. 2 v. 8°. Lond. 1870.

—— Same. 8°. Chicago. 1870.

ERTHEILER, M. Easy Lessons in German. 12°. N.Y. 1847.

ESSAI sur la Littérature Espagnole. 8°. Paris. 1810.

ESSAY on Classical Instruction. 2d ed. 16°. Lond. 1837.

ESSAYS and Reviews. 16°. Leip. 1862.

—— Same. 12th ed. 16°. Lond. 1869.

ESSAYS on Taxation and Reconstruction. By Diversity. (PC. 13.) 8°. N.Y. 1865.

ETHNOLOGICAL Society of London. Journal, New Series. v. 1, 2. 8°. Lond. 1869–70.

ETIQUETTE for Ladies. 24°. Phil. 1840.

ETON, by another "Paterfamilias." 8°. Eton. 1861.

ETON Reform; Nos. 1, 2. 8°. Lond. 1861.

ÉTUDES Sur l'Exposition de 1867. 1 e. Serie. 8°. Paris. n.d.

EUCLID. Elements; edited by Simson. 8°. Phil. 1811.

EUGENE, Prince. Memoirs, by himself. 12°. Lond. 1811.

EURIPIDES. Medea, Alcestis and Hippolytus, in Blank Verse by Williams. 12°. Lond. 1871.

—— Tragedies. Transl. by Buckley (Bohn's Ed.) 2 v. 12°. Lond. 1868.

EUTROPIUS. Breviarium Historiæ Romanæ. Ed. by Verheyk. 24°. Nuremberg. 1800.

EVANGELICAL Alliance of the U. S. Document No. 1, Constitution; Report to 5th Gen. Conference; Report on Conference at Amsterdam. 8°. N.Y 1868.

EVANGELICAL Lutheran Synod of N. Y. Constitution, etc. (PC. 6.) 8°. Alb. 1868.

EVANGELICAL Quarterly Review. v. 20, 21. 8°. Gettysburg. 1869–70.

EVANS, A. S. Our Sister Republic, Mexico. 8°. Hartford. 1870.

EVANS, E. P. Abriss der Deutschen Literaturgeschichte. 12°. N.Y. 1869.

EVANS, H. D. Christian Doctrine of Marriage. 12°. N.Y. 1870.

EVANS, R. M. Story of Joan of Arc. 12°. Lond. 1841.

EVANS, Wm. Journal of Life and Religious Services. 8°. Phil. 1870.

EVANSVILLE (Indiana). Board of Trade. Annual Report for 1867. 8°. Evansville. 1868.

EVELYN, J. Diary and Correspondence. 4 v. 12°. Lond. 1870.

EVERETT, E. Dorchester in 1630, 1776 and 1855: an Oration. Containing, also, the Proceedings in Dorchester at the Celebration of the Fourth of July, 1855. 8°. Bost. 1855.

—— Address. Gettysburg Cemetery. 8°. Bost. 1863.

—— Same. 8°. Bost. 1864.

—— Address. Inauguration of Union Club. 8°. Bost. 1863.

EVERLASTING Fortune Teller. 12°. N.Y. 1865.

EVERY Man his Own Lawyer. 12°. Poughkeepsie. 1845.

EVERY Month. v. 1–2 in 1. 4°. N.Y. 1867–9.

EVERY Saturday. v. 7–8, R. 8°. Bost. 1869.

EVILL, Wm. Winter Journey to Rome and Back. 12°. Lond. 1870.

—— Same. 12°. Lond. 1871.

EWALD, A. C. The Crown and its Advisers. 12°. Edin. 1870.

EWALD, H. Introductory Hebrew Grammar. 3d ed. Transl. by J. F. Smith. 12°. Lond. 1870.

—— History of Israel. Transl. by Carpenter. v. 3 and 4. 8°. Lond. 1871.

EWING, J. Guildry and Merchants' House of Glasgow. 12°. Glasg. 1817.

EXAMINATION of Canon Liddon's Bampton Lectures. 12°. Lond. 1871.

—— Same. 12°. Bost. 1872.

EXAMINATION of the President's Power to Remove from Office. (PC. 13.) 18°. N.Y. 1861.

EXAMINER, 1862, 1870, 2 v. f°. Lond. 1862–70.

EXCHANGE (The). v. 2. 8°. Lond. 1863.

EXPLANATORY Notices of Design, No. 30, for Central Park. (PC. 13.) 8°. N.Y. 1858.

EYFFARTH, M. Ueber die Zeit. 8°. Berlin. 1871.

EYTH, M. Wanderbuch eines Ingenieurs. 12°. Heidelberg. 1870.

FABER, F. W. Creator and Creature. 12°. Balt. 1857.

FABULÆ anonymi. *See* PHAEDRUS; Fabulæ. Deuxponts. 1784.

FAIDHERBE, L. Campagne de l'Armée du Nord, en 1870–71. 12°. Paris. 1871.

FAIRBAIRN, P. Typology of Scripture. 5th ed. 2 v. 8°. Edin. 1870.

FAIRBAIRN, W. Cast and Wrought Iron for Building. 4th ed. 8°. Lond. 1870.

FAIRBANKS, G. R. History of Florida, 1512–1842. 12°. Phil. 1871.

FAIRFIELD, E. B. Christian Patriotism; Sermon to Michigan Legislature. 8°. Lansing. 1863.

FAIRHOLT, F. W. Dictionary of Terms in Art. 12°. Lond. n.d.

—— Gog and Magog. 18°. Lond. 1869.

—— Tobacco; Its History and Associations. 12°. Lond. 1859.

FALL (The) of England. The Battle of Dorking. 12°. N.Y. 1871.

FALLET, C. Les Princes de l'Art. 12°. Bost. 1870.

—— The Princes of Art. 12°. Bost. 1870.

FAMILY Cyclopædia; or, Health in the Household. 12°. N.Y. 1871.

FAMILY Doctor. 12°. Lond. n.d.

FAMILY Friend. New Ser. v. 1. 4°. Lond. n.d.

FAMILY Save-all. 12°. Phil. n.d.

FAMILY Tutor. v. 3. 12°. Lond. n.d.

FANTON M. A. Tables of Roman Law. 4°. Lond. 1869.

FARADAY, M. Chemical History of a Candle. 12°. N.Y. 1861.

FARCY, C. Aperçu des Connaissances Humaines, au 19me Siècle. 24°. Paris. 1827.
FARLEY, F. A. What is Truth? A Discourse. 8°. N.Y. 1843.
FARMER, H. Demoniacs of the New Testament. 2d ed. 12. Lond. 1805.
FARMER'S Magazine. 3d series. v. 18, 22, 23, 26, 30, 33-39. R. 8°. Lond. 1860-71.
FARNAM, D. L. Hydraulic Apparatus. 2d ed. 8°. N.Y. 1846.
FARNINGHAM, M. Boyhood. 16°. Lond. n.d.
FARRAR, F. W. Essays on a Liberal Education. 8°. Lond. 1868.
—— Families of Speech. 12°. Lond. 1870.
—— Seekers after God. 12°. n.p. n.d.
—— Witness of History to Christ. 12°. Lond. 1871.
FASQUELLE, L. New Method of Learning French. 12°. N.Y. 1871.
FAUVEL-GOURAUD, F. First Fundamental Basis of Mnemonics. 8°. N.Y. 1844.
FAVOURITE Holiday Book for Boys. 8°. Lond. n.d.
FAVRE, J. Gouvernement de la Défense Nationale. 8°. Paris. 1871.
—— Rome et la République Francaise. 8°. Paris. 1871.
FAVRE, J. F. Nouveau Maître Italien. 16°. Turin. 1791.
FAWCETT, E. Short Poems for Short People. 12°. N.Y. 1871.
FAWCETT, H. Pauperism; its Causes and Remedies. 12°. Lond. 1871.
FEATHERSTONHAUGH, G. W. Death of Ugolino; a Tragedy. 8°. Phil. 1830.
FECHNER, H. Der deutsch-französische Krieg von 1870-1 8°. Berlin. 1871.
FELLOWES, C. D. Charles I., Cromwell, and Charles II. 4°. Lond. 1828.
FEMALE Life Among the Mormons. 12°. N.Y. 1855.
FENNELL, G. Book of the Roach. 16°. Lond. 1870.
FENWICK, S. Student's Guide to Medical Diagnosis. 16°. Lond. 1869.
—— Same. 2d ed. 16°. Lond. 1871.
FERÉ, O. Le Docteur Vampire. 8°. N.Y. 1871
FERGUSON, J. Astronomy. 2d ed. 2 v. 8°. Edin. 1821.
—— Essays and Treatises. 8°. Edin. 1823.
—— Lectures. 3d ed. 2 v. 8°. Edin. 1823.
FERGUSON, R. M. Electricity. 18°. Lond. 1867.
FERGUSON, R. S. Cumberland and Westmoreland Members of Parliament, 1660-1867. 8°. Lond. 1871.
FERGUSSON, J. Rude Stone Monuments in all Countries. 8°. Lond. 1872.
FERGUSSON, Sir W. Practical Surgery. 5th ed. 8°. Lond. 1870.
FERN, Fanny. *See* PARTON, Mrs.
FERNANDEZ, F. Spanish Grammar, 5th ed. 8°. Lond. 1809.
FERRAR, W. H. Comparative Grammar of Sanskrit, Greek, and Latin. v. 1. 8°. Lond. 1869.
FERRARI, A. Gettysburg. 16°. Leip. 1869.
FESSART, E. Manuel du Vendeur et de l'Acheteur. 24°. Paris. 1839.
FÉTIS, F. J. La Musique mise à la Portée de tout le Monde. 18°. Brussels. 1839.
FETRIDGE, W. P. Rise and Fall of the Paris Commune. 12°. N.Y. 1871.
FETTE, W. E. Dialogues from Dickens. 16°. Bost. 1870.
FEUCHTWANGER, L. Fermented Liquors. 5th ed. 12°. N.Y. 1867.
—— Water Glass, etc. 12°. N.Y. 1870.
FEUERBACH, L. Essence of Christianity. 8°. Lond. n.d.
FEUILLET, J. B. Life of St. Rose of Lima. 16°. Phil. n d.
FEUILLET, O. La Petite Comtesse. 12°. Paris. 1869.
FÉVAL, P. Capitaine Fantôme. 16°. Paris. 1867..
—— Cœur d' Acier. 2 v. 12°. Paris. 1866.
—— Les deux Femmes du Roi. 12°. Paris. 1866.
—— La Duchesse de Nemours. 12°. Paris. 1868.
—— Les Errants du Nuit. 12°. Paris. 1865.
—— La Fabrique de Mariages. 12°. Paris. 1865.
—— Les Filles de Cabanil. 12°. Paris. 1866.
—— Les Gens de la Noce. 12°. Paris. 1865.
—— Le Mari Embaumi. 2 v. 12°. Paris. 1866.

—— Les Mystères de Londres. 2 v. 12°. Paris. 1866.
—— Les Nuits de Paris. 16°. Paris. 1870.
—— Quai de la Ferraille. 2 v. 12°. Paris. 1869.
—— Roger Bontemps. 12°. Paris. 1865.
—— Mlle. Saphir. 2d ed. 12°. Paris. 1870.
—— La Tache Rouge. 8°. N.Y. 1870.
FEW (A) Remarks on the State of Church Schools. 8°. Lond. n.d.
FEYDEAU, E. Alger. 12°. Paris. 1862.
—— Amours Tragiques. 12°. Paris. 1870.
—— Les Aventures du Baron Féreste. 12°. Paris. 1869.
—— Consolation. 12°. Paris. 1872.
—— Un Début a l'Opera. 12°. Paris. 1868.
—— Le Mari de la Danseuse. 12°. Paris. 1867.
—— M. de St. Bertrand. 12°. Paris. 1864.
—— Le Secret du Bonheur. 2 v. 12°. Paris. 1868.
FFOULKES, E. S. The Athanasian Creed. 12°. Lond. n.d.
—— Is the Western Church under Anathema? 8°. Lond. n.d.
—— The Roman Index. 2d Letter to Manning. 8°. Lond. 1869.
FIELD, D. D. Suggestions on Revision of Constitution of New York. (PC. 22.) 8°. N.Y. 1867.
FIELD, F. E. The Green House as a Winter Garden. 12°. N.Y. 1870.
FIELD, G. Two Great Books of Nature and Revelation. 12°. N.Y. 1870.
FIELD, Kate. Pen Photographs of Dickens' Readings. 12°. Bost. 1871.
FIELD Lane Ragged School. 11th Annual Report, 1853. (P. 95.) 8°. Lond. 1853.
—— 12th Annual Report, 1854. (P. 96 and 97.) 8°. Lond. 1854.
FIELD, W. Stones of the Temple. 12°. Lond. 1871.
FIELDING, Sarah. L'Orpheline Angloise. French of de La Place. 4 v. 18°. Paris. 1766.
FIELDS, J. T. Yesterdays with Authors. 12°. Bost. 1872.
FIFTEEN O's and other Prayers. (Facsimile of Caxton's Print.) Sm. 4°. Lond. 1869.
FIGUIER, L. L'Alchimie, etc. 2d ed. 16°. Paris. 1856.
—— Année Scientifique, 14e et 15e Année. 2 v. 12°. Paris. 1870–2.
—— L'Homme Primitif. 8°. Paris. 1870.
—— Le Lendemain de la Mort. 12°. Paris. 1871.
—— Les Races Humaines. R. 8°. Paris. 1872.
—— Earth and Sea. L. 8°. Lond. 1870.
—— Mammalia. 8°. Lond. n.d.
—— Same. 8°. N.Y. 1870.
—— Primitive Man. 8°. Lond. 1870.
—— Same. 8°. N.Y. 1870.
—— Reptiles and Birds. 8°. N.Y. 1870.
—— The To-morrow of Death. 12°. Bost. 1872.
FINDEL, J. G. History of Freemasonry. 2d ed. 8°. Lond. 1869.
FINLASON, W. F. History of Tenures of Land in England and Ireland. 8°. Lond. 1870.
—— Report of Queen *vs.* Gurney *et al.* 8°. Lond. 1870.
FINN, M. D. Theorematical System of Painting. 16°. N.Y. 1830.
FIRE Lands Pioneer. v. 7–10. 8°. Sandusky. 1866–70.
FIRST Help in Accidents and Sickness. 12°. Bost. 1871.
FIRST Lutheran Church, Albany. Manual. 16°. Albany. 1871.
FIRST Reformed Dutch Church, Hudson N.Y. Manual and Record. (PC. 13.) 18°. Hudson. 1854.
FISCH, G. Discours; Union des Églises Evangéliques de France. 8°. Paris. 1862.
FISCHEL, E. English Constitution 8°. Lond. 1863.
FISCHER, Kuno. Commentary on Kant. Transl. by Mahaffy. 12°. N.Y. 1866.
—— Entstehung und Entwicklungsformen des Witzes. 12°. Heidelberg. 1871.
FISH, H. C. Power in the Pulpit. A Sermon. 8°. N.Y. n.d.
FISHER, E. T. Easy French Reading. 18°. N.Y. 1869.
FISHER, T. W. Plain Talk about Insanity. 8°. Bost. 1872.
FISK. Life of James Fisk, Jr. 12°. N.Y. 1871.
FITCH, G. W. Physical Geography. 12°. N.Y. 1856.

FITCHBURG Directory, to July, 1872. 8°. Fitchburg. 1871.

FITZGERALD, M. S. The Kings of Europe. 12°. Lond. 1870.

FITZGERALD, P. Comedy and Dramatic Effect. 8°. Lond. 1870.

—— The Kembles. 2 v. 8°. Lond. n.d.

FITZGERALD, W. F. V. Egypt, India and the Colonies. 12°. Lond. 1870.

FITZ-HERBERT, A. New Natura Brevium. 16°. Lond. 1652.

FITZWYGRAM, F. Horses and Stables. 8°. Lond. 1869.

FLAGG, W. J. Hand-Book of Sulphur Cure for Grapes. 16°. N.Y. 1870.

FLAMANK, J. Mind and Manner. 12°. Lond. 1870.

FLAMMARION, C. Contemplations Scientifiques. 12°. Paris. 1870.

—— Dieu dans la Nature. 16°. Paris. 1869.

—— Marvels of the Heavens. 12°. Lond. 1870.

—— Wonders of the Heavens. 16°. N.Y. 1871.

FLANDERS, H. Must the War Go On? 8°. Phil. 1863.

FLEMING, G. Animal Plagues. 8°. Lond. 1871.

—— Horse Shoes and Horse Shoeing. 8°. Lond. 1869.

FLEMING, J. Readings for Winter Gatherings. 12°. Lond. n.d.

FLEMING, J. P. Analysis of English Language. 12°. Lond. 1869.

FLETCHER, A. (of Saltoun.) Political Works. 16°. Glasg. 1749.

FLETCHER, B. Model Houses for the Industrial Classes. 8°. Lond. 1871.

FLETCHER, G. Poems. *See* FULLER Worthies' Library. v. 3.

FLETCHER, J. Poems. *See* FULLER Worthies' Library. v. 9.

FLETCHER, P. Poems. *See* FULLER Worthies' Library. v. 5–8.

FLEURIOT, Zénaïde. Alix. 2d ed. 12°. Paris. 1869.

—— Ce Pauvre Vieux. 12°. Paris. 1870.

—— Deux Bijoux. 12°. Paris. 1869.

—— Petite Belle. 12°. Paris. 1869.

FLEURY, L. Occupation et Bataille du Villiers-sur-Marne et de Plessis Lalande. 12°. Paris. 1871.

FLIGHT, E. G. True Legend of St. Dunstan and the Devil. Sq. 12°. Lond. 1871.

FLINT, A. Diseases of the Heart. 8°. Phil. 1870.

—— Diseases of Respiratory Organs. 8°. Phil. 1856.

—— Physiological Effects of Muscular Exercise. 8°. N.Y. 1871.

FLINT, A. Jr. Chemical Examination of the Urine. 12°. N.Y. 1871.

—— Physiology of Man. 3 v. 8°. N.Y. 1868–70.

FLORIAN, J. P. C. de. Estelle. 18°. Paris. 1812.

—— Guillaume Tell. 24°. Paris. 1812.

FLORIST and Pomologist. v. 1–2. L. 8°. Lond. 1867–8.

FLORUS, L. A. Rerum Romanarum Libri IV. *Also* L. Ampelii Liber Memorialis. 24°. Halle. 1762.

FLOWER, J. W. Adam's Disobedience and its Results. 2d ed. 8°. Lond. 1871.

FLOWER, W. H. Osteology of Mammalia. 12°. Lond. 1870.

FLUSHING Library Assoc'n. Catalogue of Books. Sq. 18°. Flushing. 1871.

FLY, E. M. The Bible True. 12°. Phil. 1871.

FODEN, J. Boilermakers' and Iron Ship Builders' Companion. 18°. Lond. 1869.

FOLKARD, H. C. The Sailing Boat. 4th ed. 12°. Lond. 1870.

FOLLEN, C. Deutsches Lesebuch. 3d ed. 12°. Bost. 1836.

—— German Grammar. 12°. Bost. 1831.

FONTANE, T. Kriegsgefangen. 12°. Berlin. 1871.

FONTENELLE, J. de. Manuel du Bijoutier, Joaillier, etc. 2 v. 18°. Paris 1832.

FOOD Journal. v. 1–2. 8°. Lond. 1871–2.

FOOT, S. A. Examination of the Dred Scott Case. (PC. 7.) 8°. N.Y. 1859.

FOOTE, E. B. Plain Home Talk. 12°. N.Y. 1870. Same. 1871.

FOOTE, W. H. The Huguenots. 12°. Rich. n.d.

FOOTSTEPS of St. Paul. 12°. N.Y. 1861.

FORBES, A. My Experiences of the War between France and Germany. 2 v. 8°. Lond. 1871.

FORBES, A. P. Explanation of the Nicene Creed. 2d ed. 12°. Oxford. 1866.

FORBES, R. B. Appeal on the Subject of Seamen. 8°. Bost. 1854.

—— Case Against Am. Mutual Life Ins. Co. 8°. Bost. 1861.

—— Construction of Ships for the Merchant Service. 8°. Bost. 1866.

—— Forbes (The) Rig. 8°. Bost. 1862.
—— Ocean Steam Navigation. 8°. Bost. 1855.
—— Protection of Ships from Lightning. 8°. Bost. 1848.
—— Remarks on Magnetism, etc. 8°. Bost. 1857.
—— Steam Power, etc., of U. S. Steam Sloops. 8°. Bost. 1865.
FOREIGN Protestant Pulpit. 12°. Lond. 1869.
FORMAN, A. B. Our Living Poets. 12°. Lond. 1871.
FORMBY, H. Life of Christ. 12°. N.Y. 1870.
FORREST, Mary. Women of the South. 4°. N.Y. 1861.
FÖRSTER, E. Geschichte der Italienischen Kunst. 2 v. 12°. 1869–70.
FORSTER, E. J. Pedigree and Descendants of Jacob Forster, Sen. 12°. Charlestown. 1870.
FORSTER, J. Life of Dickens. v. 1. 8°. Lond. 1872.
—— Same. 12°. Phil. 1872.
—— Life and Times of Goldsmith. 5th ed. 2 v. 8°. Lond. 1871.
—— Life of W. S. Landor. 2 v. 12°. Lond. 1869.
FORSYTH, J. Highlands of Central India. 8°. Lond. 1871.
FORSYTH, W. Constitutional Law. L. 8°. Lond. 1869.
—— Life of Cicero. 3d ed. 8°. Lond. 1869.
—— Same. 12°. N.Y. 1870. Same. 1871.
—— Novels and Novelists of the 19th Century. 12°. Lond. n.d.
—— Same. 12°. N.Y. 1871.
FORTNIGHTLY Review. New Series. v. 6–13. 8°. Lond. 1869–71.
FORVILLE, V. de. Conscrit de l'An VIII. 16°. Paris. 1860.
FORWOOD, W. S. Mammoth Cave of Kentucky. 12°. Phil. 1870.
FOSS, E. Biographical Dictionary of Judges of England. R. 8°. Lond. 1870.
—— Tabulæ Curiales. 8°. Lond. 1865.
FOSTER, B. W. Method and Medicine; an Essay. 8°. Lond. 1870.
FOSTER, E. New Cyclopædia of Illustrations Adapted to Christian Teaching. R. 8°. N.Y. 1871.
FOSTER, F. Who'd be an Author? 12°. Lond. 1869.
FOSTER, J. Critical Essays. Ed. by Ryland. 2 v. 12°. Lond. 1870–1.
FOULIS, R. Old Houses in Edinburgh. (P. 95.) 8°. Edin. 1852.
FOUQUÉ, M. de la Motte. Ondine; French of Mme. de Montolieu. 16°. Paris. 1822.
FOUR Years at Yale. 12°. N. Hav. 1871.
FOURIER, C. Theory of Universal Unity. Part 2. 16°. N.Y. n.d.
FOURTH (The); Log of the Smoothing Iron. (PC. 18.) 16°. N.Y. 1854.
FOURTH Ward Indus. School Assoc'n. 5th Report. (P. 84.) 16°. N.Y. 1859.
FOWLE, W. B. Introduction to Linear Drawing. 12°. Bost. 1839.
—— Parlor Dramas. 12°. Bost. 1857.
FOWLER Genealogy. 12°. Milwaukee. 1870.
FOWLER, O. S. Sexual Science. 8°. Phil. n.d.
FOWLER, W. W. Ten Years in Wall Street. 8°. Hartf. 1870.
FOWNES, G. Elementary Chemistry. 12°. Phil. 1847.
—— Chemistry and the Wisdom of God; A Prize Essay. 12°. N.Y. 1844.
—— Rudimentary Chemistry. 18°. Lond. 1849.
FOX, G. P. The Philosophy of Dress and Fashion. 3d ed. 8°. N.Y. 1872.
FOX, T. L. Freemasonry in England. 16°. Lond. 1870.
FOX, W. J. Finsbury Lectures. (P. 77.) 8°. Lond. 1835.
FOXE, J. Book of Martyrs, abridged. 12°. Phil. 1866.
FRAME, J. Original Sin. 12°. Lond. n.d.
FRANCATELLI, C. E. Plain Cookery Book. 16°. Lond. n.d.
FRANCE. Tableau Général de la Commerce de la France, 1834. R. 4°. Paris. 1835.
FRANCE and her People. By C. C. B. 12°. Phil. n.d.
FRANCESTOWN Academy. Exercises at the Re-union of the Teachers and Alumni. 8°. Peterboro. 1871.
FRANCIS, J. B. Lowell Hydraulic Experiments. 4°. N.Y. 1871.
—— Strength of Cast Iron Pillars. 8°. N.Y. 1865.
FRANCIS (St.) de Sales. Practical Piety. 16°. Louisville. n.d.
—— Selection from Spiritual Letters. 12°. Lond. 1871.

—— Life of. 12°. Lond. 1871.

FRANCO, S. Devotion to the Sacred Heart. 18°. Balt. 1870.

FRANÇOIS, N. Advice of a Father to his Son. (In Latin, French, Italian, German and English.) 8°. Alb. 1871.

FRANK Leslie's Illustrated Newspaper. v. 30–32. At. 4°. N.Y. 1870–1.

FRANK Leslie's Lady's Magazine. v. 24–29. 4°. N.Y. 1869–71.

FRANK Leslie's Monthly. v. 10 4°. N.Y. 1862.

FRANKLAND, C. C. Travels to Constantinople. 2d ed. 2 v. 8°. Lond. 1830.

FRANKLIN before the Privy Council, 1774. 8°. Phil. 1859.

FRANKLIN-BERGER, V. Contemporains avant, pendant et après la Guerre. 12°. Paris. 1871.

FRASER, J. B. History of Persia. 18°. N.Y. 1842.

—— Persian Princes in London. 2d ed. 2 v. 12°. Lond. 1838.

FRASER'S Magazine. Old Series. v. 8. July–Dec., 1869. 8°. Lond. n.d.

—— New Series. v. 1–4, Jan., 1870–Dec. 71. 8°. Lond. n.d.

FRAUNCE, A. Countess of Pembroke's Emanuell and Psalmes. *See* FULLER Worthies' Miscellanies.

FREDERICK the Great. Military Instructions to his Generals. 8°. Lond. 1762.

FREE Hand Drawing. 18°. Edin. 1868.

FREE Negroism; or, Results of Emancipation in the North and in the W. I. Islands. 8°. N.Y. 1862.

FREE Religion. Report of Meeting, Bost., May 30, 1867. 8°. Bost. n.d.

FREEMAN, E. A. Historical Essays. 8°. Lond. 1871.

—— Norman Conquest of England. v. 3, 4. 8°. Oxf. 1869–71.

—— Old English History for Children. 12°. Lond. 1869.

FREEMAN, W. E. New School History of England. 12°. Oxf. 1870.

FREILIGRATH, F. Poems. 16°. Leip 1869.

FRENCH, B. F. Historical Collections of Louisiana and Florida. New Series. 8°. N.Y. 1869.

FRENCH, T. V. The Old Commandment New and True in Christ. 16°. Lond. 1869.

FRENCH Love Songs. *See* CURWEN.

FRENEAU, P. Poems of the Revolution. 8°. N.Y. 1865.

FRENZEL, K. Drei Grazien. 3 v. 12° Breslau. n. d.

—— Geheimnisse. 12°. Leip. 1871.

—— Im Goldenen Zeitalter. 4 v. in 2 16°. Hanover. 1870.

—— La Pucelle. 3 v. 12°. Hanover. 1871.

—— Melusine. 12°. Breslau. 1860.

FRERE, Alice M. Antipodes and Round the World. 8°. Lond. 1870.

FRERE, John Hookham. Works, with Memoir. 2 v. 8°. Lond. 1872.

FRESENIUS, C. R. Qualitative Analysis. 7th ed. 8°. Lond. 1869.

FREYCINET, C. de. La Guerre en Province pendant le Siége de Paris. 8°. Paris. 1871.

FREYTAG, G. Die Brautfahrt. 12°. Leip. 1858.

—— Pictures of German Life in the 15th, 16th and 17th centuries. Transl. by Mr. Malcolm. 2 v. 12°. Lond. 1862.

FRIEDRICH, F. Die Frau des Ministers. 2 v. 12°. Berlin. n.d.

FRIENDLY Hands and Kindly Words. 16°. Lond. 1868.

FRIKELL, G. The Secret Out; 1,000 Tricks in Magic. 12°. Lond. n.d.

FRISWELL, J. H. Gentle Life. Sq. 12°. Lond, 1870.

—— Man's (A) Thoughts. 16°. Lond. 1872.

—— Modern Men of Letters. 12°. Lond. 1870.

FRITZE, E. Der Major. v. 1. 16°. Halle. 1869.

—— Schloss Bärenberg. 3 v. in 1. 12°. Leip. 1867.

—— Der Stille Speculant. 16°. Halle. 1870.

FROST, J. Class Book of Nature. 16°. Hartf. 1839.

—— Great Cities of the World. 12°. Auburn. 1860.

FROST, S. A. Art of Dressing Well. 16°. N.Y. n.d.

FROTHINGHAM, O. B. Allegiance and Patronage; Leaving Home and Revelations; Morality of the Rich; Sermons (bound together.) N.Y. n.d.

FROUDE, J. A. Calvinism; an Address. 8°. Lond. 1871.

—— Same. 12°. N.Y. 1871.

—— History of England. 12 v. 8°. Lond. 1858–70.

—— Same. Library ed. 12 v. 12°. N.Y. 1865–70.
—— Same. Popular ed. 12 vols. 12°. N.Y. 1870.
—— Short Studies on Great Subjects. 2d series. 8°. Lond. 1871.
—— Same. 12°. N.Y. 1871.
FUGITIVE Pieces. 12°. Lond. 1765.
FUGITIVE Slave Bill. Seizure of James Hamlet. 3d ed. 16°. N.Y. 1850.
FULLER's Telegraphic Computer. Ob. 4°. N.Y. 1852.
FULLER, T. Cambridge and Waltham Abbey. 8°. Lond. 1840.
FULLER, T. Pisgah Sight of Palestine. 12°. Lond. 1869.
FULLER, T. Poems. *See* FULLER Worthies' Library. Vol. 1.
FULLER Worthies' Library. Ed. by Grosart. 18 vols. 16°. Lond. 1868–71.
Containing:
Vol. 1. Fuller, T. Poems.
2. Washbourne, T. Poems.
3 Fletcher, G. Poems.
4. Davies, Sir J. Works. v. 1. Poems.
5–8. Fletcher, P. Poems.
9. Fletcher, J. Poems.
10. Beaumont, Sir J. Poems.
11–14. Brooke, Lord. Works.
15–18. Vaughan, H. Works.
Also, Miscellanies of the Fuller Worthies' Library.
FULTON, J. A. Peach Culture. 12°. N.Y. n.d.
FULTON, R. Torpedo War and Submarine Explosion. Ob. 4°. N.Y. 1810.
FUR, Fin and Feather. 8°. N.Y. 1868.
FURNESS, W. H. Jesus. 12°. Phil. 1870.
—— Same. 12°. Phil. 1871.
FURNISS, W. Rip Raps; or, Drift Thoughts Wide Apart. 12°. N.Y. 1871.
FUTURE (The) of the Country; by a Patriot. 8°. n.p. n.d.

GABORIAU, É. La Clique Dorée. 12°. Paris. 1871.
—— Same. 12°. Paris. 1872.
—— Les Comédiennes Adorées. 16°. Paris. 1863.
—— Les Cotillons Célèbres. 2 vols. 16°. Paris. 1869.
—— Le Crime d' Orcival. 12° Paris. 1870.
—— Le Dossier No. 113. 12°. Paris. 1869.
—— Les Esclaves de Paris. 2 v. Paris. 1869–70.
—— Les Gens de Bureau. 16°. Paris. 1870.
—— Ruses d' Amour. 16°. Paris. 1870.
—— Le 13e Hussards. 16°. Paris. 1870.
—— La Vie Infernale. 2 v. 16°. Paris. 1870.
GABOURD, A. Histoire Contemporaine. v. 7–9. 8°. Paris. 1867–70.
GAERTNER, C. The Art of Singing. L. 4°. Phil. 1871.
GAINES *vs.* Chew *et al.* The Great Gaines Case. Rep. by Walker. 8°. N.Orl. 1850.
GAIUS. Commentaries on the Roman Law. Transl. by Tomkins and Lemon. 8°. Lond. 1869.
GALAXY. v. 7–12. 8°. N.Y. 1869–71.
GALEN, P. (Pseudonym.) *See* LANGE, C. P.
GALERIA Militar Contemporanea. 2 v. R. 8°. Madrid. 1845–6.
GALIGNANI's New Paris Guide. 16°. Paris. 1839.
GALILEO, Private Life of. 12°. Lond. 1870.
—— Same. 12°. Bost. 1870.
GALL, F. J., and Spurzheim, G. Des Dispositions Innées de l'Ame et de l'Esprit. 8°. Paris. 1811.
GALLIC Gleanings. Letters descriptive of two Excursions to the French Metropolis and the Peace Congress, 1849. 12°. Lond. n.d.
GALLOWAY, R. Qualitative Analysis. 5th ed. 12°. Lond. 1870.
GALLOWAY, W. B. Physical Facts and Scriptural Record; or Eighteen Propositions for Geologists. 8°. Lond. 1872.
GALTON, F. Hereditary Genius. 8°. Lond. 1869.
—— Same. 8°. N.Y. 1870.
GAMGEE, J. Horse-Shoeing and Lameness. 8°. Lond. 1871.
GANT, F. J. The Science and Practice of Surgery. 8°. Lond. 1871.
GARCIA, Mad. E. M. de. Pablo. 16°. Paris. 1869.
GARDENER'S Monthly, v. 11–13. 18°. Phil. 1869–71.
GARDERA, F. B. Difficulties of French. 12°. N.Y. 1829.
GARDNER, A. K. Conjugal Sins. 12°. N.Y. 1870.
—— Our Children. 12°. Hartf. 1872.
GARDNER, Celia E. Stolen Waters; a Poem. 12°. N.Y. 1871

GARDNER, D. Treatise on the Law of the American Rebellion. 8°. Bost. 1862.
GARDNER, J. Christian Cyclopædia. 4°. Glasgow. 1858.
GARELLA, N. Projet d'un Canal de Panama. 8°. Paris. 1845.
GARFIELD, J. A. Oration on the Life and Character of Gen. Geo. H. Thomas. 8°. Cinc. 1871.
GARFIT, A. The Education Question. 12°. Lond. 1862.
GARIBALDI, G. Clelia. 16°. Milan. 1870.
—— Die Herrschaft des Mönchs. 2 v. 16°. Leip. 1870.
—— Mémoires. Tr. par A. Dumas. 3d. ed. 16°. Paris. 1866.
GARRICK, D. Correspondence, with Memoir. 2 v. 4°. Lond. 1831.
GARROD, A. B. Materia Medica and Therapeutics. 3d ed. 12° Lond. 1870.
GASCOIGNE, G. Poems. Ed. by W. C. Hazlitt. 2 v. Sm. 4°. n.p. 1870.
GASCOIGNE, G. Steele Glas, etc. *See* ARBER's English Reprints.
GAS-Consumers (The) Guide. 12°. Bost. 1871.
GASKIN, J. J. Varieties of Irish History. 12°. Dubl. 1869.
GASPARIN, A. de. The Family. 12°. Lond. 1867.
—— Word of Peace on the American Question. 16°. Lond. n.d.
GASPARINI, G. Attributes of Christ. 12°. N.Y. 1870.
GASTINEAU, B. L'Impératrice du Bas Empire (Théodora.) 12°. Paris. 1870.
GASTYNE, J. de. Mémoires Secrètes du Comité Central et de la Commune. 12°. Paris. 1871.
GATTY, Mrs. A. Waifs and Strays of Natural History. 16°. Lond. 1871.
GAULTIER, L. Géométrie Pratique. 16°. Paris. 1817
—— Langue Italienne. v. 1, 2d ed. 16°. Paris. 1813.
—— Méthode pour Analyser la Pensée. 24°. Paris. 1806.
—— Vers François. 16°. Paris. 1814.
GAUTIER, T. Ménagérie Intime. 16°. Paris. 1869.
—— Tableaux de Siége. 12°. Paris. 1871.
—— Voyage en Espagne. 12° Paris. 1865.
GAVAZZI, A. No Union with Rome. 12°. Lond. n.d
GAY, C. C. F. Address to Buffalo Medical Association. (PC. 8.) 8°. Buff. 1862.
—— Puerperal Eclampsia. 8°. n.p. n.d.
GAYLORD, W. L. The Soldier God's Minister; a Discourse. 8°. Fitchburg. 1862.
GAZZAM, A. W. Treatise on the Bankrupt Law for Business Men. 8°. N.Y. 1870.
GEE, S. Auscultation and Percussion. 16°. Lond. 1870.
GEER, G. J. Conversion of St. Paul. 12°. N.Y. 1871,
GEIBEL, E. Heroldsrufe. 12°. Stuttg. 1871.
GELDART, E. M. Modern Greek and Ancient Greek. 16°. Oxford. 1870.
GENELLI, Father. Life of St. Ignatius of Loyola. 12°. Lond. 1871.
GENERAL Regulations and Orders of the British Army. 8°. Lond. 1811.
GENERAL Society of Mechanics and Tradesmen. Reports, 1848–72. 8°. N.Y. n.d.
GENERAL View of the United States. 16°. Lond. 1833.
GENIN, T. H. Select Writings, with Memoir. 8°. N.Y. 1869.
GENLIS, Mme. de. Le Siége de la Rochelle. 12°. N.Y. n.d.
GENTELLES, Mme. de. Appeal to Christian Young Women. 24°. Bost. 1870.
GENTLEMAN'S Magazine. New Ser. v. 3–7. 8°. Lond. 1869–71.
GEOLOGICAL Magazine. v. 6–8. 8°. Lond. 1869–71.
GEORG, Prinz von Preussen. Glück Auf! im Fürstenhause. 12°. Berlin. 1870.
GEORGE, N. D. Annihilationism not of the Bible. 12°. Bost. 1870.
GEORGETOWN Directory. *See* WASHINGTON.
GEORGIA Historical Society. Constitution, By-Laws, etc. 8°. Savan. 1871.
GEPP, G. C. Latin Elegiac Verse. 16°. Lond. 1871.
GERMAN Conquest of England. (Same as Fall of England). 12°. Phil. 1871.
GERMAN Conversations. 16°. Lond. 1840.
GERMAN Reader for Beginners. 12°. Bost. 1831.
GERRY, E. T. Argument in the "Mumler Spirit Photograph Case." 8°. N.Y. 1869.

GERSTAECKER, F. Die Blauen und die Gelben. 12°. Jena. 1870.
—— Buntes Treiben. 3 v. 12°. Leip. 1870.
—— Die Colonie. 3 v. 12°. Leip. 1870.
—— Der Flatbootmann. 2d ed. 16°. Schwerin. 1870.
—— Die Franctireurs. 16°. Jena. n.d.
—— Gold. 3 v. 12°. Leip. 1859.
—— Im Eckfenster. 2 v. 12°. Vienna. 1871.
—— In Mexico. 2 v. 12°. Jena. 1870.
—— Irrfahrten. 12°. Berlin. n.d.
—— Kriegsbilder eines Nachzüglers. 16°. Jena. n.d.
—— Nach dem Schiffbruch. Das Wrack des Piraten. 16°. Jena. n.d.
—— Das Sonderbare Duell. 2d ed. Sq. 12°. Berlin. n.d.
—— Verhängnisse. 12°. Berlin. 1871.
—— Der Wahnsinnige. 16°. Schwerin. 1870.
GERSTNER, F. J. and F. A. de. Mechanics. 4°. Vienna. 1843.
GERVINUS, G. G. Hinterlassene Schriften. 8°. Vienna. 1872.
GESS, W. F. Scripture Doctrine of the Person of Christ. Transl. with Ad tions, by Reubelt. 12°. Andover. 1870.
GHERARDI, E. Théâtre Italien. 6 v. 16°. Paris. 1717.
GIBBONS, J. S. Banks of New York. 12°. N.Y. 1870.
GIBSON, C. B. Historical Portraits of Irish Chieftains and Anglo-Norman Knights. 8°. Lond. 1871.
GIBSON, E. Pastoral Letters; *also*, Horne: On Infidelity. 12°. N.Y. 1830.
GIBSON, R. Practical Surveying. 6th ed. 8°. Phil. 1792.
GIERLOW, J. Elements of Danish and Swedish. 12°. Camb. 1847.
—— The Holy Bible and its Relation to the Church. 16°. Chic. 1866.
GIESE, Marie. Der Kleine Probst. 12°. Berlin. 1872.
GIFFORD, H. Poems. *See* FULLER Worthies' Library.
GIFTS for Men. By X. H. 16°. Edin. 1870.
GILBART, J. W. Principles and Practice of Banking. 8°. Lond. 1871.
GILBERT, J. Cadore, or Titian's Country. 4°. Lond. 1869.
GILFILLAN, G. Life of Sir W. Scott. 12°. Edin. 1870.
GILL, C. H. Chemistry for Schools. 16°. Lond. 1869.
GILL, J. Notices of the Jews by Classic Writers. 8°. Lond. 1870.
GILL, W. F. Parlor Tableaux and Amateur Theatre. 12°. Bost. 1868.
GILLESPIE, W. M. Levelling. Topography and Higher Surveying. 8°. N.Y. 1870.
GILLMORE, P. A Hunter's Adventures in the Great West. 8°. Lond. 1871.
GILMAN, A. First Steps in English Literature. 16°. Lond. 1870.
GILMAN, D. C. Isthmus of Chocó. (PC. 13.) 8°. n.p. 1859.
GILMER, J. H. Argument in Claflin & Co. vs. Steinbock & Co. (PC. 22.) 8°. Richm. 1868.
—— War of Races. 8°. Richm. 1867.
GINSBURG, C. D. The Moabite Stone. Atl. 4°. Lond. 1870.
—— Same. 2d ed. Atl. 4°. Lond. 1871.
GIRARD, A. Carnet d'Étapes du 2e Bataillon du 4e Reg't de Marche à l'Armée du Nord. 12°. Paris. 1871.
GIRARDIN, E. de. Politique Universelle. 16°. Paris. 1854.
GIRARDIN, Mme. E. de. M. Le Marquis de Pontanges. 12°. Paris. 1866.
—— Le Vicomte de Launay. 2 v. 12°. Paris. 1868.
GIRAULT, A. N. French Student's Manual. 12°. Phil. 1848.
—— Same. 12°. Phil. 1849.
—— Same. 12°. Phil. 1850.
GIRDLESTONE, A. G. High Alps without Guides. 12°. Lond. 1870.
GIRDLESTONE, R. B. Synonyms of the Old Testament. 8°. Lond. 1871.
GLADSTONE, W. E. Juventus Mundi. 12°. Lond. 1869.
—— Same. 12°. Bost. 1869.
—— Speeches. Sm. 16°. Lond. 1870.
GLAISHER, J. Travels in the Air. 2d ed. R. 8°. Lond. 1871.
GLAZIER, W. Three Years in the Federal Cavalry. 12°. N.Y. 1870.
GLEASON, Mrs. R. B. Talks to my Patients. 12°. N.Y. 1870.
—— Same. 1871.
GLEDSTONE, J. P. Life of Whitefield. 8°. Lond. 1871.
GLEIG, G. R. Military History of Great Britain. 16°. Lond. 1845.
GLENNIE, J. S. S. Arthurian Localities. 8°. Edin. 1869.

GLOAG, P. J. Commentary on Acts. 2 v. 8°. Edin. 1870.
GLOBUS. v. 19. f°. Brunsw. 1871.
GOBRIGHT, L. A. Men and Things in Washington. 12°. Phil. 1869.
GODDARD, D. A. The Mathers Weighed in the Balances and Found Not Wanting. Sq. 18°. Bost. 1870.
GODDARD, J. Musical Development. 8°. Lond. n.d.
GODDARD, J. L. Law of Easements. 8°. N.Y. 1871.
GODDARD, S. A. Letters on the American Rebellion. 8°. Lond. 1870.
GODDARD, W. G. Writings. 2 v. 8°. Prov. 1870.
GODEY's Lady's Book. v. 16–25. 8°. Phil. 1838–42.
—— Same. v. 79–83. 8°. Phil. 1870–1.
GODIN, A. Wally. 2 v. 12°. Berl. 1871.
GODKIN, J. Land War in Ireland. 8°. Lond. 1870.
GODMAN, F. Du C. Natural History of the Azores. 8°. Lond. 1870.
GOD's Argument against Oppression. 8°. Gettysburg. 1863.
GODWIN, J. H. Gospel of St. Mark. 12°. Lond. 1869.
GODWIN, P. Out of the Past. 12°. N.Y. 1870.
GOETHE, J. W. von. Dramatic Works. 12°. Lond. 1867.
—— Egmont. 12°. Stuttg. 1868.
—— Faust. 12°. Stuttg. 1869.
—— Faust. Tr. by Hayward. 12°. Bost. 1871.
—— Faust. Pt. 1. Tr. by Talbot. 8°. Lond. 1839.
—— Faust. Tr. by Taylor. 2 v. R. 8°. Bost. 1871.
—— Gedichte. 12°. Stuttg. 1868.
—— Goetz von Berlichingen. 12°. Stuttg. 1866.
—— Hermann und Dorothee. 12°. Stuttg. 1867.
—— Hermann and Dorothea. Tr. by Miss Frothingham. 12°. Bost. 1870.
—— Poems and Ballads. Tr. by Aytoun and Martin. 16°. N.Y. 1871.
—— Theory of Colors. Tr. by Eastlake. 8°. Lond. 1840.
—— Werke. 8 v. Roy. 8°. Stuttg. 1869.
—— Wilhelm Meister. 2 v. 12°. Stuttg. 1867–70.
—— Wilhelm Meister. Tr. by Carlyle. 2 v. 18°. Lond. 1871.
GOGUÉ, A. La Cuisine Française. 4th ed. 12°. Paris. 1869.
GOLDEN Lane Ragged School. 6th An. Rep. (P. 100.) 24°. Lond. 1852.
GOLDONI, C. Opere. 31 v. 12°. Lucca. 1788–93.
GOLDSMITH, J. Biographical Class-Book. 12°. Lond. 1820.
GOLDSMITH, O. History of England, abridged. 18°. N.Y. 1817.
—— History of Greece. 12. Phil. 1865.
—— Natural History; abridged. 16°. n.p. n.d.
—— Poems. 8°. N.Y. n.d.
—— Works. Illustrated ed. R. 8°. Lond. n.d.
GOLOWIN I. Russland unter Alexander II. 8°. Leip. n.d.
GONZALÈS, E. La Belle Novice. 16°. Paris. 1870.
GOOD Girl's Annual for 1870. 12°. N.Y. 1869.
GOOD Health. v. 12. 8°. Bost. 1870–1.
GOOD Society. A Manual of Manners. 16°. Lond. 1869.
GOOD Words. 1869–71. 8.° Lond. 1869–71.
GOOD Words for the Young. v. 2–3. R. 8°. Lond. 1870–1.
GOODERE, T. M. Elements of Mechanism. 12°. Lond. 1870.
GOODRICH, C. A. Ecclesiastical Classbook. 18°. Hartf. 1835.
GOODRICH, F. B. Court of Napoleon. 8°. Phil. 1871.
GOODRICH, S. G. Pictorial History of U. S. 12°. Phil. 1869.
GOODWIN, T. S. Congregationalism. (An Essay). 8°. n.p. n.d.
GORDON, J. Charterer's Companion. 8°. Lond. 1852.
GORDON, M. M. Life of Sir D. Brewster. 12°. Edin. 1869.
GOSSE, P. H. British Sea-Anemones and Corals. 8°. Lond. 1860.
—— Introduction to Zoology. 2 v. 12°. Lond. n.d.
—— History of the Jews. 16°. Lond. n.d.
—— Land and Sea. 3d ed. 12°. Lond. 1870.
—— Letters from Alabama. 16°. Lond. 1859.
—— Life in its Lower, Intermediate and Higher Forms. 3d ed. 16°. Lond. 1870.

—— Manual of Marine Zoology for the British Isles. 2 v. 16°. Lond. 1855–56.
—— Naturalist's Rambles on the Devonshire Coast. 12°. Lond. 1853.
—— Omphalos; an Attempt to Untie th Geological Knot. 12°. Lond. 1857.
—— Rivers of the Bible. 2d ed. 12°. Lond. n.d.
GOSSON Stephen. The School of Abuse. *See* Arber's Reprints, No. 3.
GOTHAM. 8°. N.Y. 1870.
GOTTHELF, J. (Albert Bitzius.) Uli. 2 v. in 1. 12°. Berlin. 1870.
GOTTSCHALL, R. Porträts und Studien. 4 v. v. 1, 2, Literarische Charakterköpfe. v. 3, 4, Paris unter dem zweiten Kaiserreich. 12°. Leip. 1870–71.
—— Reisebilder aus Italien. 12°. Breslau. 1864.
GOUFFE, J. Book of Preserves. 8°. Lond. 1871.
GOUGH, J. B. Autobiography. 8°. Springf. 1869.
—— Man and his Masters. *See* AM. TRACT SOC. Tracts for Young Men.
GOULBURN, E. M. Cathedral System. 12°. Lond. 1870.
—— Pursuit of Holiness. 16°. Lond. 1869.
GOULD, A. A. Otia Conchologica; Descriptions of Shells and Mollusks. 8°. Bost. 1872.
GOULD, M. T. C. Art of Short Hand. 3d ed. 24°. N. Hav. 1824.
GOULD, N. D. Church Music in America. 16°. Bost. 1853.
GOULD, S. Baring. Curiosities of Olden Times. 18°. Lond. n.d.
—— Legends of Old Testament Characters. 12°. Lond. 1871.
—— Lives of the Saints. v. 1. 12°. Lond. 1872.
—— Origin and Development of Religious Belief. 2 v. 12°. N.Y. 1870.
GOUVERNEMENT (Le) en Putréfaction. 12°. Bruss. 1871.
GOUVERNEMENT (Le) qui File. Gambetta. 8°. Lond. 1870.
GOVERNING Race. By H. O. R. 8°. Wash. 1860.
GOVERNMENT School of Design, Somerset House. (P. 97.) 8°. n.p. n.d.
GRABHAM, M. C. Climate, etc., of Madeira. 16°. Lond. 1870
GRABOWSKI, Graf S. Aus Welt und Haus. 16°. Leip. 1869.
—— Haus Hohenzollern. 5 v. in 2. 12°. Berlin. n.d.
—— Des Königs und der Königin Soldat. 3 v. 12°. Leip. 1870.
—— Der Schützling des Kaisers. 16°. Berlin. 1870.
—— Nach dem Kriege. 4 v. in 2. 12°. Berlin. 1866.
—— Unter Preussen's Fahnen. 4 v. in 2. 12°. Berlin. 1867.
GRAETER, F. German and English Phrases and Dialogues. 12°. Bost. 1831.
GRAETZ, H. Influence of Judaism on the Protestant Reformation. 8°. Cinc. 1867.
GRAFFIGNY, Mme. F. de. Lettres d'une Péruvienne. 24°. Lyons. 1787.
GRAGLIA, G. A. Exercises in Italian. 2d ed. 16°. Lond. 1808.
—— Italian Grammar. 2d ed. 12°. Lond. 1808.
GRAHAM, J. Argument in the case of Wm. Winter. 8°. N.Y. n.d.
GRAHAM, J. M. Literature and Art in Great Britain. 8°. Lond. 1871.
GRAHAM, T. Elements of Chemistry. 2d ed. 2 v. 8°. Lond. 1850–58.
GRAMÁTICA de la Lengua Francesa. 8°. Bordeaux. 1816.
GRANDSAGNE, A. de, and others. Art d'Étudier, Ire Partie: Emploi du Temps. 24°. Paris. 1836.
—— Notions Générales (des Sciences). 6th ed. 24°. Paris. 1834.
GRANIER de Cassagnac, A. History of the Working and Burgher Classes. Tr. by Green. 8°. Phil. 1871.
GRANJA, J. de la. Rasgos Historicos. 12°. N.Y. 1835.
GRANT, A. Recess Studies. 8°. Edin. 1870.
— Xenophon. 16°. Phil. 1871.
GRANT, A. H. Church Seasons. Illustr. 12°. Lond. n.d.
GRANT, D. Home Politics. 8°. Lond. 1870.
GRANT, J. Memoirs of Sir J. Sinclair. 8°. Lond. 1870.
—— The Newspaper Press: Its Origin, Progress and Present Position. 2 v. 8°. Lond. 1871.
—— Sources of Joy in Seasons of Sorrow. 16°. Lond. 1871.
GRAPHIC (The). v. 1–4. At. f°. Lond. 1869–71.
GRASER, B. Norddeutschland's Seemacht. 8°. Leip. 1870.

GRATRY, A. Papal Infallibility Untenable; Three Letters. 18°. Hartf. 1870.
—— Same: Fourth Letter. 18°. Hartf. 1870. (Bound in one volume.)
GRAUVOGL, Dr. von. Text-Book of Homœopathy. 8°. Chic. 1870.
GRAVES, R. Lectures on the Four Last Books of the Pentateuch. 10th ed. 8°. Lond. 1865.
GRAY, Barry. (pseudonym.) *See* COFFIN, R. B.
GRAY, E. P. The Apostolic Treasury. 18°. San Fran. 1871.
GRAY, G. Z. Children's Crusade. 12°. N.Y. 1870.
GRAY, H. Anatomy. 5th ed., by T. Holmes. 8°. Lond. 1869.
GRAY, J. C. Bible Lore. 16°. N.Y. n.d.
—— The Biblical Museum; Notes on the Holy Scriptures. v. 1. Matthew and Mark. 12°. Lond. 1871.
GRAYJACKETS (The). By a Confederate. 8°. Richmond. n.d.
GREAT Britain. Education Commission Reports. 6 v. 8°. Lond. 1861.
—— Education. Reports of Committee of Council, 1861–2 and 1868–9. 8°. Lond. 1862–9.
—— Pilot Charts for Atlantic Ocean. f°. Lond. 1868.
—— Revised Statutes. v. 1, 2. Imp. 8°. Lond. 1870–1.
—— Schools Inquiry Commission. v. 1. 8°. Lond. 1868.
GREAT Trans-Continental Tourist's Guide. Sq. 12°. N.Y. 1870.
GREATHED, H. H. Letters during the Siege of Delhi. 12°. Lond. 1858.
GREEK Anthology. Trans. by Burgess. (Bohn's ed). 12°. Lond. 1855.
GREEK Romances of Heliodorus, Longus and Achilles Tatius. Trans. by Smith. 12°. Lond. 1855.
GREELEY, H. Political Economy. 12°. Bost. 1870.
—— What I Know of Farming. 12°. N.Y. 1871.
GREEN, Duff. How to Pay off the National Debt, etc. 12°. Phil. 1872.
GREEN, G. Mathematical Papers. 8°. Lond. 1871.
GREEN, H. Questions on English Grammar. 16°. Lond. 1846.
GREEN, H. Shakspeare and the Emblem Writers. Imp. 8°. Lond. 1870.
GREEN, Horace. Introductory Address, N. Y. Medical College. (PC. 13.) 8°. N.Y. 1850.
GREEN, J. H. The Gambler's Life. 12°. Phil. n.d.
GREEN, Mary A. E. Letters of Queen Henrietta Maria. 12°. Lond. 1857.
GREEN, N. W. Mormons, etc. 12°. Hartf. 1870.
GREEN, R. W. Scholar's Companion. 2d ed. 12°. Phil. 1836.
GREEN, Seth. Trout Culture. 12°. Caledonia, N.Y. 1870.
GREEN, S. A., M. D. Bibliography of the Massachusetts Historical Society. 8°. Bost. 1871.
—— Story of a Famous Book; an Account of Benj. Franklin's Autobiography. 8°. Bost. 1871.
GREEN, W. H. Hebrew Chrestomathy. 8°. N.Y. 1863.
—— Physical Science in Education; an Address. (PC. 13.) 8°. Easton. 1865.
GREEN Sand Marl of New Jersey. (PC. 5.) 8°. n.p. n.d.
GREEN Island Directory. *See* TROY.
GREENE, G. W. Life of Gen. Greene. v. 2, 3. 8°. N.Y. 1871.
GREENE, S. D. Broken Seal; or, The Morgan Abduction. 12°. Bost. 1870.
GREENE, Wm. B. Sovereignty of the People. 8°. Bost. 1868.
GREENER, W. Gunnery in 1858. 8°. Lond. 1858.
—— Modern Breech Loaders. 12°. Lond. n.d.
GREENLEAF, B. Elementary Algebra. 12°. Bost. 1864.
—— Elements of Geometry. 12°. Bost. 1867.
GREENWALD, E. The Lutheran Reformation. 12°. Phil. 1868.
GREENWELL, G. C. Mine Engineering. 2d ed. 4°. Newcastle. 1870.
GREENWOOD, J. Seven Curses of London. 8°. N.Y. 1869.
—— Same. 12°. Lond. n.d.
—— Wild Sports of the World. 8°. Lond. 1864.
GREENWOOD Cemetery. Exposition of Plan and Objects. 8°. N.Y. 1830.
—— Receipts and Expenditures, 1839–61. 8°. N.Y. 1861.

—— Rules and Regulations, with Suggestions Respecting the Purchase, &c., of Lots. 8°. N.Y. 1860.
—— Same, with Suggestions as to Improvements of Lots. 8°. Brookl. 1863.
—— Same, with Catalogue of Proprietors. 8°. N.Y. 1856.
—— Same, with same. 8°. N.Y. 1860 (Bound in one volume.)
GREG, W. R. The Great Duel. 12°. Lond. 1871.
—— Literary and Social Judgments. 2d ed. 12°. Lond. 1869.
—— Political Problems. 8°. Lond. 1870.
GREGOROVIUS, F. Wanderjahre in Italien. v. 4. 12°. Leip. 1871.
GREGORY, W. Hand-Book of Organic Chemistry. 16°. Lond. 1856.
GREGORY, Dr. J. Father's Legacy to his Daughters. 16°. N.Y. n.d.
—— Same. *See* PARENTAL Legacies.
GREGORY, R. Sermons on the Poorer Classes. 8°. Lond. 1869.
GREGORY Thaumaturgus. *See* ANTE-NICENE Library. v. 20.
GREMILLIET, J. J. Recueil de Problèmes. 8°. Paris. 1820.
GRENOUILLES (Les) qui Demandent un Roi. 16°. Bruss. 1871.
GRENZBOTEN, 1868–71. 14 v. 8°. Leip. 1868–71.
GRESLEY, W. Ecclesiastes Anglicanus. 2d ed. 12°. Lond. 1840.
GREVILLE, F. *See* BROOKE, Lord, in FULLER Worthies' Library. v. 11–12.
GREY, Mrs. W. Journal of a Visit to Egypt, Constantinople, etc. 8°. Lond. 1869.
GRIBBLE, T. Semi-barbarous Hebrew and Extinguished Theologian. 8°. Lond. 1871.
GRIFFIN, G. W. Studies in Literature. 16°. Balt. 1850.
GRIFFITH, G. Going to Markets and Grammar Schools, being a series of Autobiographical Sketches. 2 v. 8°. Lond. 1870.
GRIFFITH and Henfrey. Micrographical Dictionary. 2d ed. 8°. Lond. 1870.
GRIFFITH, T. Fundamentals; or Bases of Belief. 8°. Lond. 1871.
GRIMARD, E. Le Goutte de Sève. 12°. Paris. n.d
GRIMAUD de Caux, G. L'Académie des Sciences pendant le Siége de Paris. 12°. Paris. 1871.
GRIMKE, T. S. Address on Peace and War. 8°. Hartf. 1832.
GRIMM, A. T. von. Alexandra Feodorowna Empress of Russia. 2 v. Edin. 1870.
GRIMM, H. Zehn ausgewählte Essays zur Einführung in das Studium der Modernen Kunst. 12°. Berlin. 1871.
GRIMSHAW, W. History of France. 12°. Phil. 1829.
GRINDON, L. H. Life, its Nature, etc. 3d ed. 12°. Phil. 1867.
GRISCOM, J. H. Memoir of J. Griscom. 8°. N.Y. 1859.
—— Prison Hygiene; an Essay Prepared at the Request of the Prison Association of N. Y. 8°. Alb. 1868.
—— Sanitary Condition of the Laboring Population. (P. 79.) 8°. N.Y. 1845.
—— Sanitary Legislation. (P. 79.) 8°. N.Y. 1861.
GRIVEL, G. L'Isle Inconnue; ou, Mémoires du Chevalier des Gastines. 6 v. 12°. Paris. 1793–5.
GROSART, A. B. *See* FULLER Worthies' Library.
—— List of Baxter's Writings. *See* BAXTER, R. What We Must Do, etc.
—— Lord Bacon not the Author of the Paradoxes. 8°. n.p. 1865.
GROSS, Baron. Duties of an Officer in the Field. 12°. Lond. 1801.
GROSSE, J. Der neue Abälard. 12°. Leip. 1871.
—— Gegen den Strom. 3 v. 12°. Brunswick. 1871.
GROSSE Leute, Kleine Schwächen. 12°. Berlin. 1871.
GROSVENOR, W. M. Does Protection Protect? 8°. N.Y. 1870.
—— Same. 1871.
GROTE, J. A Few Words on the Educational Code. 8°. Camb. (Eng.) 1862.
GROTH, C. Quickborn. v. 1. 16°. Hamburg. 1864.
—— Same. v. 2. 12°. Leip. 1871.
GROU, J. N. The Hidden Life of the Soul. 12°. Lond. 1870.
GRÜN, Anastasius. *See* AUERSPERG.
GRUND, F. J. Merchant's Assistant. 8°. Bost. 1834.

GRÜNER, L. Garden Pavilion, Buckingham Palace. 4°. Lond. 1846.

GRÜNER, M. L. Manufacture of Steel. 8°. N. Y. 1872.

GUASCO, C. Douze Visites à Mazas pendant la Commune. 12°. n.p. n.d.

GUBBINS, M. R. Mutinies in Oudh and Siege of Lucknow. 8°. Lond. 1858.

GUÉGAN, Henri. French Grammar. 8°. Wash. 1831.

GUÉPIN, A. Économie Sociale. 24°. Paris. 1835.

GUERIN, M. de. Journal, Lettres et Poemes. 16°. Paris. 1868.

GUERRE des Communeux de Paris, 18 Mars–28 Mai, 1871. 12°. Paris. 1871.

GUERRE (La) Illustrée et Le Siége de Paris. f°. Paris. 1871.

GUEST, W. Young Man setting out in Life. 18°. N.Y. n.d.

GUETTIER, A. Practical Guide for the Manufacture of Metallic Alloys. Tr. by Fesquet. 12°. Phil. 1872.

GUIDE Book of the Central Railroad of New Jersey. 16°. N.Y. 1864.

GUIDE du Domestique. 16°. Paris. 1869.

GUIDE to English Etiquette. 18°. Lond. n d.

GUIDE to Knowledge. v. 1. 4°. Lond. 1832–3.

GUILD, C. Over the Ocean. 12°. Bost. 1871.

GUILLEMIN, A. Wonders of the Sun. 16°. N.Y. 1870.

GUILLORÉ, F. Self Renunciation. 12°. Lond. 1871.

GUINNARD, A. Three Years' Slavery among the Patagonians. 12°. Lond. 1871.

GUISET, A. de. L'Arrêt Public. 12°. Bruss. 1871.

GUIZOT, F. Christianity in Relation to the Present State of Society and Opinion. 12°. Lond. 1871.

—— Civilisation en Europe. 11th ed. 12°. Paris. 1871.

—— Le Duc de Broglie. 12°. Paris. 1872.

—— Histoire de France. v. 1. R. 8°. Paris. 1872.

—— History of Civilization. Tr. by Hazlitt. 4 v. 12°. N.Y. 1870.

—— Life of Cromwell. 12°. Lond. 1868.

—— State of Christianity. 12°. Lond. 1866.

GUMMERE, J. Surveying. 8°. Phil. 1832.

GUNN, J. C. Family Physician. 8°. Cinc. 1870.

GUNNISON, J. W. Mormons. 16°. Phil. 1856.

GURNEY, J. H. Chapters from French History. 16°. Lond. 1870.

GURNEY, W. and Wrench, J. G. Handy Dictionary of the Bible. 12°. Lond. n.d.

GUSECK, B. von. (G. von Berneck.) Im Herzen von Deutschland. 16°. Berlin. n.d.

—— Nicht aûf immer. 16°. Berlin. n.d.

—— Der Schlimmste Feind. 16°. Jena. n.d.

GUTHRIE, A. Memorial on Explosion of Steam Boilers. (PC. 2.) 8°. Wash. 1852.

GUTHRIE, F. Laws of Magnitude. 12°. Lond. 1870.

—— Plea for Ragged Schools. (P. 98.) 8°. Edin. 1848.

—— Supplement to Plea for Ragged Schools. (P. 98.) 8°. Edin. 1847.

—— and Blaikie, W. G. Saving Knowledge. 12°. N.Y. 1870.

GUTZKOW, K. Fritz Ellrodt. 3 v. 12°. Jena. 1871–2.

—— Lebensbilder. v. 1 and 2. 1. Durch Nacht zum Licht. 2. Novellen und Skizzen. 12°. Stuttg. 1870.

—— Die Ritter vom Geiste. 2 v. 12°. Berlin. n.d.

—— Die Schöneren Stunden. 12°. Stuttg. 1869.

—— Die Söhne Pestalozzis. 3 v. 12°. Berlin. 1870.

—— Der Wärwolf. 18°. Vienna. 1871.

GUY, W. A. Public Health. 12°. Lond. 1870.

GYNÆCOLOGICAL Journal. v. 1–3. 8°. Bost. 1869–70.

HACK, Maria. Stories from Grecian History. 16°. N.Y. n.d.

HACKLÄNDER, F. W. Freiwillige vor! 16°. Vienna. n.d.

—— Das Geheimniss der Stadt. 3v. in 2. 12°. Stuttg. 1868.

—— Geschichten im Zickzack. 4 v. in 2. 12°. Stuttg. 1869.

—— Hinter Blauen Brillen. 16°. Leip. n.d.

—— Der Letzte Bombardier. 8°. Phil. 1869.

—— Nahes und Fernes. 8°. Stuttg. 1870.

—— Sorgenlose Stunden in Heiteren Geschichten. 2 v. in 1. 12°. Stuttg. 1871.
—— Der Sturmvogel. 4 v. in 2. 12°. Stuttg. 1872.
—— Zwölf Zettel. 12°. Stuttg. 1868.
HACKLEY, C. W. Elements of Trigonometry. 8°. N.Y. 1838.
HADDAN, A. W. Apostolical Succession. 8°. Lond. 1869.
HADLEY, W. H. 4th and 6th Ann. Reps. of Ministry at large. Portland, Nov. 1853, and May, 1855. (P. 103.) 16°. Portl. 1853–6.
HAGEN, T. Drahtzieher. 16°. Nordhausen. 1854.
HAGENBACH, R. R. History of the Church, 18th and 19th Centuries. 2 v. 8°. N.Y. 1864.
HAKE, T. G. Madeline and other Poems. 12°. Lond. 1871.
HALE, E. E. How to Do It. 12°. Bost 1871
HALE, Mrs. Sarah J. Dictionary of Poetical Quotations. 8°. Phil. 1869.
—— Love, and other Poems. Sq. 16°. Phil. 1870.
—— Receipts for the Million. 12°. Phil. n.d.
HALF Yearly Abstract of Medical Sciences. v. 49, 50, Jan.–Dec., 1869. 12°. Lond. 1869.
—— Same. Ed. by W. D. Stone. v. 50–53, July, 1869–June, 1871. 8°. Phil. 1870–71.
HALIBURTON, T. C. High Life in New York. 12°. N.Y. 1854.
—— Letter Bag of Great Western. 12°. N.Y. 1840.
HALL, B. R. Latin Grammar. 12°. Phil. 1836.
HALL, C. H. Notes on the Gospels. 2 v. 12°. N.Y. 1871.
HALL, E. B. Discourse, Dedication of Theological Hall, Meadville. 8°. n.p. 1854.
—— Sermon, Obituary of President Harrison. 8°. Prov. 1841.
HALL, E. H. The Great West: Emigrant's Guide-Book. 16°. N.Y. 1864.
HALL, Rev. John. The Active Pity of a Queen: A Sermon. 16°. N.Y. 1871.
—— Papers for Home Reading. 12°. N.Y. 1871.
HALL, Mrs. Matthew. Royal Princesses of England, from George I. 12°. Lond. 1871.
HALL, Nathaniel. Sermon, Obituary of Dr. Thaxter. 8°. Bost. 1852.
HALL, Newman. American War: A Lecture. 12°. Bost. n.d.
—— Dignity of Labor. *See* AMER. Tract Soc.: Tracts for Young Men.
—— Liverpool to St. Louis. 16°. Lond. 1870.
HALL, R. Sermons on Various Subjects. 8°. N.Y. 1814.
HALL, S. C. Book of Memories. Sm. 4°. Lond. 1871.
HALL, Mrs. S. C. Specimens of Irish Character. 12°. Lond. n.d.
HALL, Wm. M. Bribery and Piracy. Loss of the Shooting Star. 8°. N.Y. 1870.
HALL, W. W. Bronchitis and Kindred Diseases. 12°. N.Y. 1870.
—— Coughs and Colds. 12°. N.Y. 1870.
—— Fun better than Physic. 12°. Springf. n.d.
—— The Guide-Board to Health, Peace and Competence. 8°. Springf. n.d.
—— Health and Disease, as Affected by Constipation. 12°. N.Y. 1870.
—— Health by Good Living. 12°. N.Y. 1870.
—— Health Tracts. 8°. N.Y. 1870.
—— Sleep. 12°. N.Y. 1870.
HALL'S Journal of Health. v. 1–18. 8°. N.Y. 1854–71.
HALLAM, A. H. Remains. 18°. Lond. 1869.
HALLAM, H. Student's History of Europe during the Middle Ages. By Smith. 16°. Lond. 1871.
HALLECK, F. G. Poems. 12°. N.Y. 1855.
HALLER, G. O. Dismissal from the Army; with Memoir of His Military Services. 8°. Paterson. 1863.
HALLIWELL, J. O. Dictionary of Archaic and Provincial Words. 6th ed. 2 v. 8°. Lond. 1868.
HALLOCK, Mrs. M. A. Beasts and Birds of America, Europe, Asia and Africa. Sm. 4°. N.Y. n.d.
HALSEY, L. J. Life of Rev. L. W. Green, with Select Sermons. 8°. N.Y. 1871.
HALT, R. Papiers Sauvés des Tuileries. 8°. Paris. 1871.
HAMERLING, R. Ahasver in Rom. 6th ed. 12°. Hamburg. 1870.

HAMERSLEY, L. R. Records of Living Navy and Marine Officers. 8°. Phil. 1870.

HAMERTON, P. G. Thoughts about Art. 12°. Bost. 1871.

—— Unknown River. f°. Lond. 1871.

HAMILTON, Count A. Fairy Tales. (Transl. by Lewis.) 12°. Lond. 1849.

HAMILTON, Lady Augusta. Marriage Rites. 8°. Lond. 1822.

HAMILTON, C. Life and Sport in South Eastern Africa. 12°. Lond. 1870.

HAMILTON, F. H. Military Surgery. 8°. N.Y. 1865.

—— Surgical Memoirs of the War of the Rebellion. See U. S. SANITARY COMMISSION.

HAMILTON, James, D.D. Moses the Man of God. Lectures. 2d ed. 12°. Lond. 1871.

—— Same. 12°. N.Y. 1871.

—— A Sound Mind. See AM. Tract Soc. Tracts for Young Men.

HAMILTON, Jas. A. Reminiscences. 8°. N.Y. 1869.

—— Van Buren's Calumnies Repudiated. 8°. N.Y. 1870.

HAMILTON, R. W. Sermons. 12°. N.Y. n.d.

HAMILTON, W. History of Medicine. 2 v. in 1. 8°. Lond. 1831.

HAMILTON, W. G. Useful Information for Railway Men. 24°. N.Y. 1872.

HAMLEY, E. B. Our Poor Relations. 16°. Edin. 1872.

HAMLEY, W. G. A New Sea and an Old Land (Egypt.) 8°. Edin. 1871.

HAMMOND, W. A. Diseases of the Nervous System. 8°. N.Y. 1871.

—— Physics and Physiology of Spiritualism. 12°. N.Y. 1870. Same. 1871.

—— Sleep and its Derangements. 12°. Phil. 1869.

HAMPDEN, Henrietta. Memorials of Bishop Hampden. 8°. Lond. 1871.

HANAFORD, Mrs. P. A. Life of George Peabody. 12°. Bost. 1870.

HAND-BOOK of Anglo-Saxon Orthography. 12°. N.Y. 1852.

HAND-BOOK of Archery. 2d ed. 24°. Lond. n.d.

HAND-BOOK to the Knowledge of the English Government. 16°. Lond. 1870.

HAND-BOOK of Games. Ed. by Bohn. 12°. Lond. 1867.

HAND-BOOK of Heliography. 24°. Lond. 1840.

HAND-BOOK for Immigrants. See AMERICAN Social Science Asso.

HANEY'S Manual of Sign, Carriage and Decorative Painting. 12°. N.Y. n.d.

HANNA, W. Earlier Years of Our Lord's Life. 12°. N.Y. 1870.

—— Forty Days after the Resurrection. 12°. N.Y. 1869.

—— Last Day of Our Lord's Passion. 12°. N.Y. 1868.

—— Life of Christ. 3 v. 12°. N.Y. 1871.

—— Ministry in Galilee. 12°. N.Y. 1870.

—— Our Lord's Life on Earth. 6 v. 12°. Edin. 1869.

—— The Wars of the Huguenots. 12°. Edin. 1871.

HANS, L. Second Siége de Paris. Le Comité Central et la Commune. 12°. Paris. 1871.

—— and Blanc, J. J. Guide à travers les Ruines. Paris et ses Environs. 12°. Paris. 1871.

HANSON, J. H. Latin Prose Book. 8°. N.Y. 1869.

HARBERT, W. Poems. See FULLER Worthies Library.

HARDIE, J. Account of the Fever in New York, 1805. 8°. N.Y. 1805.

HARDING, W. Universal Stenography. 18°. Lond. 1825.

HARDINGE, Emma. Modern American Spiritualism. 3d ed. 8°. N.Y. 1870.

HARDWICKE'S Science Gossip, 1869, 1870. 2 v. R. 8°. Lond. 1870–71.

HARDY, Sir F. D. Descriptive Catalogue of Materials Relative to the History of Great Britain and Ireland. v. 3. (Rolls Chron.) R. 8°. Lond. 1871.

—— Syllabus of Rymer's Fœdera. v. 1. (Rolls Chron.) R. 8°. Lond. 1869.

HARDY, R. S. Manual of Budhism. 8°. Lond. 1853.

HARE, A. J. C. Walks in Rome. 2 v. 12°. Lond. 1871.

HARGREAVES, J. G. Blunders of Vice and Folly. 12°. Lond. 1870. Same. 1871.

HARGROVE, C. Notes on Genesis; with Essays, etc. 3 v. 12°. Lond. 1870.

HÄRING, W. Die Hosen des Herrn von Bredow. 12°. Berlin. 1868.

—— Isegrimm. 2d ed. 12°. Berlin. 1871.

—— Ruhe ist die erste Bürgerpflicht. 3 v. in 2. 12°. Berl. 1861.

HARKNESS, A. First Latin Book. 12°. N.Y. 1851.
HARNEY, G. E. Stables, Outbuildings and Fences. 4°. N.Y. n.d.
—— Same. 4°. N.Y. 1870.
HARPER'S Bazaar. v. 3. 4. f°. N.Y. 1870–71.
HARPER'S Hand-Book for Travellers in Europe and the East. 12°. N.Y. 1871.
HARPER'S Illustrated Weekly. v. 14–15. f°. N.Y. 1870–71.
HARPER'S Magazine. v. 38–43. 8°. N.Y. 1869–71.
—— Index to Vols. 1–40. 8°. N.Y. 1870.
HARRIOTT, T. The Mosaic Theory. 8°. Lond. 1870.
HARRIS, C. A. Dentistry. 10th ed. Ed. by Austen. 8°. Phil. 1871.
HARRIS, E. D. Bascom Genealogy. 8°. Bost. 1870.
HARRIS, G. Theory of the Arts. 2 v. 8°. Lond. 1869.
HARRIS, H. No Royal Road to Knowledge; a Lecture. 8°. Albany. 1842.
—— Oration, July 4, 1847. 8°. Albany. 1847.
(Bound together.)
HARRIS, J. Hermes; or Universal Grammar. 5th ed. 8°. Lond. 1794.
HARRIS, J. The Pig. 12°. N.Y. n.d.
—— Same. 12°. N.Y. 1870.
HARRIS, W. Elements of Chaldee. 8°. N.Y. 1823.
HARRIS, W. S. Rudimentary Electricity. 18°. Lond. 1848.
—— Rudimentary Magnetism. 16°. Lond. 1850.
HARRIS, W. R. Epitaphs from the Old Burying Ground in Watertown. Sm. 4°. Bost. 1869.
HARRISON, W. B. Mechanic's Tool Book. 12°. N.Y. 1868.
HARRISON, W. R. Decorative Art. 4°. Lond. 1871.
HARRISSE, H. Bibliotheca Americana Vetustissima. 4°. N.Y. 1866.
HARSHA, J. W. Song of the Redeemed. 12°. Phil. 1870.
HART, A. M. The World of the Sea. 8°. Lond. n.d.
HART, Jos. E. Geographical Exercises, 18°. N.Y. 1871.
HART, John S. Bible as an Educating Power. 12°. Phil. 1862.
—— Manual of Composition and Rhetoric. 12°. Phil. 1871.
—— The Sunday-School Idea. 16°. Phil. 1871.
HARTE. F. B. East and West Poems. 16°. Bost. 1871.
—— The Heathen Chinee: Illustrated by Eytinge. Bost. 1871.
—— The Pliocene Skull. Illustrations by Shaeffer. Sm. 4°. n.p. n.d.
—— Poems. 16°. Bost. 1871.
HARTFORD Directory, 1870–71. 2 v. 12°. Hartf. 1870–71.
HARTING, J. E. Hints on Shore Shooting. 16°. Lond. 1871.
—— Ornithology of Shakespeare. 8°. Lond 1871.
HARTLEY, Florence. Ladies' Book of Etiquette. 12°. Bost. n.d.
HARTLEY, W. B. M. (Ed'r.) *See* STUART, I. W.
HARTMANN, M. Der Gefangene von Chillon. 16°. Hamburg. 1863.
—— Die Letzten Tage eines Königs. 12°. Stuttg. 1867.
—— Novellen. 2 v. 16°. Hamburg. 1863.
HARTT, C. F. Geology and Physical Geography of Brazil. 8°. Bost. 1870.
HARTWIG, G. Polar World. 8°. N.Y. 1869.
—— The Subterranean World. 8°. N.Y. 1871.
HARVARD College. Inauguration of President Eliot. 8°. Camb. 1869.
HARVEY, Mrs. Turkish Harems and Circassian Homes. 8°. Lond. 1871.
HARVEY, G. Early History of the Royal Scottish Academy. 8°. Lond. 1870.
HARVEY, R. The French Mind. 16°. Lond. 1870.
HARVEY'S Sea-Torpedo; Instructions for Management. 8°. Lond. 1871.
HASKINS, R. W. History of Phrenology. 12°. Buff. 1839.
HASSALL, A. H. Adulterations of Food. 12°. Lond. 1857.
HASSLER, F. R. Comparison of Weights and Measures. 8°. Wash. 1832.
—— Plates and Tables to System of Universe. Obl. 4°. N.Y. 1828.
HATFIELD, Julia. Bryant Homestead Book. Sm. 4°. N. Y. 1870.
HATTON, J. Reminiscences of Mark Lemon. 12°. Lond. 1871.
HAUFF, W. Lichtenstein. 12°. Berlin. 1868.
HAUSBLÄTTER. v. 4. 8°. Stuttg. 1860.

HÄUSSER, L. Deutsche Geschic te, 1786–1815. 4 v. 8°. Berlin. 1869.
—— Geschichte der französischen Revolution. 8°. Berlin. 1868.
—— Geschichte des Zeitalters der Reformation. 8°. Berlin. 1868.
HAVEN, E. O. Rhetoric. 12°. N.Y. 1869.
HAVEN, G. The Mission of America; Fast Sermon. 8°. Bost. 1863.
HAWEIS, H. R. Music and Morals. 12°. N.Y. 1872.
HAWEIS, T. Communicant's Spiritual Companion. 4th ed. 18°. N.Y. 1867.
HAWES, J. New England's Indebtedness to the Pilgrim Fathers; a Discourse. (PC. 22.) 8°. Hartf. 1859.
—— Tobacco, the Bane of the Times. 18°. Hartf. 1861.
HAWES, Mrs. Memoir of Mrs. Mary E. Van Lennep. 12°. Hartf. 1847.
HAWES, S. New Testament Manual. 16°. Bost. 1871.
—— Synchronology. 8°. Bost. 1870.
—— Same. 3d ed. 8°. Bost. 1871.
HAWTHORNE, N. Passages from English Note Books. 2 v. 12°. Bost. 1870.
—— Passages from French and Italian Note-Books. 2 v. 16°. Bost. 1872.
HAWTHORNE, Mrs. N. England and Italy. 12°. N.Y. 1869.
HAY, C. Club and Drawing-Room. 2 v. 12°. Lond. 1870.
HAY, J. Castilian Days. 12°. Bost. 1871.
—— Little Breeches. 8°. N.Y. 1871.
—— Pike County Ballads and other Pieces. 12°. Bost. 1871.
HAYDN and other Poems. 16°. N.Y. 1870.
HAYDN'S Dictionary of Dates. American Revision. 8°. N.Y. 1869.
HAYDN'S Index of Biography. Ed. by Payne. 8°. Lond. 1870.
HAYES, E. Ballads of Ireland. 4th ed. 2 v. 16°. Edin. n.d.
HAYES, I. I. The Land of Desolation. (Greenland). 12°. N.Y. 1872.
—— Progress of Arctic Discovery; an Address. (PC. 24.) 8°. N.Y. 1868.
HAYNE, J. E. G. Élémens de Topographie Militaire. 8°. Paris. 1806.
HAYNE, P. H. Legends and Lyrics. 12°. Phil. 1872.
HAYS, *et al* vs. Pa. R. R. Co. Reply to Patterson's Charges. (PC. 6.) 8°. Phil. n.d.
HAYWARD, J. Elements of Geometry. 12°. Cambr. 1829.
HAZARD, R. G. Causation and Freedom in Willing. 12°. Lond. 1869.
HAZARD, S. Cuba with Pen and Pencil. 8°. Hartf. 1870.
HAZELTINE, M. J. Clipper Chess Problem Tournament. 16°. N.Y. n.d.
HAZEN, J. A. Five Years Before the Mast. 16°. N.Y. 1869.
HAZLITT, W. English Poets and Comic Writers. 12°. Lond. 1869.
—— Literature of the Age of Elizabeth; and Characters of Shakspeare. 12°. Lond. 1869.
—— Round Table; Northcote's Conversations; Characteristics. Ed. by W. C. Hazlitt. 12°. Lond. 1871.
HAZLITT, W. C. English Proverbs. 8°. Lond. 1869.
—— New London Jest-Book. 16°. Lond. 1871.
—— Popular Antiquities of Great Britain. 3 v. 8°. Lond. 1870.
HEAD, Sir F. B. Royal Engineer. 8°. Lond. 1869.
HEAD, Sir G. Manufacturing Districts of England. 12°. N.Y. 1836.
HEADLEY, J. T. Mountain Adventures. 16°. N.Y. 1871.
HEADLEY, T. G. Elementary and Primary Views of Religion. 16°. Lond. 1871.
HEADY, M. Poems. 12°. Balt. 1869.
HEALY, Mary. Home Theatre. 12°. Bost. 1871.
HEARD, F. T. Curiosities of the Law Reporters. 12°. Bost. 1871.
HEARD, J. B. Tripartite Nature of Man. 2d ed. 12°. Edin. 1868.
HEAT and Ventilation. General Observations. 8°. Rochester. 1851.
HEATH'S Government Counterfeit Detector Sm. 4°. Bost. n.d.
HEATH, C. Practical Anatomy. 2d ed. 16°. Lond. 1869.
—— Same; ed. by Keen. 12°. Phil. 1870.
HEATHERINGTON, A. Gold Fields of Nova Scotia. 16°. Montreal. 1868.
HEATON, Mrs. C. Life of Albert Durer. L. 8°. Lond. 1870.
HEBBEL, F. Judith. 16°. Hamburg. 1841.
HEBREW Grammar. 2d ed. 8°. Camb. 1806.
HECKER, J. Wissenschaftliche Grundlage der Erziehung. 8°. N.Y. 1868.

HEDGE, F. H. Primeval World of Hebrew Tradition. 12°. Bost. 1870.
—— Prose Writers of Germany. New ed. R. 8°. Phil. 1870.
HEDGE, L. Logick. 16°. Bost. 1835.
—— Same. 16°. Buff. 1855.
HEDGES, J. A. Sorgo; or the Northern Sugar Plant. 12°. Cinc. 1863.
HEFELE, C. J. History of Councils through Nicæa. Tr. and Ed by Clark. 8°. Edin. 1871.
HEINE, H. De l'Angleterre. 12°. Paris. 1867.
—— De la France. 12°. Paris. 1867.
—— Letzte Gedichte und Gedanken. 16°. Hamburg. 1869.
—— Poëmes et Legendes. 12°. Paris. 1868.
—— Vorrede zu "Französischen Zuständen." 18. Leip. 1833.
—— Werke. v. 1–2. 12°. Phil. 1869.
HEINEMANN, O. von. Zur Erinnerung an G. E. Lessing. 12°. Leip. 1870.
HEINEMANN, W. Catechism of German Grammar. 24°. Lond. 1823.
HEINRICH, L. Der Anthropophag. 12°. Breslau. 1869.
HELE, N. F. Notes about Aldeburgh. 12°. Lond. 1870.
HELFENSTEIN, J. Grammar of Teutonic Languages. 8°. Lond. 1870.
HELIODORUS. Romances. *See* GREEK Romances.
HELLER, R. Primadonna. 12°. Berlin. 1871.
HELM, Clementine. Backfischchen's Leiden und Freuden. 2d ed. 12°. Leip. 1868.
HELMHOLTZ, H. Populäre wissenschaftliche Vorträge. 2 v. in 1. 8°. Brunswick. 1865–71.
HELMSDÖRFER, G. K. F. Becker, der Grammatiker. 8°. Frank. 1854.
HELP for the Sick and Wounded. 12°. Lond. 1870.
HELPS, A. Companions of my Solitude. 16°. Bost. 1870.
—— Conversations on War and General Culture. 12°. Bost. 1871.
—— Same. 12°. Lond. 1871.
—— Essays in the Intervals of Business. 16°. Bost. 1871.
—— Essays; and Organization in Daily Life. 12°. Bost. 1870.
—— Same. 16°. Lond. 1870.
—— Hernando Cortes. 12°. N.Y. 1871.
—— Thoughts upon Government. 12°. Lond. 1872.
—— Same. 8°. Bost. 1872.
HEMANS, C. I. Mediæval Christianity and Art in Italy. 12°. Lond. 1869.
HEMENWAY, Abigail M. Vermont Historical Gazetteer. 2 v. 8°. Burlington. 1867–71.
HENCKEL, C. and Born, W. F. Nautical and Commercial Pocket Dictionary and Dialogue Book. Obl. 8°. Copenhagen. 1836.
HENDERSON, A. Latin Proverbs and Quotations. Sm. 4°. Lond. 1869.
HENDERSON, Emily. Recollections of John Adolphus. 8°. Lond. 1871.
HENDERSON, P. Gardening for Profit. 12°. N.Y. n.d.
—— Practical Floriculture. 12°. N.Y. n.d.
HENDERSON, W. Dictionary and Concordance of Scripture Names. L. 8°. Edin. 1869.
HENLEY, R. Musings on the Revelation of St. John the Divine. 8°. Oxford. 1872.
HENRY, G. V. Military Record of Civilian Appointments. v. 1. 8°. N.Y. 1870.
HENRY the Minstrel. Wallace. Ed. by Jamieson. 12°. Glasg. 1869.
HENSEL, Octavia. Life and Letters of Gottschalk. 12°. Bost. 1870.
HENSHALL, S. Saxon and English. 4°. Lond. 1798.
HENTY, G. A. March to Magdala. 8°. Lond. 1868.
—— Out on the Pampas. 16°. Lond. 1871.
HEPWORTH, G. H. Christ and his Church. 8°. N.Y. 1872.
—— Rocks and Shoals. 16°. Bost. 1870.
HERALD of Health. New series. v. 13–18. (47–52 of Old series.) 8°. N.Y. 1869–71.
HERBERT, H. W. Complete Manual for Young Sportsmen. 12°. N.Y. n.d.
—— The Dog. 12°. N.Y. 1868.
—— Sporting Scenes and Characters. 2 v. 8°. Phil. n.d.
HERD, D. Scottish Songs. 2 v. 18°. Glasgow. 1869.
HERDER, J. G. von. Outlines of a Philosophy of Man. 2 v. Transl. by Churchill. 8°. Lond. 1803.
HERGENRÖTHER, Dr. Anti-Janus. Tr. by Robertson. 12°. Dublin. 1870.

HÉRITAGE (L') de mon Oncle. 12°. Paris. 1870.

HERODOTUS. History. Tr. by Beloe. 3 v. 24°. N.Y. 1828.

—— Same. Tr. by Rawlinson, etc. 4 v. 8°. N.Y. 1860.

—— Same. Tr. by Cary. Bohn's ed. 12°. Lond. 1867.

—— Works; Text of Baehr. Tr. by Cary. 12°. N.Y. 1868.

HEROES and Hunters of the West. 12°. Phil. 1869.

HEROINES in Obscurity. 12°. Lond. 1871.

HERSCHEL, J. F. W. Outlines of Astronomy. 10th ed. 8°. Lond. 1869.

HERTZ, H. King René's Daughter. 16°. N.Y. 1871.

—— König René's Tochter. 16°. Leip. n.d.

HERVEY, J. Theron and Aspasio. 12°. n.p. n.d.

HESEKIEL, G. Aus den Mittheilungen eines Gourmands. 12°. Berlin. 1852.

—— Bis nach Hohen-Zieritz. 3 v. 12°. Berlin. 1861.

—— Das Buch vom Grafen Bismarck. 8°. Bielefeld. 1869.

—— Der Capitain der Königin. 3 v. 12°. Berlin. 1872.

—— Krummensee I: Ueber'n Rhein nach Paris. 3 v. 12°. Berlin. 1861.

—— Same II: Heimkehr und Wiederkunft. 3 v. 12°. Berlin. 1861.

—— Life of Bismarck. Tr. by Mackenzie. 8°. Lond. 1870.

—— Same. 8°. N.Y. 1870.

—— Schellen-Moritz. 12°. Berlin. 1869.

—— Stille vor dem Sturm. 3 v. 12°. Berlin. 1863.

—— Vor Jena. 12°. Berlin. n.d.

HESEKIEL, L. Lenz Schadewacht. 2 v. 12°. Berlin. 1871.

HESIOD, Callimachus and Theognis. Tr. by Banks. (Bohn's ed.) 12°. Lond. 1871.

HESSEY, J. A. Sunday Bampton Lectures. 3d ed. 12°. Lond. 1866.

HETTNER, H. Literaturgeschichte des achtzehnten Jahrhunderts.

Part 1. Geschichte der Englischen Literatur von 1660–1770. 8°. Brunswick. 1856.

Part 2. Geschichte der Französischen Literatur im achtzehnten Jahrhundert. 8°. Brunswick. 1860.

Part 3. Geschichte der Deutschen Literatur im achtzehnten Jahrhundert. 4 v. in 2. 8°. Brunswick. 1862–70.

HEURTLEY, C. A. Sermons on Subjects of Recent Controversy. 8°. Oxf. 1871.

HEUSINGER, Ed. Eines Königs Dank. 12°. Leip. 1869.

HEUSINGER, O. Amerikanische Kriegsbilder. 12°. Leip. 1869.

HEWITSON, W. C. Exotic Butterflies. v. 1–3. 4°. Lond. 1856–66.

HEWITT, A. F. Problems of the Age. 12°. N.Y. 1868.

HEWSON, A. Earth as a Topical Application in Surgery. 12°. Phil. 1871.

HEYGATE, W. E. Poems. 16°. Lond. 1870.

HEYLLI, G. d'. Le Livre Rouge de la Commune. 12°. Paris. 1871.

HEYSE, P. Ein Neues Novellenbuch. 12°. Berlin. 1871.

—— Gesammelte Werke. v. 1. Gedichte. 12°. Berlin. 1871.

HIBBERD, S. Amateur's Flower Garden. 12°. Lond. 1871.

—— Book of the Aquarium. 16°. Lond. n.d.

—— Clever Dogs, etc. Sm. 4°. Lond. n.d.

—— The Fern Garden. 2d ed. 12°. Lond. 1869.

—— Field Flowers. 12°. Lond. 1870.

—— Rustic Adornments for Homes of Taste. Sm. 4°. Lond. 1870.

HICKIE, D. B. Catechism of Greek Accidence. 24°. Lond. 1825.

HICKOK, L. P. Creator and Creation. 8°. Bost. 1872.

HICKOK, M. J. Sermon: Conversion of Jews. (PC. 18.) 8°. N.Y. 1860.

HIGDEN, B. Polychronicon, with Transl. v. 2, 3. (Rolls Chr.) R. 8°. Lond. 1871.

HIGGINSON, E. Ecce Messias; or, The Hebrew Messianic Hope and the Christian Reality. 8°. Lond. 1871.

HIGGINSON, T. W. Atlantic Essays. 12°. Bost. 1871.

HIGGONS, B. Remarks on Burnet's History of his Own Time. 8°. Lond. 1727.

HILARIUS, F. Non Possumus. 12°. Leip. 1870.

HILEY, R. English Grammar, Abridged. 4th ed. 24°. Lond. 1841.

—— English Grammar, 3d ed. (Bound with it, is Reid's English Dictionary, N. Y. 1845.) 16°. Lond. 1840.
—— Questions on English Grammar. 3d ed. 16°. Lond. 1842.
HILL, A. F. Our Boys. 12°. Phil. 1869.
HILL, A. H. Scholar's Day Dream, etc. 16°. Lond. 1870.
HILL, Mrs. A. P. New Cook Book. 12°. N.Y. 1870.
HILL, G. H. Scenes from the Life of an Actor. 12°. N.Y. n.d.
HILL, J. Latin Synonyms. 24°. N.Y. 1809.
HILL, P. G. Life of Napoleon III. 8°. Lond. 1869.
HILLERN, Wilhelmine von. Ein Arzt der Seele. 2 v. 12°. Berlin. n.d.
—— Same. 2d ed. 2 v. 12°. Berl. 1871.
HILLGROVE, T. Art of Dancing. 16°. N.Y. 1869.
HILLHOUSE, A. L. Description of the European Olive. 4°. n.p. n.d.
HILL STREET REFUGE. Addresses, etc. (P. 101.) 24°. Lond. 1853.
HILTL, G. Die Bank des Verderbens. 2 v. 12°. Berlin. n.d.
—— Der Böhmische Krieg. 8°. Bielefeld. 1867.
—— Eine Cabinets Intrigue. 12°. Berlin. n.d.
—— Das Geheimniss des Fürstenhauses. 12°. Berlin. n.d.
—— Der Münzthurm ; I. Das Erzbild der Kurfürsten. 12°. Bielefeld. 1871.
—— Unter der rothen Eminenz. 12°. Berlin. n.d.
HINGSTON, E. P. The Genial Showman. (C. F. Browne.) 2 v. 8°. Lond. 1870.
—— Same. 8°. N.Y. 1870.
HINTON, J. Health and its Conditions. 12°. N.Y. 1871.
—— Thoughts on Health. 12°. Lond. 1871.
HINTS on the Formation, etc., of Sabbath School Unions. (P. 88 and 95.) 8°. Edin. n.d.
HINTS to Chairmen. 18°. Lond. 1837.
HINTS to Young Tradesmen. 24°. Bost. 1838.
HIPPEAU, Mme. E. L'Économie Domestique. 16°. Paris. n.d.
HIPPOLYTUS. Writings. v. 2. *See* ANTI-NICENE Christian Library. v. 9.
HIRTH, G. Tagebuch des deutsch-französischen Kriegs. v. 1. Sm. 4°. Berlin. 1871.
HISLOP, A. Adversaria, etc. 16°. Edin. n.d.
HISTOIRE de l'Armée de Chalons. 2d ed. 8°. Bruss. n.d.
HISTOIRE Généalogique des Maisons Souveraines de l'Europe. 2 v. 8°. Paris. 1811-12.
HISTOIRE de Lucie Wellers. 2 v. 16°. Lyons. 1766.
HISTOIRE de la Marquise de Terville. 16°. Lond. 1756.
HISTOIRE du Père La Chaize. 2 v. 18°. Cologne. 1694-5.
HISTORICAL Magazine. 2d ser. v. 5-7. Sm. 4°. Morrisania. 1869-70.
HISTORICAL Sketch of the College of New Jersey. 8°. Phil. 1859.
HISTORICAL Sketch of the Supervisors of N.Y. County. 8°. N.Y. 1862.
HISTORY of the Controversy in the University of N.Y. 8°. N.Y. 1838.
HISTORY of the English Church. By M. C. S. 12°. Oxf. 1869.
HISTORY of Foundation of Order of Visitation, etc. 12°. Balt. 1870.
HISTORY and Philosophy of Marriage. 12°. Bost. 1869.
HISTORY of the Railroad Conflict in the 84th Legislature of N. J. 8°. Trenton. 1860.
HITCHCOCK'S Chronological Record of the Rebellion. 8°. N.Y. 1866.
HITCHCOCK, E. Catalytic Power of the Gospel ; a Sermon. (PC. 14.) 8°. Bost. 1852.
—— 2d Report on Geol. Survey of Vermont. (PC. 21.) 8°. Burl. 1858.
HITCHCOCK, R. D. Civil Service Reform. A Discourse. 12°. N.Y. n.d.
—— Laws of Civilization ; an Address. (PC. 14.) 8°. N.Y. 1860.
—— Thanksgiving for Victories ; a Sermon. (PC. 14.) 8°. N.Y. 1864.
HITTELL, J. S. Resources of California. 5th ed. 12°. San. Fr. 1869.
HOBHOUSE, J. C. *See* BROUGHTON (Lord)
HOBLER, F. Roman Coins. 2 v. 4°. Lond. 1860.
—— Liber Mercatoris. 16°. Lond. 1838.
HÖCKER, G. Mammon and Marmor. 12°. Nuremberg. 1870.
HODDER, G. Memories of my Time. 8°. Lond. 1870.

HODGE, C. Last Hours of A. B. Dod. (PC. 14.) 8°. Princeton. n.d.
—— Systematic Theology. 2 v. 8°. N.Y. 1871-2.
HODGMAN Golden Wedding Memorial. (PC. 6.) 8°. Albany. 1865.
HODGSON, S. H. Theory of Practice. 2 v. 8°. Lond. 1870.
HODGSON, W. B. Education of Girls, and the Employment of Women. 12°. Lond. 1869.
—— Turgot, his Life and Times. 16°. Lond. 1870.
HOEFER, E. In der Welt Verloren. 4 v. in 1. 16°. Leip. 1869.
—— In Doloribus. 16°. Vienna. n.d.
—— Land und See. 12°. Breslau. 1871.
—— Neue Geschichten. 2 v. 12°. Breslau. 1867.
—— Unter Fliegenden Fahnen. 2 v. 12°. Breslau. 1872.
—— Zur linken Hand. 12°. Leip. 1872.
—— Zwei Familien. 12°. Breslau. 1869.
HOFFMAN, J. J. Japanese Grammar. L. 8°. Leyden. 1868.
HOFFMAN, W. Prophecies of our Lord and his Apostles. 12°. Lond. 1869.
HOFFMANN, E. T. W. Sämmtliche Werke. R. 8°. Paris. 1841.
HOFFMANN, G. Märchen für Jung und Alt. 12°. Berlin. n.d.
HOFFMANN, H. Californien, Nevada und Mexico. 8°. Basel. 1871.
HOGARTH'S Frolic; a Five Days' Peregrination. 4°. Lond. n.d.
HOGG, J. The Microscope. 3d ed. 12°. Lond. 1858.
—— Same. 8th ed. 12°. Lond. 1871.
—— Natural Philosophy. 12°. Lond. 1861.
HOHENTHAL, Graf. L. Der Deutsch-französische Krieg von 1870-71. 3 v. in 2. 12°. Leip. 1871.
HOLBACH, Paul Thyry [Baron d'.] System of Nature. 8°. Lond. 1850.
HOLBEACH, Henry. Student in Life and Philosophy. 2 v. 12°. Lond. 1865.
HOLBROOK, J. C. Difficulties of Infidelity; a Sermon. 8°. Homer. 1867.
HOLBROOK, M. L. Parturition without Pain. 16°. N.Y. 1871.
HOLCOMBE, J. P. Literature in Letters. 12°. N.Y. 1866.
HOLCOMBE, W. H. In Both Worlds. 12°. Phil. 1870.
—— The Other Life. 12°. Phil. 1871.
—— Our Children in Heaven. 12°. Phil. 1869.
—— Southern Voices. 16°. Phil. 1872.
HOLDICH, J. Discourse on Rev. W. Fisk. 8°. Middletown. 1839.
HOLE, S. R. Book about Roses. S. 4°. Edin. 1869.
HOLLAND, H. Recollections of Past Life. 12°. Lond. 1872.
—— Same. 12°. N.Y. 1872.
HOLLAND, H. W. National Primary Education. 12°. Lond. 1870.
HOLLAND, J. Star Streaks. 16°. Newark. 1870.
HOLLAND, T. E. Essays on the Form of the Law. 8°. Lond. 1870.
HOLLAND Memorial. Sketch of the Life of George Holland. Imp. 8°. N.Y. 1871.
HOLLENIUS, L. J. Dollars and Cents; a Comedy. 16°. N.Y. 1869.
HOLLEY, O. H. Life of Franklin. 12°. N.Y. n.d.
HOLLOWAY, Laura C. Ladies of the White House. 8°. N.Y. 1870.
HOLME, J. S. Light at Evening Tide. R. 8°. N.Y. 1870.
HOLMES, F. G. Phosphate Rocks of South Carolina. 8°. Charleston. 1870.
HOLMES, O. W. Mechanism in Thought and Morals. 16°. Bost. 1871.
—— Oration, July 4, 1863. 8°. Bost. 1863.
—— Poems. 22d ed. 16°. Bost. 1866.
—— Soundings from the Atlantic. 12°. Bost. 1866.
HOLMES, T. System of Surgery. 2d ed. 5 v. 8°. Lond. 1870-1.
HOLT, J. Fallacy of Neutrality; an Address to the People of Kentucky. 12°. N.Y. 1861.
—— Vindication from Slanders, etc. 8°. n.p. n.d.
HOLTEI, K. von. Eine alte Jungfer. 12°. Breslau. 1869.
—— Bilder aus dem häuslichen Leben. 2 v. in 1. 16°. Berlin. 1858.
—— Charpie. 2 v. in 1. 24°. Breslau. 1866.
—— Christian Lammfell. 5 v. in 2. 12°. Breslau. 1853.
—— Die Eselsfresser. 3 v. 12°. Breslau. 1860.
—— Haus Treustein. 3 v. 12°. Breslau. 1866.

—— Nachlese. 2 v. in 1. 12°. Breslau. 1870.

—— Der Obernigker Bote. 3 v. 12°. Berlin. 1854.

—— Ein Schneider. 3 v. in 1. 12°. Breslau. 1854.

—— Vierzig Jahre. 8 v. 12°. Berlin. 1843.

HOLTHOUSE, C. Hernial and other Tumours. 8°. Lond. 1870.

HOLYOKE, M. Conservation of Pictures. 12°. Lond. 1870.

HOME and Health for 1871. v. 1. 8°. N.Y. n.d.

HOME Missionary. v. 41–43. 8°. N.Y. 1869–71.

HOME Pictures of the English Poets. 12°. N.Y. 1869.

HOME Recreations and Foreign Travel. 16°. Lond. n.d.

HOMER. Works. Transl. by Buckley. (Bohn's ed.) 2 v. 12°. Lond. 1867.

—— Iliad. Transl. by Bryant. 2 v. L. 8°. Bost. 1870–1.

—— Same. 2 v. 16°. Bost. 1871.

—— Iliad. Transl. by Caldcleugh. 12°. Phil. 1870.

—— Iliad. Transl. by Cordery. 2 v. 12°. Lond. 1871.

—— Iliad. Transl. by Earl of Derby. 12°. N.Y. 1870.

—— Iliad; construed literally by Giles. v. 1. 16°. Lond. n.d.

—— Iliad. Transl. by Newman. 2d ed. R. 8°. Lond. 1871.

—— Iliad; Greek, notes by Paley. 2 v. 8°. Lond. 1866–71.

—— Iliad; transl. by Pope. 2 v. 24°. Balt. 1824.

—— Iliad; transl. by Pope. 18°. Lond. n.d.

—— Iliad, Book 1, with Interlinear Translation. 16°. Lond. 1834.

—— Odyssey. Transl. by Bryant. 2 v. L. 8°. Bost. 1871–72.

—— Odyssey, Books 1–12. Greek. Ed. by Merry. 16°. Oxford. 1870.

—— Odyssey. Transl. by Pope. 18°. Lond. 1864.

HOMES, H. A. Our Knowledge of California and the N. W. Coast one hundred years since. 8°. Albany. 1870.

—— Palatine Emigration to England in 1709. 8°. Albany. 1870. (Papers read before Albany Inst. Bound together.)

HOMILIST. Ed by Thomas. v. 28. (v. 3, Editor's series.) 12°. Lond. 1871.

HOMO versus Darwin. 12°. Phil. 1872.

HONE, P. and Lunt, G. Address and Poem to Bost. Merc. Libr. Asso. (PC. 21.) 12°. Bost. 1843.

HONEGGER, J. J. Culturgeschichte der neuesten Zeit. 4 v. 8°. Leip. 1868–71.

HONEST (An) Appeal to Every Voter (on Bible in Schools). (PC. 8.) 8°. N.Y. n.d.

HOOD, E. P. Dark Sayings on a Harp, etc. 2d ed. 12°. Lond. 1870.

—— Lamps, Pitchers and Trumpets. 1st and 2d ser. 12°. N.Y. 1869.

—— World of Moral and Religious Anecdote. 12°. Lond. 1870.

HOOD, P. Gout, Rheumatism and Allied Affections. 12°. Lond. n.d.

HOOD, T. Tales, Romances and Extravaganzas. 12°. N.Y. 1866.

—— Whimsicalities. 12°. Lond. 1870.

HOOD, W. P. Bone Setting. 12°. Lond. 1871.

HOOK, W. F. Archbishops of Canterbury. New ser., v. 3. 8°. Lond. 1869.

—— Disestablished Church of the United States. 8°. Lond. 1869.

HOOKER, W. Child's Book of Nature. Sq. 16°. N.Y. 1870.

HOOPER, G. Waterloo. 8°. Lond. 1862.

HOOPER, Lucy H. Poems. 12°. Phil. 1871.

HOPE, A. R. Book about Boys. 12°. N.Y. n.d.

HOPE, G. H. 'Till the Doctor Comes. 16°. N.Y. 1871.

HOPE, J. L. A. In Quest of Coolies. 12°. Lond. 1872.

HOPKINS, Jerome. Method for Orpheon Singing Classes. 5th ed. 8°. N.Y. n.d.

HOPKINS, M. Baccalaureate Sermon, Aug. 2, 1863. 8°. Bost. 1863.

—— Sermon, Ordination of Rev. C. M. Hyde. 8°. Bost. 1862.

HOPKINS, S. Inquiry into the Nature of True Holiness. 18°. Newport. 1791.

HOPPE, C. Percussion and Auscultation. 16°. Phil. 1869.

HOPPE, H. Katalog der Deutschen Literatur, 1801–68. 8°. St. Petersburg. 1871.
HOPPER, E. Old Horse Gray. 16°. N.Y. 1869.
HOPPIN, A. Ups and Downs on Land and Water. Obl. f°. Bost. 1871.
HORACE. Lyrics. Transl. by Baring. Sm. 4°. Lond. 1870.
—— Odes and Carmen Sæculare. Transl. by Conington. 3d ed. 16°. Lond. 1866.
—— Odes and Epodes. Transl. by Lytton. 12°. N.Y. 1870.
—— Same. 12°. Edin. 1869.
—— Odes and Epodes. Tr. by Sewell. Bohn's Ed. 12°. Lond. 1858.
—— Satires, etc. Transl. by Conington. 16°. Lond. 1870.
—— Satires. Book 1. In English Verse by Millington. 12°. Lond. 1870.
—— Satires, Epistles, Ars Poetica. In Rhythmic Prose, by Millington. 12°. Lond. 1870.
—— Works (Latin.) Ed. by Chase and Stuart. 16°. Phil. 1869.
—— Works (Latin). Ed. by Macleane. 18°. N.Y. 1860.
HORN, W. O. von. Die Spinnstube, 1870. 16°. Frankf. n.d.
—— Die Spinnstube, 1872. 16°. Frankf. n.d.
HORNE, R. H. The Poor Artist. 2d ed. 16°. Lond. 1871.
HORNE, T. H. On Infidelity. *See* GIBSON, E., Pastoral Letters.
HORSBURGH, J. India Directory. 7th ed. 4°. Lond. 1855.
HORSFORD, E. N. The Army Ration. How to Diminish its Bulk, etc. 2d ed. 8°. N.Y. 1864.
HORTICULTURIST. v. 24, 25. R. 8°. N.Y. 1869–70.
HORTON, R. Complete Measurer. 12°. Lond. 1862.
HOSACK, J. Mary Queen of Scots, and her Accusers. v. 1. 8°. Edin. 1869. Same. 1870.
HOSPITAL Days. 8°. N.Y. 1870.
HOTTEN, J. C. Literary Copyright. 12°. Lond. 1871.
HOUDIN, R. The Sharper Detected and Exposed. 12°. Lond. 1863.
HOUGH, F. B. Farm Record for 25 Years. (Blank Book.) Sm. 4°. N.Y. 1860.
HOUGH, G. W. Eclipse of Aug. 7, 1869. 8°. Albany. 1870.
—— Velocity of the Electric Current over Telegraph Wire. 8°. Albany. 1870. (Papers read before Albany Inst. Bound together.)
HOUGHTON, W. Country Walks of a Naturalist. 16°. Lond. 1869.
—— Sea Side Walks. 12°. Lond. 1870.
HOURS at Home. v. 8–11. 8°. N.Y. 1869–70.
HOUSE of Refuge, Maryland. 11th Annual Report, 1861. (P. 91.) 8°. Balt. 1862.
HOUSE of Refuge, Philadelphia. Annual Reports, 32–34. 1859–61. (P. 91.) 8°. Phil. 1862.
—— By-Laws, Charter, etc. 8°. Phil. 1860.
HOUSE of Refuge, for Western Pennsylvania. 5th Annual Report. (P. 85 and 91.) 8°. Phil. 1859.
HOUSEHOLD Book of Irish Eloquence. 8°. N.Y. 1871.
HOUSSAYE, A. L'Amour comme il Est. 16°. Paris. 1870.
—— Les Femmes comme elles Sont. 16°. Paris. 1870.
—— Histoire du 41me Fauteuil. 16°. Paris. 1858.
—— Les Parisiennes. 8°. N.Y. 1869.
—— Le Repentir de Marion. 16°. Paris. 1870.
—— Le Violon de Franjolé. 12°. Paris. 1859.
—— Voyages Humoristiques. 12°. Paris. 1856.
HOVEDEN, R. de. Chronica (Rolls Chron.) R. 8°. Lond. 1870–71.
How, Samuel B. Slaveholding not Sinful. 2d ed. 12°. New Bruns. 1856.
How New York is Governed: Frauds of the Tammany Democracy. R. 8°. N.Y. 1871.
How should the Child Criminal be Treated? (PC. 13.) 8°. Lond. 1853.
How to Amuse an Evening Party. 16°. N.Y. n.d.
How to Read Character. 12°. N.Y. n.d.
HOWARD, C. J. Conundrums and Puzzles. 16°. N.Y. n.d.
HOWARD, J. P. Fluctuations in Gold, 1862–3. Folded 12°. N.Y. n.d.
HOWARD, M. Despotic Doctrines, etc: and, Senator Dixon Unmasked. (PC. 23.) 8°. Hartf. 1863.

HOWE, G. Presbyterian Church in South Carolina. v. 1. 8°. Columbus. 1870.
HOWE, H. Adventures and Achievements of Americans. 8°. N.Y. 1859.
—— The Great West. 8°. N.Y. 1859.
—— Life and Death on the Ocean. 8°. N.Y. 1860.
—— Travels, etc., of Celebrated Travelers. 8°. N.Y. 1857.
HOWE, J. Speech on the Reciprocity Treaty. (PC. 4.). 8°. Hamilton. 1865.
HOWE, Jas. W. Emergencies and How to Treat Them. 8°. N.Y. 1871.
HOWE, M. A. D. Life of Bishop Potter. 8°. Phil. 1871.
HOWE, S. G. Sanitary Condition of Troops near Boston. (P. 79.) 8°. Wash. 1861.
HOWELL, James. Forreine Travell. *See* ARBER's Reprints, No. 16.
HOWELLS, W. D. Suburban Sketches. 12°. N.Y. 1871.
HOWIE, J. Scots Worthies. Revised by Carslaw. 8°. Edin. 1870.
HOWITT, W. The Mad War-Planet, and other Poems. 16°. Lond. 1871.
HOWS, J. A. Forest Pictures in the Adirondacks; with Poems by Street. Sm. 4°. N.Y. 1865.
HOWSON, H. American Jute. (P.C. 23.) 8°. Phil. 1862.
HOWSON, J. S. Companions of St. Paul. 12°. Lond. 1871.
—— Essays on Cathedrals. 8°. Lond. 1872.
—— and Rimmer, A. Chester as it Was. 4°. Lond. 1872.
HOWSON, W. Embanking Lands from River Floods. 8°. N.Y. 1870.
HOXTON Ragged School. Circular. (P. 97.) Sm. 4°. Lond. 1852.
HOYLE. *See* AMERICAN Hoyle.
HOYLE's Games, Improved. 24°. N.Y. 1823.
HOYT, J. S. Sermon, Obituary of Lieut. Vandeburg. 8°. Detroit, 1863.
HOZIER, H. M. British Expedition to Abyssinia. 8°. Lond. 1869.
—— Seven Weeks' War. (German War of 1866.). 2d ed. 12°. Lond. 1871.
HUBER, P. Natural History of Ants. 16°. Lond. 1820.
HUDSON, A. Lectures on Fever. 2d ed. 12°. Dubl. 1868.
HUDSON, C. F. Christ our Life. 2d ed. 12°. Bost. 1861.
—— Greek and English Concordance of the New Testament. 2d ed. 16°. Phil. 1871.
HUDSON, E. H. Queen Bertha and her Times. 12°. Lond. n.d.
HUDSON, F. Private Theatricals. 16°. N.Y. n.d.
HUDSON Directory for 1871. 12°. Hudson. 1871.
HUGGINS, W. Results of Spectrum Analysis. 12°. Lond. n.d.
HUGHES, J. S. Diseases of Prostate Gland. 16°. Dubl. 1870.
HUGHES, S. Water Works. 12°. Lond. 1870.
HUGHES, T. Alfred the Great. 12°. Lond. n.d.
HUGHES, W. Atlas of Comparative Geography. f°. Lond. 1870.
—— Manual of Geography. 16°. Lond. 1871.
HUGHES, Wm. C. American Miller. 12°. Phil. 1869.
HUGO, V. Les Chatiments. 33d ed. 12°. Paris. n.d.
—— Der Lachende Mann. 2 v. 12°. Berlin. 1869.
—— Napoléon le Petit. 16th ed. 12°. Paris. n.d.
—— Napoleon the Little. 12°. N.Y. 1870.
—— Oeuvres. 16 v. 8°. Paris. 1841–46.
—— Ruy Blas. Transl. 16°. N.Y. n.d.
HULL, E. C. P. and Mair, R. S. The European in India; with Medical Guide. 12°. Lond. 1871.
HULL, M. Question Settled. Biblical and Modern Spiritualism. 12°. Bost. 1869.
HUMBER, W. Cast and Wrought Iron Bridge Construction. 2 v. 4°. Lond. 1870.
HUMBERT, A. Le Japon Illustré. 2 v. 4°. Paris. 1870.
HUMPHREYS, H. N. History of Printing. 4°. Lond. 1868.
HUN, E. R. Trichina Spiralis. (PC. 13.) 8°. Alb. 1869.
HUN, T. Medical Systems, etc. A Lecture. 8°. Alb. 1849.
HUNNEWELL, J. F. Land of Scott. 12°. Bost. 1871.
HUNT, E. Literature of the English Language. 12°. N.Y. 1870.
HUNT, E. B. Union Foundations. American Nationality as a Fact of Science. 8°. N.Y. 1863.

HUNT, E. M. Bible Notes. 2 v. Imp. 8°. N.Y. 1870.
HUNT, Mrs. Helen. Bits of Travel. 16°. Bost. 1872.
—— Verses by H. H. 16°. Bost. 1870.
HUNT, James. Stammering and Stuttering. 7th ed. 12°. Lond. 1870.
HUNT, John. Religious Thought in England. v. 1. 8°. Lond. 1870.
HUNT, L. Autobiography. 2 v. 12°. N.Y. 1855.
—— A Day by the Fire. 16°. Bost. 1870.
—— Jar of Honey from Mt. Hybla. 16°. Lond. 1870.
—— The Seer. 2 v. 16°. Bost. 1865.
—— Wit and Humor. 12°. N.Y. n.d.
HUNT, L. M. Peeps at Brittany. 12°. Lond. 1869.
HUNT, R. Practice of Photography. 12°. Lond. 1857.
HUNT'S Merchant's Magazine. v. 63. 8°. N.Y. 1870.
HUNTER, J. Self Instruction in Book-Keeping. 18°. Lond. 1871.
HUNTER, J. K. Life Studies of Character. 12°. Lond. 1870.
HUNTER, W. W. Indian Musalmans. 2d ed. 8°. Lond. 1872.
HUNTINGTON, D. Manual of the Fine Arts. 12°. N.Y. 1870.
HUNTINGTON, E. Address on Life of Dr. E. Bartlett. (PC. 14.) Lowell. 1856.
HUNTINGTON, E. The American Penman. Obl. 8°. Hartf. 1824.
HUNTINGTON, G. The Church's Work in our Large Towns. 2d ed. 12°. Oxf. 1871.
HURLBUT, E. P. Secular View of Religion in the State. (PC. 18, 23.) 8°. Alb. 1870.
HUSBAND, H. A. Medical and Surgical Examination Questions. 18°. Lond. 1871.
HUTCHINGS, J. M. Scenes in California. 8°. N.Y. 1870.
HUTCHINS, S. C. Civil List and Forms of Government of New York. 12°. Alb. 1868.
HUTCHINSON, A. H. Try Lapland; a Fresh Field for Summer Travel. 12°. Lond. 1870.
HUTCHINSON, W. N. Dog Breaking. 5th ed. 12°. Lond. 1869.
HUTTER, L. Compend of Lutheran Theology. 12°. Phil. 1868.
HUTTON, C. Course of Mathematics. Ed. by Rutherford. 8°. Lond. 1860.
—— Mathematics. 2 v. 8°. N.Y. 1831.
HUTTON, R. D. Essays Theological and Literary. 2 v. 8°. Lond. 1871.
HUXLEY, T. H. Lay Sermons, Addresses and Reviews. 8°. Lond. 1870.
—— Same. 8°. N.Y. 1870. Same, 1871.
—— Manual of Anatomy of Vertebrated Animals. 16°. Lond. 1871.
—— Origin of Species. 12°. N.Y. 1869.
—— and Youmans, E. L. Elements of Physiology and Hygiene. 12°. N.Y. 1870
HUYSHE, G. L. The Red River Expedition. 12°. Lond. 1871.
HYACINTHE, Father. Discourses. 12°. N.Y. 1869.
—— Family and Church. 12°. N.Y. 1870.
—— France et Allemagne. 8°. Lond. 1871
—— Orations on Civil Society. 16°. Lond. n.d.
HYDE, A. Sermon, Funeral of Mr. Ball. (Repr. from 1800.) (PC. 14.) Sm. 4°. Alb. 1862.

IBN Zafer. Solwan, or Waters of Comfort. Transl. from the Arabic. 2 v. 12°. Lond. 1852.
IDE, G. B. Pious Men the Nation's Hope; A Sermon. 8°. Bost. 1863.
IDEEN, Maria A. Changing the Crosses and Winning the Crown. 16°. Phil. 1872.
IDEVILLE H. d'. Journal d'un Diplomate en Italie. Turin, 1859–62. 12°. Paris. 1872.
IHNE, W. History of Rome. 2 v. 8°. Lond. 1871.
IKHWANUS Safa; or Brothers of Purity. Transl. from the Hindustani of Maulavi Ikram 'Ali, by John Platts. 8°. Lond. 1869.
ILLINOIS. Board of Public Charities. 1st Biennial Report. 8°. Springf. 1871.
—— Comments on the School Law. 8°. Springf. 1862
—— School Law of 1861. 8°. Springf. 1861.
ILLINOIS Association of Congregationalists. Memorial on Completing a Quarter of a Century of its History. 8°. Quincy. 1863
ILLINOIS in 1837. 8°. Phil. 1837

ILLUSTRATED Christian Weekly. v. 1. April–Dec. 1871. f°. N.Y. 1871.

ILLUSTRATED London News. v. 57–59. f°. Lond. 1870–1.

ILLUSTRATED Penny Readings. 1st and 2nd Series. 2 v. 12°. Lond. n.d.

ILLUSTRATED Times. v. 17–19 and v. 20 to March, 1872. f°. Lond. 1870–72.

ILLUSTRATION Européenne. v. 1. f°. Brussels. 1871.

ILLUSTRIRTE Zeitung. v. 54. f°. Leip. 1870.

ILS en ont menti. Par un Rural. 16°. Paris. 1871.

IM neuen Reich. Erster Jahrgang. v. 1, 2. 8°. Leip. 1871.

IMBERT de Saint Amand. Les Femmes de la Cour des derniers Valois. 12°. Paris. 1870.

IMMERMANN, K. Die Epigonen. 12°. Berlin. 1854.

IN Spirit and in Truth. An Essay on the Ritual of the New Testament. 8°. Lond. 1869.

INCE, H., and Gilbert, J. English History. 12°. Lond. 1869.

—— Outlines of English History. 16°. Lond. 1870.

INDEPENDENT (The). Vols. 1–4 and 6–10. 9 v. Atl. f°. N.Y. 1848–58.

INDIAN Narratives. 12°. Claremont. 1854.

INDIANA. School Law. 8°. Indianapolis. 1861.

INDIANAPOLIS Directory, 1871–2. 2 v. 8°. Indianapolis. 1870–71.

INDUSTRIAL Resources of Tyne, Wear and Tees. 2d ed. 8°. Lond. 1864.

INFANT Education. 4th ed. (Chambers' Course). 16°. Edin. 1837.

INGELOW, Jean. Monitions of the Unseen. 16°. Bost. 1870. Same. 1871.

INGERSLEBEN, Frau von: Eleonore. 5 v. in 2. 12°. Berlin. 1871.

—— Die Haideblume. 3 v. in 2. 12°. Berlin. 1868.

INGERSOLL, C. Letter to a Friend in a Slave State. 8°. Phil. 1862.

INGERSOLL, C. M. Conversations on English Grammar. 2d ed. 12°. N.Y. 1822.

INGERSOLL, J. R. Memoir of Samuel Breck. 8°. Phil. 1863.

INGLIS, J. Thoughts on John xvii. 16°. N.Y. n.d.

INGRAM, James, D. D. Memorials of Oxford. 3 v. 8°. Oxford. 1837.

INGRAM, John. Flora Symbolica. 12°. Lond. n.d.

INMAN, T. Ancient Faiths embodied in Ancient Names. 2 v. 8°. Lond. 1868–9.

—— Myalgia. 2d ed. 8°. Lond. 1870.

—— New Theory and Practice of Medicine. 2d ed. 12°. Lond. 1861.

—— Restoration of Health. 8°. Lond. 1870.

INNER (The) Life. Hymns. 16°. Oxford. 1871.

INSIDE Paris during the Siege, by an Oxford Graduate. 12°. Lond. 1871.

INSIDE Sebastopol. 8°. Lond. 1856.

INSTITUTE of Actuaries. Journal. v. 15. 8°. Lond. 1870.

INSURANCE Monitor. v. 18–19. 4°. N.Y. 1870–71.

INSURANCE Times. v. 2–4. 4°. N.Y. 1869–71.

INTELLECTUAL Observer. v. 6, 9. 8°. Lond. 1865–6.

INTERNATIONAL Congress of Pre-historic Archæology. Transactions. 3d Sess. 8°. Lond. 1869.

INTERNATIONALE Revue. July–Dec., 1866. 8°. Vienna. 1866.

INTEROCEANIC Ship Canal, *via* Atrato and Truando (Map). (PC. 20.) Folded 8°. n.p n.d.

INVESTIGATION into the Causes of the Depressed Condition of Business. 8°. Buff. 1860.

IOWA, Annals of. Vols. 8 and 9. 2 v. in 1. 8°. Davenport. 1871.

—— Educational Laws. 8°. Des Moines. 1862.

IRON and Steel Institute Journal, No. 1; Feb. 1, 1871. 8°. Lond. n.d.

IRONS, W. J. Christianity as taught by St. Paul. 8°. Oxford. 1870.

IRVING, D. Elements of English Composition. 12°. Georgetown. 1825.

ISAAC'S Harbor Gold Co. Prospectus. (PC. 9.) 8°. N.Y. 1864.

ISAMBERT, G. Combat et Incendie de Chateaudun. 12°. Paris. 1871.

ISBISTER, A. R. Outlines of Elocution and Reading. 18°. Lond. 1870.

—— Word Builder. 18°. Lond. 1869.

ISLE Royale Mining Co. Report to Feb. 1, 1864. (PC. 9.) 8°. N.Y. 1864.

IVES, E. Jr. Musical Spelling Book. 8°. N.Y. 1846.

JACK, A. Varied Aspects of the Word of Life. 12°. Lond. 1869.
— Sanctuary Services. 12°. Edin. 1869.
JACKSON, J. C. American Womanhood. 12°. Dansville. n.d.
— How to Treat the Sick without Medicine. 12°. Dansville. 1871.
JACKSON, T. Curiosities of the Pulpit. 12°. Lond. n.d.
— Our Dumb Companions. 4th ed. Sm. 4°. Lond. n.d.
JACOB, G. A. Ecclesiastical Polity of the New Testament. 12°. N.Y. 1872.
JACOB, G. Le G. Western India before and during the Mutinies. 12°. Lond. 1871.
JACOBI, A. Inaugural Address, with Paper on Infant Asylums. 8°. N.Y. 1872.
JACOBS, F. Greek Reader. 8°. N.Y. 1827.
— Latin Reader. Part 1. 16°. Bost. 1827.
JACOLLIOT, L. The Bible in India. 8°. Lond. 1870.
— Same. 16°. N.Y. 1870.
JACOX, F. Bible Music. 12°. Lond. 1871.
— Same. 12°. Bost. 1872.
— Cues from all Quarters. 12°. Bost. 1871.
— Scripture Texts Illustrated by General Literature. 12°. N.Y. 1871.
JACQUEMART, A. Merveilles de la Céramique. v. 3. 12°. Paris. 1869.
JACQUEMONT, V. Récits Espagnols. 16°. Paris. 1870.
JACQUES, D. H. The House. 12°. N.Y. 1869.
JAEGER, B. Class Book of Zoology. 18°. N.Y. 1849.
JAHN, O. W. A. Mozart. 2d ed. 2 v. R. 8°. Leip. 1867.
JAMAICA PLAIN Directory. *See* BROOKLINE.
JAMES, H. Secret of Swedenborg. 8°. Bost. 1869.
JAMES, J. A. Young Man beginning Life. *See* AM. TRACT SOC.: Tracts for Young Men.
— Young Man Undecided in Religion. *See* AM. TRACT SOC.: Tracts for Young Men.
JAMES, W. Memoir of Rev. T. Mudge. 8°. Lond. 1871.
JAMESON, Mrs. Anna. Celebrated Female Sovereigns. 4th ed. 12°. Lond. 1869.
— Female Sovereigns. 12°. Phil. n.d.
JAMET-Massicault. Thibaud. 16°. Paris. 1870.
JANSE. Account of Anneke Janse and her Family. 16°. Alb. 1870.
JANIN, J. Les Amours du Chevalier de Fosseuse. 16°. Paris. 1867.
— L'Interne. 8°. N.Y. 1870.
JANVIER, F. D. H. The Sleeping Sentinel. A Poem. 16°. Phil. 1863.
JARDINE, John. Christian Sacerdotalism. 8°. Lond 1871.
JARVES, J. J. Art Idea. 3d ed. 16°. N.Y. 1866.
— Art Thoughts. 12°. N.Y. 1869.
JARVIS, S. F. Sermon, Ordination of Rev. A. Jackson. 8°. Hartf. 1847.
JAUFFRET, E. Le Théatre Revolutionnaire. 12°. Paris. 1869.
JAY, C. The Law. 12°. Lond. 1868.
JAY, J. La Politique Future de l'Amérique. (PC. 17.) 8°. Vienna. n.d.
— Proxy Bill and Tract Society. (PC. 1.) 8°. N.Y. 1859.
JAY, Wm. Prayers for the Use of Families. 16°. N.Y. n.d.
JAY, W. L. M. (Pseudonym.) *See* WOODRUFF, J. L. M.
JEAFFRESON, J. C. Annals of Oxford. 2 v. 8°. Lond. 1871.
— A Book about the Clergy. 2 v. 18°. Lond. 1870.
JEAN Bonhomme. 8°. Bruss. 1871.
JEANS, H. W. Nautical Astronomy and Navigation. 8°. Lond. 1870.
JEFFERS, W. N. Nautical Surveying. 8°. N.Y. 1871.
JEFFREY, E. (Lord.) Essay on Beauty: Also, Alison on Taste. 12°. Lond. 1871.
JEFFREY, Rosa V. Daisy Dare and Baby Power: Poems. Sq. 12°. Phil. 1871.
JEFFRIES, B. J. Animal and Vegetable Parasites of the Human Skin and Hair. 16°. Bost. 1872.
— The Eye in Health and Disease. 8°. Bost. 1871.
— Diseases of the Skin. 12°. Bost. 1871.
JEFFRIES, J. P. Natural History of the Human Races. 8°. N.Y. 1869.
JENKINS, E. The Coolie; his Rights and Wrongs. 12°. N.Y. 1871.

JENKINS, T. A. Barometer, Thermometer, Hygrometer, etc. 8°. Wash. 1869.
JENKS, B. Prayers and Offices of Devotion. 14th ed. 16°. Lond. 1758.
JENKS, I. C. Trial of D. F. Mayberry for Murder. (PC. 4, 17.) 12°. Janesville. 1855.
JENNINGS, H. The Rosicrucians. 12°. Lond. 1870.
JENNINGS, I. Memorials of a Century. (Hist. of Bennington, Vt.) 12°. Bost. 1869.
JENNINGS, J. K. Dialect of the West of England. 18°. Lond. 1869.
JERROLD, W. B. At Home in Paris. 2 v. 12°. Lond. 1864. Same. 1871.
—— Book for the Beach. 2 v. 12°. Lond. 1863.
—— A Brage Beaker with the Swedes. 12°. Lond. 1854.
—— Chronicles of the Crutch. 8°. Lond. 1860.
—— Cockaynes in Paris. 12°. Lond. n.d.
—— The Gavroche Party. 12°. Lond. n.d.
—— Life of D. Jerrold. 12°. Lond. n.d.
—— Signals of Distress in Refuges, etc. 16°. Lond. 1863.
JESSE, J. H. London; its Celebrated Characters, etc. 3 v. 8°. Lond. 1871.
JÉSUITE (Le). Par l'Abbé * * *. 2 v. 16°. Paris. 1865.
JEVONS, W. S. Substitution of Similars. 16°. Lond. 1869.
—— Theory of Political Economy. 8°. Lond. 1871.
JEWETT, C. Forty Years' Fight with the Drink Demon. 12°. N.Y. 1872.
—— The Temperance Cause. 8°. Chicago. 1864.
JEWETT, G. B. Critique on Bible Union Greek Testament. 8°. Salem. 1869.
JEZIERSKI, L. Bataille des 7 Jours, 21–28 Mai, 1871. 16°. Paris. 1871. *See* HANS et Blanc.
JOCELINE, Elizabeth. Mother's Legacie to her Unborne Childe. 16°. Edin. 1853.
JOCELYN, Lord. Six Months with the China Expedition. 16°. Lond. 1841.
JOHN, Eugenie. Gisèle, Comtesse de l'Empire. French of Mme. Raymond. 2 v. 12°. Paris. 1872.
—— Reichsgräfin Gisela. 2 v. Leip. 1870.
—— Thüringer Erzählungen. 12°. Leip. 1869
JOHN Jerningham's Journal. 12°. N.Y. 1871.
JOHNES, A. J. Unity and Origin of Human Race. 8°. Lond. 1846.
JOHNSON'S Family Atlas. Atlas f°. N.Y. 1870. Same. 1871.
JOHNSON, A. B. Physiology of the Senses 12°. N.Y. 1856.
JOHNSON, B. Grammar of Classical Literature. 18°. Lond. 1822.
JOHNSON, E. R., and Whitfield, J. M. Emancipation Oration and Poem. 8°. San Francisco. 1867.
JOHNSON, G. W. Gardener's Dictionary. 12°. Lond. 1870.
JOHNSON, Herrick. The Nation's Duty; Thanksgiving Sermon. 8°. Pittsburg. 1862.
JOHNSON, J. E. Monks before Christ. 16°. Bost. 1870.
JOHNSON, S. Dictionary. Ed. by Latham. 2 v. in 4. 4°. Lond. 1866–70.
JOHNSON, S. M. Free Government in England and America. 8°. N.Y. 1864.
JOHNSON, Virginia W. Travels of an American Owl. 12°. Phil. 1870.
JOHNSON, Wm. Imperial Cyclopædia of Machinery. 2 v. Atl. 8°. Glasgow. n.d.
JOHNSTON, A. K. Atlas of British History. 12°. Edin. n.d.
—— School Atlas of Classical Geography. f°. Edin. 1867
JOHNSTON, J. F. W. Application of Chemistry to Agriculture. 12°. N.Y. 1850.
—— Chemistry of Common Life. 12th ed. 2 v. 16°. N.Y. 1865.
JOHNSTON, R. Civil Service Précis. 16°. Lond. 1869.
JOHNSTONE, Miss E. British Mission of Church of Puritans. (PC. 2.) 8°. N.Y. 1861.
JOHNSTONE, R. Lectures on the Epistle of James. 12°. Edin. 1871.
JOLLIFFE, J. Petition of George Gordon for Pardon. 8°. Cinc. 1862.
JOLY, C. Napoléon III. et les Factions en 1870. 8°. St. Josse. 1870.
JONES. Una and her Paupers. Memorials of Agnes E. Jones, by her Sister. 12°. Lond. 1871.
—— Same. 12°. N.Y. 1872.
JONES, A. A. Digest of Duties of Custom House Officers. 8°. N.Y. 1836.

JONES, B. Life and Letters of Faraday. 2 v. 8°. Lond. 1870.
—— The Royal Institution; its Founder and First Professors. 12°. Lond. 1871.
JONES, C. A. History of the Church. v. 1. 16°. Lond. 1872.
JONES, E. Law of Salvage. 12°. Lond. 1870.
JONES, E. T. Book-keeping. 2d Amer. ed. 4°. N.Y. 1797.
—— Same. 4th ed. 4°. Lond. 1834.
JONES, G. Sketches of Naval Life. 2 v. 12°. New Haven. 1829.
JONES, H. L. Essays and Papers. 8°. Lond. 1870.
JONES, Jesse H. The Kingdom of Heaven; What it is; Where it is. 12°. Bost. 1871.
JONES, M. Stories of Capt. Cook's Voyages. Sq. 16°. Bost. 1870.
JONES, O. Grammar of Ornament. f°. Lond. n.d.
JONES, T. R. Animal Kingdom; and, Comparative Anatomy. 8°. Lond. 1871.
—— Natural History of Birds. 16°. Lond. 1867.
JONES, T. W. Failure of Sight from Railway Injuries. 8°. Lond. 1869.
JONES, Wm. The Broad, Broad Ocean. 12°. Lond. 1871.
JONSON, B. Works. Notes and Memoir by Gifford. Ed. by Cunningham. 3 v. 12°. Lond. n.d.
JORDAN, W. Nibelunge; Sigfridsage. 3d ed. 16°. N.Y. 1871.
JOSEPHINE, Life of. 12°. Phil. n.d.
JOSEPHUS, F. Histoire de la Guerre des Juifs. 16°. Paris. 1668.
JOSSE, A. L. Spanish Grammar. Ed. by Sales. 16°. Bost. 1822.
JOUAUST, D. Tablettes Quotidiennes du Siége de Paris. 8°. Paris. 1871.
JOUBERT, C. et Sagnier, A. Le Contrat Social de l'Avenir. 8°. Paris. 1871.
JOULIN, Dr. Les Caravanes d'un Chirurgien d'Ambulance. 12°. Paris. 1871.
JOURNAL of Botany. v. 8, 9. 8°. Lond. 1870–71.
JOURNAL des Économistes. v. 10–23. 8°. Paris. 1868–71.
JOURNAL of the Franklin Institute. 3d ser., v. 57–62. 8°. Phil. 1869–72.
JOURNAL d'une Infirmière pendant la Guerre de 1870–71. 12°. Bruss. 1871.
JOURNAL of Psychological Medicine. v. 4, 5. 8°. N.Y. 1870–71.
JOURNAL of Social Science. Nos. 1, 2, 3. 8°. N.Y. 1869–71.
JOURNAL of Speculative Philosophy. v. 1–5. 8°. St. Louis. 1867–71.
JOURNAL pour Tous. v. 1, 1855-6. 4°. Paris. 1855–6.
JOYNSON, F. H. Designing and Construction of Machine Gearing. 8°. Edin. 1868.
—— Metals Used in Construction. 16°. Edin. 1868.
JUDGED by His Words: A kind of Evidence respecting Christ. 8°. Lond. 1870.
JUKES, J. B. Letters and Extracts from Addresses and Writings. 12°. Lond. 1871.
—— Student's Manual of Geology. 3d ed., by Geikie. 12°. Edin. 1872.
JULIA. Life of the Reverend Mother Julia. 12°. N.Y. 1871.
JULIAN, George W. Speeches on Political Questions. 8°. N.Y. 1872.
JULLIEN, M. A. Essai sur l'Emploi du Tems. 4th ed. 12°. Paris. 1829.
JUNGHAUS, S. Verflossene Stunden. 12°. Leipzig. 1871.
JUSTIN, Cornelius Nepos and Eutropius; transl. by Watson. (Bohn's Ed.) 12°. Lond. 1853.
JUVENAL, Persius, Sulpicia and Lucilius; transl. by Evans. (Bohn's Ed.) 12°. Lond. 1865.
—— Satyrs. Transl. by Dryden. 16°. Lond. 1754.

KAINES, J. Love Poems of all Nations. 16°. Lond. 1870.
KALISCH, L. Heitere Stunden. 2 v. in 1. 12°. Berlin. 1872.
KALISCH, M. M. Commentary on the Old Testament. Genesis to Leviticus, Chap. 27. 4 v. 8°. Lond. 1855–72.
KANT, I. Metaphysics of Ethics. Tr. by Semple. 12°. Edin. 1869.
KAPP, F. Friedrich der Grosse und die Vereinigten Staaten. 12°. Leip. 1871.
—— Immigration and the Commissioners. 8°. N.Y. 1870.
KARR, A. Les Femmes. 12°. Paris. n.d.
—— Les Gaietés Romaines. 12°. Paris. 1870.
—— La Maison Close. 12°. Paris. n.d.

—— La Queue d'Or. 12°. Paris. 1871.
—— Roses Noires et Roses Bleues. 12°. Paris. n.d.
—— Sous les Orangers. 12°. Paris. n.d.
—— 300 Pages. 12°. Paris. n.d.
KAUFFMAN, C. H. Dictionary of Merchandise. 2d ed. 8°. Lond. 1805.
KAUFFMANN, T. American Painting Book. 4°. Bost. 1871.
KAVANAGH, J. W. Arithmetic. 16°. Dublin. 1846.
KAVANAGH, M. Origin of Language and Myths. 12°. Lond. 1871.
KAYE, J. W. Essays of an Optimist. 16°. Phil. 1871.
—— Same. 12°. Lond. 1870.
—— History of the Sepoy War in India. 2 v. 8°. Lond. 1870.
KEARY, A. The Nations Around. 12°. Lond. 1870.
—— A. and E. Heroes of Asgard. 16°. Lond. 1871.
KEATS, J. Poetical Works. 16°. Bost. 1870.
KEBBEL, T. E. The Agricultural Laborer. 12°. Lond. 1870.
KEBLE, J. Christian Year. Sq. 16°. Phil. 1870.
—— Letters of Spiritual Counsel and Guidance. 12°. Lond. 1870.
KEELER, R. Vagabond Adventures. 12°. Bost. 1870.
KEEN, W. W. Practical Anatomy; a Manual of Dissections. 12°. Phil. 1870.
KEENE, R. W. Diamond Fields of South Africa. 12°. N.Y. 1872.
KEEP, J. Sermon, Ordination of Rev. T. Woodbridge. Sm. 4°. Stockbridge. 1817.
KEIGHTLEY, H. Fairy Mythology. 12°. Lond. 1860.
KEIL, R. Frau Rath. Briefwechsel von Katharina Elisabeth Goethe. 8°. Leip. 1871.
KEIL, R. F. Introduction to Old Testament, v. 1. 8°. Edin. 1869.
KEIM, De B. R. San Domingo. 12°. Phil. 1870.
—— Sheridan's Troopers. 12°. Phil. 1870.
KEITH, T. Use of the Globes. 12°. Lond. 1828.
KELLEY, W. D. Speeches, Addresses and Letters on Industrial and Financial Questions. 8°. Phil. 1872.
KELLOGG Family Meeting and Genealogy. 8°. Bost. 1858.
KELLY, J. American Catalogue of Books. v. 2. 1866–70. 8°. N.Y. 1871.
KELLY, P. Oriental Metrology. 8°. Lond. 1832.
KELLY, W. Lectures on the Pentateuch. 12°. Lond. 1871.
KELLY, W. K. Proverbs of all Nations. 16°. Andover. 1869.
KEMPE, A. J. Church of St. Martin-le-Grand. 8°. Lond. 1825.
KENDRICK, A. C. Our Poetical Favorites. 12°. N.Y. 1871.
KENNAN, G. Tent Life in Siberia. 8°. N.Y. 1870.
KENNEDY, A. J. La Plata, Brazil and Paraguay. 12°. Lond. 1869.
KENNEDY, E. Hospitalism and Zymotic Diseases. 2d ed. 8°. Lond. 1869.
KENNEDY, E. B. Four Years in Queensland. 18°. Lond. 1870.
KENNEDY, J. C. G. Statistics of American Railroads. (PC. 2.) 8°. Wash. 1852.
KENNEDY, J. P. At Home and Abroad. 12°. N.Y. 1872.
KEOKUK Library Association. Catalogue of Library. 12°. Keokuk. 1866.
KER, J. Sermons. 8°. Edin. 1869.
KERL, Bruno. Metallurgy. 3 v. 8°. N.Y. 1869–70.
—— Repertorium der Technischen Literatur. Neue Folge. v. 1. A—K. R. 8°. Leip. 1871.
KERL, S. Composition and Rhetoric. 12°. N.Y. 1870.
KERR, R. The Gentleman's House. 3d ed. 8°. Lond. 1871.
KERR, W. C. (Pseudonym.) *See* FURNISS, W.
KERR, W. W. Law of Discovery. 8°. Lond. 1871.
KETCHUM, Mrs. Annie C. Benny. Sq. 12°. N.Y. 1870.
KEY, T. H. Philological Essays. 8°. Lond. 1868.
KEY to Souter's New Ciphering Book. 8°. Lond. 1828.
KIDDER, F. History of the Boston Massacre. 8°. Alb. 1870.
KIEPERT, H. Atlas von Hellas und den Hellenischen Colonien. f°. Berlin. 1846.
—— Hand Atlas über alle Theile der Erde. Mit Ergänzungsblättern. f°. Berlin. 1860–70.

KILLEN, W. D. The Old Catholic Church; History of the Christians, to A.D. 755. 8°. Edin. 1871.
KILLICK, A. H. Student's Hand-book of Mill's Logic. 16°. Lond. 1870.
KING, C. Mountaineering in the Nevada. 12°. Bost. 1872.
KING, E. F. Ten Thousand Wonderful Things. 12°. N.Y. n.d.
KING, Mary B. A. Looking Backward. 12°. N.Y. 1870.
KING, N. H. and H. A. Bee Keeper's Text-Book. 9th ed. Sq. 16°. N.Y. 1869.
KING, T. S. Sermon, Death of D. Webster. (PC. 14.) 8°. Bost. 1852.
—— White Hills. 8°. N.Y. 1870.
KING, W. R. Aboriginal Tribes of the Nilgiri Hills. 8°. Lond. 1870.
KINGSBURY, C. P. Artillery and Infantry. 12°. N.Y. 1849.
KINGSFORD, W. and others. History of Plank-Roads. 8°. Bost. 1851.
KINGSLEY, C. At Last; a Christmas in the West Indies. 12°. Lond 1871.
—— The Hermits. 12°. Lond. n.d.
KINLOCH, A. A. A. Large Game Shooting in Thibet and the North-west. Sm. 4°. Lond. 1869.
KINLOCH, F. Eulogy on George Washington. 4°. N.Y. 1871.
KIP, W. I. Christmas Holidays in Rome. 12°. Bost. 1869.
—— Double Witness of the Church. 12°. Phil. 1870.
—— Historical Notices of the Family of Kip. 8°. n.p. 1871.
—— Olden Times in New York. Sm. 4°. N.Y. 1872.
KIRBY, Mary and Elizabeth. The Sea and Its Wonders. Sm. 4°. Lond. 1871.
—— World at Home. Sm. 4°. Lond. 1870.
KIRBY, W. F. Synonymic Catalogue of Diurnal Lepidoptera. 8°. Lond. 1871.
KIRKE, H. The First English Conquest of Canada. 8°. Lond. 1871.
KIRKPATRICK, Mrs. Jane. Light of Other Days. 8°. New Brunswick. 1856.
KIRKWOOD, J. P. Filtration of River Water. 4°. N.Y. 1869.
KIRWAN. (Pseudonym.) *See* MURRAY, N.
KIRWAN, D. J. Palace and Hovel; or, Phases of London Life. R. 8°. Hartf. 1870.
KISTNER, O. Buddha and his Doctrine. Sm. 4°. Lond. 1869.
KITCHEL, H. D. Suppression of the Liquor Traffic. 16°. N.Y. 1870.
KITCHINER, T. Economy of the Eyes. 2 v. 12°. Lond. 1825-6.
KLAPP, M. Aus der Stadt des Concils. 16°. Berlin. 1870.
—— Revolutionsbilder aus Spanien. 12°. Hanover. 1869.
—— Zweierlei Juden. 16°. Vienna. 1870.
KLEINSTEUBER, H. Der Badewirth von Gonten. 3 v. in 2. 12°. Berlin. n.d.
KNAGGS, H. G. Lepidopterist's Guide. 12°. Lond. 1869.
KNEELAND, S. Wonders of the Yosemite Valley. R. 8°. Bost. 1871.
KNIGHT, C. Crown History of England. 12°. Lond. 1870.
—— English Cyclopædia: Supplement on Natural History. 4°. Lond. 1870.
—— Half-Hours with the Best Authors. 6 v. 12°. Phil. n.d.
—— Half-Hours with the Best Letter Writers. 2 v. 12°. Lond. 1867.
KNIGHT, Wm. Oriental Outlines. 16°. Lond. 1839.
KNORTZ, K. Märchen der Nordamerikanischen Indianer. 12°. Jena. 1870.
KNOTH, K. L. A. Hertz, Rath, Gold. f°. N.Y. 1866.
KNOX, J. Sermon, Opening of Ref. Dutch Church, Fourth Street and Lafayette Place. 8°. N.Y. 1839.
KNOX, T. W. Overland through Asia. 8°. Hartf. 1870.
KÖBERLE, G. Alles um ein Nichts. 12°. Leip. 1871.
KOCK, H. de. La Fille d'un de ces Messieurs. 12°. Paris. 1872.
—— Mlle. Croquemitaine. 12°. Paris. 1871.
KOESTER, H. Kaiser und Reich. 12°. Berlin. 1871.
KOHL, J. G. Russia. 8°. Lond. 1843.
KOHLENEGG, L. K. von. Eine Verpfuschte Saison. 12°. Leip. 1871.
KOHLRAUSCH, F. History of Germany. 8°. N.Y. 1870.
KOLLONITZ, Countess Paula. Court of Mexico. 2d ed. 8°. Lond. 1868.
KONEWKA, P. Falstaff and his Companions. 12°. Bost. 1872.
KÖNIG, E. A. Dämon Gold. 16°. Jena. n.d.

—— Durch Kampf zum Frieden. 4 v. in 2. 12°. Jena. 1871.
—— Die Geheimnisse einer Grossen Stadt. 3 v. 16°. Jena. 1870.
—— Das Princesschen. 4 v. in 2. 12°. Jena. 1872.
KÖRNER, G. Aus Spanien. 12°. Frankfort. 1867.
KORTUM, A. Die Jobsiade. 16°. Hamm. 1839.
KRAFT, Miss K. Nilometer. Diary of a Tour through Egypt, etc. 12°. N.Y. 1869.
KRAUTH, C. P. The Conservative Reformation and its Theology. 8°. Phil. 1871.
KREYSZIG, F. Shakespeare-Fragen. 12°. Leip. 1871.
—— Vorlesungen über den Deutschen Roman der Gegenwart. 12°. Berlin. 1871.
—— Vorlesungen über Shakspeare. 3 v. 12°. Berlin. 1862.
KRILOF, I. Fables. Transl. by W. R. S. Ralston. 12°. Lond. 1869.
KRUMMACHER, F. W. Autobiography. 8°. N.Y. 1869.
KULEMANN, R. Cornelie von Lentulus. 12°. Leip. 1869.
KURZ, H. Der Sonnenwirth. 12°. Frankfort. 1855.
KUSTEL, G. Concentration of Ores. 8°. San. Francisco. 1868.

LA BOISSIÈRE, de. On the United States. 12°. Phil. 1795.
LABORDE, J. V. L'Insurrection de Paris. devant la Psychologie morbide. 12°. Paris. 1872.
LABOUCHERE, H. Diary of the Besieged Resident in Paris. 8°. N.Y. 1871.
LABOULAYE, C. Encyclopédie Technologique. 2d ed. 2 v. L. 8°. Paris. 1853-4.
LABOULAYE, E. Discours Populaires. 16°. Paris. 1869.
—— Les États-Unis et la France. 8°. Paris. 1862.
——Mémoires de Franklin. 3d ed. 16°. Paris. 1870.
—— Paris en Amérique. 12°. Paris. 1863.
—— Separation war Without End. 8°. N.Y. 1863.
LA CHAPELLE, Count de. War of 1870. 12°. Lond. 1870.
LACOMBE, P. Arms and Armour. Transl. and ed. by C. Boutell. 12°. N.Y. 1870.
LACORDAIRE, R. R. F God: Conferences. 12°. N.Y. 1870.
—— Jesus Christ: Conferences. 2d ed. 12°. Lond. 1870.
—— Same. 12°. N.Y. 1870.
LA COTTIÈRE, J. de. Mes Semblables. 12°. Paris. 1871.
LACROIX, S. F. Essais sur l'Enseignement. 2d ed. 12°. Paris. 1816.
—— Trigonométrie. 2d ed. 8°. Paris. 1800.
—— and BÉZOUT, L. Trigonometry. 8°. Cambridge. 1820.
LACTANTIUS. *See* ANTE-NICENE Christian Library. v. 22.
LADIES' Repository. v. 29-31. L. 8°. Cinc. 1869-71.
LADIES' Work Table Book. 12°. Phil. n.d.
LADMIRAULT, Le Général de. Bases d'un Projet pour le Recrutement de l'Armée de Terre. 8°. Paris. 1871.
LADY'S (A) Diary of the Siege of Lucknow. 16°. Lond. 1858.
LAFAUGÈRE, L. J. Art de Faire les Armes. 8°. Paris. 1825.
LA FAYETTE, Mme. de. Henriette d'Angleterre. 16°. Amsterdam. 1742.
LA FONTAINE, J. de. Contes et Nouvelles en Vers. 2 v. 12°. n.p. 1777.
—— Fables. 8°. N.Y. 1810.
LA FOSSE, H. de. À Bâtons Rompus. 3 v. 12°. Paris. 1871.
LAGERSTROEM, A. von. Edle Frauen. 12°. Gotha. 1870.
LAGRANGE, J. L. Thèorie des Fonctions Analytiques. 4°. Paris 1797.
LA GUERRONNIÈRE, A. (le Vicomte de). L'Age de Fer ou l'Ere du Sang. 2d ed. 8°. Brussels. 1871.
—— La Commune Sanglante. 12°. Paris. 1871.
—— Les Deux Abîmes. 8°. Brussels. 1871.
—— L'Homme de Metz. 5th ed. 8°. Brussels. 1870.
—— Same. 6th ed. 8°. Brussels. 1871.
—— L'Homme de Sedan. 8th ed. 8°. Brussels. 1870.
—— Same. 10th ed. 8°. Brussels. 1870.
—— Place au Droit. 8°. Brussels. 1871.
—— La Prusse devant l'Europe. 3d ed. 8°. Brussels. 1870.
—— Same. 4th ed. 8°. Brussels. 1870.
LAING, S. H. Darwinism Refuted. 12°. Lond. 1871.

LAKESIDE Memorial of the Burning of Chicago. R. 8°. Chicago. 1872.
LALANDE, J. I. Astronomie des Dames. 6th ed. 24°. Paris. 1820.
LA MARA. Ludwig von Beethoven. 12°. Leip. 1870.
LAMARTINE, A. de. Cours Familier de Littérature. 15 v. L. 8°. Paris. 1856-63.
—— Fior d'Aliza. 16°. Paris. 1863.
—— Graziella. 12°. Paris. 1870.
—— Histoire de la Russie. 2 v. in 1. 8°. Paris. 1855.
—— Jeanne d'Arc. 12°. Paris. 1867.
—— Le Manuscrit de ma Mère. 8°. Paris. 1871.
—— Mémoires Inédits. 8°. Paris. 1870.
—— Raphaël. 16°. Paris. 1870.
—— Souvenirs et Portraits. v. 1. 12°. Paris. 1871.
—— Le Tailleur de Pierres de St. Point. 16°. Paris. 1862.
—— England in 1850. Transl. by Ouseley. 8°. N.Y. 1851.
—— French Revolution of 1848. 12°. Lond. 1865.
—— Girondists. 4 v. 12°. N.Y. 1860.
—— History of Turkey. 3 v. 12°. N.Y. 1855-7.
—— Twenty-five Years of my Life and Memoirs of my Mother. 2 v. 12°. Lond. 1872.
LAMB, C. English Dramatic Poets. 12°. Lond. 1854.
—— Essays of Elia. New ed. 16°. Lond. n.d.
—— Works, with Memoir. 4 v. 12°. Lond. 1870.
LAMB, J. Documents from MSS. at Corpus Christi Library. 8°. Lond. 1838.
LAMBERT, Miss. Ladies Complete Guide to Needlework and Embroidery. 12°. Phil. n.d.
LAMBORN, R. H. Metallurgy of Silver and Lead. 12°. Lond. 1861.
LANCASTER, J. Report of Discoveries in Education. L. 8°. [Montreal. 1833?]
LANCET. *See* LONDON Lancet.
LANDING of French Atlantic Cable. 8°. Bost. 1869.
LANDON, L. E. Works. 8°. Bost. 1859.
LANDON, M. D. Franco-Prussian War in a Nutshell. 12°. N.Y. 1871.
LANDOR, W. S. Pericles and Aspasia. 12°. Bost. 1871.
LANFREY, P. Histoire de Napoléon I. v. 3, 4. 16°. Paris. 1869-70.
—— History of Napoleon I. v. 1. 8°. Lond. 1871.
LANG, J. D. New Zealand in 1839. 8°. Lond. 1839.
LANG, N. Ballads and Lyrics of Old France. 12°. Lond. 1872.
LANGE, C. P. Der Erbe von Bettysruh. 2 v. 12°. Leip. 1866.
—— Der Friedensengel. 3 v. 12°. Berlin. 1870.
—— Der Grüne Pelz. 2 v. 2d ed. 12°. Leip. 1868.
—— Der Löwe von Luzern. 5 v. 12°. Berlin. 1869.
—— Die Tochter des Diplomaten. 2 v. 12°. Leip. 1867.
LANGE, J. P. Commentary on the Holy Scriptures.
Old Testament. v. 1. Genesis. L. 8°. N.Y. 1869.
—— v. 4. Joshua, Judges and Ruth. L. 8°. N.Y. 1872.
—— v. 10. Proverbs, Ecclesiastes and Song of Solomon. L. 8°. N.Y. 1870.
—— v. 13. Jeremiah and Lamentations. L. 8°. N.Y. 1871.
New Testament. v. 1. Matthew. L. 8°. N.Y. 1866.
—— v. 2. Mark and Luke. L. 8°. N.Y. 1870.
—— v. 3. John. L. 8°. N.Y. 1871.
—— v. 4. Acts of the Apostles. L. 8°. N.Y. 1869.
—— v. 5. Romans. L. 8°. N.Y. 1869.
—— v. 6. Corinthians. L. 8°. N.Y. 1869.
—— v. 7. Galatians, Ephesians, Philippians and Colossians. L. 8°. N.Y. 1869.
—— v. 8. Thessalonians, Timothy, Titus, Philemon and Hebrews. L. 8°. N.Y. 1868.
—— v. 9. James, Peter, John and Jude. L. 8°. N.Y. 1867.
LANGLAND. *See* EARLY Eng. Text Soc., No. 38.
—— Vision of Piers Plowman. 16°. Oxf. 1869.
LANOYE, F. de. Le Nil. 16°. Paris. 1869.
—— Egypt 3300 Years Ago. 16°. N.Y. 1870.

—— The Sublime in Nature. 16°. N.Y. 1870.

LANSING, D. C. Sermon; Dedication of Clinton Avenue Congregational Church. 8°. N.Y. 1856.

LANSING Library and Literary Association. Manual. 18°. Lansing. 1871.

LANSINGBURGH Directory. *See* TROY.

LANZI, L. History of Painting in Italy. 3 v. 12°. Lond. 1852.

LA PLACE, P. A. de. *See* FIELDING, Sarah.

LAPLACE, P. S. de. Mécanique Céleste. Transl. by Bowditch. 2 v. 4°. Bost. 1829–32.

LAPORTE, Count de. French Grammar. 8°. Bost. 1844.

LAPORTE. L'Égypte à la Voile. 12°. Paris. 1870.

LARDNER, D. Handbook of Optics. 12°. Phil. 1858.

—— Microscope. 12°. Lond. 1856.

—— Outlines of Universal History. 12°. Phil. 1835.

—— Steam Engine for Beginners. 18°. Lond. 1848.

—— Manuel du Travail des Métaux. French of Vergnaud. 2 v. 18°. Paris. 1835.

LARIMER, Mrs. S. L. Capture and Escape. 12°. Phil. 1870.

LA RIVE, W. de. Reminiscences of Cavour. Transl. by Romilly. 8°. Lond. 1862.

LA ROCHEFOUCAULD, Duke de. *See* MAXIMES et Pensées.

—— Maxims. 18°. Lond. 1868.

LA ROCHEFOUCAULD, F. J. de. Correspondence. 1744–48. 8°. Nantes. 1871.

LARWOOD, J. Book of Clerical Anecdotes. 16°. Lond. n.d.

—— Story of the London Parks. 2 v. 12°. Lond. n.d.

LA SAGRA, R. de. L'Ame. 12°. Paris. 1868.

LASCELLES, F. H. Laws on Juvenile Offenders. 8°. Lond. 1870.

LASPÉE, H. de. Calisthenics. 2d ed. S. 4°. Lond. 1865.

LASSERRE, H. Our Lady of Lourdes. 12°. N.Y. 1870.

LASTEYRIE, Mme. de. Vie de Mme. de Lafayette. 12°. Paris. 1869.

LATHAM, J. H. Theories of Philosophy and Religion. 8°. Lond. 1871.

LATHAM, R. G. English Grammar for Ladies' Schools. 16°. Lond. 1849.

—— History of English. 16°. Lond. 1849.

—— Man and his Migrations. 16°. N.Y. 1852.

LATOUR-St. Ybars. Néron. 8°. Paris. 1867.

LAUBE, H. Das Norddeutsche Theater. 12°. Leip. 1872.

LAUN, A. Washington Irving. (German.) 16°. Berlin. 1870.

LAURENCET. Physiologie de l'Homme. 24°. Paris. 1827.

LAURI, Aug. Maître Italien. 8°. Paris. 1820.

LAURIE, J. Homœopathic Domestic Medicine. 8°. N.Y. 1871.

LAURIE, P. New Buildings at Bethlem Hospital. 8°. Lond. 1838.

LAW, H. Art of Constructing Roads. 16°. Lond. 1850.

LAWLOR, D. S. Pilgrimages in the Pyrenees and Landes. 8°. Lond. 1870.

LAWRANCE, Hannah. Queens of England. 2 v. 8°. Lond. 1838.

LAWRENCE Genealogy. 8°. Bost. 1869.

LAWRENCE, H. Border and Bastile. 12°. N.Y. n.d.

LAWRENCE, J. Une Bataille dans la Pension Europe. 8°. Brussels. 1871.

LAWRENCE, Jonathan, Jr. Select Writings. 12°. N.Y. 1833.

LAWS of Etiquette. 18°. Phil. 1836.

LAWSON, G. Diseases, etc., of the Eye. 16°. Lond. 1869.

LAXTON, H. Builders' and Contractors' Tables. 4°. Lond. n.d.

LAYCOCK, John. English and German Dialogues. 2d ed. 12°. Hamburg. 1837.

LAYMAN'S Apology for Clerical Chaplains in the N. Y. Legislature. 16°. Alb. 1834.

LAZARUS, Emma. Admetus, and other Poems. 12°. N.Y. 1871.

LEA, H. C. Studies in Church History. Cr. 8°. Phil. 1869.

LEA, M. C. Manual of Photography. 8°. Phil. 1868.

LEAR, E. Journal in Corsica. R. 8°. Lond. 1870.

—— Nonsense Songs and Alphabets. 8°. Lond. 1871.

LEATHES, S. Witness of St. John to Christ. 8°. Lond. 1870.

—— Witness of St. Paul. 8°. Lond. 1869.

LEAVITT, J. Denmark and its Relations. 8°. N.Y. 1864.

—— Poland. (PC. 22.) 8°. n.p. n.d.

LEAVITT, W. S. God the Protector and Hope of the Nation: Sermon, Nov. 1862. 8°. Hudson. 1862.

LEBEAUD. Horsemanship. 24°. Phil. 1833.

LE BRETHON. French Pronunciation. 24°. N.Y. 1839.

LECKY, W. E. H. Leaders of Public Opinion in Ireland. 12°. N.Y. 1872.

—— Rationalism in Europe. 4th ed. 2 v. 12°. Lond. 1870.

LE CLERC, Jean. La Vie du Cardinal Duc de Richelieu. 2 v. 16°. Amst. 1714.

LECLERQ, É. La Guerre de 1870. 8th ed. 12°. Paris. 1871.

—— Le 2 Empire Français; Ham à Wilhelmshoehe. 12°. Brussels. 1871.

LECOMTE, A. La Logique Populaire. 24°. Paris. 1832.

LECONTE, D. F. La Guerre Franco-Allemande. 12°. Brussels. 1871.

LEDEUIL, E. Châteaudun. 2d ed. 8°. Paris. 1871.

LEE, Alec. A Sketch Romance of Motion, or a Mode of Planetary Bodies in Space. 12°. Lond. 1871.

LEE, Arthur. Army Ballads. 16°. n.p. 1871.

LEE, C. A. Physiology for Schools. 12°. N.Y. 1840.

LEE, F. G. The Christian Doctrine of Prayer for the Departed. 8°. Lond. 1872.

—— Validity of Holy Orders. 8°. Lond. 1869.

LEE, G. J. The Voice. 2d ed. Sm. 4°. Lond. 1870.

LEE, H. Life of Napoleon I. v. 1. 8°. N.Y. 1835.

LEE, H. War in the Southern Department. 8°. N.Y. 1869.

LEE, Leila. Wee Wee Songs for our Little Pets. 16°. N.Y. 1871.

LEEDS, L. W. Treatise on Ventilation. R. 8°. N.Y. 1871.

LEES, F. R. The Text-Book of Temperance. 12°. Lond. 1871.

LE FAURE, A. Les Fautes Stratégiques des Prussiens. 16°. Paris. 1872.

LEFÈBRE, M. Wonders of Architecture. 16°. N.Y. 1870.

LEFÈVRE, A. Manuel du Trigonomètre. 8°. Paris. 1819.

LEFÈVRE, E. Intervention Française en Mexique. 2 v. 8°. Brussels. 1869.

LEGENDRE, A. M. Elements of Geometry. Tr. by Farrar. 2d ed. 8°. Camb. 1825.

LEGGE, J. The Chinese Classics. v. 4. Pts. 1, 2. R. 8°. Hongkong. 1871.

LEGRET, G. P. Rudiment de la Comptabilité Commerciale. 3d ed. 12°. Paris. 1837.

LEIFCHILD, J. R. The Higher Ministry of Nature. 12°. Lond. 1872.

LEIGH, H. S. Religion of the World. 18°. Lond. 1869.

LEIGH, J. E. A. Memoir of Jane Austen. 2d ed. 12°. Lond. 1871.

LEIGHTON, J. Paris under the Commune. 12°. Lond. 1871.

LEIGHTON, R. Commentary on I. Peter. 2 v. 8°. Lond. 1870.

LEIGHTON, W. Poems. 2d ed. 18°. Lond. 1870.

LEISURE Hour, for 1869–71. 2 v. R. 8°. Lond. 1869–71.

LELAND, C. G. Hans Breitmann in Church. 8°. Phil. 1870.

—— Hans Breitmann as an Uhlan. 8°. Phil. 1871.

—— Music Lesson of Confucius. 8°. Bost. 1872.

LELAND, H. P. Gray-Bay Mare and other Sketches. 12°. Phil. 1870.

LEMELLE, J. Siége de Paris. 18°. Paris. 1871.

LEMONNYER, J. Les Journaux de Paris pendant la Commune. 12°. Paris. n.d.

LENGLÉ, P. De la République à l'Empire. Trajet Direct en 20 Heures. 12°. Paris. 1872.

LENORMANT, F., and Chevallier, E. Ancient History of the East. 2 v. 8°. Lond. 1869–70.

LEONOWENS, Anna H. English Governess at the Siamese Court. 12°. Bost. 1870.

LEPAGE, M. The French School. 5th ed. 16°. Lond. 1841.

LEPELLE de Bois-Gallais, F. Memoir of Rosa Bonheur. Tr. by Parry. 8°. N.Y. 1857.

LE PILEUR, A. Wonders of the Human Body. 16°. N.Y. 1870.

LE PLAY, F. Organization of Labor. Tr. by G. Emerson. 12°. Phil. 1871.

LEROUX, P. De l'Humanité. 2 v. 8°. Paris. 1840.

LEROY, C. G. Intelligence of Animals. 12°. Lond. 1871.

LEROY-Beaulieu, P. La Question Ouvrière au 19e Siècle. 12°. Paris. 1872.

LESCHER, F. H. Elements of Pharmacy 8°. Lond. 1869.

LESLIE, Col. Records of the Family of Leslie. 3 v. 8°. Edin. 1869.

LESLIE, C. Short and Easie Method with the Deists. 8th ed. (Bound with it, is Checkley's Speech on his Tryal.) 8°. Lond. 1723.

—— On Deism; *also*, G. West on the Resurrection. 12°. N.Y. 1830.

LESLIE, C. R. Autobiographical Recollections. Ed. by Taylor. 2 v. 12°. Lond. 1860.

LESLIE, Miss Eliza. American Girl's Book. 16th ed. 18°. N.Y. 1866.

LESLIE, J. Experiments on Air, Heat and Moisture. 8°. Edin. 1813.

LESLIE, T. E. C. Land Systems, etc., of Ireland, England and the Continent. 8°. Lond. 1870.

LESSING, G. E. Briefwechsel mit seiner Frau. 12°. Leip. 1870.

—— Nathan der Weise. 12°. Stuttg. 1869.

—— Fables, Allemand et Français. 8°. Paris. 1799.

—— Nathan the Wise. 12°. Lond. 1868.

L'ESTRANGE, A. G. Life of Miss Mitford. 3 v. 12°. Lond. 1870.

—— Same. 2 v. 12°. N.Y. 1870.

—— Literary Life of Rev. W. H. Harness. 8°. Lond. 1871.

—— Yachting Round the West of England. 8°. Lond. 1865.

LE TELLIER, C. C. Analyse Logique. 2d Part. 8th ed. 12°. Paris. 1832.

—— Nouvelle Cacographie. 16°. Paris. 1823.

—— Corrigé de la Nouvelle Cacographie. 16°. Paris. 1823.

LETHEBY, H. Lectures on Food. 12°. Lond. 1870.

LETTER from an Elder in an O. S. Presb. Church to his Son at College. 8°. N.Y. 1863.

LETTER on the Revised Code, by a Yorkshire Clergyman. 8°. Lond. 1861.

LETTER to Morrill on Knit Goods. 8°. Bost. 1866.

LETTER (A) to a Young Piano-Forte Player. 2d ed. 18°. Lond. 1830.

LETTERS from Rome on the Council. By Quirinus. 12°. Lond. 1870.

LETTERS on International Relations by the Times' Correspondent. 2 v. 8°. Lond. 1871.

LETTRE d'un Villageois sur la Guerre. 2d ed. 8°. Brussels. 1870.

LETTRES et Négociations de M. d'Estrades etc. à Nimègue. 9 v. 16°. Hague & Lond. 1710–63.

LETTS' Diary and Almanac for 1843. 12° Lond. 1842.

LEVER, T. Sermons. *See* ARBER's English Reprints. No. 12.

LEVERETT, F. P. and Bradford, T. G. Viri Romæ. 16°. Bost. 1845.

LEVESON, H. A. England Rendered Impregnable. S. 4°. Lond. 1871.

LEVI, L. Commercial Law of the World. 2 v. 4°. Lond. 1854.

—— History of British Commerce and of the Economic Progress of the British Nation, 1763–1870. 8°. Lond. 1872.

LEVIN, T. W. Six Lectures Introductory to the Philosophical Writings of Cicero. 8°. Cambr. (Eng.) 1871.

LEVIZAC, J. P. V. Lecoutz, (Abbé de). Clef de la Grammaire. 16°. Paris. 1823.

—— French Grammar. 12°. N.Y. 1829.

LEVY, W. H. Blindness and the Blind. 12°. Lond. 1872.

LEWALD, Fanny. *See* STAHR, Fanny.

LEWES, G. H. History of Philosophy. 4th ed. 2 v. 8°. Lond. 1871.

—— Life of Robespierre. 12°. Lond. 1849.

—— Same. 12°. Phil. 1849.

—— Physiology of Life. 2 v. 16°. N.Y. 1871.

—— Sea-side Studies. 12°. Edin. 1860.

LEWIS, A. N. Liabilities of Bankers and Brokers under Int. Rev. Laws. 8°. N.Y. 1869.

LEWIS, D. Our Girls. 12°. N.Y. 1871.

—— Talks about Health. 18°. Bost. 1871.

—— Talks about People's Stomachs. 12°. Bost. 1870.

LEWIS, E. G. American Sportsman. 8°. Phil. 1871.

LEWIS, Sir G. C. Letters. 8°. Lond. 1870.

LEWIS, H. English Language. 18°. Lond. 1869.

LEWIS, T. Heroic Periods in a Nation's History. 16°. N.Y. 1866.

LEWIS, W. N. People's Practical Poultry Book. 8°. N.Y. 1871.

LEYPOLDT, F. New Guide to German Conversation. 16°. N.Y. 1870.

LEYSER, J. Goethe zu Strassburg. 8°. Neustadt. 1871.

L'HERMITE, J. B. La Clef de la Correspondance Commerciale. Sq. 12°. Paris. 1846.

—— and Langhenie, J. C. B. Manual of Commercial Correspondence. German, English, French and Spanish. 12°. Hamburg. 1857.

L'HOMOND, C. F. Viri Romæ. 2d Amer. ed. 24°. Phil. 1813.

LIAÑO, H. St. A. von. Church of God and the Bishops. 12°. Lond. 1870.

LIBRARY of Education. 6 v. 24°. N.Y. 1869–70.

Containing:
- v. 1. Locke on Education.
- v. 2. Locke on Education; Milton on Education.
- v. 3. Mann's Physiology in Schools.
- v. 4. University Addresses (Mill, Froude, Carlyle).
- v. 5, 6. Bible in Public Schools.

LIBRARY of Mesmerism and Psychology. 2 v. in 1. 12°. N.Y. 1869.

Containing:
1. The Macrocosm and Microcosm, or The Universe Without and the Universe Within, by W. Fishbough.
2. Fascination, or the Philosophy of Charming, by J. B. Newman.
3. Electrical Psychology, by J. B. Dods.
4. Philosophy of Mesmerism, by J. B. Dods.
5. Psychology, or the Science of the Soul, by Joseph Haddock.

LIDDELL, H. G., and Scott, R. Greek-English Lexicon. R. 8°. N.Y. 1870.

LIDDON, H. P. The Purchas Judgment. 8°. Lond. 1871.

—— Walter Kerr Hamilton; a Sketch. 8°. Lond. 1869.

LIEBER, F. Abstraction of Moneys from the City Treasury. (PC. 8.) Sm. 4°. N.Y. 1870.

—— Changes in Constitution of New York. 8°. N.Y. 1867.

—— Fallacies of Protectionists. 4th ed. (PC. 8.) 16°. N.Y. 1870.

—— Guerilla Parties. 16°. N.Y. 1862.

LIEBETREU, C. F. Leben und Lieben. 2d ed. 12°. Berlin. 1871.

LIFE (The) and Death of Mother Shipton. Sm. 4°. Westminster. 1871.

LIGHT of the World, and other Poems. Sm. 4°. Phil. 1871.

LIGHTFOOT, J. B. The Epistle to the Galatians. Revised Text, with Introduction, Notes and Dissertations. 8°. Andover. 1870.

—— Revision of the English New Testament. 12°. Lond. 1871.

LILLIE, H. Alphabet of Monograms. 2d ed. 8°. Lond. n.d.

LINDAU, P. Harmlose Briefe eines Deutschen Kleinstädters. 12°. Leip. 1871.

—— Kleine Geschichten. 12°. Leip. 1872.

—— Literarische Rücksichtslosigkeiteu. 12° Leip. 1871.

LINDLEY, A. After Ophir: South African Gold Fields. Sm. 4°. Lond. n.d.

LINDSAY, Lord. Œcumenicity and the Church of England. 8°. Lond. 1870.

LINDSAY, C. The Evidence for the Papacy. 8°. Lond. 1870.

LINDSLEY, D. P. Elements of Tachygraphy. 16. Bost. 1869.

LINGARD, J. History of England. 6th ed. 10 v. 12°. Lond. 1855.

—— Histoire d'Angleterre. 2d ed. French of Roujoux and others. 15 v., (lacks v. 7.) 8°. Paris. 1833.

LINGG, H. Violante. 12°. Stuttgart. 1871.

LINTON, Mrs. Modern Women. 2d ser. 12°. N.Y. 1870.

LINTON, H. The Psalms of David and Solomon. 16°. Lond. 1871.

LIPPINCOTT's Dictionary of Biography. 2 v. Ed. by J. Thomas. R. 8°. Phil. 1870.

LIPPINCOTT's Magazine. v. 4-8. 8°. Phil. 1869–71.

LIREUX, A. Assemblée Nationale Comique. Illustré par Cham. 4°. Paris. 1850.

LIST of Pennsylvania Soldiers buried at Andersonville. Sm. 4°. Harrisburg. n.d.

LISTER, T. Poems. 12°. Lond. 1834.

LITERAL Prose Translations from Metastasio, Ariosto, Tasso. 2 v. 8°. Leghorn. 1826.

LITERALIST (The). 3 v. 8°. Phil. 1841.

LITERARY and Historical Society of Quebec. Transactions, 1843 to 1871. 12 parts in 10 v. 8°. Quebec. 1843–71.

LITTELL'S Living Age. v. 103–112. 8°. Bost. 1869–72.

LITTLE, W. History of Warren, N. H. 8°. Manchester. 1870.

LITTLE Folks; a Magazine for the Young. v. 1–2. Sm. 4°. N.Y. n.d.

LITTLEDALE, R. F. Commentary on the Song of Songs. 16°. Lond. 1869.

LITTRÉ, E. Dictionnaire Français. v. 2. I—P. Imp. 8°. Paris. 1869.

LIVERPOOL Free Library, North and South Districts Catalogue. 8°. Liverpool. 1855.

LIVERPOOL Industrial Ragged Schools. An. Rep's 1850–53. (P. 96 and 97.) 8°. Liverpool. 1850–54.

LIVERPOOL Ragged School Society. 5th An. Meeting. (P. 96.) 8°. Liverpool. n.d.

—— 7th An. Meeting. (P. 97.) 8°. Liverpool. n.d.

LIVES of Distinguished Shoemakers. 12°. Portland. 1849.

LIVINGSTON, E. Penal Code for the State of Louisiana. 8°. Phil. 1833.

LIVRE (Le) Noir de la Commune de Paris. 3d ed. 12°. Paris. 1871.

LIVRET de Commandemens de l'Infanterie. 2d ed. 8°. Paris. 1835.

LIVY. History of Rome. Transl. by Spillan. (Bohn's ed.) 4 v. 12°. Lond. 1862–8.

LOAN Acts of Congress, 1847–68. 8°. N.Y. n.d.

LOARING, H. J. Common Sayings. 16°. Lond. n.d.

LOBLEY, J. A. The Church and the Churches in Southern India. 8°. Cambr. (Eng.) 1870.

LOBSCHEID, W. Chinese and English Dictionary. 4°. Hongkong. 1871.

LOCH, H. B. Personal Narrative in China. 12°. Lond. 1869.

LOCK, F. La Commune; 2me Siége de Paris. 12°. Paris. 1871.

LOCKE, J. On Education. *See* LIBRARY of Education. v. 1–2.

LOCKE, R. A. Moon Hoax. 8°. N.Y. 1859.

LOCKER, F. London Lyrics. 16°. Bost. 1870.

LOCKHART, C. S. M. Guide to Isle of Wight. Sm. 4°. Lond. 1870.

LOCKYER, J. N. Elements of Astronomy. 12°. N.Y. 1870.

LOGAN, Olive. Before the Footlights and Behind the Scenes 8°. Phil. 1870.

LOK, H. Poems. *See* FULLER Worthies' Miscellanies.

LONDON Catalogue, 1800–18. 8°. Lond. 1818.

LONDON Characters, etc. 12°. Lond. n.d.

LONDON City Mission Magazine. v. 18. 8°. Lond. 1853.

LONDON Dialectical Society. Report on Spiritualism. 8°. Lond. 1871.

LONDON Directory, 1870. Imp. 8°. Lond. 1870.

LONDON, Edinburgh and Dublin Philosophical Magazine. 4th ser. v. 36–42. 8°. Lond. 1868–71.

LONDON and its Environs. 16°. Edin. n.d.

LONDON (The) Greek Grammar. 3d. ed. 16°. Lond. 1832.

LONDON Illustrated News. v. 30, 35, 36, 38, 39, 41–46, (and duplicates of 42 and 43.) 13 v. f°. Lond. 1857–65.

LONDON Lancet, 1868–71. R. 8°. N.Y. and Lond. 1868–71.

LONDON Quarterly Review. v. 31–37. 8°. Lond. 1868–71.

LONDON Review. v. 3, 4, 6, 7, 11, 12. f°. Lond. 1861–6.

LONDON Society. v. 16–20. 8°. Lond. 1869 71.

LONDON Times. *See* TIMES.

LONG, G. Decline of the Roman Republic. v. 2, 3, 4. 8°. Lond. 1866–72.

LONG, S. P. Art: Its Laws and the Reasons for Them. 12°. Bost. 1871.

LONG, T. Key to Chess Openings. 8°. Dublin. 1871.

LONGFELLOW, H. W. The Divine Tragedy. 12°. Bost. 1871.

— Evangeline. 16°. Bost. 1869.

—— Poetical Works. 18°. Bost. 1871.

LONG Island Directory, 1870. 12°. N.Y. 1870.

LONG Island Historical Society. An. Reports, May, 1864–May, 1869. 8°. Brooklyn. 1864–9.

LONGMAN, F. W. Chess Openings. 16°. Lond. 1870.

LONSDALE, H. Life of John Heysham. Sm. 4°. Lond. 1870.

—— Life and Writings of R. Knox. 12°. Lond. 1870.

LOOK, H. M. Masonic Trials. 12°. N.Y. 1870.

LORD, J. Ancient States and Empires. Sm. 8°. N.Y. 1869.

LORD, W. B., and Baines, T. Shifts and Expedients of Camp Life. R. 8°. Lond. 1871.

LORENZ, O. Catalogue Général de la Librairie Française, 1840–65. 4 v. 8°. Paris. 1867–71.

LORIMER, Mary. Among the Trees. Sm. 4°. N.Y. 1869.

LORING, F. W. The Boston Dip, and other Poems. 16°. Bost. n.d.

LOSSING, B. J. Civil War in America. 3 v. L. 8°. Phil. and Hartford. 1866–8.

—— Field Book of the Revolution. 2 v. L. 8°. N.Y. 1860.

—— Field Book of the War of 1812. L. 8°. N.Y. 1869.

—— History of England. 12°. N.Y. 1871.

—— The Home of Washington. 8°. Hartford. 1870.

—— The Hudson. Sm. 4°. N.Y. n.d.

—— Lives of Celebrated Americans. 8°. Hartford. 1869.

LOUDON, Mrs. Amateur Gardener's Calendar. Sq. 12°. Lond. 1870.

—— Plain Instructions in Gardening. 10th ed. 16°. Lond. 1869.

LOUDON, J. C. The Horticulturist. Ed. by W. Robinson. 8°. Lond. n.d.

LOUIS XIV. History of Lewis XIV. 3 v. 18°. Lond. 1742.

LOUISIANA and Mississippi Business Directory, 1870. 8°. N. Orl. 1870.

LOUISVILLE Directory for 1871. 8°. Louisville. n.d.

LOVE, W. D. Wisconsin in the Rebellion. 8°. Chicago. 1866.

LOVELL'S Canadian Dominion Directory for 1871. R. 8°. Montreal. 1871.

LOVER, S. Lyrics of Ireland. 12°. Lond. 1867.

LOW, C. R. Land of the Sun. 12°. Lond. 1870.

LOW, S., Jr. Hand-Book to Charities of London. 16°. Lond. 1870.

LOWDELL, J. L. German Evenings. 12°. Lond. 1869.

LOWELL, J. R. Among my Books. 12°. Bost. 1871.

—— The Cathedral. 12°. Bost. 1870.

—— My Study Windows. 12°. Bost. 1871.

LOWELL Directory, 1870. 8°. Lowell. 1870.

LÖWENHERZ, C. Verfehlte Ziele. 4 v. in 2. 12°. Berlin. 1869.

LOWNE, B. T. Anatomy of the Blow-Fly. 8°. Lond. 1870.

LOWREY, G. P. Defence of the Proclamation of Emancipation. 8°. N.Y. 1863.

LOYOLA, I. de. Spiritual Exercises. Ed. by Shipley. 24°. Lond. 1870.

LUBBOCK, J. Origin of Civilization. 8°. Lond. 1870.

—— Same. 12°. N.Y. 1870.

—— Same. 1871.

—— Pre-historic Times. 2d ed. 8°. Lond. 1869.

—— Same. 3d ed. 8°. Lond. 1872.

LUCAN. Pharsalia; transl. by Riley. (Bohn's ed.) 12°. Lond. 1853.

LUCAS, S. Charters of the Old English Colonies in America. 8°. Lond. 1850.

LUCIAN. Select Dialogues, with Interlinear Translation. 2d ed. 16°. Lond. 1832.

LUÇON et Mindanão. 16°. Paris. 1870.

LUCRETIUS, Carus T. On the Nature of Things. Tr. in Verse by C. F. Johnson. 12°. N.Y. 1872.

—— On the Nature of Things. Tr. by Watson and Good. 12°. Lond. 1867.

LUDLOW, F. H. Heart of the Continent. 8°. N.Y. 1870.

LUDWIG, O. Shakespeare Studien. 12°. Leip. 1872.

LUMBY, J. R. Early Dissent, etc.; three Sermons. 18°. Lond. 1870.

LUMLEY, B. Reminiscences of the Opera. 8°. Lond. 1864.

LUX, J. Le Crime du 18 Mars. 12°. Paris. 1871.

LYELL, C. Elements of Geology. 2d Am. ed. 12°. Phil. 1845.

—— Elements of Geology. 12°. Lond. 1871.

—— Principles of Geology. v. 1. 11th ed. 8°. Lond. 1872.

—— Student's Elements of Geology. 12°. N.Y. 1871.

LYLE, M. E. S. What are the Stars? 18°. Lond. 1870.

LYLES, J. H. Railway Manual, 1870–71. 8°. N.Y. n.d.

LYMAN Anniversary Proceedings, Reunion of Lyman Family. 8°. Alb. 1871.

LYNCH, T. T. Morals of Accidents and other Discourses. 12°. N.Y. 1872.

—— The Mornington Lecture. 12°. Lond. 1870.

—— Sermons for my Curates. 12°. Lond. 1871.

—— Theophilus Trinal. 16°. Lond. 1869.

LYNDON, J. W. Ninety-Three, or, the Story of the French Revolution from the Recollections of my French Tutor. 12.° Lond. 1871.

LYNDSAY, Sir David. Poetical Works. 2 v. 16°. Edin. 1871.

LYNE, A. A. The Midshipmen's Trip to Jerusalem and Cruise in Syria. 12°. Lond. 1871.

LYON, C. Wright's Narrative, etc., of Van Dieman's Land. 8°. N.Y. 1844.

LYON, W. P. Manual of Education. 18°. N.Y. 1848.

LYONNARD, N. J. Apostleship of Suffering. 16°. Lond. n.d.

LYTTON, Lord. Dramatic Works. 16°. Leip. 1860.

—— King Arthur. 12°. Lond. 1870.

—— Same. 12°. N.Y. 1871.

—— Lady of Lyons. 16°. N.Y. n.d.

—— Richelieu. 16°. N.Y. n.d.

LYTTON, R. Apple of Life. Sq. 18°. Bost. 1865.

—— Chronicles and Characters. 2 v. 12°. Lond. 1868.

—— Julian Fane: A Memoir. 12°. Lond. 1871.

—— New Poems. 2 v. 16°. Bost. 1868.

—— Lucile. Sq. 18°. Bost. 1869.

MACAULAY, Lord. Critical and Historical Essays. 12°. Lond. 1869.

—— Lays of Ancient Rome. 16°. Leip. 1851.

MCBRIDE, J. Early Settlers of Butler Co., Ohio. v. 1. 8°. Cinc. 1869.

MCCABE, J. D., Jr. Great Fortunes. 8°. Phil. 1871.

—— Paris by Sunlight and Gaslight. 8°. Phil. n.d.

—— War between Germany and France. 8°. Phil. 1871.

MCCALL, S. Culture and the Gospels. 16°. N.Y. 1871.

MCCANN, J. Anti-Darwinism. 8°. Glasgow. 1869.

MCCARTY, J. H. The American Union; a Sermon. 8°. Cinc. 1862.

MCCAUL, J. B. Hebrews. A Paraphrastic Commentary. 8°. Lond. 1871.

MCCAUSLAND, D. The Builders of Babel. 12°. Lond. 1871.

MCCLELLAN, R. H. Executor's Guide. 12°. Albany. 1862.

MCCLINTOCK, F. L. Fate of Sir J. Franklin. 3d ed. 12°. Lond. 1869.

MCCLINTOCK, J. Living Words; or, Unwritten Sermons. 12°. N.Y. 1871.

—— and Strong, J. Cyclopædia of Biblical Literature. v. 3-4. R. 8°. N.Y. 1870-72.

MCCLUNG, J. W. Minnesota in 1870. 12°. St. Paul. 1870.

MCCLURE, A. K. Three Thousand Miles through the Rocky Mountains. 12°. Phil. 1869.

MCCLURE, R. Diseases of Horses, Cattle and Sheep. 12°. Phil. 1870.

—— Gentleman's Stable Guide. 16°. Phil. 1870.

MACCOLL, M. The Ammergau Passion Play. 16°. Lond. 1870.

MCCOMBIE, W. Sermons and Lectures. 12°. Edin. 1871.

MACCORMAC, W. Notes of an Ambulance Surgeon in 1870. 12°. Lond. 1871.

MCCORRY, J. S. The Monks of Iona. 8°. Lond. 1871.

MCCOSH, J. Christianity and Positivism. 12°. N.Y. 1871.

—— The Imagination; Its Use and Abuse. *See* AM. Tract Soc. Tracts for Young Men.

—— Logic. 12°. N.Y. 1870.

MCCREA, R. B. Lost Amid the Fogs. Sketches of Life in Newfoundland. 8°. Lond. 1869.

MCCRIE, J. Autopædia; or, Instructions on Personal Education. 2d ed. 8°. Lond. 1871.

MCCULLOCH, J. M. Sermons. 2d ed. 12°. Edin. 1871.

M'CULLOCH, J. R. Commercial Dictionary. Reid's ed. 8°. Lond. 1869.

MACDONALD, A. J. Monuments, Grave-Stones, etc. 12°. Albany. 1848.

MACDONALD, Flora. Autobiography. 2 v. 12°. Edin. 1870.

MACDONALD, G. Miracles of our Lord. 12°. N.Y. 1871.

—— Same. 16°. Phil. 1871.

—— Unspoken Sermons. 16°. N.Y. 1871.

—— Within and Without. 12°. N.Y. 1872.

MACDONALD, Mrs. George. Chamber Dramas for Children. 12°. Lond. 1870.

MACDONALD, J. D. Sound and Color. 12°. Lond. 1869.
MACDONALD, J. M. Discourse on Rev. J. Carnahan. 8°. N.Y. 1860.
MACDONALD, Mrs. Mary N. Poems. 8°. N.Y. 1844.
McDONALD, R. H. Chicago and the Great Fire. 12°. N.Y. 1871.
MACDONELL, J. A Survey of Political Economy. 12°. Edin. 1871.
McDOUGALL, J. Sermons. 12°. Lond. 1871.
MACDOWALL, C. S. Parisiana. 8°. Lond. 1871.
MACDUFF, J. R. Footsteps of St. Paul. 12°. N.Y. 1870.
—— Memories of Patmos. 12°. Lond. 1871.
—— Same. 12°. N.Y. 1871.
—— St. Paul in Rome; Sermons. 12°. Lond. 1871.
McELHINNEY, J. J. Doctrine of the Church. 8°. Phil. 1871.
McELRATH, T. Dictionary of Words and Phrases used in Commerce. 8°. N.Y. 1872.
MACFARREN, G. A. Six Lectures on Harmony. 8°. Lond. 1867.
McGEE, T. D. History of Ireland. 2 v. in 1. 12°. Glasgow. n.d.
—— Poems. 12°. N.Y. 1870.
McGILCHRIST, J. Life of Bright. 16°. N.Y. n.d.
—— Life of Gladstone. 16°. N.Y. n.d.
MACGREGOR, J. The Rob Roy on the Jordan. 8°. Lond. 1869.
—— Same. 12°. N.Y. 1870.
McGUFFEY, W. H. Fourth Reader. 12°. N.Y. n.d.
McHENRY, L. J. A. Exercises in Spanish. 18°. Lond. 1814.
MACHIAVELLI, N. Works. f°. Lond. 1695.
McILVAINE, C. P. Sermon; Consecration of Bishop Polk. 8°. Hartford. 1871.
McILVAINE, J. H. Elocution. 12°. N.Y. 1870.
MACIVOR, J. Religious Progress, its Criterion, Instruments and Laws. 8°. Lond. 1872.
MACKAY, A. Facts and Dates. 16°. Edin. 1869.
MACKAY, C. Medora Leigh. 12°. Lond. 1869.
—— Same. 8°. N.Y. 1870.
MACKAY, J. A. Sermons. 8°. Lond. 1870.
MACKAY, R. W. Rise and Progress of Christianity. 12°. Lond. n.d.
McKEAN County Bituminous Coal Co. Prospectus. (PC. 9.) S. 4°. N.Y. 1864.
McKEAN and Elk Land and Improvement Co. Act of Incorporation, Report, etc. (PC. 21.) 8°. Phil. 1856.
MACKENZIE, E. M. R. View of Durham. 2 v. 4°. Newcastle. 1834.
McKENZIE, J. Instructions for Militia Artillery. 8°. Liverpool. 1870.
MACKENZIE, J. Ten Years North of Orange River. 12°. Edin. 1871.
MACKENZIE, M. Growths in the Larynx. 8°. Lond. 1871.
—— Laryngoscope in Diseases of the Throat. 8°. Lond. 1871.
MACKENZIE, R. S. Life of Charles Dickens. 12°. Phil. 1870.
—— Life of Sir W. Scott. 12°. Bost. 1871.
M'KIM, J. M. Freedom of South Carolina; an Address. 8°. Phil. 1862.
MACKINTOSH, D. Scenery of England and Wales. 16°. Lond. 1869.
MACKNIGHT, T. Life and Times of Edmund Burke. 3 v. 8°. Lond. 1858–60.
MACLACHLAN, D. Diseases and Infirmities of Advanced Life. 12°. Lond. 1863.
McLEOD, A. Trial for Murder. (PC. 17.) 8°. N.Y. 1841.
MACLEOD, D. Life of Mary Queen of Scots. 12°. N.Y. n.d.
MACLEOD, N. Days in North India. 12°. Phil. 1870.
—— Peeps at the Far East. S. 4°. Lond. 1871.
M'LETCHIE, J. Sermons, with Memoir. 8°. Edin. 1871.
MACMICHAEL, W. F. Oxford and Cambridge Boat Races. 16°. Lond. 1870.
MACMILLAN, H. Bible Teachings in Nature. 12°. Lond. 1871.
MACMILLAN'S Magazine. v. 19–25. 8°. Lond. 1869–72.
MACMULLEN, J. History of Canada. 2d ed. 8°. Lond. 1869.
McMULLEN, R. T. Down Channel from London to Lands End. 16°. Lond. 1869.
MACNAMARA, C. Asiatic Cholera. 8°. Lond. 1870.
McPHEETERS' Interest Table. Narrow. f°. Phil. 1871.
McPHERSON, E. Handbook of Politics for 1870. 8°. Wash. 1870.

—— Political History of the U. S. during the Rebellion. 8°. Wash. 1864.

MACPHERSON, S. C. Memorials of Service in India. 8°. Lond. 1865.

MACRAE, D. Americans at Home. 2 v. 12°. Edin. 1870.

—— Life of Napoleon III. 16°. Glasgow. 1870.

McVICKAR, W. A. Life of Rev. J. McVickar. 12°. N.Y. 1871.

McWATTERS, G. S. Knots Untied. 8°. Hartford. 1871.

MADAGASCAR. History of. 18°. Phil. n.d.

MADDEN, R. R. History of Irish Periodical Literature. 2 v. 8°. Lond. 1867.

MADDEN, R. R. Phantasmata. 2 v. 8°. Lond. 1857.

MADISON University. Candid Appeal. (PC. 4.) 8°. Hamilton, N.Y. 1847.

MAGASIN Pittoresque. v. 8, 9, 29, 34, 38. S. f°. Paris. 1840–1, 1861, '66, '70.

MAGASIN Théatral. v. 2–7. R. 8°. Paris. 1834–5.

MAGASIN Universel. v. 1–3. f°. Paris. 1833–6.

MAGAZINE of Horticulture. v. 34. 8°. Bost. 1868.

MAGICIAN'S Own Book. 12°. N.Y. 1868.

MAGILL, Mary T. Women; or, Chronicles of the Late War. 12°. Bost. 1871.

MAGUIRE, J. F. Pontificate of Pius IX. 12°. Lond. 1870.

MAGUIRE, T. Essays on the Platonic Ethics. 8°. Lond. 1870.

MAHAFFY, J. P. Primitive Civilizations. 18°. Lond. 1869.

—— Prolegomena to Ancient History. 8°. Lond. 1871.

MAHAN, D. H. Field Fortification. 18°. N.Y. 1836.

—— Outpost Service. 24°. N.Y. 1847.

MAHAN, M. A Church History of the First Seven Centuries. 8°. N.Y. 1872.

MAHONY, O'B. Organic Matter in Potable Water. 2d. ed. 8°. Dubl. 1869.

MAIBEN, F. Extant Epitaphs. 8°. Lond. 1870.

MAILLARD, F. Les Filles du Notaire. 16°. Lausanne. 1870.

—— Journaux à Paris pendant le Siége et sous la Commune. 12°. Paris. 1871.

MAIN, T. J., and Brown, T. Indicator and Dynamometer. 4th ed. 8°. Lond. 1864.

MAINE, H. S. Village Communities in the East and West. 8°. Lond. 1871.

MAINE. Census. 8°. Augusta. 1871.

—— Report on Jail System. 8°. Augusta. 1871.

—— Report on Recruiting Credits, 1871. 8°. n.p. n.d.

—— Revised Statutes, Jan., 1871. 8°. Portland. n.d.

MAINE Historical Society. Collections. 2d ser. 8°. Portland. 1869.

MAISTRE, X. de. Journey Round My Room. 16°. N.Y. 1871.

—— Œuvres Completes. 12°. Paris. 1866.

MAÎTRE de la Langue Allemande. 10me ed. 8°. Strasbourg. 1786.

MAJOR & Knapp's Illustrated Monthly. v. 1–2. Atl. 4°. N.Y. 1870–71.

MALET, H. P. Interior of the Earth. 8°. Lond. 1870.

MALING, E. Handbook for Ladies on Indoor Plants, Flowers and Song Birds. 16°. Lond. 1870.

MALLESON, G. B. Recreations of an Indian Official. 12°. Lond. 1872.

MALOT, H. Madame Obernin. 12°. Paris. 1870.

—— Romain Kalbris. 12°. Paris. n.d.

—— Une Bonne Affaire. 12°. Paris. 1870.

—— Les Victimes d'Amour. 3 v. 12° Paris. 1867–70.

MALTHUS, T. R. Principle of Population. 5th ed. 3 v. 8°. Lond. 1817.

MAN Next to God in his Original Status and Final Destiny. 16°. Lond. 1870.

MAN (The): the Mighty God. Outlines of Thought. 8°. Lond. 1871.

MANBY, C. W. Manual of Music. 24°. Lond. 1847.

MANCEL, G. Changement du Garnison. 16°. Paris. 1869.

MANDEVILLE, H. Course of Reading. 12°. N.Y. 1846.

—— Elements of Reading and Oratory. 8°. N.Y. 1853.

—— Primary Reader. 16°. N.Y. 1851.

—— Second Reader. 16°. N.Y. 1851.

—— Third Reader. 16°. N.Y. 1852.

MANGIN, A. Desert World. 8°. Lond. 1869.

—— Mysteries of the Ocean. 8°. Lond. 1868.

MANN, A. (Edr.) Wise, Witty and Tender Sayings in Prose and Verse, selected from the Works of Geo. Eliot. 12°. Edin. 1872.

MANN, Herman. Annals of Dedham. 8°. Dedham. 1847.

MANN, Horace, and Chase, P. E. Arithmetic Practically Applied. 12°. Phil. 1850.

MANN, W. W. Linn Base Decimal System. 16°. N.Y. 1871.

MANNING, H. E. The Ecumenical Council., etc. 8°. Lond. 1869.

—— Petri Privilegium; Three Pastoral Letters. 8°. Lond. 1871.

—— Rome the Capital of Christendom; a Sermon. 8°. Lond. 1870.

—— The Vatican Council and its Definitions. 8°. Lond. 1870.

MANUAL de Estilo Epistolar. 16°. Valencia. 1841.

MANUAL of Politeness. 24°. Phil. 1837.

MANUAL of Scientific Inquiry for Her Majesty's Navy. Ed. by Herschel. 4th ed. by Main. 12°. Lond. 1871.

MANUFACTURER and Builder. v. 1-3. 4°. N.Y. 1869-71.

MANY Things upon Money Matters. 18°. West Bradford. 1835.

MAPLE Leaves. v. 5. 4°. N.Y. 1870.

MAQUET, A. Le Beau d'Angennes. 12°. Paris. 1864.

—— La Belle Gabrielle. 3 v. in 2. 16°. Paris. 1868.

—— L'Envers et l'Endroit. 2 v. in 1. 12°. Paris. 1863.

—— La Maison du Baigneur. 2 v. 12°. Paris. 1862.

MARAH, W. H. Memoirs of Abp. Juxon. 8°. Oxford. 1869.

MARCET, Mrs. Jane. Conversations on Political Economy. 24°. N.Y. 1820.

MARCET, W. Composition of Food. 8°. Lond. 1866.

—— Diseases of the Larynx. 16°. Lond. 1869.

MARCH, D. Night Scenes in the Bible. 8°. Phil. 1869.

MARCH, F. A. Anglo-Saxon Grammar. 8°. N.Y. 1870.

—— Anglo-Saxon Reader. 8°. N.Y. 1870.

MARCHESE (Father.) Painters, etc., of Order of St. Dominic. 2 v. 12°. Dublin. 1852.

MARCOY, P. L'Amérique du Sud. 2 v. 4°. Paris. 1869.

MARCY, E. E. Life Duties. 12°. N.Y. 1869.

MARCY, R. B. Border Reminiscences. 12°. N.Y. 1871.

MARGGRAFF, H. Fritz Beutel. 12°. Frankfort. 1856.

MARGOLIOUTH, M. Hebrews in East Anglia. 8°. Lond. 1870.

—— Poetry of the Hebrew Pentateuch. 12°. Lond. 1871.

MARGUERITE. 12°. Paris. 1870.

MARGUERITE de Valois, Reine de Navarre. 12°. Paris. 1870.

MARIOLA oder Ein Blonder Dämon. 2 v. in 1. 16°. Leip. 1870.

MARION, F. Wonderful Balloon Ascents. 16°. N.Y. 1870.

—— Wonders of Optics. 12°. N.Y. 1871.

—— Wonders of Vegetation. 12°. N.Y. 1872.

MARIOTTI, L. Black Gown Papers. 2 v. 12°. Lond. 1846.

—— Fra Dolcino and his Times. 12°. Lond. 1853.

—— Italy, Past and Present. 2 v. 12°. Lond. 1848.

MARKHAM, Mrs. History of France. 12°. Lond. 1867.

—— History of Germany. 12°. Lond. 1869.

MARKHAM, C. R. Life of Lord Fairfax. 8°. Lond. 1870.

MARKHAM, G. Marie Magdalen's Lamentations for the Losse of her Master.

—— Teares of the Beloved. *See* FULLER Worthies' Miscellanies.

MARK Lane Express and Agricultural Journal. v. 25, 39 and 40. f°. Lond. 1856-71.

MARLITT, E. (Pseudonym.) *See* JOHN Eugenie.

MARMION, A. History of the Maritime Ports of Ireland. 4th ed. 8°. Lond. 1860.

MARONIER, J. H. Religious Instruction. 2 v. 16°. Bost. 1869.

MARRIAGE and Divorce. 18°. N.Y. 1870

MARRIOTT, W. B. Testimony of the Catacombs. Sq. 12°. Lond. 1870.

—— Vestments of the Church. 8°. Lond. 1869.

MARSH, J. B. Story of Harecourt, being the History of an Independent Church. 16°. Lond. 1871.

MARSHALL, C. The Canadian Dominion. 8°. Lond. 1871.

MARSHALL, E. C. Ancestry of Gen. U. S. Grant. 12°. N.Y. 1869.

MARSHALL, J. Discourse on Death of President Lincoln. 8°. Syracuse. 1865.

MARSHALL, J., (F. R. S., etc.) Description of the Human Body. 2d ed. 2 v. 4°. and f°. Lond. 1870.
MARSHALL, J. A. American Bastile. 8°. N.Y. 1871.
MARTEN, E. B. Records of Steam Boiler Explosions. 12°. Lond. 1869.
MARTENS, C. (Baron de). Guide Diplomatique. 2 v. 8°. Paris. 1837.
MARTIAL. Epigrams (Bohn's ed). 12°. Lond. 1865.
MARTIN, B. N. Choice Specimens of American Literature. 12°. N.Y. n.d.
MARTIN, C. F. Tables sur la Régulation des Calculs. 8°. Paris. 1817.
MARTIN, F. Statesman's Year Book, 1870–72. 3 v. 12°. Lond. 1870–72.
MARTIN, H. The Atonement. 8°. Lond. 1870.
MARTIN, James. Origin and History of the New Testament. 16°. Lond. 1871.
MARTIN, John H. Microscopic Objects. 8°. Lond. 1870.
MARTIN, S. Rain upon the Mown Grass. 8°. Lond. 1871.
—— Same. 2d ed. 12°. Lond. 1872.
MARTIN, T. Horace. 16°. Edin. 1870.
—— Same. 16°. Phil. 1871.
MARTINE, A. Droll Dialogues. 16°. N.Y. n.d.
MARTINEAU, R. Roots of Christianity in Mosaism; an Address. 8°. Lond. 1869.
MARVELLOUS Repository. v. 1. 18°. Bost. 1827.
MARVIN, F. R. Dream Music. 12°. N.Y. 1870.
MARVIN, W. Law of Wreck and Salvage. 8°. Bost. 1858.
MARY Stuart and the Casket Letters. By J. F. N. 16°. Edin. 1870.
MARYLAND; Constitution of 1851. 8°. Balt. 1855.
—— Constitution of 1864. 8°. Balt. 1864.
—— Constitution of 1867. 8°. Balt. 1867.
MARYLAND State Gazette and Merchants' and Farmers' Directory for Maryland and District of Columbia. R. 8°. Balt. 1871.
MASON. Consecrated Talents: or the Life of Mrs. Mary W. Mason, with an Introduction by Bishop Janes. 12°. N.Y. 1870.
MASON, C. Discourse on Daniel Webster. 8°. Bost. 1852.
MASON, F. Story of a Working Man's Life. 12°. N.Y. 1870.
MASON, Mrs. Mary. Young Housewife's Counsellor. 12°. Phil. 1871.
MASSACHUSETTS. Report of Bureau of Statistics of Labor, to March 1, 1870. 8°. Bost. 1870.
—— State Board of Health. 2d and 3d Annual Reports for 1870–71. 8°. Bost. 1871–72.
—— Report on Troy and Greenfield R.R. and Hoosac Tunnel. 8°. Bost. 1863.
MASSEY, G. A Tale of Eternity, etc. 12°. Lond. 1870.
MASSILLON, J. B. Petit Carême. L. 8°. Tours. 1862.
MASSINGER, P. Plays, notes by Gifford. 8°. N.Y. 1860.
MASSON, D. Life of Milton. v. 2. 8°. Lond. 1871.
MASSON, J. R. Petit Dictionnaire de l'Académie Française. 8th ed. Sq. 16°. Paris. 1821.
MASTERMAN, G. F. Seven Years in Paraguay. 8°. Lond. 1869.
MASTRIANI, F. I Vampiri. 18°. Naples. 1868.
MATEAUX, C. L. Home Chat with our Young Folks. Sm. 4°. N.Y. n.d.
MATHESON, J. England to Delhi. Sm. 4°. Lond. 1870.
MATTHÆI, G. Wendische Grammatica. 16°. Budissin. 1721.
MATTHIÆ, A. Greek Grammar, abridged by Edwards. 4th ed. 16°. Lond. 1834.
MATTHIEU de Boulogne. Napoleon IV: Chroniques de l'Avenir. 16°. Paris. 187–.
MATTISON, H. Romanism; its General Decline and Present Condition. 8°. N.Y. 1870.
MATTOCKS, B. Minnesota as a Home for Invalids. 16°. Phil. 1871.
MAUDIT (Le). Par l'abbé * * *. 2 v. Sq. 18°. Paris. 1864.
MAUDSLEY, H. Body and Mind. 12°. N.Y. 1871.
MAUDUIT, A. R. Leçons de Géometrie. 2 v. 8°. Paris. 1807.
MAUNDEVILE, J. Voiage and Trauaile. Ed. by Halliwell. 8°. Lond. 1866.

MAURICE, F. D. Patriarchs and Lawgivers of the Old Testament. 12°. Lond. 1867.
—— Prophets and Kings of the Old Testament. (Sermons). 12°. Lond. 1871.
—— Social Morality. 8°. Lond. 1869.
MAURY, M. F. Sailing Directions. 4th ed. 4°. Wash. 1852.
MAVERICK. A. H. J. Raymond and the New York Press. 8°. Hartford. 1870.
MAXIMILIAN, I. On the Wing. Tr. by Lushington. 8°. Lond. 1868.
MAXIMES et Pensées. La Rochefoucauld, Montesquieu, Vauvenargues. 12°. Paris 1855.
MAXTON, J. Workman's Manual of Engineering Drawing. 16°. Lond. 1871.
MAXWELL, J. C. Theory of Heat. 12°. Lond. 1871.
MAY's London Press Directory. 8°. Lond. 1871.
MAY, T. E. Constitutional History of England, 1760-1860. 3d ed. 3 v. 12°. Lond. 1871.
—— Same. 4 v. 12°. N.Y. 1865.
MAYNARD, J. C. Naturalist's Guide. 12°. Bost. 1870.
MAZZINI, G. Life and Writings. v. 6. 12°. Lond. 1870.
MEADE, H. Disturbed Districts of New Zealand. 8°. Lond. 1870.
MEADE, R. W. Naval Architecture. 8°. Phil. 1869.
MEARS, J. W. The Church and Temperance; a Sermon. 12°. N.Y. 1871.
MECHANICS' Institute, Montreal. Catalogue of Library. 18°. Montreal. 1855.
—— Catalogue of Library. 18°. Montreal. 1869.
MECHANICS' Library Association, Lancaster, Pa. Catalogue of Books. 18°. Lancaster. 1870.
MECHANICS' Magazine. New Ser., v. 10, 21-23. Sm. f°. Lond. 1863, '69-'70.
MEDBERY, J. K. Mysteries of Wall street. 12°. Bost. 1870.
MEDICAL Gazette. v. 3-6. 4°. N.Y. 1869-71.
MEEK, A. B. Romantic Passages in Southwestern History. 3d ed. 12°. Mobile. 1857.
MEIDINGER, J. V. Grammaire Allemande. 8°. Metz. 1832.
MEISSNER, A. Die Kinder Roms. 4 v. in 2. 12°. Berlin. 1870.
—— Rococo-Bilder. 12°. Gumbinnen. 1871.
MELIA, P. Hints and Facts on the Origin of Man. 12°. Lond. 1872.
—— History of the Waldenses. L. 8°. Lond. 1870.
MELINE, J. F. Commercial Traveling. 8°. Cambr. 1869.
—— Mary Queen of Scots and her latest English Historian. 12°. N.Y. 1871.
MELIORA. v. 10-12. 8°. Lond. 1867-9.
MELS, A. Erlebtes und Erdachtes. 12°. Stuttgart. 1869.
—— Gebilde und Gestalten. 12°. Leip. 1869.
—— Seltsame Schicksale. 2 v. 12°. Berlin. 1871.
—— Von der Elbe bis zur Tauber. Sm. 4°. Bielefeld. 1867.
MELVILL, H., and others. One Hundred Sermons. 8°. Lond. n.d.
MEMMINGER, R. W. What is Religion? 12°. Phil. 1872.
MÉMOIRES d'une Idéaliste. 12°. Geneva. 1869.
MÉMOIRES Secrets du Second Empire. 8°. Brussels. 1871.
MEMOIRS of the Court of Louis XIV. 3 v. in 1. 8°. Lond. 1819.
MEMORABILIA of the City of Perth. 8°. Perth. 1806.
MEMPHIS. Annual Directory for 1870-71. 8°. St. Louis. 1870-71.
MEN who Advertise. R. 8°. N.Y. 1870.
MÉNAGE (Le) Impérial. Lui et Elle en Apparence et en Realité. 8°. Brussels. 1871.
MENAULT, E. Intelligence of Animals. 16°. N.Y. 1869.
MENDELSSOHN, M. Phædon; or the Death of Socrates. 12°. Lond. 1789.
MENDÉS, C. Les 73 Journées de la Commune. 5th ed. 12°. Paris. 1871.
MENGES, P. Abendstunden eines Handwerkers. 24°. Saratoga. 1868.
MENSCH, G. L. van Beethoven. 12°. Leip. 1871.
MENZEL, W. Geschichte des französischen Kriegs, 1870-1. 2 v. 12°. Stuttgart. 1871.
—— History of Germany. Tr. by Mrs. Horrocks. 12°. Lond. 1869.
MERCANTILE Library Association of Boston. Index to the Catalogue. R. 8°. Bost. 1869.

MERCANTILE Library Association of Portland. Catalogue. 8°. Portland. 1859.
MERCANTILE Library Association of Portsmouth (N. H.) Catalogue of Library. 18°. Portsmouth. 1870.
MERCANTILE Library of Baltimore. Catalogue of Additions, 1851–8. 8°. Balt. 1858.
MERCANTILE Library of Philadelphia. Catalogue. Imp. 8°. Phil. 1871.
MERCEIN, Imogen. Conversations on Palestine. 24°. N.Y. 1840.
MERCER, C. Waterloo Campaign. 2 v. 8°. Edin. 1870.
MERCHANT and Ship-Master's Assistant. 8°. North Shields. 1833.
MERCHANTS' Magazine. v. 59–62. 8°. N.Y. 1868–70.
MERCIER. La Recluse Angloise. 2 v. 16°. Amsterdam. 1770.
MERCIER, L. Outlines of the Life of the Lord Jesus Christ. 2. v. 12°. Lond. 1871.
MEREDITH, L. P. The Teeth, and How to Save Them. 16°. Phil. 1871.
MERLIN, Countess de. Memoir and Letters of Malibran. 2 v. 12°. Phil. 1840.
MERRETT, H. S. Land and Engineering Surveying. R. 8°. Lond. 1863.
MERRIFIELD, C. W. Technical Arithmetic and Mensuration. 16°. Lond. 1872.
MERRILL, J. Cosmogony; or Thoughts in Philosophy. 16°. n.p. n.d.
MERRILL, W. E. Iron Truss Bridges for Railroads. 4°. N.Y. 1870.
MÉRY, J. Constantinople, et la Mer Noire. L. 8°. Paris. 1855.
MERYON, E. History of Medicine. v 1. 8°. Lond. 1861.
MESHULLAM; or, Tidings from Jerusalem. 12°. n.p. 1850.
MESNARD, J. Merveilles de l'Exposition de 1867. f°. Paris. 1867.
METCALF, R. Letter and Spirit. 16°. Bost. 1870.
METCALFE, F. History of German Literature. 12°. Lond. 1858.
METEYARD, Eliza. A Group of Englishmen. The Wedgwoods and their Friends. 8°. Lond. 1871.
—— Hallowed Spots of Ancient London. Sm. 4°. Lond. 1870.
MÉTHODE pour Apprendre à Lire par le Système Phonétique. 8°. Paris. 1853.
METHODIST Quarterly Review. v. 51–3. 8°. N.Y. 1869–71.
METROPOLITAN Art Museum in N.Y. Meeting, Nov. 23, 1869. 8°. N.Y. 1869.
MEUNIER, V. Great Hunts. 16°. N.Y. 1869.
MEW, W. M. Report to the Secretary of the Treasury on Life-Saving Inventions. 8°. Wash. 1868.
MEXICAN Gulf and Henderson R.R. Prospectus. (PC. 10.) 8°. N.Y. 1857.
MEXICANISCHE Typen und Skizzen. 16°. Berlin. 1870.
MEYER, M. Electricity and Practical Medicine. Tr. by Hammond. 8°. N.Y. 1869.
MEYR, M. Duell und Ehre. 12°. Leip. 1870.
MEZGER, G. C. Geschichte der Bibliothek in Augsburg. 8°. Augsburg. 1842.
MEZIÈRES, A. Récits de l'Invasion. 12°: Paris. 1871.
MICHAUD, J. F. Histoire des Croisades. 4 v. 8°. Paris. 1860.
MICHEL, A. Le Siége de Paris, 1870–1. 12°. Paris. n.d.
MICHELET, J. La Femme. 16°. Paris. 1867.
—— La France devant l'Europe. 2d ed. 16°. Florence. 1871.
—— La Mer. 5th ed. 16°. Paris. 1869.
—— Nos Fils. 16°. Paris. 1870.
—— The Bird. R. 8°. Lond. 1869.
—— France before Europe. 12°. Lond. 1871.
—— Same. 12°. Bost. 1871.
—— Roman Republic. Transl. by Hazlitt. 12°. Lond. 1847.
MICHELL, E. B. Siege Life in Paris. 8°. Lond. n.d.
MICHIELS, A. Peinture Flamande et Hollandaise. 4 v. 8°. Paris. 1847.
—— Rubens et l'École d'Anvers. 8°. Paris. 1854.
MICHIGAN. School Funds and School Laws. 8°. Lansing. 1859.
MICHIGAN State Library. Catalogue for 1871–2. 8°. Lansing. 1870.
MICROSCOPIC Objects. 12°. Lond. 1847.
MIDDLETON, E. E. Cruise of the Kate. 12°. Lond. 1870.
MIDOSI, L. F. Portuguese and English Grammar. 8°. Lond. 1832.
MIFFLIN, J. H. Fine Arts in America; an Address. 8°. Phil. 1833.

MILES, G. Christine, and Other Poems. 12°. N.Y. 1866.

MILES, H. A. Picture Writing in the Bible. 12°. Bost. 1870.

MILL, J. S. Contest in America. 2d ed. 16°. Bost. 1862.

—— Irish Land Question. 12°. Lond. 1870.

—— Principles of Political Economy. 2 v. 8°. Lond. 1865.

—— Same 12°. Lond. 1866.

—— Subjection of Women. 12°. Phil. 1869.

—— University Address. *See* LIBRARY of Education. v. 4.

—— and Hare, T. True and False Democracy. 8°. Bost. 1862.

MILLARD, J. Grammar of Elocution. 18°. Lond. 1869.

MILLER'S New Guide to Hudson River. 16°. N.Y. 1871.

MILLER, E. P. Dyspepsia. 12°. N.Y. 1870.

—— Exhausted Vitality. 12°. N.Y. 1867.

MILLER, H. Headship of Christ, and Rights of Christian People. Ed. by Bayne. 12°. Bost. 1865.

MILLER, J. Christianum Organum. 12°. Lond. 1870.

MILLER, J. Songs of the Sierras. 12°. Bost. 1871.

MILLER, W. A. Magnetism and Electricity. 8°. N.Y. 1871.

—— Elements of Chemistry. 8°. N.Y. 1864.

MILLINGEN, F. Wild Life among the Koords. 8°. Lond. 1870.

MILLINGEN, J. G. History of Duelling. 2 v. 8°. Lond. 1841.

MILMAN, A. (Ed'r.) English and Scotch Historical Ballads. 16°. Lond. 1871.

MILMAN, H. H. Essays. 8°. Lond. 1870.

—— Latin Christianity. 8 v. 12°. N.Y. 1870.

MILNE, A. Materia Medica. 18°. Edin. 1869.

—— Midwifery and Diseases of Women. 16°. Edin. 1861.

MILNE, J. D. Industrial Employment of Women. 12°. Lond. 1870.

MILNER, J. End of Religious Controversy. 16°. Dubl. 1867.

MILTON, J. Treatise of Education. *See* LIBRARY of Education, v. 2.

—— Paradise Lost; Notes by Boyd. 12°. N.Y. 1857.

MILTON, Lord, and Dr. Cheadle. Northwest Passage by Land. 12°. Lond. n.d.

MILWAUKEE Directory, 1870–1. 8°. Milwaukee. 1870.

MINIFIE, W. Text-book of Geometrical Drawing. 8°. N.Y. 1869.

MINNESOTA. School Law of 1862. 8°. St. Paul. 1862.

MINNESOTA; its Advantages to Settlers. 8°. St. Paul. 1869.

MINNESOTA; its Progress and Capabilities. 8°. St. Paul. 1862.

MINNESOTA Historical Society. Collections. v. 2. 8°. n.p. n.d.

Collections. v. 3. Part 1. 8°. St. Paul. 1870.

MINNESOTA Statistics for 1869. 8°. St. Paul. 1870.

MINTO, Wm. A Manual of English Prose Literature. 12°. Edin. 1872.

MINTON, S. Glory of Christ in the Creation and Reconciliation of All Things. 16°. Lond. 1869.

MIRABEAU, Marquis de. Memoirs. 4 v. 8°. Lond. 1835–6

MIRANDA, A. de. Un Diner chez Bismarck. 8°. Brussels. 1870.

MIRECOURT, E. de. Comment les Femmes se Perdent. 12°. Paris. 1870.

—— La Marquise de Courcelles. 12°. Paris. 1871.

MISSIONARY Herald, v. 64–66. 8°. Cambr. 1868–71.

MISSISQUOI Copper Mine. Reports on (PC. 9.) 8°. Bost. 1864.

MITCHELL'S New General Atlas. Atl. 4°. Phil. 1871. Same. 1872.

MITCHELL, E. Five Thousand a Year. 12°. Bost. 1870.

MITCHELL, G. Journal des deux Mondes pendant le Siége de Paris. 8°. Paris. 1871.

MITCHELL, S. A. School Geography. 16°. Phil. 1851.

MITCHELL, S. W. Injuries of Nerves and their Consequences. 8°. Phil. 1872.

—— Wear and Tear; or, Hints for the Overworked. 16°. Phil. 1871.

MITCHELL, T. Manual of Architecture. 12°. Lond. 1870.

MIVART, St. G. Genesis of the Species. 12°. N.Y. 1871.

—— Same. 12°. Lond. 1871.

MOBERLY, G. Brighstone Sermons. 12°. Lond. 1869.

—— Way of Faith; or, Sayings of the Great 40 Days; Five Discourses. 12°. Lond. 1871.

MOBILE. Directory for 1870, 1871. 2 v. 8°. Mobile. 1871–2.

MODERN Thinker (The). v. 1. No. 1. 8°. N.Y. 1870.

MOFFAT, J. C. Comparative History of Religions. Part 1: Ancient Sculptures. 12°. N.Y. 1871.

MOINE (Le). Par l'Abbé * * *. 16°. Paris. 1869.

MOLAND, Louis. Par Ballon Monté. Lettres Envoyées de Paris pendant le Siége. 12°. Paris. 1871.

MOLESWORTH, W. N. History of England from 1830. v. 1. 8°. Lond. 1871.

MOLIÈRE, J. B. P. de. Œuvres. 8 v. 24°. Paris. 1753.

MOLINARI, M. G. de. Les Clubs Rouges pendant le Siége de Paris. 12°. Paris. 1871.

MÖLLHAUSEN, B. Das Hundertguldenblatt.
1. Der Bürgerkrieg. 3 v. in 1. 12°. Berlin. 1870.
2. Der Kunstsammler. 3 v. in 1. 12°. Berlin. 1870.

—— Der Piratenlieutenant. 4 v. in 2. 12°. Berlin. 1870.

MOLLOY, G. Geology and Revelation. 12°. Lond. 1870.

—— Passion Play at Ober-Ammergau in 1871. 12°. Lond. 1871.

MOMMSEN, T. History of Rome. 3 v. 12°. N.Y. 1870.

MOMMSEN, Strauss, etc. War between Germany and France. 12°. Lond. 1871.

MONIER, M. Wonders of Pompeii. 16°. N.Y. 1870.

MONITOR (The) Post Office and Shippers' Guide. Imp. 8°. N. Y. 1872.

MONNIN, A. Life of the Curé d'Ars (M. Vianney.) 12°. Baltimore. 1870.

MONROE, L. B. Physical and Vocal Training. 12°. Phil. 1869.

—— Public and Parlor Readings. 12°. Bost. 1872.

MONSELET, C. Chanvallon. 12°. Paris. 1872.

—— François Soleil. 12°. Paris. 1866.

MONSELL, J. S. B. Paris Musings; or, Devotional Poems. 16°. Lond. 1871.

MONSIEUR Napoléon et sa Cour. 4th ed. 8°. Brussels. 1871.

MONTAGU, E. W. Autobiography. 3 v. 12°. Lond. 1869.

—— Same. 12°. Phil. 1870.

MONTAGUE, Lady M. W. Works. 5 v. 18°. Lond. 1803.

MONTAIGNE, M. Essais (variorum ed.) 4 v. 18°. Paris. 1854.

MONTALEMBERT, Count. Monks of the West. 5 v. 8°. Edin. 1861–7.

—— Same, v. 1, 2. 8°. Bost. 1872.

MONTE, A. G. Four Hundred Millions; Chapters on the Chinese. 12°. Lond. 1871.

MONTEITH, A. H. Lessons in German. 8°. Phil. n.d.

MONTÉPIN, X. de. La Maison Maudite. 12°. Paris. n.d.

—— Les Pirates de la Seine. 12°. Paris. n.d.

MONTESQUIEU. *See* MAXIMES et Pensées.

MONTEZ, Lola. Anecdotes of Love. 12°. N.Y. n.d.

—— Lectures. 12°. N.Y. 1858.

MONTGOMERY, W. F. Signs and Symptoms of Pregnancy. 8°. Phil. 1857.

MONTHLY Magazine. v. 1. Apr.–Dec. 1799. 8°. N.Y. 1800.

MONTHLY Religious Magazine, v. 41–3. 8°. Bost. 1870.

MONTREAL Directory, 1870–1. 8°. Montreal. 1870.

MONUMENTA Juridica. Black Book of the Admiralty. Ed. by Sir J. Twiss. v. 1. (Rolls' Chronicles). 8°. Lond. 1871.

MOODY, Joel. The Science of Evil. 12°. Topeka. 1871.

MOORE, C. H. What to Read and How to Read. 12°. N.Y. 1871.

MOORE, D. Sermons on Special Occasions. 12°. Lond. 1871.

MOORE, F. Grounds of Humiliation and Hope; Fast Sermon. 8°. Phil. 1863.

MOORE, James. Sir John Moore's Campaign in Spain. 2d ed. 4°. Lond. 1809.

MOORE, T. Letters and Journals of Lord Byron; with Notices of his Life. 2 v. 8°. Phil. 1869.

—— Memoir of Sheridan. 2 v. 12°. N.Y. 1866.

MORALE de l'Invasion Prussienne. 12°. Paris. 1871.

MORDAUNT *vs.* Mordaunt *et al.* Official Report. 8°. Lond. 1870.

MORDENTE, J. E. Exercises in Spanish. 16°. Lond. 1811.

MORE. Life of Hannah More. 12°. Lond. 1856.

MOREL, C. Authority and Conscience; a Debate on Dogmatic Theology and Faith. 12°. Lond. 1871.

MOREL, H. Le Pilori des Communeux. 12°. Paris. 1871.

MORELET, A. Travels in Central America. 12°. N.Y. 1871.

MORENO, J. Viage á Constantinopla. f°. Madrid. 1790.

MORFIT, C. Treatise on Manufacture of Soaps. 8°. N.Y. 1871.

MORFORD, H. Short Trip Guide to Europe. 16°. N.Y. 1870. Same. 1871.

MORGAN, D. T. Hymns of the Latin Church. 12°. Lond. 1871.

MORGAN, G. C. Scientific Table for Knowledge. 18°. Lond. 1826.

MORGAN, H. J. Celebrated Canadians. 8°. Montreal. 1865.

MORGAN, J. A. Macaronic Poetry. 16°. N.Y. 1872.

MORGAN, N. Phrenology, and How to Use it in Analyzing Character. 12°. Lond. 1871.

MORGAN, R. C. At Jesus' Feet. 16°. Phil. 1871.

MORGAN, W. Manual of Mining Tools. Atl. 16°. and 4°. Lond. 1871.

MORIAC, E. Paris sous la Commune. 12°. Paris. 1871.

MORIN, G. Histoire Critique de la Commune. 12°. Paris. 1871.

MORLEY, C. Guide for Lyceums, etc. 18°. N.Y. 1841.

MORLEY, H. Clement Marot. 2 v. 12°. Lond. 1871.

—— Jerome Cardan. 2 v. 8°. Lond. 1854.

—— Life of Pallissy. 16°. Lond. n.d.

—— Tables of English Literature. f°. Lond. 1870.

MORLEY, J. Critical Miscellanies. 8°. Lond. 1871.

—— Voltaire. 8°. N.Y. 1872.

MORRIS, D. Class-Book History of England. 16°. Lond. 1871.

MORRIS, F. O. Difficulties of Darwinism. 8°. Lond. 1869.

—— Dogs and their Doings. R. 8°. Lond. n.d.

MORRIS, J. Condition of Catholics under James I; Father Gerard's Narrative of the Gunpowder Plot. 8°. Lond. 1871.

MORRIS, R. English Accidence. 18° Lond. 1872.

MORRIS, Robt. Courtship and Matrimony. 12°. Phil. n.d.

MORRIS, T. British Carpentry; Gothic Roofs. 8°. Lond. 1871.

—— A House for the Suburbs. 8°. Lond. 1870.

MORRIS, W. Earthly Paradise. Parts 3, 4. 12°. Bost. 1869–71.

MORRIS, W. O. Land Question of Ireland. 12°. Lond. 1870.

MORRISON, J. Alliance with the Great Mogul. 12°. Lond. 1774.

MORRISON, J. Book-keeping. 3d ed. 4°. Lond. 1828.

MORSE, J. and K. C. Traveler's Guide. 2d ed. 16°. New Haven. 1826.

MORSE, S. F. B. Academies of Arts; a Discourse. 8°. N.Y. 1827.

MORSE, Sidney E. Geographical, Statistical and Ethical View of the American Slaveholders' Rebellion. 8°. N.Y. 1863.

MOSELEY, H. Lectures on Astronomy. 4th ed. 16°. Lond. 1864.

MOSENTHAL, S. H. Maryna. 16°. Leip. 1871.

MOSSMAN, S. Our Australian Colonies. 16°. Lond. n.d.

MOTHER Goose's Melodies for Children. 8°. N.Y. 1871.

MOTHER Goose's Melodies. With Illustrations by Miss Chase. 4°. Phil. n.d.

MOTTOES and Aphorisms from Shakspeare. 8°. Lond. n.d.

MOULS, J. Art of Speaking French. 16°. N.Y. 1836.

MOUNT Alpine Gold Co. Prospectus. (PC. 9.) 8°. Providence. 1864.

MOUNT WASHINGTON in Winter. 12°. Bost. 1871.

MOUNTAIN Adventures. 12°. Bost. 1869.

MOUNTFORD, W. Miracles, Past and Present. 12°. Bost. 1870.

MOWBRAY, G. M. Nitro-Glycerine in Construction of Hoosac Tunnel. 8°. n.p. n.d.

MOWRY, S. Arizona and Sonora. 12°. N.Y. 1871.

MRS. Jerningham's Journal. 16°. Lond. 1870.

MUDGE, Z. A. Witch Hill; a History of Salem Witchcraft. 16°. N.Y. n.d.

MUDIE, R. Popular Mathematics. 16°. 1836.

MÜGGE, T. Afraja. 16°. Breslau. 1862.

—— Erich Randall. 12°. Frankfort. 1856.

—— Der Voigt von Silt. 2d ed. 2 v. in 1. 18°. Berlin. 1858.

MÜHLBACH, Louise. (Pseudonym.) *See* MUNDT, Clara.

MÜHLENBERG, W. A. The Woman and her Accusers; a Sermon. 24°. N.Y. n.d.

MÜHLFELD, J. Für's Vaterland. 12°. Jena. 1866.

—— Im Bann der Schuld. 12°. Gumbinnen. 1870.

—— Matthisson und Adelaide. 15°. Berlin. 1872.

MUIR, J. Original Sanskrit Texts. v. 4, 5. 8°. Lond. 1863–70.

MUIR, R. Bills of Exchange and Promissory Notes. 16°. Edin. 1836.

MUIRHEAD, J. P. Inventions of J. Watt. 3 v. 4°. Lond. 1854.

MULDER, L. Leesbock over de Mestmakerij. 18°. Deventer. 1854.

MULFORD, E. The Nation. 8°. N.Y. 1870.

MULHALL, M. G. and E. T. River Plate. v. 1. 8°. Buenos Ayres. 1869.

MÜLLER, F. Facts and Arguments for Darwin. Tr. by Dallas. 12°. Lond. 1869.

MULLER, G. F. and Pallas, P. S. Conquest of Siberia, and the History of the Transactions, Wars, etc., between Russia and China. 12°. Lond. 1843.

MÜLLER, H. Im Wartesalon erster Klasse. *See* ELZ, A. Er ist nicht, etc.

MÜLLER, H. L. Commerce du Globe. Ob. 4°. Paris. 1839.

MÜLLER, J. Fortification. 2d ed. 8°. Lond. 1764.

—— Same. 3d ed. 8°. Lond. 1774.

MÜLLER, Max. Chips from a German Workshop. 3 v. 8°. Lond. 1868-70.

—— Same. 3 v. 12°. N.Y. 1869–71.

—— Essays. 3. v. (in German, by F. Liebrecht.) 12°. Leip. 1869–72.

—— Lectures on Language. 6th ed. 2 v. 12°. Lond. 1871.

—— Same. 12°. N.Y. 1871.

—— Lectures on the Science of Religion. 12°. N.Y. 1872.

MÜLLER, O. Der Professor von Heidelberg. 12°. Stuttgart. 1870.

MULLIGAN, J. Grammatical Structure of English. 12°. N.Y. 1852.

MULLINS, J. D. Free Libraries and News-rooms. 18°. Lond. 1869.

MUNDT, Clara (L. Mühlbach). Damenalmanach. 16°. Leip. 1870.

—— Deutschland gegen Frankreich. 4 v. in 2. 12°. Jena. 1868.

—— Frankreich gegen Deutschland. 5 v. in 2. 12°. Jena. 1868.

—— Kaiser Joseph und sein Landsknecht. Abth. 1. 4 v. in 2. 12°. Leip. 1870.

—— Same. Abth. 2. 4 v. in 2. 12°. Leip. 1871.

—— Kaiserburg und Engelsburg. 16°. Jena. 1871.

—— Maria Theresia und der Pandurenobrist Trenck. Abth. 2. 2 v. in 1. 12°. Brunn. 1862.

—— Mohammed Ali und sein Haus. 4 v. in 2. 12°. Jena. 1871.

—— Mohammed Ali's Nachfolger. 4 v. in 2. 12°. Jena. 1872.

—— Die Opfer des Religiösen Fanatismus. v. 1, 2. 12°. Prague. 1871.

—— Reisebriefe aus Aegypten. 2 v. in 1. 12°. Jena. 1870.

—— Von Solferino bis Königgrätz:
Abth. 1. Kirchenfürsten und Weltfürsten. 4 v. in 2. 12°. Berlin. 1869.
" 2. Solferino. 4 v. in 2. 12°. Berlin. 1870.
" 3. Die Nebenbuhler um Deutschland. 4 v. in 2. 12°. Berlin. 1870.

MUNN, D. Theory of Arithmetic. 12°. Edin. 1871.

MUNSELL, J. Collections on the History of Albany. v. 3, 4. L. 8°. Alb. 1870–1.

—— Chronology of Paper and Paper Making. 4th ed. 8°. Alb. 1870.

MURGER, H. Le Roman du Capucin 16°. Paris. 1869.

MURPHY, J. G. Commentary on Exodus. 8°. Edin. 1866.

MURPHY, J. J. Sermons on Various Subjects. 12°. Lond. 1871.

MURPHY, J. N. Ireland. 12°. Lond. 1870.

MURRAY'S Hand-book; Constantinople. 16°. Lond. n.d.

—— Same; Rome and Environs. 10th ed. 12°. Lond. 1871.

MURRAY, G. W. History of Himself, etc. (PC. 8.) 16°. Springfield. n.d.

MURRAY, James. The Prophet's Mantle. 12°. Edin. 1870.

MURRAY, J. C. Outline of Hamilton's Philosophy. 8°. Bost. 1870.

MURRAY, J. H. Travels in Uruguay. 12°. Lond. 1871.

MURRAY, J. P. Life of John Banim. 12°. N.Y. 1869.

MURRAY, L. English Grammar. 16°. Windsor. 1834.

MURRAY, N. Kirwan's Letters to Hughes. 12°. N.Y. 1855.

—— Parish and other Pencillings. 12°. N.Y. 1854.

MURRAY, W. H. H. Music-Hall Sermons. 16°. Bost. 1870.

—— Park Street Pulpit Sermons. 12°. Bost. 1871.

MUSAEUS, Tieck, Richter. Tales. Tr. by T. Carlyle. 8°. Lond. 1871.

MUSÉE des Familles. v. 1–5. f°. Paris. 1834–8.

MUSEUM and English Journal of Education. v. 5. L. 8°. Lond 1869.

MUSGRAVE, G. Ramble into Brittany. 2 v. 12°. Lond. 1870.

MUSICAL Anecdotes and Stories. 18°. Bost. 1841.

MUSSET, A. de. Select Prose and Poetry. 16°. N.Y. 1870.

MUSSET, P. de. Lui et Elle. 16°. Paris. 1865.

MUSTERS, G. C. At Home with the Patagonians. 8°. Lond. 1871.

MÜTZELBURG, A. Die Enterbten. 16°. Berlin. n.d.

MYERS, H. M., and P. V. M. Life and Nature under the Tropics. 12°. N.Y. 1871.

MYERS, T. B. Letters and MSS. of Signers of the Declaration of Independence. Sm. 4°. N.Y. 1871.

MYERS, Mrs. V. Letters to Mr. Hoyt. (PC. 17.) 8°. Phil. 1847.

MYSTERIES of Washington City. 18°. Wash. 1844.

MYSTERY (The) Finished; the Negro has a Soul. 12°. Memphis. 1868.

NACK, J. The Immortal, and other Poems. 12°. N.Y. 1850.

NANGLE, Edward. History of the Reformation, for Children. 3 v. 18°. Achill. 1851.

NAPHEGYI, G. Album of Language. Imp. 4°. Phil. 1869.

—— Among the Arabs. 12°. Phil. 1868.

—— Ghardaia. 12°. N.Y. 1871.

—— Grand Review of the Dead. 8°. N.Y. 1869.

NAPHEYS, G. H. Physical Life of Women. 12°. Phil. 1870.

—— Transmission of Life. 12°. Phil. 1871.

NAPIER, C. O. G. Book of Nature and of Man. 8°. Phil. 1870.

NAPIER, Mark. Wigtown Martyrs. 8°. Edin. 1870.

NAPOLEON I. Memoirs and Historical Miscellanies dictated to Gourgaud and Montholon. 7 v. 8°. Lond. 1823.

—— Correspondence with King Joseph. 2 v. 8°. Lond. 1855.

NAPOLEON III. Napoleonic Ideas. 12°. N.Y. 1859.

NAPOLEON III. from Popular Caricatures. 12°. Lond. n.d.

NAPOLÉON, Jerome (Le Prince.) La Verité à mes Calomniateurs. 8°. Paris. 1871.

NARBROUGH, J. Voyages. *See* COREAL, F.

NARRAGANSETT Club. Publications. v. 4. Bloody Tenent yet more Bloody; by R. Williams. Sm. 4°. Providence. 1870.

NARRATIVE of certain Occurences at the late Special Convention of the Diocese of New York. (PC. 1.) 8°. N.Y. 1851.

NASH, H. A. Student's Compendium of the Book of Common Prayer. 16°. Lond. 1871.

NASH, J. British Song Birds. 12°. Lond. 1872.

NASHVILLE Directory, 1870–71. 2 v. 8°. Nashville. 1870–1.

NASON, E. Memoir of Mrs. Rowson. 8°. Alb. 1870.

NAST'S Illustrated Almanac for 1872. 12°. N.Y. 1872.

NATION (The). v. 13. July–Dec. 1871. 4°. N.Y. 1871.

NATION, W. H. C. Apple Blossoms. 16°. Lond. 1870.

NATIONAL Asso. for the Promotion of Social Science. Transactions, 1868–71. 4 v. 8°. Lond. 1869–72.

NATIONAL Board of Fire Underwriters. Proceedings of the Annual Meetings and of the Sessions of the Executive Committee, Feb. 1867–April, 1871. 8°. N.Y. n.d.

—— Remarks of the President, Henry A. Oakley, Esq., at the 5th Annual Meeting, April 19, 1871. 8°. N.Y. 1871.

NATIONAL Education Union Conference, Leeds, Dec., 1869. 8°. Lond. 1869.

NATIONAL Elementary Education and the New Code. 8°. Lond. 1871.

NATIONAL Guard. First Golden Anniversary. Sq. 12°. N.Y. 1869.

NATIONAL Insurance Convention of the U. S. Official Reports of Proceedings, by Olcott. 2 v. 8°. N.Y. 1871.

NATIONAL Quarterly Review. v. 18–23. 8°. N.Y. 1869–71.

NATIONAL Stock Exchange. Constitution and By-Laws. (PC. 2.) 8°. N.Y. 1869.

NATURAL Science, Religious Creeds and Scripture Truth. 8°. Edin. 1870.

NATURE. 1–5. Imp. 8°. Lond. 1870–2.

NAUTICAL Magazine, v. 38, 39. 8°. Lond. 1869–70.

—— New Series. v. 1. 8°. Lond. 1871.

NAVAL Chronicle, v. 1–40. 8°. Lond. 1799–1818.

NAVILLE, E. Problem of Evil. 12°. Edin. 1871.

NAYLER, B. S. Common Sense on Rules Regarding English. 8°. Melbourne. 1869.

NAZARETH. 12° Lond. 1872.

NAZET, H. et Spoll, E. A. Blocus et Capitulation de Metz. 8°. Brussels. 1870.

NEAL, J. Great Mysteries and Little Plagues. 16°. Bost. 1870.

NEAL, R. H. Memorial of Rev. B. Stow. 18°. Bost. 1870.

NEALE, J. M. Three Groups of Sermons; on the Apocalypse, the Holy Name, and the Last Chapter of Proverbs. 16°. Lond. n.d.

NEFTEL, W. B. Galvano-Therapeutics. 12°. N.Y. 1871.

NEILL, E. D. English Colonization of America during the 17th Century. 8°. Lond. 1871.

—— Pocahontas and her Companions. Sm. 4°. Alb. 1869.

—— Virginia Company of London. Sm. 4°. Alb. 1869.

NELSON, Lord. Life of, by the Old Sailor. 16°. Lond. 1867.

NEUMANN, J. *Text-Book of Skin Diseases. Tr. by Pullar. 8°. Lond. 1871.

NEVILLE, C. and M. The Cross, and Verses of Many Years. 16°. Oxford. 1870.

NEVINS, R. P. Black Robes; or Sketches of Missions and Ministers in the Wilderness and on the Border. 16°. Phil. 1872.

NEVINS, Wm. Pensamientos sobre el Papismo. In Spanish by Rule. 18°. Gibraltar. 1839.

NEWARK Directory, 1870. 8°. Newark. 1870.

NEWARK Library Association. Catalogue. 8°. Newark. 1857.

NEW Bedford Directory, 1869–70. 8°. New Bedford. 1869.

NEWBURGH Free Library. Catalogue. 8°. Newburgh. 1868.

NEWELL, R. H. O. C. Kerr Papers. 12°. N.Y. 1871.

—— Versatilities. 12. Bost. 1871.

NEW ENGLAND Historical-Genealogical Register. v. 20–25. 8°. Bost. 1866–71.

NEW ENGLAND Medical Gazette. v. 5, 6. 8°. Bost. 1870–1.

NEW Englander. v. 27–30. 8°. New Haven. 1868–71.

NEW Era. v. 1. Oct. 1870–Sept. 1871. 8°. N.Y. 1871.

NEW Fashioned Girl; a Poem. 16°. N.Y. 1870.

NEWHALL, J. B. Sketches of Iowa. 18°. N.Y, 1841.

NEW HAMPSHIRE. Catalogue of State Library. 8°. Concord. 1857.

NEW HARTFORD Directory. *See* UTICA.

NEW HAVEN Directory, 1870–2. 2 v. 12°. and 8°. New Haven. 1870–1.

NEWHOUSE, S., etc. Trappers' Guide. 8°. N.Y. 1869.

NEW JERSEY. Annual Report of State Geologist, for 1869, 1870. 2 v. 8°. Trenton and New Brunswick. 1870–71.

—— Geology, with Maps. 2 v. 8°. and 4°. Newark. 1862.

NEW JERSEY State Business Directory, 1870–71. 8°. Alb. 1870.

NEW Letter Writer. 16°. Phil. n.d.

NEWMAN, E. British Butterflies. Imp. 8°. Lond. 1871.

NEWMAN, F. W. Cure of the Great Social Evil. 8°. Lond. 1869.

—— Dictionary of Modern Arabic. 2 v. 12°. Lond. 1871.

—— Europe of the Near Future. 16°. Lond. 1871.

—— Grammar of Assent. 12°. N.Y. 1870.

—— Hiawatha, rendered into Latin, with Abridgment. 16°. Lond. 1862.

—— Miscellanies; chiefly Addresses, Academical and Historical. 8°. Lond. 1869.

—— Orthoepy. 8°. Lond. 1839.

—— Regal Rome. 12°. N.Y. 1852.

NEWMAN, J. B. Natural History of Man. 12°. N.Y. 1852.

NEWMAN, J. H. Discussions and Arguments of Various Subjects. 12°. Lond. 1872.

—— Essays, Critical and Historical. 2v. 12°. Lond. 1871.

—— Essays on Miracles. 2d ed. 12°. Lond. 1870.

—— Miscellanies. 12°. Lond. 1870.

—— History of my Religious Opinions. 12°. Lond. 1869.

—— Sermons on Subjects of the Day. 12°. Lond. 1869.

NEWMAN, J. P. Self Denial for the Promotion of Temperance a Duty and Pleasure; a Sermon. 12°. N.Y. 1871.

NEW Monthly Magazine. v. 144–9. 8°. Lond. 1867–71.

NEW ORLEANS Directory, 1870–1. 2 v. 8°. New Orleans. 1870–1.

NEW Palace at Westminster. 15th ed. 8°. Lond. 1858.

NEWPORT, David. Indices to Revision of the Scripture. 16°. Phil. 1871.

NEW (The) Reign of Terror in the Slaveholding States. 12°. N.Y. 1860.

NEWSPAPER Press Directory for 1857. (Mitchell's.) R. 8°. Lond. 1857.

NEW System of Practical Domestic Economy. 3d ed. 12°. Lond. 1823.

NEW YORK [City]. Board of Education. Report on Bible in Schools. (PC. 5.) 8°. N.Y. 1859.

—— Same. 24th, 26th, 28th and 29th Annual Reports for 1865–67–69 and 70. 4 v. 8°. N.Y. 1866–71.

—— Board of Health of the Health Department of the City of New York. 1st Annual Report. 8°. N.Y. 1871.

—— Central Park. 13th Annual Report of the Commissioners. 8°. N.Y. 1870.

—— City Inspector's Report for 1860. 8°. N.Y. 1861.

—— Commissioners of Public Charities and Correction. 8th, 10th, and 11th Ann. Reports for 1867, '69 and '70. 3 v. 8°. Alb. and N.Y. 1867–71.

—— Commissioners of Public Parks. 1st Annual Report. 8°. N.Y. 1871.

—— Comptroller's Annual Report for 1846. 8°. N.Y. 1847.

—— Department of Docks. Public Meetings. 8°. N.Y. 1870.

—— Enrollment Lists, 18th Ward. 4°. N.Y. 1863.

—— Fire Department. Constitution. 8°. N.Y. 1839.

—— Manual of the Common Council, 1850, 1853. 2 v. 12°. N.Y. 1850–3.

—— Manual of the Corporation, 1868–69. 2 v. 8°. N.Y. n.d.

—— Mayor, etc., of New York *vs.* Erben. Synopsis of the Case. 8°. N.Y. 1863.

—— Metropolitan Board of Health. 3d and 4th Annual Reports. 8°. Alb. and N.Y. 1869–70.

—— Same. Manual. 18°. N.Y. 1869.

—— Same. Memorial on Compulsory Vaccination. 8°. N.Y. 1862.

—— Metropolitan Fire Department. 3d, 4th and 5th Annual Reports. 3 v. 8°. Alb. and N.Y. 1868–70.

—— Metropolitan Police Department. Annual Reports of the Commissioners, 1865–70. 6 v. 8°. N.Y. 1865–70.

—— Names, etc., of the Common Council. 8°. N.Y. 1837.

—— Police Department of the City of New York. 1st Annual Report. 8°. N.Y. 1871.

—— Public Documents for 1868. 10 v. 8°. N.Y. 1869.

NEW YORK (State). Assembly Documents. 92d and 93d Sessions, 1869–70. 24 v. 8°. Alb. 1869–70.

—— Assembly Journal. 92d and 93d Sessions. 1869–70. 4 v. 8°. Alb. 1869–70.

—— Banking Department. Annual Report on Savings Banks. 8°. Alb. 1870.

—— Cabinet. Reports on. Nos. 17–20 and 22. 5 v. 8°. Alb. 1864–9.

—— Calendar of Historical Manuscripts in the Office of the Secretary of State. Ed. by O'Callaghan. Pt. 1. Dutch Manuscripts. Pt. 2. English Manuscripts. 2 v. Imp. 8°. Alb. 1865–6.

—— Calendar of Historical Manuscripts relating to the War of the Revolution in the office of the Secretary of State. 2 v. Imp. 8°. Alb. 1864.

—— Calendar of N. Y. Colonial Manuscripts indorsed Land Papers in the office of the Secretary of State, 1643–1803. 8°. Alb. 1864.

—— Census of 1865. f°. Alb. 1867.

—— Commissioners of Emigration. Annual Reports, 1868–71. 4 v. 8°. N.Y. 1869–72.

—— Debate on Slavery. Assembly, Jan. 23, 1850. (PC. 15.) 8°. N.Y. 1850.

—— Geological Survey. Palaeontology. v. 4, part 2. 4°. Alb. 1867.

—— Index of the Laws. v. 3. 8°. Alb. 1867.

—— Law Library. First Supplementary Catalogue. 8°. Alb. 1865.

—— Laws Passed at 92d, 93d and 94th Sessions of the Legislature. 6 v. 8°. Alb. 1869–71.

—— Legislative Manual, 1862, 1870. 2 v. S. 16°. Alb. 1862–70.

—— Library. Reports of Trustees. 6 v. 8°. Alb. 1864–9.

—— Local Taxation. Report of Commission. 8°. N.Y. 1871.

—— Militia Law of 1828. 16°. n.p. n.d.

—— Poor Laws. 8°. Alb. 1871.

—— Quarantine. Report, 1848, on Removal of. 8°. n.p. n.d.

—— Savings Banks, Special Reports on, by Keyes. 8°. Alb. 1868.

—— Senate Documents. 92d and 93d Sessions, 1869–70. 14 v. 8°. Alb. 1869–70.

—— Senate Journal. 92d and 93d Sessions. 1869–70. 2 v. 8°. Alb. 1869-70.

—— State Surveyor and Engineer's Annual Report, 1867–8. 8°. Alb. 1869.

—— Vattemare's Report on the Paris Exhibition. (PC. 15.) 8°. N.Y. 1856.

New York. Complete Guide to the City of New York. 16°. N.Y. n.d.

New York City Directory, 1870, 1871–2. 2 v. 8°. N.Y. 1870–1.

New York, Doggett's City Co-Partnership Directory, 1846–7; and 1850–1. 2 v. 8°. N.Y. n.d.

New York, Doggett's Street Directory, 1850–1. 8° .N.Y. 1851.

New York City during the American Revolution. From Original Papers in the Mercantile Library. Sm. 4°. N.Y. 1861.

New York. The Great Metropolis for 1846; same, 1848. 2 v. 24°. N.Y. 1846–8.

New York. Stranger's Key to New York. 24°. N.Y. 1830.

New York. Wilson's Business Directory. 1871–2. 16°. N.Y. 1871.

New York Albion. v. 49. Jan.–Dec. 1871. f°. N.Y. 1871.

New York Astronomical Observatory. Charter and By-Laws. (PC. 5; PC. 15.) 8°. N.Y. 1859.

New York Athenæum. To the Publick. (Report on the Constitution, 1825.) 8°. N.Y. 1824.

New York Chamber of Commerce. Report on Harbor Encroachments. (PC. 5.) 8°. N.Y. 1864.

—— 12th and 13th Annual Reports, 1869–70, 1870–1. 2 v. 8°. N.Y. 1870–1.

New York City Mission and Tract Society. Year Book, 1870. 8°. N.Y. 1870.

New York Corn Exchange. Charter and By-Laws. (PC. 15.) 12°. N.Y. n.d.

New York and Erie R. R. Address of Convention. 12°. Auburn. 1837.

—— Reports to Stockholders, 1840, 1853, 1855. 8°. N.Y. 1841–56.

—— Truths on N. Y. and Erie R. R. By E. Williams. 12° N.Y. 1842.

New York Fire Ins. Co. *vs.* Howell *et al.* Respondents' Case, Court of Errors. 8°. N.Y. n.d.

New York Free Press. Aug.–Dec. 1870. f°. N.Y. 1871.

New York Genealogical and Biographical Record. v. 1 and 2. 8°. N.Y. 1870–1.

New York and Harlem R. R. Co. Memorial to N. Y. City. (PC. 6.) 8°. N.Y. 1855.

New York Herald (Daily), July 1869–Dec. 1871. 7 v. f°. N.Y. 1869–71.

New York Medical Journal. v. 8–13. 8°. N.Y. 1868–71.

New York Medico-Legal Society. Report of Committee on Criminal Abortion. 8°. N.Y. 1872.

New York Mills Directory. *See* Utica.

New York Observer. Year Book and Almanac. 8°. N.Y. 1871

New York Prison Association. *See* Prison Association.

New York Sanitary and Chemical Compost Co. Prospectus. (PC. 20.) 8°. N.Y. 1865.

NEW YORK-Staatszeitung (Daily). v. 37. Jan.-Dec. 1871. Mit Sonntagsblatt, vol. 23. Atl. f°. N.Y. 1871.

NEW YORK Standard (Daily). 1870-Dec. 1871. 4 v. Atl. f°. N.Y. 1871.

NEW YORK State Inebriate Asylum. 8°. N.Y. 1871.

NEW YORK Sun. *See* SUN.

NEW YORK Teacher. New Series. v. 3, 4. 8°. 1862-3. For volumes subsequent to 1863, *see* AMERICAN EDUCATIONAL MONTHLY.

NEW YORK Times (Daily). July 1869 to Dec. 1871. 7 v. Atl. f°. N.Y. 1869-71.

NEW YORK Tribune (Daily). July 1869 to Dec. 1871. 7 v. Atl. f°. N.Y. 1869-71.

NEW YORK Underwriter. v. 13-15. 4°. N.Y. 1868-71.

NEW YORK World. *See* WORLD.

NEW YORK Yacht Club. Constitution, etc. 24°. N.Y. 1870.

NIAGARA Ship Canal and Reciprocity. Papers of J. D. Hayes, and Speech of I. T. Hatch, published by Buffalo Board of Trade. 8°. Buff. 1865.

NICHOLAS, T. Pedigree of the English People. 2d ed. 8°. Lond. 1871.

NICHOLLS, J. F. Life of Cabot. Sq. 12°. Lond. 1869.

NICHOLS, J. R. Fireside Science. 12°. N.Y. 1872.

NICHOLS, T. Handy-Book of the British Museum. 8°. Lond. 1870.

NICHOLS, T. L. Religions of the World. 8°. Cinc. n.d.

NICHOLSON, H. A. Advanced Text-Book of Zoology. 12°. Edin. 1870.

—— Manual of Zoology. v. 2. Vertebrata. 12°. Edin. 1870.

NIEMEYER, F. von. Text-Book of Practical Medicine. 2 v. 8°. N.Y. 1870.

NIENDORF, M. A. Die Randschrift eines Königs. 12°. Berlin. n.d.

—— Rittergut Marderheim. 2 v. in 1. 12°. Berlin. 1872.

NIGHTINGALE, Florence. Introductory Notes on Lying-in Institutions. 8°. Lond. 1871.

NINETEENTH Century. v. 3. R. 8°. Phil. 1870.

NITZSCH, G. W. Anmerkungen zu Homer's Odyssee. 3 v. in 2. 8°. Hanover. 1826-40.

NOAD, H M. Rudimentary Magnetism. 16°. Lond. 1872.

NOAILLES, Baroness de. Memoirs of the Marquise de Montagu. 12°. Lond. 1870.

NOBLE, F. A. Blood the Price of Redemption; Thanksgiving Sermon. 8°. St. Paul. 1862.

NODIER, C. Les Sept Chateaux du Roi de Bohême. 16°. Paris. 1852.

NOËL et Chapsal. Grammaire Française. 23d ed. 12°. Paris. 1835.

NOEL, Hon. R. Beatrice and other Poems. 16°. Lond. 1868.

NOHL, L. Beethoven's Brevier. 16°. Leip. 1870.

—— Neue Bilder aus dem Leben de Musik. 12°. Munich. 1870

NORDHEIMER, I. Hebrew Grammar. v. 1. 8°. N.Y. 1838.

NORIAC, Jules. La Bêtise Humaine. 12°. Paris. 1864.

NORMANDY, A. Introduction to Ross's Chemical Analysis. 8°. Lond. 1849.

NORRIS, E. Assyrian Dictionary. Parts 1 and 2. 2 v. R. 8°. Lond. 1868-70.

NORRIS, J. P. Key to the Four Gospels. 16°. Lond. 1869.

—— Key to the Narrative of the Acts of the Apostles. 16°. Lond. 1871.

NORRIS, T. American Angler's Book. 8°. Phil. n.d.

—— Fish Culture. 12°. Phil. 1868.

NORRIS, W. Ancient Slavery disapproved of God. 12°. Phil. 1862.

NORTH, J. W. History of Augusta, Maine. 8°. Augusta. 1870.

NORTH American Review. v. 108-113. 8°. Bost. 1869-71.

NORTH British Review. v. 48-53. 8°. Edin. and Lond. 1868-71.

NORTHCOTT, W. H. Lathes and Turning. 8°. Lond. 1868.

NORTHEND, C. Child's Speaker. 18°. N.Y. 1870.

NORTHERN Pacific R.R. Petition to Canada Legislature. (PC. 19.) f°. Quebec. 1854.

NORTHERN Traveler. (Niagara, Quebec, and the Springs). 18°. N.Y. 1825.

NORTON. T. The Hermit, a Poem. 8°. Lond. 1872.

NORWAY and the Vöring-Fos. 16°. Dublin. 1870.

NOS Sauveurs. 12°. Brussels. 1871.

NOTES and Queries. 4th Ser. v. 3-7. Sm. 4°. Lond. 1869-71.

NOTES of Travel at Majunga, Zanzibar, etc. 12°. Salem. 1854.
NOTICIOSO de Ambos Mundos. No. 1 and Nos. 135–165. f°. N.Y. 1835–9.
NOTT, E. Lectures on Biblical Temperance. 12°. Lond. 1863.
—— Resurrection of Christ. 12°. N.Y. 1872.
NOURSE, J. E. Maritime Canal of Suez. 8°. Wash. 1869.
NOUVELLE Académie des Jeux. 2d ed. 16°. Paris. 1818.
NOUVELLE Lettre de Junius à son Ami A. D. 8°. Paris. 1871.
Novo (O) Mundo. v. 1. f°. N.Y. 1870–1.
NOYE, W. Maxims. 16°. Alb. 1870.
NOYES, J. H. History of American Socialisms. 8°. Phil. 1870.
NOYES, W. C. Argument on Trial of Mr. Tallmadge. 8°. N.Y. 1858.
—— Speech on Washington's Birthday. (PC. 15.) 8°. N.Y. 1860.
NUGENT, E. Optics. 12°. N.Y. 1868.
NUGENT, E. C. Country House Charades. Sq. 12°. Lond. n.d.
OAKLEY, F. The Priest on the Mission. 12°. Lond. 1871.
OBEN, J. von. Des Hauses Eckstein. 3 v. in 1. 12°. Leip. 1870.
O'BRENNAN, M. A. Archbishop Mac Hale: a Lecture. 8°. Chicago. 1870.
O'CALLAGHAN, J. C. Irish Brigades in France. 8°. Glasgow. 1870.
O'CONNOR, W. A. Commentary on Romans. 12°. Lond. 1871.
O'DEA, J. J. Development of Religious Ideas. 8°. N.Y. 1872.
—— Sphere, Rights and Obligations of Medical Experts. 8°. N.Y. 1871.
ODLING, W. Outlines of Chemistry. 12°. Lond. 1870.
O'DRISCOLL, W. J. Memoir of Maclise. 8°. Lond. 1871.
OELSCHLÄGER, H. Wunderliche Leute. 3 v. in 1. 12°. Leip. 1869.
OESER, Ch. Briefe an eine Jungfrau über die Hauptgegenstände der Aesthetik (Aesthetische Briefe). Herausgegeben von Grube. 12th ed. 12°. Leip. 1871.
OETTINGER, Ed. M. Die Nordische Semiramis. 3 v. 12°. Berlin. 1863.
OFFICER'S Manual in the Field. Sq. 16°. Lond. 1798.
OFFICES of Prayer for Private Devotion. 24°. Lond. 1843.
O'FLANAGAN, J. R. Lord Chancellors of Ireland. 2 v. 8°. Lond. 1870.
O'GORMAN, Edith. Trials and Persecutions; or, Convent Life Unveiled. 12°. Hartford. 1871.
OHIO. School Laws of 1862. 8°. Columbus. 1862.
—— GEOLOGICAL Survey, by Newberry. Report of Progress in 1870. 8°. Columbus. 1870.
OLD Book Collector's Miscellany; or, a Collection of Readable Reprints of Literary Rarities. Ed. by C. Hindley. v. 1. 8°. Lond. 1871.
OLD and New. v. 1–4. 8°. Bost. 1870–1.
OLDHAM, C. H. What is Malaria? 8°. Lond. 1871.
OLFERS, Marie von. Novellen. 12°. Berlin. 1872.
OLIPHANT, L. Piccadilly. 12°. Edin. 1870.
OLIPHANT, Mrs. St. Francis of Assisi. 12°. Lond. n.d.
—— Sketches of the Reign of George II. 2 v. 8°. Edin. 1869.
OLIVER Optic's Magazine. v. 7. R. 8°. Bost. 1871.
OLIVIER, U. Jean Laroche. 18°. Lausanne. 1870.
OLLANTA. An Ancient Ynca Drama. Transl. from the Quichua by C. R. Markham. 12°. Lond. 1871.
OLLENDORFF, H. G. Key to Ollendorff's French Method. 12°. N.Y. 1848.
—— Method, for French; by Jewett. 12°. N.Y. 1846.
—— Same, by Value. 12°. N.Y. 1851.
—— New Method for German (Adler's). 12°. N.Y. 1870.
—— New Method for Learning Italian. 12°. N.Y. 1870.
OLMSTED, M. N. Universal Path-Finder. 18°. N.Y. 1866.
O'MEARA, R. Napoleon in Exile. 4th ed. 2 v. 8°. Lond. 1822.
ONCE a Week. v. 1. f°. N.Y. 1871.
ONEIDA Circular. v. 8. f°. Oneida Community. 1871.
ONEIDA Institute. Manual Labor Meeting. 8°. N.Y. 1831.
O'NEILL, C. Chemistry of Calico Printing and Dyeing. 8°. Manch. (Eng.) 1860.
—— Dictionary of Calico Printing and Dyeing. 8°. Lond. 1862.
ONLY Once. Original Papers, by various Contributors. 4°. N.Y. 1862.
ONWARD. v. 1–2. 8°. N.Y. 1869.

OPINIONS Concerning the Bible Law of Marriage. 12°. Phil. 1871.
OPPENHEIM, H. B. Friedensglossen zum Kriegsjahr. 8°. Leip. 1871.
ORAM, E. English Grammar and Composition. 12°. N.Y. 1846.
ORDENANZAS de Bilbao. 8°. Paris. 1837.
ORDERICUS Vitalis. Ecclesiastical History of England and Normandy. Transl. by Forester. 4 v. 12°. Lond. 1854.
ORDRE der Texten op de Feestdagen voor Paaschen; Boek der Psalmen; Catechismus. 16°. Hague. n.d.
O'REILLY, A. G. The Martyrs of the Coliseum. 16°. Balt. 1872.
O'RIELLY, H. C. Colles and the Telegraph. (PC. 5.) Sm. 4°. Morrisania. 1869.
ORIENT (L') Ancien et Moderne. v. 1. 8°. Paris. 1842.
ORMATHWAITE, Lord. Astronomy and Geology Compared. 12°. Lond. 1872.
ORME, T. A. Science of Heat. 18°. Lond. 1870
ORMSBY, R. Life of St. Francis de Sales. 16°. N.Y. 1871.
ORSINI, C. L'Alliance Latine. 12°. Paris. 1871.
ORTOLAN, J. J. E. History of Roman Law. Tr. by Pritchard and Nasmith. 8°. Lond. 1871.
ORTON, J. Andes and Amazon. 12°. N.Y. 1870.
ORTON, W. Argument on Postal Telegraph. *See* WESTERN UNION TELEGRAPH CO.
OSBORN, H. S. Metallurgy of Iron and Steel. 8°. Phil. 1869.
OSBORN, S. Poems. 16°. Bost. 1823.
OSBORN, V. R. Key to Latin and Greek. 16°. New Haven. 1829.
OSBORNE, Mrs. C. J. Memorials of Lady Osborne. 2 v. 8°. Dublin. 1870.
OSSIAN. Poems; Gaelic, with translation by Clarke. 2 v. 8°. Edin. 1870.
OSSOLI, Margaret F. Works and Memoirs. 6 v. 12°. N.Y. 1869.
OTTO, F. Gallerie hervorragender Kaufleute und Förderer des Handels. 1ste Sammlung. Das Buch berühmter Kaufleute. 8°. Leip. 1868. 2te. Sammlung. Der Kaufmann zu allen Zeiten. 8°. Leip. 1869.
OTTO, Louise. Deutsche Wunden. 4 v. in 2. 12°. Bremen. 1872.
OTWAY, T. Venice Preserved. Revised by J. P. Kemble. [*Not Circulated; Kemble's own copy, with his Autograph Notes.*] 4°. Lond. 1811.
OUR Boys and Girls, for 1871. R. 8°. 8°. Bost. 1871.
OUR Campaign around Gettysburg. 16°. Brooklyn. 1864.
"OUR Established Church" and "The Unestablished Church." 8°. N.Y. 1870.
OUR Eternal Home. 12°. Bost. 1868.
OUR First Year of Army Life (1st Conn. Heavy Artillery.) 8°. New Haven. 1862.
OUR Monthly. v. 1–4. R. 8°. Cinc. 1870–1.
OUR Society. v. 1–3. f°. N.Y. 1870–2.
OUR Young Folks. v. 5–7. 8°. Bost. 1869–71.
OUT of Town. An Account of the Suburban Towns and Residences of Chicago. 8°. Chicago. 1869.
OVERLAND Monthly. v. 1–7. 8°. San Francisco. 1868–71.
OVID, Metamorphoses, Book 1, with Interlinear Translation. 2d ed. 16°. Lond. 1831.
—— Metamorphoses, in Blank Verse, by H. King. 8°. Lond. 1871.
—— Works. Transl. by Riley. (Bohn's Ed.) 2 v. 12°. Lond. 1864–8.
OWEN, C. H. Modern Artillery. 8°. Lond. 1871.
OWEN, R. D. The Debatable Land between this World and the Next. 12°. N.Y. 1872.
—— Policy of Emancipation. 12°. Phil. 1863.
OXBERRY'S British Theatre. 17 v. 18°. Bost. 1822.
OXENDEN, A. Counsel to the Awakened. 18°. Phil. 1857.
OXENHAM, H. N. Recollections of Ober Ammergau in 1871. 16°. Lond. 1871.

PAALZOW, Frau. Godwie Castle. 16°. Breslau. 1855.
—— Jacob van der Nees. 16°. Breslau. 1855.
—— Ste. Roche. 16°. Breslau. 1855.
—— Thomas Thyrnau. 16°. Breslau. 1855.
PACIFIC, R. R. of Missouri. Documents on Organization, Condition, etc. 8°. N.Y. 1853.

PACKARD, A. S., Jr. Guide to the Study of Insects. 8°. Salem. 1870.
PACKARD's Monthly. New ser. v. 1. 8°. N.Y. 1869.
PAGE, D. Earth's Crust; an Outline of Geology. 16°. Edin. 1865.
PAGE, D. P. Theory and Practice of Teaching. 12°. N.Y. 1850.
PAGET, J. Surgical Pathology. 3d ed., by Turner. 8°. Lond. 1870.
PAINE, M. Institutes of Medicine. 8th ed. 8°. N.Y. 1868.
—— Same. 9th ed. 8°. N.Y. 1870.
—— Physiology of the Soul and Instinct as distinguished from Materialism. 8°. N.Y. 1872.
PAINTER, Gilder and Varnisher's Companion. 16°. Phil. 1850.
PALERMO, E. The Amusing Practice of the Italian language. 8°. Lond. 1779.
—— Works. 5 v. 8°. Lond. 1837.
PALIKAO, Cousin de Montauban (le Comte de). Un Ministère de la Guerre de 24 Jours. 8°. Paris. 1871.
PALLISER, Mrs. B. Brittany and its Byways. 12°. Lond. 1869.
—— Historic Devices, Badges and War Cries. 8°. Lond. 1870.
PALL Mall Gazette. v. 12. f°. Lond. 1870.
PALMER's Index to the London Times. *See* TIMES.
PALMER, E. H. The Desert of the Exodus. 2 v. 8°. Camb. (Eng.) 1871.
PALMER, G. Kidnapping in the South Seas. 8°. Edin. 1871.
PALMER, J. W. Folk Songs. Sm. 4°. N.Y. 1867.
—— Poetry of Compliment and Courtship. 12°. Bost. 1868.
PALMER, R. Our Country must be Saved. 8°. N.Y. 1867.
PALMERSTON (Lord). Selections from Private Journals of Tours in France. 8°. Lond. 1871.
PALMETTO Pictures. 16°. N.Y. 1863.
PAPIERS Secrets du Second Empire. Nos. 1–13. 8°. Brussels. 1870–1.
PARECBOLAE sive Excerpta Statutorum Universitatis Oxoniensis. 16°. Oxford. 1832.
PARENTAL Legacies: viz., Advice from a Lady of Quality to her Children, and Gregory's Father's Legacy to his Daughters. 16°. New Brunswick. 1808.
PARE, W. Co-operative Agriculture. 12°. Lond. 1870.
PARIS, E. L'Art Naval à l'Exposition Universelle en 1867. With Atlas. 8°. & L. fol. Paris. 1869.
PARIS, L. P. Comte de. Les Associations Ouvrières en Angleterre. (Trades' Unions.) 16°. Paris. 1869.
—— The Trades' Unions of England. 16°. Lond 1869.
PARIS Directory and Visitors' Guide. 18°. Paris. 1837.
PARK, R. Pantology. 8°. Phil. 1841.
PARKER, E. H. Handbook for Mothers. 12°. N.Y. 1867.
PARKER, J. Ad Clerum. Advice to a Young Preacher. 12°. Lond. 1870.
—— Same. 16°. Bost. 1871.
—— The City Temple. Sermons Preached in Poultry Chapel, London. 1st and 2d ser. 2 v. 8°. Lond. 1870–71.
—— Homiletic Analysis of the New Testament. v. 1. 8°. Lond. 1870.
PARKER, L. Syphilitic Diseases. 5th ed. 8°. Lond. 1871.
PARKER, R. G. Natural Philosophy. 12°. Bost. 1839.
PARKER, S. E. Logic. 8°. Phil. 1837.
PARKER, S. P. The Church's Law of Interpretation of Scripture; a Sermon. 18°. Hartford. 1870.
PARKER, T. Historic Americans. 12°. Bost. 1870.
—— Sermon of Immortal Life. 2d ed. 12°. Bost. 1850.
PARKES, E. A. Practical Hygiene. 8°. Phil. 1868.
PARKINSON, J. C. Ocean Telegraph to India. 12°. Edin. 1870.
—— Places and People. 12°. Lond. 1869.
—— Under Government. 5th ed. 16°. Lond. 1869.
PARKMAN, F. Discovery of the Great West. 8°. Bost. 1869.
PARLOR Magic. 12°. N.Y. n.d
PARLOR Theatricals. 16°. N.Y. n.d.
PARMELE, H. Key to First Chart of Masonic Mirror. 24°. New Haven. 1825.
PARNELL, J. Poems. 16°. Dublin. 1776.
PARR, H. Echoes of a Famous Year. 12°. Lond. 1872.
PARRINO, A. Guide di Pozzuoli. 24°. Naples. 1751.
PARRISH, E. Pharmacy. 3d ed. 8°. Phil. 1867.

PARRISH, J. Intemperance and Disease. (PC. 23). 8°. n p. n.d.
PARRISH, R. A., Jr. Unpaid Claim on France. 8°. Phil. 1869.
PARSONS, T. The Infinite and the Finite. 12°. Bost. 1872.
—— Laws of Business. 8°. Hartford. 1869.
—— Slavery: its Origin, Influence and Destiny. 16°. Bost. 1863.
PARTON, J. Does it Pay to Smoke? 16°. Lond. n.d.
—— Humorous Poetry of the English Language. 12°. Bost. 1870.
—— Peoples Book of Biography. R. 8°. Hartford. 1869.
—— Topics of the Time. 12°. Bost. 1871.
—— Triumphs of Enterprise, Ingenuity and Public Spirit. 8°. Hartford. 1871.
PARTON, Mrs. Sarah. Folly as it Flies. 12°. N.Y. 1868.
—— Ginger-Snaps. 12°. N.Y. 1870.
PARTRIDGE, J. A. From Feudal to Federal. 8°. Lond. 1872.
PASCAL, C. A travers l'Atlantique. 2d ed. 16°. Paris. 1870.
PASCHKOWSKY, D. von. Christine. 3 v. in 1. 12°. Hanover. 1870.
PASQUÉ, E. Goldengel von Köln. 2 v. 12°. Berlin. 1867.
PASSENGER and Health Laws of New York and the United States. 8°. N.Y. 1846–7.
PAST, Present and Future of the Society of Friends. 8°. n.p. 1870.
PATENT Law and Practice. 16°. Lond. 1871.
PATENT Office. (of U. S.) Rules and Directions. 8°. n.p. n.d.
PATON, A. A. Egyptian Revolution. 2d ed. 2 v. 8°. Lond. 1870.
PATRIARCH (The) and the Tsar. Replies of the Humble Nicon. Transl. from the Russ by Palmer. 8°. Lond. 1871.
PATTERSON, A. J. The Magyars. 2 v. 12°. Lond. 1869.
PATTERSON, R. The American Sabbath. 18°. Phil. n.d.
PATTERSON, R. Reporter's Assistant. 18°. Phil. 1849.
PATTERSON, R. H. The State, the Poor and the Country. 8°. Lond. 1870.
PATTERSON, Wm. J. Home and Foreign Trade of Canada. 8°. Montreal. 1871.
PATTON, W. Laws of Fermentation. 12°. N.Y. 1871.

PAUL of Tarsus. 16°. Bost 1872.
PAYNE, J. Masque of Shadows and other Poems. 16°. Lond. 1870.
PAYNTER, C. T. Voyages in the Black Sea and Sea of Azoff. 16°. St. Louis. 1852.
PEABODY, A. P. Lessons from the Rebellion; an Address. 8°. Bost. 1867.
PEABODY, E. Address, Centennial, Wilton, N. H. 8°. Bost. 1839.
—— Sermon; Installation of Rev. S. Osgood. 8°. Providence. 1842.
PEABODY, Elizabeth P. Identification of the Artizan and Artist. 8°. Bost. 1869.
—— Polish-American System of Chronology. 16°. Bost. 1850.
PEABODY, S. H. Cecil's Book of Beasts. 12°. Phil. 1870.
—— Cecil's Book of Birds. 12°. Phil. 1870.
—— Cecil's Book of Insects. 12°. Phil. 1870.
PEAK, Gewilem. (Pseudonym.) *See* POPE, Henry.
PEALE, R. Graphics. 2d ed. 12°. Phil. 1838.
PEARSON, C. H. Historical Maps of England. 2d ed. f°. Lond. 1870.
PEARSON, E. Angler's Garland for 1870. 12°. Westminster. 1870.
PEARSON, Emily C. Gutenberg and the Art of Printing. 12°. Bost. 1871.
PEARSON, Emma M. and MacLaughlin, Louisa E. Our Adventures during the War of 1870. 2 v. 12°. Lond. 1871.
PEARSON, Jona. Contributions for Genealogies of First Settlers of Albany County. Sm. 4° Alb. 1872.
PEARSON, J. B. Creed or no Creed; three Sermons. 16°. Cambr. (Eng.) 1871.
PECH, J. Influence of Liberty on Taste. 8°. N.Y. 1869.
PECK, Geo. W. Adventures of one Terence MacGrant. 12°. N.Y. 1871.
PECK, I. B. Peck Genealogy. 8°. Bost. 1868.
PECK, J. T. Central Idea of Christianity. 12°. Bost. 1856.
PECK, W. G. Elements of Mechanics. 12°. N.Y. 1868.
PEDDER, H. C. Man and Woman. 12°. N.Y. 1871.
PEDDIE, Mrs. R. Second Reformation in Spain. 12°. Lond. 1871.

PEEBLES, J. M. Seers of the Ages. 8°. Bost. 1870.

PÉGOT-OGIER, E. The Fortunate Isles; or, The Canaries. Tr. by Locock. 2 v. 8°. Lond. 1871.

PEIRCE, B. Physical and Celestial Mechanics. 4°. Bost. 1855.

—— Plane and Spherical Trigonometry. 8°. Bost. 1852.

PEIRCE, B. K. Word of God Opened. 12°. N.Y. n.d.

PEIRCE, O. B. English Grammar. 12°. Buff. 1839.

—— English Grammar. 12°. Watertown. 1843.

PELLETAN, E. Jean Jarousseau, the Pastor of the Desert. 16°. Lond. 1872.

PELLICO, S. My Prisons. 16°. Bost. 1868.

PELZ, E. Das Mississipi Gesenke. 8°. Leip. 1871.

PEMBER, E. H. Tragedy of Lesbos. 16°. Lond. 1870.

PEMBROKE (Earl of), and Kingsley, Dr. South Sea Bubbles. 8°. N.Y. 1872.

PENDLETON, Mrs. H. Parents' Guide. 12°. N.Y. 1871.

PENN Monthly Magazine. v. 1, 2. 8°. Phil. 1870-1.

PENNELL, H. C. Modern Practical Angler. 12°. Lond. 1870.

PENNSYLVANIA. Common School Laws. 8°. Harrisburg. 1862.

PENNSYLVANIA Relief Association for East Tennessee. Report to Contributors. (PC. 8.) 8°. Phil. 1864.

PENSACOLA. The City of Pensacola. (PC. 23.) 4°. n.p. 1870.

PEOPLE'S Library, Newport. Catalogue. 8°. Providence. 1870.

PEOPLE'S Magazine. New series. v. 5-8. R. 8°. Lond. 1870-71.

PÉPÉ, G. Événemens à Naples, 1820-1. 8°. Paris. 1822.

PEPPER, J. H. Cyclopædic Science Simplified. Sq. 12°. Lond. 1869.

—— Playbook of Metals. 12°. Lond. 1869.

PEPYS, S. Diary and Correspondence. — 12°. Lond. 1870.

—— Memoirs and Diary. 16°. Lond. n.d. *See also* WILSON, JAMES GRANT.

PÉQUÉGNOT, A. Géométrie des Arts. R. 8°. Paris. 1853.

PERCY Anecdotes. 12°. Lond. n.d.

PERCY Folio MS. *See* EARLY ENGLISH TEXT SOCIETY.

PERCY, J. Manufacture of Russian Sheet Iron. 8°. Lond. 1871.

—— Metallurgy of Lead. 8°. Lond. 1870.

PEREIRA, J. Elements of Materia Medica and Therapeutics. Ed. by Bently and Redwood. 8°. Lond. 1872.

PEREZ, Juan. Epistola Consolatoria. 12°. Lond. 1871.

PEREZ de Hita, G. Historia de las Guerras Civiles de Granada. 16°. Barcelona. 1757.

PERFECT (The) Ceremonies of Craft Masonry. Sq. 12°. n.p. 1871.

PERING, P. Churches and their Creeds. 12°. Lond. 1871.

PERKINS, E. E. Haberdashery and Hosiery. 3d ed. 24°. Lond. 1834.

PERKINS, F. B. Charles Dickens. 12°. N.Y. 1870.

PERKINS, G. R. Primary Arithmetic. 8°. Hartford. 1850.

PERNY, P. Deux mois de Prison sous la Commune. 16°. Paris. 1871.

PERRIN, J. French and English Conversation. 18°. Phil. 1830.

—— French Grammar. 12°. N.Y. 1829.

PERROT d' Ablancourt, N. Les Apophtegmes des Anciens 16°. Amsterdam. 1730.

PERSOZ, J. Traité de l'Impression des Tissus, and Atlas. 3 v. 8°. and 4°. Paris. 1846.

PERSIUS. Satires, transl. by Dryden. *See* JUVENAL.

PERTZ, G. H. Das Leben des Feldmarschalls Grafen Neithardt von Gneisenau. v. 1-3 8°. Berlin. 1864-69.

PESCHIER, A. Causeries Parisiennes. 16°. Stuttgart. 1861.

PESTALOZZI, H. Lienhard und Gertrud. 2 v. Sq. 16°. Langensalza. 1870.

—— Wie Gertrud ihre Kinder Lehrt. Sq. 16°. Langensalza. 1870.

PESTI (A.) "Kereskedö Ifjak Társulata." Evkönyve I., 1866-9: II., 1870. 12°. Pesth. 1870-1.

PETERMANN'S Geographische Mittheilungen. v. 16. 4°. Gotha. 1870.

PETERSEN, F. A. Military Review of the Campaign in Virginia and Maryland. 8°. N.Y. 1862.

PETERSON'S Magazine. v, 59, 60. 8°. Phil. 1871.

PETHERICK, J. and B. H. Central Africa. 2 v. 8°. Lond. 1869.

PETIT, P. Guide-Récueil de Paris Brulé. 12°. Paris. 1871.

PÉTITION d'un Bossu à l'Assemblée Nationale. 16°. Paris. 1871.

PETITS (Les.) Papiers Secrets des Tuileries et St. Cloud. 12°. Brussels. 1870.

PETO, Sir S. M. Taxation. 8°. N.Y. 1866.

PETTIGREW, A. Handy Book of Bees. 12°. Edin. 1870.

PEVERELEY, C. A. Book of American Pastimes. 2d ed. 12°. N.Y. 1868.

PEYTON, J. L. Over the Alleghanies. 12°. Lond. 1869.

PFAFF, A. "La Grande Nation" in ihren Reden und Thaten. 8°. Cassel. 1871.

PFNOR, R. Ornamentation Usuelle de toutes les Époques dans les Arts Industriels et en Architecture. 2 v. L. 4°. Paris. 1866-8.

PHAEDRUS. Fabulae. Etiam P Syri Sententiae; Aviani et anonymi Fabulae. 8°. Deuxponts. 1784.

PHARMACEUTICAL Journal. 2d ser. v. 10; 3d ser. v. 1. 8°. Lond. 1869-71.

PHARMACOPŒIA of the U. S. 12°. Phil. 1869.

PHASES of Party. 8°. Lond. 1869

PHELPS' New York City Guide. 24°. N.Y. 1853.

PHELPS, Mrs. A. L. Familiar Lectures on Botany. 12°. N.Y. 1860.

PHELPS, R. H. Newgate of Connecticut. 3d. ed. 8°. Hartford. 1844.

PHELPS, W. D. Fore and Aft. 16°. Bost. 1871.

PHILADELPHIA. Burley's Business Directory, 1871. 8°. Phil. 1871.

PHILADELPHIA Board of Health. Reports for 1869-70. 8°. Phil. 1870-71.

PHILADELPHIA Directory, 1870. 8°. Phil. 1870.

PHILADELPHIA Photographer. v. 8. 8°. Phil. 1871.

PHILIPON de la Madelaine, L. Manuel Epistolaire. 12th ed. 16°. Paris. 1830.

PHILLIPPO, J. M. Jamaica, its Past and Present. 8°. Phil. 1843.

PHILLIPS, G. S. Divine Evolution of the Churches. 16°. Phil. 1871.

PHILLIPS, J. Geology of Oxford and the Valley of the Thames. 8°. Oxford. 1871.

PHILLIPS, L. B. Dictionary of Biographical Reference. Imp. 8°. N.Y. 1871.

PHILLIPS, R. Story of Gautama Buddha, and his Creed. 16°. Lond. 1871.

PHILLIPS, W. Inventor's Guide. 12°. Bost. 1837.

PHIPPS, J. Treatise on Indigo. R. 8°. Calcutta. 1832.

PHONOGRAPHIC Teacher, (in Phonetics), by Sunergos. 18°. Lond. 1847.

PHOTOGRAPHIC Art Journal for 1870. 4°. Lond. 1870.

PHOTOGRAPHIC Times. v. 1. 8°. N.Y. 1871.

PHRENOLOGICAL Journal. New ser. v. 1-4. 8°. N.Y. 1870-1.

PIATT, J. J. Landmarks and other Poems. 16°. N.Y. 1872.

PIATT, Mrs. S. M. B. A Woman's Poems. 16°. Bost. 1871.

PICARD, L. B. The Parasite; a Comedy. 16°. Phil. 1872.

PICHAT, L. Cartes sur Table. 12°. Paris. 1855.

PICHON, L. L'Amant de la Morte. 12°. Paris. 1872.

PICK, E. Etymological Dictionary of the French Language. 8°. Lond. 1869.

PICKET, A. and J. W. Geographical Grammar. 8°. N.Y. 1816.

PICTURES of Hungarian Life. 12°. Lond. 1869.

PICTURES from Paris in War and Siege, by an American Lady. 12°. Lond. 1871.

PIDDINGTON, H. Memoirs on Law of Storms. 8°. Calcutta. 1840-2.

PIEDAGNEL, A. Les Ambulances de Paris pendant le Siége. 12°. Paris. 1871.

PIERCE, H. M. Address to First Graduating Class Rutgers Female College. 8°. N.Y. 1867.

PIEROTTI, E. Decrets de la Commune de Paris et du Gouvernement à Versailles. 18°. Paris. 1871.

—— Rapports Militaires Officiels du Siége de Paris, 1870-1. 18°. Paris. 1871.

PIERROT, J. Cours d'Éloquence Française. 8°. Paris. 1822.

PIETZKER, M. A. Life of Menschikoff. 16°. Lond. 1870.

PIKE, G. H. Ancient Meeting-Houses in London. 12°. Lond. 1870.

PILKINGTON, H. W. Musical Dictionary. 16°. Bost. 1812.

PILLET, R. M. L'Angleterre. 8°. Paris. 1815.

PILPAY's Fables. 12°. N.Y. 1872.
PINART, D. Nourishment of the Christian Soul. 16°. Lond. 1865.
PINDAR. Odes. Transl. by Turner and Moore. 12°. Lond. 1868.
PINE, G. W. Beyond the West. 2d. ed. 8°. Utica. 1871.
PINNEY, N. First Book in French. 18°. N.Y. 1849.
PIONEERS of Civilization. 16°. N.Y. n.d.
PIOTROWSKI, R. Souvenirs d'un Sibérien. 12°. Paris. 1870.
PIPER, H. Profitable and Ornamental Poultry. 16°. Lond. 1871.
PISEMSKI, A. Tausend Seelen. 2 v. in 1. 12°. Berlin. 1870.
PITMAN, I. Exercises in Phonography. 8th ed. 18°. Lond. 1849.
—— Manual of Phonography. 8th ed. 18°. Lond. 1849.
—— Reporter's Companion. 3d ed. 18°. Lond. 1849.
PITTSBURGH and Allegheny Directory, 1870-1. 8°. Pittsburgh. 1870.
PLA Y TORRES, C. Diccionario de la Lengua Castellana. 16°. Paris. 1826.
PLAN of the Theological Seminary of the Presbyterian Church in the U. S. 2d ed. 8°. Elizabethtown. 1816.
PLATO. Dialogues, transl. and ed. by Jowett. 4 v. 8°. Oxford. 1871.
—— Gorgias. Notes by Thompson. 8°. Lond. 1871.
—— Opera. (Bekker's and variorum notes). 11 v. 8°. Lond. 1826.
—— Summary of Dialogues and Index. By Day. 12°. Lond. 1870.
—— Works; transl. by Cary and others. (Bohn's ed.) 6 v. 12°. Lond. 1868.
PLATTNER, C. F. Manual of Analysis with the Blowpipe. Ed. by Richter. Transl. by Cornwall and Caswell. 8°. Lond. 1872.
—— Use of the Blowpipe in Examination of Minerals, Ores, etc. Ed. by Muspratt. 8°. Lond. 1850.
PLAUTUS. Comedies transl. by Riley. (Bohn's ed.) 2 v. 12°. Lond. 1867.
PLAYFAIR, J. Elements of Geometry. 8°. N.Y. 1830.
PLEA (A) for Impartial Suffrage. 8°. Chicago. 1868.
PLEASURE: A Holiday Book of Prose and Verse. 8°. N.Y. 1871.
PLINY. Natural History. (Bohn's ed.) Transl. by Bostock and Riley. 6 v. 12°. Lond. 1866-7.
PLINY the Younger. Select Letters. Latin, with Notes by Church and Brodribb. 12°. Lond. 1871.
PLUMER, W. S. Studies in the Book of Psalms. R. 8°. Phil. 1870.
PLUMTRE, C. J. Lectures on Elocution. 8°. Lond. 1870.
PLUMTRE, E. H. Biblical Studies. 12°. Lond. 1870.
PLUTARCH. Lives. Langhorne's transl. R. 8°. N.Y. 1859.
—— Morals; transl. and ed. by Goodwin. 5 v. 8°. Bost. 1870.
POCKET Book in Arithmetic, Astronomy, etc. 16°. Lond. n.d.
POCOCK, N. Records of the Reformation; The Divorce, 1527-33. 2 v. 8°. Oxford. 1870.
POE, E. A. Conchologist's First Book. 2d ed. 16° Phil. 1840.
—— Poems. 12°. N.Y. 1869.
—— Tales. 2 v. 12°. N.Y. 1867.
POETS (The) and Poetry of America: A Satire. 18°. Phil. 1847.
POITEVIN, P. Littérature Française. 2 v. 16°. Paris. 1865.
POKE, W. Cornish Pumping Engine. 4°. Lond. 1844.
POLE, W. Theory of the Modern Scientific Game of Whist. 12°. N.Y. 1872.
POLIDORI, C. Grammaire Italienne. 16°. Lond. 1809.
POLITICAL Economy. Pamphlets on. 4 v. 8°. Lond. and Oxford. v.d.
POLITICAL Situation; a Herald Interview. 8°. N.Y. n.d.
POLKO, Elise. Freudvoll und Leidvoll. 12°. Leip. 1871.
—— Frische Blätter. 12°. Lelp. 1870.
—— Im Vorübergehen. 12°. Leip. 1872.
—— Sie schreibt. 12°. Leip. 1871.
POLLARD, E. A. The Southern Spy. 16°. Wash. 1859.
—— Virginia Tourist. 12°. Phil. 1870.
POLLARD, W. Stanleys of Knowsley. 12°. Liverpool. 1868.
POLO. The Book of Ser Marco Polo. Transl. and ed. by Yule. 2 v. 8°. Lond. 1871.
POLYTECHNISCHES Journal. v. 190-202. 8°. Augsburg. 1869-71

POMEROY, M. M. Brick-Dust. 12°. N.Y. 1871.
—— Gold Dust. 12°. N.Y. 1871.
—— Our Saturday Nights. 12°. N.Y. 1870.
POND, E. The Seals Opened; or, The Apocalypse Explained. 12°. Portland. 1871.
PONSON du Terrail, P. A. de. La Bohémienne du Grand Monde.
1. La Bohémienne du Grand Monde. 12°. Paris. 1867.
2. Le Drame de Planche Mibray. 12°. Paris. 1867.
3. L' Héritage de Corinne. 12°. Paris. 1867.
—— Les Contes du Drapeau.
1. Les Cosaques à Paris. 12°. Paris. 1866.
2. La Mère Michel. 12°. Paris. 1866.
—— La Dame aus Gant Noir. 12°. Paris. 1868.
—— Les Drames de Paris.
1. L' Héritage Mystérieux. 12°. Paris. 1868.
2. Le Club des Valets de Cœur. 12°. Paris. 1868.
3. Turquoise la Pécheresse. 12°. Paris. 1869.
—— Le Forgeron de la Cour-Dieu. 2 v.
1. La Pupille des Moines. 12°. Paris. 1869.
2. L' Empoissonneuse. 12°. Paris. 1869.
—— Le Maître Rossignol. 12°. Paris. 1869.
—— Les Misères de Londres. 4e Partie Un Drame dans le Southwark. 12°. Paris. 1869.
—— Mon Village.
1. Mlle. Mignonne. 12°. Paris. 1867.
2. La Mère Miracle. 12°. Paris. 1867.
3. Le Brigadier La Jeunesse. 12°. Paris. 1867.
—— Le Secret du Docteur Rousselle. (Suite de "Mon Village.")
1. Maubert le Boiteux. 12°. Paris. 1868.
2. La Chevrette. 12°. Paris. 1868.
—— Les Voleurs du Grand Monde.
1. Cartahut ou la Barque-Fantome. 12.° Paris. 1869.
2. Le Mystère du Passage du Soleil. 12°. Paris. 1870.
3. Le Seigneur de la Montagne. 12°. Paris. 1870.
4. Le Dévouement de Jeanne. 12°. Paris. 1870.
PONTMARTIN, A. de. Lettres d'un Intercepté. 12°. Paris. 1871.
—— Le Radeau de la Méduse. 12°. Paris. 1871.
PONTON, M. The Beginning; its When and its How. 12°. Lond. 1871.
POOK, S. M. Draughting Vessels. 8°. N.Y. 1866.
POOLE, F. Queen Charlotte Islands. 8°. Lond. 1872.
POOR, H. W. Manual of the Railroads of the U. S. 8°. N.Y. 1871.
POOR, J. A. Transcontinental Railway. 8°. Portland. 1869.
POPE, A. Works, ed by Croker and Elwin. v. 1–7. 8°. Lond. 1871.
POPE, F. L. Modern Practice of the Electric Telegraph. 8°. N.Y. 1870.
POPE, G. U. Text-Book of Indian History. Sm. 4°. Lond. 1871.
POPE, Henry. The Struggle for Existence. 16°. N.Y. 1872.
POPE and the Council. By Janus. 12°. Lond. 1869.
—— Same. 16°. Bost. 1870.
POPULAR Science Review. v. 4, 8–10. 8°. Lond. 1865, '69–71.
PORTAL, A. Poems. 8°. Lond. 1781.
PORTER, F. J. Appeal for Re-examination. 8°. Morristown. 1869.
—— Reply to Mr. Chandler. (PC. 18.) 8°. Morristown. 1870.
PORTER, J. K. Argument in Parish Will Case. 8°. Alb. 1862.
PORTER, J. L. Life and Times of Henry Cooke. 8°. Lond. 1871.
PORTER, N. American Colleges. 16°. New Haven. 1870.
—— Books and Reading. 12°. N.Y. 1870.
—— Same. 1871.
—— Elements of Intellectual Science. 12°. N.Y. 1871.
—— The Science of Nature *vs.* the Science of Man. 16°. N.Y. 1871.
PORTER, Rose. Summer Driftwood. 16°. N.Y. 1870.
PORTER, W. S. Musical Cyclopædia. 18°. Bost. 1834.
PORTFOLIO; an Artistic Periodical. f°. Lond. 1870.

PORTLAND. (Me.) Directory, 1871. 8°. Portland. 1871.

PORTLAND Public Library. Finding List and Supplement. 8°. Portland. 1869.

PORTLAND, Rutland, Oswego and Chicago R.R. Co. First Annual Report. 8°. Portland. 1871.

PORTSMOUTH (N. H.) Directory for 1871. 8°. Portsmouth. 1871.

POTTER, A. Drinking Usages. 16°. N.Y. 1870.

POTTER, Alonzo. Religious Philosophy. 8°. Phil. 1872.

POTTER, E. R. Address to Rhode Island Historical Society. 8°. Providence. 1851.

POTTER, H. L. D. Manual of Reading. 12°. N.Y. 1872.

POTTER, W. B. Spiritualism as it Is. 8°. Coventry. 1866.

POUCHET, F. The Universe. R. 8°. N.Y. 1870.

POULTRY Book for the Many. 16°. Lond. n.d.

POUND, W. Story of the Gospels Combined. 2 v. 8°. Lond. 1869.

POWELL, J. Two Years in the Pontifical Zouaves. 8°. Lond. 1871.

POWELL, T. W. Analysis of American Law. 8°. Phil. 1870.

POWELL, W. B. Canoe Traveling; Log of a Cruise on the Baltic. Sq. 12°. Lond. 1871.

POWER, J. Handy-Book about Books. 8°. Lond. 1870.

POWER, J. C. History of Springfield, Ill. 8°. Springfield. 1871.

PRACTICAL Mechanic's Journal. 3d ser., v. 4. 5. 4°. Lond. 1869–70.

PRACTICAL Use of the Blowpipe. 12°. N.Y. 1868.

PRACTICE with Science. Agricultural Papers. v. 2. 8°. Lond. 1869.

PRACTIONER (The). v. 2–5. 8°. Lond. 1869–71.

PRATT, N. A. Ashley River Phosphates. 8°. Phil. 1868.

PRAVAL, C. French Syntax. Ed. by d'Oisy. 16°. Lond. 1818.

PRAYER Book *vs.* Prayer Book. 8°. Phil. 1869.

PREACHER's Lantern. v. 1. 8°. Lond. 1871.

PRECHT, V. Die Deutschen in Amerika. und die Deutsch-Amerikanischen Friedensfeste. 8°. N.Y. 1871.

PRENDERGAST, T. Mastery Series. French. 12°. N.Y. 1870.

PRENTICE, G. D. Life of Clay. 16°. N.Y. 1831.

—— Prenticeana. 12°. Phil. 1870.

PRESBYTERIAN Reunion; a Memorial Volume. 8°. N.Y. 1870.

PRESCOTT, G. B. History of the Electric Telegraph. 12°. Bost. 1866.

PRESCOTT, H. P. Strong Drink and Tobacco Smoke. 8°. Bost. 1869.

PRESCOTT, W. Prescott Memorial; a Genealogical Memoir. 8°. Bost. 1870.

PRESCOTT Consolidated Mining Co. Prospectus. (PC. 9.) 8°. N.Y. 1865.

PRESSENSÉ, Edmond de. Early Years of Christianity. Transl. by Annie Harwood. v. 1. Apostolic Era. 8°. Lond. 1869.

—— Same. 12°. N.Y. 1870.

v. 2. Martyrs and Apologists. 8°. Lond. 1871.

—— Same. 12°. N.Y. 1871.

—— Rome and Italy. 12°. N.Y. 1870.

PRESSENSÉ, Mme. E. de. Scènes d'Enfance et de Jeunesse. 12°. Paris. 1870.

PRESTON, Margaret J. Old Song and New. 12°. Phil. 1870.

PRESTON, T. S. Christ and the Church. 12°. N.Y. 1870.

—— The Vicar of Christ. 12°. N.Y. 1872.

PRÉVEL, J. Un Mari qui Pleure 16°. Paris. 1869.

PREVENTION (The) of War. 12°. Lond. 1871.

PRÉVOST d'Exilis, A. F. Histoire de Marion Lescaut. Ed. by St. Beuve. 12°. Paris. 1857.

—— Marion Lescaut. Transl. by Moylan, illustrated by Johannot. 8°. Lond. 1841.

PRÉVOST-PARADOL, L. A. France. 8°. Edin. 1869.

PRICHARD, I. Chronicles of Budgepore. 2 v. 16°. Lond. n.d.

PRIESTCRAFT Unmasked. v. 1. 8°. N.Y. 1830.

PRIESTLEY, J. History of the Corruptions of Christianity. 12°. Lond. 1871.

PRIME, E. D. G. Around the World. 12°. N.Y. 1872.

PRIMEVAL Man Unveiled; or, The Anthropology of the Bible. 12°. Lond. 1871.

PRINCIPLES at Stake. Edited by Sumner. 8°. Lond. 1868.
PRINGLE, R. O. Veterinary Hand-book. 12°. Dublin. 1871.
PRIOR, R. C. A. Popular Names of British Plants. 12°. Lond. 1870.
PRISON Association of New York. 24th, 25th and 26th Annual Reports. 3 v. 8°. N.Y. 1869-71.
PRO Aris et Focis. (A Plea for Our Altars and Hearths.) 16°. N.Y. n.d
PROBLEM (The) of the Church and the World Reconsidered. 8°. Lond. 1871.
PROBYN, J. W. National Self-Government. 12°. Lond. 1870.
PROCTER, Adelaide A. Legends and Lyrics. 12th ed. 18°. Lond. 1870.
PROCTER, F. History of the Book of Common Prayer. 9th ed. 12°. Lond. 1870.
PROCTOR, E. D. A Russian Journey. 12°. Bost. 1871.
PROCTOR, L. B. Bench and Bar of New York. 8°. N.Y. 1870.
PROCTOR, R. A. Light Science for Leisure Hours. 12°. Lond. 1871.
—— New Star Atlas. 12°. Lond. 1872.
—— Other Worlds than Ours. 8°. Lond. 1870.
—— Same. 12°. N.Y. 1871.
—— Saturn and Its Systems. 8°. Lond. 1865.
—— The Sun. 12°. Lond. 1871.
PROLIX, P. Peregrination through Pennsylvania. 18°. Phil. 1836.
PROPERTIUS, Petronius, Secundus, Aristaenetus. Transl. (Bohn's ed.) 12°. Lond. 1854.
PROSPECT (The); a Review of Politics. By Mountaineer. 8°. Buff. 1862.
PROTESTANT Episcopal Church of the U. S. Hymnal. 16°. Alb. 1872.
—— Prières Publiques. 8°. N.Y. 1803.
—— Same. Ed. by Verren. 12°. N.Y. 1831.
—— Diocese of Long Island. Journal of Convention, Nov. 1868. 8°. Brooklyn. 1869.
PROTOPLAST (The); a Series of Papers. 4th ed. 12°. Lond. 1870.
PROUDFIT, J. Sermon, Installation of Rev. W. Irwin. 8°. N.Y. 1862.
PROVIDENCE Directory and R. I. Business Directory, 1870. 8°. Providence. 1870.
PROVIDENCE Directory for 1871-2. 8°. Providence. 1871.
PRUSSE et France; un Trait de Plumes, Sept. 1870. 8°. Brussels. 1870.
PRUTZ, R. Aus der Heimat. 12°. Leip. 1868.
PRYDE, D. Great Men of European History. 16°. N.Y. n.d.
PRYME, G. Autobiographic Recollections. 8°. Cambr. (Eng.) 1870.
PSEAUMES de David. Avec Musique. 24°. No title.
PSEAUMES de David. Á Quatre Parties. 18°. Lausanne. 1813.
PSEAUMES de David. Avec Musique. 24°. Paris. 1817.
PUBLIC Library of Cincinnati. Catalogue. R. 8°. Cinc. 1871.
PUBLIC Library of Detroit. Catalogue. 8°. Detroit. 1868.
PUBLIC School Latin Grammar. 12°. Lond. 1871.
PUBLISHERS' Circular. v. 1-7. R. 8°. Lond. 1837-44.
PUFENDORF, S. Les Devoirs de l'Homme et du Citoien. 8°. Amsterdam. 1735.
PULLEN, H. W. Fight at Dame Europa's School. 16°. N.Y. 1871.
—— Same. Illustrated by Nast. 16°. N.Y. 1871.
PULPIT Analyst. v. 4. 12°. Lond. 1869.
PULSFORD, J. Christ and His Seed. Sm. 4°. Lond. 1870.
—— Quiet Hours. 12°. Lond. 1870.
PUMPELLY, R. Across America and Asia. 8°. N.Y. 1870.
PUNCH (London). v. 1-11. New Library Series. 4°. Lond. n.d.
PUNCHINELLO. v. 1. f°. N.Y. 1870.
PURTON, W. Sacramental System of the Church of England. 18°. Lond. 1870.
PUSEY, E. B. Is Healthful Reunion Impossible? 8°. Oxford. 1870.
—— The Real Presence of the Body and Blood of Jesus Christ. 8°. Oxford. 1857.
—— Sermon on the Eucharist. 8°. N.Y. 1843.
PUTLITZ, G. zu. Die Alpenbraut. 12°. Berlin. 1870.
—— Funken unter der Asche. 12°. Berlin. 1871.
—— Walpurgis. 12°. Berlin. 1870.
PUTNAM, S. Sequel to Analytical Reader. 12°. Dover. 1831.

PUTNAM's Magazine. v. 2–5. 8°. N.Y. 1868–70.

PUTTENHAM, G. Art of English Poetrie. *See* ARBER's Reprints. v. 7.

PÜTZ, W. Hand-book of Ancient Geography and History. 12°. Lond. 1849.

PYLODET, L. (Pseudonym.) *See* LEYPOLDT, F.

PYNCHON, T. R. Chemical Forces. 12°. Hartford. 1870.

PYNE, H. England and France in the 15th Century. 8°. Lond. 1870.

QUACKENBOS, G. P. Natural Philosophy. 12°. N.Y. 1869.

QUARLL. Surprising Adventure of Philip Quarll. 18°. Lond. 1869.

QUARTERLY Journal of Psychological Medicine. v. 3. 8°. N.Y. 1869. For other volumes *See* JOURNAL of Psychological Medicine.

QUARTERLY Journal of Science. v. 5–8. 8°. Lond. 1868–71.

QUARTERLY Review. v. 126–131. 8°. Lond. 1869–71.

QUARTZ Hill Gold Co. Report, June 7, 1864. (PC. 10.) 8°. N.Y. 1864.

QUATREFAGES, A. de. La Race Prussienne. 12°. Paris. 1871.

QUEEN; the Lady's Newspaper and Court Chronicle. v. 49. f°. Lond. 1871.

QUEL est notre Nom? N, ou M? 3d ed. 8°. Brussels. 1870.

QUESTION (La) de l'Esclavage aux Etats Unis. 8°. Hague. 1862.

QUESTIONS on Grimshaw's Goldsmith's Rome, with Key. 2 v. 16°. Phil. 1826.

QUETELET, A. Astronomie Populaire. 24°. Brussels. 1827.

QUICK, Robert H. Essays on Educational Reformers. 12°. Lond. 1868.

QUICKSILVER Mining Co. Charter, Report, etc. (PC. 10.) 8°. N.Y. 1864.

QUILLET, C. Callipaedia. Transl. by Rowe. 12°. Lond. 1712.

QUIN, E. Atlas of Ancient and Mediæval History. f°. Lond. n.d.

QUINCY Mining Co. Report for 1863. (PC. 10.) 8°. N.Y. 1864.

QUINET, E. Le Siége de Paris et la Défense Nationale. 12°. Paris. 1871.

QUINN, P. T. Money in the Garden. 12°. N.Y. 1871.

—— Pear Culture. 12°. N.Y. 1869.

—— Same. 1871.

QUINTILIAN. Institutes of Oratory. 2 v. Transl. (Bohn's ed.) 12°. Lond. 1854.

RAABE, W. (Pseudonym). *See* CORVIN, J. von.

RABELAIS, F. Works. Illustrated by Doré. 12°. Lond. n.d.

RABON, C. Le Capitaine Lambert. 12°. Paris. 1861.

RACINE, J. The Suitors. Transl. by Browne. 12°. N.Y. 1871.

RACKSTROW, B. Observations on Electricity. 8°. Lond. 1748.

RADAU, R. Wonders of Acoustics. 16°. N.Y. 1870.

RADCLIFFE, C. B. Dynamics of Nerve and Muscle. 12°. Lond. 1871.

RADCLIFFE, J. N. Fiends, Ghosts and Spirits. 12°. Lond. 1854.

RADICAL. v. 5–9. 8°. Bost. 1869–71.

RAE, J. (Edr.) Statutes of Henry VIII. in Fac-simile from the original print of Caxton. 4°. Lond. 1869.

RAE, W. F. Westward by Rail. 12°. Lond. 1870.

—— Same. 12°. N.Y. 1871.

RAFFLES, T. Lectures on Practical Religion. 12°. Liverpool. 1820.

RAILROAD Gazette. 4th ser. v. 3, (15th year). f°. N.Y. 1871.

RAILROAD from St. Louis to San Francisco. Boston Plan. (PC. 5.) 8°. Bost. 1849.

RAINEY, T. Ocean Steam Navigation and the Ocean Post. 8°. N.Y. 1858.

RAISSON, H. Code Galant. 5th ed. 18°. Paris. 1834.

RALEIGH, W. Guiane. *See* COREAL, F.

RALSTON, W. R. S. Songs of the Russian People. 8°. Lond. 1872.

RAM, J. Science of Legal Judgment. Ed. by Townshend. 8°. N.Y. 1871.

—— Treatise on Facts. 8°. N.Y. 1870.

RAMBAUD, L. Le Testament d'un Latin. 12°. Paris. 1872.

RAMBLES in Cuba. 16°. N.Y. 1870.

RAMBOSSON, J. Histoire des Météores. 2d ed. 8°. Paris. 1870.

—— Les Pierres Précieuses. 8°. Paris. 1870.

RAMSAY, E. B. Reminiscences of Scottish Life and Character. 20th ed. 8°. Edin. 1871.

RAMSAY, G. M'J. Cosmology. 12°. Bost. 1870.

RANC, A. Le Roman d'une Conspiration. 12°. Paris. 1869.

RAND, B. H. Medical Chemistry. 12°. Phil. 1871.

RAND, E. S. Seventy-five Popular Flowers. 12°. Bost. 1870.

RANDALL, P. M. Quartz Operator's Hand book. 12°. N.Y. 1871.

RANDALL, S. S. History of the Common School System of New York. 8°. N.Y. 1871.

—— History of New York State. 12°. N.Y. 1870.

RANDOLPH, J. Lectures on Theology. 3 v. 8°. Lond. 1869–70.

RANDOLPH, Sarah N. Domestic Life of Thomas Jefferson. 8°. N.Y. 1871.

RANKE, L. v. Die Deutschen Mächte und der Fürstenbund. 2 v. 8°. Leip. 1871–2.

—— Geschichte Wallensteins. 8°. Leip. 1869.

—— Der Ursprung des Siebenjährigen Kriegs. 8°. Leip. 1871.

—— History of the Popes. 3 v. 12°. Lond. 1868–9.

RANKIN, W. Battles of the Revolution. 12°. N.Y. 1849.

RANKINE, W. J. M. Cyclopædia of Machine and Hand Tools. 4°. Lond. 1869.

RANYARD, Mrs. L. N. The Book and its Story. 12°. Lond. 1871.

—— Fresh Leaves in the Book and its Story. 12°. N.Y. 1871.

RAPHALL, M. J. Bible View of Slavery. 16°. N.Y. 1861.

RASCH, G. Berlin bei Nacht. 12°. Berlin. n.d.

RAU, H. Deutschlands Kassandra. 12°. Stuttg. 1871.

RAUCH, J. H. Intramural Interments. 8°. Chicago. 1866.

RAUE, C. G. Annual Record of Homœopathic Literature. 8°. N.Y. 1870.

RAUE, G. Elements of Psychology, 4th ed., by Dressler. 12°. Oxford. 1871.

RAUMER, F. von. Historisches Taschenbuch. 4th Ser. v. 10. 12°. Leip. 1869.

—— Same. 5th Ser. v. 1. Ed. by W. H. Riehl. 12°. Leip. 1871.

RAVENSTEIN, E. G. Denominational Statistics of England and Wales. 12°. Lond. 1870.

RAWLINSON, G. Five Great Monarchies of the Eastern World. 2d ed. 3 v. 8°. N.Y. 1871.

—— Historical Illustrations of the Old Testament. 16°. Lond. n.d.

—— Manual of Ancient History. 8°. Oxford. 1869.

—— Same. 12°. N.Y. 1871.

RAYMOND, G. Chronicles of England; a Metrical History. 8°. Lond. 1842.

RAYMOND, Ida. (Pseudonym). *See* TARDY, Mrs. Mary T.

RAYMOND, O. Art and Fishing. 16°. Lond. 1866.

RAYMOND, R. W. Mines of the West. 8°. N.Y. 1871.

—— Mines, Mills and Furnaces of Pacific States and Territories. 8°. N.Y. 1871.

—— Statistics of Mines, West of Rocky Mountains. 8°. Wash. 1870. *See also* UNITED STATES.

RAYMUND, G. Ein Hartes Herz. 12°. Hanover. n.d.

—— Schloss Elkrath. 3 v. in 2. 12°. Hanover. 1866.

—— Zweimal Vermählt. 3 v. in. 2. 12. Hanover. 1868.

RAYNAL, T. G. F. European Settlements in the Indies. Translated by Justamond. 5 v. 8°. Lond. 1777.

READ, D. Nathan Read and the Steam Engine. 12°. N.Y. 1870.

READ, N. S. Astronomical Dictionary. 16°. New Haven. 1817.

READ, W. F. Theory of Navigation. 8°. Lond. 1869.

READER (The). v. 6., 1865. f°. Lond. 1865.

REAL Cedula, Sept. 19, 1783. Ordenanzas de los 5 Gremios de Madrid. f°. Madrid. 1783.

REALITÉS de la Vie Domestique présentées aux jeunes Femmes. 12°. Paris. 1870.

REASON Why. 12°. N.Y. n.d.

REASONS for Returning to the Church of England. 12°. Lond. 1871.

REAVIS, L. U. The New Republic. 2d ed. 8°. St. Louis. 1867.

REBOLD, E. Free Masonry in Europe. Tr. by Brennan. 8°. Cinc. 1867.

RECENT Discussions on Abolition of Patents. 8°. Lond. 1869.

RECLUS. É. Histoire d'un Ruisseau. 16°. Paris. n.d.

—— The Earth. Transl. by Woodward. 2 v. 8°. Lond. 1871.
—— Same. 8°. N.Y. 1871.
RECORD (The) of Zoological Literature, 1866–9. v. 4–6. 8°. Lond. 1867–70.
RECREATIONS of a Recluse. 2 v. 8°. Lond. 1870.
RÉCUEIL concernant le Quiétisme. 16°. Amsterdam. 1688.
RÉCUEIL de Decrets, etc., concernant le Régime de la Bibliothêque Royale. 8°. Paris. 1848.
REDDING, C. Personal Reminiscences. 3 v. 12°. Lond. 1867.
REDE, L T. Art of Money Getting. 18°. Lond. 1828.
REDWITZ, O. von. Amaranth. 12°. Mentz. 1871.
—— Das Lied vom Neuen Deutschen Reich. 12°. Phil. n.d.
REED, E. J. Our Iron-clad Ships. 8°. Lond. 1869.
REED, H. The Public Debt. 8°. Cinc. 1868.
REED, J. Man and Woman. 16°. Bost. 1870.
REED, M Manual of Systematic History. 12°. Lond. 1871.
REED, T. A. Reporter's Guide. 16°. Lond. 1869.
REED, W. B. Among my Books. 16°. N.Y. 1861.
REES-Lestienne, C. F. Correspondance Commerciale. 2d ed. 16°. Brussels. 1839.
REEVES, J. History of English Law, v. 3. 8°. Lond. 1869.
REFLECTIONS on Ancient Beauty. 24°. N.Y. 1832.
REICHEL, O. J. See of Rome in the Middle Ages. 8°. Lond. 1870.
REID, A. English Dictionary. 16°. N.Y. 1845.
See HILEY, R. English Grammar.
REID, G. W. Catalogue of the Works of George Cruikshank, with an Essay on his Genius, by Bell. 3 v. 4°. Lond. 1871.
REID, H. Treatise on Concrete. 12°. Lond. 1869.
REID, H. G. Past and Present; or, Social and Religious Life in the North. 12°. Edin. n.d.
REID, J. Sorrow. 12°. N.Y. 1870.
REID, J. T. Art Rambles in Shetland. S. 4°. Edin. 1869.
REID, T. Clock and Watch Making. 3d ed. 8°. Glasgow. 1847.
REID, W. Law of Storms. R. 8°. Lond. 1849.
REIDE, T. Staff Officer's Manual. 18°. Lond. 1806.
REINER, C. Lessons on Number. 16°. Lond. 1835.
RELLSTAB, L. Drei Jahre von Dreissigen. 3 v. 8°. N.Y. 1858.
REMARKABLE Men. 12°. Lond. n.d.
REMBRANDT, P. Life and Works of. At. f°. n.p. n.d.
RENAN, E. Le Cantique des Cantiques. 8°. Paris. 1861
—— La Monarchie Constitutionelle en France. 16°. Paris. 1870.
—— De l'Origine du Langage. 4th ed. 8°. Paris. 1864.
—— La Réforme Intellectuelle et Morale. 8°. Paris. 1872.
—— Constitutional Monarchy in France. 16°. Bost. 1870.
—— Life of Jesus. 12°. N.Y. 1869.
RENNIE, J. Alphabet of Scientific Chemistry. 18°. Lond. 1833.
RENWICK, J. Familiar Illustrations of Natural Philosophy. 18°. N.Y. 1840.
—— First Principles of Chemistry. 16°. N.Y. 1840.
RÉORGANISATION des Forces Militaires de la France. 8°. Paris. 1871.
RÉPERTOIRE du Théâtre François. Par Petitot et Fiévée. 23 v. 8°. Paris. 1803–4.
REPLY to Mill on Subjection of Women. 12°. Phil. 1870.
REPUBLIC. v. 3. R. 8°. N.Y. 1852.
RETCLIFFE, Sir J. Biarritz; 1. Gaëta–Warschau-Düppel. 4 v. in 2. 12°. Berlin. 1869.
—— Nena Sahib. 3 v. 8°. Berlin. n.d.
—— Puebla; 1. Der Schatz der Ynkas. 3 v. 12°. Berlin. 1866–70.
RETROSPECT of Medicine and Surgery. *See* BRAITHWAITE.
REUTER, F. Sämmtliche Werke. 13 v. 12°. Wismar. 1865–70.
REVELATIONS; a Companion to the "New Gospel of Peace." 16°. N.Y. 1863.
RÉVILLE, A. The Devil; his Origin, Greatness and Decadence. 16°. Lond. 1871.
—— History of the Doctrine of the Deity of Jesus Christ. 12°. Lond. 1870.

RÉVILLON, T. Le Faubourg St. Antonie. 12°. Paris. 1872.

REVOLUTION (The). v. 1–4 in 2. 4°. N.Y. 1868–9.

RÉVOLUTION (La) Plébéienne; Lettres à Junius. 8°. Paris. 1871.

REVUE Contemporaine. v. 64–75. 8°. Paris. 1868–70.

REVUE des Deux Mondes. v. 78–98. 8°. Paris. 1868–72.

REVUE Française. v. 1–5 in 2. 8°. N.Y. 1834–6.

REVUE Moderne. v. 49–55. 8°. Paris. 1868–9.

REYNOLDS, E. W. Tangletown Letters. 12°. Buff. 1856.

REYNOLDS, F. Glaphyra, and other Poems. 12°. Lond. 1870.

REYNOLDS, J. G. Marine Corps in Mexico. 8°. N.Y. 1853.

REYNOLDS, J. R. System of Medicine. v. 1. 2d ed. 8°. Phil. 1870.

REYNOLDS, L. E. Mysteries of Masonry. 12°. Phil. 1870.

REYNOLDS, S. History of Williamsburgh. 16°. Williamsburgh. 1852.

RHODE ISLAND. Acts relating to the Public Schools. 8°. Providence. 1857.

—— Acts and Resolves, May Session, 1861; January Session, 1862. 2 v. 8°. Providence. 1861–2.

RHODES, M. J. Visible Unity of the Catholic Church. 2 v. 8°. Lond. 1870.

RHYMESTER'S Run through Italy. 16°. Lond. 1871.

RICARDUS de Cirencestria. Speculum Historiale de Gestis Regum Angliae. (Rolls Chronicles.) 2 v. R. 8°. Lond. 1863–9.

RICE, H. Letters from the Pacific Slope. 12°. N.Y. 1870.

RICH, A. J. Historical Discourse, Westminster, Mass. 8°. Springfield. 1869.

RICHARDS, A. B. Medea; a Poem. Sm. 4°. Lond. 1869.

RICHARDS, S. T. Perils of our Prosperity; Thanksgiving Sermon. 8°. Hartford. 1854.

RICHARDS, W. C. Retrorsum; a Poem. 18°. N.Y. 1869.

RICHARDSON, Mrs. Abby S. Percy's Year of Rhymes. Sq. 12°. N.Y. 1867.

RICHARDSON, C. J. The Englishman's Home. 2d ed. 12°. Lond. n.d.

RICHARDSON, F. (Ed'r.) *See* VÁLMIKÍ.

RICHARDSON, J. G. Medical Microscopy. 12°. Phil. 1871.

RICHARDSON, W. H. Journal with Col. Doniphan. 12°. Balt. 1848.

RICHARDSON, W. R. From London Bridge to Lombardy. 8°. Lond. 1869.

RICHEBOURG, E. Les Francs-Tireurs de Paris. La Fille du Maire. 12°. Paris. 1872.

RICHER, E. Religion of Good Sense. 16°. Bost. 1870.

RICHMOND Directory, 1870–1. 8°. Richmond. 1870.

RICHMOND (Me.) Directory. *See* BATH.

RICHMOND and Louisville Medical Journal. v. 7, 9–11. Louisville. 1869–71.

RICHTER, T. Plattner's Manual. *See* PLATTNER.

RICHTERS, E. F. Manual of Harmony. 8°. N.Y. n.d.

RICKARD, F. I. Resources of the Argentine Republic in 1869. 8°. Lond. 1870.

RIDDLE, J. E. Latin-English Lexicon. 2d ed. S. 4°. Lond. 1851.

RIEHL, W. H. Naturgeschichte des Volkes. v. 4. Wanderbuch. 8°. Stuttg. 1869

RIGG, A. Harmony of the Bible with Experimental Sciences. 16°. Lond. 1869.

RIGG, J. H. Sabbath and Sabbath Law. 8°. Lond. 1869.

RIGHTS of Great Britain Asserted. 7th ed. 16°. Lond. 1776.

RIKART, C, von. Menes and Cheops Identified. 8°. Lond. 1869.

RILEY, H. T. Classical Quotations. 12°. Lond. 1866.

RILEY, J. C. Materia Medica and Therapeutics. 12°. Phil. 1869.

RIMMEL, E. Book of Perfumes. L. 12°. Phil. 1866.

—— Paris Exhibition of 1867. 8°. Phil. n.d.

RING, Max; Aus dem Tagebuche eines Berliner Arztes. 16°. Leip. 1870.

—— Götter und Götzen. 4 v. in 2. 12°. Berlin. n.d.

—— In der Schweiz. Reisebilder und Novellen. 2 v. in 1. 12°. Leip. 1870.

—— Lieben und Leben. 3 v. in 2. 12°. Berlin. 1869.

—— Lorbeer und Cypresse. 16°. Berlin. n.d.

—— Die Seelenfreunde. 3 v. 12°. Berlin. 1871.

—— Verirrt und Erlöst. 2 v. in 1. 12°. Leip. 1870.

—— Die Weltgeschichte ist das Weltgericht! L. N. Bonaparte. 12°. Berlin. 1870.

RINGWALT, J. L. American Encyclopædia of Printing. S. 4°. Phil. 1871.

RINK, F. T. and Vater, J. S. Arabisches, Syrisches und Chaldäisches Lese buch. 8°. Leip. 1802.

RIPPINGHAM, J. English Composition. 5th ed. 16°. Lond. 1825.

—— Speaking Extempore. 3d ed. 12°. Lond. 1819.

RISSÉ, J. F. Schubert und seine Lieder I; Müllerlieder. 12°. Hanover. 1872.

RITCHIE, Mrs. A. C. M. Italian Life and Legends. 12°. N.Y. 1870.

RITCHIE, J. E. Religious Life of London. 8°. Lond. 1870.

RITSON, J. Scotish Songs, 2 v. 12°. Glasgow. 1869.

RITT, O. Histoire de l'Isthme de Suez. 8°. Paris. 1869.

RITTER, F. L. History of Music. 1st ser. 16°. Bost. 1870.

RIVERSIDE Magazine, v. 3. 8°. N.Y. 1870.

RIVIÈRE, H. La Grande Marquise. 12°. Paris. 1869.

—— Mlle. d'Avremont; Monsieur Margerie. 12°. Paris. 1872.

—— Pierrot; Caïn; l'Envoutement. 12°. Paris. 1870.

ROBBINS, Eliza. Guide to Knowledge. 16°. N.Y. 1853.

ROBERT Emmett. 12°. Lond. n.d.

ROBERTS, J. Billiards. 12°. Lond. n.d.

ROBERTS, R. Glenmâhra. 12°. Lond. 1870.

ROBERTS, R. House Servant's Directory. 2d ed. 16°. Bost. 1828.

ROBERTSON, A. Conversation on Anatomy, etc. 2 v. 18°. Phil. 1828.

ROBERTSON, J. Elements of Navigation. 6th ed. 2 v. R. 8°. Lond. 1796.

ROBERTSON, J. A. Gaelic Topography of Scotland. 12°. Edin. 1869.

ROBERTSON, J. C. How shall we Conform the Liturgy? 3d ed. 12°. Lond. 1869.

ROBERTSON, T. Cours de Langue Anglaise. 6th ed. 8°. Paris. 1850.

—— Nouveau Cours de Langue Anglaise. Part 3. 8°. Paris. 1850.

ROBINSON, C. J. Castles of Herefordshire. 4°. Lond. 1869.

ROBINSON, D. The Priest, Calvin and Wesley. 12°. N.Y. 1872.

ROBINSON, E. Biblical Researches in Palestine. 4 v. 8°. Bost. 1868.

ROBINSON, E. G. The Church and the Bible; an Address. 8°. Rochester. 1866.

ROBINSON, G. F. Fall of Metz. 8°. Lond. 1871.

ROBINSON, H. P. Pictorial Effect in Photography. S. 4°. Lond. 1869.

ROBINSON, J. Universal Modern History. 16°. Lond. 1822.

ROBINSON, S. Guano, for Farmers. 8°. N.Y. 1853.

—— How to Live. 12°. N.Y. 1870.

ROBINSON, W. Alpine Flowers for English Gardens. 12°. Lond. 1870.

—— Gleanings from French Gardens. 12°. Lond. 1869.

—— Hardy Flowers. Sq. 16°. Lond. 1871.

—— Mushroom Culture. 12°. Lond. 1870.

—— Parks, Promenades, and Gardens of Paris. 8°. Lond. 1869.

—— Subtropical Garden. 12°. Lond. 1871.

—— The Wild Garden. 12°. Lond. 1870.

ROBOLSKI, H. Paris während der Belagerung, 1870-1. 8°. Berlin. 1871.

ROCA, G. Les Droits à l'Avancement des Officiers Prisonniers de Guerre. 8°. Paris. 1871.

ROCHESTER Directory, 1870. 8°. Rochester. 1870-1.

RODENBERG, J. Die Neue Sündfluth. 4 v. in 2. 12°. Berlin. 1865.

—— Von Gottes Gnaden. 5 v. in 2. 16°. Berlin. 1870.

RODNEY, R. B. Alboin and Rosamond. Sq. 16°. Phil. 1870.

RODWELL, Anne. Juvenile Pianist. Sq. 18°. Lond. 1836.

RODWELL, G. F. Dictionary of Science. 12°. Lond. 1871.

ROGEARD, A. Sayings of Labienus. (The Suppressed Critique on Napoleon's "Julius Cæsar.") 8°. N.Y. 1865.

ROGERS, C. A Century of Scottish Life. 12°. Edin. 1871.

—— Life and Songs of Baroness Nairne, with Memoir and Poems of Caroline Oliphant. 12°. Lond. 1869.

—— Scotland, Social and Domestic. 8°. Lond. 1869.

ROGERS, James. Present State of Therapeutics. 8°. Lond. 1870.
ROGERS, J. E. T. Historical Gleanings. 12°. Lond. 1869.
—— Same. 2d Series. 12°. Lond. 1870.
ROGGE, B. The Chaplain in the Field of War. Transl. by Geo. Gladstone. 12°. Lond. 1870.
ROHLFS, G. Land und Volk in Afrika. 12°. Bremen. 1870.
—— Von Tripolis nach Alexandrien. 12°. Bremen. 1871.
ROLANDO, G. Modern Art of Fencing. 18°. Lond. 1822.
ROLES, J. Inside Views of Slavery. 8°. N.Y. 1864.
ROLLESTON, F. Mazzaroth; and, Mizraim. 8°. Lond. 1862-5.
ROLLIN, C. Œuvres Complètes. 30 v. 8°. Atlas, 2 v. 4°. Paris. 1823-5.
ROLLS Chronicles (Chronicles and Memorials of Great Britain and Ireland). Separate works as follows:
—— Amundesham, J. Annales Monasterii S. Albani. 2 v. R. 8° Lond. 1870-71.
—— Ancient Laws of Ireland. Senchus Mor. 2 v. R. 8°. Lond. 1865-69.
—— Hardy, Sir F. D. Descriptive Catalogue of Materials Relative to the History of Great Britain and Ireland. v. 3. R. 8°. Lond. 1871.
—— Higden, R. Polychronicon. v. 2, 3. R. 8°. Lond. 1869 71.
—— Hoveden, R. de. Chronica. 4 v. R. 8°. Lond. 1868-71.
—— Monumenta Juridica. Black Book of the Admiralty. v. 1. R. 8°. Lond. 1871.
—— Ricardus de Cirencestria. Speculum Historiale de Gestis Regum Angliæ. 2 v. R. 8°. Lond. 1863-69.
—— Walsingham, T. Gesta Abbatum Monasterii S. Albani. 3 v. R. 8°. Lond. 1867-69.
—— Willelmus Malmesbiriensis. De Gestis Pontificum Anglorum Libri Quinque. R. 8°. Lond. 1870.
ROLLWYN, J. A. S. Astronomy Simplified 8°. Lond. n.d.
ROMANCE of Travel. 12°. Phil. 1869.
ROMANCERO del Cid. Nueva Edicion, por Carolina Michaelis. 12°. Leip. 1871.
ROMANOFF, H. C. Historical Narratives from the Russian. 12°. Lond. 1871.
—— Liturgy of St. John Chrysostom. 16°. Lond. 1871.
—— Rites and Customs of the Greco-Russian Church. 12°. Lond. 1868.
ROMANOS, R. M. Escenas Matritenses. 2d Series. 12°. Madrid. 1862.
RÖMHELD, A. Anna Braun. 2 v. in 1. 16°. Leip. 1870.
ROOPER, G. Thames and Tweed. 12°. Lond. n.d.
ROOSMALEN, A de. L'Orateur; ou, Cours de Débit et d'Action. 2d ed. Imp. 8°. Paris. 1842.
ROQUEPLAN, F. Parisine. 9th ed. 16°. Paris. n.d.
ROQUETTE, O. Heinrich Falk. 3 v. 12°. Breslau. 1858.
—— Welt und Haus. 12°. Brunswick. 1871.
RÖRDANSZ, C. W. European Commerce. 8°. Bost. 1819.
ROSCOE, H. E. Elementary Chemistry. 18°. Lond. 1871.
ROSCOE, W. Life of Lorenzo de Medici. 2 v. 8°. Phil. 1842.
ROSE, S. Loyola and the Early Jesuits. 2d ed. 8°. Lond. 1871.
ROSENTHAL, T. von. German Scholar's Hand-Book. 24°. Lond. n.d.
ROSS, W. P. M. Book-Keeping. f°. 8°. Phil. 1847.
ROSSEL, L. N. Abrégé de l'Art de la Guerre. 12°. Paris. 1871.
—— Posthumous Works. 12°. Lond. 1872.
ROSSETTI, D. G. Poems. 12°. Lond. 1870.
—— Same. 16°. Bost. 1870.
ROSSETTI, Maria F. A Shadow of Dante. 12°. Lond. 1871.
—— Same. 12°. Bost. 1872.
ROSSITER, W. Elementary Handbook of Physics. 12°. Edin. 1871.
ROTH, M. On Paralysis in Infancy, Childhood and Youth. 8°. Lond. 1869.
ROTHENFELS, E. von. [Pseudonym.] *See* INGERSLEBEN, Frau von.
ROTHSCHILD, C. and A. de. History and Literature of the Israelites. 2 v. 12°. Lond. 1870.
—— Same. Abridged. 16°. Lond. 1872.
ROUILLON, M. de. French Grammar. 6th ed. 12°. Lond. 1839.
ROUND Table. v. 2-9. L. 4°. N.Y. 1865-9.
ROUSE, E. S. Bugle Bast. 12°. Phil. 1864.
ROUSSEAU, J. J. Émile. 12°. Paris. 1866.
—— Confessions. 12°. Lond. 1861.
—— Same. 12°. Lond. 1871.

ROUSSEL, J. B. ainé. Connaissances des Marchandises. 5 v. 8°. Bordeaux. 1846.
ROUSSEL, N. Scènes Bibliques. 8°. Paris. 1841-2.
—— Scènes Patriarchales. 8°. Paris. 1841.
ROWBOTHAM, J. German Grammar. 16°. Lond. 1832.
ROWELL & Co's. American Newspaper Directory. 8°. N.Y. 1869.
ROWLANDS, D. Sermons on Historical Subjects. 16°. Lond. 1870.
ROWLETT, J. Tables of Discount. 4°. Phil. 1802.
ROWSON, Susanna. Miscellaneous Poems. 12°. Bost. 1804.
ROY, J. E. Manual of the Congregational Churches. 16°. Chicago. 1869.
ROYAL Decrees of Scanderoon. 16°. N.Y. 1870.
ROYAL Geographical Society. Journal. v. 38-40. 8°. Lond. 1868-70.
ROYAL Society of Northern Antiquaries.
—— Antiquarisk Tidsskrift, 1852-60. 3 v. 8°. Copenhagen. 1854-60.
—— Mémoires, 1843-60. 4 v. 8°. Copenhagen. 1844-60.
—— Reports of Anniversary Meetings 1838-9. 8°. Copenhagen. 1839.
ROZAN, C. La Bonté. 16°. Paris. n.d.
RÜFFER, C. T. Grammaire Allemande. 3d ed. 12°. Geneva. 1836.
RUGGLES, H. J. Shakspeare as Artist. 16°. N.Y. 1870.
RULE, W. H. Councils, Ancient and Modern. 24°. Lond. 1870.
—— History of the Karaite Jews. 12°. Lond. 1870.
—— Holy Sabbath. 12°. Lond. n.d.
RULLOFF, E. H., the Man of Two Lives. 8°. N.Y. 1871.
RUMFORD, Benjamin Thompson, (Count). Essays. 8°. Bost. 1798-1804.
—— Works. v. 1. R. 8°. Bost. 1870.
RUPPANER, A. Reply to Dr. Sayre. (PC. 16.) 8°. N.Y. 1870.
RUSCHENBERGER, W. S. M. Conchology. 16°. Phil. 1844.
—— Elements of Botany. 12°. Phil. 1844.
—— Elements of Entomology. 12°. Phil. 1845.
—— Elements of Mammalogy. 12°. Phil. 1844.
—— First Book of Natural History. 12°. Phil. 1844.
—— Herpetology and Ichthyology. 16°. Phil. 1844.
—— Ornithology. 16°. Phil. 1844.
RUSHTON, W. L. Shakspeare Illustrated by the Lex Scripta. Part 1. 12°. Lond. 1870.
—— Shakspeare's Euphuism. 12°. Lond. 1871.
RUSKIN, J. Ethics of the Dust. 12°. Lond. 1867.
—— Fors Clavigera. Letters to the Workmen and Labourers of Great Britain. 12°. N.Y. 1871.
—— Same. Part 2. 12°. N.Y. 1872.
—— Lectures on Art. 12°. Oxford. 1870.
—— Same. 12°. N.Y. 1870.
—— Modern Painters. v. 1-5. R. 8°. Lond. 1860-7.
—— Munera Pulveris. Six Essays on the Elements of Political Economy. 12°. N.Y. 1872.
—— Works. Revised edition. v. 1, 2, 3. 8°. Lond. 1871-2.
RUSSELL, Count H. Pau and the Pyrenees. 12°. Lond. 1871.
RUSSELL, John (Earl). Foreign Policy of England. 8°. Lond. 1871.
—— Speeches and Despatches. 2 v. 8°. Lond. 1870.
RUSSELL, J. S. Naval Architecture. 3 v. L. f°. Lond. n.d.
RUSSELL, M. History of Barbary States. 18°. N.Y. 1835.
—— Palestine. 18°. N.Y. 1835.
RUSSELL, Wm. Grammar of Composition. 16°. New Haven. 1823.
RUSSELL, W. C. Representative Actors. 12°. Lond. n.d.
RUSSELL, W. H. Diary in the East. 8°. Lond. 1869.
RUST, J. Druidism Exhumed. 12°. Edin. 1871.
RÜSTOW, W. Der Krieg von 1866 in Deutschland und Italien. 8°. Zurich. 1866.
—— War for the Rhine Frontier, 1870. 3 v. 8°. Edin. 1871-2.
RUTGERS Female College. Proceedings at Inauguration. 8°. N.Y. 1867.
RUTTENBER, E. M. History of the Indian Tribes of Hudson's River. 8°. Alb. 1872.
RUXTON, G. Mexico and the Rocky Mountains. 12°. N.Y. 1848.
RUYSDAEL, J. Life and Works of Art. f°. n.p. n.d.

RYAN, J. Elements of Astronomy. 18°. N.Y. 1826.
—— Key to Algebra. 16°. N.Y. 1825.
RYLAND, J. Life and Death of Rev. A. Fuller. 8°. Charlestown. 1818.
RYLAND, J. E. Wholesome Words. 18°. Lond. n.d.
RYLE, J. C. Thoughts on the Gospels: John. 2 v. 12°. N.Y. 1868–70.
SAAVEDRA, Faxardo D. de. Corona Gotica Castellana y Austriaca. 6 v. (v. 5 missing). 16°. Madrid. 1789–90.
SABINE, R. History of the Electric Telegraph. 2d ed. 12°. N.Y. 1869.
SABONADIÈRE, W. Coffee-Planter of Ceylon. 12°. Lond. 1870.
SACCHETTI, F. Cento Novelle. 12°. Verona. 1821.
SACHER-MASOCH. Das Vermächtniss Kains: I. Die Liebe. 2 v. in 1. Stuttg. 1870.
SADLER, M. F. Abundant Life, and other Sermons. 16°. N.Y. 1871.
—— Sacrament of Responsibility. (Holy Baptism.) 16°. N.Y. 1871.
SADLER, M. T. The Bible the People's Charter. 8°. Lond. 1869.
SADLER, P. L'Art de la Correspondance Anglaise et Française. 2d ed. 2 v. in 1. 12°. Paris. 1836.
—— Same. 6th ed. 2 v. 12°. Paris. 1865.
—— Grammaire Pratique de la Langue Anglaise. 2d ed. 16°. Paris. 1835.
—— Manuel Classique de Conversations Françaises et Anglaises. 8th ed. 18°. Paris. 1869.
—— Manuel de Phrases Françaises et Anglaises. 26th ed. 18°. Paris. 1870.
SADLER, T. Edwin Wilkins Field; a Memorial Sketch. 12°. Lond. 1872.
SADLIER'S Catholic Directory, Almanac, and Ordo for 1870, 71 and 72. 3 v. 12°. N.Y. 1870–72.
SAELTZER, A. Treatise on Acoustics. 16°. N.Y. 1872.
SAILOR'S Magazine. v. 40–43. 8°. N.Y. n.d.
SAINT ABE and his Seven Wives. 16°. N.Y. 1872.
SAINT-AMAND, I. de. L'Abbé Deguerry. 12°. Paris. 1871.
ST. BARTHOLOMEW'S Hospital Reports. v. 3–6. 8°. Lond. 1867–70.
ST. CLAIR, Lady H. Dainty Dishes. 12°. Edin. 1870.
SAINT-EDME, E. La Science pendant le Siége de Paris. 12°. Paris. 1871.
ST. GEORGE'S Society. Constitution. 18°. N.Y. 1853.
SAINT-GERMAIN, M. T. de. La Guerre de Sept Mois. 12°. Paris. 1871.
ST. JAMES' Magazine. New series, v. 3–8. 8°. Lond. 1869–72.
SAINT JOSEPH City Directory for 1871. 8°. Saint Joseph. 1871.
ST. LEONARDS, Lord. Handy Book of Property Law. 8th ed. 12°. Edin. 1869.
ST. LOUIS Directory, 1870, 71. 2 v. 8°. St. Louis. 1870–1.
ST. LOUIS Public School Library Catalogue. R. 8°. St. Louis. 1870.
SAINT MARS, Mme. Cisterne de (Comtesse Dash): L'Arbre de la Vierge. 12°. Paris. 1872.
—— Un Secret de Famille. 12°. Paris. 1872.
ST. PAUL'S Magazine. v. 3–8. 8°. Lond. 1869–71.
SAINT SIMON, Duke de. Memoirs; abridged by St. John. 4 v. 12°. Lond. 1857.
SAINT VICTOR, P. de. Barbares et Bandits. 12°. Paris. 1871.
SAINTE BEUVE, C. A. Le Général Jomini. 12°. Paris. 1869.
—— Nouveaux Lundis. v. 11, 12, 13. 12°. Paris. 1869–70.
—— Poésies Complètes. 2 v. in 1. 12°. Paris. 1863.
—— Port-Royal. 3d ed. 6 v. 12°. Paris. 1867.
—— Portraits Contemporains. 5 v. 12°. Paris. 1870–71.
—— Portraits de Femmes. 12°. Paris. 1856.
—— Souvenirs et Indiscretions. Le Diner du Vendredi Saint. 12°. Paris. 1872.
—— Volupté. 12°. Paris. 1869.
SAINTINE, X. B. Les Trois Reines. 12°. Paris. 1859.
SALKELD, J. First Book in Spanish. 12°. N.Y. 1848.
SALLUST. Catiline and Jugurthine War. (Latin). Ed. by Anthon. 12°. Bost. 1833.
SALLUST, Florus, and Velleius Paterculus. Transl. by Watson. (Bohn's ed.) 12°. Lond. 1869.
SALON für Literatur, Kunst und Gesellschaft. v. 7, 8, 9. 8°. Leip. n.d.

SALTER, T. W. Field's Chromatography. 8°. Lond. n.d.

SAMPSON, M. B. Central America and Ocean Transit. 8°. N.Y. 1850.

SAMUELSON, J. Views of the Deity. 12°. Lond. 1871.

SAMUELSON, S. The German Working Man. 12°. Lond. 1869.

SAND, George. (Pseudonym.) *See* DUDEVANT, Mme. A.

SAND, M. Six Mille Lieues à toute Vapeur. 12°. Paris. 1863.

SANDEAU, J. Marianna. 12°. Paris. 1865.

SANDERS, C. W. Spelling Book. 16°. Cazenovia. 1849.

SANDERS, G. W. Uses and Trusts. 2d Am. ed. 8°. Phil. 1855.

SANFORD. In Memoriam Mrs. and Mr. Sanford. (PC. 16.) 8°. N.Y. 1862.

SANFORD, E. History of Berkley, Mass. 8°. N.Y. 1872.

SANGSTER, Wm. Umbrellas and their History. 12°. Lond. n.d

SANSEVERINO, M. D. Histoire de Bianca Capello. 8°. Lausanne. 1779.

SAPHIR, A. The Lord's Prayer. 16°. Lond. 1870.

SARCEY, F. Le Siége de Paris. 12°. Paris. 1871.

—— Paris during the Siege. 12°. Lond. 1871.

SARDOU, V. Patrie! 3d ed. 12°. Paris. 1870.

SARGANT, W. L. Essays of a Birmingham Manufacturer. 3 v. 8°. Lond. 1869–71.

SARGENT, E. Woman who Dared. 16°. Bost. 1869.

SARGENT, F. Compendium of Biblical Criticism. 8°. Lond 1871.

SARGENT, H. W. Skeleton Tours. 18°. N.Y. 1870.

SARGENT, J. Y. and Dallas, T. F. Greek and Latin Prose Composition. 12°. Lond. 1870.

SARGENT, W. History of Braddock's Expedition against Fort Du Quesne. 8°. Phil. 1856.

—— Life of Major André. 8°. N.Y. 1871.

SARJEANT, T. Short Hand. 18°. Phil. 1789.

SATAN in Society. By a Physician. 12°. Cinc. 1871.

SATCHEL (A) Guide for the Vacation Tourist in Europe. 16°. N.Y. 1872.

SATURDAY Review. v. 29, 31 and 32. f°. Lond. 1870–1.

SAUNDERS, F. Evenings with the Sacred Poets. 12°. N.Y. 1870.

—— Salad for the Solitary and the Social. 8°. N.Y. 1872.

SAUVESTRE, Mme. C. Guide Pratique pour les Écoles Professionnelles de jeunes Filles. 8°. Paris. 1868.

SAUZAY, A. Marvels of Glass Making. 12°. Lond. 1870.

—— Wonders of Glass Making. 16°. N.Y. 1870.

SAVAGE, J. The Librarian. 3 v. 8°. Lond. 1868.

SAVANNAH Directory, 1870. 8°. Savannah. 1870.

SAVARY, C. Letters on Egypt. 3d ed. 2 v. 8°. Lond. 1799.

SAVILLE, B. W. Truth of the Bible. 12°. Lond. 1871.

SAWYER, J. Physical Diagnosis of Lungs and Heart. 12°. Lond. 1870.

SAXE, J. G. Fables and Legends of Many Countries Rendered in Rhyme. 16°. Bost. 1872.

—— Poems; Highgate ed. 16°. Bost. 1871.

SAYRE, L. A. The Alleged Malpractice Suit of Walsh *vs.* Sayre. 8°. N.Y. 1870.

—— Answer to Dr. Ruppaner. 8°. N.Y. 1870.

—— Review of Dr. Ruppaner's Case. (PC. 16.) 8°. N.Y. 1870.

SCALPEL. v. 11–12 in 1 v. 8°. N.Y. n.d.

SCANLAN, M. Love and Land. Poems. 16°. Bost. 1869.

SCARAMELLI, J. B. Directorium Asceticum, or Guide to the Spiritual Life. 4 v. 12°. Dublin. 1870–71.

SCARRON, Paul. Le Roman Comique. 2 v. in 1. 8°. Paris. 1858.

—— Théâtre Complet. 3 v. 16°. Hague. 1775.

SCHADE, C. B. German Grammar. 4th ed. 12°. Leip. 1828.

SCHAEFFER, C. Early History of the Lutheran Church in America. 12°. Phil. 1868.

SCHANZ, J. Der Montcenis Tunnel. 12°. Vienna. 1872.

SCHEFFEL, J. V. Frau Aventiure. 2d ed. 12°. Stuttg. 1869.

—— Gaudeamus. 16°. Stuttg. 1870.

—— Gaudeamus. Transl. by C. G. Leland. 18°. Bost. 1872.
—— Der Trompeter von Säkkingen. 12°. Stuttg. 1863
SCHELIHA, Von. Coast Defence. R. 8°. Lond. 1868.
SCHELLEN, H. Spectrum Analysis. 8°. Lond. 1872.
—— Same. 8°. N.Y. 1872.
SCHERR, J. Allgemeine Geschichte der Literatur. 3d ed. 2 v. 8°. Stuttg. 1869.
—— Dämonen. 12°. Leip. 1871.
—— Farrago. 12°. Leip. 1870.
—— Geschichte der Deutschen Frauenwelt. 2 v. in 1. 12°. Leip. 1865.
—— Michel. 4 v. in 2. 16°. Prague. 1858.
—— Same. 2d ed. 4 v. in 2. 12°. Leip. 1871.
—— Schiller und seine Zeit. 3 v. in 1. 12°. Leip. 1862.
—— Studien. 3 v. 12°. Leip. 1865.
—— Das Trauerspiel in Mexico. 12°. Leip. 1868.
—— Von '48 bis '51. v. 1, 2. 8°. Leip. 1868–70.
—— Die Waise von Wien. 3 v. 12°. Stuttg. 1847.
SCHERZER, K. von. Circumnavigation of the Globe in the Novara. 3 v. 8°. Lond. 1861.
—— Travels in the Free States of North America. 2 v. 12°. Lond. 1857.
SCHIEFERDECKER, C. C. Horrors of Vaccination. 16°. N.Y. 1870.
SCHILLER, E. Hand Book of Progressive Philosophy. 12°. N.Y. 1871.
SCHILLER, F. von. Sämmtliche Schriften. Historisch-kritische Ausgabe. Herausgegeben von K. Goedeke. v. 1–9. 8°. Stuttg. 1867–70.
—— Sämmtliche Werke. 12 v. 8°. Stuttg. 1835–6.
—— Early Dramas and Romances. 12°. Lond. 1867.
—— History of the Thirty Years' War. Transl. by Morrison. 12°. Lond. 1870.
—— Poems and Ballads. Transl. by Lytton. 18°. N.Y. n.d.
—— Works. Transl. 12°. Lond. 1868.
SCHILLER-Feier, 10 Nov., 1859. (PC. 18.) 4°. N.Y. 1859.
SCHIMMELPENNINCK, Mrs. Mary Anne. Autobiography. Edited by Hankin. 4th ed. 12°. Lond. 1860.
SCHINZ, C. Blast Furnace. 12°. Lond. 1870.
—— Same. 12°. Phil. 1871.
SCHIRMER, A. Die Spionin. 4 v. in 1. 12°. Leip. 1869.
SCHLÄGEL, M. von. Gefangen und Belagert. 12°. Jena. n.d.
—— Die Helden der Arbeit. 12°. Bielefeld. 1871.
—— Nach uns die Sündflut! 1st Abth. 4 v. in 2. 12°. Leip. 1872.
—— Stereoscopen. 12°. Munich. 1872.
—— Von Sünde zu Sünde. 3 v. in 2. 12°. Berlin. 1870.
—— Wildes Blut. 12°. Berlin. n.d.
SCHLAGINTWEIT, H., A. and R. von. India and High Asia: Atlas. Parts 1, 2, 3. Elephant f°. Leip. 1861–63.
SCHLAGINTWEIT, R. von. Californien; Land und Leute. 12°. Cologne. 1871.
—— Die Pacific-Eisenbahn in Nordamerika. 12°. Cologne. 1870.
SCHLEGEL, F. History of Literature. 12°. N.Y. 1841.
SCHLEGEL, H., and Verster de Wulverhorst, A. H. Traité de Fauconnerie. Atl. f°. Leyden. 1844–58.
SCHLEICHER, A. Darwinism Tested. 12°. Lond. 1869.
SCHMEIZELIUS, M. M. Præcognita Historiæ Ecclesiasticæ. 4°. Jena. 1721.
SCHMID, C. F. Biblical Theology of the New Testament. 8°. Edin. 1870.
SCHMID, H. Mütze und Krone. 5 v. in 2. 12°. Leip. 1869.
SCHMIDT, J. Bilder aus dem Geistigen Leben unserer Zeit. 2 v. 8°. Leip. 1870–1.
SCHMIDT-Weissenfels. Hinter Schloss und Riegel. 12°. Berlin. 1866.
—— Die Schöne Gefangene. 12°. Leip. n.d.
—— Strassburg. 12°. Berlin. n.d.
SCHMITZ, L. Elementary Latin Grammar. 16°. Edin. 1852.
SCHMUCKER, S. S. Fraternal Appeal to American Churches. 2d ed. 12°. N.Y. 1839.
SCHNAASE, C. Geschichte der Bildenden Künste. v 3, 4. 8°. Düsseldorf. 1869–71.

SCHNÉEGANS, A. La Guerre en Alsace. 1re Partie: Strasbourg. 12°. Neuchatel. n.d.
SCHOEDLER, F. Elements of Botany. Ed. by Medlock. 12°. Lond. 1851.
SCHOELCHER, P. La Nouvelle Armée. Also Truchy, J.: L'Armée Française en 1871. 8°. Paris. 1871.
SCHOLAR'S Reference Book. 12°. Phil. 1836.
SCHRADER, A. Auf den Wogen des Lebens. 3 v. 12°. Leip. 1871.
—— Kunst und Liebe. 2 v. 12°. Leip. 1871.
—— Der Untergang des alten Regime. 12°. Leip. 1871.
—— Das Verhängniss. 3 v. 12°. Leip. 1871.
—— Der Weg zum Glücke. 12°. Leip. 1871.
SCHROEDER, A. Schicksale der Protestanten in Frankreich. 8°. Gotha. 1871.
SCHROEDER van der Kolk, J. L. C. Mental Diseases. Tr. by Rudall. 8°. Lond. 1870.
SCHÜCKING, L. Filigran. 12°. Hanover. 1869.
—— Same. Neue Folge. 12°. Hanover. 1872.
—— J. J. Rousseau. 16°. Leip. 1869.
—— Luther in Rom. 3 v. in 2. 12°. Hanover. 1870.
—— Verschlungene Wege. 3 v. 12°. Hanover. 1871.
SCHULTE, J. F. von. Die Macht der Römischen Päpste. 8°. Prague. 1871.
SCHUYLER, A. Logic. 12°. Cinc. n.d.
SCHWAB, G. Fünf Bücher Deutscher Lieder und Gedichte. 4th ed. 12°. Leip. 1857.
SCHWARTZ, M. S. Arbeit adelt den Mann. 16°. Stuttg. n.d.
—— Blätter aus dem Frauenleben. 16°. Stuttg. n.d.
—— David Walden. 16°. Stuttg. n.d.
—— Der Ehestand. 16°. Stuttg. n.d.
—— Eines Eiteln Mannes Frau. 16°. Stuttg. n.d
—— Ellen oder Ein Jahr. 16°. Stuttg. n.d.
—— Geburt und Bildung. 16°. Stuttg. n.d.
—— Gold und Name. 16°. Stuttg. n.d.
—— Jugenderinnerungen. 16°. Stuttg. n.d.
—— Die Kinder der Arbeit. 16°. Stuttg. n.d.
—— Die Leidenschaften. 16°. Stuttg. n.d.
—— Der Mann von Geburt. 16°. Stuttg. n.d.
—— Mathilde. 16°. Stuttg. n.d.
—— Meine Lebensschicksale. 16°. Stuttg. n.d.
—— Ein Opfer der Rache. 16°. Stuttg. n.d.
—— Schuld und Unschuld. 16°. Stuttg. n.d.
—— Die Schutzlosen. 16°. Stuttg. n.d.
—— Sein oder Nichtsein. 12°. Berlin. 1867.
—— Die Söhne des Drehorgelmanns. 16°. Stuttg. n.d.
—— Die Tochter des Edelmanns. 16°. Stuttg. n.d
—— Die Wittwe und ihre Kinder. 16°. Stuttg. n.d.
—— Wilhelm Stjernhelm. 16°. Stuttg. n.d.
—— Zwei Familienmütter. 16°. Stuttg. n.d.
—— Ein Zweifaches Lebensziel. 16°. Stuttg. n.d.
SCIENCE of Etiquette. 24°. Glasgow. 1836.
SCIENCE of Money. 16°. Phil. 1871.
SCIENTIFIC American. v. 22 and 24. f°. N.Y. 1870–1.
SCOFFERN, J. Stray Leaves of Science and Folk-Lore. 8°. Lond. 1870.
SCOTT, A. M. Chronicles of the Rebellion. 12°. Cinc. 1864.
SCOTT, C. Drawing Room Plays. 12°. Lond. 1870.
SCOTT, D. B. School History of the U. S. 12. N.Y. 1870.
SCOTT, F. Letters from a Layman. 8°. Lond. 1869.
SCOTT, G. G. Intellectual First Cause. 12°. Cambr. (Eng.) 1870.
SCOTT, Sir Walter. Ivanhoe. French of Dumas. 12°. Paris. 1862.
—— Rokeby. 24°. Phil. 1813.
SCOTT, W. B. Albert Durer and his Works. L. 8°. Lond. 1869.
SCOTTISH Liturgies. Ed. by G. W. Spratt. 12°. Edin. 1871.
SCOTTISH University Addresses. *See* LIBRARY of Education, v. 4.
SCOVEL, S. F. Always Thankful; a Thanksgiving Sermon. 8°. Springfield. (O.) 1862.

SCOVILLE, J. L. Old Merchants of New York. 5th Series. 12°. N.Y. 1870.
SCRIBNER'S Monthly. v. 1-3. 8°. N.Y. 1870-72
SCRIPTURE Atlas. 4°. Phil. 1809.
SCUDDER, J. M. Diseases of Children. 8°. Cinc. 1869.
—— Eclectic Practice in Diseases of Children. 8°. Cinc. 1869.
SEABURY, S. Testimony of Eusebius in Regard to St. Peter's Visit to Rome. 16°. N.Y. 1871.
SEAMAN, E. American System of Government. 12°. N.Y. 1870.
SEARS, D. Contrabands and Vagrants. 16°. n.p. n.d.
SEARS, E. H. The Fourth Gospel; the Heart of Christ. 12°. Bost. 1872.
SEATON. W. W. Seaton, of the National Intelligencer. A Biographical Sketch. 12°. Bost. 1871.
SEBERUS, W. Index Vocabulorum in Homero. 8°. Oxford. 1780.
SECESSIAD (The). A Poem. 18°. Pittsburg. 1862.
SECOND, L. Nouvelles Soirées Chrétiennes. 12°. Geneva. 1871.
SECOND Armada. 16°. Phil. 1871.
SECOND (A) Collection of Poems, etc. against Popery and Tyranny. Sm. 4°. Lond. 1869.
SECRET Documents of the Second Empire. Transl. by Curry. 12°. Lond. 1871.
SECRETI, L. Grammaire Italienne. 18°. Geneva. 1787.
SECRETS of Internal Revenue. Ed. by Felton. 8°. Phil. 1870.
SEDGWICK. Dedication of Statue of Gen. Sedgwick. 8°. N.Y. 1869.
SEE, G. von. (Pseudonym.) *See* STRUENSEE, G. von.
SEE, I. M. The Rest of Faith. 16°. N.Y. 1871.
SEELEY, I. R. Lectures and Essays. 8°. Lond. 1870.
—— Roman Imperialism. 16°. Bost. 1871.
SEGUIER, F. P. Dictionary of Works of Painters. R. 8°. Lond. 1870.
SÉGUR, Comtesse S. de. Après la Pluie le Beau Temps. 12°. Paris. 1872.
—— Un Bon Petit Diable. 12°. Paris. 1869.
—— Les Deux Nigauds. 12°. Paris. 1868.
—— Diloy le Chemineau. 12°. Paris. 1869.
—— La Fortune de Gasparin. 12°. Paris. 1866.
—— François le Bossu. 12°. Paris. 1866.
—— Mémoires d'un Ane. 12°. Paris. 1869.
—— Pauvre Blaise. 12°. Paris. 1869.
—— Quel Amour d'Enfant! 12°. Paris. 1867.
—— La Sœur de Gribouille. 12°. Paris. 1870.
SEISS, J. A. Apocalypse. v. 1. 12°. Phil. 1869.
—— Ecclesia Lutherana. 3d ed. 12°. Phil. 1869.
SEIZE Saintes dediées aux Jeunes Demoiselles. (Plates.) 4°. Paris. 1823.
SELF-Formation. (Attributed to Capel Lofft.) 12°. Bost. 1846.
SELLAR, J. A. Church Discipline and Practice. Sermons. 12°. Edin. 1869.
SEMPRONIUS. Histoire de la Commune de Paris en 1871. 12°. Paris. n.d.
SEN, Keshub Chunder. English Visit. 12°. Lond. n.d.
SENIOR, N. W. Journals in France and Italy. 2 v. 12°. Lond. 1871.
SEOANE, M. Spanish and English Dictionary. 5th ed. (Not Circulated; interleaved, with MS. additions.) 2 v. 4°. Lond. 1837.
SERIES of Woman's Rights Tracts. 16°. Rochester. n.d.
SERMON on the Mount, and Parables (in Phonetics). 2d ed. 18°. Lond. 1849.
SERMONS during Lent, at Oxford, 1868, 1869. 2 v. 8°. Oxford. 1869-70.
SETON, G. Letters and Letter-Writers. 16°. Edin. 1870.
SEUME, J. G. Werke. 6th ed. 8 v. in 4. Sq. 16°. Leip. 1863.
SÉVIGNÉ, Mme. M. de. Lettres Choisies. Ed. by Regnier. R. 8°. Paris. 1870.
SEWELL, E. M. Poems of Bygone Years. 16°. Lond. 1871.
—— and Yonge, C. M. European History. 2 v. 12°. Lond. 1870.
SEWELL, R. Analytical History of India. 12°. Lond. 1870.
SEYMOUR, Horatio, and Blair, F., Jr. Lives of. 12°. Phil. n.d.
SEYMOUR, M. H. The Confessional. 16°. Lond. 1870.
SEYMOUR, R. A. Pioneering on the Pampas. 12°. Lond. 1869.

SEYMOUR, S. Western Incidents. 12°. N.Y. 1867.
SHADOW of the Rock and other Religious Poems. 24°. N.Y. n.d.
SHAFFNER, T. P. Telegraph Manual. 8°. N.Y. 1867.
SHAFTESBURY, Lord. Characteristics. Ed. by Hatch. v. 1. 8°. Lond. 1870.
SHAIRP, J. C. Culture and Religion. 16°. Edin. 1871
—— Same. 16°. N.Y. 1872.
—— Studies in Poetry. 2d ed. 12°. Edin. 1872.
—— Same. 16°. N.Y. 1872.
SHAKSPEARE, W. As You Like It. 16°. N.Y. 1848.
—— Hamlet. (Booth's ed.) 8°. N.Y. n.d.
—— King Henry VIII. Ed. by Rolfe. 16°. N.Y, 1872.
—— Merchant of Venice. Ed. by Rolfe. 12°. N.Y. 1871.
—— Readings, by Kemble. 3 v. 12°. Lond. 1870.
—— Richard III.; Acting Edition. 18°. Phil. n.d.
—— Sonnets and Lover's Complaint. From ed. of 1609. 8°. Lond. 1870.
SHAND, A. J. On the Trail of the War. 8°. N.Y. 1870.
SHARMAN, H. P. Handy Book for Life Assurance Agents. 18°. Lond. n.d.
SHARPE, E. The Ornamentation of the Transitional Period of British Architecture. (A.D. 1145–1190.) Pt. 1. f°. Lond. n.d.
—— Seven Periods of English Architecture. 2d ed. 8°. Lond. 1860.
SHARPE, S. Decree of Canopus. 8°. Lond. 1870.
—— History of Egypt. 5th ed. 2 v. 12°. Lond. 1870.
—— The Rosetta Stone. 8°. Lond. 1871.
—— Texts Explained by Ancient Monuments. 12°. Lond. 1869.
SHARPE'S London Magazine. New ser. v. 33–37. L. 8°. Lond. n.d.
SHARSWOOD, G. Lectures introductory to the Study of the Law. 12°. Phil. 1870.
SHAW, E. M. Records of the Late London Fire Establishment. f°. Lond. 1870.
SHAW, H. W. Josh Billings' Allminax, 1871, 1872. 8°. N.Y. 1871–2.
SHAW, R. Exposition of the Westminster Confession. 12°. Phil. n.d.
—— Visits to High Tartary, Yârkand and Kâshghar. 8°. Lond. 1871.
SHAW, S. Chemistry of Pottery. R. 8°. Lond. 1837.
SHEDD, W. G. T. Sermons to the Natural Man. 12°. N.Y. 1871.
—— The Union and the War; a Sermon. 16°. N.Y. 1863.
SHELLEY, P. B. Works, ed. by Rossetti. 2 v. 12°. Lond. 1870.
—— Poetical Works. 1st ser. 16°. Lond. n.d.
SHEPARD, T. P. Receipts for Calico Printing. 8°. Providence. 1872.
SHEPHEARD, H. Traditions of Eden. 8°. Lond. 1871.
SHEPPARD, N. Shut up in Paris. 16°. Leip. 1871.
SHERIDAN, T. Powers of Parliament. Edited by Bannister. Sm. 4°. Lond. 1870.
SHERLOCK, W. Discourse on a Future Judgment. 12°. N.Y. 1834.
SHERMAN, J. Philosophy of Language Illustrated. 16°. Trenton Falls. 1826.
SHERWOOD, J. D. Comic History of the U. S. 12°. Bost. 1870.
SHEW, J. Midwifery and Diseases of Women. 12°. N.Y. 1869.
—— Water-Cure Manual. 12°. N.Y. 1849.
SHIMEALL, R. C. The Unseen World. 12°. N.Y. 1870.
SHIPLEY, O. Four Cardinal Virtues. (Sermons.) 16°. Lond. 1871.
—— Glossary of Ecclesiastical Terms. 12°. Lond. 1872.
SHIPPING and Commercial List. v. 22–29. f°. N.Y. 1836–43.
SHORTT, J. Law Relating to Works of Literature and Art. 8°. Lond. 1871.
SHRIMPTON, C. British Army and Miss Nightingale. 8°. Paris. 1864.
SHUTTLEWORTH, J. K. Four Periods of Public Education. 8°. Lond. 1862.
—— Letter to Earl Granville on the Revised Code. 8°. Lond. 1861.
SIBREE, J., Jr. Madagascar and its People. 12°. Lond. n.d.
SIBREE, Marie. Sermons from the Studio. 12°. Lond. 1867.
SICKELS, D. Freemason's Monitor. 32°. N.Y. 1870.

SIGERSON, G. Land Tenure of Ireland. 12°. Lond. 1871.
—— Modern Ireland. 2d ed. 12°. Lond. 1869
SILJESTRÖM, P. A. Bidrag til Skol-Arkitekturen. Forster Haftet. 4°. Stockholm. 1856.
SILVER, A. Discourses on the Rationality of the Christian World. 12°. Bost. 1870.
SIMEON, C. Horæ Homileticæ; or, Discourses Digested into One Continued Series, and Forming a Commentary upon every Book in the Old and New Testament. 21 v. 8°. Lond. 1848-55.
SIMMS, F. W. Mathematical Drawing Instruments. 16°. Lond. 1837.
—— Levelling. 5th ed. 8°. N.Y. 1870.
—— Treatise on Mathematical Instruments. 8°. Lond. 1834.
SIMON, F. N. Tenue des Livres. 2 v. 8°. Paris. 1832.
SIMONIN, L. Mines and Miners. R. 8°. Lond. n.d.
SIMONNE, T. Metodo para aprender el Frances. 12°. N.Y. 1853.
SIMPSON, Sir James Y. Works. 3 v. 8°. Edin. 1871-2.
—— Same. 3 v. 8°. N.Y. 1871-2.
SIMPSON, T. Algebra. 6th ed. 8°. Lond. 1790.
SIMS, C. S. Clark and Rose Pedigrees. 8°. Prescott, (Canada.) 1870.
SIMS, J. M. Silver Sutures in Surgery. 8°. N.Y. 1858.
SIXPENNY Magazine. New ser., v. 1-4. 8°. Lond. 1868-9.
SIZER, N. What to Do and Why; and How to Educate each Man for his Proper Work. 12°. N.Y. 1872.
SKEAT, W. W. Specimens of English Literature. 16°. Oxford. 1871.
SKEFFINGTON, S. W. The Sinless Sufferer; Six Sermons. 3d ed. 12°. Lond. 1872.
SKENE, W. F. Coronation Stone. S. 4°. Edin. 1869.
SKETCHES of Eminent Medical Men. 8°. Phil. n.d.
SKETCHES of History, Life, and Manners in the United States. 12°. New Haven. 1826.
SKETCHES of Obscure Poets. 16°. Lond. 1833.
SLACK, H. J. Marvels of Pond Life. 12°. Lond. 1861.
SLAFTER, E. F. Memorial of J. Slafter. 8°. Bost. 1869.
SLAGG, John, Jr. Cotton Trade of Lancashire and the Treaty of 1860. 8°. Lond. 1870.
SLEEMAN, W. H. Rambles and Recollections of an Indian Official. 2 v. 8°. Lond. 1844.
SMART, B. H. Accidence of English Grammar. 16°. Lond. 1841.
—— Key to Exercises in English. 16°. Lond. 1847.
—— Manual of Grammar. 16°. Lond. 1847.
—— Manual of Rhetoric. 18°. Lond. 1848.
—— Principles of English Grammar. 16°. Lond. 1847.
SMART, W. S. Last Sermon in 1st Cong. Church. 8°. Alb. 1868.
SMEATON, A. C. Builder's Pocket Manual. 16°. Lond. 1836.
SMEATON, G. The Atonement. 8°. Edin. 1870.
SMILES, S. (Edr.) A Boy's Voyage round the World. 12°. Lond. 1871.
—— Same. 12°. N.Y. 1871.
—— Character. 12°. Lond. 1871.
—— Self-Help. 12°. Bost. 1869.
SMITH, Adam. Essays. 12°. Lond. 1869.
—— Wealth of Nations. 12°. Lond. 1870.
SMITH, Agnes. Eastern Pilgrims; or, Travels of Three Ladies. 8° Lond. 1870.
SMITH, Albert. Mont Blanc. With Memoir by Yates. 18°. Lond. n.d.
—— Wassail Bowl. 2 v. in 1. 12°. Lond. 1843.
SMITH, Rev. Alfred Chas. Tour in Portugal. 12°. Lond. 1870.
SMITH, Chas. J. Manual of English Grammar. 16°. Lond. 1846.
—— Synonyms Discriminated. 8°. N.Y. 1871.
SMITH, Charles Perrin. Lloyd and Carpenter Family. 4°. Camden. 1870.
SMITH, E. Delafield. Argument in the Peterhoff Case. 8°. N.Y. 1863.
SMITH, Eustace. Wasting Diseases of Children. 2d ed. 8°. Lond. 1870.
SMITH, F. B. Asleep. 12°. Brooklyn. n.d.
SMITH, F. P. Materia Medica and Natural History of China. Imp. 8°. Shanghai. 1871.

—— Vocabulary of Proper Names, Chinese and English. Imp. 8°. Shanghai. 1870.
SMITH, F. S. Poems for the Million. 16°. N.Y. 1871.
SMITH, George. History of Assurbanipal, from the Cuneiform Inscriptions. R. 8°. Lond. 1871.
SMITH, G. V. The Bible and Popular Theology. 8°. Lond. 1871.
SMITH, Hely. The MacCallum More; a History of the Argyll Family. 16°. Lond. 1871.
SMITH, Henry B. The Reformed Churches; an Address to Presb. Hist. Soc. 8°. Phil. 1855.
SMITH, H. and J. Rejected Addresses. 18°. Lond. 1869.
SMITH, Col. James. Captivity with the Indians. Notes by Darlington. 8°. Cinc. 1870.
SMITH, John. Domestic Botany. 12°. Lond. 1871.
SMITH, J. A. Letters on Natural Magic 12°. Lond. 1868.
SMITH, J. Calvin. Map of North America; *Also*, Doggett's Map of the United States. Folded 18°. N.Y. 1849.
SMITH, J. G. Examination of Medical Witnesses. 16°. Lond. 1829.
SMITH, Joshua T. Comparative View of Ancient History. 8°. Bost. 1839.
SMITH, Matthew H. Twenty Years in Wall Street. 8°. Hartford. 1870.
SMITH, Maj-Gen. M. W. Modern Tactics of the Three Arms. 8°. Lond. 1869.
SMITH. P. Ancient History of the East. 12°. N.Y. 1871.
—— Student's Ancient History. 12°. Lond. 1871.
SMITH, R. Payne. Prophecy a Preparation for Christ. 12°. Bost. 1870.
SMITH, Stephen. Doctor in Medicine, and other Papers. 16°. N.Y. 1872.
SMITH, Rev. Thomas. Abridgment of Walker's Dictionary. Sq. 16°. N.Y. 1818.
SMITH, Wm. History of New York. 8°. Albany. 1814.
SMITH, Rev. Wm. Dictionary of the Bible. Ed. by Hackett. v. 3, 4. L. 8°. N.Y. 1870.
—— Dictionary of Greek and Roman Geography. 2 v. 8°. Lond. 1856.
—— Smaller Scripture History. 16°. N.Y. 1871.
—— Student's Gibbon. 12°. N.Y. 1871.
—— and Hall, T. English-Latin Dictionary. R. 8°. N.Y. 1871.
SMITH, Wm. L. American Arguments for British Rights. 8°. Charlestown. 1806.
SMITH, Wm. Prescott. History of Baltimore and Ohio R. R. 8°. Baltimore. 1853.
—— Railway Celebrations of 1857. 12°. N.Y. 1858.
SMITHSONIAN Institution. Annual Report. 8°. Wash. 1871.
—— Contributions to Knowledge. v. 16, 17. 4°. Wash. 1870-1.
—— Miscellaneous Collections. v. 8, 9. 8°. Wash. 1869.
SMYTH, A. Christian Culture in Public Schools; a Lecture. 12°. Bost. 1852.
SMYTH, C. P. Antiquity of Intellectual Man. 12°. Edin. 1868.
—— Equal Surface Projection for Maps of the World. 8°. Edin. 1870.
SMYTH, R. B. Gold Fields of Victoria. R. 8°. Melbourne. 1869.
SNOWE, J. The Rhine; Legends, Traditions, History. 2 v. 8°. Lond. 1839.
SOBIESKI, John, and Stuart, Charles Edward. Lays of the Deer Forest. 2 v. 12°. Edin. 1848.
SOCIABLE (The). 12°. N.Y. n.d.
SOCIÉTÉ Historique de Montreal. Mémoires, etc., relatifs à l'Histoire du Canada. R. 8°. Montreal. 1859.
SOCIÉTÉ Impériale des Antiquaires de la France. Annuaire, 1853. 18°. Paris. n.d.
SOCIÉTÉ Royale des Antiquaires du Nord. *See* ROYAL Society of Northern Antiquaries.
SOCIETY of Arts. Journal, v. 16-18. R. 8°. Lond. 1868-70.
SOCIETY of Engineers. Transactions, 1868. 8°. Lond. 1869.
SOLER, J. El Serrano de las Alpujarras; el Cuadro Misterioso. 16°. N.Y. 1842.
—— Spanish Grammar. 16°. N.Y. 1842.
—— Spanish Guide for Conversation. 16°. N.Y. 1843.
SOMERS, R. Southern States since the War. 8°. Lond. 1871.
SOMERSET, Duke of. Christian Theology and Modern Skepticism. 16°. N.Y. 1872.

SOMERVILLE, Mrs. Physical Geography. 12°. Lond. 1838.

SOMERVILLE, W. C. Letters from an American in Paris on the French Revolution. 8°. Balt. 1822.

SONGS of the Heart. 12°. N.Y. 1872.

SONGS of Scotland. 12°. Lond. n.d.

SONREL, L. The Bottom of the Sea. 16°. Lond. 1870.

—— Same. 16°. N.Y. 1871.

SOPHOCLES. Electra. Translated. 18°. n.p. n.d.

—— Philoctetes. Revised by Blaydes. 8°. Lond. 1870.

—— Tragedies; Oxford translation. (Bohn's ed.) 12°. Lond. 1863.

—— Works. (Greek text and notes by Wunder.) 2 v. 8°. Lond. 1864.

SOPHOCLES, E. A. Greek Lexicon, Roman and Byzantine Periods. R. 8°. Bost. 1870.

SOPWITH, T. Plans and Drawings. 2d ed. 16°. n.p. 1841.

SOREL, A. La Grande Falaise. 12°. Paris. 1872.

SORIN, E. Les Martyrs du Siége de Paris. 12°. Paris. 1872.

SORR, A. de. Jeanne et sa Suite. 12°. Paris. 1870.

SORRENTO Wood Carving. Sq. 12°. Bost. 1870.

SOULÉ, F., Gihon, J. H. and Nisbet, J. Annals of San Francisco. 8°. N.Y. 1855.

SOULE, R. Dictionary of English Synonymes. 12°. Bost. 1871.

SOULIÉ, F. Le Chateau des Pyrenées. 2 v. 12°. Paris. 1865.

—— Le Comte de Toulouse. 12°. Paris. 1870.

—— Les Drames Inconnus. 5 v. 16°. Paris. 1857.

—— Le Lion Amoureux. 12°. Paris. 1870.

—— La Lionne. 12°. Paris. 1863.

—— Les Mémoires du Diable, 3 v. 12°. Paris. 1863–9.

—— Si Jeunesse Savait, si Vieillesse Pouvait. 2 v. 12°. Paris. 1867.

SOUTER's New Ciphering Book, No. 2. 4°. Lond. 1827.

SOUTH, R. Sermons. v. 3–5. 8°. N.Y. 1870–71.

SOUTH CAROLINA Tax Payer's Convention. Proceedings. 8°. Charleston. 1871.

SOUTH CAROLINA Institute. Premium List, 1870. Containing also a Sketch of Charleston. 8°. Charleston. 1870.

SOUTHARD, L. H. Elements of Thorough Bass and Harmony. 12°. Bost. n.d.

SOUTHERN History of the War; Official Reports of Battles. 8°. N.Y. 1864.

SOUTHERN Magazine. (Formerly New Eclectic.) v. 8, 9 for 1871. 8°. Balt. n.d.

SOUTHERN Notes for National Circulation. 12°. Bost. 1860.

SOUTHERN Pacific Railroad. Survey on 32d Parallel. 8°. Cinc. 1856.

SOUTHERN Review. v. 5–9. 8°. Balt. 1869–71.

SOUTHEY, R. Poet's Pilgrimage to Waterloo. 18°. Bost. 1866.

SOUTHGATE, H. Noble Thoughts in Noble Language. 8°. Lond. n.d.

—— What Men have Said about Women. 12°. Lond. 1868.

SOUVENIRS Numismatiques de la Révolution de 1848. 4°. Paris. n.d.

SOUVENIRS d'un Prisonnier de Guerre. 8°. Brussels. 1871.

SPALDING, H. G. Rational Temperance. (PC. 23.) 8°. Bost. n.d.

SPALDING, M. J. D'Aubigné's History of the Great Reformation in Germany and Switzerland Reviewed. 12°. Balt. 1844.

SPALDING, S. J. Spalding Memorial; Edward Spalding and his Descendants. 8°. Bost. 1872.

SPANISH-English Dictionary. R. 8°. No title.

SPANISH Pictures with Pen and Pencil. 4°. Lond. 1870.

SPARKS, W. H. Memories of Fifty Years. 8°. Phil. 1870.

SPAULDING, E. G. History of Legal Tender. 8°. Buff. 1870.

SPEAKER's Commentary. *See* BIBLE, with commentary, ed. by Cook.

SPEAKMAN, F. H. Divisions in the Society of Friends. 18°. Phil. 1869.

SPECIMENS of Fancy Turning. By an Amateur. Sm. 4°. Phil. 1869.

SPECTACLE (Le) de la Nature. 8 v. 16°. Utrecht and Hague. 1733–53.

SPECTACLE de la Nature; or, Nature Display'd. 5th ed. 12°. Lond. 1740.

SPECTATOR. v. 34, 35, in 4 v. and v. 44. f°. Lond. 1861–71.

SPEER, W. Oldest and Newest Empire. China and the U. S. 8°. Hartford. 1870.
SPENCE, J. Lectures on Surgery. 2 v. 8°. Edin. 1871.
SPENCER, Countess. East and West. 12°. Lond. 1871.
SPENCER, C. H. Americanism and other Isms. 8°. New Haven. 1870.
SPENCER, H. Classification of the Sciences. 8°. N.Y. 1870.
—— Education: Intellectual, Moral and Physical. 12°. N.Y. 1872.
—— Essays: Moral, Political and Æsthetic. 12°. N.Y. 1872.
—— First Principles of a New System of Philosophy. 12°. N.Y. 1872.
—— Illustrations of Universal Progress. 12°. N.Y. 1872.
—— Principles of Biology. 2 v. 12°. N.Y. 1872.
—— Principles of Psychology. v. 1. 12°. N.Y. 1871.
—— Recent Discussions. 12°. N.Y. 1871.
—— Social Statistics. 12°. N.Y. 1872.
SPENDER, E. Fjord, Isle and Tor. 12°. Lond. 1870.
SPENSER, E. Faerie Queene. 16°. N.Y. 1871.
SPIELHAGEN, F. Allzeit voran! 3 v. 12°. Berlin. 1872.
—— Auf der Düne. 12°. Berlin. 1866.
—— Deutsche Pioniere. 12°. Berlin. 1871.
—— In Reih' und Glied. 3 v. Berlin. 1868.
—— Vermischte Schriften. 2 v. in 1. 12°. Berlin. 1868.
SPILSBURY, W. H. Lincoln's Inn. 16°. N.Y. 1850.
SPINDLER, C. Der Jude. 4 v. in 2. 16°. Stuttg. 1854.
SPIRIT of Missions. v. 36. 8°. N.Y. 1871.
SPIRITUAL Magazine. New ser., v. 3–6. 8°. Lond. 1868–71.
SPONS' Dictionary of Engineering. Ed. by Byrne. Divisions 1–4. A–F. 4 v. R. 8°. Lond. 1870–1.
SPOONER, S. Guide to Sound Teeth. 16°. N.Y. 1836.
SPOONER, T. Wm. Spooner and Descendants. R. 8°. Cinc. 1871.
SPRINGFIELD, (Mass.) Directory, 1870–71–72. 2 v. 8°. Springfield. 1870–1.
SPRUNER, K. von. Historico-Geographical Hand-Atlas. Ob. f°. Lond. 1861.
SPURGEON, C. Feathers for Arrows. 16°. Lond. 1870.
—— John Ploughman's Talk. 16°. N.Y. 1869.
—— Treasury of David. 2 v. 8°. Lond. 1870–1.
SPUYTEN Duyvel (The) Chronicle. 12°. N.Y. 1856.
SQUIER, E. G. Honduras. 12°. Lond. 1870.
STAB, R. L. Auf Dornigem Pfade. 18°. Berlin. 1869.
STAEL, Mme. de. Corinne. 12°. Paris. 1865.
—— De l'Allemagne. 12°. Paris. 1867.
—— Delphine. 12°. Paris. 1869.
STAFFORD, A. The Female Glory; or, the Life and Death of the Holy Virgin Mary. (Rep. from ed. of 1635.) 16°. Lond. 1869.
STAHL, A. Historische Bilder aus der Alten Welt. 16°. Vienna. 1870.
STAHL, P. J. Les Bonnes Fortunes Parisiennes. 16°. Paris. n.d.
STAHR, A. Agrippina. 8°. Berlin. 1867.
—— Aus der Jugendzeit. 12°. Schwerin. 1870.
—— Cleopatra. 8°. Berlin. 1864.
—— Lessing, sein Leben und Werke. 6th ed. 8°. Berlin. 1869.
—— Tacitus' Geschichte der Regierung von Tiberius. 8°. Berlin. 1871.
—— and Stahr, F. Ein Winter in Rom. 8°. Berl. 1869.
STAHR, Fanny. Nella. 12°. Berlin. 1870.
—— Von Geschlecht zu Geschlecht. 4 v. in 2. 12°. Berlin. 1871.
STAINER, J. A Theory of Harmony founded on the Tempered Scale. 8°. Lond. 1871.
STAMM, A. T. Die Erlösung der Darbenden Menschheit. 12°. Zurich. 1871.
STANDARD Atlas of Classical Geography. 8°. Lond. 1861.
STANDARD Library Cyclopædia. 2 v. 16°. Lond. 1860.
STANHOPE, Earl. History of England, 1701–13. 8°. Lond. 1870.
STANLEY, A. P. Athanasian Creed. 12°. Lond. 1871.
—— The Eastern Church. 4th ed. 8°. Lond. 1869.
—— Essays on Church and State. 8°. Lond. 1870.
—— Lectures on the History of the Church of Scotland. 8°. Lond. 1872.

—— Life and Correspondence of Dr. Arnold. 12°. Bost. 1870.

—— Memorials of Westminster Abbey. 3d ed. 8°. Lond. 1869.

—— National Thanksgiving Sermons. 16°. Lond. 1872.

—— Sinai and Palestine in Connection with their History. 8°. Lond. 1871.

STANLEY, E. History of Birds. 12°. Lond. 1865.

STANLEY, W. O. Memoirs on Remains of Ancient Dwellings in Holyhead Islands. 8°. Lond. 1871.

STAPLES, N. A. Sermons, with Memoir. 16°. Bost. 1870.

STARR, F., Jr. People of Color; a Discourse. 8°. Alb. 1862.

STATEMENT of Facts, etc., on New London as a Naval Station. (PC. 22.) 8°. New London. 1862.

STATISTICAL Society of London. Journal. v. 31–33. 8°. Lond. 1868–70.

STATISTICS of Trade of United Kingdom. Imp. 8°. Lond. 1869.

STAUNTON, H. Chess Player's Hand-book. 16°. Lond. 1868.

—— The Great Schools of England. 12°. Lond. 1869.

STAVELEY, E. F. British Insects. 12°. Lond. 1871.

STEADMAN, E. The Southern Manufacturer. 8°. Gallatin. 1858.

STEARNS, E. J. Afterpiece to the Comedy of Convocation. 16°. Hartford. 1870.

STEARNS, J. G. Inquiry into Freemasonry. 6th ed. 18°. Utica. 1858.

—— Letters on Freemasonry. 18°. Utica. 1860.

STEBBING, T. R. R. Essays on Darwinism. 12°. Lond. 1871.

STEEL, D., Jr. Ship-Master's Assistant. 8th ed. 8°. Lond. 1799.

STEELE, Mrs. E. Memoirs of Mrs. Baddeley. 6 v. 16°. Lond. 1787.

STEELE, J. D. Answers to Questions in Fourteen Weeks' Courses. 12°. N.Y. 1870.

STEELE, R. H. Historical Discourse, 1st Ref. Dutch Church. 8°. New Brunswick. 1867.

STEELE, S. S. Drawing-Room Plays. 12°. Phil. 1865.

STEEN, I. Mental Arithmetic. 18°. Lond. 1846

STEFFENS, A. Arthur Fromm. 4 v. in 2. 12°. Leip. 1871.

—— Ein Wechsel. 3 v. in 1. 12°. Leip. 1869.

STEINMETZ, A. The Gaming Table. 2 v. 8°. Lond. 1870.

STELLE, J. P. American Watchmaker and Jeweler. 12°. N.Y. n.d.

STEMS and Twigs; or Sermon Framework. 2d Ser. 12°. Lond. 1872.

STENHOUSE, Mrs. T. B. H. Exposé of Polygamy in Utah; a Lady's Life among the Mormons. 16°. N.Y. 1872.

STEPHEN, Caroline E. The Service of the Poor. 12°. Lond. 1871.

STEPHEN, Sir G. The Life of Christ. 12°. Lond. 1871.

STEPHEN, J. Lectures on the History of France. 8°. N.Y. n.d.

STEPHEN, L. The Playground of Europe. 12°. Lond. 1871.

STEPHENS, A. H. War between the States. 2 v. 8°. Phil. n.d.

STEPHENS, J. B. Convict Once; a Poem. 16°. Lond. 1871.

STERN, S. Representative Government. 12°. Phil. 1871.

STEVENS, A. H. Dissertation on Inflammation. 8°. Phil. 1811.

STEVENS, G. T. Life as a Physical Phenomenon. 8°. Alb. 1869.

STEVENS, H. Bibliotheca Historica: Library of H. Stevens, Sr. 12°. Bost. 1870.

—— The Cabots. Sq. 18°. Bost. 1870.

—— Historical and Geographical Notes, 1453–1530. 8°. New Haven. 1869.

—— Tehuantepec. 8°. N.Y. 1869.

STEVENS, Wm. Methodist Plans of Sermons. 12°. Lond. 1870.

STEVENS, W. B. (Edr.) The Bow in the Cloud. Sm. 4°. Phil. 1871.

—— Sermon, Obituary of Bishop Boone. 8°. Phil. 1865.

STEVENSON, D. and Scribner, T. T. Indiana's Roll of Honor. 2 v. 8°. Indianapolis. 1864–6.

STEVENSON, T. Light-house Illumination. 2d ed. 8°. Edin. 1871.

STEVENSON, W. F. Lives and Deeds worth Knowing About. 12°. Lond. 1870.

—— Same. 12°. N.Y. 1870.

STEWART, T. G. Bright's Disease. 2d ed. 8°. Edin. 1871.

STICKNEY, M. A. The Stickney Family. 8°. Salem. 1869.

STILES, H. R. History of Brooklyn. v. 2, 3. 8°. Brooklyn. 1869–70.
—— History of Bundling. 12°. Alb. 1871.

STILL, Wm. The Underground Railroad. 8°. Phil. 1872.

STILLÉ, C. J. Historical Development of American Civilization. 8°. New Haven. 1863.
—— Northern Interests and Southern Independence. 8°. Phil. 1863.

STIRLING, J. H. As Regards Protoplasm. 16°. New Haven. 1870.

STITH, Wm. History of Discovery and Settlement of Virginia. 8°. N.Y. 1865.

STÖCKHARDT, A. Chemistry. 12°. Cambr. 1850.

STOCQUELER, J. H. History of the British Army, from 1860. Sm. 4°. Lond. 1871.

STODDARD, A. F. Slavery or Freedom in America. 18°. Glasgow. 1863.

STODDARD, R. H. The Book of the East, and other Poems. 12°. Bost. 1871.

STOFFEL, (Le Colonel Baron). Rapports Militaires Écrits de Berlin, 1866–70. 8°. Paris. 1871.

STOKES, J. Cabinet-maker and Upholsterer's Companion. 12°. Phil. 1869.

STONE, E. M. Memoir of T. A. Tefft. 8°. Providence. 1869.

STONE, J. B. History of Lichfield Cathedral. Sq. 12°. Lond. 1870.

STONE, J. K. Invitation Heeded; Return to Catholic Unity. 12°. N.Y. 1870.

STONE, W. L. Life of Red Jacket. 8°. Alb. 1866.

STONEY, B. B. Strains in Girders. v. 2. 8°. Lond. 1869.

STORCH, A. Die Geheimnissvollen. 2d ed. 4 v. in 2. 8°. Pesth. 1869.
—— Die Katakomben von Wien. 2d ed. 4 v. in 2. 8°. Vienna. 1870.
—— Ein Kind des Volkes. 2d ed. 3 v. in 1. 8°. Pesth. 1869.
—— Mexiko. 5th ed. 4 v. in 2. 8°. Pesth. 1868.

STORER, H. R. Reflex Insanity in Women. 12°. Bost. 1871.

STOREY, W. D. View of St. Anthony Falls. 8°. Minneapolis. 1867.

STORIES from German Writers, with Interlinear Translation. 2d ed. 16°. Lond. 1838.

STORIES from Italian Writers, with Interlinear Translation. 16°. Lond. 1830.

STORMONTH, J. Dictionary of the English Language. 12°. Edin. 1871.

STORY, I. Yarico to Inkle; an Epistle. 12°. Hartford. 1792.

STORY, R. H. Life and Remains of R. Lee, D.D. 3 v. 8°. Lond. 1870.

STORY, W. W. Graffiti d'Italia. 16°. Lond. 1868.
—— Roba di Roma. 6th ed. 8°. Lond. 1871.
—— Roman Lawyer in Jerusalem. 18°. Bost. 1870.

STORY of Nala. (Sanscrit). Ed. by Williams, with Translation by Milman. 8°. Oxford. 1860.

STOUGHTON, J. Ecclesiastical History of England; Church of the Restoration. 2 v. 8°. Lond. 1870.

STOWE, Mrs. H. B. Lady Byron Vindicated. 12°. Bost. 1870.
—— Onkel Tom's Hütte. 12°. Vienna. 1853.

STOWELL, H. The Law of Labor a Law of Love. *See* AM. Tract Soc. Tracts for Young Men.

STOWITS, G. H. History of the 100th Reg. N. Y. S. Volunteers. 12°. Buff. 1870.

STRABO. Geography. Transl. by Hamilton and Falconer. (Bohn's ed.) 3 v. 12°. Lond. 1854.

STRANG, J. Confession and Execution. (PC. 17.) 12°. N.Y. 1827.

STRANGE, T. L. The Bible: Is It the Word of God? 8°. Lond. 1871.
—— The Speaker's Commentary Reviewed. 12°. Lond. 1871.

STRANGE Visitors. 12°. N.Y. 1869.

STRASBOURG! 40 Jours de Bombardement. Par un Réfugié Strasbourgeois. 12°. Neuchatel. 1871.

STRAUSS, D. F. Krieg und Friede; Zwei Briefe an E. Renan nebst dessen Antwort. 12°. Berlin. 1870.
—— Voltaire. 2d ed. 12°. Leip. 1870.

STRECKFUSS, A. Der tolle Hans. 12°. Berlin. n.d.

STREET, A. B. Poems. *See* How's Forest Pictures.

STREET, G. E. Gothic Architecture in Spain. 2d ed. 8°. Lond. 1869.

STREETS (The) and Lanes of a City. 12°. Lond. 1871.
STRICKLAND, Agnes. Lives of the Queens of England. Abridged. 12°. N.Y. 1867.
—— Lives of the Last Four Princesses of the Royal House of Stuart. 12°. N.Y. 1872.
STRICTURES on Prof. McVickar's Pamphlet. (PC. 16.) 8°. N.Y. 1829.
STRODTMANN, A. H. Heine's Leben und Werke. 3 v. 8°. Berlin. 1867–9.
—— Immortellen Heinrich Heine's. 16°. Berlin. 1871.
STRONG, M. M. Territorial Legislation in Wisconsin; an Address. 8°. Madison. 1870.
STRONG, P. R. Awful, and Other Jingles. 12°. N.Y. 1871.
STRONG and Free. 8°. Lond. 1869.
STROUD, W. New Greek Harmony of the Four Gospels. 4°. Lond. 1853.
—— Physical Cause of the Death of Christ. 2d ed. 12°. Lond. 1871.
STRUENSEE, G. von. Erzählungen eines alten Herrn. 2 v. 12°. Breslau. 1860–3.
—— Falkenrode. 4 v. in 2. 12°. Hanover. 1870.
—— Heimathlos. 4 v. in 2. 12°. Breslau. 1867.
—— Krieg und Friede. 4 v. in 2. 12°. Berlin. 1872.
—— Neue Novellen. 12°. Hanover. 1869.
—— Ost und West. 4 v. in 2. 16°. Breslau. 1865.
—— Radowa. 4 v. in 2. 12°. Hanover. 1870.
—— Vor fünfzig Jahren. 3 v. 12°. Breslau. 1859.
—— Zwei gnädige Frauen. 3 v. 12°. Breslau. 1860.
STRUHNNECK, F. W. Herrschaft und Priesterthum. 12°. Berlin. 1871.
STUART, B. The Successful Engineer. 16°. Edin. 1868.
STUART, C. B. Civil and Military Engineers of America. 8°. N.Y. 1871.
STUART, Isaac W. Hartford in the Olden Time. 8°. Hartford. 1853.
STUBBS, Wm. Select Charters and other Illustrations of English History. 12°. Oxford. 1870.
STUCKLE, H. Interoceanic Canals. 8°. N.Y. 1870.
STUDENT and Intellectual Observer. v. 3–5. 8°. 1869–71.
STURGES, E. B. Druggist's Legal Directory. R. 8°. Phil. n.d.
STYFFE, K. Iron and Steel. 8°. Lond. 1869.
SUE, E. La Bonne Aventure. 2 v. in 1. 12°. Paris. 1861.
—— Le Diable Médecin.
1. Adèle Verneuil. 12°. Paris. 1865.
2. La Grande Dame. 12°. Paris. 1866.
3. Clémence Hervé. 12°. Paris. 1866.
—— Les Fils de Famille. 3 v. in 2. 12°. Paris. 1861.
—— Gilbert et Gilberte. 3 v. 12°. Paris. 1860.
—— Les Sept Péchés Capitaux.
1. L'Orgueil. 2 v. in 1. 12°. Paris. 1870.
2. L'Envie; La Colère. 2 v. in 1. 12°. Paris. 1866.
3. La Luxure; La Paresse. 12°. Paris. 1866.
4. L'Avarice; La Gourmandise. 12°. Paris. 1865.
SUETONIUS. Works. Transl. by Thomson and Forester. 12°. Lond. 1855.
SUFFOLK, W. T. Microscopical Manipulation. 16°. Lond. 1870.
SUICIDE d'une Dynastie. 8°. Brussels. 1871.
SULLIVAN, E. Happy England. 8°. Lond. 1871.
—— Protection to Native Industry. 8°. Lond. 1870.
SULLIVAN, G. L. Report on R. R. Route from the Hudson. (PC. 3.) N.Y. 1831.
SULLIVAN, W. Political Class Book. 16°. Bost. 1839.
SUMMERS, J. Rudiments of Chinese. 16°. Lond. 1864.
SUMNER, C. Duel between France and Germany: a Lecture. 8°. N.Y. 1870.
—— The Rebellion; Its Origin and Main-Spring. R. 8°. N.Y. 1861.
—— Works. 4 v. 8°. Bost. 1870–1.
SUMNER, J. B. Apostolical Preaching and Ministerial Duty. 12°. N.Y. 1830.
SUN. July–Dec., 1870; Jan.–Dec., 1871. f°. N.Y. 1870–1.
SUNDAY at Home, for 1870–1. 2 v. R. 8°. Lond. n.d.

SUNDAY Magazine. v. 5–7. 8°. Lond. 1869–71.

SUN Pictures. f°. Lond. 1872.

SURENNE, G. New French Manual. 12°. N.Y. 1869.

SURTEES, R. History of Durham. 4 v. f°. Lond. 1816–40.

SUTPHEN, M. C. Sermon; Obituary of Rev. J. McDowell; with Address. 8°. Phil. 1863.

SUTTON, F. Systematic Hand-book of Volumetric Analysis. 2d ed. 8°. Lond. 1871.

SVITZER, E. Annotationes in Colotomiam. 16°. Copenhagen. 1827.

SWAHILI Tales, with Translation by Steere. 12°. Lond. 1870.

SWAIN, W. P. Injuries and Diseases of the Knee-Joint. 8°. Lond. 1869.

SWAN, W. D. Primary Spelling Book. 18°. Phil. 1851.

—— Spelling Book. 16°. Phil. 1853.

SWAN Point Cemetery. Charter, By-Laws, etc. 8°. Providence. 1869.

SWAYNE, G. C. Herodotus. 16°. Phil. 1870.

SWEETMAN, W. The Daughters of the King, and other Poems. 12°. Lond. 1871.

SWEET, J. B. Memoir of H. Hoare. 8°. Lond. 1869.

SWETCHINE, Mme. Sophie de. Writings. 16°. Bost. 1869.

SWIFTIANA. 2 v. 16°. Dublin. n.d.

SWINBURNE, A. C. Songs before Sunrise. 12°. Bost. 1871.

—— Same. 12°. Lond. 1871.

SWINDELL, J. G. Wells and Pumps. 16°. Lond. n.d.

SWINTON, W. History of the 7th Regiment. 8°. N.Y. 1870.

—— The "Times" Review of McClellan. 8°. N.Y. 1864.

SWOOPE, H. B. Literary Character of the Bible; a Lecture. 8°. Phil. 1867.

SYBEL, H. von. History of the French Revolution. v. 3, 4. 8°. Lond. 1869.

SYED Ahmed Khan Bahador. Essays on the Life of Mohammed. 8°. Lond. 1870.

SYLVESTER, J. J. Laws of Verse. 12°. Lond. 1870.

SYNOPTICAL Table of Egyptian and Sacred History. R. 8°. No title.

SYPHER, J. R., and Apgar, E. A. History of New Jersey. 12°. Phil. 1870.

SYRACUSE and Onondaga Co. Directory, 1870–1, '71–2. 2 v. 8°. Syracuse. 1870–1.

SYRUS, P. Sententiæ. *See* PHÆDRUS; Fabulæ. (Deuxponts, 1784.)

SZAJNOCHA, C. Le Chateau de Zolkiew. 12°. Paris. 1870.

TABLAS de Cambio. (Manuscript). 4°. No title.

TABLEAU Historique de la Guerre Franco-Allemande. 8°. Berlin. 1871.

TABLES Astronomiques, méridien de Paris. v. 1. 4°. No title.

TABLES of Discount and Interest, $1. to $1.000. Ob. 8°. Portland. 1825.

TACITUS. Annals. Books 1, 2. Transl. by Beesly. 8°. Lond. 1870.

—— Annals; Latin, with Commentary by Frost. 8°. Lond. 1872.

TAINE, H. De l'Intelligence. 2 v. 8°. Paris. 1870.

—— Notes sur l'Angleterre. 12°. Paris. 1872.

—— Philosophie de l'Art en Grèce. 16°. Paris. 1869.

—— Philosophie de l'Art dans les Pays-Bas. 16°. Paris. 1869.

—— Un Séjour en France de 1792 à 1795. Traduit de l'Anglais. 12°. Paris. 1872.

—— Du Suffrage Universel et de la Manière de Voter. 12°. Paris. 1872.

—— Art in Greece. 12°. N.Y. 1871.

—— Art in the Netherlands. 12°. N.Y. 1870.

—— History of English Literature. Tr. by H. Van Laun. 2 v. 8°. N.Y. 1871.

—— Intelligence. Transl. by Haye. 2 v. 8°. Lond. 1871.

—— Same. 8°. N.Y. 1871.

—— Selections; edited by H. Van Laun. 16°. Lond. 1869.

TALBOT, G. F. Analysis of the Organization of the Prussian Army. 8°. Lond. 1871.

TALKS with a Child on the Beatitudes. 18°. Phil. 1870.

TALKS with a Philosopher. 16°. Phil. 1871.

TALLEYRAND, C. M. Commerce of the U. S. with Europe. 8°. Bost. 1809.

TALMAGE, T. D. W. Abominations of Modern Society. 12°. N.Y. 1872.

—— Crumbs Swept Up. 12°. Phil. 1871.

—— The Evil Beast; a Sermon. 16°. N.Y. 1871.

—— Sermons. 12°. N.Y. 1872.

TANDON, M. The World of the Sea. Tr. by Hart. L. 8°. Lond. n.d.

TANNER, H. S. American Traveler. 3d ed. 24°. Phil. 1837.

TANNER, J. Practical Midwifery and Obstetrics. 16°. Lond. 1871.

TANNER, T. P. H. Clinical Medicine. 2d ed. 16°. Lond. 1869.

—— Practice of Medicine. 6th ed. 2 v. 8°. Lond. 1869.

TAPPAN, Cora L. V. Hesperia. 12°. n.p. 1871.

TAPPAN, H. P. Growth of Cities; a Discourse. 8°. N.Y. 1855.

TAPPAN, L. Life of A. Tappan. 12°. N.Y. 1870.

TARDY, Mrs. M. T. Living Female Writers of the South. 8°. Phil. 1871.

—— Southland Writers. 2 v. 8°. Phil. 1870.

TARN, E. W. Science of Building. 8°. Lond. 1870.

TARR, A. D. American Reader. 12°. Phil. 1858.

TARVER, J. C. Dictionnaire des Verbes Français. 8°. Lond. 1821.

TASTU, Mme. A. Éducation Maternelle. f°. Paris. 1836.

TATE, I. Outlines of Experimental Chemistry. 16°. Lond. 1850.

TATE, W. Counting House Guide: Part 1. 16°. Lond. 1849.

TAYLER, C. B. Memorials of English Martyrs. 12°. Bost. n.d.

TAYLOR, A. S. Medical Jurisprudence. 8°. Phil. 1845.

TAYLOR, B. Japan in our Days. 12°. N.Y. 1872.

—— The Masque of the Gods. 16°. Bost. 1872.

—— Travels in Arabia. 12°. N.Y. 1872.

TAYLOR, C. H. Funeral Oration on S. A. Douglas. 8°. Alton. 1861.

TAYLOR, G. H. Diseases of Women. 12°. Phil. 1871.

—— Illustrated Sketch of the Movement Cure. 16°. N.Y. 1866.

TAYLOR, G. L. Autobiography. v. 1. 4°. Lond. 1870.

TAYLOR, Jeremy. Poems. *See* FULLER Worthies' Library; Miscellanies.

—— Readings for Every Day in Lent. 18°. N.Y. 1868.

TAYLOR, J. O. H. Chess Brilliants. 12°. Norwich, Eng. 1869.

TAYLOR, Meadows. Student's Manual of the History of India. 12°. Lond. 1870.

TAYLOR, S. H. Classical Study. 12°. Andover. 1870.

TAYLOR, Wm. Life of C. C. Mackintosh. 12°. Edin. 1831.

TAYLOR, W. C. History of the Civil Wars of England. 2 v. 18°. Edin. 1831.

—— Natural History of Society. 2 v. 12°. Lond. 1840.

TAYLOR, W. H. The Book of Travels of a Doctor of Physic. 12°. Phil. 1871.

TEACHINGS from the Church's Year. 12°. Oxford. 1870.

TECHNOLOGIST. v. 1, 2. f°. N.Y. 1870–71.

TEGETMEIER, W. B. Pigeons. L. 8°. Lond. '68.

TEMME, J. D. H. Bankrott. 2 v. in 1. 12°. Berlin. n.d.

—— Die Erbgrafen. 4 v. in 2. 12°. Leip. 1869.

—— Die Frau des Rebellen. 12°. Leip. 1870.

—— Das Recht auf Erden. 12°. Leip 1871.

—— Ein Verworfener. 12°. Berlin. n.d.

TEMPLE Bar. v. 25–33. 8°. Lond. 1869–71.

TENCH, W. Narrative of Expedition to Botany Bay. 16°. N.Y. 1789.

TENNANT, C. People's Blue Book: Taxation As It Is, and As It Ought to Be. 12°. Lond. 1872.

TENNESSEE (State of). Acts, 1871. 8°. Nashville. 1871.

—— Catalogue of the General and Law Library. 8°. Nashville. 1871.

—— House Journal of the First Session of the Thirty-seventh General Assembly. 8°. Nashville. 1871.

—— Senate Journal of the First Session of the Thirty-seventh General Assembly. 8°. Nashville. 1871.

TENNYSON, A. The Holy Grail, and other Poems. 12°. Bost. 1870.

—— The Last Tournament. 16°. Bost. 1872.

—— Poems. 8°. N.Y. 1870.

TÉNOT, E. Campagnes des Armées de l'Empire en 1870. 12°. Paris. 1872.
—— Paris in 1851. 12°. N.Y. 1870.
TERENCE and Phædrus. Works, transl. (Bohn's ed.) 12°. Lond. 1867.
TERHUNE, Mrs. M. V. Common Sense in Housekeeping. 8°. N.Y. 1871.
TERNAUX, M. Histoire de la Terreur. 7 v. 8°. Paris. 1867–9.
TERRE HAUTE Directory, 1871–2. 8°. Terre Haute. 1871.
TERRESTRIAL Magnetism. 8°. Edin. 1871.
TERTULLIAN. Writings. v. 3. *See* ANTE-NICENE Christian Library. v. 18.
TESTAMENTS of the Twelve Patriarchs. *See* ANTE-NICENE Christian Library. v. 22.
TESTIMONY on Abuses in Cambridge Jail. 8°. Bost. 1860.
TESTIMONY of Christ's Second Appearing. Exemplified by the Church of Christ. 8°. Alb. 1869.
TESTUT, O. L'Internationale. 12°. Paris. 1871.
TEXAS Almanac, 1871. 12°. Galveston. 1871.
TEXT-BOOK of Freemasonry. 16°. Phil. n.d.
TEXT-BOOK for the Republican Campaign. 16°. N.Y. 1868.
THACKERAY, W. M. Miscellanies. 2 v. 12°. Bost. 1871.
THARAU, H. Novellen. 4 v. in 2. 12°. Bielefeld. 1871.
THAYER, W. M. Communion Wine. 12°. N.Y. 1869.
THAXTER, Celia. Poems. 18°. N.Y. 1872.
THÉÂTRE de la Foire. v. 5. 16°. Paris. 1724.
THEOCRITUS, Bion and Moschus. Idylls and the War Songs of Tyrtaeus. Transl. (Bohn's ed.) 12°. Lond. 1864.
THEOLOGICAL REVIEW. v. 8. 8°. Lond. 1871.
THEOPHRASTUS. Characters from, by R. C. Jebb. 16°. Lond. 1870.
THESES nec non Disputatio ex Universa Vinosophia. 18°. n.p. 1860.
THIELE, J. M. Thorwaldsen and his Works. 4 v. 4°. N.Y. 1869.
THIERS, L. A. Déposition de Monsieur Thiers sur le 18 Mars, 1871. 16°. Paris. 1872.
THIN, G. The Tientsin Massacre. 16°. Edin. 1870.
THINGS New and Old Relative to Life. (Sermons.) By T. H. 12°. Lond. n.d.
THOLUCK, A. Commentary on the Sermon of the Mount. 8°. Edin. 1869.
—— Hours of Christian Devotion. 12°. Edin. 1870.
THOM'S Irish Almanac and Directory for 1870. 8°. Dublin. 1870.
THOMAS, D. Homiletic Commentary on Acts. 8°. Lond. 1870.
THOMAS, E. Chronicles of Pathan Kings of Delhi. 8°. Lond. 1871.
THOMAS, J. Lippincott's Dictionary of Biography. 2 v. R. 8°. Phil. 1870.
THOMAS, J., Jr. Cottage Architecture. 8°. N.Y. 1855.
—— Illustrated Annual Register of Rural Affairs for 1872. 12°. Alb. 1872.
THOMAS, J. S. The Case of Gen. Fremont. 8°. St. Louis. 1862.
THOMAS, W. C. Mural Decoration. 8°. Lond. n.d.
THOMAS, Wm. The Pilgrim; a Dialogue on Henry VIII. Ed. by Froude. 8°. Lond. 1861.
THOMAS Aquinas (St.). Catena Aurea; Commentary on the Four Gospels. Collected out of the Works of the Fathers. 8 v. 8°. Lond. 1864–5.
THOMPSON, E. H. Life of St. Stanislas Kostka. 12°. Phil. 1870.
THOMPSON, H. M. Sin and Penalty; or, Future Punishment. 2d ed. 16°. Milwaukee. 1871.
THOMPSON, H. P. and Messler, A. Discourses, Funeral of Rev. A. Van Liew. 8°. New Brunswick. 1869.
THOMPSON, Sir Henry. Practical Lithotomy and Lithotrity. 2d ed. 8°. Lond. 1871.
THOMPSON, J. History of Leicester in the 18th Century. 8°. Leicester. 1871.
THOMPSON, J. P. Home Worship. R. 8°. Bost. n.d.
—— Man in Genesis and in Geology. 12°. N.Y. 1870.
—— Thanksgiving Sermon, Nov. 27, 1862. 8°. N.Y. 1863.
—— Theology of Christ. 12°. N.Y. 1870.
THOMPSON, M. L. P. Discourse, Obituary of Mrs. Hopkins. 8°. Buff. 1858.
THOMSON, Mrs. A. T. Life of Villiers, Duke of Buckingham. 3 v. 12°. Lond. 1860.

THOMSON, E. Our Oriental Missions. 2 v. 16°. Cinc. 1870.
THOMSON, G. The Discovery of a New World of Being. 12°. Lond. 1871.
THOMSON, J. The Seasons. 32°. N.Y. 1812.
THOMSON, T. Organic Chemistry; Vegetables. L. 8°. Lond. 1838.
THOMSONBY'S Cricketers in Council. 16°. Lond. 1871.
THORNBURY, G. W. Monarchs of the Main. (Buccaneers.) 3 v. in 1. 8°. Lond. 1855.
THORNTON, W. T. Labour. 8°. Lond. 1869.
THOROWGOOD, J. C. Notes on Asthma. 12°. Lond. 1870.
THOUGHTS about the City of St. Louis. 8°. St. Louis. 1854.
THOUGHTS on Annexation of Texas. 8°. N.Y. 1844.
THOUGHTS on the Moral Physiology and Pathology of Liquor Drinking. 8°. Bost. 1862.
THREE Letters to the Cornhill Magazine on Public School Education, by Paterfamilias. 16°. Lond. 1861.
THRILLING Stories of the Forest and Frontier. 12°. Phil. 1869.
THUCYDIDES. Analysis and Summary. Ed. by Wheeler. 12°. Lond. 1855.
—— Peloponnesian War. Transl. by Dale. 2 v. 12°. Lond. 1868.
THURLOW, T. J. H. Trades' Unions Abroad. 8°. Lond. 1870.
THURSTON, C. M. Thurston and Pitman Genealogies. 8°. N.Y. 1865–8.
TIARKS, J. G. German Grammar. 16°. Bost. 1834.
TIBULLUS, Albius. Elegies. Transl. into English Verse by Cranstoun. 12°. Edin. 1872.
TIECK, L. Sämmtliche Werke. R. 8°. Paris. 1841.
TILESTON, Edward. Hand-book of the Administration of the U. S. 16°. Bost. 1871.
TILLOTSON, J. Palestine, its Holy Sites and Sacred Story. 8°. Lond. n.d.
TILT, E. J. Change of Life, in Health and Disease. 8°. Phil. 1871.
TILTON, T. Sanctum Sanctorum. 12°. N.Y. 1870.
—— Golden Age Tracts. 18°. N.Y. 1871.
TILTON'S Journal of Horticulture. v. 5–9. 8°. Bost. 1869–71.
TIMBS, J. Abbeys, Castles, and Ancient Halls of England and Wales. 12°. Lond. n.d.
—— Anecdote Lives of Hogarth, Reynolds, Gainsborough, Fusell, Lawrence and Turner 12°. Lond. 1865.
—— Anecdote Biography of Pitt and Burke. 12°. Lond. 1862.
—— Eccentricities of the Animal Creation. 12°. Bost. 1869.
—— Lady Bountiful's Legacy. 12°. Lond. 1868
—— Nooks and Corners of English Life. 12°. N.Y. 1863.
—— Notabilia; or, Curious and Amusing Facts. 12°. Lond. 1872.
—— Year Book of Facts. 16°. Lond. 1871.
—— Same. 16°. Lond. 1872.
TIMES (London). Daily, 1869–71. 12 v. Atlas f°. Lond. 1869–71.
—— Index to the Times by Palmer, from Oct. 1, 1867 to Dec. 30, 1871. 17 v. Sm. 4°. Lond. 1867–72.
TIMLOW, H. R. The Light of the House. (Mrs. E. P. Adams.) 4°. N.Y. 1867.
TINGRY, P. F. Painter's and Colorman's Guide. 12°. Phil. 1831.
TINSLEY'S Magazine. v. 3–9. 8°. Lond. 1869–71.
TISCHENDORF, C. When were our Gospels Written? 3d ed. 8°. Lond. 1867.
TISSANDIER, G. En Ballon! pendant le Siége de Paris. 12°. Paris. 1871.
—— La Houille. 12°. Paris. 1869.
—— Wonders of Water. 12°. N.Y. 1871.
TITE, W. Antiquities found at the New Exchange. 8°. Lond. 1848.
TO SAN FRANCISCO and Back. 16°. Lond. n.d.
TOBIN, J. The Honeymoon; a Play. 16°. N.Y. n.d.
TODD, J. Congregationalism; a Sermon. 8°. Phil. 1837.
—— Mountain Flowers. 16°. Northampton. 1869.
—— Student's Manual. 16°. Northampton. 1842.
—— Sunset Land. 16°. Bost. 1870.
TODD, R. B. and others. Anatomy and Physiology of Man. Part 2 of v. 1. 8°. Lond. 1871.
TODD, S. E. Apple Culturist. 12°. N.Y. 1871.
—— Young Farmer's Manual. 2 v. 12°. N.Y. 1870.

TOLLEMACH, W. A. Spanish Towns and Spanish Pictures. L. 8°. Lond. 1870.

TOLSTOI, A. R. Death of Ivan the Terrible. 16°. Lond. 1869.

TOMKINS, F. J. and Jencken, H. D. Modern Roman Law. 8°. Lond. 1870.

TOMLINSON, C. Cyclopædia of Useful Arts. 3 v. R. 8°. Lond. 1868.

—— Pneumatics. 18°. Lond. 1848.

TOMLINSON, W. Landscape Paintings in Oil Colors. 12°. Lond. n.d.

TONDINI, C. The Pope of Rome and the Popes of the Oriental Orthodox Church. 12°. Lond. 1871.

TOPIN, M. The Man with the Iron Mask. 12°. Lond. 1870.

TORRENS, R. Letter to Lord Melbourne. 2d ed. 8°. Lond. 1837.

TORRENS, W. M. Empire in Asia; How we came by it. 8°. Lond. 1872.

TORREY, J., and others. Report on N.Y. and Phila. Gases. (PC. 16.) 16°. N.Y. 1851.

TOTTEN, B. J. Naval Text Book and Dictionary. 12°. N.Y. 1862.

TOURRIER, J. French as it is Spoken. 12th ed. 16°. Lond. n.d.

TOVEY, Chas. Champagne, its History, Properties and Manufactures. 16°. Lond. 1870.

TOWER, D. B., and Tweed, B. F. Grammar of Composition. 12°. N.Y. 1856.

TOWLE, G. M. American Society. 2 v. 12°. Lond. 1870.

TOWNDROW, T. Guide to Short Hand. 16°. Bost. 1837.

—— Guide to Stenography. 2d ed. 16°. New Haven. 1832.

TOWNSEND, C. Compendium of Commercial Law. 8°. Bost. 1872.

TOWNSEND, C. H. Religious Opinions. 12°. Lond. 1869.

TOWNSEND, G. A. New World compared with Old. 8°. Hartford. 1870.

TOWNSEND, G. H. Every-day Book of Modern Literature. 12°. Lond. n.d.

TOWNSEND, L. T. God-Man. 16°. Bost. 1872.

—— Sword and Garment. 16°. Bost. 1871.

TOWNSHEND, F. T. Cruise in Greek Waters. 8°. Lond. 1870.

TOWRY, M. H. Clanship and the Clans. 18°. Edin. n.d.

TRACT Society of the Methodist Episc. Church. 8°. N.Y. n.d.

TRACY, C., and Helmer, C. D. Oration and Poem to Phi Beta Kappa. 8°. New Haven. 1862.

TRACY, W. Hand-book of Law. 8°. N.Y. 1871.

TRADE Circular Annual for 1871. R. 8°. N.Y. 1871.

TRAFTON, Adeline. An American Girl Abroad. 16°. Bost. 1872.

TRALL, R. T. Alcoholic Controversy. 12°. N.Y. 1856.

—— Sexual Physiology. 12°. N.Y. 1870.

TRANSATLANTIC Magazine. v. 3, 4. 8°. Phil. 1871.

TREDGOLD, T. Elementary Carpentry. 5th ed. 4°. Lond. 1870.

—— Elementary Carpentry. Revised by Hurst. 12°. Lond. 1871.

TREES, Plants and Flowers. 16°. Phil. 1870.

TREGELLES, S. P. Heads of Hebrew Grammar. 16°. Lond. n.d.

TREITSCHKE, H. Von. Fire Test of the North German Confederation. Tr. by Hyndman. 16°. Lond. 1871.

—— What we Demand from France. 12°. Lond. 1870.

TRENCH, R. C. Deficiencies in English Dictionaries. 8°. Lond. 1860.

—— English, Past and Present. 7th ed. 12°. N.Y. 1871.

—— Notes on the Miracles. 8°. N.Y. 1872.

—— Notes on the Parables of Our Lord. 8°. N.Y. 1872.

—— On the Study of Words. 25th ed. 16°. N.Y. n.d.

—— Synonyms of the New Testament. 7th ed. 8°. Lond. 1871.

TREVELYAN, G. O. The Competition Wallah. 2d ed. 12°. Lond. 1866.

—— Ladies in Parliament, and Other Pieces. 12°. Camb. (Eng.) 1869.

TRIBUNE Almanac, 1869–71. 12°. N.Y. 1869–71.

TRIBUNE's Exhibit of Industry of Minneapolis and St. Anthony. 8°. Minneapolis. 1871.

TRISTRAM, H. B. Topography of the Holy Land. 12°. Lond. n.d.

TROCHU (Le Général.) L'Armée Française en 1867. 20th ed. 8°. Paris. 1870.

TROLLOPE, A. Cæsar. 16° Edin. 1870.

—— Same. 16°. Phil. 1870.

TROLLOPE, Mrs. F. Domestic Manners of the Americans. 8°. Lond. 1832.
TROLTSCH, A. von. Diseases of the Ear. 8°. N.Y. 1869.
TRONSON, L. Examination of Conscience. Ed. by Shipley. 12°. Lond. 1870.
TROTTER, J. P., and others. Flowers from Fatherland. 16°. Edin. 1870.
TROWBRIDGE, J. T. The Vagabonds, and Other Poems. 12°. Bost. 1869.
—— Same. 4°. N.Y. 1868.
TROWBRIDGE, Mrs. L. Excelsior Cook Book. 12°. N.Y. 1870.
TROY, West Troy and Cohoes Directory, 1870. 8°. Troy. 1870.
TROY, Lansingburgh, West Troy, Cohoes and Green Island Directory, 1871. 8°. Troy. n.d.
TRUCHY, J. L'Armeé Française en 1871. *See* Schoelcher, E., La Nouvelle Armée. 8°. Paris. 1871.
TRUE Picture of a Modern Whig Reviv'd. 16°. Lond. 1707.
TRUE Statement of the Public School Meetings in Hoboken, Feb. 1854. 8°. N.Y. 1854.
TRUE Story of Mrs. Shakspeare's Life. 12°. Bost. 1870.
TRURAN, W. Iron Manufacture of Great Britain. 18°. N.Y. 1867.
TSCHAGGENY, B. Commerce de la France avec l'Europe. 8°. Paris. 1817.
TUCKER, Wm. Family Dyer and Scourer. 16°. Phil. 1831.
TUCKERMAN, H. T. Life of John P. Kennedy. 12°. N.Y. 1871.
TUKE, T. Holy Eucharist and Popish Breaden God. *See* FULLER Worthies' Miscellanies.
TUNNER, P. A. Roll Turning for the Manufacture of Iron, with Atlas of Plates. 8°. and f°. N.Y. 1869.
TUPPER, M. F. A Creed, etcetera. 8°. Lond. 1870.
—— Poems. 16°. N.Y. n.d.
TURF, Field and Farm. v. 13. July–Dec. 1871. f°. N.Y. 1871.
TURGENJEW, I. Das Adelige Nest; Drei Portraits. 12°. Mitau. 1870.
—— Drei Novellen. 12°. Vienna. 1872.
—— Visionen; Helene. 12°. Mitau. 1871.
TURNER, C. E. Our Great Writers. 2 v. in 1. 8°. St. Petersburg. 1864.
TURNER, D. W. Analysis of the History of Germany. 2d ed. 16°. Lond. 1867.
TURNER, Eliza S. Out-of-Door Rhymes. 16°. Bost. 1872.
TURRELL, H. J. Manual of Logic. 16°. Lond. 1870.
TUSON, R. V. Veterinary Pharmacopœia. 12°. Lond. 1869.
TUTTLE, H. Arcana of Spiritualism. 12°. Bost. 1871.
TWELLS, L. Demoniacks in the New Testament. 8°. Lond. 1737.
TWELVE (The) Stars of the Republic: Our Nation's Gift-Book to her Young Citizens. 8°. N.Y. 1850.
TWINING, T. Science for the People. 8°. Lond. 1870.
TWO Consciences; or, Conscience the Moral Law and Conscience the Witness. 12°. Phil. 1870.
TWO Months in Palestine. 12°. Lond. 1870.
TWOMBLY, A. S. Merry Maple Leaves. Sm. 4°. N.Y. 1872.
TYAS, R. The Weather Glass. 16°. Lond. n.d.
—— Companion to the Weather Glass. 16°. Lond. n.d.
TYERMAN, L. Life and Times of John Wesley. 3 v. 8°. Lond. 1870–1.
—— Same. 3. v. 8°. N.Y. 1871–2.
TYLOR, E. B. Primitive Culture. 2 v. 8°. Lond. 1871.
TYNDALL, J. Diamagnetism and Magne-Crystallic Action. 8°. Lond. 1870.
—— Faraday as a Discoverer. 12°. Lond. 1870.
—— Fragments of Science for Unscientific People. 12°. Lond. 1871.
—— Same. 12°. N.Y. 1871.
—— Hours of Exercise in the Alps. 12°. Lond. 1871.
—— Same. 12°. N.Y. 1871.
—— Imagination in Science. 8°. Lond. 1870.
—— Light and Electricity. 12°. N.Y. 1871.
—— Notes on Electricity. 12°. Lond. 1870.
—— Notes on Light. 12°. Lond. 1870.
TYNG, S. H. Memoir of Rev. G. T. Bedell. 12°. Phil. 1826.
TYPICAL Selections from English Authors. 16°. Oxford. 1869.
TYSON, J. The Cell Doctrine. 12°. Phil. 1870.
TYTLER, A. F. Elements of General History. Revised by Robbins. 2d ed. 12°. Hartford. 1821.

TYTLER, Sarah, and Thomson, J. L. Songstresses of Scotland. 2 v. 12°. Lond. 1871.

"UBIQUE" (Pseudonym). *See* GILLMORE, P.

UEBER Land und Meer. v. 21-25. 4°. Stuttg. 1869-71.

UEBERWEG, F. History of Philosophy. v. 1; Ancient and Mediaeval Philosophy. 8°. N.Y. 1872.

—— System of Logic and History of Logical Doctrines 8°. Lond. 1871.

UCHARD, M. La Comtesse Diane. 12°. Paris. 1864.

—— Raymond. 12°. Paris. 1865.

ULBACH, L. La Cocarde Blanche. 12°. Paris. 1868.

—— La Voix du Sang. 12°. Paris. 1858.

ULE, O. Aus der Natur. Essays. 2 v. 12°. Leip. 1871.

ULLIAC-Trémadeure, Mlle. S. Étienne et Valentin. 12°. Paris. 1868.

ULLOA, A. de. Voyage to South America. 2 v. 8°. Lond. 1758.

UNION College; Inauguration of Prof. Aiken. 8°. Alb. 1870.

UNION Copper Land and Mining Co. Statement of Property. (PC. 20.) 8°. Bost. 1863.

UNION des Églises Évangéliques de France. 8me Synode. 1862. 8°. Paris. 1862.

UNION League Club. Proceedings, Death of Gov. Andrew. (PC. 20.) 8°. N.Y. 1867.

UNION Prayer-Book. 12°. N.Y. 1871.

UNION Questions. v. 1. Life of Christ. 24°. Phil. n.d.

—— Same, 1831.

UNITARIAN National Conference. Fourth Meeting. 8°. Bost. 1870.

UNITED Mines of Zacatecas. Prospectus. (PC. 10.) S. 4°. N.Y. n.d.

UNITED STATES: Public Documents (alphabeted by subjects), viz. :

—— Agriculture. Report of Commissioner, 1867, 1868, 1870. 3 v. 8°. Wash. 1868-70.

—— Army. Act Establishing Rules and Articles of War. 18°. N.Y. 1812.

—— Same. Infantry Tactics. 2d ed. 8°. Wash. 1825.

—— Same. General Regulations for the Army. 8°. Wash. 1825.

—— Astronomical and Meteorological Observations, 1867-9. 3 v. 4°. Wash. 1870-2.

—— Banks. Report of the Secretary of the Treasury, Jan. 1, 1850. 8°. Wash. 1850.

—— Same. National Bank Act. With Amendments. 8°. N.Y. 1870.

—— British America. Relations with N. W. British America. 8°. Wash. 1862.

—— Catacazy, Constantine. Correspondence in Relation to. 8°. Wash. n.d.

—— Census. Ninth Census; Statistics of Population. 4°. Wash. 1871.

—— Central American Affairs, and the Enlistment Question. Documents. 8°. Wash. 1856.

—— Coast Survey. Annual Reports of Superintendent, 1865-66-67 and 68. 4 v. 4°. Wash. 1867-71.

—— Same. Harbor Charts. Atl. f°. n.p. n.d.

—— Same. Map of Alaska. 24x33 in. Wash. 1870.

—— Commerce and Navigation. Annual Report of Bureau of Statistics, 1867-69 and '70. 3 v. 8°. Wash. 1869-71

—— Commercial Relations. Annual Reports, Sept. 30, 1869 and 1870. 2 v. 8°. Wash. 1871.

—— Congressional Directory of 41st Congress. 8°. Wash. 1870.

—— Congressional Documents, 1866-7, 67-8, 68-9. 73 v. 8°. Wash. 1867-9.

—— Consuls. Opinion of Attorney-General on Authority of. (PC. 2.) 8°. Wash. 1855.

—— Defences of Washington. 4°. Wash. 1871.

—— Diplomatic Correspondence. (*See* FOREIGN AFFAIRS below.)

—— Education. Circular of Information, July, 1871. 8°. Wash. 1871.

—— Same. Report of Commissioner for 1870-1. 2 v. 8°. Wash. 1870-1.

—— Engineers. Annual Report of Chief for 1868-9-70. 3 v. 8°. Wash. v.d.

—— Same. Papers on Practical Engineering, No. 9. Limes, Hydraulic Cements and Mortars. By Q. A. Gillmore. 8°. N.Y. 1872.

—— Same. Professional Papers, No. 19. Report on Béton Aggloméré, by Q. A. Gillmore. 8°. Wash. 1871.

—— Enlistments. *See* above. Central America.

—— Fessenden. Addresses on Death of Mr. Fessenden. L. 8°. Wash. 1870.

—— Finances. Reports for 1869–70–71. 3 v. 8°. Wash. 1869–71.

—— Foreign Affairs. Papers Relating to; for 1868, 1870, and 1871. 4 v. 8°. Wash. 1869–71.

—— Same. Senate Report on the Foreign Service. (PC. 4.) 8°. Wash. 1868.

—— Geological Exploration of 40th Parallel. By King. v. 3. Mining Industry, with Atlas of Plates. v. 5, Botany. 3 v. 8°. and Obl. f°. Wash. 1870–1.

—— Immigration. Special Report on. 8°. Wash. 1871.

—— Land Office. Reports for 1866–7–8. 3 v. 8°. Wash. 1866–8.

—— Library of Congress. Catalogue of Additions, 1869–70. 2 v. Imp. 8°. Wash. 1870–1.

—— Same. Catalogue. (Index of Subjects.) 2 v. Imp. 8°. Wash. 1869.

—— Lincoln. Assassination of Mr. Lincoln. 4°. Wash. 1867.

—— Merchant Vessels of the U. S.; List of, June 30, 1870. 8°. Wash. 1871.

—— Message and Documents (abridged). 2d Sess., 41st Cong. 8°. Wash. 1870.

—— Message and Documents (abridged). 3d Sess., 41st Cong. 8°. Wash. 1871.

—— Mineral Resources. Raymond's Reports for 1869–70. 2 v. 8°. Wash. 1869–70.

—— Mint, Philadelphia. Annual Report. (PC. 16.) 8°. Phil. 1860.

—— Money Order System. 8°. Wash. 1864.

—— Naval Observatory. Observations during 1868. 4°. Wash. 1871.

—— Navy. Regulations, 1865. 12°. Wash. 1865.

—— Same. 12°. Wash. 1870.

—— Navy. Register. 8°. Wash. 1870.

—— Navy. Report of Secretary, and of Postmaster General for 1870. 8°. Wash. 1870.

—— Panama Congress. Message, March 17, 1826.

—— Paris Exhibition of 1867. Reports of Commissioners. Ed. by W. P Blake. 6 v. 8°. Wash. 1870.

v. 1.—Containing:
1. Introduction by Beckwith.
2. General Survey of the Exhibition.
3. Report on Fine Arts by Leslie.
4. Extracts from Committee's Report on Weights and Measures.
5. Bibliography of the Exposition.
6. General Alphabetical Index to the Reports.

v. 2.—Containing:
1. Production of Iron and Steel, by Hewitt.
2. Precious Metals, by Blake.
3. Progress ot Industrial Chemistry

v. 3.—Containing:
1. Barnard's Report on Machinery, etc.

v. 4.—Containing:
1. Telegraphy, by Morse.
2. Steam Engineering, by Auchincloss.
3. Engineering and Public Works, by Blake.
4. Béton Coignet, by Beckwith.
5. Asphalt and Bitumen, by Beckwith.
6. Buildings and Building Materials, by Bowen.
7. Mining and Ores, by D'Aligny and others.

v. 5.—Containing:
1. Quantities of Cereals produced Compared, by Rugby.
2. Cereal Products Exhibited, by Hazard.
3. Preparation of Food, by Johnston.
4. Beet Root Sugar and Alcohol, by D'Aligny.
5. Culture of the Vine, etc., by Wilder and others.
6. School Houses, by Freese.
7. Munitions of War, by Norton and Valentine.
8. Instruments of Medicine, Surgery, etc., by Evans.
9. Musical Instruments, by Stevens.

v. 6.—Containing:
1. Wool and Manufactures of Wool, by Mudge and Hayse.
2. Cotton, by Mudge and Nourse.
3. Silk and Silk Manufactures, by Cowdin.
4. Clothing and Woven Fabrics, by Stevens.
5. Education, by Hoyt.
6. List of the Reports.

—— Patents. Report, 1859, Mechanics. 2 v. 8°. Wash. 1860.
—— Same. Report, 1867. 4 v. 8°. Wash. 1868.
—— Same. Report, 1868. 4 v. 8°. Wash. 1869.
—— Same. Report for 1869, v. 1, 3. 8°. Wash. 1871.
—— Same. Report for 1870, v. 1, Alphabetical List of Patentees and Patents. 8°. Wash. 1871.
—— Same. Specifications and Drawings, July 4, 1871 to Jan. 23, 1872. 30 v. 4°. Wash. 1871-2.
—— Railroads. Report on Aid to Additional Railroads to the Pacific. 8°. Wash. 1869.
—— Rebellion. Report on Conduct of War (1865-6.) 4 v. 8°. Wash. 1865-6.
—— Register. 12°. Wash. 1841.
—— Revenue. Report of Special Commissioner for 1869. 8°. Wash. 1870.
—— Same. Bill for Codification of Revenue Laws. 4°. Wash. 1869.
—— Same. Internal Revenue Act, June 30, 1864. 8°. Wash. 1864.
—— Session Documents. *See* above. Congressional Documents.
—— Statistics. Monthly Reports of Bureau, Nos. 1-20. Nov. 1866; Aug. 1868. 4°. Wash. 1866-8.
—— Surgeon-General's Office. Circulars, Nos. 1-4. 3 v. 4°. Wash. 1868-70.
—— Same. Circulars, Nos. 2, 5, 7. 3 v. 4°. Wash. 1871.
—— Tariff of 1861. 8°. N.Y. 1861.
—— Tariff Revised to Feb. 24, 1869, by Ogden. 8°. N.Y. 1869.
—— Tariff Revised to July 14, 1870, by Ogden. 8°. N.Y. 1870.
—— Tax Law, amended to March 7, 1863. 18°. Milwaukee. 1863.
—— Tax Law, June 30, 1864. 18°. N.Y. 1864.
—— Treasury. *See* FINANCES above.
—— Whittlesey's Report in Carmick & Ramsey's Case. (PC. 16.) 8°. Wash. 1857.
UNITED States. History of the U. S. By a Citizen of Massachusetts. 2d ed. 12° Keene. 1821.
UNITED States Anti-Masonic Convention, Phil., Sep. 11, 1830. Proceedings. 8. Phil. 1830.
UNITED States, Europ. and West Va. Land and Mining Co. Petition and Prospectus. (PC. 10.) 8°. N.Y. 1867.
UNITED States Register (Disturnell's) for 1870. 12°. N.Y. 1870.
UNITED States Register or Blue Book for 1872. 8°. Phil. n.d.
UNITED States Sanitary Commission. Bulletin. 3 v. in 1. 8°. N.Y. 1866.
—— Documents, Nos. 1-95. 3 v. 8°. N.Y. 1866.
—— Surgical Memoirs of the Rebellion. Ed. by Hamilton. 8°. N.Y. 1870.
UNITED States Stamp Tax Law, as to Banking; N. Y. Meeting. (PC. 21.) S. 4°. N.Y. 1862.
UNITY of Italy. R. 8°. N.Y. 1871.
UNIVERS (L') Pittoresque. (Partial set). 23 v. 8°. Paris. 1835-48.
UNIVERSALIST Quarterly. New ser., v. 6, 8. 8°. Bost. 1869-71.
UNIVERSITY Addresses. *See* LIBRARY of Education. v. 4.
UNIVERSITY of Albany; History of Medical College. 8°. Alb. 1867.
UNIVERSITY of Glasgow. Addresses at Opening Session, 1870-71. 16°. Edin. 1870.
UNIVERSITY of Minnesota Almanac for 1871 and 1872. 2 v. 8°. Minneapolis. 1871-2.
UNIVERSITY (The) Question (of Michigan). (PC. 16.) 8°. n.p. n.d.
UNWIN, W. C. Wrought Iron Bridges and Roofs. 8°. Lond. 1869.
UPHAM, F. W. The Wise Men. 16°. N.Y. 1869.
UPTON, E. Tactics for Non-Military Bodies. 18°. N.Y. 1870.
URE, A. The Cotton Manufacture of Great Britain. 2 v. 12°. Lond. 1861.
—— Dictionary of Arts, Manufactures, and Mines. 6th ed. 3 v. R. 8°. Lond. 1867.
—— Same, with Supplement of 1845. L. 8°. Lond. 1839-45.
—— The Philosophy of Manufactures. 3d ed. 12°. Lond. 1861.
URLIN, R. D. John Wesley's Place in Church History. 18°. Lond. 1870.
URQUHART, D. La Turquie. 2 v. 18°. Brussels. 1837.
USEFUL Metals and their Alloys. 8°. Lond. 1866.

UTICA, Clinton, Deerfield, New Hartford, New York Mills, Whitesboro and Yorkville Directory, 1871. 8°. Utica. 1871.

UZOKHILAIN, P. Wobanaki Kimzowi Awighighan, (*i.e.* Abnaki Spelling Book.) 24° Bost. 1830.

VACANO, E. and Stadion, Graf. E. Dornen. 2 v. in 1. 12°. Pesth. 1869.

VACCINE. Information on Prevention of Small Pox. (PC. 1.) 8°. N.Y. 1859.

VALDES, G. Bando de Gobernacion de Cuba. 2d ed. 8°. Havana. 1843.

VALENTIA, George (Lord). Atlas to Voyages. Ob. 4°. Paris. 1813.

VALENTIN, W. G. Laboratory Text Book of Practical Chemistry. 8°. Lond. 1871.

VALENTINE, Mrs. R. Home Book. 12°. Lond. 1868.

—— Nobility of Life. 4°. Lond. 1869.

VALFREY, J. Diplomatie du Gouvernement de la Défense Nationale. Pts. 1, 2. 8°. Paris. 1871-2.

VALLEJO. Resources of. (PC. 20.) 8°. n.p. 1869.

VÁLMÍKI. Rámáyan. Translated by Griffith. 2 v. 8°. Lond. 1870-1.

—— The Iliad of the East. (Rāmāyana.) Ed. by Frederika Richardson. 12°. Lond. 1870.

VAN BRUYSSEL, E. Population of an Old Pear-Tree. 12°. N.Y. 1870.

VAN CHOATE, S. F. Ocean Telegraphing. 4°. Cambridge. 1865.

VANDENHOFF, G. Elocution. 12°. N.Y. 1851.

VANDERDECKEN. The Yacht Sailor. 3d ed. 12°. Lond. 1868.

VANDEVELDE, L. Description des Fortifications de Paris. 8°. Brussels. 1870.

VAN DYKE, H. J. The Lord's Prayer. 12°. N.Y. 1871.

VANES, B. British Mail Trade. Ob. 4°. Lond. n.d.

VANITY Fair. v. 1-3. f°. Lond. 1868-70.

VAN LENNEP, H. J. Travels in Little-Known Parts of Asia Minor. 2 v. 12°. Lond. 1870.

VAN LIEW, J. Discourse, Dedication of Reformed Prot. Dutch Church. Readington, N. J. 8°. N.Y. 1865.

VAN NAME, A. Contributions to Creole Grammar. 8°. n.p. n.d.

VAN NEST, A. R. Jr. Ministerial Responsibility; 11th Anniversary Sermon. 8°. N.Y. 1859.

VAN NOSTRAND. Eclectic Engineering Magazine. v. 3, 4. 4°. N.Y. 1870-1.

VAN OOSTERZEE, J. J. Theology of the New Testament, 12°. Lond. 1870.

—— Same. 12. N.Y. 1871.

VAN RENSSELAER, C. Religious Instruction in Colleges; a Discourse. 8. Phil. 1853.

VAN WART, I., Jr. Golden Cross, and other Poems. Sm. 4°. N.Y. 1870.

VAN ZANDT, N. B. Description of the Military Lands between the Mississippi and the Illinois Rivers, and Map. 2 v. 8°. Wash. 1818.

VARNHAGEN von Ense. Biographische Portraits. 8°. Leip. 1871.

VASSAR Female College. Report on Organization. L. 8°. N.Y. 1859.

VAUGHAN, C. J. Half Hours in Temple Church. 16°. Lond. 1871.

—— The Revised Code of the Committee on Education Dispassionately Considered. 8°. Camb. (Eng.) 1861.

VAUGHAN, H. Works. *See* FULLER Worthies' Library.

VAUGHAN, J. Sermons to Children, 4th ed. 12°. Lond. 1871.

VAUGHAN, R. B. Life and Labours of S. Thomas of Aquin. 2 v. 8°. Lond. 1871-2.

VAUVENARGUES. *See* MAXIMES et Pensées.

VAYSE de Villiers, R. J. F. Itinéraire Descriptive de la France. 13 v. 8°. Paris. 1813-35.

VEITCH, J Memoir of Sir W. Hamilton. 8°. Edin. 1869.

VEITCH, Zepherina P. Hand-book for Nurses for the Sick. 12. Lond. 1870.

VEITH, J. E. Life Pictures of the Passion of Christ. 12°. Bost. 1870.

VELOCIPEDE (The). By J. F. B. Sq. 16°. Lond. 1869.

VENEDEY, J. Die Deutschen Republikaner unter der Französischen Republik. 8°. Leip. 1870.

VERDI, T. S. Maternity 12°. N.Y. 1870.

—— Same. 1871.

VEREKER, C. S. Scenes in the Sunny South. (North Africa). 2 v. 12°. Lond. 1871.
VERENA, S. Ueber Alles die Pflicht. 3 v. in 2. 12°. Berlin. 1870.
VEREY, J. The Open Air. 12°. Lond. 1869.
VERITY, R. Subject and Object, as Connected with our Double Brain. 8°. Edin. 1870.
VERMONT Historical Gazeteer. *See* HEMENWAY.
VERMONT Historical Society; Collections. v. 1, 2. 8°. Montpelier. 1870–1.
VERMONT State Business Directory for 1870. 8°. Bost. 1870.
VERNE, J. Les Anglais au Pole Nord. 12°. Paris. n.d.
—— Autour de la Lune. 12°. Paris. n.d.
—— Cinq Semaines en Ballon. 12°. Paris. n.d.
—— De la Terre à la Lune. 12°. Paris. n.d.
—— Le Désert de Glace. 12°. Paris. n.d
—— Les Enfants du Capitaine Grant. 3 v. 12°. Paris. n.d.
—— Vingt Mille Lieues sous les Mers. 2 v. 12°. Paris. n.d.
—— Voyage au Centre de la Terre. 12°. Paris. n.d.
—— Journey to the Centre of the Earth. 12°. N.Y. 1872.
VÉRON, L. Mémoires d'un Bourgeois de Paris. 5. v. in 2. 16°. Paris. 1856–7.
VÉSINIER, P. History of the Commune of Paris. 12°. Lond. 1872.
VEUILLOT, L. La Legalité. 18°. Paris. 1871.
—— Paris pendant les deux Siéges. 8°. Paris. 1871.
—— Rome pendant le Concile, 1869–70. 2 v. 8°. Paris. 1872.
VIARDOT, L. Merveilles de Sculpture. 12°. Paris. 1869.
—— Wonders of European Art. 12°. Lond. 1871.
—— Same. 12°. N.Y. 1871.
—— Wonders of Italian Art. 12°. Lond. 1870.
—— Wonders of Sculpture. Sm. 4°. Lond. 1872.
VICTOR, Francis F. Rivers of the West. 8°. Hartford. 1870.
VICTORIA Magazine. v. 13–16. 8°. Lond. 1868–72.
VICTORINUS Writings. *See* ANTE-NICENE. Christian Library. v. 18.
VIETS, A. P. Discourse, Re-interment of Deacon Case. (PC. 22.) 8°. Hartford. 1851.
VIEYRA, A. Portuguese Grammar. 9th ed. 8°. Lond. 1813.
VIGNON, C. Un Naufrage Parisien. 16°. Paris. 1869.
VILBORT, J. L'Œuvre de M. de Bismarck. 12°. Paris. 1869.
VILLALOBOS, F. L. de. Medical Works. Ed with Memoir, by Gaskoin. 12°. Lond. 1870.
VILLETARD, E. Histoire de l'Internationale. 12°. Paris. 1871.
VINCE, S. Principles of Fluxions. 8°. Phil. 1812.
VINCENT, Mlle. Un Frère Adoptif. 12°. Geneva. 1870.
VINCENT, F. History of Delaware. v 1. 8°. Phil. 1870.
—— Union of Great Britain and the United States. An Essay. 16°. Wilmington. 1870.
VIOLLET-le-Duc, E. E. Mémoires sur la Défense de Paris, avec un Atlas. 2 v. 8°. and f°. Paris. 1871.
VIRGIL, P. M. Aeneid (Latin); notes by Chase. 16°. Phil. 1868.
—— Same, Book 1. With Interlinear. Translation. 5th ed. 16°. Lond. 1832.
—— Works. Latin; notes by Conington and Nettleship. 3 v. 8°. Lond. 1865–72.
—— Works. Transl. by Davidson. (Bohn's Ed.) 12°. Lond. 1870.
—— Works. Transl. by Lonsdale and Lee. 12°. Lond. 1871.
VITET, L. Lettres sur le Siége de Paris. Nrs. 1–7. 18°. Paris. 1871.
VOGEL, A. Diseases of Children. Transl. by Raphael. 8°. N.Y. 1870.
VOGT, C. Altes und Neues aus Thier-und Menschenleben. 2 v. in 1. Frankfort. 1859.
—— Natürliche Geschichte der Schöpfung. 2d ed. 8°. Brunswick. 1858.
—— Physiologische Briefe. 3 ed. 8°. Giessen. 1861.
VOGT, C. F. Letters on Chess. 16°. Lond. 1848.
VOICE (A) from the Newsboys. 16°. N.Y. n.d.

VOITURE, V. de. Œuvres, ed. by Ubicini. 2 v. 12.°. Paris. 1855.

VOLCKHAUSEN, A. Das Kind aus dem Ebräergang. 2 v. in 1. 12°. Stuttg. 1870.

VOLTAIRE, F. M. A. de. Henriade. 8°. Paris. 1814.

—— Age of Louis XIV. and XV. Transl. by Griffith. 3 v. 8°. Lond. 1799–81.

—— Annals of the [German] Empire. 8°. Lond. 1871.

—— History of Charles XII. Transl. by Kenrich; *also*, Life of Peter the Great. 8°. Lond. 1780.

—— Philosophical Dictionary. R. 8°. Bost. 1856.

—— Toleration; The Ignorant Philosopher; Commentary on Beccaria. Transl. by Williams. 8°. Lond. 1779.

—— Universal History; or, Essay on the Manners and Spirits of Nation. 5 v. 8°. Lond. 1780.

VON ACHTEN der Letzte. 12°. Wiesbaden. 1871.

VOYAGE and Venture. 12°. Phil. 1869.

VOYSEY, C. The Sling and the Stone. v. 3–5. 8°. Lond. 1868–72.

VYNER, R. T. Notitia Venatica; a Treatise on Fox-Hunting. 6th ed. 8°. Lond. n.d.

WACHENHUSEN, H. Haut Ihm! 12°. Berlin. n.d.

—— Tagebuch vom Französischen Kriegs schauplatz. 12°. Berlin. n.d.

—— Unter dem Weissen Adler. 12°. Berlin. 1866.

—— Vom Armen Egyptischen Mann. 12°. Berlin. n.d.

—— Vom Neuen Babylon. 12°. Berlin. 1872.

WADDELL, W. H. Greek Grammar for Beginners. 12°. N.Y. 1869.

WADE, H. Rod-Fishing in Clear Waters. 16°. Lond. n.d.

WADSWORTH, C. A Mother's Sorrow. *See* AM. Tract Society; Tracts for Young Men.

WAGGONER, J. H. The Atonement. 16°. Battle Creek. 1668.

WAGNER, Richard. Beethoven. 12°. Leip. 1870.

WAILLY, A. de. Principes de la Langue Française. 16°. Paris. 1823.

WAIT, W. Justices and County Courts. 2 v. 8°. Alb. 1868.

WAIT, W. B. Plans and Illustrations of New Public School System. L. 8°. Bost. 1861.

WAKELEY, J. B. Anecdotes of the Wesleys. 18°. Lond. n.d.

WAKEMAN, Mrs. Anna R. In Memoriam George Wakeman. 8°. N.Y. 1870.

WALCKENAER, Baron. Mémoires touchant la Vie et les Écrits de Mme. de Sévigné. 3d ed. 6 v. in 3. 16°. Paris. 1856.

WALCOT, Mrs. E. C. Traditions and Customs of Cathedrals. 12°. Lond. 1872.

WALDEGRAVE, James (Earl). Memoirs, 1754–58. 12°. Phil. 1827.

WALDMÜLLER, R. (Pseudonym.) *See* DUBOC, E.

WALFORD, E. County Families of the United Kingdom. 5th ed. Imp. 8°. Lond. 1870.

—— Same. 6th ed. Imp. 8°. Lond. 1871.

WALFORD, Th. (Edr.). Letters and Journals of James, Eighth Earl of Elgin. 8°. Lond. 1872.

WALKER, Amasa. The Science of Wealth. 12°. Phil. 1872.

WALKER, A. F. Vermont Brigade in Shenandoah Valley. 12°. Burlington, Vt. 1869.

WALKER, C. M. History of Athens Co., Ohio. 8°. Cinc. 1869.

WALKER, C. V. Electrotype Manipulation. 2d Am. ed. 16°. Phil. 1852.

WALKER, E. Military Elements. 2d ed. 12°. Lond. 1868.

WALKER, James B. Doctrine of the Holy Spirit. 12°. Phil. 1870.

—— Living Questions of the Age. 12°. Phil. 1870.

—— Philosophy of the Plan of Salvation. 12°. Bost. 1870.

WALKER, John. Key to the Classical Pronunciation of Greek, Latin and Scripture Proper Names. 8°. Phil. 1808.

—— Rhetorical Grammar. 3d ed. 8°. Lond. 1801.

WALKER, Mary E. Hit. 12°. N.Y. 1871.

WALKER, T. Elements of Geometry. 12°. Bost. 1829.

WALKER, W. B. Cyclical Deluges. 12°. Lond. 1871.

WALKER, Wm. Lessons on Animals and Figures. Imp. 8°. Lond. n.d.
WALLACE, A. R. Natural Selection. 12°. Lond. 1870.
—— Review of Descent of Man. 18°. N.Y. 1871.
—— Travels on the Amazon and Rio Negro. 8°. Lond. 1870.
WALLACE, E. D. England's Last Queen. 16°. N.Y. 1871.
—— A Woman's Experiences in Europe. 8°. N.Y. 1872.
WALLACE, J. H. American Trotting Register. 8°. N.Y. 1871.
WALLACE, R. Geometry. 12°. Glasgow. 1831.
WALLACE, W. C. Treatise on the Eye. 4th ed. 16°. N.Y. 1846.
—— Wonders of Vision. 12°. N.Y. 1841.
WALLACE, W. R. Poems. 2d ed. 16°. N.Y. 1851.
WALLAS, J. Manual of Plain Devotions. 2d ed. 18°. Lond. 1869.
—— Holy Baptism. 12°. Lond. 1869.
WALLER, J. F. Revelations of Peter Brown, Poet and Peripatetic. 16°. Lond. n.d.
WALLINGTON, N. Reign of Charles I. 2 v. 12°. Lond. 1869.
WALLIS, S. T. Discourse on Mr. Peabody. 8°. Baltimore. 1870.
WALMSLEY, H. M. Ruined Cities of Zulu Land. 2 v. 12°. Lond. 1869.
WALPOLE, H. Anecdotes of Painting. 12°. Lond. 1871.
WALSH, J. H. The Horse. 8°. Lond. 1869.
—— Short Gun and Sporting Rifle. 12°. Lond. 1862.
WALSINGHAM, T. Gesta Abbatum Monasterii S. Albani. Rolls Chronicles. 3 v. R. 8°. Lond. 1867–69.
WALTON, E. Flowers from the Upper Alps. f°. Lond. 1869.
—— and Bonney, T. G. Coast of Norway. Obl. f°. Lond. 1870.
WANKLYN, J. A., and E. T. Chapman. Water Analysis; Potable Water. 16°. Lond. 1868.
WANOSTROCHT, N. French Grammar. 16°. Havre. 1795.
—— La Liturgie (Church of England). 32°. Lond. 1806.
WAR Correspondence of the Daily News. 2 v. 12°. Lond. 1871.
—— Same. 2d ed. 12°. Lond. 1871.
WARBURTON, A. F. Trial of Crew of Savannah. 8°. N.Y. 1862.
WARD, Mrs. The Microscope. 3d ed. 12°. Lond. 1869.
—— The Telescope. 3d ed. 12°. Lond. 1869.
WARD, A. (Pseudonym.) *See* BROWNE, C. F.
WARD, E. C. New Lunar Tables. R. 8°. N.Y. 1849.
WARD, J. H. Steam for the Million. 8°. N.Y. 1867.
WARD, W. French Importer's Ready Calculator. 12°. N.Y. 1844.
WARDNER, N. Nature's God and His Memorial. (Sabbath.) 18°. Westerly. 1867.
WARING, E. J. Manual of Practical Therapeutics. 3d ed. 16°. Lond. 1871.
—— Practical Therapeutics. 2d Amer. ed. 8°. Phil. 1871.
WARING, G. E., Jr. Earth Closets. 2d ed. 16°. N.Y. 1869.
—— Earth Closets and Earth Sewage. 8°. N.Y. 1870.
—— Handy-Book of Husbandry. 8°. N.Y. 1870.
WARINGTON, G. Can we Believe in Miracles? 16°. Lond. n.d.
WARNER, C. D My Summer in a Garden. 12°. Bost. 1871.
—— Same. Illustrated. Sq. 16°. Bost. 1872.
—— Saunterings. 16°. Bost. 1872.
WARNER, T. How to Keep the Clock Right. 8°. Lond. 1869.
WARREN, H. Painting in Water Colors.
WARREN, Ira. Household Physician. R. 8°. Bost. 1870.
WARREN, J. L. Rehearsals: A Book of Verses. 12°. Lond. 1870.
WARREN, S. Introduction to Law Studies. Ed. by Thompson. 12°. Alb. 1870.
WARREN, S. E. Elements of Machine Construction and Drawing. 8°. N.Y. 1870.
—— Plates to Machine Construction. Sm. 4°. N.Y. n.d.
WARREN, T. R. Dust and Foam; or, Three Oceans. 12°. N.Y. n.d.
—— Shooting, Boating and Fishing. 12°. N.Y. 1871.
—— Yachtman's and Amateur Sailor's Primer. 12°. N.Y. 1863.
WARREN, W. These for Those. 12°. Portland. 1870.

WARTENSLEBEN, Graf H. von. Die Operationen der Süd-Armee im Jan. und Feb. 1871. 8°. Berlin. 1872.

WARTON, T. History of English Poetry. Ed. by Hazlitt. 4 v. 8°. Lond. 1871.

WARWICK, E. Nosology. 12°. Lond. 1848.

WASHBOURNE, T. Poems. *See* FULLER Worthies' Library. v. 2.

WASHBURN, C. A. History of Paraguay. 2 v. 8°. Bost. 1871.

WASHINGTON, G. Words of Washington. Selected by J. Parton. Sq. 18°. Bost. 1872.

WASHINGTON'S Birth-day, Vienna, Feb. 22, 1870. 8°. Vienna. 1870.

WASHINGTON, Georgetown and Alexandria Directory, 1870, 71. 2 v. 8°. Wash. 1870-1.

WATERBURY, J. B. Memoir of Rev. J. Scudder. 12°. N.Y. 1870.

WATERHOUSE, S. Resources of Missouri. 8°. St. Louis. 1867.

WATERLAND, D. Index to his Works. 8°. Oxford. 1828.

WATERTON, C. Essays in Natural History. 12°. Lond. 1871.

WATIN, J. F. L'Art du Peintre, Doreur Vernisseur et du Fabricant de Couleurs. 8°. Lyons. 1823.

WATSON, E. P. Manual of the Hand Lathe. 12°. Phil. 1869.

—— Modern Practice of American Machinists and Engineers. 12°. Phil. 1871.

WATSON, H. C. Compendium of Cybele Britannica. 8°. Lond. 1870.

WATSON, H W. Elements of Plane and Solid Geometry. 16°. Lond. 1871.

WATSON, J. F. Historic Tales of Olden Time. 16°. N.Y. 1832.

WATSON, J. S. Biographies of Wilkes and Cobbett. 12°. Edin. 1870.

—— Reasoning Power in Animals. 12°. Lond. 1867.

WATSON, J. W. Beautiful Snow, and other Poems. Enlarged Edition. 12°. Phil. n.d.

WATSON, R. Theological Institutes. 7th ed. 3 v. 8°. Lond. 1842.

WATSON, T. Lectures on the Principles and Practice of Physic. 5th ed. 2 v. 8°. Lond. 1871.

WATSON, W. C. History of Essex County, N. Y. 8°. Alb. 1869.

WATSON'S Art Journal. v. 14. 4°. N.Y. 1870.

WATT, A. Electro-Metallurgy. 16°. Lond. 1869.

WATTS, H. A. Dictionary of Chemistry. (Supplement.) 8°. Lond. 1872.

WATTS, I. Logick. Sq. 16°. Leeds. 1792

WATTS, W. M. Index of Spectra. With a Preface by Roscoe. 8°. Lond. 1872.

WAYSIDE Pillars. 12°. Lond. 1866.

WEARING of the Green Song Book. 24°. Bost. 1869.

WEBB, F. C. Up the Tigris to Bagdad. 8°. Lond. 1870.

WEBBE, S. W. English Poetrie. *See* ARBER'S English Reprints.

WEBER, J. Memoirs of Maria Antoinetta. 3 v. 8°. Lond. 1805-12.

WEBER, J. J. Illustrirter Kalender für 1870, '71, '72. 3 v. 8°. Leip. 1869-71.

WEBSTER, J. G. Epidemic Cholera. 12°. N.Y. 1866.

WEBSTER, N. Observations on Language and on Commerce. 12°. New Haven. 1839.

WEDGWOOD, H. Dictionary of English Etymology. 8°. Lond. 1872.

WEDGWOOD, Julia. John Wesley and the Evangelical Reaction of the Eighteenth Century. 12°. Lond. 1871.

WEEDEN, T. English Grammar. 16°. Lond. 1848.

WEEKS, R. K. Episodes and Lyric Pieces. 12°. N.Y. 1870.

WEIDENMANN, J. Beautifying Country Homes. L. 4°. N.Y. 1870.

WEIR, A., and Maclagan, W. D. The Church and the Age. 8°. Lond. 1870.

WEISBACH, J. Lehrbuch der Ingenieur- und Maschinen-Mechanik. Pt. 2. Statik der Bauwerke und Mechanik der Umtriebsmaschinen. 4th ed. 8°. Brunswick. 1865.

—— Manual of the Mechanics of Engineering and of the Construction of Machines. v. 1. Theoretical Mechanics. 8°. N.Y. 1870.

—— Principles of the Mechanics of Machinery and Engineering. v. 2. 8°. Lond. 1848.

WEISS, J. American Religion. 12°. Bost. 1871.

WEITTRECHT, Rev. J. J. Memoir of. 12°. N.Y. 1856.

WELCH, F. G. Moral, Intellectual and Physical Culture. 12°. N.Y. 1869.

WELD, C. R. Notes on Burgundy, 12°. Lond. 1869.

WELDON, G. W. Unity in Variety. Sm. 4°. Lond. n.d.

—— Same. 16°. N.Y. 1872.

WELLMER, A. Bruder Studio. 12°. Berlin. 1871.

WELLS, D. A. Recent Financial, Industrial and Commercial Experiences of the U. S. 8°. N.Y. 1872.

WELLS, S. R. New Physiognomy. 8°. N.Y. 1872.

WELLS, W. Water Power of Maine. 8°. Augusta. 1869.

WELSH, William. Women Helpers in the Church. 12°. Phil. 1872.

WELTAUSSTELLUNG ZU Paris, 1867. Bericht des Österreichischen Central-Comité. 6 v. Mit Atlas zum zweiten Bande. 8°. Vienna. 1869.

v. 1. I. Einleitung.
II. Die Kunstwerke und die Histoire du Travail.
III. Instrumente für Kunst und Wissenschaft.

v. 2. IV. Werkzeuge und Maschinen.
V. Verkehrsmittel. (Atlas mit 40 Tafeln.)

v. 3. VI. Chemisch-Metallurgische Industrie.
VII. Nahrungsmittel und Getränke.

v. 4. VIII. Garne, Gewebe, Bekleidungs-Gegenstände und Papier.
IX. Kunstgewerbe, Möbel und Einrichtungsstücke.

v. 5. X. Land-und Forstwissenschaft.

v. 6. XI. Social-Ökonomische Abtheilung.
Nachträge. Inhaltsverzeichniss.

WENDT, E. E. Papers on Maritime Legislation. 2d ed. 8°. Lond. 1871.

WESLEY. His own Biographer. 12°. Lond. 1871.

WESLEYAN Methodist Magazine. v. 93, 94. 8°. Lond. 1871.

WEST, C. Nervous Disorders in Childhood. 12°. Lond. 1871.

WEST, G. The Resurrection. *See* LESLIE, C., on Deism.

WESTCHESTER County Directory, 1869-70. 12°. N.Y. 1869.

WESTCOTT, B. F. General Survey of the History of the Canon of the New Testament. 3d ed. 12°. Lond. 1871.

—— Introduction to the Study of the Four Gospels. 4th ed. 12°. Lond. 1872.

WESTERMANN'S Illustrirte Deutsche Monatshefte. v. 24-31. 8°. Brunswick. 1868-72.

WESTERN Monthly. v. 3. 8°. Chic. 1870.

WESTERN Union Telegraph Co. Annual Report, July 13, 1869. 8°. N.Y. 1869.

—— Mr. Orton's Argument on Postal Telegraph. R. 8°. N.Y. 1870.

—— Proposed Union of Telegraph and Postal Systems. 8°. Camb. 1869.

WESTHALL, C. Modern Training. 4th ed. 24°. Lond. n.d.

WESTLAKE, J. W. Success; a Poem. 18°. Phil. 1860.

WESTMINSTER Review. New ser., v. 35-40. 8°. Lond. 1869-71.

WESTON, D. The Baptist Movement of One Hundred Years Ago. 8°. Bost. 1868.

WESTON, E. P. The Pedestrian; a Walk from Boston to Washington. 8°. N.Y. 1862.

WESTON, J. Stenography Completed. 8°. Lond. 1738.

WEST Roxbury Directory. *See* BROOKLINE.

WEST Troy Directory. *See* TROY.

WEY, F. Chronique du Siége de Paris. 12°. Paris. 1871.

WHARTON, J. Arithmetic and Mensuration. 16°. Lond. 1847.

WHARTON, J. J. S. Laws relating to the Women of England. 8°. Lond. 1853.

WHARTON, T. J. Address, Opening of Philadelphia Athenæum. 8°. Phil. 1847.

WHAT Happened after the Battle of Dorking. 16°. N.Y. 1871.

WHATELY, Miss E. J. Life of Calvin. 16°. Lond. n.d.

—— Life of Wycliffe. 16°. Lond. n.d.

—— Story of Luther. 16°. Lond. n.d.

—— Story of Zwingli. 2d ed. 16°. Lond. 1868.

WHATELY, M. L. Among the Huts in Egypt. 12°. Lond. 1871.

WHATLEY, R. Errors of Romanism. 8°. Phil. 1843.
—— Logic. 12°. N.Y. 1832.
—— Rhetoric. 12°. N.Y. 1833.
WHEATLEY, H. B. Round about Piccadilly. 8°. Lond 1870.
WHEELER, C. H. Ten Years on the Euphrates. 16°. Bost. n.d.
WHEELER, G. The Choice of a Dwelling; Hiring, Buying or Building a House. 12°. Lond. 1871.
—— Homes for the People. 12°. N.Y. n d.
WHEELWRIGHT, H. W. Sporting Sketches at Home and Abroad 12°. Lond. n.d.
WHICH; The Right or the Left? 12°. N.Y. 1855.
WHIPPLE, C. K. Relations of American Board to Slavery. 12°. Bost. 1861.
WHIPPLE, E. P. Essays and Reviews. 2 v. 12°. Bost. 1870.
—— Literature of the Age of Elizabeth. 12°. Bost. 1869.
—— Literature and Life. Enlarged edition. 12°. Bost. 1871.
—— Success and its Conditions. 12°. Bost. 1871.
WHIST Player's Hand-Book. 18°. Phil. 1844.
WHITAKER, J. Mary Queen of Scots Vindicated. 3 v. 8°. Lond. 1787.
WHITAKER, J. Almanac for 1870. 12°. Lond. 1870.
—— Same, 1872. 12°. Lond. n.d.
WHITE, C. Ecce Femina. 16°. Hanover, N.H. 1870.
WHITE, Rev. Jas History of France. 8°. N.Y. 1870.
WHITE, John. Sketches from America. 8°. Lond. 1870.
WHITE, J. J. Cranberry Culture. 12°. N.Y. 1870.
WHITE, J. W. Taking Impressions of the Mouth. 8°. Phil. 1871.
WHITE, R. History of the Battle of Bannockburn. 8°. Edin. 1871.
WHITE, R. G. Chronicles of Gotham. Books 1, 2. 12°. N.Y. 1871–72.
—— The Fall of Man. 12°. N.Y. 1871.
—— Words and their Uses. 12°. N.Y. 1870.
WHITEHEAD, J. Lives of Rev. John and of Rev. Charles Wesley. 12°. Lond. 1843.
WHITEHEAD, S. Spanish Grammar. 12°. Lond. 1820.
WHITESBORO Directory. *See* UTICA.
WHITESIDE, J. Early Sketches of Eminent Persons. 12°. Dublin. 1870.
WHITFIELD, F. Earthly Shadows of the Heavenly Kingdom. 16°. Lond. 1872.
WHITING, W. War Powers under the Constitution. 8°. Bost. 1871.
WHITMAN, W. After All, Not to Create Only. 12°. Bost. 1871.
—— Leaves of Grass. 12°. Wash. 1871.
WHITMORE, W. H. Massachusetts' Civil List, 1630–1774. 8°. Bost. 1870.
WHITNEY, Mrs. A. D. T. Mother Goose for Grown Folks. 12°. Bost. n.d.
—— Pansies. 16°. Bost. 1872.
WHITNEY, J. P. Colorado. R. 8°. Lond. 1867.
WHITNEY, W. D. German Grammar. 12°. N.Y. 1860.
WHITTIER, J. G. Child Life. 12°. Bost. 1871.
—— Miriam, and Other Poems. 12°. Bost. 1870.
—— Poems, 2 v. 16°. Bost. 1869.
—— Poetical Works. 2 v. 12°. Bost. 1870.
WHITTLE, J. L. Catholicism and the Vatican. 12°. Lond. 1872.
WHO is Responsible for the War? By Scrutator. 12°. Lond. 1871.
WHY is a New Code Wanted? By Omega. 8°. Lond. 1861.
WHYMPER, E. Scrambles amongst the Alps. R. 8°. Lond. 1871.
WHYTE, Wm. A. A Land Journey from Asia to Europe. 8°. Lond. 1871.
WICHERT, E. Hinter den Coulissen. 3 v. 12°. Berlin. 1872.
—— Kleine Romane. 3 v. 12°. Berlin. 1871.
WICKEDE, J. von. Herzog Wallenstein in Mecklenburg, 2 v. 12°. Jena. 1865.
—— Ein Husarenofficier Friedrichs des Grossen. 12°. Jena. 1866.
—— Joachim Slüter. 2 v. 16°. Berlin. n.d.
—— Kriegsbilder des Jahres 1870. 12°. Hanover. 1871.
WICKHAM, W. Correspondence. 2 v. 8°. Lond. 1870.
WIELAND, C. M. Oberon. 12°. Berlin. 1866.

WIENER, W. Nach dem Orient. 12°. Vienna. 1870.

WIGGINS, R. New York Expositor. 18°. N.Y. n.d.

WIGHT, O. W. Philosophy of Sir W. Hamilton. 8°. N.Y. 1866.

WILBERFORCE, S. Heroes of Hebrew History. 12°. N.Y. 1870.

—— Sermons to the University of Oxford. 3d ser. 8°. Oxford. 1871.

WILCOCKS, A. Influence of Ether in the Solar System. 4°. Phil. 1864.

WILD Flower. 8°. N.Y. n.d.

WILDER, M. P. Address to N. E. Historical-Genealogical Society. 8°. Bost. 1870.

WILEY, C. A. Elocution and Oratory. 12°. N.Y. 1869.

WILEY, H. North Carolina Reader, No. 3. 12°. N.Y. 1857.

WILHELMI, A. Einer muss heirathen. *Also*, Benedix, R. Eigensinn. 12°. N.Y. n.d.

WILKESON, S. How our National Debt may be a National Blessing. 8°. Phil. 1865.

WILKINS, A. S. The Light of the World. 12°. Lond. 1869.

—— Same. 2d ed. 12°. Lond. 1870.

—— Phœnicia and Israel; an Historical Essay. 12°. Lond. 1871.

WILKINS, H. St. C. Reconnoitring in Abyssinia. 8°. Lond. 1870.

WILKINSON, Jas. J. G. The Human Body and its Connexion with Man. 2d ed. 12°. Lond. 1860.

WILKINSON, M. M. U. False Discontinuity. 8°. Camb. (Eng.) 1871.

WILKINSON, W. English Country Houses. 4°. Lond. 1870.

WILKINSON, W. C. Dance of Modern Society. 16°. N.Y. 1869.

WILLARD, Emma. Universal History in Perspective. 8°. N.Y. 1870.

WILLARD, S. The Columbian Union. 12°. Alb. 1815.

WILLARD, S. Some Miscellany Observations Respecting Witchcraft. S. 4°. Bost. 1869.

WILLELMUS Malmesbiriensis. De Gestis Pontificum Anglorum Libri Quinque. R. 8°. Lond. 1870.

WILLET, J. E. Wonders of Insect Life. 12°. Phil. 1872.

WILLEY, S. H. Discourse, Closing Exercises at Howard Presb. Church. (PC. 22.) 8°. Lond. 1867.

WILLIAMS, Annie M. Wax Flower Modelling Made Easy. 16°. Lond. 1871.

WILLIAMS, B. S. Orchid Grower's Manual. 4th ed. 12°. 1871.

WILLIAMS, C. J. B. and C. T. Pulmonary Consumption. 12°. Lond 1871.

WILLIAMS, C. K. Centennial Celebration, Rutland, Vt. 8°. Rutland. 1870.

WILLIAMS, C. P. Review of the Financial Situation. 8°. Alb. 1868.

WILLIAMS, C. T. Climate of the South of France. 2d ed. 12°. Land. 1869.

WILLIAMS, E. Truths on N.Y. and Erie R. R. *See* NEW YORK and Erie R. R.

WILLIAMS, G. The Holy City. 2d ed. 2 v. 8°. Lond. 1871.

—— Preciousness of Redemption; a Sermon. 12°. Hartford. 1809.

WILLIAMS, H. T. Window Gardening. 8°. N.Y. 1872.

WILLIAMS, I. Characters of the Old Testament. 16°. Lond. 1869.

—— Commentary on the Gospel Narrative. 12°. Lond. 1870.

—— Our Lord's Nativity. 12°. Lond. 1869.

WILLIAMS, Jane. History of Wales. 8°. Lond. 1869.

WILLIAMS, J. F. Bibliography of Minnesota. 8°. St. Paul. 1870.

—— History of Newspaper Press of St. Paul. 8°. n.p. 1871.

WILLIAMS, J. J. Report on Tehuantepec Railway and Ship Canal. 8°. N.Y. 1870.

WILLIAMS, R. Bloody Tenant yet more Bloody. *See* NARRAGANSETT Club; Publications. v. 4.

WILLIAMS, T. Fiji and the Fijians. 12°. Lond. 1870.

WILLIAMS, W. M. The Fuel of the Sun. 8°. Lond. 1870.

WILLIAMSON, A. Journeys in North China. 2 v. 12°. Lond. 1870.

WILLIAMSON, B. An Elementary Treatise on the Differential Calculus. 12°. Lond. 1872.

WILLIAMSON, R. S. Meteorology and Hypsometry. 4°. N.Y. 1869.

WILLIS, R. Principles of Mechanism. 2 ed. 8°. Lond. 1870.
—— Spinoza. 8°. Lond. 1870.
WILLIS, R. S. Our Church Music. 12°. N.Y. 1856.
WILLKOMM, E. Die Familie Ammer. 12°. Frankfort. 1855.
WILLMOTT, R. A. Pleasures of Literature. 16°. Lond. 1866.
WILLSON, Forceythe. Old Sergeant, and Other Poems. 16°. N.Y. 1867.
WILLSON, M. History of the United States. 16°. N.Y. 1846.
WILMOT, A., and Chase, J. C. History of Cape Colony. 8°. Lond. 1869.
WILMOT, J. E. Reminiscences of Assheton Smith. 12°. Lond. 1862.
WILSON, D. Chatterton; a Biographical Study. 12°. Lond. 1869.
WILSON, E. Churchman's Manual of Apostolical Doctrine. 16°. Lond. 1871.
WILSON, E. Lectures on Dermatology. 8°. Lond. 1871.
WILSON, G. Inorganic Chemistry; Revised by Madan. 12°. Lond. 1871.
WILSON, H., and Caulfield, J. Wonderful Characters. 12°. Lond. n.d.
WILSON, H. H. Works. v. 11, 12. Theatre of the Hindus. 3d ed. 2 v. 8°. Lond. 1871.
—— Memorial of Chief Justice Kirkpatrick. 8°. N.Y. 1870.
WILSON, J. G. Mr. Secretary Pepys and his Diary. 12°. N.Y. 1869.
WILSON, J. M. Presb. Historical Almanac, 1861. 8°. Phil. 1861.
WILSON, W. Democracy, *vs.* Doulocracy. 8°. Cinc. 1848.
WILSON, W. Poems. 16.° Poughkeepsie. 1869.
WILSON, Warren, etc. Recovery of Jerusalem. 8°. Lond. 1871.
—— Same. 8°. N.Y. 1871.
WIMPFFEN, (Le Général de). Sedan. 2d ed. 8°. Paris. 1871.
WIMPFFEN, (Le Général de). Réponse au Général Ducrot par un Officier Supérieur. 8°. Paris. 1871.
WINANS, R. One Religion: Many Creeds. 8°. Baltimore. 1870.
WINCHELL, A. Sketches of Creation. 12°. N.Y. 1870.
WINCKELMANN, J. History of Ancient Art. Transl. by H. Lodge. v. 3. R. 8°. Bost. 1872.
WINCKLER, W. Die Deutschen Kleinstädter in America. 12°. Leip. 1871.
WINFIELD, C. H. History of the Land Titles of Hudson County, N.J., 1609–71. With Maps. 2 v. Imp. 8°. N.Y. 1872.
WINN, C. A. What I saw of the War. 12°. Edin. 1870.
WINSLOW, E. S. Commercial Calculator. 2d ed. 16°. Bost. 1854.
WINSLOW, F. Anatomy of Suicide. 8°. Lond. 1840.
WINTER, W. My Witness (Poems). 12°. Bost. 1871.
WINTERFELD, A. von. Der Elephant. 4 v. in 2. 12°. Leip. 1870.
—— Die Fanatiker der Ruhe. 4 v. in 2. 12°. Leip. 1867.
—— Ein Gemeuchelter Dichter. 4 v. in 2. 12°. Jena. 1867.
—— Herr von Filz. 12°. Leip. 1868.
—— Humoresken. 5 v. in 3. 16°. Berlin. 1868–71.
—— Humoristische Soldaten—Novellen. 13 v. in 4. 12°. Berlin. 1867.
—— Moderne Odyssee. 3 v. in 1. 12°. Jena. 1871.
—— Der Stille Winkel. 4 v. in 2. 12°. Berlin. 1865.
—— Der Winkelschreiber. 3 v. in 1. 12°. Jena. 1869.
WINTERFELD, K. Der Deutsch-Französische Krieg von 1870–1. 12°. Berlin. 1871.
WIRGMAN, T. Principles of the Kantesian Philosophy. 2d ed. 8°. Lond. 1832.
WIRTH, J. G. A. Die Geschichte der Deutschen. Revised and Continued by Zimmermann. 4 v. 12°. Stuttg. 1865.
WISCONSIN. Laws on Common Schools. 8°. Madison. 1859.
WISE, I. M. Origin of Christianity. 16°. Cinc. 1868.
WISEMAN, N. Recollections of Four Popes. 12°. Lond. n.d.
WOLF, A. Deux Empereurs (1870–1871). 12°. Brussels. 1871.
WOLFF, J. Researches and Missionary Labours. 12°. Phil. 1837.
WOLTMANN, A. Holbein und seine Zeit (Supplement). 8°. Leip. 1868.
WOOD, A. Class-Book of Botany. 12°. Paris. 1[illegible]

WOOD, F. Early Life of Fernando Wood. By a Citizen of New York. 12°. N.Y. 1855.
WOOD, G. B. Historical and Biographical Memoirs. 8°. Phil. 1872.
WOOD, J. G. Bible Animals. 8°. Lond. 1869.
—— Same. 8°. N.Y. 1870.
—— Common Moths of England. 16°. Lond. 1870.
—— Insects at Home; an Account of British Insects. 8°. Lond. 1872.
—— Same. 8°. N.Y. 1872.
—— Natural History of Man. 2 v. R. 8°. Lond. 1868–70.
—— Common Objects of the Microscope. 16°. Lond. 1864.
—— Strange Dwellings. 12°. Lond. 1871.
—— Uncivilized Races of Men. 2 v. R. 8°. Hartford. 1870.
WOOD, Mary A. E. Letters of Royal and Illustrious Ladies of Great Britain. 3 v. 12°. Lond. 1846.
WOOD, O. E. West Point Scrap Book. 8°. N.Y. 1871.
WOOD, S. Plain Path to Good Gardening. 12°. Lond. n.d.
WOOD, W. Manual of Physical Exercises. 12°. N.Y. 1867.
WOODBURY, I. B. Elements of Musical Composition. 12°. Bost. 1847.
—— Self-Instructor in Musical Composition. 16°. N.Y. n.d.
WOODGATE, H. O. "Essays and Reviews" Considered, etc. 8°. Lond. 1863.
WOODHEAD, H. Memoirs of Christina, Queen of Sweden. 2 v. 12°. Lond. 1863.
WOODRUFF, C. S. Intellectual Freedom. 12°. N.Y. n.d.
WOODRUFF, J. L. M. My Winter in Cuba. 12°. N.Y. 1871.
WOODS, Caroline H. Woman in Prison. 16°. N.Y. 1869.
WOODS, L. Sermon; Obituary of Moses Brown. 8°. Andover. 1827
WOODS, N. A. Prince of Wales in Canada and the United States. 12°. Lond. 1861.
WOODWARD, A. Life of Gen. Lyon. 12°. Hartford. 1862.
—— History of Franklin, Conn. 8°. New Haven. 1869.
WOOLMAN, J. Journal. With an Introduction by Whittier. 12°. Bost. 1871.
WOOLRYCH, H. W. Lives of Eminent Serjeants-at-Law of the English Bar. 2 v. 8°. Lond. 1869.
WOOLSEY, T. D. Essay on Divorce. 12°. N.Y. 1869.
—— Eulogy on C. C. Felton. 8°. Wash. 1862.
—— The Religion of the Present and the Future; Sermons. 12°. N.Y. 1871.
WORCESTER, J. E. Elements of Geography. 12°. Bost. 1832.
WORCESTER, S. Fourth Reader. 12°. Bost. 1837.
WORCESTER Directory for 1870–1. 2 v. 8°. Worcester. 1870–1.
WORDS of Cheer for the Master's Workers. Sq. 16°. N.Y. n.d.
WORDS of Weight on the Woman Question. 12°. Lond. 1871.
WORK for All. Sq. 12°. N.Y. 1872.
WORKING (The) Farmer. v. 1–11, in 4 v. 8°. N.Y. 1849–56.
WORKSHOP (The). v. 1–4. 4°. N.Y. 1869–71.
WORLD (Daily). July, 1869—Dec. 1871. 6 v. Atl. f°. N.Y. 1869–71.
WORLD Almanac, 1871–2. 2 v. 12°. N.Y. 1871–2.
WORLD of Wonders. 4°. Lond. n.d.
WORMAN, J. H. L'Écho de Paris. The French Echo or Dialogues to Teach French Conversation. 12°. N.Y. 1870.
WORMELL, R. Course of Natural Philosophy. 18°. Lond. 1871.
—— Elementary Mechanics. 16°. Lond. 1869.
WRAY, L. Practical Sugar Planter. 8°. Lond. 1848.
WRECK-Elections of a Busy Life. Ob. 4°. N.Y. 1867.
WRIGHT, A. S. Practical Receipts. 12°. N.Y. n.d.
WRIGHT, B. H. Origin of the Erie Canal. Services of B. Wright. 8°. Rome. 1870.
WRIGHT, D. Executor's Guide. 12°. Auburn. 1845.
WRIGHT, Elizur. A Curiosity of Law. 12°. Bost. 1866.
WRIGHT, Rev. G. N. Life of Louis Philippe. 8°. Lond. n.d.
WRIGHT, H. B. Practical Treatise on Labor. 12°. N.Y. 1871.
WRIGHT, H. C. Empire of the Mother. 12°. Bost. 1863.

WRIGHT, L. Brahma Fowl. 12°. Lond. 1870.

WRIGHT, T. History of the English Language; a Lecture. 8°. Liverpool. 1857.

—— Womankind in Western Europe. S. 4°. Lond. 1869.

WUNDERLICH, C. A. and Seguin, E. Medical Thermometry and Human Temperature. 12°. N.Y. 1871.

WYATT, M. D. Fine Art. 4°. Lond. 1870

WYCLIF, J. Select English Works. Ed. by P. Arnold. 3 v. 8°. Oxford. 1869.

WYLD, J. Map of India. Folded 8°. Lond. 1842.

—— Map of Overland Route to India. Folded 8°. Lond. n.d.

—— Map of the War in China. Folded 16°. Lond. 1842.

WYLDE, J. Book of Trades. 16°. Edin. 1870.

WYLIE, J. A. Daybreak in Spain. 12°. Lond. n.d.

—— Road to Rome *via* Oxford. 12°. Lond. 1868.

WYLIE, S. B. Memoir of Alex. McLeod. 8°. N.Y. 1855.

WYNN, Miss F. W. Diaries of a Lady of Quality. 2d ed. 12°. Lond. 1864.

WYNTER, A. Curiosities of Toil. 2 v. 12°. Lond. 1870.

WYSE, T. Impressions of Greece. 8°. Lond. 1871.

WYTHE, J. H. Agreement of Science and Revelation. 12°. Phil. 1872.

XENOPHON, Selections (Greek) with Notes by Phillpotts. 16°. Oxford. 1871.

—— Anabasis. Transl. by Watson. (Bohn's ed.) 12°. Lond. 1867.

—— Cyropædia. Transl. by Watson. (Bohn's ed.) 12°. Lond. 1861.

—— Minor Works. Transl. by Watson. (Bohn's ed.) 12°. Lond. 1857.

YALE College. Addresses, Inauguration of Pres. Porter. 8°. N.Y. 1871.

YATES, E. The Gospels Interwoven. 8°. Pittsfield. 1862.

YEAMAN, G. H. Study of Government. 8°. Bost. 1871.

YEAR-Book and Almanac of British North America, 1867–70. 12°. Montreal. 1869.

YEAR-Book of Unitarian Churches, 1870–71. 12°. Bost. 1870–71.

YEATS, J. Natural History of Commerce. 12°. Lond. 1870.

YEO, J. B. Season at St. Moritz. 12°. Lond. 1870.

YONGE, C. D. English–Greek Lexicon. R. 8°. N.Y. 1870.

—— History of England. 12°. Lond. 1871.

—— History of France under the Bourbons. 4 v. 8°. Lond. 1866–67.

—— Three Centuries of English Literature. 12°. Lond. 1872.

—— Same. 12°. N.Y. 1872.

YONGE, Charlotte M. Book of Golden Deeds. 12°. Lond. 1871.

—— Book of Worthies. 12°. Lond. 1869.

—— Cameos from English History. Wars with France. 2d ser. 12°. Lond. 1871.

—— Musings over the Christian Year. 12°. Oxford. 1871.

—— Same. 16°. N.Y. 1871.

—— Pioneers and Founders in the Mission Field. 12°. Lond. n.d.

—— Scripture Readings for Schools and Families. 12°. Lond. 1871.

YORKE, O. Secret History of "The International" Working Men's Association. 12°. Lond. 1872.

YORKVILLE Directory. *See* UTICA.

YOUATT, W. The Dog. 8°. N.Y. n.d.

YOUNG, E. Labor and Subsistence in the U. S. in 1869. 8°. Wash. 1870.

YOUNG, J. Creator and Creation. 12°. Lond. 1870.

YOUNG, J. C. Memoir of Charles M. Young. 12°. Lond. 1871.

YOUNG, J. R. Analytical Geometry. 8°. Phil. 1833.

—— Integral Calculus. 8°. Phil. 1833.

—— Trigonometry. 8°. Phil. 1833.

YOUNG, W. B. Arithmetical Dictionary. R. 8°. N.Y. 1844.

YOUNG Debater. 16°. N.Y. 1869.

YOUNG Lady's Equestrian Manual. 18°. Phil. 1839.

YOUNG Lady's New Grammar. 16°. Lond. 1847.

YOUNG Man, Succeeding or Failing in Business. *See* AM. TRACT SOC. Tracts for Young Men.

YOUNG Mechanic. 12°. Lond. 1871.

—— Same. Sq. 12°. N.Y. 1871.

YOUNG Men's Association of Buffalo. Annual Reports, 1–34; By-Laws, 1842; 25th Anniversary. 2 v. 8°. Buff. 1837–70.

—— Catalogue of the Library. R. 8°. Buff. 1871.

YOUNG Men's Mercantile Library Association of Cincinnati. Catalogue of Library. 8°. Cinc. 1869.

YOUNG Men's Mercantile Library Association of Pittsburgh. Catalogue of Library. 8°. Pittsburgh. 1867.

YRIARTE, C. Les Prussiens à Paris et le 18me Mars. 8°. Paris. 1871.

YULE, H. Cathay and the Way Thither. 2 v. 8°. Lond. 1866.

ZELL's Popular Encyclopædia. 2 v. 4°. Phil. 1869–70.

ZELLER, E. Die Philosophie der Griechen in ihrer Geschichtlichen Entwicklung. 5 v. 18°. Leip. 1869.

—— Stoics, Epicureans and Sceptics. 12°. Lond. 1870.

ZENKER, W. Der Suez Canal. 2d ed. 8°. Bremen. 1869.

ZERFFI, G. C. Spiritualism and Animal Magnetism. 16°. Lond. 1871.

ZINCKE, F. B. Egypt of the Pharaohs and of the Kedivé. 8°. Lond. 1871.

ZOLA, E. Les Rougon-Macquart. 1. La Fortune des Rougon. 12°. Paris. 1871.

—— Same. 2. La Curée. 12°. Paris. 1871.

ZOTTI, R. Le Nouvean Vénéroni; or Grammaire Italien. 8th ed. 16°. Paris. 1823

ZUNDEL, J. Harmony and Modulation. 8°. N.Y. 1862.

ZURCHER and Margollé. Meteors. Transl. by Lackland. 12°. N.Y. 1870.

CLASSIFIED INDEX.

SYNOPSIS OF THE CLASSIFIED INDEX.

(DEPARTMENTS AND CLASSES.)

THEOLOGY.

1. Sacred Books; Exegesis.
2. Church History; Historical Theology.
3. Systematic and Polemic Theology.
4. Homiletics; Pastoral Theology.
5. Philosophy of Religion.
6. Devotional and Practical.
7. Collected Works.
8. Spiritism; Witchcraft.

MENTAL AND MORAL SCIENCE.

1. History of Philosophy.
2. Mental Philosophy.
3. Moral Philosophy.
4. Educational Treatises.
5. Educational Systems.
6. Instruction.

POLITICAL SCIENCE.

1. Government and Law.
2. Political Economy.
3. Commerce and Trade.
4. Social Science.

LITERATURE.

1. History of Literature.
2. Philology.
3. Poetry, Drama, Fiction.
4. Taste and Criticism.
5. Literary Miscellany.
6. Classics.
7. Periodical Literature.
8. Bibliography.
9. Encyclopædias.

HISTORY, GEOGRAPHY AND TRAVELS.

1. Universal Geography and Travels.
2. Universal History.
3. Historical Collaterals.
4. Ancient History.
5. Mediæval History.
6. European History.
7. Asia, Africa, South Seas.
8. North and South America.
9. United States.

BIOGRAPHY.

1. Collective Biography.
2. Individual Biography.
3. Genealogy and Names.

MATHEMATICS.

(SUBDIVIDED BY SECTIONS, BUT NOT BY CLASSES.)

NATURAL SCIENCES.

1. General Treatises.
2. Cosmology.
3. Natural Philosophy.
4. Astronomical Science.
5. Chemistry.
6. Natural History.
7. Botany.
8. Geology.

MEDICAL SCIENCE.

1. General Medicine.
2. Anatomy and Physiology.
3. Hygiene.
4. Materia Medica.
5. Pathology and Therapeutics.
6. Surgery.
7. Medical Jurisprudence.
8. Mental Disorders.
9. Animal Magnetism.

THE ARTS.

1. General Treatises.
2. Civil Engineering.
3. Architecture and Carpentry.
4. Military and Naval Arts.
5. Mechanic Arts and Trades.
6. Agriculture and Domestic Arts.
7. Fine Arts.
8. Games and Amusements.

CLASSIFIED INDEX.

DEPARTMENT A.—THEOLOGY.

Class I.—Sacred Books and Exegesis.

Bible and Parts of Bible.

Rheims and Douay Version. *Bible.*
Abridged Bible. *Budinger.*
Greek Testament, with Vulgate. *Bible.*
First Printed English New Testament, by Tyndale. (Arber's Fac-Simile.) *Bible.*
New Testament in Danish. *Bible.*
New Testament in Spanish. *Bible.*
Nuovo Testamento. *Bible.*
Hebrew Prophets; translated by Williams. *Bible.*
Daniel and the Minor Prophets. Ed. by Wordsworth. *Bible.*
Critical New English Testament. *Bible.*
New Testament; Noyes' Transl. *Bible.*
New Testament. (Gospels and Acts.) Notes by Warren. *Bible.*
New Translations of the Psalms. Part 2. *Didham.*
Psalms; transl. by W. Kay. *Bible.*
Psalms; Conant's Version. *Bible.*

Apocrypha.

Apocrypha, Greek and English. *Bible.*
New Testament; The Suppressed Gospels and Epistles. *Bible.*
Apocryphal Acts of the Apostles. Ed. by Wright.

Commentaries; Whole Bible.

Bible, with Commentary. (Speaker's Commentary.)
Commentary on the Bible. *Clarke.*
Bible Notes. *Hunt.*
Commentary on the Bible. *Lange.*
Biblical Studies. *Plumptre.*
Literary Character of the Bible; a Lecture. *Swoope.*

Commentaries; Old Testament.

Pentateuch and Joshua critically examined. *Colenso.*
Lectures on the Pentateuch. *Kelly.*
Commentary on the Old Testament; Genesis to Leviticus. *Kalisch.*
Notes on Genesis, with Essays, and Addresses. *Hargrove.*
Commentary on Genesis. *Lange.*
Lectures on Four Last Books of the Pentateuch. *Graves.*
Commentary on Exodus. *Murphy.*
The Idol in Horeb. *Beke.*
Commentary on Joshua, Judges and Ruth. *Lange.*
Job; transl. with Notes. *Coleman.*
Commentary on Psalms. *Delitzsch.*
Psalms of David and Solomon. *Linton.*
Studies in Psalms. *Plumer.*
Treasury of David. *Spurgeon.*
Proverbs, Ecclesiastes, and the Song of Solomon, with Notes. *Cowles.*
Commentary on Proverbs, Ecclesiastes and Song of Solomon. *Lange.*
Commentary on the Song of Songs. *Littledale.*
Le Cantique des Cantiques. *Renan.*
Commentary on Jeremiah and Lamentations. *Lange.*
Prophets during the Assyrian Empire; Version by R. Williams. *Bible.*
Notes on Amos, with Translation. *Drake.*

Commentaries; New Testament.

Notes on the Gospels. *Hall.*
Key to the Four Gospels. *Norris.*
Catena Aurea. *Thomas Aquinas.*
Introduction to the Study of the Four Gospels. *Westcott.*
Commentary on the Gospel Narrative. *Williams.*
Gospel of Matthew Expounded. *Adamson.*
Commentary on Matthew. *Lange.*
Gospel of St. Mark. *Godwin.*
Last 12 Verses of Mark Vindicated. *Burgon.*

Commentary on Mark and Luke. *Lange.*
Commentary on John. *Lange.*
Fourth Gospel the Heart of Christ. *Sears.*
Thoughts on John xxii. *Inglis.*
Thoughts on the Gospels; John. *Ryle.*
On the Sermon on the Mount. *Tholuck.*
Commentary on Acts. *Gloag.*
Commentary on Acts of the Apostles. *Lange.*
Key to the Narrative of the Acts of the Apostles. *Norris.*
Commentary on Romans. *O'Connor.*
Commentary on Romans. *Lange.*
Commentary on Corinthians. *Lange.*
Galatians. New Transl. Notes by Godwin. *Bible.*
Epistle to the Galatians. *Lightfoot.*
Commentary on Galatians, Ephesians, Philippians and Colossians. *Lange.*
Commentary on Thessalonians, Timothy, Titus, Philemon and Hebrews. *Lange.*
Jewish Temple and Christian Church. *Dale.*
Commentary on Hebrews. *Delitzsch.*
Hebrews; a Paraphrastic Commentary. *McCaul.*
Commentary on Epistles for Sundays and Holydays. *Denton.*
Commentary on James, Peter, John and Jude. *Lange.*
Lectures on the Epistle of James. *Johnstone.*
Commentary on Peter. *Leighton.*
Revelation of John, with Notes. *Cowles.*
Memoirs of Patmos. *Macduff.*

Biblical Encyclopædias.

Bible Dictionary. *Boutell.*
Christian Cyclopædia. *Gardner.*
Handy Dictionary of the Bible. *Gurney and Wrench.*
Cyclopædia of Biblical and Theological Literature. *McClintock.*
Dictionary of the Bible. *Smith.*

History of the Bible.

Plain Account of the English Bible. *Blunt.*
Book and Its Story. *Ranyard.*
Fresh Leaves in the Book and its Story. *Ranyard.*
Historical Illustrations of the Old Testament. *Rawlinson.*
Scènes Bibliques. *Roussel.*
Scènes Patriarchales *Roussel.*
Origin and History of the New Testament. *Martin.*
When were our Gospels Written? *Tischendorf.*
History of the Canon of the New Testament. *Westcott.*

Other Biblical Aids.

Bible Student.
Bible Lore. *Gray.*
Biblical Museum; Notes on the Scriptures. *Gray.*
Apostolic Treasury. *Gray.*
Study of the Bible. *Dunn.*
Introduction to the Old Testament. *Davidson.*
Introduction to Old Testament. *Keil.*
New Testament Manual. *Hawes.*
Cruden's Concordance. Ed. by Youngman.
Dictionary and Concordance of Scripture Names. *Henderson.*
Greek and English Concordance of the New Testament. *Hudson.*
Synonyms of the New Testament. *Trench.*
Synonyms of the Old Testament. *Girdlestone.*
Story of the Gospels Combined. *Pound.*
New Greek Harmony of the Four Gospels. *Stroud.*
Gospels Interwoven. *Yates.*

Exegetical Works.

Church's Law of Interpretation of Scripture. *Parker.*
Word of God Opened. *Peirce.*
Compendium of Biblical Criticism. *Sargent.*
The *Literalist.*
Misread Passages of Scripture. *Brown.*
Lectures on the Parables. *Cumming.*
Talks with a Child on the Beatitudes.
Poetry of the Hebrew Pentateuch. *Margoliouth.*
Typology of Scripture. *Fairbairn.*
The Wise Men. *Upham.*
Demoniacs of the New Testament. *Farmer.*
Speaker's Commentary Reviewed. *Strange.*
New Bible Commentary Critically Examined. *Colenso.*
Indices to Revision of the Scripture. *Newport.*
Critique on Bible Union Greek Testament. *Jewett.*
Revision of the New Testament. *Ellicott.*
Revision of the English New Testament. *Lightfoot.*

CLASS II.—CHURCH HISTORY; HISTORICAL THEOLOGY.

Biblical Antiquities.

Smaller Scripture History. *Smith.*
Texts Explained by Ancient Monuments. *Sharpe.*
Moabite Stone. *Ginsburg.*
Mazzaroth, and Mizraim. *Rolleston.*
Legends of Old Testament Characters. *Gould.*

Biblical Geography and Natural History.

Scripture Atlas.
Rivers of the Bible. *Gosse.*
Desert of the Exodus. *Palmer.*
Pisgah Sight of Palestine. *Fuller.*
Biblical Researches in Palestine. *Robinson.*
Sinai and Palestine in Connection with their History. *Stanley.*
Bible Animals. *Wood.*

Sacred Biography.

Characters of the Old Testament. *Williams.*
Heroes of Hebrew History. *Wilberforce.*
Patriarchs and Law Givers of the Old Testament. *Maurice.*
Prophets and Kings of the Old Testament. *Maurice.*
Moses, the Man of God. *Hamilton.*
Prophet's Mantle. *Murray.*
Lives of the Saints. *Gould.*
Life of St. Paul. *Conybeare.*
Conversion of St. Paul. *Howson.*
Footsteps of St. Paul. *Macduff.*

Prophecy, Generally.

Prophecies of Our Lord and His Apostles. *Hoffman.*

Prophecy; Second Advent.

Prophecy, a Preparation for Christ. *Smith.*
Testimony of Christ's Second Appearing.

Prophecy; Apocalypse.

Cities of the Nations Fell. *Cumming.*
Fall of Babylon Foreshadowed. *Cumming.*
Seventh Vial. *Cumming.*
John; or, the Apocalypse. *Desprez.*
The Seals Opened; or, the Apocalypse Explained. *Pond.*
Apocalypse. *Seiss.*

Christology.

Life of Jesus, the Christ. *Beecher.*
Jesus; his Life and Work. *Crosby.*
Jesus. *Deems.*
Life of Our Lord. *Ellicott.*
Examination of Liddon's Bampton Lectures.
Witness of History to Christ. *Farrar.*
Life of Christ. *Formby.*
The Old Commandment New and True in Christ. *French.*
Jesus. *Furness.*
Attributes of Christ. *Gasparini.*
Scripture Doctrine of the Person of Christ. *Gess.*
Ecce Messias. *Higginson.*
Life of Christ. *Hanna.*
Our Lord's Life on Earth. *Hanna.*
Earlier Years of Our Lord's Life on Earth. *Hanna.*
Last Day of Our Lord's Passion. *Hanna.*
Judged by his Words.
Witness of St. John to Christ. *Leathes.*
Witness of St. Paul to Christ. *Leathes.*
Man (The): The Mighty God.
Outlines of the Life of Christ. *Mercier.*
Glory of Christ. *Minton.*
Nazareth.
Resurrection of Christ. *Nott.*
Christ and the Church. *Preston.*
Life of Jesus. *Renan.*
History of the Doctrine of the Deity of Christ. *Réville.*
Life of Christ. *Stephen.*
God-Man. *Townsend.*
Union Questions; Life of Christ.
The Light of the World. *Wilkins.*
Our Lord's Nativity. *Williams.*

Church History, Generally.

Præcognita Historiæ Ecclesiasticæ. *Schmeizelius.*
Origin of Christianity. *Wise.*
Rise and Progress of Christianity. *Mackay.*
History of the Church. *Jones.*
Studies in Church History. *Lea.*
Councils; Ancient and Modern. *Rule.*
Christian Sacerdotalism. *Jardine.*
History of the Corruptions of Christianity. *Priestley.*
Book of Martyrs; abridged. *Foxe.*
Ecclesiastical Class Book. *Goodrich.*

Church History; Apostolic and Primitive.

The Training of the Twelve. *Bruce.*
Paul of Tarsus.
Hippolytus and His Age. *Bunsen.*
History of Councils through Nicæa. *Hefele.*
Old Catholic Church, to A.D. 755. *Killen.*
Early Years of Christianity. *Pressensé.*
Latin Christianity. *Milman.*
Testimony of the Catacombs. *Marriott.*
Mediaeval Christianity. *Hemans.*

Testimony of Eusebius in Regard of St. Peter's Visit to Rome. *Seabury*.
Catechism of the Ancient Schools. *Berrian*.
Historia Ecclesiastica. *Bede*.
Ecclesiastical History. *Bede*.

Church History; Modern.

History of the Church, 18th and 19th Centuries. *Hagenbach*.
Christianity in Relation to Society and Opinion. *Guizot*.
Ecclesiastical History of England and Normandy. *Ordericus Vitalis*.
Monks of Iona. *M'Corry*.
Ecclesiastical History of England; Church of the Restoration. *Stoughton*.
Lectures on History of Church of Scotland. *Stanley*.
Memorials of the English Martyrs. *Tayler*.
Religious Thought in England. *Hunt*.
Religious Life of London. *Ritchie*.
Denominational Statistics of England and Wales. *Ravenstein*.
Schicksale der Protestanten in Frankreich. *Schroeder*.
Religious Life in Germany. *Baur*.
Second Reformation in Spain. *Peddie*.
Daybreak in Spain. *Wylie*.
Document No. 1, Constitution, etc., of *Evangelical* Alliance of the U. S.
Fraternal Appeal to American Churches. *Schmucker*.
Disestablished Church of the U. S. *Hook*.
Discourse on Morals in New Haven. *Cleaveland*.
Annals of the First African Church. *Douglass*.
Commemorative Discourse, Church of Holy Trinity. *Drowne*.
Discourse; Dedication of Theological Hall, Meadville. *Hall*.
Minutes of *Christian* Convention, Aurora, Ill., 1867.
Union des Églises Évangeliques de France.

Patristics.

Ante-Nicene Christian Library.
Apostolical Constitutions. *Ante-Nicene*, etc., v. 17.
Archelaus. *Ante-Nicene*, v. 20.
Arnobius Adversus Gentes. *Ante-Nicene*, etc., v. 20.
Clementine Homilies. *Ante-Nicene* etc., v. 17.
Writings of Commodianus. *Ante-Nicene*, etc., v. 18.
Cyprianus. *Ante-Nicene*, etc., v. 13.
Dionysius of Alexandria. *Ante-Nicene*, etc., v. 20.
Fragments of 2d and 3d Centuries. *Ante-Nicene*, etc., v. 22.
Gregory Thaumaturgus. *Ante-Nicene*, v. 20.
Writings of Hippolytus. *Ante-Nicene*, etc., v. 9.
Lactantius. *Ante-Nicene*, etc., v. 21, 22.
Methodius. *Ante-Nicene*, etc., v. 14.
Writings of Tertullian, v. 3. *Ante-Nicene*, v. 18.
Testaments of Twelve Patriarchs. *Ante-Nicene*, etc., v. 22.
Writings of Victorianus. *Ante-Nicene*, etc., v. 18.

Historical Theology.

Glossary of Ecclesiastical Terms. *Shipley*.
Religions of the World. *Nichols*.
Dictionnaire des Hérésies.
Traditions and Customs of Cathedrals. *Walcot*.
Comparative History of Religions, Pt. 1. Ancient Sculptures *Moffat*.
Origin and Development of Religious Belief. *Gould*.
God in History *Bunsen*.
Ancient Faiths embodied in Ancient Names. *Inman*.
Ten Great Religions. *Clarke*.
Lecture on Ecumenical Councils. *Coit*.
History of Protestant Theology. *Dorner*.
Devil; his Origin, Greatness and Decadence. *Réville*.
Religion of the World. *Leigh*.
The Church and the Bible; an Address. *Robinson*.
Churches and their Creeds. *Pering*.
Athanasian Creed. *Ffoulks*.
Athanasian Creed. *Stanley*.
The Priest, Calvin and Wesley. *Robertson*.
Religion of the Present and the Future. *Woolsey*.
Problem of the Church and the World.
Religious Progress; its Criterion, Instruments and Laws. *MacIvor*.
The Church and the Age. *Weir*.

Class III.—Systematic and Polemic Theology; Sects.

Doctrinal and Systematic Theology Generally.

Bible Lessons. *Abbott.*
Antidote to "The Gates Ajar."
Gospel Doctrine Vindicated. *Austin.*
Our Seven Churches. *Beecher.*
Progress of Doctrine in the New Testament. *Bernard.*
Human Power in the Divine Life. *Bishop.*
Household Theology. *Blunt.*
Key to Christian Doctrine and Practice. *Blunt.*
Bremen Lectures on Religious Questions.
First Principles of Ecclesiastical Truth. *Brown.*
Seed-Truths. *Church.*
Complete Triumph of Moral Good over Evil.
Voice of God. *Cowie.*
Church and World. *Craik.*
Deus Semper.
Divine Kingdom on Earth as It Is in Heaven.
Selections from Unpublished Writings. *Edwards.*
The Spiritual Order. *Erskine.*
Essays and Reviews.
Creator and Creature. *Faber.*
Essence of Christianity. *Feuerbach.*
Explanation of Nicene Creed. *Forbes.*
Calvinism; an Address. *Froude.*
Saving Knowledge. *Guthrie and Blaikie.*
Elementary and Primary Views of Religion. *Headley.*
Christ and His Church. *Hepworth.*
Theron and Aspasio. *Hervey.*
Sermons on Subjects of Recent Controversy. *Heurtley.*
Systematic Theology. *Hodge.*
Inquiry into the Nature of True Holiness. *Hopkins.*
Christianity as taught by St. Paul. *Irons.*
Doctrine of the Church. *McElhinney.*
Roots of Christianity in Mosaism. *Martineau.*
What Is Religion? *Memminger.*
Christianum Organum. *Miller.*
Way of Faith. *Moberly.*
Lectures on the Science of Religion. *Müller.*
Problem of Evil. *Naville.*
Development of Religious Ideas. *O'Dea.*
Central Idea of Christianity. *Peck.*
Divine Evolution of the Churches. *Phillips.*
Lectures on Theology. *Randolph.*
Views of the Deity. *Samuelson.*
Biblical Theology of the New Testament. *Schmid.*
The Rest of Faith. *See.*
Sin and Penalty. *Thompson.*
Religious Opinions. *Townsend.*
Theology of the New Testament. *Van Osterzee.*
Index to Works of *Waterland.*
Theological Institutes. *Watson.*
One Religion: Many Creeds. *Winans.*
Essays and Reviews Considered. *Woodgate.*
Religion of the Present and the Future. *Woolsey.*

Natural Theology.

Higher Ministry of Nature. *Leifchild.*
Bible Teachings in Natnre. *Macmillan.*
Unity in Variety. *Weldon.*

Religion and Science.

Harmonic Maxims of Science and Religion. *Baker.*
Science, Philosophy and Religion. *Bascom.*
Life Theories and Religious Thoughts. *Beale.*
Two Great Books of Nature and Revelation. *Field.*
Dieu dans la Nature. *Flammarion.*
Chemistry and the Wisdom of God. *Fownes.*
Physical Facts and Scriptural Record. *Galloway.*
Semi-barbarous Hebrew and Extinguished Theologian. *Gribble.*
Culture and the Gospels. *McCall.*
Geology and Revelation. *Molloy.*
Lectures on the Science of Religion. *Müller*
Natural Science, Religious Creeds and Scripture Truth.
Primeval Man Unveiled; or, the Anthropology of the Bible.
Harmony of the Bible with the Experimental Sciences. *Rigg.*
Culture and Religion. *Shairp.*
Man in Genesis and Geology. *Thompson.*
Agreement of Science and Revelation. *Wythe.*

Evidences of Christianity.

Religious Philosophy. *Potter.*
Traditions of Eden. *Shepheard.*

Inspiration of the Bible.

Peep into Sacred Tradition. *Abbott.*
Ad Fidem. *Burr.*
Bridge of History over the Gulf of Time. *Cooper.*
Inspiration of the Scriptures; a Sermon. *Dix.*
Bible True. *Fly.*
Holy Bible and its Relation to the Church. *Gierlow.*
The Bible the People's Charter. *Sadler.*
Truth of the Bible. *Saville.*
The Bible and Popular Theology. *Smith.*
The Bible; Is it the Word of God? *Strange.*

Miracles.

Miracles of our Lord. *MacDonald.*
Miracles, Past and Present. *Mountford.*
Essays on Miracles. *Newman.*
Miracles of our Lord. *Trench.*
Can we Believe in Miracles? *Warington.*

Christ; Atonement; Holy Spirit.

Christ the Consoler.
Doctrine of Scripture on the Atonement. *Crawford.*
Dialogue on the Atonement.
Sunday Bampton Lectures. *Hessey.*
Christ our Life. *Hudson.*
The Atonement. *Martin.*
Headship of Christ and Rights of Christian Peoples. *Miller.*
Christ and his Seed. *Pulsford.*
Atonement. *Smeaton.*
Theology of Christ. *Thompson.*
Atonement. *Waggoner.*
Philosophy of the Plan of Salvation. *Walker.*
Doctrine of the Holy Spirit. *Walker.*

Depravity.

Adam's Disobedience and its Results. *Flower.*
Original Sin. *Frame.*

Immortality; Future State.

State of the Dead. *Badger.*
Resurrection of the Dead. *Cochrane.*
Philosophy of a Future State. *Dick.*
Le Lendemain de la Mort. *Figuier.*
The To-Morrow of Death. *Figuier.*
Annihilationism not of the Bible. *George.*
In Both Worlds. *Holcombe.*
Other Life. *Holcombe.*
Our Children in Heaven. *Holcombe.*
Kingdom of Heaven; What it is; Where it is. *Jones.*
Resurrection, by West. *Leslie* on Deism.
Our Eternal Home.
Discourse on a Future Judgment. *Sherlock.*
The Unseen World. *Shimeall.*
Earthly Shadows of the Heavenly Kingdom. *Whitfield.*

Church of Rome; History.

History of the Popes. *Ranke.*
Martyrs of the Coliseum. *O'Reilly.*
Fables respecting the Popes of the Middle Ages. *Döllinger.*
See of Rome in the Middle Ages. *Reichel.*
Récueil concernant le Quiëtisme.
Recollections of Four Popes. *Wiseman.*
Pontificate of Pius IX. *Maguire.*
Letters from Rome on the Councils, by Quirinus.
Macht der Römischen Päpste. *Schulte.*
Herrschaft und Priesterthum. *Struhnneck.*
Catholicism and the Vatican. *Whittle.*

Church of Rome; Theology, etc.

Catholic World.
Abécédaire Religieux.
Catechism of the Christian Faith.
Genius of Christianity. *Chateaubriand.*
Mass and Rubrics of Roman Catholic Clergy. *Cotter.*
Devotion to the Sacred Heart. *Franco.*
Apostolical Succession. *Haddan.*
Anti-Janus. *Hergenröther.*
Problems of the Age. *Hewitt.*
Our Lady of Lourdes. *Lasserre.*
Apostleship of Suffering. *Lyonnard.*
Evidence for the Papacy. *Lindsay.*
Ecumenical Council. *Manning.*
Petri Privilegium; Three Pastoral Letters. *Manning.*
Rome, the Capital of Christendom. *Manning*
Vatican Council and its Definitions. *Manning.*
Petit Carême. *Massillon.*
End of Religious Controversy. *Milner.*
Priest on the Mission. *Oakley.*
Pope and Council. By Janus.
Vicar of Christ. *Preston.*
Real Presence of the Body and the Blood of Christ. *Pusey.*
Visible Unity of the Catholic Church. *Rhodes.*
Directorium Asceticum. *Scaramelli.*
Letters from a Layman. *Scott.*
The Confessional. *Seymour.*

The Femall Glory; or, Life and Death of the Holy Virgin Mary. *Stafford.*
Invitation Heeded; Return to Catholic Unity. *Stone.*
La Legalité. *Veuillot.*
Rome pendant le Concile. *Veuillot.*

Church of Rome; Opposers.

Romanism as it Is. *Barnum.*
The Great Apostasy Identical with Papal Rome. *Berg.*
Is the Western Church under Anathema? *Ffoulkes.*
The Roman Index. *Ffoulkes.*
No Union with Rome. *Gavazzi.*
Papal Infallibility Untenable. *Gratry.*
Church of God and the Bishops. *Liãno.*
Romanism, its General Decline and Present Condition. *Mattison.*
Kirwan's Letters to Hughes. *Murray.*
Pensamientos sobre el Papismo. *Nevins.*
"*Our* Established Church" and "The Unestablished Church."
Rome and Italy. *Pressensé.*
Holy Eucharist and Popish Breaden God, by Túke. *Fuller* Worthies' Library, Miscellanies.
Errors of Romanism. *Whately.*

Monastic Orders.

Annales Monasterii St. Albani. *Amundesham.*
Beggynhof, or City of the Single.
Mysteries of Neapolitan Convents. *Caracciolo.*
Charlestown Convent; Its Destruction by a Mob.
Cloister Legends; or, Convents and Monasteries in the Olden Time.
Life of St. *Dominic*, with Sketch of the Dominican Order.
History of Foundation of Order of Visitation.
Monks before Christ. *Johnson.*
Hermits. *Kingsley.*
Monks of the West. *Montalembert.*
Port Royal. *Sainte-Beuve.*
Gesta Abbatum S. Albani. *Walsingham.*
Inquisition. *Berg.*
Ignatius Loyola, and the Early Jesuits. *Rose.*

Greek and Eastern Churches.

Patriarch and Tsar. Replies of the Humble Nicon.
The Eastern Church. *Stanley.*
Pope of Rome and Popes of Oriental Orthodox Church. *Tondini.*

Reformation.

Reformation in the 16th Century. *Aubigné.*
D'Aubigné's Reformation Reviewed. *Spalding.*
Lutheran Reformation. *Greenwald.*
History of the Reformation, for Children. *Nangle.*
Records of the Reformation. *Pocock.*
Geschichte der Reformation. *Häusser.*
Reformed Churches. *Smith.*
Select English Works. *Wyclif.*
Reply to Cobbett's History of the Reformation in England and Ireland. *Collette.*
Wigtown Martyrs. *Napier.*
Huguenots. *Foote.*
History of the Waldenses. *Melia.*

Church of England.

Common Prayer Book of Edward VI.
Students' Compendium of the Book of Common Prayer. *Nash.*
La Liturgie (Church of England), *Wanostrocht.*
History of the Book of Common Prayer. *Procter.*
Prayer-Book *vs.* Prayer-Book.
Exposition of the Thirty-nine Articles. *Boultbee.*
Church Discipline and Practice. *Sellar.*
Churchman's Manual of Apostolical Doctrine. *Wilson.*
Constitutional History of the Church briefly Examined. *Crosslé.*
History of the English Church.
Church of England, its Apostolical Foundations. By a Presbyter of Tennessee.
Dogma; or what is Our Faith.
Ecclesia; Church Problems Considered.
Cathedral System. *Goulburn.*
Essays on Cathedrals. *Howson.*
Stones of the Temple. *Field.*
Ecclesiastes Anglicanus. *Gresley.*
Œcumenicity and Church of England. *Lindsay.*
Principles at Stake.
Is Healthful Reunion Impossible? *Pusey.*
Reasons for Returning to the Church of England.
Afterpiece to the Comedy of Convocation. *Stearns.*

Road to Rome *via* Oxford. *Wylie.*

English Dissent.

Early Dissent, etc. Three Sermons. *Lumby.*

Story of Harecourt. *Marsh.*

The Sling and the Stone. *Voysey.*

Protestant Episcopal Church of U. S.

Livre des Prières Publiques. *Prot.* Episc. Church.

Prières Publiques. *Prot.* Episc. Church of the U. S.

American Quarterly Church Review.

Evangelical Quarterly Review.

Narrative of Certain Occurences at the late Special Convention of the Diocese of New York.

Journal of Convention of Diocese of Long Island, 1868. *Prot. Epis. Ch.*

How shall we Conform the Liturgy? *Robertson.*

Double Witness of the Church. *Kip.*

Essay on True Catholic Liberty. *Bolles.*

Letters to Dr. Miller. *Bowden.*

Commemorative Discourse. *Drowne.*

The Church's Work in our Large Towns. *Huntington.*

Presbyterians.

American Presbyterian Review.

Biblical Repertory and Princeton Review.

Bibliotheca Sacra.

Exposition of the Westminster Confession. *Shaw.*

Presbyterian Church in South Carolina. *Howe.*

Presbyterian Reunion.

Plan of the Theological Seminary of the Presbyterian Church in the U. S.

Congregationlists.

Congregational Quarterly.

Congregational Review.

New Englander.

Congregationalism. *Goodwin.*

Congregationalism; a Sermon. *Todd.*

Manual of the Congregational Churches. *Roy.*

Sermon, 25th Anniversary of Pastorate. *Brainerd.*

150th Anniversary of *Congregational* Church, Columbia, Conn.

British Mission of Church of Puritans. *Johnstone.*

Sermon, Dedication of Clinton Ave. Cong. Church. *Lansing.*

Methodists.

Methodist Quarterly Review.

Wesleyan Methodist Magazine.

Baptists; Baptism.

Baptist Quarterly.

Baptist History. *Cramp.*

Baptist Movement of 100 Years Ago. *Weston.*

Holy Baptism. *Wallas.*

Sacrament of Responsibility (Holy Baptism). *Sadler.*

Unitarians; Trinity.

Doctrine of the Trinity Defended. *Eagar.*

Christian Examiner.

Monthly Religious Magazine.

Tracts, Army Series. *Amer.* Unitarian Asso.

Discussion on the Trinity. *Beach and Hickey.*

Steps of Belief. *Clarke.*

Letter and Spirit. *Metcalf.*

Unitarian National Conference. Fourth Meeting.

Year-Book of Unitarian Churches.

Universalist; Future Punishment.

Universalist Quarterly.

Creator and Creation. *Young.*

Swedenborgians.

New View of Hell. *Barrett.*

Swedenborgian Delusion. *Burgess.*

Present State of Christendom. *Clissold.*

Prophetic Spirit. *Clissold.*

Dialogues on the Writings of Swedenborg.

Dictionary of Correspondences.

Secret of Swedenborg. *James.*

Discourses on Rationality of Christian Religion. *Silver.*

Quakers.

Portraiture of Quakerism. *Clarkson.*

Past, Present and Future of the Society of Friends.

Divisions in the Society of Friends. *Speakman.*

Lutherans.

Augsburg Confession.

Compend of Lutheran Theology. *Hutter.*

Conservative Reformation and its Theology. *Krauth.*

Ecclesia Lutherana. *Seiss.*

Early History of the Lutheran Church in America. *Schaeffer.*

Manual of *First* Lutheran Church, Albany.

Constitution, etc., of *Evangelical* Lutheran Synod of N. Y.

Reformed Church.

Religious Instruction. *Maronier.*
Manual and Record, *First* Ref. Dutch Church, Hudson, N.Y.
Manual of Reformed Church. *Corwin.*
Discourse; Opening of Ref. Dutch Church. *Dewitt.*
Sermon; Opening of Ref. Dutch Church. *Knox.*
Historical Discourse; 1st Ref. Dutch Church. *Steele.*
Discourse; Dedication of Church at Readington. *Van Liew.*

Mormons.

Female Life Among the Mormons.
Mormons. *Green.*
Exposé of Polgamy in Utah. *Stenhouse.*

Heathen Religions.

Chinese Classics. *Legge.*
The Wheel of the Law. *Alabaster.*
Catena of Buddhist Scriptures from the Chinese. *Beal.*
Hand-Book for the Student of Chinese Buddhism. *Eitel.*
Three Lectures on Buddhism. *Eitel.*
Manual of Buddhism. *Hardy.*
Buddha and his Doctrines. *Kistner.*
Story of Gautama Buddha. *Phillips.*
Druidism Exhumed. *Rust.*

Church Polity; Eccles. Trials.

Ecclesiastical Polity of the New Testament. *Jacob.*
Validity of Holy Orders. *Lee.*
Checkley's Speech on his Trial. *Leslie.*
Purchas Judgment. *Liddon.*

Church and State.

Secular View of Religion in the State. *Hurlbut.*
Layman's Apology for Clerical Chaplains in the N. Y. Legislature.
Williams' Bloody Tent yet more Bloody. *Narragansett.*
Essays on Church and State. *Stanley.*

Rites and Ceremonies.

Clergyman's Assistant in Reading the Liturgy.
Church Vestments. *Dolby.*
In Spirit and in Truth.
Vestments of the Church. *Marriott.*
Ordre der Texten op de Feestdagen voor Paschen, etc.
Liturgy of St. John Chrysostom. *Romanoff.*
Scottish Liturgies.

Ordinances.

Chemical Change in the Eucharist *Abbadie.*
Holy Eucharist. *Cahill.*
Sacramental System of Churches of England. *Purton.*
Sermon on the Eucharist. *Pusey.*
Communion Wine. *Thayer.*

Religious Supertitions, etc.

Children's Crusade. *Gray.*
Phantasmata. *Madden.*

CLASS IV.—HOMILETICS AND PASTORAL THEOLOGY.

Homiletics.

Preparation and Delivery of Sermons. *Broaddus.*
Sacred Rhetoric. *Dabney.*
Power in the Pulpit; a Sermon. *Fish.*
New Cyclopædia of Illustrations Adapted to Christian Teaching. *Foster.*
Lamps, Pitchers and Trumpets. *Hood.*
Curiosities of the Pulpit. *Jackson.*
Homiletic Analysis of Matter. *Parker.*
Pulpit Analyst.
Feathers for Arrows. *Spurgeon.*
Stems and Twigs; or, Sermon Framework.
Methodist Plans of Sermons. *Stevens.*
Homiletic Commentary on Acts. *Thomas.*

Pastoral Theology.

Statement on Ministers' Salaries. *Brooks.*
Pastoral Letters. *Gibson.*
Ad Clerum. *Parker.*
Apostolical Preaching and Ministerial Duty. *Sumner.*
Sword and Garment. *Townsend.*
Ministerial Responsibility: a Sermon. *Van Nest.*

CLASS V.—PHILOSOPHY OF RELIGION.

Philosophy of Religion.

Theories of Philosophy and Religion. *Latham.*
Authority and Conscience. *Morel.*
Religious Philosophy. *Potter.*

Infidelity.

Horne: On Infidelity. *Gibson.*
Difficulties of Infidelity: a Sermon. *Holbrook.*
Rationalism in Europe. *Lecky.*

Short and Easie Method with the Deists. *Leslie.*
Christian Theology and Modern Skepticism. *Somerset.*

Infidel and Rationalist Books.

Free Religion. Report of Meeting, Bost. May 30th, 1867.
De l'Humanité. *Leroux.*
Priestcraft Unmasked. v. 1.
Philosophical Dictionary. *Voltaire.*
American Religion. *Weiss.*
Intellectual Freedom. *Woodruff.*

CLASS VI.—DEVOTIONAL AND PRACTICAL.

Prayer.

The Model Prayer. *Baldwin.*
Morning and Evening Exercises. *Beecher.*
Prayers. *Bunsen.*
Prayers and Devotional Meditations from the Psalms. *Burritt.*
Fifteen O's and other Prayers.
Communicant's Spiritual Companion. *Hawes.*
Prayers for the Use of Families. *Jay.*
Prayers and Offices of Devotion. *Jenks.*
Christian Doctrine of Prayers for the Departed. *Lee.*
Spiritual Exercises. *Loyola.*
Offices of Prayers for Private Devotion.
The Lord's Prayer. *Saphir.*
House of Christian Devotion. *Tholuck.*
Home Worship. *Thompson.*
Union Prayer-Book.
Lord's Prayer. *Van Dyke.*
Manual of Plain Devotions. *Wallas.*

Meditations, etc.

The Origin of the two Cities, Heavenly and Earthly. *St. Augustine.*
City of God. *St. Augustine.*
Comforting Thoughts for the Weak and Weary. *Bickersteth.*
Life and Truth; or, Bible Thoughts and Themes. *Bonar.*
Devout Christian's Help. *Carter.*
Footsteps of Christ. *Caspers.*
End of Life.
Eikon Basilike.
Selections from Spiritual Letters of *St. Francis de Sales.*
Practical Piety. *St. Francis de Sales.*
Gifts for Men, by X. H.
Sources of Joy in Seasons of Sorrow. *Grant.*
Hidden Life of the Soul. *Grou.*
Self-Renunciation. *Guilloré.*
Song of the Redeemed. *Harsha.*
Musings on the Revelation of St. John the Divine. *Henley.*
Light at Evening Time. *Hoam.*
Changing the Crosses and Winning the Crown. *Ideen.*
Night Scenes in the Bible. *March.*
Epistola Consolatoria. *Perez.*
Nourishment of the Christian Soul. *Pinart.*
Sorrow. *Reid.*
Wholesome Words. *Ryland.*
Asleep. *Smith.*
Bow in the Cloud. *Stevens.*
Writings. *Swetchine.*
Readings for Every Day in Lent. *Taylor.*
Teachings from the Church's Year.
Examination of Conscience. *Tronson.*
Life Pictures of the Passion of Christ. *Veith.*
Preciousness of Redemption. *Williams.*
Musings over the Christian Year. *Yonge.*
Scripture Readings for Schools and Families. *Yonge.*

Practical Theology, Generally.

Young Man Undecided in Religion, by James. *Amer. Tract Soc.*
Higher Christian Life. *Boardman.*
Pursuit of Holiness. *Goulburn.*
Letters of Spiritual Counsel and Guidance. *Keble.*
At Jesus' Feet. *Morgan.*
Counsel to the Awakened. *Oxenden.*
Lectures on Practical Religion. *Raffles.*
Religion of Good Sense. *Richer.*

Theological Essays.

Essays on Christian Unity. *Bannerman.*
Radical Problems. *Bartol.*
Ecclesia; a Second Series of Essays on Theological and Ecclesiastical Questions.
Church Seasons. *Grant.*
Scripture Texts Illustrated by General Literature. *Jacox.*
Mornington Lecture. *Lynch.*
Theophilus Trinal. *Lynch.*
Quiet Hours. *Pulsford.*
John Ploughman's Talk. *Spurgeon.*
Talks with a Philosopher.
Living Questions of the Age. *Walker.*

Foreign Missions.

Missionary Herald.
Spirit of Missions.
Mission to the Jews. *Bonar*.
Sermon to Foreign Missionary Societies. *Cheever*.
Martyr Church of Madagascar. *Ellis*.
Bible in India. *Jacolliott*.
Church and the Churches in Southern India. *Lobley*.
Our Oriental Missions. *Thomson*.
These for Those. *Warren*.

Home Missions, Bible Societies, etc.

Discourse for City Missions. *Cuyler*.
Home Missionary.
Proxy Bill and Tract Society. *Jay*.
London City Mission Magazine.
Black Robes; or, Missions and Ministers in the Wilderness and on the Border. *Nevins*.
Year Book of *N. Y.* City Mission and Tract Soc.
Discourse to Amer. Home Miss. Soc. *Smith*.
East and West. *Spencer*.
Discourse to Home Miss. Soc. *Storrs*.
Manual of the *Tract Society* of the Methodist Episcopal Church.
Women Helpers in the Church. *Welsh*.

Sunday Schools.

Sunday School Speaker. *Cheney*.
Sunday School Idea. *Hart*.
Hints on the Formation of Sabbath School Unions.
New York Sunday School Institute.

Sabbath Question.

Sabbath Manual. *Edwards*.
American Sabbath. *Patterson*.
Sabbath and Sabbath Law. *Rigg*.
Holy Sabbath. *Rule*.
Nature's God and his Memorial. *Wardner*.

Peace Question.

Address on Peace and War. *Grimke*.
Prevention of the War.

Class VII.—Collected Works.

Religious Periodicals.

Christian Observer.
Christian Work.
Christian World.
Illustrated Christian Weekly.
Independent.
Monthly Religious Magazine.
Sunday at Home.
Sunday Magazine.
Theological Review.

Sermons.

Sermon; Ordination of the Rev. S. Kingsbury. *Adams*.
Sermon; Ordination of Rev. J. Moore. *Adams*.
Ordination of Rev. J. Wyeth. *Adams*.
Sermons, by Lever. *Arber's*.
A Year with Great Preachers. *Ashley*.
Sermons; 4th ser. *Beecher*.
Consoler and Sufferer. *Bosanquet*.
Sunday Afternoon. *Brown*.
Sermon at the Ordination of Rev. T. A. Farley. *Channing*.
Crown of Thorns. *Chapin*.
Sermons; The Hour which Cometh and Now Is. *Clarke*.
Life (The) that Now Is. *Collyer*.
East and West; Inaugural Discourses. *Conway*.
Morals of Bethesda. *Cooke*.
Sermons, Notes, etc. *Cowan*.
Conflict of Races; a Sermon. *Cowles*.
Ten Commandments. *Dale*
Sermons. *Deems*.
Discourse, Fast Day, July 23, 1812. *Dwight*.
Scriptural Discourses. *Eldridge*.
What is Truth? a Discourse. *Farley*.
Discours, Union des Églises Évangeliques de France. *Fisch*.
Foreign Protestant Pulpit.
Two Sermons; Leaving Home, and Revelations. *Frothingham*.
Sermons on the Poorer Classes. *Gregory*.
Active Pity of a Queen. *Hall*.
Sermons on Various Subjects. *Hall*.
Life of Rev. L. W. Green, with Select Sermons. *Halsey*.
Sermons. *Hamilton*.
Catalytic Power of the Gospel. *Hitchcock*.
Homilist.
Dark Sayings on a Harp. *Hoad*.
Baccalaureate Sermon. *Hopkins*.
Sermon; Ordination of C. M. Hyde. *Hopkins*.
Discourses. *Hyacinthe*.
Family and Church. *Hyacinthe*.
Pious Men the Nation's Hope. *Ide*.
Sanctuary Services. *Jack*.
Varied Aspects of the Word of Life. *Jack*.

Sermon; Ordination of Rev. A. Jackson, and Vindication of his Chronology. *Jarvis.*
Sermons. *Ker.*
God. *Lacordaire.*
Jesus Christ. *Lacordaire.*
Morals of Accidents, and other Discourses. *Lynch.*
Sermons for my Curates. *Lynch.*
Living Words; or, Unwritten Sermons. *McClintock.*
Sermons and Lectures. *McCombie.*
Sermons. *McCulloch.*
Unspoken Sermons. *MacDonald.*
Sermons. *McDougall.*
St. Paul in Rome; Sermon. *Macduff.*
Sermon, Consecration of Bishop Polk. *McIlvaine.*
Sermons. *Mackay.*
Sermons, with Memoir. *McLetchie.*
Rain upon the Mown Grass. *Martin.*
One Hundred Sermons. *Melvill.*
Brightstone Sermons. *Moberly.*
Sermons on Special Occasions. *Moore.*
Women and Her Accusers. *Mühlenberg.*
Sermons. *Murphy.*
Music Hall Sermons. *Murray.*
Park Street Pulpit: Sermons. *Murray.*
Three Groups of Sermons. *Neales.*
Sermon on Subjects of the Day. *Newman.*
City Temple; Sermons Preached in the Poultry Chapel. *Parker.*
Sermon of Immortal Life. *Parker.*
Sermon, Installation of Rev. S. Osgood. *Peabody.*
Creed, or No Creed; Three Sermons. *Pearson.*
Preacher's Lantern.
Sermon, Installation of Rev. W. Irwin. *Proudfit.*
Sermon on the Eucharist. *Pusey.*
Perils of our Prosperity; Thanksgiving Sermon *Richards.*
Sermons on Historical Subjects. *Rowlands.*
Abundant Life and other Sermons. *Sadler.*
Always Thankful; Thanksgiving Sermon. *Scovel.*
Sermons during Lent, at Oxford.
Sermons to the Natural Man. *Shedd.*
The Union and the War; a Sermon. *Shedd.*
Four Cardinal Virtues. *Shipley.*
Horæ Homileticæ. *Simeon.*
The Sinless Sufferer; Six Sermons. *Skeffington.*
Last Sermon in 1st Cong. Church. *Smart.*
Sermons. *South.*
National Thanksgiving Sermons. *Stanley.*
Sermons, with Memoir. *Staples.*
The Evil Beast; a Sermon. *Talmage.*
Sermons. *Talmage.*
Things New and Old Relative to Life.
Thanksgiving Sermon. *Thompson.*
Sermon to Children. *Vaughan.*
Half Hours in the Temple Church. *Vaughan.*
Sermons to the University of Oxford. *Wilberforce.*
Discourse, Closing Exercises at Havard Presb. Church. *Willey.*

Class VIII.—Spirits, Witchcraft.

Spiritualism.

Spiritualism Magazine.
Spiritualism Answered by Science. *Cox.*
Death and After Life. *Davis.*
The Fountain. *Davis.*
Great Harmonia. *Davis.*
Physics and Physiology of Spiritualism. *Hammond.*
Modern American Spiritualism. *Hardinge.*
Question Settled. *Hull.*
Report on Spiritualism, *London* Dialectical Society.
Spiritualism as it Is. *Potter.*
Debatable Land between this World and the Next. *Owen.*
Strange Visitors.
Arcana of Spiritualism. *Tuttle.*
Spiritualism and Animal Magnetism. *Zerffi.*

Witchcraft, etc.

Everlasting Fortune Teller.
Witch Hill; a History of Salem Witchcraft. *Mudge.*
Fiends, Ghosts and Spirits. *Radcliffe.*
Some Miscellany Observations Respecting Witchcraft. *Willard.*

DEPARTMENT B.—MENTAL AND MORAL SCIENCE.

CLASS I.—HISTORY OF PHILOSOPHY.

History of Philosophy.

London, Edinburgh and Dublin Philosophical Magazine.
History of Philosophy. *Lewes.*
History of Philosophy. *Ueberweg.*

Greek and Roman Philosophy.

Christianity and Greek Philosophy. *Cocker.*
Six Lectures Introductory to the Philosophical Writings of Cicero. *Levin.*
Philosophie der Griechen. *Zeller.*
Stoics, Epicureans and Sceptics. *Zeller.*

CLASS II.—MENTAL PHILOSOPHY.

Ontology; Biology.

Basic Outline of Universology. *Andrews.*
Gillespie's Argument for a First Cause. *Barrett.*
Creator and Creation. *Hickok.*
System of Nature. *Holbach.*
The Science of Nature *vs.* The Science of Man. *Porter.*
Intellectual First Cause. *Scott.*
Illustrations of Universal Progress. *Spencer.*
Classification of the Sciences. *Spencer.*
Principles of Biology. *Spencer.*

Psychology.

Psychology. *Cousin.*
Fundamentals; or Bases of Belief. *Griffith.*
Tripartite Nature of Man. *Heard.*
Outlines of a Philosophy of Man. *Herder.*
L'Ame. *La Sagra.*
Man next to God.
Elements of Psychology. *Raue.*
Principles of Psychology. *Spencer.*
Recent Discussions. *Spencer.*
Discovery of a New World of Being. *Thomson.*

Metaphysics.

Inquiries Concerning the Intellectual Powers. *Abbott.*
Senses and Intellect. *Bain.*
Grammar of Philosophy. *Blair.*
Opera Philosophica. *Descartes.*
Matter for Materialists. *Doubleday.*
Ueber die Zeit. *Eyffarth.*
Entstehung und Entwicklungsformen des Witzes. *Fischer.*
Commentary on Kant. *Fischer.*
Méthode pour Analyser la Pensée. *Gaultier.*
Journal of Speculative Philosophy.
Phaedon. *Mendelssohn.*
Scientific Table for Knowledge. *Morgan.*
Outline of Hamilton's Philosophy. *Murray.*
Grammar of Assent. *Newman.*
Elements of Intellectual Science. *Porter.*
The Infinite and the Finite. *Parsons.*
Hand-Book of Progressive Philosophy. *Schiller.*
First Principles of a New System of Philosophy. *Spencer.*
De l'Intelligence. *Taine.*
Intelligence. *Taine.*
Philosophy of Sir W. Hamilton. *Wight.*
Principles of the Kantesian Philosophy. *Wirgman.*
Intellectual Freedom. *Woodruff.*

Positivism.

Positive Philosophy. *Comte.*
Christianity and Positivism. *McCosh.*
Modern Thinker.

Phrenology.

Hand-Book of Phrenology. *Donovan.*
Des Dispositions Innées de l'Ame et de l'Esprit. *Gall and Spurzheim.*
History of Phrenology. *Haskins.*
How to Read Character.
Phrenology, and How to Use It. *Morgan.*
Phrenological Journal.

Mind and Body.

Mind and Brain. *Duncan.*
Hereditary Genius. *Galton.*
Mechanism in Thought and Morals. *Holmes.*
Body and Mind. *Maudsley.*
Physiology of the Soul and Instinct, as distinguished from Materialism. *Paine.*
Subject and Object, and the Double Brain. *Verity.*
New Physiognomy. *Wells.*

Class III.—Moral Philosophy.

Moral Philosophy, Generally.

Ethics. *Aristotle.*
Grammar of Moral Philosophy. *Baker*
Four Phases of Morals. *Blackie.*
Théories et Idées Morales dans l'Antiquité. *Denis.*
Metaphysics of Ethics. *Kant.*
Essays on the Platonic Ethics. *Maguire.*
Science of Evil. *Moody.*
La Réforme Intellectuelle et Morale. *Renan.*
La Bonté. *Rozan.*
Two Consciences; or Conscience the Moral Law, and Conscience the Witness.

Practical Ethics, Generally.

Imagination, by Welsh. *Amer. Tract Soc.*
Life a Race, by Dwight. *Amer. Tract Soc.*
Economia della Vita Umana. *Dodsley.*
Économie de la Vie Humaine. *Dodsley.*
Education of the Heart. *Ellis.*
Blunders of Vice and Folly. *Hargreaves.*
Theory of Practice. *Hodgson.*
Mother's Legacie to her Unborne Childe. *Joceline.*
Life Duties. *Marcy.*
Social Morality. *Maurice.*
Parental Legacies.
Advice from a Lady of Quality to her Children. *Parental Legacies.*
Satan in Society.
Character. *Smiles.*
Self-Help. *Smiles.*
Nobility of Life. *Valentine.*

Morals, Amusements.

Gambler's Life. *Green.*
Dance of Modern Society. *Wilkinson.*

Morals; Stimulants and Narcotics.

Man and His Masters, by Gough. *Amer. Tract Soc.*
Crime of Drunkenness; a Discourse. *Anderson.*
Discourse on the Traffic in Spirituous Liquors. *Bacon.*
Tobacco, the Bane of the Times. *Hawes.*
Temperance Cause. *Jewett.*
Suppression of the Liquor Traffic. *Kitchel.*
Self-Denial for Promotion of Temperance, a Duty and Pleasure. *Newman.*
Strong Drink and Tobacco Smoke. *Prescott.*
Thoughts on the Moral Physiology and Pathology of Liquor Drinking.

Morals; Business.

Defaulters, by Brown. *Amer. Tract Soc.*
Dignity of Labor, by Hall. *Amer. Tract Soc.*
Law of Labor a Law of Love, by Stowell. *Amer. Tract Soc.*
Young Man, Succeeding or Failing in Business. *Amer. Tract Soc.*
Lawyer and Client. *Butler.*
Hints to Young Tradesmen.

Morals; Marriage and Divorce.

Argument of Domesticus on Marrying Deceased Wife's Sister.
Christian Mother.
Christian Doctrine of Marriage. *Evans.*
The Family. *Gasparin.*
History and Philosophy of Marriage.
Marriage and Divorce.
Opinions concerning the Bible Law of Marriage.

Morals; Young Men.

Independence of Mind. By Dwight. *Amer. Tract Soc.*
Mother's Sorrow. By Wadsworth. *Amer. Tract Soc.*
Sound Mind. By Hamilton. *Amer. Tract Soc.*
Tracts for Young Men. *Amer. Tract Soc.*
Young Man beginning Life. By James. *Amer. Tract Soc.*
Boyhood. *Farningham.*
Young Man Setting out in Life. *Guest.*
Rocks and Shoals. *Hepworth.*

Morals; Women.

What Now? *Deems.*
Daughters of England. *Ellis.*
Appeal to Christian Young Women. *Gentelles.*
Father's Legacy to his Daughters. *Gregory.*
Same. *Parental* Legacies.
Cure of the Great Social Evil. *Newman.*

Etiquette.

Canons of Good Breeding.
Book of Politeness. *Celnart.*
Letters to his Son. *Chesterfield.*
Remarks on Chesterfield's Letters. *Crawford.*
Science des Personnes du Cour. *Chevigni.*
Etiquette for Ladies.
Good Society; a Manual of Manners.
Guide to English Etiquette.
Ladies' Book of Etiquette. *Hartley.*
Laws of Etiquette.
Manual of Politeness.
Code Galant. *Raisson.*
Science of Etiquette.

Class IV.—Educational Treatises.

Education, Generally.

Schools for the People. *Bartley.*
Education of the People; a Letter. *Coleridge.*
What Shall my Son be? *Davenant.*
Report of Manchester (Eng.) *Educational* Congress.
Education Question. *Garfit.*
Art d'Étudier. *Grandsagne.*
Wissenschaftliche Grundlage der Erziehung. *Hecker.*
Library of Education.
Locke on Education. *Library* of Education
Milton on Education. *Library* of Education
Scottish University Addresses. *Library* of Education
University Addresses, by Mill, Froude, Carlyle. *Library* of Education.
Manual of Education. *Lyon.*
Nos Fils. *Michelet.*
National Education Union Conference, Leeds.
Theory and Practice of Teaching. *Page.*
What to Do, and Why. *Sizer.*
Education. *Spencer.*
Moral, Intellectual and Physical Culture. *Welch.*

Home Education.

Gentle Measures in the Management of the Young. *Abbott.*
Complete Governess.
Education Maternelle. *Tastu.*

Self-Education.

How to Do it. *Hale.*
Essai sur l'Emploi du Tems. *Jullien.*
Autopædia; or, Instructions on Personal Education. *McCrie.*
Self-formation.
Student's Manual. *Todd.*

Infant Education.

Kindergarten. *Douai.*
Infant Education.

Female Education.

Woman's Profession as Mother and Educator. *Beecher.*
Education of Girls, and the Employment of Women. *Hodgson.*
Address to Graduates, Rutgers Female College. *Pierce.*
Guide Pratique pour les Écoles Professionnelles de jeunes Filles. *Sauvestre.*
Report on Organization of *Vassar* Female College.

Education of Teachers.

History of Teachers' Association in New York City. *Batchelor.*
Teachers' Institutes. *Bates.*
Rules and Course of Study, *California* State Normal School.

Education, Classical and Real.

Classical and Scientific Studies, and the Great Schools of England. *Atkinson.*
Systems, etc., of Scientific Instruction. *Barnard.*
Essay on Classical Instruction.
Essays on a Liberal Education. *Farrar.*
Physical Science in Education. *Green.*
Mann's Physiology in Schools. *Library* of Education
Oneida Institute. Manual Labor Meeting.
Classical Study. *Taylor.*

Education, Religious and Secular.

Bible in Common Schools. *Cheever.*
Question for the Hour. *Clarke.*
Bible as an Educating Power. *Hart.*
Honest Appeal to every Voter on Bible in Schools.
Bible in Public Schools. *Library* of Education.
Report on Bible in Schools. *New York* City.
Culture and Religion. *Shairp.*
Christian Culture in Public Schools. *Smyth.*

Class V.—Systems of Education.

Public Education, Generally.

National Primary Education. *Holland.*
National Education; Systems, etc. *Barnard.*
Four Periods of Public Education. *Shuttleworth.*

Public Education; American.

Reports and Papers of *Educational* Association of Virgina, July, 1867.
History of the Common School System of New York. *Randall.*

True Statement of the Public School Meetings in Hoboken, Feb., 1854.
University (The) Question of Michigan.
Plans and Illustrations of New Public School System. *Wait.*

Public Education; Foreign.

Brief Comments on the Revised Speech of Mr. Lowe, Feb. 13, 1862.
Letter to Mr. Lowe on the Education Code. *Bromby.*
Revised Education Code; Letter to Earl Granville. *Bromby.*
Education Question. Revision a Necessity. *Collins.*
Education Commission Report. *Great Britain.*
Report of Committee of Council on Education. *Great Britain.*
Report on Education. *Great Britain.*
Schools Inquiry Commissions. *Great Britain.*
Few Words on the Educational Code. *Grote.*
Letter on the Revised Code; by a Yorkshire Clergyman.
National Elementary Education and the New Code.
Letter to Earl Granville on the Revised Code. *Shuttleworth.*
Three Letters to the Cornhill Magazine, by Paterfamilias.
Revised Code Dispassionately Considered. *Vaughan.*
Why is a New Code Wanted? By Omega.

Educational Institutions.

Inauguration of President Barnard. *Columbia* College.
Eton; by another "Paterfamilias."
Eton Reform.
Four Years at Yale.
Inauguration of President Eliot. *Harvard College.*
Historical Sketch of the College of New Jersey.
History of the Controversy in University of New York.
Documents from MSS. at Corpus Christi Library. *Lamb.*
Candid Appeal for *Madison* University.
American Colleges. *Porter.*
Parecbolae sive Excerpta Statutorum Universitatis Oxoniensis.
Proceedings at Inauguration, *Rutgers* Female College.
The Great Schools of England. *Staunton.*
Inauguration of Prof. Aiken. *Union College.*
Address at Opening of *University* of Glasgow, 1870–1.
Instruction in Colleges; A Discourse. *Van Rensselaer.*
Addresses; Inauguration of Pres. Porter. *Yale College.*

Societies for Mental Improvement, etc.

Constitution of *Calliopean* Society.
Reports, *General* Society of Mechanics and Tradesmen.
Guide for Lyceums, etc. *Morley.*

Educational Periodicals.

American Educational Monthly.
American Journal of Education.
Connecticut Common School Journal.
Museum and English Journal of Education.
New York Teacher.

Education; Public Documents.

Reports of Superintendents of Common Schools in *Connecticut.*
Report of the Board of Education of *Connecticut.*
28th Annual Report of *Detroit* Board of Education.
Comments on the School Law. *Illinois.*
School Law of 1861. *Illinois.*
School Law. *Indiana.*
Educational Laws. *Iowa.*
School Funds and School Laws. *Michigan.*
School Law of 1862. *Minnesota.*
Reports of Board of Education. *N. Y. City.*
Ohio School Laws of 1862.
Pennsylvania Common School Laws.
Rhode Island Acts relating to the Public Schools.
United States Bureau of Education; Circular of Information, July, 1871.
Report of *U. S.* Commissioner of Education for 1870.
Wisconsin Laws on Common Schools.

CLASS VI.—INSTRUCTION.

Systems of Instruction.

Essais sur l'Enseignement. *Lacroix.*
Report of Discoveries in Education. *Lancaster.*

Logic.

Logic. *Bain.*
Logic. *Condillac.*
Logick. *Hedge.*
Student's Hand-Book to Mill's Logic. *Killick.*
Logique Populaire. *Lecomte.*
Analyse Logique. *Le Tellier.*
Logic. *McCosh.*
Logic. *Parker.*
Logic. *Schuyler.*
Manual of Logic. *Turrell.*
System of Logic and History of Logical Doctrines. *Ueberweg.*
Logick. *Watts.*
Logic. *Whatley.*

Rhetoric and Eloquence.

Treatise on Gesture. *Barber.*
Rhetoric and Belles-Lettres. *Blair.*
Elements of Rhetoric and Criticism. *Boyd.*
Youth's Speaker. *Cathcart.*
Rhetoric. *Haven.*
Speaking Extempore. *Rippingham.*
Orateur. *Roosmalen.*
Manual of Rhetoric. *Smart.*
Rhetorical Grammar. *Walker.*
Rhetoric. *Whatley.*
Young Debater.

Spelling.

Spelling turned Etymology *Arnold.*
Orthoepy and Orthography of English. *De Levante.*
Spelling Book. *Sanders.*
Primary Spelling Book. *Swan.*
Spelling Book. *Swan.*

Composition and Letter-Writing.

English Composition. *Edwards.*
Manual of Composition and Rhetoric. *Hart.*
Elements of English Composition. *Irving.*
Composition and Rhetoric. *Kerl.*
Manual de Estelo Epistolar.
Manuel Epistolaire. *Philipon.*
English Composition. *Rippingham*
Grammar of Composition. *Russell.*
Grammar of Composition. *Tower.*
Laws of Verse. *Sylvester.*

Elocution; Reading.

A. B. C. Buch; Erstes Buch.
Select Reader. *Angell.*
Child's Book of Reading. *Blair.*
Public School Speaker and Reader. *Carpenter.*
System of Elocution. *Comstock.*
Dialogues from Dickens. *Fette.*
Stammering and Stuttering. *Hunt.*
Outlines of Elocution and Reading. *Isbister.*
Fourth Reader. *MacGuffey.*
Elocution. *McIlvaine.*
Course of Reading. *Mandeville.*
Primary Reader. *Mandeville.*
First, Second and Third Readers. *Mandeville.*
Droll Dialogues. *Martine.*
Grammar of Elocution. *Millard.*
Public and Parlor Readings. *Monroe.*
Orthoepy. *Newman.*
Child's Speaker. *Northend.*
Lectures on Elocution. *Plumptre.*
Sequel to Analytical Reader. *Putnam.*
American Reader. *Tarr.*
Elocution. *Vandenhoff.*
Elocution and Oratory. *Wiley.*
North Carolina Reader. *Wiley.*
Fourth Reader. *Worcester.*

Mnemonics.

First Fundamental Basis of Mnemonics. *Fauvel-Gouraud.*

Penmanship.

Dolbear's Penmanship.
The American Penman. *Huntington.*
Catalogue of Autographs. *Putnam.*

Short-Hand; Phonetics.

Phonographic Class-Book. *Andrews and Boyle.*
Phonographic Reader. *Andrews and Boyle.*
Reading Lessons in Steno-Phonography. *Burns*
Self-Instruction in Steno-Phonography. *Burns.*
Philosophic Alphabet. *Edmonds.*
Charlie's House. *Ellis.*
Phonography in Foreign Languages. *Ellis.*
Phonetic Primer. *Ellis.*
Plea for Phonetic Spelling. *Ellis.*
Méthode pour Apprendre à Lire par le Système Phonétique.
Art of Short Hand. *Gould.*
Universal Stenography. *Harding.*
Elements of Tachygraphy. *Lindsley.*

Reporter's Assistant. *Patterson.*
Phonographic Teacher. By Sunergos.
Exercises in Phonography. *Pitman.*
Manual of Phonography. *Pitman.*
Reporter's Companion. *Pitman.*
Reporter's Guide. *Reed.*
Short Hand. *Sarjeant.*
Sermon on the Mount, and Parables. (Phonetics).
Guide to Short Hand. *Towndrow.*
Guide to Stenography. *Towndrow.*
Stenography Completed. *Weston.*

DEPARTMENT C.—POLITICAL SCIENCE.

Class I.—Government and Law.

General Treatises.

Ancient Laws of Ireland (Rolls Chronicles).
Theory of Legislation. *Bentham.*
Art of Negotiating with Princes. *Callières.*
Nationality. *Cockburn.*
History of Government. *Dunganne.*
Constitutional Law. *Forsyth.*
Politique Universelle. *Girardin.*
Political Problems. *Greg.*
Thoughts Upon Government. *Helps.*
Free Government in England and America. *Johnson.*
Village Communities in the East and West. *Maine.*
True and False Democracy. *Mill.*
Napoleonic Ideas. *Napoleon III.*
From Feudal to Federal. *Partridge.*
National Self-Government. *Probyn.*
Devoirs de l'Homme et du Citoien. *Pufendorf.*
Du Suffrage Universel et de la Manière de Voter. *Taine.*

English Government.

Constitutional Progress. *Burrows.*
Administration of Great Britain. *Carr.*
Crown and its Advisers. *Ewald.*
English Constitution. *Fischel.*
Political Works. *Fletcher.*
Hand-book of the English Government.
Constitutional History of England. *May.*
Powers of Parliament. *Sheridan.*
Competition Wallah. *Trevelyan.*

United States' Government.

Jubilee of the Constitution. *Adams.*
Federal Judiciary; a Discourse. *Boardman.*
Are we a Nation? *Bundy.*
History of the Union and the Constitution. *Burr.*
View of the Constitution. *Du Ponceau.*
Examination of the President's Power to Remove from Office.
Suggestions on Revision of Constitution of New York. *Field.*
Sovereignty. *Greene.*
Union Foundations. *Hunt.*
Civil List and Forms of Government of New York. *Hutchins.*
Changes in Constitution of New York. *Lieber.*
Charters of the Old English Colonies in America. *Lucas.*
Constitutions of 1851, 1864, 1867. *Maryland.*
The Nation. *Mulford.*
Plea for Impartial Suffrage.
American System of Government. *Seaman.*
Representative Government. *Stern.*
Political Class Book. *Sullivan.*
War Powers under the Constitution. *Whiting.*
Study of Government. *Yeaman.*

French Government.

La Monarchie Constitutionelle en France. *Renan.*
Constitutional Monarchy in France. *Renan.*

International Law.

Struggle for Neutrality in America. *Adams.*
Neutrality of Great Britain during the American Civil War. *Bernard.*
Laws of Naturalization. *Cutler.*
Syllabus of Rymer's Fœdera. *Hardy.*
Les États-Unis et la France. *Laboulaye.*
Letters on International Relations, by the Times Correspondent.
Guide Diplomatique. *Martens.*
Foreign Policy of England. *Russell.*
American Arguments for British Rights. *Smith.*
Opinion of Attorney-General on Authority of Consuls, etc. *U. S.*

Roman Laws.

Commentaries on Roman Law. *Gaius.*
History of Roman Law. *Ortolan.*
Modern Roman Law. *Tomkins and Jencken.*

Common Law, Generally.

American Law Review.
First Book of the Law. *Bishop.*
Executor's and Administrator's Instructor. *Brotherson.*
Law of Negligence. *Campbell.*
The Counsellor. *Crowell.*
Compendium of the Laws of England. *Enfield*
Every Man his Own Lawyer.
New Natura Brevium. *Fitz-Herbert.*
Law of Easements. *Goddard.*
Curiosities of the Law Reporters. *Heard.*
Essays on the Form of the Law. *Holland.*
Law of Discovery. *Kerr.*
Executor's Guide. *McClellan.*
Maxims. *Noye.*
Analysis of American Law. *Powell.*
Science of Legal Judgment. *Ram.*
Treatise on Facts. *Ram.*
English Law. *Reeves.*
Uses and Trusts *Sanders.*
Lectures introductory to the Study of the Law. *Sharswood.*
Hand-book of Law. *Tracy.*
Justices and County Courts. *Wait.*
Introduction to Law Studies. *Warren.*
The Columbian Union. *Willard.*
Executor's Guide. *Wright.*

Law of Real Property.

Testamentary Law of Maryland. *Dorsey.*
History of Tenures of Land in England and Ireland. *Finlason.*
Land Systems, etc., of Ireland, England and the Continent. *Leslie.*
Handy Book of Property Law. *St. Leonards.*

Commercial Law.

Law of Private Corporations Aggregate. *Angell and Ames.*
Rights of Seamen. *Butts.*
American Commercial Law. *Chamberlin.*
Commercial Laws of the States.
Collection Laws of Indiana. *Davis.*
Law of Shipping. *Dixon.*
Essays on Brokers and Factors. *Edwards.*
Bankrupt Law for Business Men. *Gazzam.*
Liber Mercatoris. *Hobler.*
Law of Salvage. *Jones.*
Commercial Law of the World. *Levi.*
Liabilities of Bankers and Brokers. *Lewis.*
Law of Wreck and Salvage. *Marvin.*
Commercial Traveling. *Meline.*
Bills of Exchange and Promissory Notes. *Muir.*
Ordenanzas de Bilbao.
Laws of Business, *Parsons.*
Compendium of Commercial Law. *Townsend.*
Papers on Maritime Legislation. *Wendt.*

Military Law.

Reply to Binney on Habeas Corpus. *Brown.*
Law of Commerce in Time of War. *Castle.*
Enemy's Territory and Alien Enemies *Dana.*
Guerilla Parties *Lieber.*

Codes, Statutes, Digests.

Digest of N. Y. Statutes and Reports, 3d Supplement. *Abbott.*
Codigo Civil. *Argentine Republic.*
Revised Statutes. *Great Britain.*
Penal Code. *Livingston.*
Revised Statutes, Jan. 1871. *Maine.*
Index of the Laws. *New York.*
Laws, 94th Session of Legislature. *New York.*
Session Laws, 1870. *New York.*
Statutes of Henry VII. *Rae.*
Acts and Resolves, May 1861, Jan. 1862. *Rhode Island.*

Parliamentary Law.

Parliamentary Manual. *Cushing.*
Hints to Chairmen.
New York (State.) Legislative Manual, 1862, 1870.

Administration.

Civil Service Reform. *Hitchcock.*
Civil Service Précis. *Johnston.*

Crime and Punishment.

Increase of Crime and its Cause. *Boone.*
Capital Punishment. *Cheever.*
How should the Child-Criminal be treated?
Laws on Juvenile Offenders. *Lascelles.*

Criminal Cases.

Remarkable Trials and Notorious Characters. *Benson.*
Remarkable Trials. *Dunphy and Cummins.*
Trial of Col. Henley. *Chandler.*
Trial of W. *Cobbett.*
Report, Queen *vs.* Gurney *et al.* *Finlason.*
Argument, Case of Wm. Winter. *Graham.*
Petition of George Gordon for Pardon. *Jolliffe.*
Trial of A. *McLeod* for Murder.
Report, *Mordaunt vs.* Mordaunt, *et al.*
Confession and Execution of Jesse *Strang.*
Trial of Crew of Savannah. *Warburton.*

Civil Cases.

Argument in Relf *et al. vs.* Gaines. *Duncan.*
Examination of the Dred Scott Case. *Foot.*
Argument in Claflin & Co. *vs.* Steinbock & Co. *Gilmer.*
Mayor, etc., of *New York vs.* Erben. Synopsis of Case.
Respondents' Case, *New York Fire Insurance Co., vs.* Howell *et al.*
Argument in the Peterhoff Case. *Smith.*
Argument; Trial of Mr. Tallmage. *Noyes.*
Argument in Parish Will Case. *Porter.*
Whittlesey's Report in Carmick and Ramsey's Case. *U. S.*
Report of *Gaines vs.* Chew *et al.*, by Walker.
Curiosity of Law. *Wright.*

Class II.—Political Economy.

General Treatises.

Principles of Social Science. *Carey.*
Junius Tracts. *Colton.*
Logic of Political Economy. *De Quincey.*
Economist.
Questions of the Day, Economic and Social. *Elder.*
Volkswirthschaftliche Aufsätze. *Eras.*
Political Economy. *Greeley.*
Theory of Political Economy. *Jevons.*
Journal des Économistes.
Speeches, etc., on Industrial and Financial Questions. *Kelley.*
Survey of Political Economy. *MacDonell.*
Conversations on Political Economy. *Marcet.*
Principles of Political Economy. *Mill.*
Pamphlets on *Political Economy.*
Munera Pulveris. *Ruskin.*
Wealth of Nations. *Smith.*
Science of Wealth. *Walker.*
Die Erlösung der Darbenden Menschheit. *Stamm.*
Happy England. *Sullivan.*

Taxation; Revenue; Finance.

National Debts. *Baxter.*
Taxation of the United Kingdom. *Baxter.*
Argument in Excise Law. *Clinton.*
Revenue Digest and Custom House Guide. *Cone.*
Internal Revenue and Tariff Laws. *Dresser.*
How to Pay Off the National Debt, etc. *Green.*
Digest of Duties of Custom House Officers. *Jones.*
Letter to Morrill on Knit Goods.
Report of *New York* State Commission on Local Taxation.
Taxation. *Peto.*
Public Debt. *Reed.*
People's Blue Book; Taxation as it is and as it ought to be. *Tennant.*
Loan Acts of Congress.
Essays on Taxation and Reconstruction, by Diversity.
Bill for Codification of Revenue Laws. *U. S.*
Internal Revenue Act, June 30, 1864. *U. S.*
Finance Report for 1869, 70, 71. *U. S.*
Report of Special Commissioner of Revenue for 1869. *U. S.*
Tariff of 1861. *U. S.*
Tariff Revised to Feb. 24, 1869. *U. S.*
Tariff Revised to July 14, 1870. *U. S.*
Tax Law, 1863 and '64. *U. S.*
Secrets of Internal Revenue. Ed. by Felton.
Our National Finances. *Walker.*
How Our National Debt may be a National Blessing. *Wilkeson.*
Review of the Financial Situation. *Williams.*

Protection and Free Trade.

Protection to Native Industry. *Sullivan.*
Sophisms of the Protectionists. *Bastiat.*
Does Protection Protect? *Grosvenor.*
Fallacies of Protectionists. *Lieber.*

Labor and Wages.

Claims of Labour.
Appeal on the Subject of Seamen. *Forbes.*
History of the Working and Burgher Classes. *Granier de Cassagnac.*
In Quest of Coolies. *Hope.*
Coolie. *Jenkins.*
Agricultural Laborer. *Kebbel.*
Question Ouvrière au 19e Siècle. *Leroy-Beaulieu.*
Report of *Massachusetts* Bureau of Statistics of Labor, to March 1, 1870.
Fors Clavigera. *Ruskin.*
The German Working Man. *Samuelson.*
Labour. *Thornton.*
Work for All.
Practical Treatise on Labor. *Wright.*

Labor and Subsistence in the U. S. in 1869. *Young.*

Pauperism; the Poor.

Pauperism; its Causes and Remedies. *Fawcett.*
Reports of Ministry at Large. *Hadley.*
Poor Laws. *New York.*
State, Poor and Country. *Patterson.*
Service of the Poor. *Stephen.*
Streets and Lanes of a City.

Copyright and Patents.

Law of Copyright. *Copinger.*
Literary Copyright. *Hotten.*
Law Relating to Works of Literature and Art. *Shortt.*
Patent Law and Practice.
Rules and Directions. *Patent Office.*
Inventor's Guide. *Phillips.*
Recent Discussions on Abolition of Patents.
Patent Reports. *U. S.*

CLASS III.—COMMERCE AND TRADE.

Commerce and Trade Generally.

Commercial Resources, etc., of British India.
Commerce du Globe. *Müller.*
Gallerie hervorragender Kaufleute und Förderer des Handels. *Otto.*
Central America and Ocean Transit. *Sampson.*
Natural History of Commerce. *Yeats.*

Commerce; Great Britain and Europe.

Commercial and Financial Chronicle.
Tableau Général de la Commerce de la *France.*
Industrial Resources of Tyne, Wear and Tees.
History of British Commerce, 1763–1870. *Levi.*
Mark Lane Express and Agricultural Journal.
Haberdashery and Hosiery. *Perkins.*
Real Cedula; Ordenanzas de los 5 Gremios de Madrid.
European Commerce. *Rördansz.*
Statistics of Trade of United Kingdom.
Commerce de la France avec l'Europe. *Tschaggeny.*
British Mail Trade. *Vanes.*

Commerce; United States.

American Exchange and Review.
Commercial and Financial Register.
The *Exchange.*
Hunt's Merchant's Magazine.
Merchant's Magazine.
Real Estate Transactions. *Aub.*
Commerce of the U. S. and Mediterranean. *Baker.*
Trade and Commerce of Buffalo, 1869–70. *Buffalo* Board of Trade
2d Annual Statement of *Chicago* Board of Trade for 1859.
Memorial of *Chicago* Convention for River and Harbor Improvements.
Annual Report of *Evansville* Board of Trade, 1867.
Investigation into the Causes of the Depressed Condition of Business (1860).
Incorporation, etc., of *McKean* and Elk Land, etc., Co.
Niagara Ship Canal and Reciprocity.
Annual Reports of *New York* Chamber of Commerce.
Charter and By-Laws, *N. Y. Corn* Exchange.
Prospectus of *New York Sanitary* and Chemical Compost Co.
Home and Foreign Trade of Canada. *Patterson.*
Southern Manufacturer. *Steadman.*
Commerce of the U. S. with Europe. *Talleyrand.*
Tribune's Exhibit of Industry of Minneapolis and St. Anthony.
Annual Report of *U. S.* Bureau of Statistics on Commerce and Navigation, June 30, 1870.
Commercial Relations; Annual Reports to Sept. 30, 1869, and 1870. *U. S.*
List of Merchant Vessels of the *U. S.*, June 30, 1870.
Recent Financial, Industrial and Commercial Experiences of the U. S. *Wells.*

Mining Corporations.

Organization, etc., of *Clute* Lead Mining Co.
Acts of Incorporation; *Connecticut* and Schuylkill Iron and Coal Co.

Prospectus, etc., of *Dover* Marble Co.
Prospectus of *Eagle* Gold Co.
Prospectus of *Isaac's* Harbor Gold Co.
Report of *Isle Royale* Mining Co.
Prospectus of *McKean* Co. Bituminous Coal Co.
Reports on *Missisquoi* Copper Mine.
Prospectus of *Mount* Alpine Gold Co.
Report of *Quartz* Hill Gold Co.
Charter, Report, etc., of *Quicksilver* Mining Co.
Report of *Quincy* Mining Co.
Statement of Property of *Union* Copper Land and Mining Co.
Prospectus of *United* Mines of Zacatecas.
Petition and Prospectus of *U. S.*, Europe and West Va. Land Mining Co.

Railroads; History.

Origin and History of the Pacific Railroad. *Breese.*
History of Railroad Conflict in Legislature of New Jersy.
Statistics of American Railroads. *Kennedy.*
Railway Manual. *Lyles.*
Prospectus of *Mexican* Gulf and Henderson R. R.
Address of Convention 1837 on *N. Y. and Erie* R. R.
Reports to Stockholders on *N. Y. and Erie* R. R.
Truths on *N. Y. and Erie* R. R., by Williams.
Memorial of *N. Y. and Harlem* R. R. Co.
Petition to Canada Legislature of *Northern* Pacific R. R. Co.
Documents on Organization, Condition, etc., of *Pacific* Railroad of Missouri.
Transcontinental Railway. *Poor.*
First Annual Report of *Portland*, Rutland, Oswego and Chicago R. R. Co.
Railroad from St. Louis to San Francisco, Boston Plan.
History of Baltimore & Ohio R. R. *Smith.*
Railway Celebrations. *Smith.*
Report on Aid to Additional Railroads to the Pacific. *U. S.*

Banks and Banking.

Account of Mississippi Repudiation.
Bank Torpedo.
Banker's Magazine and Statistical Register.
Bank of the United States.
Constitutional Law; Decisions on Taxation of Bank Stock.
The NationalBanks. *Delmar.*
Banks of New York. *Gibbons.*
Principles and Practice of Banking. *Gilbart.*
Special Reports on Savings Banks. *New York.*
National Bank Act, with the Amendments. *U. S.*
Report on Banks, Jan. 1, 1850. *U. S.*

Weights and Measures.

Metric System. *Barnard.*
Metric System. *Davies.*
Comparison of Weights and Measures. *Hassler.*
Complete Measurer. *Horton.*
Oriental Metrology. *Kelly.*

Currency and Money.

The Royal Mint. *Ansell.*
Interest Tables. *Breban.*
Tables of Discount on British Sterling. *Chase.*
Tables of Gold, by Act of March, 1843. *Dixon.*
Revised Weights and Silver Currency. *Du Bois.*
Heath's Government Counterfeit Detector.
Interest Table. *McPheeters.*
Many Things upon Money Matters.
Science of Money.
History of Legal Tender. *Spaulding.*
Tablas de Cambio.
Tables of Discount and Interest.
Letter to Lord Melbourne. *Torrens.*
United States Mint Philadelphia. *U. S.*
U. S. Money Order System.
French Importer's Ready Calculator. *Ward.*
Fluctuations in Gold, 1862-3. *Howard.*

Stocks, Stock Exchange.

Ten Years in Wall Street. *Fowler.*
Mysteries of Wall Street. *Medbery.*
Constitution and By-Laws, *National* Stock Exchange.
Twenty Years in Wall Street. *Smith.*

Bookkeeping.

Bryant and Stratton's Commercial Bookkeeping.
New Method of Keeping Accounts. *Cotheal.*

Teneduria de Libros. *Degrange.*
Tenue des Livres. *Degrange.*
Self-Instruction in Bookkeeping. *Hunter.*
Bookkeeping. *Jones.*
Rudiment de la Comptabilité Commerciale. *Legret.*
Bookkeeping. *Morrison.*
Bookkeeeping. *Ross.*
Tenue des Livres. *Simon.*

Insurance.

Assurance Magazine.
Insurance Monitor.
Insurance Times.
New York Underwriter.
Life and Accident Insurance Cases. *Bigelow.*
Proceedings; *National* Insurance Convention of the U. S.
Annual Meeting, *National* Board Fire Underwriters.
National Board of Fire Underwriters. Remarks of the President, April 19, 1871.
Marine Insurance. *Dixon.*
Handy-Book for Life Assurance Agents. *Sharman.*

Mercantile Manuals.

Commercial Dictionary. *McElrath.*
Ready Reckoner. *Brisbane.*
Nouveau Manuel Epistolaire. *Cas.*
Clef de la Correspondance Commerciale Anglaise et Française.
Clerk's Assistant.
Spanish Commercial Correspondent. *Dann and Gonzalez.*
How to Make Money. *Davies.*
American Ready Reckoner. *Day.*
Manuel du Vendeur et de l'Acheteur. *Fessart.*
Charterer's Companion. *Gordon.*
Merchants' Assistant. *Grund.*
Dictionary of Merchandise. *Kauffman.*
Clef de la Correspondance Commerciale. *L'Hermite.*
Manual of Commercial Correspondence. *L'Hermite.*
Merchant and Ship-Master's Assistant.
Monitor Post Office and Shipper's Guide.
Art of Money Getting. *Rede.*
Correspondance Commerciale. *Rees-Lestienne.*
Connaissances des Marchandises. *Roussel.*
Tables of Discount. *Rowlett.*
L'Art de la Correspondance Anglaise et Française. *Sadler.*
Counting House Guide. *Tate.*
Commercial Calculator. *Winslow.*

Cotton Trade.

Report on Cotton Manufacture. *Atkinson.*
Cotton Trade of Lancashire, and the Treaty of 1860. *Slagg.*

Class IV.—Social Science.

Sociology, Generally.

Progressive Lessons in Social Science. *Ellis.*
Theory of Universal Unity. *Fourier.*
Seven Curses of London. *Greenwood.*
Économie Sociale. *Guépin.*
Journal of Social Science. *American* Social Science Association.
Hertz, Rath, Gold. *Knoth.*
Meliora.
Transactions, 1868–71, of *National* Asso. for Social Science.
American Socialisms. *Noyes.*
Social Statics. *Spencer.*
Strong and Free.
Abomination of Modern Society. *Talmage.*

Association.

Association Monthly.
Organization of Labor. *Le Play.*
Trades Unions. *Paris.*
Les Associations Ouvrières en Angleterre. *Paris.*
Internationale. *Testut.*
Trades Unions Abroad. *Thurlow.*
Histoire de l'Internationale. *Villetard.*
Secret History of the "International." *Yorke.*

Women's Rights.

Law of Married Women. *Bishop.*
Woman Suffrage. *Blake.*
Women's Suffrage. *Bushnell.*
Married Women. *Child.*
Nature's Aristocracy. *Collins.*
Rights of Married Women. *Cord.*
Woman's Worth and Worthlessness. *Dodge.*
Subjection of Women. *Mill.*
Industrial Employment of Women. *Milne.*
Pro Aris et Focis.
Series of Woman's Rights Tracts.

What Men Have Said about Women. *Southgate.*

Reply to Mill on Subjection of Women.

Laws Relating to the Women of England. *Wharton.*

Ecce Femina. *White.*

Essay on Divorce. *Woolsey.*

Words of Weight on the Woman Question.

Empire of the Mother. *Wright.*

Public Charities.

1st Special Report of *Chicago* Relief and Aid Society.

Hill Street Refuge: Addresses, etc.

Maryland, Philadelphia and Western Pennsylvania *House of Refuge* Reports.

Hoxton Ragged School Circular.

Illinois Board of Public Charities, 1st. Biennial Report.

Signals of Distress in Refuges, etc. *Jerrold.*

5th and 7th Annual Meetings of *Liverpool* Ragged School Society.

Annual Reports of *Liverpool* Industrial Ragged Schools.

Hand-book to Charities of London. *Low.*

Constitution, etc. of *St. George's* Society.

Lady Bountiful's Legacy. *Timbs.*

Reform and Correctional Institutions.

Prison Hygiene. *Griscom.*

Report on Jail System. *Maine.*

Newgate of Conneticut. *Phelps.*

Annual Reports N. Y. *Prison* Association.

Testimony on Abuses in Cambridge Jail.

Woman in Prison. *Woods.*

Police, Fire Department, etc.

Knots Untied. *Mc Watters.*

Constitution and Laws of *N. Y. City* Fire Department.

Fire Department Reports. *N. Y. City.*

New York (City) Metropolitan Police Annual Report, Oct. 31, 1869.

Records of the Late London Fire Establishment. *Shaw.*

Public Health.

Sanitary Condition of Laboring Population. *Griscom.*

Sanitary Legislation. *Griscom.*

Public Health. *Guy.*

2d Annual Report of *Massachusetts* State Board of Health, for 1870.

1st Annual Report, *New York* (City) Board of Health.

Manual of Metropolitan Board of Health. *N. Y. City.*

Report of Metropolitan Board of Health. *N. Y. City.*

Report, on Removal of Quarantine. *N. Y. State.*

Report of *Philadelphia* Board of Health, for 1870.

Cemeteries; Burial.

Cemetery of Cypress Hills.

Exposition of Plan and Objects of *Greenwood* Cemetery.

Receipts and Expenditures of *Greenwood* Cemetery.

Rules and Regulations of *Greenwood* Cemetery.

Intramural Interments. *Rauch.*

Charter, By Laws, etc. of *Swan* Point Cemetery.

Population; Censuses.

Population of Massachusetts. *Chickering.*

Census of 1871. *Maine.*

Principle of Population. *Malthus.*

Census of 1865. *N. Y. State.*

Ninth Census; Statistics of Population. *U. S.*

Emigration; Colonization.

African Repository.

Hand-Book for Emigrants. *Amer. Soc. Sci. Asso.*

Immigration, its Evils and Consequences. *Busey.*

Immigration and the Commissioners. *Kapp.*

Report of Commissioners of Emigration. *N. Y. State.*

Passenger and Health Laws of New York and the United States.

Special Report on Immigration. *U. S.*

Slavery, Generally.

Slavery and the Slave Trade Ancient and Modern. *Blake.*

Kidnapping in the South Seas. *Palmer.*

Bible View of Slavery. *Raphall.*

American Slavery and Abolition.

Future of the Colored Race in America. *Aikman.*

Duty to the Fugitive Slave; Sermon. *Arvine.*

Picture of Slavery in the U. S. *Bourne.*

Black Man. *Brown.*

Fellowship with Slaveholders. *Cheever.*
Account of Slave Insurrections. *Coffin.*
Slavery Abolished. *Conkling.*
Methodist Episcopal Church and Slavery. *De Vinné.*
Curse of Canaan Rightly Interpreted. *Edgar.*
Relations of the Federal Government and Slavery. *Edgerton.*
Free Negroism; or Results of Emancipation.
Fugitive Slave Bill.
Governing Race.
Slaveholding not Sinful. *How.*
Emancipation. (Oration and Poem.) *Johnson and Whitfield.*
Mystery Finished; the Negro has a Soul.
New Reign of Terror in the Slave-holding States.
Debate on Slavery, Asembly, Jan. 23, 1850. *N. Y. State.*
Ancient Slavery disapproved of God. *Norris.*
Policy of Emancipation. *Owen.*
Slavery, its Origin, Influence and Destiny. *Parsons.*
Question de l'Esclavage aux États-Unis.
Inside Views of Slavery. *Roles.*
Southern Notes for National Circulation.
Underground Railroad. *Still.*
People of Color; a Discourse. *Starr.*
Slavery or Freedom in America. *Stoddard.*
Relations of American Board to Slavery. *Whipple.*
Democracy *vs.* Doulocracy. *Wilson.*

Statistics.

Annual Register for 1869–70.
Statesman's Year Book, 1870–72. *Martin.*
Journal of the *Statistical* Society of London.
United States Bureau of Statistics, Monthly Reports.
United States Register.

Almanacs.

Almanach Français des États-Unis, 1852.
Almanach de Gotha, 1870–72.
Almanach du Marin pour 1840.
Almanacs for 1871.
Australian Hand-Book and Almanac for 1872.
British Almanac for 1870–72.
Carl Pretzel's Vedder Brognostdikador Almineck Kalinder.
Comic Almanac, by Cruikshank.
Connaissance des Tems, 1802, 1830, 1834.
Secular Diary. *Cresswell.*
Era Almanach and Annual.
Letts' Diary and Almanac, 1843.
Nast's Illustrated Almanac for 1872.
N. Y. Observer Year Book and Almanac, 1871.
Sadlier's Catholic Directory, Almanac and Ordo for 1870, 71, 72.
Josh Billings' Allminax, 1871–72. *Shaw.*
Thom's Irish Almanac and Directory for 1870.
Illustrated Annual Register of Rural Affairs for 1872. *Thomas.*
Tribune Almanac, 1869–71.
University of Minnesota Almanac for 1871 and 1872.
Illustrirter Kalender für 1870, 71, 72. *Weber.*
Whitaker's Almanack, 1870–72.
Presbyterian Historical Almanac. *Wilson*
World Almanac, 1871, 72.
Year Book and Almanac of British North America, 1867–70.

Secret Societies.

American Odd Fellow.
Ritual of Freemasonry. *Allyn.*
Swedenborg Rite and Masonic Leaders. *Beswick.*
Old Constitutions of the Free Masons. *Cox.*
True Masonic Chart. *Cross.*
History of Freemasonry. *Findel.*
Freemasonry in England. *Fox.*
Broken Seal; the Morgan Abduction. *Greene.*
Rosicrucians. *Jennings.*
Masonic Trials. *Look.*
Perfect Ceremonies of Craft Masonry.
Key to First Chart of Masonic Mirror. *Parmele.*
Free-Masonry in Europe. *Rebold.*
Mysteries of Masonry. *Reynolds.*
Freemason's Monitor. *Sickles.*
Letters on Freemasonry. *Stearns.*
Inquiry into Freemasonry. *Stearns.*
Text Book of Freemasonry.
Proceedings of *U. S. Anti-Masonic* Convention, Phil., Sept. 11, 1830.

DEPARTMENT D.—LITERATURE.

Class I.—History of Literature.

General History of Literature.

History of Literature. *Schlegel.*
Allgemeine Geschichte der Literatur. *Scherr.*
Literaturgeschichte des 18ten Jahrhunderts. *Hettner.*
Grundsteine einer Allgemeinen Culturgeschichte der Neuesten Zeit. v. 3, 4. *Honegger.*
Cours Familier de Littérature. *Lamartine.*
History of Political Literature. *Blakey.*
Origin and Progress of Writing. *Astle.*

History of Ancient Literature.

Original Sanskrit Texts. *Muir.*
Encyclopédie Classique. *Boutmy.*
Classical Literature. *Cleveland.*
Grammar of Classical Literature. *Johnson.*

History of Modern European Literature.

Abriss der Deutschen Literaturgeschichte. *Evans.*
Prose Writers of Germany. *Hedge.*
History of German Literature. *Metcalfe.*
Essai sur la Littérature Espagnole.
Cours Pratique de la Littérature Francaise. Dix Neuvième Siècle. *Poitevin.*
Bilder aus dem Geistigen Leben unserer Zeit. *Schmidt.*

History of English Literature.

Annual Review and History of Literature.
Dictionary of Authors. *Allibone.*
Tables of English Literature. *Morley.*
History of English Literature. *Collier.*
History of English Literature. *Taine.*
Manual of English Prose Literature. *Minto.*
History of English Poetry. *Warton.*
Literature of the Age of Elizabeth. *Whipple*
Three Centuries of English Literature. *Yonge.*
English Literature of 19th Century. *Cleveland.*
Novels and Novelists of the 19th Century. *Forsyth.*
Literature and Art in Great Britain. *Graham.*
First Steps in English Literature. *Gilman.*
Literature of English Language. *Hunt.*
Arber's English Reprints.
Publications of *Chaucer* Society.
Publications of *Early* English Text Society.
Fuller Worthies' Library.
Catnach Press.

History of American Literature.

American Literature. *Cleveland.*
Living Writers of the South. *Davidson.*
Living Female Writers of the South. *Tardy.*
Southland Writers. *Tardy.*

Class II.—Philology.

Philology, Generally.

American Philological Association. Proceedings, 1st, 2d and 3d Annual Sessions, 1870–72.
Discours sur la Manière d'apprendre les Langues. *Anaya.*
Essai de Traduction de cinq Langues. *Boulard.*
Essay on Language. *Cardell.*
Dialoghi Francesi, Italiani, Tedeschi ed Inglesi.
Families of Speech. *Farrar.*
Comparative Grammar of Sanskrit, Greek and Latin. *Ferrar.*
Advice of a Father to his Son; Latin, French, Italian, German and English. *François.*
Hermes; or, Universal Grammar. *Harris.*
Origin of Language and Myths. *Kavanagh.*
Philological Essays. *Key.*
Chips from a German Workshop. *Müller.*
Essays (in German.) *Müller.*
Lectures on Language. *Müller.*
Album of Language. *Naphegyi.*
Mastery Series. *Prendergast.*
De l'Origine du Langage. *Renan.*
Philosophy of Language Illustrated. *Sherman.*

Oriental Languages.

Dictionary of Modern Arabic. *Newman.*
Arabisches, Syrisches und Chaldäisches Lesebuch. *Rink.*
Armenian and English Grammar. *Aucher.*

Assyrian Dictionary. *Norris.*
Elements of Chaldee. *Harris.*
Vocabulary of Proper Names, Chinese and English. *Smith.*
Chinese and English Dictionary. *Lobscheid.*
Rudiments of Chinese. *Summers.*
China's Place in Philology. *Edkins.*
The Rosetta Stone. *Sharpe.*
Decree of Canopus. *Sharpe.*
Hebrew Grammar. *Dunham.*
Introductory Hebrew Grammar. *Ewald.*
Hebrew Chrestomathy. *Green.*
Hebrew Grammar.
Hebrew Grammar. *Nordheimer.*
Heads of Hebrew Grammar. *Tregelles.*
Picture Writing in the Bible. *Miles.*
Japanese Grammar. *Hoffman.*
Syriac Miscellanies. *Cowper.*

American Languages.

Wobanaki Kimzowi Awighigan, (*i. e.* Abnaki Spelling Book). *Uzokhilain.*
Contributions to Creole Grammar. *Van Name.*

Greek.

Modern Greek and Ancient Greek. *Geldart.*
Greek-English Lexicon. *Liddell and Scott.*
Greek Lexicon, Roman and Byzantine Periods. *Sophocles.*
English-Greek Lexicon. *Yonge.*
Index Vocabulorum in Homero. *Seberus.*
Catechism of Greek Accidence. *Hickie.*
Greek Grammar. *Matthiæ.*
Greek Grammar for Beginners. *Waddell.*
London Greek Grammar.
Elucidation of the Student's Greek Grammar. *Curtius.*
First Greek Lessons. *Arnold.*
Méthode pour la Langue Grecque. *Burnouf.*
Greek Prose Composition. *Arnold.*
Greek and Latin Prose Composition. *Sargent and Dallas.*
Greek Reader. *Jacobs.*
Select Dialogues from *Lucian;* with Interlinear Translation.
Iliad of *Homer*, Book 1, with Interlinear Translation.

Latin.

Latin-English Dictionary. *Entick.*
Latin-English Lexicon. *Riddle.*
English-Latin Dictionary. *Smith and Hall.*
Ainsworth's Dictionary, abridged by Dymock and Anthon.
Dictionary to Cæsar's Gallic War. *Creak.*
Clavis Ciceroniana. *Ernesti.*
Latin Synonyms. *Hill.*
Latin Grammar. *Abeille.*
Latin Grammar. *Hall.*
Public School Latin Grammar.
Elementary Latin Grammar. *Schmitz.*
Key to Latin and Greek. *Osborn.*
Freddie's Latin Lessons. *Albert.*
First Lessons in Latin. *Andrews.*
First Latin Book. *Harkness.*
First and Second Latin Book. *Arnold.*
Latin Reader. *Jacobs.*
Latin Prose-Book. *Hanson.*
Latin Translator. *Cubi i Soler.*
Latin Prose Composition. *Arnold.*
Æsop's Fables with Interlinear Translation.
Metamorphoses of *Ovid*, Book 1, with Interlinear Translation.
Æneid of *Virgil*, Book 1, with Interlinear Translation.
Viri Romæ. *Leverett.*
Viri Romæ. *L'Homond.*

German.

German Grammar. *Bachmair.*
German Grammar. *Bernays.*
Nature and Genius of the German Language. *Boileau.*
Treasury of English and German. *Cauvin.*
German Course. *Comfort.*
German Reader. *Comfort.*
Easy Lessons in German. *Ertheiler.*
Deutsches Lesebuch. *Follen.*
German Grammar. *Follen.*
German Conversations.
German Reader for Beginners.
German and English Phrases and Dialogues. *Graeter.*
Catechism of German Grammar. *Heinemann.*
Grammar of Teutonic Languages. *Helfenstein.*
English and German Dialogues. *Laycock.*
New Guide to German Conversation. *Leypoldt.*
Maître de la Langue Allemande.
Grammaire Allemande. *Meidinger.*
Lessons in German. *Monteith.*
New Method for German (Adler's). *Ollendorf.*
German Scholar's Hand-Book. *Rosenthal.*
German Grammar. *Rowbotham.*
Grammaire Allemande. *Rüffer.*
German Grammar. *Schade.*
Stories from German Writers, with Interlinear Translation.

German Grammar. *Tiarks.*
German Grammar. *Whitney.*
Wendische Grammatica. *Matthaei.*

Scandinavian Languages.

Elements of Danish and Swedish. *Gierlow.*
Icelandic Grammar. *Bayldon.*
Icelandic-English Dictionary. *Cleasby.*

Anglo-Saxon.

Anglo-Saxon Grammar. *March.*
Anglo-Saxon Reader. *March.*
Hand-Book of Anglo-Saxon Orthography.
Saxon and English. *Henshall.*

English, Generally.

Proceedings of *American* Philological Association.
Patronymica Cornu-Britannica. *Charnock.*
Early English Pronunciation, by Ellis. *Chaucer Society.*
Studies in English. *De Vere.*
Analysis of English Language. *Fleming.*
History of English. *Latham.*
English Language. *Lewis.*
English, Past and Present. *Trench.*
Observations on Language. *Webster.*
History of the English Language; a Lecture. *Wright.*

English Grammar.

English Grammar. *Arnold.*
Analytic Grammar. *Barnard.*
American Grammar. *Brown.*
English Grammar. *Brown.*
English Grammar. *Bullions.*
Gramatica Inglesa *Casey.*
Study of English. *Cavert.*
English Grammar. *Champlin.*
Grammar. *Clark.*
Grammaire Anglaise. *Cobbett and Perrin.*
English Grammar. *Covell.*
Questions on English Grammar. *Green.*
Scholar's Companion. *Green.*
English Grammar. *Hiley.*
English Grammar abridged. *Hiley.*
Questions on English Grammar. *Hiley.*
Conversations on English Grammar. *Ingersoll.*
English Grammar for Ladies' Schools. *Latham.*
English Accidence. *Morris.*
English Grammar. *Murray.*
Grammatical Structure of English. *Mulligan.*
English Grammar and Composition. *Oram.*
English Grammar. *Peirce.*
Cours de Langue Anglaise. *Robertson.*
Nouveau Cours de Langue Anglaise. *Robertson.*
Grammaire Anglaise. *Sadler.*
Accidence of English Grammar. *Smart.*
Key to Exercises in English. *Smart.*
Manual of Grammar. *Smart.*
Principles of English Grammar. *Smart.*
Manual of English Grammar. *Smith.*
English Grammar. *Weeden.*
Young Lady's New Grammar.

English Dictionaries.

Deficiencies in English Dictionaries. *Trench.*
Johnson's Dictionary, ed. by Latham.
English Dictionary. *Reid.*
Abridgment of Walker's Dictionary. *Smith.*
Dictionary of the English Language. *Stormouth.*
Dictionary of English Etymology. *Wedgwood.*
New York Expositor. *Wiggins.*
Dictionary of Oldest Words in the English Language. *Coleridge.*
Dictionary of Archaic and Provincial Words. *Halliwell.*

English Etymology, Dialects, etc.

English Lessons for English People. *Abbott and Seeley.*
Common Sense on Rules Regarding English. *Nayler.*
Word Builder. *Isbister.*
Words and their Uses. *White.*
Synonyms. *Crabb.*
Synonyms Discriminated. *Smith.*
Dictionary of English Synonymes. *Soule.*
Dialect of West of England. *Jennings.*
Americanisms. *De Vere.*

French; Courses and Methods.

Pronouncer and Key. *Andrews.*
Nouvelles Conversations, Françaises, Anglaises et Allemandes. *Bellenger.*
Guide to French Conversations. *Bellenger and Witcomb.*
Curso de Temas Franceses. *Berbrugger.*
French Reader. *Boeuf.*
Colloquial Phrases. *Bolmar.*
Fables, with Key. *Bolmar.*
Complete French Master. *Boyer.*
Exercises in French. *Chambaud.*
Themes. François et Anglois. *Chambaud.*
Conversations and Dialogues. *Chouquet.*
Conversations in French. *Chouquet.*
Manual of Conversation. *Clifton and Dufriche Desgenettes.*
Traducteur François. *Cubi i Soler.*

Catechism of French Grammar. *Delavoye.*
Dialogues Français et Allemands.
French Tutor. *Du Moulin.*
Comparison of French and English. *Duverger.*
New Method of Learning French. *Fasquelle.*
Easy French Reading. *Fisher.*
Difficulties of French. *Gardera.*
French Student's Manual. *Girault.*
French Pronunciation. *Le Brethon.*
French School. *Lepage.*
Art of Speaking French. *Mouls.*
Ollendorff's Method for French, by Jewett.
Ollendorff's Method for French, by Value.
Key to *Ollendorff's* French Method.
French and English Conversation. *Perrin.*
Causeries Parisiennes. *Peschier.*
Cours d'Éloquence Française. *Pierrot.*
Manuel Classique de Conversations Françaises et Anglaises. *Sadler.*
Manuel de Phrases Françaises et Anglaises. *Sadler.*
Art de la Correspondance Anglaise et Française. *Sadler.*
Metodo para aprender el Frances. *Simonne.*
New French Manual. *Surenne.*
French as it is Spoken. *Tourrier.*
Principes de la Langue Française. *Wailly.*
L'Écho de Paris. *Worman.*

French Grammars.

Grammatica Francese. *Biagioli.*
Corrigé des Exercises Grammaticaux. *Boniface.*
Grammaire Française. *Boniface.*
Vers François. *Gaultier.*
Gramática de la Lengua Francesa.
French Grammar. *Guégan.*
French Grammar. *Laporte.*
Nouvelle Cacographie. *Letellier.*
Corrigé de la Nouvelle Cacographie. *Letellier.*
Clef de la Grammaire. *Levizac.*
French Grammar. *Levizac.*
Grammaire Française. *Noël et Chapsal.*
French Grammar. *Perrin.*
First Book in French. *Pinney.*
French Syntax. *Praval.*
French Grammar. *Rouillon.*
French Grammar. *Wanostrocht.*

French Dictionaries.

French Word-Book. *Bossut.*
Dictionnaire Français - Anglais; abrégé par Salmon. *Boyer.*
Dictionnaire Français. *Littré.*
Petit Dictionnaire de l'Académie Française. *Masson.*
Etymological Dictionary of the French Language. *Pick.*
Dictionnaire des Verbes Français. *Tarver.*

Spanish.

Diccionario de la Lengua Castellana. *Play Torres.*
Spanish and English Dictionary. *Seoane.*
Spanish-English Dictionary.
Spanish Grammar. *Del Mar.*
Grammaire Espagnole. *Chalumeau de Verneuil.*
Spanish Grammar. *De Vere.*
Spanish Grammar. *Fernandez.*
Spanish Grammar. *Josse.*
Spanish Grammar. *Soler.*
Spanish Grammar. *Whitehead.*
Lengua Castellana. *Borras.*
English Translator (from Spanish). *Cubi i Soler.*
Traductor Español. *Cubi i Soler.*
Exercises in Spanish. *McHenry.*
Exercises in Spanish. *Mordente.*
First Book in Spanish. *Salkeld.*
Spanish Guide for Conversation. *Soler.*

Portuguese.

Spanish and Portuguese Languages. *Bachi.*
Portuguese and English Grammar. *Midosi.*
Portuguese Grammar. *Vieyra.*

Italian.

Italian and English Dictionary. *Baretti.*
Grammaire Italienne. *Biagioli.*
Italian Grammar. *Graglia.*
Grammaire Italienne. *Polidori.*
Grammaire Italienne. *Secreti.*
Nouveau Vênéroni; ou Grammaire Italienne. *Zotti.*
Introduction to Italian. *Baretti.*
Collection of Italian Colloquial Phrases.
Langue Italienne. *Gaultier.*
Exercises in Italian. *Graglia.*
Nouveau Maître Italien. *Favre.*
Maître Italien. *Lauri.*
New Method for Italian. *Ollendorff.*
Amusing Practice of the Italian Language. *Palermo.*
Stories from Italian Writers, with Interlinear translation.

CLASS III.—POETRY ; DRAMA ; FICTION.

Greek Poets.

Medea, Alcestis and Hippolytus. Tr. by Williams. *Euripides*.
Tragedies. *Euripides*.
Hesiod, Callimachus and Theognis.
Iliad. *Homer*.
Odyssey. *Homer*.
Works of *Homer*.
Odes of *Pindar*.
Electra. *Sophocles*.
Philoctetes of *Sophocles*, revised by Blaydes.
Tragedies. *Sophocles*.
Works. *Sophocles*.
Theocritus, Bion and Moschus, Idylls and the War songs of Tyrtaeus.

Latin Poets.

Poems and Fragments. Tr. by Ellis. *Catullus*.
Poems of *Catullus* and Tibullus and the Vigil of Venus.
Lyrics. *Horace*.
Satires, Book I. *Horace*.
Satires, Epistles, Ars Poetica. *Horace*.
Works. *Horace*.
Juvenal, Persius, Sulpicia and Lucilius.
Satyrs. Transl. by Dryden. *Juvenal*.
Pharsalia. *Lucan*.
On the Nature of Things. *Lucretius*.
Epigrams. *Martial*.
Metamorphoses of *Ovid*, in Verse by King.
Works. Transl. by Riley. *Ovid*.
Satires of Persius. *Juvenal*.
Propertius, Petronius, J. Secundus. Aristaenetus.
Elegies of *Tibullus*. Transl. by Cranstoun.
Works. *Virgil*.
Æneid. *Virgil*.

Macaronics, Modern Latin Verse.

Hiawatha rendered into Latin. *Newman*.
Latin Elegiac Verse. *Gepp*.
Macaronic Poetry. *Morgan*.

Irish and Scotch Poetry.

Ballads of Ireland. *Hayes*.
Wearing of the Green Song Book.
Ballad Minstrelsy of Scotland.
Poems of *Ossian;* with Transl. by Clarke.
Scottish Songs. *Ritson*.
Scottish Songs. *Herd*.
Songs of Scotland.
Wallace. *Henry* the Minstrel.

English Poetical Collections.

Beeton's Great Book of Poetry.
Early Ballads. *Bell*.
English and Scotch Historical Ballads. *Milman*.
Folk Songs. *Palmer*.
Household Book of Poetry. *Dana*.
Household Book of Songs. *Bowman*.
Humorous Poetry of the English Language. *Parton*.
Library of Poetry and Song. *Bryant*.
Love Poems of All Nations. *Kaines*.
Our Poetical Favorites. *Kendrick*.
Poetry of Compliment and Courtship. *Palmer*.
Poets of America. *Cheever*.
Southern Amaranth. *Brock*.

Early English Poetry.

Canterbury Tales by Chaucer. *Chaucer* Society.
Collection of Old Ballads.
Destruction of Troy. *Early* English.
Percy Folio M.S. *Early* English.
Second Collection of Poems against Popery and Tyranny.
Vision of Piers Plowman. *Langland*.
Vision of Piers Plowman, by Langland. *Early* English.

Poetical Works.

Admetus, and other Poems. *Lazarus*.
Angler's Garland for 1870. *Pearson*.
Apple Blossoms. *Nation*.
Army Ballads. *Lee*.
Autumn Dreams. *Castlen*.
Awful, and other Jingles. *Strong*.
Beatrice. *Noel*.
Beautiful Snow, and other Poems. *Watson*.
Book of the East, and other Poems. *Stoddard*.
Boston Dip, and other Poems. *Loring*.
Child-Life. *Whittier*.
Christine, and other Poems. *Miles*.
Chronicles and Characters. *Lytton*.
Coila's Whispers.
Come to the Woods, and other Poems. *Cornish*.
Countess of Pembroke's Emanuell, etc., by Fraunce. *Fuller* Worthies' Library, Miscellanies.
Cross, and Verses of Many Years. *Neville*.
Daisy Dare and Baby Power. *Jeffrey*.

Daughter of the King, and other Poems. *Sweetman.*
Dream Music. *Marvin.*
East and West Poems. *Harte.*
Episodes and Lyric Pieces. *Weeks.*
Essay on American Poetry, with Poems. *Brown.*
Fables and Legends of Many Countries. *Saxe.*
Fallacies and Tendencies of the Age. *Dean.*
Glaphyra, and other Poems. *Reynolds.*
Golden Cross, and other Poems. *Van Wart.*
Haydn, and other Poems.
Hesperia. *Tappan.*
Holy Grail, and other Poems. *Tennyson.*
Immortal, and other Poems. *Nack.*
Ladies in Parliament, and other Pieces. *Trevelyan.*
Landmarks, and other Poems. *Piatt.*
Lays of Ancient Rome. *Macaulay.*
Lays of the Deer Forest. *Sobieski.*
Leaves of Grass. *Whitman.*
Legends and Lyrics. *Hayne.*
Legends and Lyrics. *Procter.*
Life and Songs of Baroness Nairne; with Memoir and Poems of Caroline Oliphant. *Rogers.*
Light from the Star of Bethlehem. *Dawes.*
Light of the World, and other Poems.
London Lyrics. *Locker.*
Love and Land. *Scanlan.*
Love, and other Poems. *Hale.*
Love Songs. *De Vere.*
Lover's Diary. *Cary.*
Mad-War-Planet, and other Poems. *Howitt.*
Madeline, and other Poems. *Hake.*
Masque of the Gods. *Taylor.*
Masque of Shadows, and other Poems. *Payn.*
Miriam, and other Poems. *Whittier.*
Miscellaneous Poems. *Rowson.*
Monitions of the Unseen. *Ingelow.*
Mother Goose for Grown Folks. *Whitney.*
Mother Goose in a New Dress.
Music Lesson of Confucius. *Leland.*
My Witness. *Winter.*
Nebraska Legends and Poems. *Dake.*
New Poems. *Lytton.*
Old Sergeant, and other Poems. *Willson.*
Old Song and New. *Preston.*
Out-of-Door Rhymes. *Turner.*
Palmetto Pictures.
Percy's Year of Rhymes. *Richardson.*
Pike County Ballads, and other Pieces. *Hays.*
Poems of Lord Bacon. *Fuller* Worthies.
Poems. *Bell.*
Poems. *Brincklé.*
Poems. *Bryant.*
Poems. *Burleigh.*
Poems. *Butler.*
Poetical Works. *Campbell.*
Poems. *Carew.*
Poetical Works. *Chatterton.*
Poetical Works. *Cook.*
Poems of Sir J. Davies. *Fuller* Worthies.
Poems. *Davidson.*
Poems, with Life. *Davis.*
Poems. *Dorr.*
Poems of Progress. *Doten.*
Poetical Works. *Dryden.*
Poems. *Embury.*
Poems. *Gascoigne.*
Poems of G. J. and P. Fletcher. *Fuller* Worthies.
Poems. *Freiligrath.*
Poems. *Freneau.*
Poems of Gascoigne. *Arber's* Reprints.
Poems by Gifford. *Fuller* Worthies.
Poems. *Halleck.*
Poems by Harbert. *Fuller* Worthies.
Poems. *Harte.*
Poems. *Heady.*
Poems. *Heygate.*
Poems. *Holmes.*
Poems. *Hooper.*
Poetical Works. *Keats.*
Poems. *Leighton.*
Poems, *Lister.*
Poems of H. Lok. *Fuller* Worthies.
Poetical Works. *Longfellow.*
Poetical Works. *Lyndsay.*
Poems. *McDonald.*
Poems. *McGee.*
Poems. *Osborn.*
Poems. *Parnell.*
Poems. *Poe.*
Poems. *Portal.*
Poems. *Rossetti.*
Poems. *Saxe.*
Poetical Works. *Shelley.*
Poems of Bygone Years. *Sewell.*
Poems for the Million. *Smith.*
Poems. *Tennyson.*
Poems. *Thaxter.*
Poems. *Tupper.*
Poems. *Wallace.*
Poems of Washbourne. *Fuller* Worthies.
Poems. *Whittier.*
Poetical Works. *Whittier.*
Poems. *Wilson.*

Poets and Poetry of America; a Satire.
Prologue, Knight's Tale, etc. *Chaucer.*
Puck's Nightly Pranks. *Bund.*
Radical Rhymes. *Denton.*
Rehearsals; a Book of Verses. *Warren.*
Rejected Addresses. *Smith.*
Revelations of Peter Brown, Poet and Peripatetic. *Waller.*
Scholar's Day Dream. *Hill.*
Seers of the Ages. *Peebles.*
Short Poems for Short People. *Fawcett.*
Soldier's Songs. *Edgell.*
Songs before Sunrise. *Swinburne.*
Songs of the Heart.
Songs of the Sierras. *Miller.*
Sonnets and Lovers Complaint. *Shakspeare.*
Southern Voices. *Holcombe.*
Star Streaks. *Holland.*
Struggle for Existence. *Pope.*
Tales. *Crabbe.*
Thirty Poems. *Bryant.*
Thistle-Down. *Boyle.*
Thoughts in Verse. *Cooper.*
Thoughts in Verse. *Elliott.*
Two Brothers, and other Poems. *Bickersteth.*
Vagabonds, and other Poems. *Trowbridge.*
Versatilities. *Newell.*
Verses by H. H. *Hunt.*
Warp and Woof. *Duffield.*
Wee Wee Songs for our Little Pets. *Lee.*
A Woman's Poems. *Piatt.*
Works of Anne *Bradstreet.*
Works. *Byron.*
Works. *Pope.*
Works. *Shelley.*
Works of H. Vaughan. *Fuller* Worthies.

Single Poems.

After All, not to Create Only. *Whitman.*
Alboin and Rosamond. *Rodney.*
Apple of Life. *Lytton.*
Art of Preserving Health. *Armstrong.*
The Baby's Things. *Abbott.*
Balaustion's Adventure. *Browning.*
Benny. *Ketchum.*
Cathedral. *Lowell.*
Clytie and Zenobia; a Poem. *Clarke.*
Collegiad.
Convict Once; a Poem. *Stephens.*
Cream of Tartar; a Lay of Alexis.
Divine Tragedy. *Longfellow.*
Earthly Paradise. Parts 3, 4. *Morris.*
Evangeline. *Longfellow.*
Faerie Queene. *Spenser.*
Grand Review of the Dead. *Naphegyi.*
Hans Breitmann as an Uhlan. *Leland.*
Hans Breitmann in Church. *Leland.*
Heathen Chinee. *Harte.*
Hermit. *Norton.*
John Jerningham's Journal.
King Arthur. *Lytton.*
Last Tournament. *Tennyson.*
Little Breeches. *Hay.*
Ludibria Lunæ. *Courthope.*
Medea. *Richards.*
Mrs. Jerningham's Journal.
Napoleon Fallen; a Lyrical Drama. *Buchanan.*
New Fashioned Girl.
Nothing to Wear. *Butler.*
Old Horse Gray. *Hopper.*
Paradise Lost. *Milton.*
Pliocene Skull. *Harte.*
Poet's Pilgrimage to Waterloo. *Southey.*
Prince Hohenstiel Schwangau. *Browning.*
Retrorsum. *Richards.*
Rhymester's Run through Italy.
Rokeby. *Scott.*
Roman Lawyer in Jerusalem. *Story.*
Royal Decrees of Scanderoon.
Seasons. *Thomson.*
Sleeping Sentinel. *Janvier.*
Song of the Sower. *Bryant.*
Stolen Waters; a Poem. *Gardner.*
Story of the Fountain. *Bryant.*
Tale of Eternity. *Massey.*
True Legend of St. Dunstan and the Devil. *Flight.*
Wanderer. *Channing.*
Warning of War. *Congdon.*
Wilde's Summer Rose. *Barclay.*
Within and Without. *MacDonald.*
Woman who Dared. *Sargent.*
Yarico to Inkle. *Story.*

Epigrams, Acrostics.

Acrostics from across the Atlantic.
Epigrammatists. *Dodd.*

Sacred Poetry.

Christian Year. *Keble.*
A Creed, etcetera. *Tupper.*
Evenings with the Sacred Poets. *Saunders.*
Hymnal of *Protestant* Episc. Church.
Hymns for all Christians. *Deems and Cary.*
Hymns of the Latin Church. *Morgan.*
Inner Life. Hymns.
Man and Woman. *Reed.*

Marie Magdalen's Lamentations, etc., by Markham. *Fuller* Worthies
Methodist Hymnology. *Creamer.*
Parish Musings, or Devotional Poems. *Monsell.*
Poems of Jeremy Taylor. *Fuller* Worthies.
Pseaumes de David, avec Musique.
Pseaumes de David, à Quatre Parties.
Revival Melodies. *Dadmun.*
Shadow of the Rock, and other Religious Poems.
Songs of the Church. *Davies.*
Teares of the Beloved, by Markham. *Fuller* Worthies.
Temptacyon of Jesus, by Bale. *Fuller* Worthies.
Words of Cheer for the Master's Workers.
Yesterday, To-day and Forever. *Bickersteth.*

German Poetry.

Abendstunden eines Handwerkers. *Menges.*
Ahasver in Rom. *Hamerling.*
Amaranth. *Redwitz.*
Aus der Heimat. *Prutz.*
Book of German Songs. *Dulcken.*
Dornrosen; Erstlingsblüthen Deutscher Lyrik in Amerika.
Eusebius Hützler's einfältige Selbstbekenntnisse. *Duboc.*
Flowers from Fatherland. *Trotter.*
Frau Aventiure. *Scheffel.*
Fünf Bücher Deutscher Lieder und Gedichte. *Schwab.*
Gaudeamus. *Scheffel.*
Gaudeamus. Transl. by Leland. *Scheffel.*
Gedichte. *Goethe.*
Gesammelte Werke. V. 1. Gedichte. *Heyse.*
Hermann und Dorothea. *Goethe.*
Hermann and Dorothee. *Goethe.*
Heroldsrufe. *Geibel.*
Jobsiade. *Kortum.*
Kaiser und Reich. *Koester.*
Last Knight. *Auersperg.*
Letzte Gedichte und Gedanken. *Heine.*
Lied vom neuen Deutschen Reich. *Redwitz.*
Nibelunge; Sigfridsage. *Jordan.*
Oberon. *Wieland.*
Poems et Legends. *Heine.*
Poems. *Freiligrath.*
Poems and Ballads. *Schiller.*
Poems and Ballads. *Goethe.*
Quickborn. *Groth.*
Sämmtliche Werke. V. 1, 2, 6, 7, 11. *Reuter.*
Trompeter von Säkkingen. *Scheffel.*
War Songs of the Germans. *Blackie.*

Italian Poetry.

Literal Prose Translations from Metastasio, Ariosto, Tasso.
Divine Comedy. *Dante.*
A Shadow of Dante. *Rossetti.*
Orlando Furioso. *Ariosto.*

French Poetry.

Ballads and Lyrics of Old France. *Lang.*
Chatiments. *Hugo.*
Contes et Nouvelles en Vers. *La Fontaine.*
Echoes from the French Poets. *Curwen.*
Fables. *La Fontaine.*
French Love Songs.
Henriade. *Voltaire.*
Poésies Complètes. *Sainte-Beuve.*

Poems of Other European Nations.

Lilja; an Icelandic Poem. *Asgrimsson.*
Songs of the Russian People. *Ralston.*
Lusiad. *Camoens.*
Romancero del Cid.

Oriental Poetry.

Iliad of the East (Rāmāyana). *Válmíki.*
Rámáyan. *Válmíki.*
Kusa Jatakaya. *Alagiyavanna Mohottāla.*
Story of Nala.

Dramatic History, Biography and Criticism.

English Drama under Tudors and Stuarts.
History of the American Stage. *Brown.*
History of the American Theatre. *Dunlap.*
Actors' Protective Union.
Théatre Révolutionnaire. *Jauffret.*
Norddeutsches Theater. *Laube.*
Representative Actors. *Russell.*
Essays on the Drama. *Donne.*
Comedy and Dramatic Effect. *Fitzgerald.*
Before the Footlights and Behind the Scenes. *Logan.*
Edwin *Booth* in Twelve Dramatic Characters.

English Drama; Collected Works.

Oxberry's British Theatre.
Comic Dramas by Miss Edgeworth. *Patronage* (with Novels.)
Works of *Jonson.*
Dramatic Works. *Lytton.*
Plays. *Massinger.*
English Dramatic Poets. *Lamb.*

Private Theatricals. *Hudson.*
Drawing-Room Plays. *Scott.*
Drawing-Room Plays. *Steele.*
Parlor Dramas. *Fowle.*
Social Stage. *Baker.*
Chamber Dramas for Children. *MacDonald.*
Home Theatre. *Healy.*
Country House Charades. *Nugent.*

Single English Dramas.

Death of Ugolino. A Tragedy. *Featherstonhaugh.*
Dollars and Cents. *Hollenius.*
Honeymoon. *Tobin.*
Lady of Lyons. *Lytton.*
Parasite; a Comedy. *Picard.*
Po–ca–hon–tas. *Brougham.*
Richelieu. *Lytton.*
Tragedy of Lesbos. *Pember.*
Venice Preserved. *Otway.*

Shakspeare Editions.

Readings, by Kemble. *Shakspeare.*
As You Like It. *Shakspeare.*
Hamlet, Booth's ed. *Shakspeare.*
King Henry VIII. Ed. by Rolfe. *Shakspeare.*
Merchant of Venice. Ed. by Rolfe. *Shakspeare.*
Richard III. Acting ed. *Shakspeare.*

Shakspeare, Commentaries, etc.

Shakspeare in Germany. *Cohn.*
Shakspeare and the Emblem Writers. *Green.*
Ornithology of Shakspeare. *Harting.*
Shakspeare Fragen. *Kreyszig.*
Vorlesungen über Shakspeare. *Kreyszig.*
Shakspeare Studien. *Ludwig.*
Mottoes and Aphorisms from Shakspeare.
Shakspeare as Artist. *Ruggles.*
Shakspeare's Euphuism. *Rushton.*
Shakspeare Illustrated by the Lex Scripta. *Rushton.*

French Dramas.

Les Aristocraties. *Arago.*
Changement du Garnison. *Mancel.*
Lions et Renards. *Augier.*
Magasin Théatral.
Un Mari qui Pleure. *Prével.*
Œuvres. *Molière.*
Parasite. *Picard.*
Patrie! *Sardou.*
Post Scriptum. *Augier.*
Princesse Georges. *Dumas.*
Répertoire du Théâtre François.
Ruy Blas. *Hugo.*
Suitors. *Racine.*
Théatre Complet. *Dumas* (fils.)
Théatre Complet. *Scarron.*
Théâtre de la Foire.
Théatre de Nohant. *Dudevant.*

German Dramas.

Art in the Mountains. *Blackburn.*
To and from the Passion Play in 1871. *Doane.*
The Ammergau Passion Play. *Maccoll.*
Passion Play at Ober-Ammergau. *Molloy.*
Recollections of Ober-Ammergau. *Oxenham.*
Brautfahrt. *Freytag.*
Dramatic Works. *Goethe.*
Egmont. *Goethe.*
Eigensinn, by Benedix. *Wilhelmi.*
Einer muss heirathen. *Wilhelmi.*
Er ist nicht eifersüchtig. *Elz.*
Faust. *Goethe.*
Goetz von Berlichingen. *Goethe.*
Im Wartesalon erster Klasse, by Müller. *Elz.*
Judith; eine Tragödie. *Hebbel.*
König René's Tochter. *Hertz.*
Maryna. *Mosenthal.*
Nathan der Weise. *Lessing.*
Nathan the Wise. *Lessing.*
Torquato Tasso. *Gœthe.*
Violante. *Lingg.*
Weiberfeind, by Benedix. *Elz.*

Italian Dramas.

Dramme, con Memorie. *Da Ponte.*
Théatre Italien. *Gherardi.*
Opere. *Goldoni.*

Dramas from other Nations

Death of Ivan the Terrible. *Tolstoi.*
King Renés Daughter. *Hertz.*
Ollanta. An Ancient Ynca Drama.
Mahá–Virá–Charita. *Bhavabuti.*
Theatre of the Hindus. *Wilson.*

English Prose Fiction.

Popular Romances of the Middle Ages. *Cox* and Jones.
Fairy Fancies. *Eden.*
Greek Romances of Heliodorus, Longus and Achilles Tatius.
Italian Life and Legends. *Ritchie.*
Tales. *Musaeus.*
Tales. *Poe.*
Tales, by Richter. *Musaeus.*
Tales, by Tieck. *Musaeus.*
Specimens of Irish Character. *Hall.*
Sporting Scenes and Characters. *Herbert.*

Tales, Romances and Extravaganzas. *Hood.*
Solwan. *Ibn Zafer.*
Spuytenduyvel Chronicle.
Surprising Adventure of Philip *Quarll.*
Traits and Stories of the Irish Peasantry. *Carleton.*
Wilhelm Meister. *Goethe.*

French Novels.

Abdallah. *Laboulaye.*
Acté. *Dumas.*
Adèle Verneuil. *Sue.*
Alix. *Fleuriot.*
Amant de la Morte. *Pichon.*
Amélie Mansfield.
Amour comme il est. *Houssaye.*
Amours du Beau Gustave. *Bréhat.*
Amours du Chevalier de Fosseuse. *Janin.*
Amours Tragiques. *Feydeau.*
André. *Dudevant.*
Anglais au Pole Nord. *Verne.*
Anne Séverin. *Craven.*
Antonia. *Dudevant.*
Antonine. *Dumas.*
Après la Pluie le Beau Temps. *Ségur.*
Arbre de la Vierge. *St. Mars.*
Article 47. *Belot.*
Autour de la Lune. *Verne.*
Autour d'une Source. *Droz.*
Aventure d'Amour. *Dumas.*
Aventures d'un jeune Naturaliste. *Biart.*
Aventures du Baron de Féreste. *Feydeau.*
Aventurier. *Assolant.*
Bal de l'Opéra. *Bréhat.*
Bâtard de Mauléon. *Dumas.*
Beau d'Angennes. *Maquet.*
Beau Laurence. *Dudevant.*
Belle Gabrielle. *Maquet.*
Belle Novice. *Gonzalès.*
Bêtise Humaine. *Noriac.*
Bohémienne du Grand Monde. *Ponson du Terrail.*
Bon petit Diable. *Ségur.*
Bonne Affaire. *Malot.*
Bonne Aventure. *Sue.*
Bonnes Fortunes Parisiennes. *Stahl.*
Buveurs de Cendres. *Du Camp.*
Capitaine Fantome. *Féval.*
Capitaine Lambert. *Rabou.*
Cartes sur Table. *Pichat.*
Ce Pauvre Vieux. *Fleuriot.*
Césarine Dietrich. *Dudevant.*
Chanvallon. *Monselet.*
Chasse à l'Idéal. *Achard.*
Chasseurs d'Hommes. *Bréhat.*
Chateau des Pyrenées. *Soulié.*
Chateau Rouge. *Dumas.*
Chateau de Zolkiew. *Szajnocha.*
Chauffeurs Indiens. *Bréhat.*
Chemin de la Fortune. *Conscience.*
Cinq Semaines en Ballon. *Verne.*
Citadins et Campagnards. *De Witt.*
Clémence Hervé. *Sue.*
Clique Dorée. *Gaboriau.*
Clotilde. *Pontmartin.*
Cocarde Blanche. *Ulbach.*
Cœur d'Acier. *Féval.*
Comment les Femmes se Perdent. *Mirecourt.*
Comte de St. Germain. *Capendu.*
Comte de Toulouse. *Soulié.*
Comte de Warrens. *Aimard* and Crisafulii.
Comtesse Diane. *Uchard.*
Comtesse de Monte-Christo.
Comtesse de Rudolstadt. *Dudevant.*
Conscrit de l'An VIII. *Forville.*
Constance Verrier. *Dudevant.*
Consuelo. *Dudevant.*
Contes Drôlatiques. *Balzac.*
Contes de Famille. *Ducray-Duminil.*
Contes des Fées. *Ducray-Duminil.*
Corinne. *Staël.*
Cosaques à Paris. *Ponson du Terrail.*
Cousin aux Millions. *Bréhat.*
Cousine Bette; le Cousin Pons. *Balzac.*
Création et Rédemption. *Dumas.*
Crime d'Orcival. *Gaboriau.*
Curée. *Zola.*
Dame au Gant Noir. *Ponson du Terrail.*
De la Terre à la Lune. *Verne.*
Début dans la Vie; Maître Cornelius. *Balzac.*
Début a l'Opéra. *Feydeau.*
Décameron. *Boccaccio.*
Delphine. *Staël.*
Demoiselles Tourangeau. *Champfleury.*
Dernières Fées. *Féval.*
Désert de Glace. *Verne.*
Deux Amis. *Bréhat.*
Deux Bijoux. *Fleuriot.*
Deux Dianes. *Dumas.*
Deux Femmes du Roi. *Féval.*
Deux Nigauds. *Ségur.*
Diable à Paris.
Diable Médecin. *Sue.*
Dieu Dispose. *Dumas.*
Diloy le Chemineau. *Ségur.*
Docteur Vampire. *Féré.*
Dossier, No. 113. *Gaboriau.*

Drame de Planche Mibray. *Ponson du Terrail.*
Drame de la Rue de Paix. *Belot.*
Drame à Trouville. *Bréhat.*
Drames Inconnus. *Soulié.*
Duchesse de Nemours. *Féval.*
Duperies de l'Amour. *Daudet.*
Émile. *Rousseau.*
Enfants du Capitaine Grant. *Verne.*
Envers et Endroit. *Maquet.*
Errants du Nuit. *Féval.*
Esclaves de Paris. *Gaboriau.*
Estelle. *Florian.*
Étienne et Valentin. *Ulliac-Trémadeure.*
Fabrique de Mariages. *Féval.*
Famille de Germandre. *Dudevant.*
Fanny. *Feydeau.*
Faubourg St. Antoine. *Révillon.*
Fellah. *About.*
Femmes. *Karr.*
Femmes comme elles sont. *Houssaye.*
Femmes qui Aiment. *Fortunio.*
Fille du Régent. *Dumas.*
Fille d'un de ces Messieurs. *Kock.*
Filles de Cabanil. *Féval.*
Filles du Notaire. *Maillard.*
Fils de Famille. *Sue.*
Fior d'Aliza. *Lamartine.*
Fleurange. *Craven.*
Forgeron de la Cour Dieu. *Ponson du Terrail.*
Fortune de Gasparin. *Ségur.*
Fortune des Rougon. *Zola.*
François le Bossu. *Ségur.*
François Soleil. *Monselet.*
Francs-Tireurs de Paris. *Richebourg.*
Frère Adoptif. *Vincent.*
Frères de la Côte. *Gonzalès.*
Gens de Bureau. *Gaboriau.*
Gens de la Noce. *Féval.*
Gil Blas. *Le Sage.*
Gilbert et Gilberte. *Sue.*
Gisèle, Comtesse de l'Empire. *John.*
Grande Dame. *Sue.*
Grande Falaise. *Sorel.*
Grande Marquise. *Rivière.*
Graziella. *Lamartine.*
Guillaume Tell. *Florian.*
Habitude et Souvenir. *Belot.*
Héritage d'un Banquier. *Deligny.*
Héritage de Corinne. *Ponson du Terrail.*
Héritage de mon Oncle.
Histoire de Lucie Wellers.
Histoire de la Marquise de Terville.
Histoire d'un Sous-Maître. *Erckmann-Chatrian.*
Houilleurs de Polignies. *Berthet.*
Indiana. *Dudevant.*
Infâme. *About.*
Interne. *Janin.*
Isabel de Bavière. *Dumas.*
Isle Inconnue. *Grivel.*
Ivanhoe. French of Dumas. *Scott.*
Jean Laroche. *Olivier.*
Jeanne et sa Suite. *Sorr.*
Jésuite. Par l'Abbé * * *
Lettres de mon Moulin. *Daudet.*
Lettres d'une Péruvienne. *Graffigny.*
Lion Amoureux. *Soulié.*
Lionne. *Soulié.*
Louis XV. et sa Cour. *Dumas.*
Louis XVI. et la Révolution. *Dumas.*
Lui et Elle. *Musset.*
Madame Obernin. *Malot.*
Madame Thérèse. *Erckmann-Chatrian.*
Madeleine. *Sandeau.*
Mlle. Croquemitaine. *Kock.*
Mlle. D'Avremont. *Rivière.*
Mlle. Saphir. *Féval.*
Maison du Baigneur. *Maquet.*
Maison Close. *Karr.*
Maison Maudite *Montépin.*
Maître d'Armes. *Dumas.*
Maître Pierre. *About.*
Maître Rossignol. *Ponson du Terrail.*
Maitres Sonneurs. *Dudevant.*
Maitresses du Diable. *Bréhat.*
Malgrétout. *Dudevant.*
Manon Lescaut. *Prévost.*
Marcelle. *Achard.*
Marguerite.
Marguerite de Valois, Reine de Navarre.
Mari de la Danseuse. *Feydeau.*
Mari Embaumé. *Féval.*
Mariages de Paris. *About.*
Marianna. *Sandeau.*
Marquis de Pontanges. *Girardin.*
Marquise de Courcelles. *Mirecourt.*
Maudit. Par l'Abbé * * *
Mauprat. *Dudevant.*
Maxence Humbert. *Achard.*
Mémoires d'un Ane. *Ségur.*
Mémoires d'une Aveugle. *Dumas.*
Mémoires du Diable. *Soulié.*
Ménagerie Intime. *Gautier.*
Mère Michel. *Ponson du Terrail.*
Mille et un Fantomes. *Dumas.*
Misères de Londres. *Ponson du Terrail.*
Moine. Par l'Abbé * * *
Mon Villlage. *Ponson du Terrail.*
M. Lecoq. *Gaboriau.*

Monsieur, Madame et Bébé. *Droz.*
M. de St. Bertrand. *Feydeau.*
M. Sylvestre. *Dudevant.*
Mystères de Londres. *Féval.*
Narcisse. *Dudevant.*
Naufrage Parisien. *Vignon.*
Nœud du Ruban. *Ancelot.*
Nouveaux Contes Turcs et Arabes. *Digeon.*
Nouvelles Napolitaines. *Boubée.*
Nouvelles Soirées Chrétiennes. *Second.*
Nuits de Paris. *Féval.*
Oeuvres Complètes. *Balzac.*
Oeuvres Complètes. Xavier de *Maistre.*
Olympe de Mezières; Le Mari de Delphine. *Achard*
Ondine. *Fouqué.*
Orpheline Angloise. *Fielding.*
Paquet de Lettres. *Droz.*
Paris en Amérique. *Laboulaye.*
Parisiennes. *Houssaye.*
Parisine. *Roqueplan.*
Paul Méré. *Cherbuliez.*
Pauvre Blaise. *Ségur.*
Peau du Lion; La Chasse aux Amants. *Bernard.*
Père Goriot. *Balzac.*
Perles Noires. *Enault.*
Petite Belle. *Fleuriot.*
Petite Comtesse. *Feuillet.*
Petits Romans. *Bréhat.*
Pierre qui Roule. *Dudevant.*
Pierrot; Cain; l'Envoutement *Rivière.*
Pile et Face. *Biart.*
Pirates de la Seine. *Montépin.*
Prince Max à Paris. *Beaumont-Vassy*
Princesse de Monaco. *Dumas.*
Quai de la Ferraille. *Féval.*
Quel Amour d'Enfant. *Ségur.*
Queue d'Or. *Karr.*
Raphaël. *Lamartine.*
Raymon. *Uchard.*
Réalités de la Vie Domestique, presentées aux jeunes Femmes.
Récit d'une Soeur. *Craven.*
Recluse Angloise. *Mercier.*
Régence. *Dumas.*
Regent Mustel. *Dumas.*
Reine Margot. *Dumas.*
Repentir de Marion. *Houssaye*
Riches et Pauvres. *De Witt.*
Roger Bontemps. *Féval.*
Romain Kalbris. *Malot.*
Roman du Capucin. *Murger.*
Roman Comique. *Scarron.*
Roman d'une Conspiration. *Ranc.*
Roman d'une Honnête Femme. *Cherbuliez.*
Roman d'une jeune Fille. *Daudet.*
Roses Noires et Roses Bleues. *Karr.*
Ruses d'Amour. *Gaboriau.*
San Felice. *Dumas.*
Scènes d'Enfance et de Jeunesse. *Pressensé.*
Scènes d'Histoire et de Famille. *De Witt.*
Scènes de la Vie Contemporaine. *Bréhat.*
Secret du Bonheur. *Feydeau.*
Secret de Famille. *Saint Mars.*
Secret de M. de Boisonnange. *Deligny*
Sept Chateaux du Roi de Bohème. *Nodier.*
Sept Péchés Capitaux. *Sue.*
Si Jeunesse Savait, si Vieillesse Pouvait. *Soulié.*
Siége de la Rochelle. *Genlis.*
Sœur de Gribouille. *Ségur.*
Sophie Printems. *Dumas.*
Sous les Orangers. *Karr.*
Tache Rouge. *Féval.*
Tailleur de Pierres de St. Point. *Lamartine.*
Talisman de Robert Nels. *Deligny.*
Tamaris. *Dudevant.*
Terre Chaude. *Biart.*
Terre Tempereé. *Biart.*
Testament de la Comtesse. *Bréhat.*
Thibaud. *Jamet-Massicault.*
Le 13e Hussards. *Gaboriau.*
Trois Reines. *Saintine.*
Ursule de Mirouët. *Balzac.*
Vengeance d'un Mulâtre. *Bréhat.*
Vénus de Gordes. *Belot.*
Vicomte de Launay. *Girardin.*
Victimes d'Amour. *Malot.*
Vie Aventureuse. *Foudras.*
Vie Infernale. *Gaboriau.*
Vieille Roche. *About.*
Violon de Franjolé. *Houssaye.*
Vingt Mille Lieues sous les Mers. *Verne.*
Voix du Sang. *Ulbach.*
Voleurs du Grand Monde. *Ponson du Terrail.*
Volupté. *Sainte-Beuve.*
Voyage au Centre de la Terre. *Verne.*
Voyages Humoristiques. *Houssaye.*

German Novels.

Abenteuer eines jungen Peruaners. *Bibra.*
Adeliges Nest; Drei Portraits. *Turgenjew.*
Aegyptische Königstochter. *Ebers.*
Afraja. *Mügge.*

Alles um ein Nichts. *Köberle.*
Allzeit voran! *Spielhagen.*
Alpenbraut. *Putlitz.*
Alte Jungfer. *Holtei.*
Anna Braun. *Römheld.*
Anthropophag. *Heinrich.*
Arbeit adelt den Mann. *Schwartz*
Arthur Fromm. *Steffens.*
Arzt der Seele. *Hillern.*
Auf Dornigem Pfade. *Stab.*
Auf dem Wiener Congress. *Bacher.*
Auf den Wogen des Lebens. *Schrader.*
Auf der Düne. *Spielhagen.*
Aus dem Tagebuch eines Berliner Arztes. *Ring.*
Aus Deutschen Gauen. *Bodenstedt.*
Aus Drei Jahrhunderten. *Brachvogel.*
Aus Welt und Haus. *Grabowski.*
Backfischchen's Leiden und Freuden. *Helm.*
Badewirth von Gonten. *Kleinsteuber.*
Bank des Verderbens. *Hiltl.*
Bankrott. *Temme.*
Beaumarchais. *Brachvogel.*
Benoni. *Brachvogel.*
Biarritz. *Retcliffe.*
Bilder aus dem häuslichen Leben. *Holtei.*
Bis nach Hohen Zieritz. *Hesekiel.*
Blätter aus dem Frauenleben. *Schwartz.*
Blaue und Gelbe. *Gerstaecker.*
Bruder Studio. *Wellmer.*
Buntes Treiben. *Gerstaecker.*
Bürgerkrieg. *Möllhausen.*
Cabinets Intrigue. *Hiltl.*
Capitain der Königin. *Hesekiel.*
Charlotte Ackermann. *Müller.*
Christian Lammfell. *Holtei.*
Christine. *Paschkowsky.*
Colonie. *Gerstaecker.*
Cornelie von Lentulus. *Kulemann.*
Dämon Gold. *König.*
Damenalmanach. *Mundt.*
David Walden. *Schwartz.*
Des Hauses Eckstein. *Oben.*
Des Königs und der Königin Soldat. *Grabowski.*
Deutsche Kleinstädter in America. *Winckler.*
Deutsche Pioniere. *Spielhagen.*
Deutsche Wunden. *Otto.*
Deutscher Novellenschatz.
Deutschland gegen Frankreich. *Mundt.*
Deutschlands Kassandra. *Rau.*
Dornen. *Vacano und Stadion.*
Drahtzieher. *Hagen.*
Drama in Californien. *Almeira.*
Draümling. *Corvin.*
Drei Grazien. *Frenzel.*
Drei Jahre von Dreissigen. *Rellstab.*
Drei Novellen. *Turgenjew.*
Duell und Ehre. *Meyr.*
Dunkelgraf. *Bechstein.*
Durch Kampf zum Frieden. *König.*
Durch Nacht zum Licht. *Gutzkow.*
Durch die Zeitung. *Dincklage.*
Ehestand. *Schwartz.*
Eines eiteln Mannes Frau. *Schwartz.*
Eleonore. *Ingersleben.*
Elephant. *Winterfeld.*
Ellen oder ein Jahr. *Schwartz.*
Enterbte. *Mützelburg.*
Epigonen. *Immermann.*
Erb-und Gerichtsherr. *Avé-Lallemant.*
Erbe von Bettysruh. *Lange.*
Erbgrafen. *Temme.*
Erich Randall. *Mügge.*
Erlebtes und Erdachtes. *Mels.*
Erzählungen eines alten Herrn. *Struensee.*
Eselsfresser. *Holtei.*
Falkenrode. *Struensee.*
Familie Ammer. *Willkomm.*
Fanatiker der Ruhe. *Winterfeld.*
Filigran. *Schücking.*
Flatbootmann. *Gerstaecker.*
Fliegender Holländer. *Brachvogel.*
Franctireurs. *Gerstaecker.*
Frankreich gegen Deutschland. *Mundt.*
Frau des Ministers. *Friedrich.*
Frau des Rebellen. *Temme.*
Freiwillige vor! *Hackländer.*
Freudvoll und Leidvoll. *Polko.*
Friedensengel. *Lange.*
Frische Blätter. *Polko.*
Fritz Beutel. *Marggraff.*
Fritz Ellrodt. *Gutzkow.*
Frühling. *Corvin.*
Funken unter der Asche. *Putlitz.*
Für's Vaterland. *Mühlfeld.*
Gebilde und Gestalten. *Mels.*
Geburt und Bildung. *Schwartz.*
Gefangene von Chillon. *Hartmann.*
Gegen den Strom. *Grosse.*
Geheimniss des Fürstenhauses. *Hiltl.*
Geheimniss der Stadt. *Hackländer.*
Geheimnisse. *Frenzel.*
Geheimnisse einer Grossen Stadt. *König.*
Geheimnissvolle. *Storch.*
Gehrt Hansen. *Duboc.*
Geliebte des Prinzen. *Dedenroth.*
Gemeuchelter Dichter. *Winterfeld.*
Geschichten in Zickzack. *Hackländer.*
Gettysburg. *Ferrari.*

Glancarty. *Brachvogel.*
Glück auf! im Fürstenhause. *Georg* Prinz von Preussen.
Glücks Peter. *Andersen.*
Godwie Castle. *Paalzow.*
Gold. *Gerstaecker.*
Gold und Name. *Schwartz.*
Goldelse. *John.*
Goldengel von Köln. *Pasqué.*
Götter und Götzen. *Ring.*
Grüner Pelz. *Lange.*
Grüne Straücher aus dem Schweizerlande. *Bitter.*
Haideblume. *Ingersleben.*
Hartes Herz. *Raymund.*
Haus Hohenzollern. *Grabowski.*
Haus Treustein. *Holtei.*
Heimathlos. *Strueensee.*
Heimliche und unheimliche Geschichten. *Gerstaecker.*
Heinrich Falk. *Roquette.*
Heinrich Heines Erste Liebe. *Diez.*
Heitere Stunden. *Kalisch.*
Helden der Arbeit. *Schlägel.*
Herr von Filz. *Winterfeld.*
Herrschaft des Mönchs. *Garibaldi.*
Herzog Wallenstein in Mecklenburg. *Wickede.*
Hinter Blauen Brillen. *Hackländer.*
Hinter den Coulissen. *Wichert.*
Hosen des Herrn von Bredow. *Häring.*
Humoresken. *Winterfeld.*
Humoristische Soldaten-Novellen. *Winterfeld.*
Hundertguldenblatt. *Möllhausen.*
Husarenofficier Friedrichs des Grossen. *Wickede.*
Im Bann der Schuld. *Mühlfeld.*
Im Eckfenster. *Gerstaecker.*
Im Goldenen Zeitalter. *Frenzel.*
Im Herzen von Deutschland. *Guseck.*
Im Vorübergehen. *Polko.*
In Doloribus. *Hoefer.*
In Mexico. *Gerstaecker.*
In Reih und Gleid. *Spielhagen.*
In der Schweiz. *Ring.*
In der Welt Verloren. *Hoefer.*
Irrfahrten. *Gerstaecker.*
Isegrimm. *Häring.*
Jacob van der Nees. *Paalzow.*
J. J. Rousseau. *Schücking.*
Joachim Slüter. *Wickede.*
Jude. *Spindler.*
Jugenderinnerungen. *Schwartz.*
Kaiser Joseph und sein Landsknecht. *Mundt.*
Kaiserburg und Engelsburg. *Mundt.*
Karfunkel. *Becker.*
Katakomben von Wien. *Storch.*
Kind aus dem Ebräergang. *Volckhausen.*
Kind des Volkes. *Storch.*
Kinder der Arbeit. *Schwartz.*
Kinder Roms. *Meissner.*
Kirchenfürsten und Weltfürsten. *Mundt.*
Kleine Geschichten. *Lindau.*
Kleiner Probst. *Giese.*
Kleine Romane. *Wichert.*
König August und sein Goldschmidt. *Carion.*
Königs Dank. *Heusinger.*
Kreuz und Quer. *Gerstaecker.*
Krieg und Friede. *Struensee.*
Krösus von Philadelphia. *Armand.*
Krummensee I. Ueber'n Rhein nach Paris *Hesekiel.*
Krummensee II. Heimkehr und Wiederkunft. *Hesekiel.*
Kunst und Liebe. *Schrader.*
Kunstsammler. *Möllhausen.*
Lachender Mann. *Hugo.*
Land und See. *Hoefer.*
Landhaus am Rhein. *Auerbach.*
Leben und Lieben. *Liebetreu.*
Lebensbilder. *Gutzkow.*
Leidenschaften. *Schwartz.*
Lenz Schadewacht. *Hesekiel.*
Letzter Bombardier. *Hackländer.*
Letzte Tage eines Königs. *Hartmann.*
Lichtenstein. *Hauff.*
Lieben und Leben. *Ring.*
Lienhard und Gertrud. *Pestalozzi.*
Löwe von Luzern. *Lange.*
Ludwig XIV. *Brachvogel.*
Luther in Rom. *Schücking.*
Major. *Fritze.*
Mammon und Marmor. *Höcker.*
Mann von Geburt. *Schwartz.*
Märchen für Jung und Alt. *Hoffmann.*
Maria Theresia und Pandurenobrist Trenck. *Mundt.*
Mariola oder ein Blonder Dämon.
Marotte. *Baudissin.*
Mathilde. *Schwartz.*
Matthisson und Adelaide. *Mühlfeld.*
Meine Lebensschicksale. *Schwartz.*
Melusine. *Frenzel.*
Mexiko. *Storch.*
Michel. *Scherr.*
Moderne Odyssee. *Winterfeld.*
Mohammed Alis Nachfolger. *Mundt.*
Mohammed Ali und sein Haus. *Mundt.*

Münzthurm. 1st Pt. *Hiltl.*
Mütze und Krone. *Schmid.*
Nach dem Kriege. *Grabowski.*
Nach dem Schiffbruch; Wrack des Piraten. *Gerstaecker.*
Nach Uns die Sündflut. *Schälgel.*
Nahes und Fernes. *Hackländer.*
Nebenbuhler um Deutschland. *Mundt.*
Nella. *Stahr.*
Nenah Sahib. *Retcliffe.*
Neuer Abälard. *Grosse.*
Neue Erzählungen. *Erckmann-Chatrian.*
Neue Geschichten. *Hoefer.*
Neue Novellen. *Struensee.*
Neue Sündfluth. *Rodenberg.*
Neues Novellenbuch. *Heyse.*
Nicht auf Immer. *Guseck.*
Nixenfischer. *Becker.*
Nomaden. *Bayer.*
Non Possumus. *Hilarius.*
Nordische Semiramis. *Oettinger.*
Novellen. *Hartmann.*
Novellen. *Olfers.*
Novellen. *Tharau.*
Novellen und Skizzen. *Gutzkow.*
Obernigker Bote. *Holtei.*
Olle Kamellen. *Reuter.*
Onkel Tom's Hütte. *Stowe.*
Opfer der Rache. *Schwartz.*
Opfer des Religiösen Fanatismus. v. 1, 2. *Mundt.*
Ost und West. *Struensee.*
Paso de las Animas. *Bibra.*
Piratenlieutenant. *Möllhausen.*
Primadonna. *Heller.*
Prinzesschen. *König.*
Professor von Heidelberg. *Müller.*
Pucelle. *Frenzel.*
Puebla; Der Schatz des Ynkas. *Retcliffe.*
Rabbi's Vermächtniss. *Becker.*
Radowa. *Struensee.*
Randschrift eines Königs. *Niendorf.*
Räthsel von Hildburghausen. *Brachvogel.*
Recht auf Erden. *Temme.*
Regenbogen. *Corvin.*
Reichsgräfin Gisela. *John.*
Ritter vom Geiste. *Gutzkow.*
Rittergut Marderheim. *Niendorf.*
Ruhe ist die Erste Bürgerpflicht. *Häring.*
Ste. Roche. *Paalzow.*
Sämmtliche Werke. *Hoffmann.*
Sämmtliche Werke. *Tieck.*
Sara. *Dincklage.*
Schellen-Moritz. *Hesekiel.*
Schlimmster Feind. *Guseck.*
Schloss Bärenberg. *Fritze.*
Schloss Elkrath. *Raymund.*
Schneider. *Holtei.*
Schöne Gefangene. *Schmidt-Weissenfels.*
Schubert und seine Zeitgenossen. *Brachvogel.*
Schuld und Unschuld. *Schwartz.*
Schützling des Kaisers. *Grabowski.*
Schutzlose. *Schwartz.*
Schwarzwälder Dorfgeschichten. *Auerbach.*
Scelenfreunde. *Ring.*
Sein oder Nichtsein. *Schwartz.*
Seltsame Schicksale. *Mels.*
Sie schreibt. *Polko.*
Söhne des Drehorgelmanns. *Schwartz.*
Söhne Pestalozzi's. *Gutzkow.*
Solferino. *Mundt.*
Soll und Haben. *Freytag.*
Sonderbares Duell. *Gerstaecker.*
Sonnenwirth. *Kurz.*
Sorgenlose Stunden. *Hackländer.*
Sphinx. *Bayer.*
Spinoza. *Auerbach.*
Spionin. *Schirmer.*
Stereoscopen. *Schlägel.*
Stiefkinder. *Baudissin.*
Stiller Speculant. *Fritze.*
Stille vor dem Sturm. *Hesekiel.*
Stille Winkel. *Winterfeld.*
Strassburg. *Schmidt-Weissenfels.*
Sturmvogel. *Hackländer.*
Tausend Seelen. *Pisemski.*
Thomas Thyrnau. *Paalzow.*
Thron und kein Geld. *Bölte.*
Thüringer Erzählungen. *John.*
Thurmkätherlein. *Becker.*
Tochter des Diplomaten. *Lange.*
Tochter des Edelmanns. *Schwartz.*
Toller Hans. *Streckfuss.*
Trödler. *Brachvogel.*
Ueber Alles die Pflicht. *Verena.*
Uli. *Gotthelf.*
Unter Fliegenden Fahnen. *Hoefer.*
Unter Preussen's Fahnen. *Grabowski.*
Unter der Rothen Eminenz. *Hiltl.*
Unter dem Weissen Adler. *Wachenhusen.*
Untergang des alten Regime. *Schrader.*
Verfehlte Ziele. *Löwenherz.*
Verflossene Stunden. *Junghans.*
Verhängniss. *Schrader.*
Verhängnisse. *Gerstaecker.*
Verirrt und Erlöst. *Ring.*
Vermächtniss Kains. *Sacher-Masoch.*
Vermächtniss des Millionärs. *Duboc.*
Verpfuschte Saison. *Kohlenegg.*
Verschlungene Wege. *Schücking.*

Verworfener. *Temme.*
Visionen; Helene. *Turgenjew.*
Voigt von Silt. *Mügge.*
Vom Hofe Elisabeths and Jacobs. *Bodenstedt.*
Von Geschlecht zu Geschlecht. *Stahr.*
Von Gottes Gnaden. *Rodenberg.*
Von Solferino bis Königgratz. *Mundt.*
Von Sünde zu Sünde. *Schlägel.*
Vor fünfzig Jahren. *Struensee.*
Vor Jena. *Hesekiel.*
Wahnsinnige. *Gerstaecker.*
Waise von Wien. *Scherr.*
Wally. *Godin.*
Walpurgis. *Putlitz.*
Wärwolf. *Gutzkow.*
Wechsel. *Steffens.*
Weg zum Glücke. *Schrader.*
Welt und Haus. *Roquette.*
Wie Gertrud ihre Kinder Lehrt. *Pestalozzi.*
Wildes Blut. *Schlägel.*
Wilhelm Meister. *Goethe.*
Wilhelm Stjernhelm. *Schwartz.*
Winkelschreiber. *Winterfeld.*
Wittwe und ihre Kinder. *Schwartz.*
Wunderliche Leute. *Oehlschläger.*
Zur linken Hand. *Hoefer.*
Zwei Familien. *Hoefer.*
Zwei Familienmütter. *Schwartz.*
Zwei Gnädige Frauen. *Struensee.*
Zweierlei Juden. *Klapp.*
Zweifaches Lebensziel. *Schwartz.*
Zweimal Vermählt. *Raymund.*
Zwischen Zwei Nationen. *Bayer.*
Zwölf Zettel. *Hackländer.*

Novels in Italian and Spanish.

Cento Novelle. *Sacchetti.*
Clelia. *Garibaldi.*
Decameron. *Boccaccio.*
Escenas Matritenses. *Romanos.*
Fabulas Morales. *Balmaseda.*
Fontana de Oro. *Galdos.*
Serrano de las Alpujarras. *Soler.*
Vampiri. *Mastriani.*

Class IV.—Taste and Criticism.

Aesthetics; Collective Criticisms.

Essays on Taste, by Alison. *Jeffrey.*
Æsthetics. *Bascom.*
Essay on Beauty. *Jeffrey.*
Reflections on Ancient Beauty.
Influence of Liberty on Taste. *Pech.*
Essays in Criticism. *Arnold.*
Our Living Poets. *Forman.*
Novels and Novelists. *Forsyth.*
Harmlose Briefe eines Deutschen Kleinstädters. *Lindau.*
Literarische Rücksichtslosigkeiten. *Lindau.*
Aesthetische Briefe. *Oeser.*
Nouveaux Lundis. *Sante-Beuve.*
Portraits Contemporains. *Sainte-Beuve.*
Studies in Poetry. *Shairp.*
Our Great Writers. *Turner.*
Art of English Poetrie, by Puttenham. *Arber's.*
Apologie for Poetrie, by Sidney. *Arber's.*
Discourse of English Poetrie, by Webbe. *Arber's.*

Individual Criticism.

Æschylus. *Copleston.*
Harmony of Bacon's Essays. *Arber.*
Lord Bacon not the Author of the Paradoxes. *Grosart.*
Remarks on Burnet's History of his own Time. *Higgons.*
Cæsar. *Trollope.*
Coleridge and his Writings.
Shadow of Dante. *Rossetti.*
Pen Photographs of Dickens' Readings. *Field.*
Concordance to Keble's Christian Year.
Herodotus. *Swayne.*
Juventus Mundi. *Gladstone.*
Homer; Iliad and Odyssey. *Collins.*
Anmerkungen zu Homer's Odyssee. *Nitzsch.*
Horace. *Martin.*
Waverley Manual. *Cornish.*
Sophocles. *Collins.*
Tacitus 'Geschichte der Regierung von Tiberius. *Stahr.*
Virgil. *Collins.*
Xenophon. *Grant.*

Class V.—Literary Miscellany.

Courses of Reading.

Best Reading; with Classified Bibliography.
Choice of Books. *Carlyle.*
Course of Reading. *Mandeville.*
What to Read and How to Read. *Moore.*
Books and Reading. *Porter.*
Manual of Reading. *Potter.*

Essays and Sketches.

Causeries. *About.*
Chapters of Erie, and other Essays. *Adams.*
Musings of a Middle-Aged Woman. *Ailenroc.*
Friendship's Garland. *Arnold.*
Stranger's Gift. *Bokum.*
Present Day Thoughts. *Boyd.*
Rook's Garden. *Bradley.*
Anatomy of Melancholy. *Burton.*
California Mail Bag.
Heroes and Hero-Worship. *Carlyle.*
Sartor Resartus. *Carlyle.*
Scenes and Studies. *Clayton.*
Castles in the Air. *Coffin.*
Earthward Pilgrimage. *Conway.*
Scenes in the South. *Creecy.*
Nouvelles Études Historiques et Littéraires. *Cuvillier-Fleury.*
Odd Hours of a Physician. *Darby.*
Colloquia Peripatetica. *Duncan.*
Bores, by Miss Edgeworth. See *Harington* (with novels).
Physician's Problems. *Elam.*
Society and Solitude. *Emerson.*
Micro-Cosmographie, by Earle. *Fuller* Worthies.
Yesterdays with Authors. *Fields.*
Mind and Manner. *Flamank.*
Critical Essays. *Foster.*
The *Fourth.* Log of the Smoothing Iron.
Gentle Life. *Friswell.*
A Man's Thoughts. *Friswell*
Modern Men of Letters. *Friswell.*
Short Studies on Great Subjects. *Froude.*
Fugitive Pieces.
Out of the Past. *Godwin.*
Porträts und Studien, v. 1, 2. *Gottschall.*
Rasgos Historicos. *Granja.*
Recess Studies. *Grant.*
Literary and Social Judgments. *Greg.*
Studies in Literature. *Griffin.*
Die Schöneren Stunden. *Gutzkow.*
Papers for Home Reading. *Hall.*
Round Table; Northcote's Conversations, etc. *Hazlitt.*
Vorrede zu den "Französischen Zuständen." *Heine.*
Companions of my Solitude. *Helps.*
Conversations on War and General Culture. *Helps.*
Essays, and Organization in Daily Life. *Helps.*
Atlantic Essays. *Higginson.*
Adversaria. *Hislop.*
Henry *Holbeach*, Student in Life and Philosophy.
Soundings from the Atlantic. *Holmes.*
Charpie. *Holtei.*
Forreine Travell, by Howell. *Arber's Reprint.*
Suburban Sketches. *Howells.*
Day by the Fire. *Hunt.*
Jar of Honey from Mt. Hybla. *Hunt.*
Seer. *Hunt.*
Wit and Humor. *Hunt.*
Life Studies of Character. *Hunter.*
Essays, Theological and Literary. *Hutton.*
Book for the Beach. *Jerrold.*
Chronicles of the Crutch. *Jerrold.*
Essays and Papers. *Jones.*
Sketches of Naval Life. *Jones.*
Gaietés Romaines. *Karr.*
Femmes. *Karr.*
300 Pages. *Karr.*
Essays of an Optimist. *Kaye.*
At Home and Abroad. *Kennedy.*
Light of Other Days. *Kirkpatrick.*
Mes Semblables. *La Cottière.*
Souvenirs et Portraits. *Lamartine.*
Eliana. *Lamb.*
Essays of Elia. *Lamb.*
Pericles and Aspasia. *Landor.*
Select Writings. *Lawrence.*
Modern Women. *Linton.*
London Characters, etc.
Among my Books. *Lowell.*
My Study Windows. *Lowell.*
Critical and Historical Essays. *Macaulay.*
Journey Round my Room. *Maistre.*
Essays. *Milman.*
Essais. *Montaigne.*
Courtship and Matrimony. *Morris.*
Great Mysteries and Little Plagues. *Neal.*
Discussions and Arguments. *Newman.*
Essays, Critical and Historical. *Newman.*
Miscellanies. *Newman.*
Piccadilly. *Oliphant.*
Only Once, Original Papers by various Contributors.
Places and People. *Parkinson.*
Folly as it Flies. *Parton.*
Ginger-Snaps. *Parton.*
Topics of the Time. *Parton.*
Triumphs of Enterprise, Ingenuity and Public Spirit. *Parton.*
Brick-Dust. *Pomeroy.*
Gold-Dust. *Pomeroy.*
Our Saturday Nights. *Pomeroy.*
Summer Driftwood. *Porter.*

Recreations of a Recluse.
Among my Books. *Reed*.
Tangletown Letters. *Reynolds*.
Lorbeer und Cypresse. *Ring*.
Essays. *Rumford*.
Works. *Rumford*.
Essays of a Birmingham Manufacturer. *Sargant*.
Nouveaux Lundis. *Ste. Beuve*.
Port Royal. *Ste. Beuve*.
Portraits de Femmes. *Ste. Beuve*.
Portraits Contemporains. *Ste. Beuve*.
Souvenirs et Indiscretions, etc. *Sainte Beuve*.
Labor for the Solitary and the Social. *Saunders*.
Dämonen. *Scherr*.
Farrago. *Scherr*.
Studien. *Scherr*.
Stray Leaves of Science and Folk-Lore. *Scoffern*.
Lectures and Essays. *Seeley*.
Characteristics. *Shaftesbury*.
Doctor in Medicine, and other Papers. *Smith*.
Essays. *Smith*.
Wassail Bowl. *Smith*.
The Rhine; Legends, Traditions, History. *Snowe*.
Americanism and other Isms. *Spencer*.
Essays, Moral, Political and Æsthetic. *Spencer*
Vermischte Schriften. *Spielhagen*.
Crumbs Swept Up. *Talmage*.
Miscellanies. *Thackeray*.
Characters from *Theophrastus*, by Jebb.
Sanctum Sanctorum. *Tilton*.
Open Air. *Verey*.
Toleration: The Ignorant Philosopher: Commentary on Beccaria. *Voltaire*.
Hit. *Walker*.
My Summer in a Garden. *Warner*.
Essays and Reviews. *Whipple*.
Literature and Life. *Whipple*.
Success and its Conditions. *Whipple*.
Pleasures of Literature. *Willmott*.
Curiosities of Toil. *Wynter*.

Comic and Satirical Works.

Account of Abimelech Coody, etc.
American Tour of Brown, Jones and Robinson.
Andy's Trip to the West, etc.
Attic Wit, from the Pens of Tom Taylor, and others.
Flush Times of Alabama and Mississippi. *Baldwin*.
Comic History of England. *Beckett*.
Complete Works of Artemus Ward. *Browne*.
More Happy Thoughts. *Burnand*.
Mirthfulness. *Clark*.
Mark Twain's Autobiography. *Clemens*.
Roughing It. *Clemens*.
Broad Grins. *Colman*.
Comic English Grammar.
Table-Book. *Cruikshank*.
Essay on Irish Bulls, by Miss Edgeworth. *Castle Rackrent* (with novels).
High Life in New York. *Haliburton*.
Letter-Bag of the Great Western. *Haliburton*.
New London Jest-Book. *Hazlitt*.
Hogarth's Frolic; a Five Days' Peregrination.
Whimsicalities. *Hood*.
Travels of an American Owl. *Johnson*.
Bataille dans la Pension Europe. *Lawrence*.
Nonsense Songs and Alphabets. *Lear*.
Assemblée Nationale Comique. *Lireux*.
Moon Hoax. *Locke*.
Miss Columbia's Public School.
O. C. Kerr Papers. *Newell*.
Adventures of One Terence MacGrant. *Peck*.
Prenticeana. *Prentice*.
Fight at Dame Europa's School. *Pullen*.
Works. Illustrated by Doré. *Rabelais*.
Revelations. A Companion to the "New Gospel of Peace."
Comic History of U. S. *Sherwood*.
Theses, etc., ex Universa Vinosophia.
True Story of Mrs. Shakspeare's Life.
Merry Maple Leaves. *Twombly*.
Chronicles of Gotham. *White*.
Fall of Man. *White*.
Wreck-Elections of a Busy Life.

Anecdotes, Maxims, Proverbs.

Cyclopædia of Anecdotes. *Arvine*.
Bench and Bar. *Bigelow*.
Book of Blunders.
World of Moral and Religious Anecdote. *Hood*.
Book About the Clergy. *Jeaffreson*.
Book of Clerical Anecdotes. *Larwood*.
Anecdotes of Love. *Montez*.
Percy Anecdotes.
Bench and Bar of New York. *Proctor*.

Reminiscences of Scottish Life and Character. *Ramsay.*
Swiftiana.
Book of Golden Deeds. *Yonge.*
Maximes de La Rochefoucauld. *Maximes.*
Maxims. *La Rochefoucauld.*
Maximes et Pensées.
Pensées de Montesquieu. *Maximes.*
Apophtègmes des Anciens. *Perrot* d'Ablancourt.
Maximes de Vauvenargues. *Maximes.*
Words of *Washington*, Selected by Parton.
Bohn's Handbook of Proverbs.
Latin Proverbs and Quotations. *Henderson.*
Proverbs of all Nations. *Kelly.*

Fables and Legends.

Fairy Legends. *Croker.*
Wonderful Stories from Northern Lands. *Goddard.*
Legends of Old Testament Characters. *Gould.*
Fairy Tales. *Hamilton.*
Primeval World of Hebrew Tradition. *Hedge.*
Märchen für Jung und Alt. *Hoffmann.*
Fairy Mythology. *Keightley.*
Märchen etc der nordamerikanischen Indianer. *Knortz.*
Fables. *Krilof.*
Fables, Allemand et Français. *Lessing.*
Life and Death of Mother Shipton.
Pilpay's Fables.
Swahili Tales.

Entertaining Collections.

Boy's Annual. *Beeton.*
Fact, Fiction, History and Adventure. *Beeton.*
Wonderful Escapes. *Bernard.*
Cases and Queries.
Cassell's Illustrated Readings.
Readings for Winter Gatherings. *Fleming.*
Good Girl's Annual, 1870.
Curiosities of Olden Times. *Gould.*
Spinnstube. *Horn.*
Illustrated Penny Readings.
Marvellous Repository.
Home Chat. *Mateaux.*
Novels, Tales and Poetry, by various Authors.
Old Book Collector's Miscellany.
Nooks and Corners of English Life. *Timbs.*
Notabilia; or, Curious and Amusing Facts. *Timbs.*
World of Wonders.

Books of Quotations.

Dictionary of Practical Quotations. *Hale.*
Flora Symbolica. *Ingram.*
Classical Quotations. *Riley.*

Selections, Beauties.

Readings in English Literature. *Chambers.*
Studies in Poetry and Prose. *Cleveland.*
Trozos Selectos de Literatura. *Cosson.*
Readings for Winter Gatherings. *Fleming.*
Half Hours with the Best Authors. *Knight.*
Choice Specimens of American Literature. *Martin.*
Select Prose and Poetry. *Musset.*
Beethoven's Brevier. *Nohl.*
Pleasure; a Holiday Book of Prose and Verse.
Salad for the Solitary and the Social. *Saunders.*
Specimens of English Literature. *Skeat.*
Noble Thoughts in Noble Language. *Southgate.*
Selections from *Taine*, ed. by Van Laun.
Wise, etc. Sayings from George Eliot. *Mann.*
Immortellen H. Heine's. *Strodtmann.*
Every-day Book of Modern Literature. *Townsend.*
Typical Selections from English Authors.

Complete Works and Collections.

Works. Ed. by Fraser. *Berkeley.*
Brooke, Lord. Works. *Fuller* Worthies.
Oeuvres. *Chateaubriand.*
Publications of *Chaucer* Society.
Poems and Prose Remains. *Clough.*
Scisma d'Inghilterra, etc. *Davanzati.*
Œuvres Choisies. *Diderot.*
Prose Works. *Emerson.*
Works of J. H. *Frere*, with Memoir.
Select Writings. *Genin.*
Hinterlassene Schriften. *Gervinus.*
Writings. *Goddard.*
Werke. *Goethe.*
Journal, Lettres, Poèmes. *Guérin.*
Remains. *Hallam.*
Werke. *Heine.*

Gesammelte Werke. *Heyse.*
Sämmtliche Werke. *Hoffmann.*
Works, with Memoir. *Lamb.*
Works. *Landon.*
Works of *Machiavelli.*
Oeuvres Complètes. *Maistre.*
Life and Writings of *Mazzini.*
Works. *Montague.*
Works and Memoirs of Margaret F. *Ossoli.*
Works. *Pope.*
Oeuvres Complètes. *Rollin.*
Posthumous Works. *Rossel.*
Works. *Rumford.*
Works. *Ruskin.*
Sämmtliche Schriften. *Schiller.*
Sämmtliche Werke. *Schiller.*
Works. *Schiller.*
Werke. *Seume.*
Works of Charles *Sumner.*
Sämmtliche Werke. *Tieck.*
Works of Vaughan. *Fuller* Worthies.

Speeches, Collected.

Reden. *Bismarck.*
Cromwell's Letters and Speeches. *Carlyle.*
Speeches. *Cobden.*
Speeches, Letters and Sayings. *Dickens.*
Elgin Speeches. *Duff.*
Speeches. *Erskine.*
Speeches. *Gladstone.*
Household Book of Irish Eloquence.
Speeches on Political Questions. *Julian.*
Miscellaneous Addresses. *Newman.*
Speeches and Despatches. *Russell.*
Washington's Birth-day. Vienna.

Single Speeches and Addresses.

Centenary Address, N. Y. Hospital. *Beekman.*
Oration, July 4, 1867. *Clarke.*
Address before Governor and Legislature of Conn. *Clerc.*
Address to Whig and Cliosophic Societies. *Dayton.*
Address to Alumni of N. Y. City University. *Draper.*
Address to His Early Companions. *Elliott.*
Address at Gettysburg Cemetery. *Everett.*
Address, Inauguration of Union Club. *Everett.*
God's Argument against Oppression.
No Royal Road to Knowledge. *Harris.*
Oration, July 4, 1847. *Harris.*
Oration, July 4, 1863. *Holmes.*
Address and Poem to Bost. Merc. Lib. Asso. *Hone and Lunt.*
Inaugural Address. *Jacobi.*
Speech, Washington's Birth-day. *Noyes.*
Destiny of America; a Speech. *Seward.*
Oration and Poem to Phi Beta Kappa. *Tracy* and Helmer.
Address, Opening of Philadelphia Athenaeum. *Wharton.*

Lectures, Etc.

Protective Policy in Literature. *Coggeshall.*
Finsbury Lectures. *Fox.*
Discours Populaires. *Laboulaye.*
Lectures. *Montez.*

Lectures; Correspondence.

Private Correspondence. *Clay.*
Letters and other Writings. *Denison.*
Correspondence, with Memoir. *Garrick.*
Letters of Queen Henrietta Maria. *Green.*
Literature in Letters. *Holcombe.*
Letters and Extracts. *Jukes.*
Half Hours with Best Letter Writers. *Knight.*
Correspondance. *La Rochefoucauld.*
Lessing's Briefweehsel mit seiner Frau.
Letters. *Lewis.*
Letters to Mr. Hoyt. *Myers.*
Letters and MSS. of Signers of the Declaration of Independence. *Myers.*
Napoleon's Correspondence with King Joseph.
New Letter Writer.
Letters and Letter-Writers. *Seton.*
Lettres Choisies. *Sévigné.*
Oeuvres. *Voiture.*
Letters and Journals of James, Eighth Earl of Elgin. *Walford.*
Letters of Royal and Illustrious Ladies of Great Britain. *Wood.*

CLASS VI.—CLASSICS.

Greek Prose Classics.

Oration on the Crown. *Demosthenes.*
Orations of *Demosthenes.* (Bohn's transl.)
History. Transl. by Beloe. *Herodotus.*
History. Transl. by Rawlinson. *Herodotus.*
History. (Bohn's transl.) *Herodotus.*
Works of *Herodotus.* Text of Baehr, Transl. by Cary.

Dialogues of *Plato*, transl. and ed. by Jowett.
Gorgias of *Plato*; notes by Thompson.
Opera. Ed. by Bekker. *Plato*.
Works of *Plato*. (Bohn's transl.)
Summary and Index to *Plato's* Dialogues. By Day.
Lives. Transl. by Longfellow. *Plutarch*.
Morals. Transl. by Goodwin. *Plutarch*.
Peloponnesian War. Transl. by Dale. *Thucydides*.
Analysis and Summary of *Thucydides*, by Wheeler.
Anabasis. (Bohn's transl.) *Xenophon*.
Cyropædia. (Bohn's transl.) *Xenophon*.
Minor Works. (Bohn's transl.) *Xenophon*.
Selections (Greek, notes by Phillpotts.) *Xenophon*.

Latin Prose Classics.

Commentaries of *Cæsar*. Ed. by Moberley.
Commentaries. (Bohn's transl.) *Cæsar*.
Opera. *Cæsar*.
Cato Major, and Lælius of *Cicero*; Latin, notes by Barker.
De Claris Oratoribus; vel Brutus. *Cicero*.
De Officiis. *Cicero*.
Opera. *Cicero*.
Orationes Selectæ, ed. Klotz. *Cicero*.
De Oratore of *Cicero*, Calvert's transl.
Orations of *Cicero* against Catiline. Tr. and Ed. by Wilkins and Hahn.
Select Letters (Latin) with notes by Watson *Cicero*.
Select Orations (Latin, ed. Anthon.) *Cicero*.
Works of *Cicero*. (Bohn's transl.)
Breviarium Historiæ Romanæ. *Eutropius*.
Rerum Romanarum Libri IV. *Florus*.
Ampelii Liber Memorialis. *Florus*.
Justin, Cornelius Nepos and Eutropius. (Bohn's transl.)
History of Rome (Bohn's transl). *Livy*.
Anonymi Fabulæ. *Phædrus*.
Aviani Fabulæ. *Phædrus*.
Fabulæ. *Phædrus*.
Syri Sententiæ. *Phædrus*.
Comedies. (Bohn's transl.) *Plautus*.
Natural History. (Bohn's transl.) *Pliny*.
Select Letters of *Pliny* the Younger, notes by Church and Brodribb.
Institutes of Oratory. (Bohn's transl.) *Quintilian*.
Catiline and Jugurthine War. Ed. by Anthon. *Sallust*.
Sallust, Florus, et Vellejus Paterculus. (Bohn's transl.)
Geography. (Bohn's transl.) *Strabo*.
Works. *Suetonius*.
Annals. With Commentary, by Frost. *Tacitus*.
Annals. Books 1, 2. Transl. by Beesly. *Tacitus*.
Terence and Phædrus. (Bohn's transl.)

Class VII.—Periodical Literature.

[For periodicals on special subjects, see under those subjects.]

Magazines.

History of Irish Periodial Literature. *Madden*.
Academy.
Aldine Press.
All the Year Round.
American Review.
Argosy.
Atlantic Monthly.
Ballou's Monthly Magazine.
Beecher's Magazine.
Belgravia.
Bentley's Miscellany.
Bizarre.
Blackwood's Edinburgh Magazine.
Boston Miscellany of Literature and Fashion.
British Controversialist.
British Quarterly Review.
Broadway.
Cassell's Magazine.
Chambers' Journal.
Chatterbox.
Contemporary Review.
Cornhill Magazine.
Daheim.
Dark Blue.
De Bow's Review.
De la Salle Monthly.
Demorest's Illustrated Monthly.
Demorest's Young America.
Dublin Review.
Dublin University Magazine.
Eclectic Magazine.
Edinburgh Review.
Englishwoman's Domestic Magazine.

Every Month.
Every Saturday.
Family Friend.
Fortnightly Review.
Frank Leslie's Lady's Magazine.
Frank Leslie's Monthly.
Frazer's Magazine.
Galaxy.
Gentleman's Magazine.
Godey's Lady's Book.
Good Words.
Good Words for the Young.
Graphic.
Grenzboten.
Harper's Magazine.
Hausblätter.
Herald of Health.
Hours at Home.
Im Neuen Reich.
Internationale Revue.
Ladies' Repository.
Leisure Hour.
Lippincott's Magazine.
Littell's Living Age.
Little Folks.
London Quarterly Review.
London Review.
London Society.
Macmillan's Magazine.
Magasin Pittoresque.
Magasin Universel.
Major & Knapp's Illustrated Monthly.
Maple Leaves.
Monthly Magazine.
Musée des Familles.
National Quarterly Review.
New Era.
New Monthly Magazine.
Nineteenth Century.
North American Review.
North British Review.
Notes and Queries.
Old and New.
Oliver Optic's Magazine.
Once a Week.
Onward.
Our Boys and Girls.
Our Monthly.
Our Young Folks.
Overland Monthly.
Packard's Monthly.
Penn Monthly.
Peoples' Magazine.
Peterson's Magazine.
Putnam's Magazine.
Quarterly Review.
Radical.
Republic.
Revue Contemporaine.
Revue des Deux Mondes.
Revue Française.
Revue Moderne.
Riverside Magazine.
Sailor's Magazine.
St. James Magazine.
St. Paul's Magazine.
Salon für Literatur, Kunst und Gesellschaft.
Scribner's Monthly.
Sharpe's London Magazine.
Shipping and Commercial List.
Sixpenny Magazine.
Southern Magazine.
Southern Review.
Sunday at Home.
Temple Bar.
Tinsley's Magazine.
Transatlantic Magazine.
Victoria Magazine.
Westermann's Illustrirte Deutsche Monatshefte.
Western Monthly.
Westminster Review.

Newspapers.

The Newspaper Press; its Origin, Progress, and Present Position. *Grant*.
May's London Press Directory.
Newspaper Press Directory for 1857.
Rowell & Co.'s American Newspaper Directory.
History of Newspaper Press of St. Paul. *Williams*.
Appleton's Journal.
Athenæum.
Canadian Illustrated News.
Critic.
Daily News.
Deutsche Ausstellungs-Zeitung.
Diario de Lisboa, Jan.–June 1866.
Examiner.
Frank Leslie's Illustrated Newspaper.
Harper's Bazaar.
Illustrated London News.
Illustrated Times.
Illustration Europénne.
Illustrirte Zeitung.
Journal pour Tours.
London Illustrated News.
London *Times*.
Nation.
N. Y. Evening Post.

N. Y. Free Press.
N. Y. Herald.
N. Y. Staatszeitung.
N. Y. Standard.
N. Y. Times.
N. Y. Tribune.
Noticioso de Ambos Mundos.
Novo Mundo.
Oneida Circular.
Our Society.
Pall Mall Gazette.
Punchinello.
Queen ; the Lady's Newspaper and Court Chronicle.
Reader.
Revolution.
Round Table.
Saturday Review.
Spectator.
Sun.
Times (London).
Index to the London *Times.*
Ueber Land und Meer.
Vanity Fair.
World.

General Bibliography.

Bookworm.
How to Tell a Caxton. *Blades.*
Dictionnaire de Géographie Ancienne et Moderne à l'Usage du Libraire. Par un Bibliophile.
Booksellers' Directory, 1869, 1870. *Dingman.*
Katalog der Deutschen Literatur. *Hoppe.*
American Catalogue of Books. *Kelly*
London Catalogue, 1800–1818.
English Catalogue for 1869 ; for 1870.
Catalogue Général de la Librairie Française. *Lorenz.*
Handy-Book about Books. *Power.*
Librarian. *Savage.*

Library Management, etc.

17th, 18th and 19th Annual Reports of *Boston* Public Library.
Reports and Catalogues, *Charlestown* Public Library.
Memories of the British Museum. *Cowtan.*
Founders of the British Museum. *Edwards.*
Free Town Libraries. *Edwards.*
Manual of *Lansing* Library.
Geschichte der Bibliothek in Augsburg. *Mezger.*
Free Libraries and Newsrooms. *Mullins.*
Pesti Kereskedö Ifjak Társulata.
Report of Trustees of State Library. *N. Y.* State.
Récueil de Decrets, etc., concernant la Bibliothèque Royale.
Reports, By-Laws, etc., of *Young Men's* Asso. of Buffalo.

Special Bibliography.

Lincoln Bibliography. *Boyd.*
Encyclopædia Bibliographica. *Darling.*
Bibliotheca Americana Vetustissima. *Harrisse.*
Bibliotheca Historica. *Stevens.*
Bibliography of Minnesota. *Williams.*

Library Catalogues.

California State Library Catalogue.
Catalogue of *City* Library of Lowell.
Catalogue of Library of *Detroit* Young Men's Society.
Catalogue of *Keokuk* Libr. Asso. Library.
Catalogue of *Liverpool* Free Library.
Catalogue of Library, *Mechanics'* Institute, Montreal.
Catalogue of Books of *Mechanics'* Library Association, Lancaster, Pa.
Catalogue of *Mercantile* Library, Baltimore.
Index to the Catalogue of *Mercantile* Library Association of Boston.
Catalogue of *Mercantile* Library of Philadelphia.
Catalogue of *Mercantile* Library, Portland.
Catalogue of *Mercantile* Library, Portsmouth, N. H.
Catalogue of *Michigan* State Library.
Catalogue of *Newark* Library Association.
Catalogue, *Newburgh* Free Library.
Catalogue of *New Hampshire* State Library.
Catalogue of State Law Library. *N. Y.* State.
Handy-Book of the British Museum. *Nichols.*
Catalogue of *People's* Library, Newport.
Finding List and Supplement of *Portland* Public Library.
Catalogue of *Public* Library of Cincinnati.
Catalogue of *Public* Library, Detroit.
Catalogue of *St. Louis* Public School Library.

Catalogue of Additions to Library of Congress. *U. S.*

Index of Subjects, Catalogue of *U. S.* Congressional Library.

Catalogue of Library, *Young* Men's Association of Buffalo.

Catalogue of Library, *Young* Men's Mercantile Library Association of Cincinnati.

Catalogue of Library, *Young* Men's Mercantile Library Association of Pittsburgh.

Sale Catalogues; Publishers' Lists.

Livres Grecs, Latins, etc. *Bossange.*

Publishers' Uniform Trade List Directory. *Challen.*

Publishers' Circular.

Trade Circular Annual for 1871.

Class IX.—Encyclopædias.

Encyclopædias.

American Annual Cyclopædia.

Family Cyclopædia.

Pantology. *Park.*

Standard Library Cyclopædia.

Zell's Popular Encyclopædia.

Technical Dictionaries.

Abrégé du Grand Dictionnaire de Technologie.

Dictionary of Terms in Art. *Fairholt.*

Nautical and Commercial Pocket Dictionary, etc. *Henckel and Born.*

Repertorium der Technischen Literatur. *Kerl.*

Encyclopédie Technologique. *Laboulaye.*

Commercial Dictionary. *M'Culloch.*

Dictionary of Science. *Rodwell.*

Collections of Useful Knowledge.

Dr. Chase's Recipes. *Chase.*

Family Tutor.

Guide to Knowledge.

Ten Thousand Wonderful Things. *King.*

Common Sayings. *Loaring.*

Facts and Dates. *Mackay.*

Universal Path-Finder. *Olmsted.*

Guide to Knowledge. *Robbins.*

Scholar's Reference Book.

DEPARTMENT E.—HISTORY, GEOGRAPHY, TRAVEL.

Class I.—Universal Geography.

Universal Geography.

Dictionnaire de Géographie.

System of Geography. *Bell.*

Manual of Geography. *Hughes.*

Elements of Geography. *Worcester.*

Geographical Exercises. *Hart.*

Geographical Grammar. *Picket.*

School Geography. *Mitchell.*

Names of Places. *Edmunds.*

Tour du Monde. *Dufrénoy.*

Applications de la Géographie à l'Histoire. *Bescherelle.*

Hand-Book of Ancient Geography and History. *Pütz.*

Dictionary of Greek and Roman Geography. *Smith.*

Geographical Periodicals.

Petermann's Geographische Mittheilungen.

Globus.

Journal of *Royal* Geographical Society.

Atlases and Maps.

Atlas of Comparative Geography. *Hughes.*

New General Atlas. *Mitchell.*

Johnson's Family Atlas.

Student's Atlas. *Bartholomew.*

Atlas of Ancient and Mediæval History. *Quin*

Historico-Geographical Hand Atlas. *Spruner.*

School Atlas of Classical Geography. *Johnston.*

Standard Atlas of Classical Geography.

Hand-Atlas. *Kiepert.*

Use of the Globes. *Keith.*

Equal Surface Projection for Maps of the World. *Smyth.*

Map of North America. *J. C. Smith.*

Doggett's Map of the U. S., with Map of North America. *J. C. Smith.*

Accompaniment to Mitchell's Map of the U. S.
Coast Survey Map of Alaska. *U. S.*
Carte de la Théâtre de la Guerre en Italie. *Bacler d'Albe.*
Atlas von Hellas. *Kiepert.*
Map of Overland Route to India. *Wyld.*
Map of India. *Wyld.*

Hydrography and Charts.

Nautical Surveying. *Jeffers.*
Coast Survey Report for 1865, 66, 67 and 68. *U. S.*
Coast Survey. Harbor Charts. *U. S.*
Introduction, etc. *Coast Survey.*
Reply to Official Defence. *Coast Survey.*
India Directory. *Horsburgh.*

Circumnavigations.

Voyage Round the World. *Adams.*
Voyage Round the World. *Beauvoir.*
Antipodes and Round the World. *Frere.*
Cruise Round the World, 1869–70, under Admiral Hornby.
Around the World. *Prime.*
Circumnavigation of the Globe in the Novara. *Scherzer.*
A Boy's Voyage Round the World. *Smiles.*

Miscellaneous Travels and Voyages.

Wandering in Every Clime. *Ainsworth.*
Incidents on Land and Water. *Bates.*
Illustrated Travels. *Bates.*
Voyageurs Anciens et Modernes. *Charton.*
Mountain Adventures. *Headley.*
Mountain Adventures.
Home Recreations and Foreign Travel.
Travels, etc., of Celebrated Travelers. *Howe.*
Romance of Travel.
Thrilling Stories of the Forest and Frontier.
Voyage and Venture.
Stories of Cook's Voyages. *Jones.*
Mutineers of the Bounty. *Belcher.*
Innocents Abroad. *Clemens.*
On the Wing. *Maximilian.*
Voyage de Narbrough. *See* Voyages, etc , par *Coreal.*
Canoe Traveling on the Baltic. *Powell.*
Across America and Asia. *Pumpelly.*
Atlas to Voyages. *Valentia.*
Dust and Foam. *Warren.*
Researches and Missionary Labors. *Wolff.*

General Guide Books; Travelers' Manuals.

[For local guide-books, etc., see names of localities.]

Shifts and Expedients of Camp Life. *Lord and Baines.*
Our Ocean Highways. *Dempsey.*
Skeleton Tours. *Sargent.*
Travelers' Guide. *Davison.*
Satchel Guide for the Vacation Tourist in Europe.
Short Trip Guide to Europe. *Morford.*
Hand-Book for Travelers in Europe and the East. *Harper.*
Travelers' Manual for Conversation. *Baedeker.*
Appleton's European Guide Book.
Great Trans-Continental Tourist's Guide.
Northern Traveler.

CLASS II.—UNIVERSAL HISTORY.

Philosophy of History.

Study and Use of History. *Bigland.*
Essays on Historical Truth. *Bisset.*
Discours sur l'Histoire Universelle. *Bossuet.*
Philosophy of Universal History. *Bunsen.*
Laws of Human Progress; a Lecture. *Dewey.*
History and Theory of Revolutions. *Clark.*
Growth of Cities; a Discourse. *Tappan.*

History of Civilization.

Aryan Civilization. *Barker.*
History of Civilization. *Dean.*
Fallacies and Tendencies of the Age. *Dean*
L'Homme Primitif. *Figuier.*
Primitive Man. *Figuier.*
History of Civilization. *Guizot.*
Civilisation en Europe. *Guizot.*
Laws of Civilization (Address). *Hitchcock.*
Orations on Civil Society. *Hyacinthe*
Origin of Civilization. *Lubbock.*
Pre-historic Times. *Lubbock.*
Builders of Babel. *McCausland.*
Primitive Culture. *Tylor.*
Universal History; or Essay on the Manners and Spirit of Nations. *Voltaire.*

Universal History.

Weltgeschichte. Ed. by Schmidt, continued by Arndt. *Becker.*

Outlines of Universal History. *Lardner.*
Historisches Taschenbuch. *Raumer.*
Manual of Systematic History. *Reed.*
Elements of General History. *Tytler.*
Universal History in Perspective. *Willard.*
Historical Essays. *Freeman.*
Histoire Contemporaine. *Gabourd.*
Great Cities of the World. *Frost.*

Class III.—Historical Collaterals.

Ethnography.

Journal of *Ethnological* Society of London.
Transactions, *International* Congress of Pre-historic Archæology.
Oneness of the Race. *Bersier.*
Descent of Man. *Darwin.*
Review of Descent of Man. *Wallace.*
Homo versus Darwin.
Les Races Humaines. *Figuier.*
Unity and Origin of Human Race. *Johnes.*
Man and his Migrations. *Latham.*
Hints and Facts on the Origin of Man. *Melia.*
Natural History of Man. *Newman.*
Pedigree of the English People. *Nicholas.*
Naturgeschichte des Volkes. *Riehl.*
Antiquity of Intellectual Man. *Smyth.*
Natural History of Man. *Wood.*
Uncivilized Races of Men. *Wood.*
Asiatic Affinities of the Old Italians. *Ellis.*

Chronology.

Synchronology. *Hawes.*
Haydn's Dictionary of Dates.
Polish-American System of Chronology. *Peabody.*

Antiquities; Heraldry.

Arms and Armor. *Lacombe.*
Anniversary Meetings of *Royal* Society of Northern Antiquaries.
Antiquarisk Tidsskrift. *Royal* Society, etc.
Mémoires. *Royal* Society, etc.
Great Pyramid. *Day.*
Historic Devices, Badges and War Cries. *Palliser.*
Remains of Ancient Dwellings in Holyhead Islands. *Stanley.*
Rude Stone Monuments in all Countries, *Fergusson.*
Catalogue of MSS. and Relics, Washington's Headquarters.
Antiquities of Heraldry. *Ellis.*

Numismatics.

Gold and Silver Coins. *Eckfeldt and Du Bois.*
Roman Coins. *Hobler.*
Souvenirs Numismatigues de la Révolution de 1848.

Manners and Customs.

History of Bundling. *Stiles.*
History and Philosophy of Marriage.
Marriage Rites. *Hamilton.*
Cups and their Customs.
Drinking Usages. *Potter.*
Club and Drawing Room. *Hay.*
Natural History of Society. *Taylor*
American Society. *Towle.*
History of the Rod. *Cooper.*
Customs and Manners of the Bedouins.
History of Duelling. *Millingen.*
Life and Death of the Sublime Society of Beef Steaks. *Arnold.*
Umbrellas and their History. *Sangster.*
Philosophy of Dress and Fashion. *Fox.*
Art of Dressing Well. *Frost.*
Womankind in Western Europe. *Wright.*

Class IV.—Ancient History.

Ancient History, Generally.

Prolegomena to Ancient History. *Mahaffy.*
Ancient History of the East. *Lenormant.*
Ancient States and Empires. *Lord.*
Manual of Ancient History. *Rawlinson.*
Comparative View of Ancient History. *Smith.*
Student's Ancient History. *P. Smith.*
Historische Bilder aus der Alten Welt. *Stahl.*
Synoptical Table of Egyptian and Sacred History.

Jews.

History of Israel. *Ewald.*
Notices of the Jews by Classic Writers. *Gill*
Histoire de la Guerre des Juifs. *Josephus.*
History and Literature of the Israelites. *Rothschild.*
Phœnicia and Israel. *Wilkins.*

Eastern Empires.

The Nations Around, *Keary*.
Orient Ancien et Moderne.
Five Great Monarchies. *Rawlinson*.
History of Assurbanipal. *Smith*.
Ancient History of the East. *Smith*.

Ancient Egypt.

Egypt 3,300 Years ago. *Lanoye*.
Menes and Cheops Identified. *Rikart*.
History of Egypt. *Sharpe*.
Egypt of the Pharaohs and of the Kedivé. *Zincke*.

Ancient Greece.

History of Greece. *Curtius*.
History of Greece. *Goldsmith*.
Stories from Grecian History. *Hack*.

Rome; Regal, Republican; City.

Questions on Grimshaw's Goldsmith's Rome; with Key.
History of Rome. *Mommsen*.
History of Rome. *Ihne*.
Decline of the Roman Republic. *Long*.
Regal Rome. *Newman*.
Roman Republic. *Michelet*.

Rome; Empire.

Roman Imperialism. *Seeley*.
Students' Gibbon. *Smith*.

Greek and Roman Antiquities.

Classical Dictionary. *Anthon*.
Compendium of Grecian Antiquities. *Cleveland*
Charicles. *Becker*.
Gallus. *Becker*.
Wonders of Pompeii. *Monier*

Mythology.

Mythology of the Aryan Nations. *Cox*.
Hand-Book of Legendary and Mythologic Art. *Clement*.
Heroes of Asgard. *Keary*

Class V.—Mediæval History.

Crusades.

Histoire des Croisades. *Michaud*.
Student's History of Europe During the Middle Ages. *Hallam*.

Modern Jews.

The Jews. *Alexander*.
History of the Jews. *Gosse*.
History of the Karaite Jews. *Rule*.
Hebrews in East Anglia. *Margoliouth*.

Modern History; Generally.

Annals of Europe.
Universal Modern History. *Robinson*
Studien. *Scherr*.

Class VI.—Modern Europe.

Great Britain; Generally.

Illustrated History of England. *Cassell*.
History of England. *Creasy*.
Short History of England. *Davys*.
Child's History of England. *Dickens*.
New School History of England. *Freeman*
Old English History for Children. *Freeman*.
History of England abridged. *Goldsmith*.
English History. *Ince*.
Outlines of English History. *Ince*.
Atlas of British History. *Johnston*.
Knight's Crown History of England.
Histoire d'Angleterre. *Lingard*.
History of England. *Lingard*.
History of England. *Lossing*.
Class-Book History of England. *Morris*.
Historical Maps of England. *Pearson*.
Chronicles of England; a Metrical History. *Raymond*.
Descriptive Catalogue, for History of Great Britain and Ireland, by *Hardy*. (Rolls Chron.)
History of England. *Stanhope*.
Select Charters and other Illustrations of English History. *Stubbs*.
Civil Wars of England. *Taylor*.
History of England. *Yonge*.
Cameos from English History; Wars with France. *Yonge*.

Great Britain, to Conquest.

Before the Conquest. *Adams*.
Polychronicon, with Transl. *Higden*.
Chronica. *Hoveden*.
Speculum Historiale. *Ricardus*.
De Gestis Pontificum Anglorum. *Willelmus* of Malmesbury.

Great Britain; Conquest, to Stuarts.

History of Norman Conquest. *Freeman*.
Norman Kings of England. *Cobbe*.
Life and Reign of *Edward I*.
England and France in the 15th Century. *Pyne*.
England under the Tudors. *Birchall*.
History of England. *Froude*.
The Pilgrim; Dialogue on Henry VIII. *Thomas*.

Great Britain; Stuarts and Cromwell.

History and Literature of the Stuart Period. *Davies.*
Narrative of Gunpowder Plot, by Gerard. *Morris.*
Condition of Catholics under James I. *Morris.*
Reign of Charles I. *Wallington.*
Charles I, Cromwell, and Charles II. *Fellowes.*

Great Britain; Recent.

True Picture of a Modern Whig Revived.
Reign of George II. *Oliphant.*
History of England from 1830. *Molesworth.*
England's Last Queen. *Wallace.*
Home Politics. *Grant.*
Phases of Party.

English Local History, etc.

Notes about Aldeburgh. *Hele.*
Cambridge and Waltham Abbey. *Fuller.*
Chester as it Was. *Howson.*
View of Durham. *Mackenzie.*
History of Durham. *Surtees.*
History of Leicester. *Thompson.*
History of Lichfield Cathedral. *Stone.*
Annals of Oxford. *Jeaffreson.*
Memorials of Westminster Abbey. *Stanley.*
Abbeys, Castles, and Ancient Halls of England and Wales. *Timbs.*
Castles of Herefordshire. *Robinson.*

English Military and Naval History.

Military History of Great Britain. *Gleig.*
History of the British Army. *Stocqueler.*
Military Forces of the Crown. *Clode.*
Monumenta Juridica; Black Book of the Admiralty.
Naval Chronicle.
Waterloo. *Hooper.*
Waterloo Campaign. *Mercer.*
Fall of England? Battle of Dorking.
German Conquest of England.
What Happened after the Battle of Dorking.
Second Armada.

English Statistics, Public Documents, etc.

Hand-Book of the Administrations of Great Britain. *Carr.*
Under Government. *Parkinson.*
Tabulæ Curiales. *Foss.*

British Antiquities.

Coronation Stone. *Skene.*
Domesday Book (Lincolnshire and Rutlandshire).
Antiquities found at the New Exchange. *Tite.*
Gog and Magog. *Fairholt.*

Scotland.

History of Scotland. *Burton.*
Arthurian Localities. *Glennie.*
Clanship and the Clans. *Towry.*
History of the Battle of Bannockburn. *White.*
Gaelic Topography of Scotland. *Robertson.*
Past and Present. *Reid.*
A Century of Scottish Life. *Rogers.*
Scotland, Social and Domestic. *Rogers.*
Guildry and Merchants' House of Glasgow. *Ewing.*
Memorabilia of the City of Perth.
Land of Lorne. *Buchanan.*
Iona. *Argyll.*
Art Rambles in Shetland. *Reid.*

Ireland.

Student's Manual of Irish History. *Cusack.*
History of Ireland. *McGee.*
Varieties of Irish History. *Gaskin.*
Ireland. *Murphy.*
Modern Ireland. *Sigerson.*
History of the Kingdom of Kerry. *Cusack.*
History of the Maritime Ports of Ireland. *Marmion.*
Irlande et France. *Duquet.*
Irish Land. *Campbell.*
Land War in Ireland. *Godkin.*
Irish Land Question. *Mill.*
Land Question of Ireland. *Morris.*
Land Tenures of Ireland. *Sigerson.*

England; Travels.

English Note Books. *Hawthorne.*
Manufacturing Districts of England. *Head.*
De l'Angleterre. *Heine.*
Memorials of Oxford. *Ingram.*
England in 1850. *Lamartine.*
Yachting round the West of England. *L'Estrange.*
Guide to Isle of Wight. *Lockhart.*
Scenery of England and Wales. *Mackintosh.*
Down Channel from London to Lands End. *McMullen.*
L'Angleterre. *Pillet.*
English Visit. *Sen.*
Notes sur l'Angleterre. *Taine.*
History of Wales. *Williams.*

London.

London Directory.
London and its Environs.
Palace and Hovel; Phases of London Life. *Kirwan.*

London; its Celebrated Characters. *Jesse.*
Hallowed Spots of Ancient London. *Meteyard.*
Letters from London. *Dallas.*
Persian Princes in London. *Fraser.*
Her Majesty's Tower. *Dixon.*
Hand-Book to Charities of London. *Low.*
New Palace at Westminster.
Ancient Meeting Houses in London. *Pike.*
Lincoln's Inn. *Spilsbury.*
Round about Piccadilly. *Wheatley.*

France, Generally.

France, its History and Revolutions. *Chambers.*
History of France. *Grimshaw.*
Histoire de France. *Guizot.*
History of France. *Markham.*
History of France. *White.*
Lectures on the History of France. *Stephen.*
Wars of the Huguenots. *Hanna.*
France under the Bourbons. *Yonge.*
France and Hereditary Monarchy. *Bigelow.*
Hinter Schloss und Riegel. *Schmidt-Weissenfels.*
Femmes de la Cour des derniers Valois. *Imbert de St. Amand.*

France, Louis XIV.

Chapters from French History. *Gurney.*
Secret History of French Court. *Cousin.*
History of Louis XIV. *Abbott.*
Age of Louis XIV and XV. *Voltaire.*
History of Lewis XIV. *Louis XIV.*
Memoirs of the Court of Louis XIV.
Revolt of the Protestants of the Cevennes. *Bray.*
Protestant Exiles from France under Louis XIV. *Agnew.*

French Revolution.

French Revolution. *Carlyle.*
Histoire Musée de la République Française. *Challamel.*
Girondists. *Lamartine.*
Ninety-three. *Lyndon.*
La Terreur. *Ternaux.*
Un Séjour en France. 1792–1795. *Taine.*
Geschichte der Französischen Revolution. *Häusser.*
History of the French Revolution. *Sybel.*

Consulate; Empire.

Court of Napoleon. *Goodrich.*
Histoire de Napoléon I. *Lanfrey.*
History of Napoleon I. *Lanfrey.*

France; Recent History.

Mémoires d'une Idéaliste.
French Revolution of 1848. *Lamartine.*
French Mind. *Harvey.*
France. *Prévost-Paradol.*
Second Empire Français. *Leclerq.*
L'Empire, les Bonaparte et la Cour. *Claretie.*
Ménage Imperial.
Courtisanes du Second Empire.
Mémoires Secrets du Second Empire.
Papiers Secrets du Second Empire.
Sayings of Labienus. *Rogeard.*
Paris in 1851. *Ténot.*
Armée Française en 1867. *Trochu.*
At Home in Paris. *Jerrold.*
Secret Documents of the Second Empire.
Petits Papiers Secrets des Tuileries et St. Cloud.
Ma Mission en Prusse. *Benedetti.*
Là France et la Prusse avant la Guerre. *Gramont.*
La Verité à mes Calomniateurs. Prince *Napoleon.*

France, War 1870–1; Generally.

Diary of the War of 1870–71. *Allnutt.*
Guerre Étrangère et Guerre Civile. *Beaussire.*
Great European Conflict. *Bible.*
Year of Battles; Franco-German War of 1870–71. *Brockett.*
Campaign of 1870, Reprinted from the Times.
Campagne de 1870, Traduit du Times par Allou.
Wanderings in War Time; France and Germany, 1870–1. *Capper.*
In France with the Germans. *Corvin.*
France in 1870–1. *Cowdin.*
Guerre de 1870. *Debrit.*
Histoire de la Campagne de France 1870–1. *Delaunay.*
Deutsch-Französischer Krieg. *Fechner.*
Great Duel. *Greg.*
Guerre Illustrée et le Siége de Paris.
Tagebuch des Deutsch-Französischen Kriegs. Vol. I. *Hirth.*
Geschichte des Deutsch-Französischen Kriegs. *Hohenthal.*
War of 1870. *La Chapelle.*
Franco-Prussian War in a Nutshell. *Landon.*
Guerre Franco-Allemande. *Leconte.*
Guerre de 1870. *Leclerq.*
War between Germany and France. *Mc Cabe*
Geschichte des Französischen Kriegs. *Menzel.*

Echoes of a Famous Year. *Parr*
War for the Rhine Frontier. *Rüstow*.
Guerre de Sept Mois. *Saint-Germain*.
Duel between France and Germany. *Sumner*.
Tableau Historique de la Guerre Franco-Allemande.
Campagnes des Armées de l'Empire en 1870. *Ténot*.
Tagebuch vom Französischen Kriegsschauplatz. *Wachenhusen*.
War Correspondence of the Daily News.
Kriegsbilder des Jahres 1870. *Wickede*.
Deutsch-Französischer Krieg von 1870–1. *Winterfeld*.

War of 1870-1; Battles, etc.

Operationen der Deutschen Heere. *Blume*.
De Frœschwiller à Paris. *Delmas*.
Guerre en Alsace. *Schnéegans*.
Corps Cathelineau pendant la Guerre. *Cathelineau*.
Histoire de l'Armée de Chalons.
Campagne de la Loire et de la Sarthe. *Breuillac*.
Première Armée de la Loire. *Aurelle* de Paladines.
Deuxième Armée de la Loire. *Chanzy*.
Campagne de l'Armée du Nord. *Faidherbe*.
L'Armée du Rhin. *Bazaine*.
Rapport Sommaire sur les Opérations de l'Armée du Rhin. *Bazaine*.
Fall of Metz. *Robinson*.
Blocus et Capitulation de Metz. *Nazet*.
Chateaudun. *Ledeuil*.
Combat et Incendie de Chateaudun. *Isambert*.
Sedan. *Wimpffen*.
Des *Causes* qui ont Amené la Capitulation de Sedan.
Journée de Sedan. *Ducrot*.
Le Général de *Wimpffen!* Réponse au Général Ducrot par un Officier Supérieur.
Strasbourg! 40 Jours de Bombardement.
Journal du Siége de Strasbourg. *Du Casse*.
Occupation et Bataille de Villiers-sur-Marne et de Plessis-Lalande. *Fleury*.
Guerre en Province pendant le Siége de Paris. *Freycinet*.
Garibaldi et l'Armée des Vosges. *Bordone*.
Garibaldi, ses Opérations, à l'Armée de Vosges. *Middleton*.
Südarmee im Jan. und Feb. 1871. *Wartensleben*.

War of 1870-1; Military Publications.

Général Trochu devant l'Histoire. *Borrego*.
Réorganisation de l'État Militaire. *Chareton*.
Carnet d'Étapes du 2e Bataillon du 4e Regiment. *Girard*.
Un Ministère de la Guerre de 24 Jours. *Palikao*.
Bases d'un Projet pour le Recrutement de l'Armée de Terre. *Ladmirault*.
Fautes Stratégiques des Prussiens. *Le Faure*.
Des *Causes* qui ont Amené les Désastres de l'Armée Française.
Droit à l'Avancement des Officiers Prisonniers de Guerre. *Roca*.
Nouvelle Armée. *Schoelcher*.
L'Armée Française en 1871. Par Truchy. *Schoelcher*.
Rapports Militaires Écrits de Berlin, 1866–70. *Stoffel*.
Description des Fortifications de Paris. *Vandenvelde*.
Critiques Militaires, par un Officier Inférieur.
Cavalerie Française. *Bonie*.
Military Resources of Prussia and France. *Chesney and Reeve*.
Réorganisation des Forces Militaires de la France.
Caravanes d'un Chirurgien. *Joulin*.
Notes of an Ambulance Surgeon in 1870. *MacCormac*.

War of 1870-1; German Publications.

War between Germany and France. *Mommsen, Straus, etc*.
Krieg und Friede. *Strauss*.
Die Deutschen in America und die Friedensfeste. *Precht*.
Haut Ihm! *Wachenhusen*.
Wieder unser. *Auerbach*.
Während des Kriegs. *Braun*.
Kriegsgefangen. *Fontane*.
Kriegsbildereines Nachzüglers. *Gerstaecker*.
Hinterlassene Schriften. *Gervinus*.

Friedensglossen Zum Kriegsjahr. *Oppenheim.*

"La Grande Nation" in ihren Reden und Thaten. *Pfaff.*

Die Weltgeschichte ist das Weltgericht. *Ring.*

Farrago. *Scherr.*

Hammerschläge und Historien. *Scherr.*

Gefangen und Belagert. *Schlaegel.*

Fire Test of the North German Confederation. *Treitschke.*

What we Demand from France. *Treitschke.*

War of 1870-1; Government of National Defence.

Gouvernement du 4 Sept., et la Commune de Paris. *Andréoli.*

Dictature de Gambetta. *Blandeau.*

Collection Générale des Lois et Décrets du Gouvernement Français. *Charriaut.*

Journée du 4 Sept. au Corps Législatif. *Dréolle.*

Gouvernement de la Défense Nationale. *Favre.*

Rome et la République Française. *Favre.*

Siége de Paris et la Défense Nationale. *Quinet.*

Diplomatie du Gouvernement de la Défense Nationale. *Valfrey.*

War of 1870-1. Siege of Paris.

Mémorial du Siége de Paris. *Arsac.*

Journal of the Siege of Paris. *Bingham.*

Siéges de Paris. *Borel d'Hauterive.*

Defense of Paris. *Bowles.*

Debâcle. *Claretie.*

Paris Assiegé. *Claretie.*

Les Ballons pendant le Siége de Paris. *Clerval.*

Libres Paroles d'un Assiegé. *Coquerel.*

Tableaux de Siége. *Gautier.*

L'Académie des Sciences pendant le Siége de Paris. *Grimaud de Caux.*

Inside Paris during the Siege, by an Oxford Graduate.

Tablettes Quotidiennes du Siége de Paris. *Jouaust.*

Diary of Besieged Resident in Paris. *Labouchere.*

Siége de Paris. *Lemelle.*

Journaux de Paris pendant le Siége. *Lemonnyer.*

Parisiana. *Macdowall.*

Journaux à Paris pendant le Siége et sous la Commune. *Maillard.*

Siége de Paris. *Michel*

Siege Life in Paris. *Michell.*

Journal des Deux Mondes pendant le Siége de Paris. *Mitchell.*

Par Ballon Monté. *Moland.*

Clubs Rouges pendant le Siége de Paris. *Molinari.*

Pictures from Paris in War and Siege. By an American Lady.

Ambulances de Paris pendant le Siége. *Piedagnel.*

Rapports Militaires Officiels du Siége de Paris, 1870–1. *Pierotti.*

Paris während der Belagerung 1870–1. *Robolsky.*

Science pendant le Siége de Paris *Saint-Edme.*

Siége de Paris. *Sarcey.*

Paris during the Siege. *Sarcey.*

Shut Up in Paris. *Sheppard.*

Martyrs du Siége de Paris. *Sorin.*

En Ballon! pendant le Siége de Paris. *Tissandier.*

Paris pendant les deux Siéges. *Veuillot.*

Mémoires sur la Défense de Paris. *Viollet-le-Duc.*

Lettres sur le Siége de Paris. *Vitet.*

Chronique du Siége de Paris. *Wey.*

War of 1870-1; The Commune.

Agonie de la Commune.

Histoire Intime de la Révolution du 18 Mars. *Audebrand.*

Affaire Rossel. *Bizet.*

Paris under the Commune. *Brockett.*

Bulletin des Lois de la Commune de Paris.

Les Hommes de la Commune. *Clère.*

Paris pendant le Siége et les 65 Jours de la Commune. *Dalsème.*

Agonie de la Commune. *Daudet.*

Rise and Fall of the Paris Commune. *Fetridge.*

Mémoires Secrètes du Comité Central et de la Commune. *Gastyne.*

Douze Visites à Mazas pendant la Commune. *Guasco.*

Guerre des Communeux de Paris, 18 Mars.—28 Mai. 1871.

Bataille des 7 Jours, 21–28 Mai, 1871, par Jezierski. *Hans et Blanc.*

Second Siége de Paris. Le Comité Central et la Commune. *Hans.*

Livre Rouge de la Commune. *Heylli.*

Commune Sanglante. *La Guéronnière.*

L'Insurrection de Paris devant la Psychologie Morbide. *Laborde.*

Paris under the Commune. *Leighton.*

Livre Noir de la Commune de Paris.

Commune; Deuxième Siége de Paris. *Lock.*
Crime du 18 Mars. *Lux.*
73 Journées de la Commune. *Mendès.*
Pilori des Communeux. *Morel.*
Paris sous la Commune. *Moriac.*
Histoire Critique de la Commune. *Morin.*
Deux Mois de Prison sous la Commune. *Perny.*
Décrets de la Commune de Paris et du Gouvernement à Versailles. *Pierotti.*
Histoire de la Commune de Paris en 1871. *Sempronius.*
Déposition de Monsieur *Thiers* sur le 18 Mars.
History of the Commune of Paris. *Vésinier.*
Vom Neuen Babylon. *Wachenhusen.*
Les Prussiens à Paris et le 18 Mars. *Yriarte.*

War of 1870-1; Controversies, Etc.

Récits d'un Soldat. *Achard.*
Les *Allemands* en France. Huit Jours en Seine-et-Oise.
Litérature Française pendant la Guerre 1870–1. *Borchardt.*
France Envahie. *Claretie.*
La *Clef.* Journal Politique.
Convention Boiteuse.
Foi et Patrie. *Dhombres.*
Dialogue aux Enfers entre Charles X. et Louis-Philippe Ier.
Journal d'un Voyageur pendant la Guerre. *Dudevant.*
Lettre sur les Choses du Jour. *Dumas.*
Administration et Propagande Prussiennes en Alsace. *Dumont.*
Un Barde au XIXme Siécle. *Duprez.*
Empire et l'Opposition devant la France.
Consolation. *Feydeau.*
My Experiences of the War between France and Germany. *Forbes.*
Grenouilles qui Demandent Un Roi.
Arrêt Public. *Guiset.*
Gouvernement en Putréfaction.
Gouvernement qui file. Gambetta.
France et Allemagne *Hyacinthe.*
Ils en ont Menti. Par un Rural.
Jean Bonhomme.
Napoleon III, et les Factions en 1870. *Joly.*
Journal d'une Infirmière pendant la Guerre de 1870–71.
A Batons Rompus. *La Fosse.*
Age de Fer. *La Guéronnière.*
Deux Abîmes. *La Guéronnière.*
L'Homme de Metz. *La Guéronnière.*
L'Homme de Sédan. *La Guéronnière.*
Place au Droit. *La Guéronnière.*
Prusse devant l'Europe. *La Guéronnière.*
De la République à l'Empire. *Lenglé.*
Lettre d'un Villageois sur la Guerre.
Napoleon IV. Chroniques de l'Avenir. *Matthieu de Boulogne.*
Récits de l'Invasion. *Mezières.*
France devant l'Europe. *Michelet.*
France before Europe. *Michelet.*
Un Diner chez Bismarck. *Miranda.*
Monsieur Napoleon et sa Cour.
Morale de l'Invasion Prussienne.
Nos Sauveurs.
Nouvelle Lettre de Junius à Son Ami A— D—.
Our Adventures during the War of 1870. *Pearson and Maclaughlin.*
Pétition d'un Bossu à l'Assemblée Nationale.
Prussse et France.
Lettres d'un Intercepté. *Pontmartin.*
Le Radeau de la Méduse. *Pontmartin.*
Quel est Votre Nom.
Testament d'un Latin. *Rambaud.*
Révolution Plébeienne; Lettres à Junius.
Chaplain in the Field of War. *Rogge.*
Barbares et Bandits. *Saint-Victor.*
Suicide d'une Dynastie.
Souvenirs d'un Prisonnier de Guerre.
What I saw of the War. *Winn.*
Who is Responsible for the War?
Deux Empereurs. *Wolf*

France; Travels.

Itinéraire Descriptive de la France. *Vaysse de Villiers.*
France and the French. *Chamier.*
Fair France. *Craik.*
France and her People.
De la France. *Heine.*
Selections from Private Journals of Tours in France. *Palmerston.*
Unknown River. *Hamerton.*
Pardon of Guingamp. *De Quetteville.*
Peeps at Brittany. *Hunt.*
Ramble into Brittany. *Musgrave.*
Brittany and its By-Ways. *Palliser.*
Notes on Burgundy. *Weld.*
Pyrenees and Landes. *Lawlor.*
Pau and the Pyrenees. *Russell.*
Cicerone de Versailles
Memories of French Palaces. *Challice.*

Paris.

Hand-Book; Paris. *Baedeker.*
Paris Directory and Visitors' Guide.
Galignani's New Paris Guide.
Gallic Gleanings.
Porträts und Studien v. 3, 4. Paris unter dem zweiten Kaiserreich. *Gottschall.*
Paris by Sunlight and Gaslight. *McCabe.*
Nos Ruines. Par Angot. *Hans et Blanc.*
Guide à travers les Ruines. *Hans et Blanc.*
Sketches of Modern Paris. *Ebeling.*
At Home in Paris. *Jerrold.*
Cockaynes in Paris. *Jerrold*
Guide Récueil de Paris Brulé. *Petit.*
Letters of an American in Paris. *Somerville.*
Vom Neuen Babylon. *Wachenhusen.*

Continental Europe--History.

History of Modern Europe. *Dyer.*
European History. *Sewell and Yonge.*
Lettres et Negociations de M. d'Estrades, etc., à Nimègue.
History of Charles XII, also Life of Peter the Great. *Voltaire.*
Von '48 bis '51. *Scherr.*
Europe of the Near Future. *Newman.*
L'Alliance Latine. *Orsini.*

Continental Europe--Travels.

Pictures of Travel. *Andersen.*
Poets' Bazaar. *Andersen.*
Bubbles and Ballast. *Bouligny.*
Life in the Old World. *Bremer.*
France, Germany, and Switzerland. *Buffum.*
Search for Winter Sunbeams. *Cox.*
Old World seen with Young Eyes. *Dyer.*
Europe; or, Scenes in England, etc. *Eddy.*
Over the Ocean. *Guild.*
England and Italy. *Hawthorne.*
French and Italian Note-Books. *Hawthorne.*
Lands of Scott. *Hunnewell.*
Bits of Travel. *Hunt.*
From London Bridge to Lombardy. *Richardson.*
Journals in France and Italy. *Senior.*
Playground of Europe. *Stephen.*
Book of Travels of a Doctor of Physic. *Taylor.*
New World Compared with Old. *Townsend.*
American Girl Abroad. *Trafton*
Woman's Experiences in Europe. *Wallace.*
Saunterings. *Warner.*

Spain--History.

Historia de los Arabes en España. *Conde.*
Revolutionsbilder aus Spanien. *Klapp.*
Récits Espagnols. *Jacquemont.*
Historia de las Guerras Civiles de Granada. *Perez de Hita.*
Corona Gotica Castellana y Austriaca. *Saavedra.*
Daybreak in Spain. *Wylie.*
Sir John Moore's Campaign in Spain. *Moore.*

Spain and Portugal--Travels.

In Spain and Portugal. *Andersen.*
Voyage en Espagne. *Gautier.*
Castilian Days. *Hay.*
Aus Spanien. *Körner.*
Tour in Portugal. *Smith.*
Spanish Pictures with Pen and Pencil.
Spanish Towns and Spanish Pictures. *Tollemach.*

Italy--History.

History of Piedmont. *Gallenga.*
Italy, Past and Present. *Mariotti.*
Événemens à Naples, 1820–21. *Pépé.*
Journal d'un Diplomate en Italie, 1859–62. *Ideville.*
Two Years in the Pontifical Zouaves. *Powell.*
Unity of Italy.

Italy--Travels.

Riviera. *Alford.*
Pictures from Sicily. *Bartlett.*
Rome and the Campagna. *Burn.*
Wintering at Mentone. *Chambers.*
Cadore. *Gilbert.*
Reisebilder aus Italien. *Gottschall.*
Wanderjahre in Italien. *Gregorovius.*
Journal in Corsica. *Lear.*
Guida di Pozzuoli. *Parrino.*
Italian Life and Legends. *Ritchie.*
Graffiti d'Italia. *Story.*
Hand-Book; Italy. *Baedeker.*

City of Rome.

Murray's Hand-Book of Rome and Environs.
Contemporary Annals of Rome.
Journey to Rome and Back. *Evill.*
Walks in Rome. *Hare.*
Christmas Holidays in Rome. *Kip.*
Aus der Stadt des Concils. *Klapp.*
Ein Winter in Rom. *Stahr.*
Roba di Roma. *Story.*

Switzerland; Alps.

Alpine Journal.
Atlas to Guide to Switzerland. *Ebel.*
Switzers. *Dixon.*
High Alps without Guides. *Girdlestone.*
Mont Blanc. *Smith.*
Hours of Exercise in the Alps. *Tyndall.*
Scrambles among the Alps. *Whymper.*

Germany.

Deutsche Geschichte. *Häusser.*
History of Germany. *Kohlrausch.*
History of Germany. *Markham.*
History of Germany. *Menzel.*
Annals of the (German) Empire. *Voltaire.*
Geschichte der Deutschen, revised by Zimmermann. *Wirth.*
Ursprung des Siebenjährigen Kriegs. *Ranke.*
Deutsche Mächte und der Fürstenbund. *Ranke.*
History of the Thirty Years' War. *Schiller.*
De l'Allemagne. *Staël.*
Deutsche Republikaner unter der Französischen Republik. *Venedey.*
Böhmischer Krieg von 1866. *Hiltl.*
Deutscher Krieg von 1866. *Blankenburg.*
Seven Weeks' War. *Hozier.*
Von der Elbe bis zur Tauber. *Mels.*
Krieg von 1866 in Deutschland und Italien. *Rüstow.*
Norddeutschlands Seemacht. *Graser.*
Among the Goths and Vandals. *Blaikie.*
Pictures of German Life. *Freytag.*
Geschichte der Deutschen Frauenwelt. *Scherr.*
Rhine and Northern Germany. *Baedeker.*
Southern Germany. *Baedeker.*

Prussia.

Friedrich der Grosse und die Vereinigten Staaten. *Kapp.*
Race Prussienne. *Quatrefages.*
Berlin bei Nacht. *Rasch.*
L'Œuvre de M. de Bismarck. *Vilbort.*

Holland and Belgium.

Baedeker's Hand-Book for Belgium and Holland.
Geschiedenis van den Oorlog 1793–1802. Van der *Aa.*

Hungary; Poland.

Austro-Hungarian Empire and the Policy of Count Beust.
Magyars. *Patterson.*
Pictures of Hungarian Life.
Poland. *Leavitt.*

Scandinavia.

Pictures of Travel in Sweden. *Anderson.*
How to See Norway. *Campbell.*
A Brage-Beaker with the Swedes. *Jerrold.*
Norway and the Vöring-Fos.
Fjord, Isle and Tor. *Spender.*
Coast of Norway. *Walton and Bonney.*
Try Lapland: A Fresh Field for Summer Travel. *Hutchinson.*
Peasant Life in Sweden. *Lloyd.*
Denmark and its Relations. *Leavitt.*

Russia.

Histoire de la Russie. *Lamartine.*
Historical Narratives from the Russian. *Romanoff.*
Russland unter Alexander II. *Golovin.*
Russia. *Kohl.*
Modern Russia. *Eckardt.*
Russia in 1870. *Barry.*
Free Russia. *Dixon.*
A Russian Journey. *Proctor.*
Black Sea and Sea of Azoff. *Paynter.*
Capoue en Crimée.
Inside Sebastopol.

Modern Greece.

La Grèce Contemporaine. *About.*
Cruise in Greek Waters. *Townshend.*
Impressions of Greece. *Wyse.*
Visit to Constantinople and Athens. *Colton.*

Turkey.

Länder an der Untern Donau. *Brennecke.*
History of Turkey. *Lamartine.*
Turquie. *Urquhart.*
War between Turkey and Russia. *Schimmelpenninck.*
Turkish Harems and Circassian Homes. *Harvey.*
Murray's Hand-Book; Constantinople.
Travels to Constantinople. *Frankland.*
Viage á Constantinopla. *Moreno.*
Constantinople, et la Mer Noire. *Méry.*
Plates to Journey through Albania. *Broughton.*

Class VII.—Asia; Africa; South Seas.

Holy Land.

Mountains of Palestine. *Alexander.*
Sensaciones en Oriente. *Arosemena.*
Voyage en Terre Sainte. *Bovet.*
Midshipmen's Trip to Jerusalem and Cruise in Syria. *Lyne.*
Rob Roy on the Jordan. *Macgregor.*
Conversations on Palestine. *Mercein.*
Biblical Researches in Palestine. *Robinson.*
Palestine. *Russell.*
Palestine, its Holy Sites and Sacred Story. *Tillotson.*
Two Months in Palestine.
Ancient Edom.
Walks about Jerusalem. *Bartlett.*
Jerusalem, the City of Herod and Saladin. *Besant and Palmer.*
Meshullam; or, Tidings from Jerusalem.
Topography of the Holy Land. *Tristram.*
The Holy City. *Williams.*
Recovery of Jerusalem. *Wilson, Warren, etc.*

East, Generally.

Heathen and Holy Lands. *Briggs.*
Letters from the East. *Bryant.*
Far East. *Burt.*
Greece, Egypt, and the Holy Land. *Clarke.*
Reisebilder aus dem Orient. *Dalton.*
Ten Months' Tour in the East. *De Burton.*
Morning Lands. *Dicey.*
Egypt, India, and the Colonies. *Fitzgerald.*
Egypt, Constantinople, etc. *Grey.*
Voiage and Trauaile of Sir J. *Maundeville.*
Diary in the East. *Russell.*
Eastern Pilgrims. *Smith.*
Nach dem Orient. *Wiener.*

Egypt.

The Nile without a Dragoman. *Eden.*
New Sea and Old Land. *Hamley.*
Nilometer. *Kraft.*
Le Nil. *Lanoye.*
Egypt à la Voile. *Laporte.*
Reisebriefe aus Ægypten. *Mundt.*
Maritime Canal of Suez. *Nourse.*
Egyptian Revolution. *Paton.*
Histoire de l'Isthme de Suez. *Ritt.*
Letters on Egypt. *Savary.*
Vom Armen Egpytischen Mann. *Wachenhusen.*
Among the Huts in Egypt. *Whately.*
Suez-Canal. *Zenker.*

Abyssinia.

March to Magdala. *Henty.*
British Expedition to Abyssinia. *Hozier.*
Reconnoitring in Abyssinia. *Wilkins.*

Africa, General & Northern.

History of *Africa.*
Land und Volk in Afrika. *Rohlfs.*
Von Tripolis nach Alexandrien. *Rohlfs.*
History of Barbary States. *Russell.*
Scenes in the Sunny South. *Vereker.*
Algérie. *Behaghel.*
Alger. *Feydeau.*
Ghardaia. *Naphegyi.*
Among the Arabs. *Naphegyi.*
Histoire de Maroc. *Chénier.*
Fortunate Isles; or the Canaries. *Pégot-Ogier.*

Africa, Western.

Journey to Musardu. *Anderson.*
Appendix to Journey to Musardu. *Anderson.*
Country of the Dwarfs. *Du Chaillu.*
Equatorial Africa. *Du Chaillu.*
Lost in the Jungle. *Du Chaillu.*
My Apingi Kingdom. *Du Chaillu.*
Stories of the Gorilla Country. *Du Chaillu.*
Wild Life under the Equator. *Du Chaillu.*

Africa, Eastern.

Ost-Afrika. *Bechtinger.*
Zanzibar. *Burton.*
Notes of Travel at Majunga, Zanzibar, etc.
Central Africa. *Petherick.*
Madagascar and its People. *Sibree.*
History of *Madagascar.*

Africa, Southern.

History of Cape Colony. *Wilmot and Chase.*
Cape of Good Hope Association.
Lion Hunter of South Africa. *Cumming.*
Life and Sport in South-Eastern Africa. *Hamilton.*
Diamond Fields of South Africa. *Keene.*
After Ophir; South African Gold Fields. *Lindley.*
Ten Years North of Orange River. *Mackenzie*

Asia, Generally.

Land Journey from Asia to Europe. *Whyte.*
The Book of Ser Marco *Polo.*
Overland through Asia. *Knox.*
India and High Asia. *Schlagintweit.*
Luçon et Mindanão.
Visits to High Tartary, Yârkand and Kâshgar. *Shaw.*
Travels in Asia Minor. *Van Lennep.*
Ten Years on the Euphrates. *Wheeler.*

Arabia, Persia, Armenia.

Travels in Arabia. *Taylor.*
Land of the Sun. *Low.*
History of Persia. *Fraser.*
Wild Life among the Koords. *Millingen.*
Up the Tigris to Bagdad. *Webb.*

Hindostan.

Text-Book of Indian History. *Pope.*
Analytical History of India. *Sewell.*
Student's Manual of the History of India. *Taylor.*
Chronicles of Pathan Kings of Delhi. *Thomas.*
Ancient Geography of India. *Cunningham.*
Empire in Asia; How we Came by it. *Torrens.*
Alliance with the Great Mogul. *Morrison.*
Races of North-Western India. *Elliot.*
Aboriginal Tribes of the Nilgiri Hills. *King.*
European in India; with Medical Guide. *Hull and Mair.*
Letters during Siege of Delhi. *Greathed.*
Mutinies in Oudh and Siege of Lucknow. *Gubbins.*
Western India before and during the Mutinies. *Jacob.*
Sepoy War. *Kaye.*
Lady's Diary of the Siege of Lucknow.
Eastern Experiences. *Bowring.*
Land of the Veda. *Butler.*
Planter in the Jungles of Mysore. *Elliot.*
Highlands of Central India. *Forsyth.*
Indian Mususlmans. *Hunter.*
Days in North India. *Macleod.*
Peep at the Far East. *Macleod.*
Recreations of an Indian Official. *Malleson.*
England to Delhi. *Matheson.*
Chronicles of Budgepore. *Prichard.*
Coffee-Planter of Ceylon. *Sabonadière.*
Rambles and Recollections of an Indian Official. *Sleeman.*
Duke of Edinburgh in Ceylon. *Capper.*

East Indies.

Voyages aux Indes Orientales. *Coreal.*
European Settlements in the Indies. *Raynal.*
English Governess at the Siamese Court. *Leonowens.*
Map of India. *Wyld.*

China.

Reisen in China. *Bastian.*
Journey through the Interior of China. *Bickmore.*
De Pékin à Shanghai. *Buissonet.*
Rambles of a Naturalist in the China Sea. *Collingwood.*
Why and How; Chinese Emigration. *Conwell.*
Travels of a Pioneer of Commerce. *Cooper.*
Six Months with the China Expedition. *Jocelyn.*
Personal Narrative in China. *Loch.*
Four Hundred Millions; Chapters on the Chinese. *Monte.*
Oldest and Newest Empire. *Speer.*
Tientsin Massacre. *Thin.*
Journeys in North China. *Williamson.*
Map of the War in China. *Wyld.*
Cathay and the Way Thither. *Yule.*

Japan.

Japan. *Dickson.*
Japon Illustré. *Humbert.*
Japan in Our Days. *Taylor.*

Siberia.

Conquest of Siberia. *Muller and Pallas.*
Reindeers, Dogs and Snow Shoes. *Bush.*
Tent Life in Siberia. *Kennan.*

Australia; New Zealand.

Colonial Adventures and Experiences.
Four Years in Queensland. *Kennedy.*
Our Australian Colonies. *Mossman.*
Narrative of Expedition to Botany Bay. *Tench.*
Gold Fields of Victoria. *Smyth.*
Wright's Narrative of Van Diemen's Land. *Lyon.*
New Zealand in 1839. *Lang.*
Station Life in New Zealand. *Barker.*
Disturbed Districts of New Zealand. *Meade.*

Pacific and Islands.

Fiji and the Fijians. *Williams.*
Queen Charlotte Islands. *Poole.*
South Sea Bubbles. *Pembroke and Kingsley.*

CLASS VIII.—NORTH AND SOUTH AMERICA.

South America, Generally.

Isthmus of Chocó. *Gilman.*
L'Amèrique du Sud. *Marcoy.*
Life and Nature under the Tropics. *Meyers.*
Andes and Amazon. *Orton*
Voyage to South America. *Ulloa.*

Guiana, Venezuela, Brazil, Peru.

Guiane, par Raleigh. *See* Voyages, etc., par. *Coreal.*
Venezuela. *Eastwick.*
Travels on the Amazon and Rio Negro. *Wallace.*
Lima; or Sketches of the Capital of Peru. *Fuentes.*

Paraguay, Argentine Republic, Etc.

Resources of the Argentine Republic. *Rickard.*
River Plate. *Mulhall.*
La Plata, Brazil and Paraguay. *Kennedy.*
Seven Years in Paraguay. *Masterman.*
History of Paraguay. *Washburn.*
Out on the Pampas. *Henty.*
Pioneering on the Pampas. *Seymour.*
Travels in Uruguay. *Murray.*
At Home with the Patagonians. *Musters.*

West Indies.

At Last; a Christmas in the West Indies. *Kingsley.*
Cuba with Pen and Pencil. *Hazard.*
Rambles in Cuba.
Bando de Gobernacion de Cuba. *Valdes.*
My Winter in Cuba. *Woodruff.*
San Domingo. *Keim.*
Jamaica, its Past and Present. *Phillippo.*

Central America.

Travels in Central America. *Morelet.*
Honduras. *Squier.*
Tehuantepec. *Stevens.*

Mexico.

Mexico; its Revolutions. *Church.*
Our Sister Republic. *Evans.*
Mexico. *Ruxton.*
Court of Mexico. *Kollonitz.*
Intervention Française en Mexique. *Lefèvre.*
Trauerspiel in Mexico. *Scherr.*
Aventures d'un jeune Naturaliste en Mexique. *Biart.*
Terre Chaude. *Biart.*
Terre Temperée. *Biart.*
Young Naturalist in Mexico. *Biart.*
Mexicanische Typen und Skizzen.

Arctic Explorations.

Progress of Arctic Discovery; an Address. *Hayes.*
Northwest Passage, by Land. *Milton.*
Fate of Sir J. Franklin. *McClintock.*
Land of Desolation (Greenland). *Hayes.*

British America.

History of Canada. *Bell.*
New France. *Charlevoix.*
History of Canada. *MacMullen.*
Canadian Dominion. *Marshall.*
First English Conquest of Canada. *Kirke.*
Lovell's Canadian Dominion Directory for 1871.
Transactions of *Literary* and Historical Society of Quebec.
Mémoires Relatifs à l'Histoire du Canada. *Societé* Historique de Montreal.
Red River Expedition. *Huyshe.*
Chiploquorgan (Canada and Newfoundland). *Dashwood.*
Lost Amid the Fogs. *McCrea.*

America, Natives, Discovery, Settlements.

Ancient America. *Baldwin*
Antiquities of Central America and Discovery of America by the Northmen. *Davis.*
Northmen in Maine. *De Costa.*
Relation of *Cabeça* de Vaca, transl. by Smith.
Historical and Geographical Notes. *Stevens.*
Sailing Directions of Henry Hudson. *De Costa.*
Colonization of America during the 17th Century. *Neill.*
North American Indians. *Catlin.*
Indian Tribes of Hudson's River. *Ruttenber.*

North America; Travels.

Transatlantic Sketches. *Chester.*
Travels in U. S. and Canada. *De Roos.*
Sketches from America. *White.*
Prince of Wales in Canada and the United States. *Woods.*
Californien, Nevada und Mexiko. *Hoffmann.*

Class IX.—United States.

U. S. Travels.

General View of the United States.
United States. *La Boissière.*
A travers l'Atlantique. *Pascal.*
Sketches of History, Life and Manners in the United States.
Six Mille Lieues à toute Vapeur. *Sand.*
Travels in the Free States of North America. *Scherzer.*
Americans at Home. *Macrae.*
Domestic Manners of the Americans. *Trollope.*
American Traveler. *Tanner.*
Liverpool to St. Louis. *Hall.*
Rip Raps. *Furniss.*
Heart of the Continent. *Ludlow.*
Westward by Rail. *Rae.*
South and West. *Deedes.*
Over the Alleghanies. *Peyton.*

U. S. Guide Books, Gazetteers, Etc.

Traveler's Guide. *Morse.*
Great West. *Hall.*
Mammoth Cave. *Binkerd.*
Mammoth Cave of Kentucky. *Forwood.*
Guide-Book of the Central R. R. of New Jersey.
List of Post Offices. *Disturnell*

U. S. Directories.

Albany Directory.
Alexandria Directory. *Washington.*
Baltimore Directory.
Bangor and Brewer Directory.
Bath, Brunswick and Richmond Directory.
Boston Directory.
Brewer Directory. *Bangor.*
Brookline, Jamaica Plain and West Roxbury Directory.
Brooklyn Directory.
Brunswick Directory. *Bath.*
Buffalo City Directory.
Burlington (Vt.) Directory.
Cambridge Directory.
Charleston Directory.
Charlestown Directory.
Chicago Directory.
Cincinnati Directory.
Cleveland Directory.
Clinton Directory. *Utica.*
Cohoes Directory. *Troy.*
Columbus Directory.
Davenport Directory.
Deerfield Directory. *Utica.*
Detroit Directory.
District of Columbia Merchants' and Farmers' Directory. *Maryland.*
Fitchburg Directory.
Georgetown Directory. *Washington.*
Green Island Directory. *Troy.*
Hartford Directory.
Hudson Directory.
Indianapolis Directory.
Jamaica Plain Directory. *Brookline.*
Lansingburgh Directory. *Troy.*
Long Island Directory.
Louisiana and Mississippi Business Directory.
Louisville Directory.
Lowell Directory.
Maryland State Gazette and Merchants' and Farmers' Directory for Maryland and District of Columbia.
Memphis Annual Directory.
Milwaukee Directory.
Mobile Directory.
Montreal Directory.
Nashville City Directory.
Newark Directory.
New Bedford Directory.
New Hartford Directory. *Utica.*
New Haven Directory.
New Jersey State Business Directory.
New Orleans Directory.
New York Business Manual. *Disturnell.*
New York Directory.
New York, Doggett's City Co-Partnership Directory, 1846–7, 1850–1.
New York City, Doggett's Street Directory.
Complete Guide to the City of *New York.*
New York City Wilson's, Business Directory.
Phelps' New York City Guide.
New York Mills Directory. *Utica.*
Philadelphia, Burley's Business Directory.
Philadelphia Directory.
Pittsburgh and Alleghany Directory.
Portland (Me.) Directory.
Portsmouth (N. H.) Directory.
Providence Directory, and R. I. Business Directory.
Richmond Directory.
Rochester Directory.

St.Joseph City Directory.
St. Louis Directory.
Savannah Directory.
Springfield (Mass.) Directory.
Syracuse and Onondaga Co. Directory.
Terre Haute Directory.
Troy, Lansingburgh, West Troy, Cohoes and Green Island Directory.
Troy, West Troy and Cohoes Directory.
Utica, Clinton, Deerfield, New Hartford, New York Mills, Whitesboro' and Yorkville Directory.
Vermont State Business Directory.
Washington, Georgetown and Alexandria Directory.
Westchester County Directory.
West Roxbury Directory. *Brookline.*
West Troy Directory. *Troy.*
Whitesboro' Directory. *Utica.*
Worcester Directory.
Yorkville Directory. *Utica.*

U. S. General History.

Historical Magazine.
Change for American Notes.
Child's History of the U. S. *Bonner.*
Pictorial History of the U. S. *Goodrich.*
History of the Boston Massacre. *Kidder.*
School History of the U. S. *Scott.*
U. S. History of the U. S. by a Citizen of Massachusetts.
History of the U. S. *Willson.*

U. S. Colonial History.

Virginia Company of London. *Neill.*
Indian Narratives.
Epistola ad J. Wintrop. *Dreuillettes.*
French and Indian Wars. *Drake.*
New England's Indebtedness to the Pilgrim Fathers. *Hawes.*
History of Braddock's Expedition. *Sargent.*

U. S. Revolutionary War.

Field-Book of Revolution. *Lossing.*
Calendar of Revolutionary Papers. *N. Y. State.*
War in the Southern Department. *Lee.*
Address on Battle of Hubbardton. *Clark.*
Campaign in Ilinois, 1778–9. *Clarke.*
Speech on American Taxation. *Burke.*
Rights of Great Britain Asserted.
Twelve Stars of the Revolution.

U. S. War of 1812; Mexican War.

Field-Book of 1812. *Lossing.*
Marine Corps in Mexico. *Reynolds.*
Journal with Col. Doniphan. *Richardson.*

U. S. Rebellion; Generally.

Hitchcock's Chronological Record of the Rebellion.
Synopsis of the American War. *Balme.*
Civil War in America. *Draper.*
Geographical, Statistical and Ethical Review of the Rebellion. *Morse.*
Letters on the American Rebellion. *Goddard.*
Gray Jackets. By a Confederate.
Civil War in America. *Lossing.*
Chronicles of the Rebellion. *Scott.*
War between the States. *Stephens.*
Reports on Conduct of the War. *U. S.*
Southern History of the War; Official Report of Battles.
Southern Spy. *Pollard.*
Military Record of Civilian Appointments. *Henry.*
Four Years of Fighting. *Coffin.*

U. S. Rebellion; States.

Illinois in the War for the Union. *Eddy.*
Indiana's Roll of Honor. *Stevenson.*
List of Pennsylvania Soldiers Buried at Andersonville.
Wisconsin in the Rebellion. *Love.*

U. S. Rebellion; Campaign, etc.

Peninsular Campaign. *Barnard.*
Patriots and Guerrillas. *Brents.*
Three Years in the Federal Cavalry. *Glazier.*
Amerikanische Kriegsbilder. *Heusinger.*
Our Boys. *Hill.*
Sheridan's Troopers. *Keim.*
Our Campaign around Gettysburgh.
Our First Year of Army Life.
Military Review of the Campaign in Virginia and Maryland. *Petersen.*
Bugle Blast. *Rouse.*
On the Trail of the War. *Shand.*
History of the 100th Regiment N. Y. S. Volunteers. *Stowits.*
Von Achten der Letzte.
Vermont Brigade in Shenandoah Valley. *Walker.*

U. S. Rebellion; Documents, Addresses, etc.

Address to Legislature, Jan. 3. 1862. *Andrew.*
New York City. Enrollment Lists, 18th Ward.
Gov. Buckingham's Message, 1862, with Number of Drafted Men. *Connecticut.*
Report on Recruiting Credits, 1871. *Maine.*

Report of *Pennsylvania* Relief Association for East Tennessee.
Address to Christians, etc., by the Clergy of the Confederate States.
Address of the Ohio Soldiers in the Army of the Cumberland.
Past, Present and Future of the U. S.; a Sermon. *Armitage*.
Alabama Claims. *Beaman*.
Thoughts for the Times. *Bishop*.
Addresses, April 14, 16, 19, 1865. *Boardman*.
God's Hand in the War. *Boynton*.
Patriotism Aiding Piety; a Fast Sermon. *Brainerd*.
Great and Grave Questions. *Broom*.
The Hour, the Peril, etc.; an Address. *Carrington*.
American Crisis. *Chase*.
Speeches in Ohio, etc., in 1863. *Chase*.
Christian Politics; a Fast Sermon. *Chesebrough*.
Christian Courage; a Sermon. *Clark*.
Our National Restoration. *Clark*.
Discourse; Aspects of the War. *Clarke*.
Services of the Freed People to the U. S. Army. *Colyer*.
Complicity of Democracy with Treason in Ohio.
Confederate States *vs.* J. H. Gilmer.
Proceedings, *Convention* of Loyal League, May 26, 1863.
Sermon on the Origin of the War. *Cook*.
Copperhead Catechism.
Correspondence between Gov. Andrew and Gen. Butler.
Crisis.
Fortress of the Rebellion. *Crozier*.
The War; a Sermon. *Dean*.
Humiliation and Hope; a Discourse. *Duffield*.
Hope for Our Country; a Sermon. *Dwinell*.
Echoes from the South.
Our Nation; an Address. *Emerson*.
Christian Patriotism; a Sermon. *Fairfield*.
Must the War Go On? *Flanders*.
Future of the Country.
Law of the American Rebellion. *Gardner*.
Soldier, God's Minister; a Discourse. *Gaylord*.
War of Races. *Gilmer*.
American War; a Lecture. *Hall*.
Thanksgiving for Victories; a Sermon. *Hitchcock*.
Fallacy of Neutrality. *Holt*.
Sanitary Condition of Troops near Boston. *Howe*.
Letter to a Friend in a Slave State. *Ingersoll*.
The Nation's Duty; a Sermon. *Johnson*.
Separation, War without End. *Laboulaye*.
Border and Bastile. *Lawrence*.
God the Protector and Hope of the Nation; a Sermon. *Leavitt*.
Letter from an Elder in an Old School Presbyterian Church to his Son at College.
Heroic Periods in a Nation's History. *Lewis*.
Defence of the Proclamation of Emancipation. *Lowrey*.
American Union; a Sermon. *McCarty*.
Political History of U. S. during Rebellion. *McPherson*.
Freedmen of South Carolina; an Address. *M'Kim*.
American Bastile. *Marshall*.
Contest in America. *Mill*.
Grounds of Humiliation and Hope; a Sermon. *Moore*.
Blood the Price of Redemption. Thanksgiving Sermon. *Noble*.
Our Country must be Saved. *Palmer*.
Lessons from the Rebellion; an Address. *Peabody*.
Question de l'Alabama et Droit des Gens. *Pradier-Fodéré*.
The *Prospect*: a Review of Politics, by Mountaineer.
Union and the War; a Sermon. *Shedd*.
Northern Interests and Southern Independence. *Stillé*.
The Rebellion, its Origin and Mainspring. *Sumner*.
"Times" Review of McClellan. *Swinton*.

Reconstruction.

Report on Vacated Territory. *Contrabands'* Relief Commission.
Southern States since the War. *Somers*.

Political History.

Historical Development of American Civilization. *Stillé*.
Congressional Globe, 38th to 42d Congress, 1863 to 1871.
Congressional Directory, 41st Congress. *U. S.*
Hand-Book of the Administration of the U. S. *Tileston*.
Hand-Book of Politics. *McPherson*.
Civil Service of the U. S.

15

United States Register or Blue-book for 1872.
Fortieth Congress. *Barnes.*
True and False Democracy. *Mill and Hare.*
Party Divisions; a Lecture. *Duer.*
Mission of America; Sermon. *Haven.*
Message on Panama Congress, March 17, 1826. *U. S.*
Signs of the Times (1832). *Carey.*
Speech on Polk's Veto of the French Spoliation Bill. *Clayton.*
Review of Pierce's French Spoliation Veto. *Causten.*
Proceedings of the *Democratic* National Convention, Baltimore, June, 1852.
Text-Book for the Republican Campaign.
Speeches, *Eighteenth* Ward Republican Festival.
Political Situation; a Herald Interview.
Despotic Doctrines, etc. *Howard.*
Documents on Central America and British Enlistments. *U. S.*
U. S. Relations with N. W. British America.
Foreign Affairs. *U. S.*
Papers on Foreign Relations. *U. S.*
Senate Report on the Foreign Service. *U. S.*
Diplomatic Correspondence 1865. *U. S.*
Correspondence in Relation to C. Catacazy. *U. S.*
Politique Future de l'Amèrique. *Jay.*

Statistics; Public Documents.

Graduates, etc., of West Point. *Cullum.*
U. S. Navy Register.
Message and Documents, 2d Sess., 41st Cong. *U. S.*
Message and Documents, 3d Sess., 41st Cong. *U. S.*
Message and Documents, 1868–9. *U. S.*
Congressional Documents, 1866–7, '67–8. *U. S.*
Session Documents, 3d Sess., 40th Cong. *U. S.*
Report of Secretary of the Navy and Postmaster-General. *U. S.*
Land Office. Report 1868. *U. S.*

Southern States.

Historical Collections of Louisiana and Florida. *French.*
Romantic Passages in South-Western History. *Meek.*

Western States.

A travers l'Amérique. Le "Far West." *Audouard.*
Seat of Empire. *Coffin.*
Heroes and Hunters of the West.
Great West. *Howe.*
Mountaineering in the Sierra Nevada. *King.*
Three Thousand Miles through the Rocky Mountains. *McClure.*
Discovery of the Great West. *Parkman.*
Mississippi Gesenke. *Pelz.*
Beyond the West. *Pine.*
Letters from the Pacific Slope. *Rice.*
Pacific-Eisenbahn in Nord-Amerika. *Schlagintweit.*
Western Incidents. *Seymour.*
Description of the Military Lands, and Map. *Van Zandt.*
River of the West. *Victor.*

Maine.

Collections of *Maine* Historical Society.
History of Augusta, Maine. *North.*
Rambles in Mt. Desert. *De Costa.*

New Hampshire.

Mount Washington in Winter.
History of Old Chester. *Chase.*
White Hills. *King.*
History of Warren, N. H. *Little.*
Address, Centennial, Wilton, N. H. *Peabody.*

Vermont.

History of Vermont. *Carpenter.*
Vermont Historical Gazetteer. *Hemenway.*
Collections of *Vermont* Historical Society.
Address to Vermont Historical Society. *Butler.*
Memorials of a Century. *Jennings.*
Centennial Celebration of Rutland, Vt. *Williams.*

Massachusetts.

History of Massachusetts. *Carpenter.*
Bibliography of Local History of Massachusetts. *Colburn.*
Massachusetts Civil List, 1630—1774. *Whitmore.*
Annual Meeting of *Bunker* Hill Monument Association, June 11th, 1871.
History of Berkley, Mass. *Sanford.*
Annals of Dedham. *Mann.*
Dorchester in 1630, 1776 and 1855.
History of Essex County. *Watson.*
History of Fair Haven, Mass. *Adams.*

Historical Discourse to Hollis Association. *Davis.*
Power Loom, and Origin of Lowell. *Appleton.*
Historical Discourse, Westminster, Mass. *Rice.*

Rhode Island.

Address to Rhode Island Historical Society. *Potter.*

Connecticut.

History of Connecticut. *Carpenter.*
Colonial Records of *Connecticut* (Hoadly's), 1706–16.
History of Franklin, Conn. *Woodward.*
Hartford in the Olden Time. *Stuart.*
Statement of Facts, etc., on New London as a Naval Station.
Historical Address, Stamford, Conn. *Alvord.*
History of Wallingford and Meriden. *Davis.*

New York State.

History of the State of New York. *Brodhead.*
History of New York. *Carpenter.*
Olden Times in New York. *Kip.*
History of New York State. *Randall.*
History of New York. *Smith.*
New York State Register. *Disturnell.*
Annual Reports of *Long Island* Historical Society.
Collections on History of Albany. *Munsell.*
History of Brooklyn. *Stiles.*
History of Rye. *Baird.*
History of Williamsburgh. *Reynolds.*
Hudson. *Lossing.*
Miller's New Guide to Hudson River.
Calendar of Land Papers. *N. Y. State.*
Senate Documents, 92d and 93d Sess. (1869 and 1870). *N. Y. State.*
Legislative Documents, 92d, 93d and 94th Sess. *N. Y. State.*
Calendar of Historical MSS. *N. Y. State.*
Senate Journal, 92d and 93d Sess. (1869 and 1870). *N. Y. State.*
Assembly Journal, 92d and 93d Sess. (1869 and 1870). *N. Y. State.*
Assembly Documents, 92d and 93d Sess. (1869 and 1870). *N. Y. State.*
Historic Tales of Olden Time. *Watson.*

New York City.

New York Tax-Book. *Darling.*
N. Y. City, Names, etc., of Common Council.
The Great Metropolis; a Guide to *New York.*
Manual of Corporation. *N. Y. City.*
Stranger's Key to *New York.*
Historical Sketch of the Supervisors of N. Y. County.
Report of City Inspector for 1860. *N. Y. City.*
Comptroller's Report for 1846. *N. Y. City.*
New York City during the American Revolution.
Dangers and Defenses of New York. *Barnard.*
Central Park under Ring Leader Rule.
Civil Rights; the Hibernian Riot and Insurrection of the Capitalists.
Public Meetings, Department of Docks. *N. Y. City.*
How New York is Governed; Frauds of the Tammany Democracy.
Abstraction of Moneys from City Treasury. *Lieber.*
Few Words of Warning on a Railroad in Fifth Avenue. *Bristed.*
To the Publick; Report on the Constitution. *N. Y. Athenæum.*

New Jersey.

History of New Jersey. *Carpenter.*
History of New Jersey. *Sypher and Apgar.*
History of the Land Titles of Hudson County, N. J., 1609–1871. *Winfield.*

Pennsylvania; Delaware.

History of Pennsylvania. *Carpenter.*
Peregrination through Pennsylvania. *Prolix.*
Petrolia. *Cone.*
History of Delaware. *Vincent.*

Washington City.

Mysteries of Washington City.
Men and Things in Washington. *Gobright.*
Bohn's Hand-Book of Washington.

Virginia.

History of Virginia. *Carpenter.*
History of Discovery and Settlement of Virginia. *Stith.*
Virginia Tourist. *Pollard.*
Sketches and Recollections of Lynchburg. *Cabell.*
Home of Washington. *Lossing.*

South Carolina.

Proceedings, Taxpayer's Convention of *South Carolina*, May, 1871.
Sketch of Charleston, S. C.
South Carolina Inst. Prem. List.
Description of *Aiken*, S. C.

Georgia.

History of Georgia. *Carpenter*.

Mortuary Record of Savannah. *Duncan*.

Florida.

History of Florida, 1512–1842. *Fairbanks*.

City of *Pensacola*.

Louisiana and Texas.

Tableaux of New Orleans. *Dowler*.

Thoughts on Annexation of Texas.

Tennessee and Kentucky.

History of Tennessee. *Carpenter*.

History of Kentucky. *Carpenter*.

Pioneer Life in Kentucky. *Drake*.

Ohio; Michigan.

History of Ohio. *Carpenter*.

Early Settlers of Butler Co., Ohio. *McBride*.

History of Athens Co., Ohio. *Walker*.

Fire Lands Pioneer.

Illinois.

History of Illinois. *Carpenter*.

Illinois in 1837.

Out of Town; Suburban Towns, etc., of Chicago.

Chicago and the Great Fire. *McDonald*.

Lakeside Memorial of Burning of Chicago.

History of Springfield, Ill. *Power*.

Minnesota.

Collections of *Minnesota* Historical Society.

Minnesota in 1870. *McClung*.

Minnesota, its Progress and Capabilities.

Minnesota Statistics, 1869.

Minnesota; its Advantages to Settlers.

View of St. Anthony Falls. *Storey*.

Kansas, Arizona, Colorado, Nevada.

Arizona and Sonora. *Mowry*.

Resources of *Arizona* Territory.

Colorado. *Whitney*.

Mountaineering in the Nevada. *King*.

Utah; Mormons.

Mormons. *Gunnison*.

Geschichte der Mormonen. *Busch*.

California and Alaska.

Resources of California. *Hittell*.

Californien. *Schlagintweit*.

Our Knowledge of California, etc., 100 Years ago. *Homes*.

Surveyor-General's Report. *California*.

Sunset Land. *Todd*.

Scenes in California. *Hutchings*.

Two Years before the Mast. *Dana*.

Annals of St. Francisco. *Soulé*.

To San Francisco and Back.

Resources of *Vallejo*.

Wonders of the Yosemite Valley. *Kneeland*.

Alaska and its Resources. *Dall*.

DEPARTMENT OF BIOGRAPHY.

CLASS I.—COLLECTIVE BIOGRAPHY.

Collective Biography, Generally.

Beeton's Dictionary of Universal Biography.

Biographical Class-Book. *Goldsmith*.

Dictionary of Biographical Reference. *Phillips*.

Haydn's Index of Biography.

Lippincott's Biographical Dictionary.

Biographische Portraits. *Varnhagen von Ense*.

People's Book of Biography. *Parton*.

Book of Memories. *Hall*.

Book of Worthies. *Yonge*.

Contemporains avant, pendant et après la Guerre. *Franklin-Berger*.

Drawing-Room Portrait Gallery of Eminent Personages.

Early Sketches of Eminent Persons. *Whiteside*.

Great Men of European History. *Pryde*.

Historical Portraits of Irish Chieftains and Anglo-Norman Knights. *Gibson*.

Lives and Deeds worth Knowing About. *Stevenson*.

Plutarch's Lives; Langhorne's Translation.

Portraits Contemporains. *Sainte-Beuve*.

Remarkable Men.

Pioneers of Civilization.

Triumphs of Enterprise, Ingenuity and Public Spirit. *Parton*.

Wonderful Characters. *Wilson*.

Collective Biography; British.

Anecdote Biography of Pitt and Burke. *Timbs.*
Biographies of Wilkes and Cobbett. *Watson.*
British Heroes and Worthies.
British Statesmen.
Cumberland and Westmoreland Members of Parliament. *Ferguson.*
Dictionary of Judges of England. *Foss.*
English Premiers, Walpole to Peel. *Earle.*
Group of Englishmen; the Wedgwoods and their Friends. *Meteyard.*
Historical Gleanings. *Rogers.*
Lions, Living and Dead. *Dix.*
Lives of Lyndhurst and Brougham. *Campbell.*
Lord Chancellors of Ireland. *O'Flanagan.*
Leaders of Public Opinion in Ireland. *Lecky.*
Men at the Helm. *Adams.*
Scots Worthies. *Howie.*
Worthies of Warwickshire. *Colvile*

Collective Biography; American.

Dictionary of American Biography. *Drake.*
Adventures and Achievements of Americans. *Howe.*
Confederate Soldier (G. M. and B. W. Harris). *Edwards.*
Court Circles of the Republic. *Ellet.*
Fremont and McClellan. *Denslow.*
Great Fortunes. *McCabe.*
Historic Americans. *Parker.*
Lives of Celebrated Americans. *Lossing.*
Lives of Horatio *Seymour* and F. Blair, Jr.
Old Merchants of N. Y. *Scoville.*
Records of Living Navy and Marine Officers. *Hamersley.*
Twelve Stars of the Republic.
William's Biographical Annals. *Durfee.*
Celebrated Canadians. *Morgan.*

Collective Biography; Literary and Professional.

Essays on Educational Reformers. *Quick.*
Home Pictures of the English Poets.
Kembles. *Fitzgerald.*
Lives of the Philosophers, by *Diogenes* Laertius.
Seekers after God. *Farrar.*
Sketches of Eminent Medical Men.
Sketches of Obscure Poets.
Songstresses of Scotland. *Tytler.*
Yesterdays with Authors. *Fields.*
Lives of Eminent Serjeants-at-Law of the English Bar. *Woolrych.*

Collective Biography; Artists.

Anecdote Lives of Hogarth, Reynolds, Gainsborough, Fusell, Lawrence and Turner. *Timbs.*
Les Princes de l'Art. *Fallet.*
The Princes of Art. *Fallet.*
Painters, etc., of Order of St. Dominic. *Marchese.*

Collective Biography; Merchants.

Civil and Military Engineers of America. *Stuart.*
Men who Advertise.
Lives of Distinguished Shoemakers.

Collective Biography; Soldiers and Sailors.

The Cabots. *Stevens.*
Galeria Militar Contemporanea.
Life and Death on the Ocean. *Howe.*
Lives of the Warriors, 1648–1704. *Cust.*
Monarchs of the Main. (Buccaneers.) *Thornbury.*

Collective Biography; Clergy.

Archbishops of Canterbury. *Hook.*
Biographical Sketches and Anecdotes of Friends.
Lives of the Saints. *Butler.*
Pioneers and Founders in the Mission Field. *Yonge.*
Lives of J. and C. Wesley. *Whitehead.*
Anecdotes of the Wesleys. *Wakeley.*

Collective Biography; Royal.

Celebrated Female Sovereigns. *Jameson.*
The Kings of Europe. *Fitzgerald.*
Last Four Princesses of House of Stuart. *Strickland.*
Queens of England. *Lawrance.*
Queens of England. *Strickland.*
Royal Princesses of England from George I. *Hall.*
Marie-Thérèse et Marie-Antoinette. *Armaillé.*

Collective Biography; Women.

Les Comédiennes Adorées. *Gaboriau.*
Les Cotillons Célèbres. *Gaboriau.*
Edle Frauen. *Lagerstroem.*
Ladies of the White House. *Holloway.*
A Life's Motto. *Dale.*
Memoirs of Celebrated Women. *Abrantes.*
Model Women. *Anderson.*
Portraits de Femmes. *Sainte Beuve.*
Transplanted Flowers (Mrs. Rumpf and Duchess de Broglie). *Baird.*
Women of the South. *Forrest.*

CLASS II.—INDIVIDUAL BIOGRAPHY.

The Light of the House (Mrs. E. P. Adams). *Timlow.*
Life of John Adams. *Adams.*
Recollections of John Adolphus. *Henderson.*
Agrippina. *Stahr.*
Alexandra Feodorowna Empress of Russia. *Grimm.*
Alfred the Great. *Hughes.*
Story of my Life. *Anderson.*
Life of Major André. *Sargent.*
Proceedings *Union* League Club. Death of Gov. Andrew.
St. Anselm. *Church.*
Life and Correspondence of Dr. Arnold. *Stanley.*
Memoir of Jane Austen. *Leigh.*
Memoir of Rev. S. Bacon. *Ashmun.*
Memoirs of Mr. Baddeley. *Steele.*
Sermon; Funeral of Mr. Ball. *Hyde.*
Life of Banim. *Murray.*
Life of R. H. Barham. *Barham.*
Life of Sir C. Barry. *Barry.*
Address; Life of Dr. E. Bartlett. *Huntington.*
Memoir of Rev. G. T. Bedell. *Tyng.*
Ludwig von Beethoven. *Lamara.*
L. von Beethoven. *Mensch.*
Beethoven. *Wagner.*
Lord G. Bentinck. *Disraeli.*
K. F. Becker, der Grammatiker. *Helmsdörfer.*
Belden the White Chief. *Brisbin.*
Gustave Bergenroth. *Cartwright.*
Retrospections of the Stage. *Bernard.*
Queen Bertha and her Times. *Hudson.*
Life of Count *Beugnot.*
Life and Letters of *Bewick.*
Memoir of Thomas *Bewick* by himself.
Story of Count Bismarck's Life. *Bullen.*
Buch vom Grafen Bismarck. *Hesekiel.*
Life of Bismarck. *Hesekiel.*
Fifty Years in the Magic Circle. *Blitz.*
Joseph Bonaparte. *Abbott.*
Memoirs and Letters of C. *Boner.*
Memoir of Rosa Bonheur. *Lepelle de Bois-Gallais.*
Life of A. Bonwicke. *Bonwicke.*
Sermon; Obituary of Bishop Boone. *Stevens.*
Nat the Navigator (Bowditch). *Cheney.*
Reminiscences of Fifty Years. *Boyd.*
Life of Rev. T. Brainerd. *Brainerd.*
Memoirs of J. *Brasbridge.*
Memoir of Samuel Breck. *Ingersoll.*
Life, Letters and Posthumous Works. *Bremer.*
Life of Sir D. Brewster. *Gordon.*
Life of Bright. *McGilchrist.*
Duc de Broglie. *Guizot.*
Life and Times of Lord *Brougham*, by himself.
Sermon; Obituary of Moses Brown. *Woods.*
Genial Showman (C. F. Browne). *Hingston.*
Life of I. K. Brunel. *Brunel.*
Bryant Homestead Book. *Hatfield.*
Life of Villiers, Duke of Buckingham. *Thomsen.*
C. C. J. von Bunsen (in German). *Bunsen.*
Memoir of Baron Bunsen. *Bunsen.*
Life and Times of Edmund Burke. *Macknight.*
Tribute to Mr. Burlingame. *Cowdin.*
Lord Byron (in German). *Elze.*
Lord Byron; a Biography. *Elze.*
Life of Byron. *Moore.*
True Story of Lord and Lady *Byron.*
Vindication of Lady *Byron.*
Story of Lady Byron Vindicated. *Stowe.*
Life of Cabot. *Nicholls.*
Life of Calvin. *Whately.*
Histoire de Bianca Capello. *Sanseverino.*
Discourse on Rev. J. Carnahan. *Macdonald.*
Jerome Cardan. *Morley.*
Memoir of John Carpenter. *Brewer.*
Life of Archbishop Carroll. *Brent.*
Life of Kit Carson. *Burdett.*
Discourse; Reinterment of Deacon Case. *Viets.*
The Great Empress (Catharine II). *De Vere.*
Reminiscences of Cavour. *La Rive.*
Thomas Chalmers; a Biographical Study. *Dodds.*
Memoir of R. Chambers. *Chambers.*
Chatterton; a Biographical Study. *Wilson.*
Memoirs of Christina, Queen of Sweden. *Woodhead.*
Life of Cicero. *Forsyth.*
Life of Clay. *Prentice.*
Cleopatra. *Stahr.*
Biographia Literaria. *Coleridge.*

Memoir of D. Conolly. *Clark.*
Life and Times of Henry Cooke. *Porter.*
Life of Anthony Ashley Cooper, First Earl of Shaftesbury. *Christie.*
Hernando Cortes. *Helps.*
Life of Adventure. *Corvin.*
Memoir of Bishop Cotton. *Cotton.*
Life of John J. Crittenden. *Coleman.*
Life of Cromwell. *Guizot.*
Empty Crib. *Cuyler.*
Memoir of Ulric Dahlgren. *Dahlgren.*
Life and Writings of A. J. Dallas. *Dallas.*
Reminiscences of S. H. *Dana.*
Biter Bit; or Dana's Sun.
Proceedings of Croton Department at Death of Mr. *Dean.*
Life of Richard Deane. *Deane.*
Abbé Deguerry. *Saint-Amand.*
Varieties of Vice Regal Life. *Denison.*
Charlotte de la Trémouille, Comtesse de Derby. *De Witt.*
Lady of Latham (Derby). *De Witt.*
Charles *Dickens;* the Story of his Life.
Life of Charles Dickens. *Forster.*
Life of Charles Dickens. *Mackenzie.*
Charles Dickens. *Perkins.*
Last Hours of A. B. Dod. *Hodge.*
Battle of the Books. *Dodge.*
Fra. Dolcino and his Times. *Mariotti.*
Aus meinem Leben. *Dorn.*
Reply to an Anonymous Letter. *Douglas.*
Eulogy on S. A. Douglas. *Cox.*
Life and Speeches of S. A. *Douglas.*
Funeral Oration on S. A. Douglas. *Taylor.*
Review of Autobiography of T. *Douglas.*
Silver Wedding of Mr. and Mrs. *F. P. Draper.*
Life of A. Dürer. *Heaton.*
Albert Durer and his Works. *Scott.*
Robert *Emmett.*
Memoirs of Prince *Eugene*; by himself.
Journal of the Life and Services of Wm. *Evans.*
Diary and Correspondence. *Evelyn.*
Eulogy on E. Everett. *Davis.*
Life of Lord Fairfax. *Markham.*
Julian Fane; a Memoir. *Lytton.*
Life and Letters of Faraday. *Jones.*
Faraday as a Discoverer. *Tyndall.*
Eulogy on C. C. Felton. *Woolsey.*
Address, on Death of Mr. Fessenden. *U. S.*
Edwin W. Field; a Memorial Sketch. *Sadler.*
Life of James *Fisk, Jr.*
Discourse on Rev. W. Fisk. *Holdich.*
Who'd be an Author? *Foster.*
Francis I. *Cochrane.*
Francis of Assisi. *Oliphant.*
Life of *Francis* de Sales.
Life of St. Francis de Sales. *Ormsby.*
Life of St. Francis Xavier. *Bohurs.*
Life of Franklin *Holley.*
Mémoires de Franklin *Laboulaye.*
Franklin before the Privy Council, 1774.
History of Frederick the Great. *Abbott.*
History of Frederick the Great. *Carlyle.*
Case of Gen. Fremont. *Thomas.*
Life and Death of Rev. A. Fuller. *Ryland.*
Private Life of *Galileo.*
Life of Col. Gardiner. *Doddridge.*
Mémoires de *Garibaldi.*
Life of J. Gibson. *Eastlake.*
Life of Gladstone. *McGilchrist.*
Feldmarchall von Gneisenau. *Pertz.*
Frau Rath (Goethe). *Keil.*
Goethe zu Strassburg. *Leyser.*
Life and Times of Goldsmith. *Forster.*
Life and Letters of Gottschalk. *Hensel.*
Autobiography *Gough.*
Life of Gen. Greene. *Greene.*
Going to Market. *Griffith.*
Memoir of J. Griscom. *Griscom.*
Sermon—Obituary of Mme. Ursula Griswold. *Devotion.*
Life and Religious Experiences of Lady *Guion.*
Dismissal from the Army; with Memoir. *Haller.*
Van Buren's Calumnies Repudiated. *Hamilton.*
Reminiscences. *Hamilton.*
Memoir of Sir W. Hamilton. *Veitch.*
W. K. Hamilton. *Liddon.*
Memorials of Bishop Hampden. *Hampden.*
Literary Life of Rev. W. H. Harness. *L'Estrange.*
Sermon, Obituary of Pres. Harrison. *Hall.*
Madame de Hautefort. *Cousin.*
Life of Sir H. Havelock. *Brock.*
H. Heine's Leben. *Strodtmann.*
Henriette d'Angleterre. *La Fayette.*
Life of John Heysham. *Lonsdale.*
Scenes from Life of an Actor. *Hill.*
Memoir of H. Hoare. *Sweet.*
Memories of my Time. *Hodder.*
Holbein und seine Zeit. *Woltmann.*
Recollections of Past Life. *Holland.*

Holland Memorial. Life of George Holland.
Vindication from Slanders, etc. *Holt.*
Discourse, Obituary of Mrs. Hopkins. *Thompson.*
History of Queen Hortense. *Abbott.*
Autobiography. *Hunt.*
Washington Irving (German). *Laun.*
Memoir of Washington Irving. *Adams.*
Jean Jarousseau, the Pastor of the Desert. *Pelletan.*
Law; What I have Seen, &c. *Jay.*
Current Fictions, etc. (Jay & Dawson, Corr). *Dawson.*
Jeanne d'Arc. *Lamartine.*
Story of Joan of Arc. *Evans.*
Domestic Life of Thomas Jefferson. *Randolph.*
Life of Douglas Jerrold. *Jerrold.*
Forty Year's Fight with the Drink Demon. *Jewett.*
Le Général Jomini. *Sainte Beuve.*
Una and her Paupers; Memorials of Agnes E. Jones. *Jones.*
Life of Empress *Josephine*, Wife of Napoleon I.
Life of Dr. Judson. *Bonar.*
Life of the Reverend Mother *Julia.*
Handwriting of Junius Professionally Investigated. *Chabot and Twistleton.*
Memoirs of Apb. Juxon. *Marah.*
History of Gen. Kearney. *De Peyster.*
Memoir of J. Keble. *Coleridge.*
Vagabond Adventures. *Keeler.*
Life of John P. Kennedy. *Tuckerman.*
Life of the Duke of Kent. *Anderson.*
Addresses, etc., of Bar of New York, on Death of Wm. Kent.
Looking Backward. *King.*
Memorial of Chief Justice Kirkpatrick. *Wilson.*
Life and Writings of R. Knox. *Lonsdale.*
Autobiography. *Krummacher.*
Histoire du Père La Chaize.
Vie de Mme. de Lafayette. *Lasteyrie.*
Manuscrit de ma Mère. *Lamartine.*
Mémoires Inédits. *Lamartine.*
Twenty-five Years of my Life, and Memoirs of my Mother. *Lamartine.*
Life of W. S. Landor. *Forster.*
Capture and Escape. *Larimer.*
Hugh Latimer. *Demaus.*
Souvenirs. *Le Brun.*
Life and Remains of R. Lee. *Story.*
Medora Leigh. *Mackay.*
Reminiscences of Mark Lemon. *Hatton.*
Autobiographical Recollections of Charles R. *Leslie.*
Zur Erinnerung an G. E. Lessing. *Heinemann.*
Lessing, sein Leben und seine Werke. *Stahr.*
Assassination of Mr. Lincoln. *U. S.*
Discourse on Death of Pres. Lincoln. *Marshall.*
History of Lewis XIV. *Louis XIV.*
History of Louis XIV. *Abbott.*
History of Louis Philippe. *Abbott.*
Life of Louis Philippe. *Wright.*
Life of St. Ignatius of Loyola. *Genelli.*
Story of Luther. *Whately.*
Life of Gen. Lyon. *Woodward.*
Autobiography. *Macdonald.*
Sermon—Obituary of Rev. J. McDowell, with Addresses. *Sutphen.*
Archbishop Mac Hale. *O'Brennan.*
Life of C. C. Mackintosh. *Taylor.*
Memoir of Alexander McLeod. *Wylie.*
Memoir of Maclise. *O'Driscoll.*
Memorials of Service in India. *Macpherson.*
Life of Rev. J. McVickar. *Mc Vickar.*
Vie de Mahomed. *Boulainvilliers.*
Memoir and Letters of Malibran. *Merlin.*
The Man with the Iron Mask. *Topin.*
Border Reminiscences. *Marcy.*
Memoirs of Maria Antoinetta. *Weber.*
Clement Marot. *Morley.*
Mary, Queen of Scots and her Accusers. *Hosack.*
Mary Stuart and the Casket Letters.
Life of Mary, Queen of Scots. *MacLeod.*
Mary, Queen of Scots and her Latest English Historian. *Meline*
Mary, Queen of Scots Vindicated. *Whitaker.*
Story of a Working Man's Life. *Mason.*
Life of Mrs. Mary W. *Mason.*
Life of Lorenzo de Medici. *Roscoe.*
Rococo-Bilder. (A. G. Meissner.) *Meissner.*
Life of Menschikoff. *Pietzker.*
Life and Letters of Hugh Miller. *Bayne.*
John Milton. *Edmonds.*
Life of Milton. *Masson.*
Memoirs. *Mirabeau.*
Life of Miss Mitford. *L'Estrange.*
Life of Mohammed. *Syed Ahmed.*
Memoirs of Marquise de Montagu. *Noailles.*
Autobiography. *Montagu.*
Life of Hannah *More.*

W. A. Mozart. *Jahn.*
Memoir of Rev. T. Mudge. *James.*
History of Himself, etc. *Murray.*
Memoirs of *Napoleon* I, dictated to Gourgaud and Montholon.
Histoire de Napoléon I. *Lanfrey.*
History of Napoleon I. *Lanfrey.*
Life of Napoleon I. *Lee.*
Napoleon in Exile. *O'Meara.*
Napoléon le Petit. *Hugo.*
Napoleon the Little *Hugo.*
Napoleon III, from Popular Caricatures.
Life of Napoleon III. *Hill.*
Life of Napoleon III. *Macrae.*
Le Dernier des Napoléon. *Napoléon III.*
La Verité à mes Calomniateurs. Prince *Napoléon.*
Life of *Nelson*, by the Old Sailor.
Néron. *Latour St. Ybars.*
My Religious Opinions. *Newman.*
Trials and Persecutions. *O'Gorman.*
Memorials of Lady Osborne. *Osborne.*
Robert Owen, the Founder of Socialism in England. *Booth.*
Life of Palissy. *Morley.*
Life of Lord Palmerston. *Bulwer.*
Unpaid Claim on France. *Parrish.*
Life of George Peabody. *Hanaford.*
Discourse on Mr. Peabody. *Wallis.*
My Prisons. *Pellico.*
Mr. Secretary Pepys and his Diary. *Wilson.*
Diary and Correspondence. *Pepys.*
Souvenirs d'un Sibérien. *Piotrowski.*
Pocahontas and her Companions. *Neill.*
The Marquis of Pombal. *Carnota.*
Appeal for Re-examination. *Porter.*
Reply to Chandler. *Porter.*
Life of Bishop Potter. *Howe.*
Autobiographic Recollections. *Pryme.*
H. J. Raymond and the N. Y. Press. *Maverick.*
Nathan Read and the Steam Engine. *Read.*
Personal Reminiscences. *Redding.*
Life of Red Jacket (Sa-Go-Ye-Wat-Ha). *Stone.*
Life and Works of *Rembrandt.*
Vie du Cardinal Duc de Richelieu. *Le Clerc.*
Life of Robespierre. *Lewes.*
Amye Robsart and the Earl of Leicester. *Adlard.*
Life of St. Rose of Lima. *Feuillet.*
Life of Rossini. *Edwards.*
Confessions. *Rousseau.*
Memoir of Mrs. Rowson. *Nason.*
Rulloff, the Man of Two Lives.
Memoir of Count Rumford. *Ellis.*
Life and Works of *Ruysdael.*
Saint Simon and Saint Simonism. *Booth.*
Memoirs; abridged by St. John. *Saint-Simon.*
In Memoriam Mrs. and Mr. *Sanford.*
Schiller und seine Zeit. *Scherr.*
Schiller-Feier, 1859.
Autobiography of Mrs. Mary Anne *Schimmelpenninck*, ed. by Hankin.
Life of Sir W. Scott. *Gilfillan.*
Life of Sir W. Scott. *Mackenzie.*
Memoir of Rev. J. Scudder. *Waterbury.*
Way Rev. M. L. Scudder secured a Cottage. *Clark.*
W. W. *Seaton:* a Sketch.
Life and Letters of Cathe. M. Sedgwick. *Dewey.*
Dedication of Statue of Gen. *Sedgwick.*
Mémoires sur Mme. de Sévigné. *Walckenaer.*
Sermon Commemorative of Rev. G. A. Shelton. *Currie.*
Memoir of Sheridan. *Moore.*
Memoirs of Sir J. Sinclair. *Grant.*
Memorial of J. Slafter. *Slafter.*
Reminiscences of Assheton Smith. *Wilmot.*
Captivity with the Indians. *Smith.*
Memories of Fifty Years. *Sparks.*
Spinoza. *Willis.*
Aus der Jugendzeit. *Stahr.*
Life of St. Stanislas Kostka. *Thompson.*
Life of John Sterling. *Carlyle.*
Memorial of Rev. B. Stow. *Neal.*
Life of A. Tappan. *Tappan.*
Autobiography. *Taylor.*
Memoir of T. A. Tefft. *Stone.*
Sermon; Obituary of Dr. Thaxter. *Hall.*
Impératrice du Bas Empire. (Théodora.) *Gastineau.*
Life and Character of Gen. Thomas. *Garfield.*
Life of Thomas of Aquin. *Vaughan.*
Discourse; Obituary of H. Townsend, M. D. *Clark.*
Turgot, his Life and Times. *Hodgson.*
Sermon; Obituary of Lieut. Vandeburg. *Hoyt.*
Memoirs of Mrs. Mary E. Van Lennep. *Hawes.*

Discourses; Funeral of Rev. A. Van Liew. *Thompson and Messler.*
Mémoires d'un Bourgeois de Paris. *Véron.*
G. C. Verplanck; an Address. *Daly.*
Proceedings of *Century* Association, in Memory of Mr. Verplanck.
Rev. A. Verren judged by his Works. *Barthelemy.*
Life of the Curé d'Ars (M. Vianney). *Monnin.*
Life of St. Vincent de Paul. *Bedford.*
Voice (A) from the Newsboys.
Voltaire. *Morley.*
Voltaire. *Strauss.*
In Memoriam George Wakeman. *Wakeman.*
Memoirs of James Earl *Waldegrave.*
Geschichte Wallenstein's *Ranke.*
Eulogy on George Washington. *Kinloch.*
Life of D. Webster. *Curtis.*
Sermon on Death of D. Webster. *King.*
Discourse on Daniel Webster. *Mason.*
Memoir. *Weittrecht.*
Wesley his own Biographer.
Life and Times of John Wesley. *Tyerman.*
John Wesley's Place in Church History. *Urlin.*
Wesley and the Evangelical Reaction. *Wedgwood.*
Life of Whitefield. *Gladstone.*
Correspondence. *Wickham.*
Memoir of Rev. M. Wiggleworth. *Dean.*
Victoria C. Woodhull. *Tilton's* Golden Age Tracts.
Early Life of Fernando *Wood.*
Sermon; Ordination of Rev. T. Woodbridge. *Keep.*
Journal of John *Woolman.*
Life of Wycliffe. *Whately.*
Diaries of a Lady of Quality. *Wynn.*
Memoir of Chas. M. Young. *Young.*
Story of Zwingli. *Whately.*

Class III.—Genealogy and Names.

Genealogy.

New England Historical-Genealogical Register.
History of N. E. Historical-Genealogical Register. *Dean.*
N. Y. Genealogical and Biographical Record.
Address to N. E. Historical-Genealogical Society. *Wilder.*
Genealogies of First Settlers of Albany County. *Pearson.*
Dormant and Extinct Peerages. *Burke.*
Peerage and Baronetage. *Burke.*
Royal Descents and Pedigrees of Founder's Kin. *Burke.*
Debrett's Illustrated Baronetage for 1870.
Debrett's Illustrated Peerage for 1870.
Dod's Peerage, Baronetage and Knightage, for 1871 and for 1872.
County Families of the United Kingdom. *Walford.*
Histoire Généalogique des Maisons Souveraines de l'Europe.
MacCallum More; a History of the Argyll Family. *Smith.*
Nathaniel Baldwin and Descendants. *Baldwin.*
Bascom Genealogy. *Harris.*
History of the Bill Family. *Bill.*
Carver Centenary.
Clark and Rose Pedigrees. *Sims.*
Clarke Descendants. *Clarke.*
Family Record. *Coe.*
Curtis Descendants. *Clarke.*
Pedigree and Descendants of Jacob Forster, Sr. *Forster.*
Fowler Genealogy.
Fuller Decendants. *Clarke.*
Ancestry of Gen. U. S. Grant. *Marshall.*
Hodgman Golden Wedding Memorial.
Account of Anneke *Janse* and her Family.
Kellogg Family Meeting and Genealogy.
Historical Notices of the Family of Kip. *Kip.*
Lawrence Genealogy.
Records of Family of Leslie. *Leslie.*
Lloyd and Carpenter Family. *Smith.*
Lyman Anniversary Proceedings.
The Mathers. *Goddard.*
Peck Genealogy. *Peck.*
Penn Pedigree. *Coleman.*
Prescott Memorial. *Prescott.*
Spalding Memorial. *Spalding.*
Wm. Spooner and Descendants. *Spooner.*
Stanleys of Knowsley. *Pollard.*
The Stickney Family. *Stickney.*

Decendants of Elder John Strong. *Dwight.*
Thurston and Pitman Genealogies. *Thurston.*

Epitaphs.

Epitaphs from St. Pancras. *Cansick.*
Epitaphs from Watertown. *Harris.*
Extant Epitaphs. *Maiben.*
Monuments, Grave-Stones, etc. *Macdonald.*

Names.

Key to Pronunciation of Greek, Latin, and Scripture Proper Names. *Walker.*

DEPARTMENT OF MATHEMATICS.

General Treatises.

Course of Mathematics. *Hutton.*
Mathematics. *Hutton.*
Logic of Mathematics. *Davies.*
Popular Mathematics. *Mudie.*
Mathematical Papers. *Green.*
Arithmetic and Mensuration. *Wharton.*
Technical Arithmetic and Mensuration. *Merrifield.*
Elementary Treatise on Mathematical Instruments.
Treatise on Mathematical Instruments. *Simms.*
Mathematical Drawing Instruments. *Simmons.*
Récueil de Problémes. *Gremilliet.*

Arithmetic.

Arithmetic. *Adams.*
Fractional Arithmetic. *Clifford.*
Systematic Arithmetic. *Cruttenden.*
Arithmetic. *Emerson.*
Arithmetic. *Kavanagh.*
Arithmetic Practically Applied. *Mann.*
Linn-Base Decimal System. *Mann.*
Theory of Arithmetic. *Munn.*
Primary Arithmetic. *Perkins.*
Pocket Book in Arithmetic, Astronomy, etc.
Lessons on Numbers. *Reiner.*
Souter's New Ciphering Book.
Key to Souter's New Ciphering Book.
Mental Arithmetic. *Steen.*
Arithmetical Dictionary. *Young.*

Algebra.

Elementary Algebra. *Greenleaf.*
Key to Algebra. *Ryan.*
Algebra. *Simpson.*

Geometry.

Treatise on the Chylindre, by Chaucer. *Chaucer Society.*
Descriptive Geometry. *Davies.*
Legendre's Geometry and Trigonometry. *Davies.*
Géométrie Descriptive. *Duchesne.*
Euclid's Elements, ed. by Simson.
Géométrie-Pratique. *Gaultier.*
Elements of Geometry. *Greenleaf.*
Elements of Geometry. *Hayward.*
Elements of Geometry. *Legendre.*
Leçons de Géometrie. *Mauduit.*
Géometrie des Arts. *Péquegnot.*
Elements of Geometry. *Playfair.*
Elements of Geometry. *Walker.*
Geometry. *Wallace.*
Elements of Plane and Solid Geometry. *Watson.*
Analytical Geometry. *Young.*

Trigonometry.

Elements of Trigonometry. *Hackley.*
Trigonométrie. *Lacroix.*
Trigonometry. *Lacroix and Bézout.*
Manuel du Trigonomètre. *Lefèvre.*
Plane and Spherical Trigonometry. *Peirce.*
Trigonometry. *Young.*

Calculus; Tables.

Differential and Integral Calculus. *Bézout.*
Elementary Treatise on Differential Calculus. *Williamson.*
False Discontinuity. *Wilkinson.*
Integral Calculus. *Young.*
Principles of Fluxions. *Vince.*
Substitution of Similars. *Jevons.*
Théorie des Fonctions Analytiques. *Lagrange.*
Telegraphic Computer. *Fuller.*
Tables sur la Régulation des Calculs. *Martin.*

DEPARTMENT H.—NATURAL SCIENCES.

Class I.—General Works.

Treatises and Dictionaries.

Aperçu des Connaissances Humaines au 19me. Siécle. *Farcy.*
Cours des Sciences et des Arts.
Cyclopædic Science Simplified. *Pepper.*
Notions Générales des Sciences. *Grandsagne.*
Spectacle de la Nature.
Manual of Scientific Inquiry for Her Majesty's Navy, by Herschel.
Science Record for 1872. *Beach.*
Address on Natural Sciences. *De Kay.*
Answers to Questions in Fourteen Weeks' Courses. *Steele.*
Contemplations Scientifiques. *Flammarion*
Conversations on Nature and Art
Fireside Science. *Nichols*
Fragments of Science. *Tyndall*
Imagination in Science. *Tyndall.*
Letters on Natural Magic. *Smith.*
Light Science for Leisure Hours. *Proctor.*
Populäre wissenschaftliche Vorträge. *Helmholtz.*
Practice with Science.
Reason Why.
Science for the People. *Twining.*
Royal Institution; its Founders and First Professors. *Jones.*
Miscellaneous Collections. *Smithsonian.*
Contributions to Knowledge. *Smithsonian.*
Journal of Researches into Natural History and Geology. *Darwin.*

Periodicals; Transactions.

American Journal of Science and Arts.
Année Scientifique, 1865–72. *Figuier.*
Annual of Scientific Discovery.
Annual Report of *Smithsonian* Institution.
British Association for Advancement of Science. Reports 38th, 39th, 40th, and 41st Meetings.
Cosmos.
Hardwicke's Science Gossip.
Intellectual Observer.
Journal of *Society* of Arts.
Journal of the Franklin Institute.
Nature.
Popular Science Review.
Practical Mechanic's Journal.
Quarterly Journal of Science.
Student and Intellectual Observer.
Year Book of Facts, 1871 and 1872. *Timbs.*

Class II.—Cosmology and Physical Geography.

Cosmology.

Reign of Law. *Argyll.*
Forces of the Universe. *Berwick.*
Plates and Tables to System of Universe. *Hassler.*
Sketch Romance of Motion. *Lee.*
Cosmogony. *Merrill.*
Astronomy and Geology Compared. *Ormathwaite.*
Beginning; Its When and Its How. *Ponton.*
Universe. *Pouchet.*
Cosmology. *Ramsay.*
Cyclical Deluges. *Walker.*
Sketches of Creation. *Winchell.*

Physical Geography.

Physical Geography. *Fitch.*
Alphabet of Physical Geography.
Physical Geography. *Somerville.*
Univers Pittoresque.
Earth Delineated. *Ainsworth.*
Sur Terre et sur Mer. *Drouët.*
Earth and Sea. *Figuier.*
Earth. *Reclus.*
Water and Land. *Abbott.*
Polar World. *Hartwig.*
The Sublime in Nature. *Lanoye.*
Desert World. *Mangin.*
Drame du Vésuve. *Beulé.*
Histoire d' un Ruisseau. *Reclus.*

The Sea.

World of the Sea. *Hart.*
Broad, broad Ocean. *Jones.*
Sea, and Its Wonders. *Kirby.*
Mysteries of the Ocean. *Mangin.*
La Mer. *Michelet.*
The Bottom of the Sea. *Sonrel.*
The World of the Sea. *Tandon.*
Wonders of Water. *Tissandier.*

Class III.—Natural Philosophy.

General Treatises.

Grammar of Natural Philosophy. *Blair.*
Natural Philosophy. *Deschanel.*
Traité Élémentaire de Physique. *Despretz.*
Natural Philosophy. *Hogg.*
Natural Philosophy. *Parker.*
Light Science for Leisure Hours. *Proctor.*
Natural Philosophy. *Quackenbos.*
Familiar Illustrations of Natural Philosophy. *Renwick.*
Elementary Hand-Book of Physics. *Rossiter.*
Course of Natural Philosophy. *Wormell.*
Lectures. *Ferguson.*
Essays and Treatises. *Ferguson.*
Fragments of Science for Unscientific People. *Tyndall.*
Aunt Rachel's Letters about Water and Air.
Sound and Color. *Macdonald.*
Light and Electricity. *Tyndall.*

Heat.

Science of Heat. *Orme.*
Theory of Heat. *Maxwell.*
Heat. *Box.*
Heat. *Abbott.*

Pneumatics.

Experiments on Air, Heat and Moisture. *Leslie.*
Pneumatics. *Tomlinson.*
Practical Hydraulics. *Box.*

Acoustics and Optics.

Wonders of Acoustics. *Radau.*
Acoustics. *Saeltzer.*
Theory of Colors. *Goethe.*
Hand-Book of Optics. *Lardner.*
Optics. *Nugent.*
Light. *Abbott.*
Results of Spectrum Analysis. *Huggins.*
Spectrum Analysis. *Schellen.*
Index of Spectra. *Watts.*
Dipleidoscope. *Dent.*
Wonders of Optics. *Marion.*
Notes on Light. *Tyndall.*
Wonders of Vision. *Wallace.*
Economy of the Eyes. *Kitchiner.*

Electricity.

Manuel d'Electricité. *Demonferrand.*
Electricity. *Ferguson.*
Observations on Electricity. *Rackstrow.*
Notes on Electricity. *Tyndall.*
Electrical Tables and Formulæ. *Clark and Sabine.*
Velocity of the Electric Current. *Hough.*

Magnetism.

Magnetism. *Airy.*
Rudimentary Magnetism. *Harris.*
Terrestrial Magnetism.
Magnetism and Electricity. *Miller.*
Rudimentary Magnetism. *Noad.*
Diamagnetism and Magne-Crystallic Action. *Tyndall.*

Meteorology; Ballooning.

Handy Book of Meteorology. *Buchan.*
Introductory Text-Books of Meteorology. *Buchan.*
Atmospheric System. *Butler.*
Meteorology and Hypsometry. *Williamson.*
Psychrometrical Table for Aqueous Vapor. *Coffin.*
Directions for Reading the Hygrometer. *Cameron.*
Barometer, Thermometer, Hygrometer, etc. *Jenkins.*
Weather Glass. *Tyas.*
Companion to Weather Glass. *Tyas.*
Mount Washington in Winter.
Memoirs on Law of Storms. *Piddington.*
Law of Storms. *Reid.*
Travels in the Air. *Glaisher.*
Wonderful Balloon Ascents. *Marion.*
Art of Flying. *Andrews.*

Mechanics.

Power in Motion. *Armour.*
Experimental Mechanics. *Ball.*
Compendium of Mechanics. *Brunton.*
Mechanical Philosophy. *Carpenter.*
Mechanics. *Courtenay.*
Mechanics. *Gerstner.*
Laws of Magnitude. *Guthrie.*
Elements of Mechanics. *Peck.*
Elementary Mechanics. *Wormell.*

Class IV.—Astronomical Science.

Mécanique Céleste. *Laplace.*
Physical and Celestial Mechanics. *Peirce.*
Spherical Astronomy. *Brünnow.*
Astronomical Dictionary. *Read.*
Elements of Astronomy. *Ryan.*
Popular Astronomy. *Arago.*
Astronomy without Mathematics. *Denison.*
Astronomy. *Ferguson.*
Outlines of Astronomy. *Herschel.*

Astronomie des Dames. *Lalande.*
Elements of Astronomy. *Lockyer.*
Lectures on Astronomy. *Moseley.*
Astronomie Populaire. *Quetelet.*
Astronomy Simplified. *Rollwyn.*
U. S. Naval Observatory, Observations, 1868.
Astronomical and Meteorological Observations, 1867–69. *U. S.*
Charter and By-laws, *N. Y.* Astron. Observatory.
Longitude Tables. *Elford.*
Tables Astronomiques, Méridien de Paris.
On the Astrolabe. *Chaucer.*
Telescope. *Ward.*
Wonders of the Sun. *Guillemin.*
Sun. *Proctor.*
Fuel of the Sun. *Williams.*
Eclipse of Aug. 7, 1869. *Hough.*
Saturn and its System. *Proctor.*
Meteoric Theory of Saturn's Rings. *Davies.*
What are the Stars? *Lyle.*
Marvels of the Heavens. *Flammarion.*
Wonders of the Heavens. *Flammarion.*
Midnight Sky. *Dunkin.*
Other Worlds than Ours. *Proctor.*
New Star Atlas. *Proctor.*
Influence of Ether in the Solar System. *Wilcocks.*
Histoire des Météores. *Rambosson.*
Meteors. *Zurcher and Margollé.*

Class V.—Chemistry.

General Treatises.

Dictionary of Chemistry. *Watts.*
Grammar of Chemistry. *Blair.*
Rudimentary Chemistry. *Fownes.*
Chemistry for Schools. *Gill.*
Elements of Chemistry. *Graham.*
Outlines of Chemistry. *Odling.*
Alphabet of Scientific Chemistry. *Rennie.*
First Principles of Chemistry. *Renwick.*
Elementary Chemistry. *Roscoe.*
Chemistry. *Attfield.*
Chemistry. *Fownes.*
Hand-Book of Organic Chemistry. *Gregory.*
Chemistry. *Miller.*
Chemistry. *Stöckhardt.*
Chemical Forces. *Pynchon.*
L'Alchimie, etc. *Figuier.*

Chemical Analysis.

Select Methods in Chemical Analysis. *Crookes.*
Introduction to Ross' Chemical Analysis. *Normandy.*
Outlines of Experimental Chemistry. *Tate.*
Laboratory Text Book of Chemistry. *Valentin.*
Systematic Hand-Book of Volumetric Analysis. *Sutton.*
Qualitative Analysis. *Crafts*
Qualitative Analysis. *Fresenius.*
Qualitative Analysis. *Galloway.*
Use of the Blowpipe. *Plattner.*
Manual of Blowpipe Analysis. Ed. by Richter. *Plattner.*
Practical Use of the Blowpipe.
Organic Matter in Potable Water. *Mahony.*
Water Analysis; Potable Water. *Wanklyn and Chapman.*
Chemical History of a Candle. *Faraday.*
Chemical Examination of the Urine. *Flint.*

Chemistry, Organic & Inorganic.

Chemistry, Inorganic and Organic. *Bloxam.*
Organic Chemistry; Vegetables. *Thomson.*
Inorganic Chemistry. *Wilson.*

Class VI.—Natural History.

General Treatises.

English Cyclopædia; Supplement on Natural History. *Knight.*
Methods of Study in Natural History. *Agassiz.*
Naturalist's Guide. *Maynard.*
First Book of Natural History. *Ruschenberger.*
Altes und Neues aus Thier-und Menschenleben. *Vogt.*
Natürliche Geschichte der Schöpfung. *Vogt.*
Physiologische Briefe. *Vogt.*
Spectacle de la Nature (French).
Spectacle de la Nature or, Nature Displayed.

Abrégé de l'Histoire Naturelle, après Buffon.
Class-Book of Nature. *Frost.*
Natural History; abridged. *Goldsmith.*
Cassell's Popular Natural History.
Child's Book of Nature. *Hooker.*
Circle of the Year. *Adams.*
World at Home. *Kirby.*
Book of Nature and Man. *Napier.*
Land and Sea. *Gosse.*
Country Walks of a Naturalist. *Houghton.*
Sea Side Walks. *Houghton.*
Minéralogie et Botanique. *Duméril.*
Letters from Alabama. *Gosse.*
Lay Sermons, etc. *Huxley.*
Aus Natur und Wissenschaft. *Büchner.*
Stellung des Menschen. *Büchner.*
Aus der Natur. *Ule.*
Leaves from the Book of Nature. *De Vere.*
Waifs and Strays of Natural History. *Gatty.*
Essays on Natural History. *Waterton.*

Local Treatises.

Contributions to the Natural History of the U. S. *Agassiz.*
Geology and Zoology of Abyssinia. *Blanford.*
Jardin des Plantes. *Boitard.*
Natural History of the Strait of Magellan. *Cunningham.*
Natural History of the Azores. *Godman.*
Manual of Marine Zoology for the British Isles. *Gosse.*
Reports on State Cabinet. *N. Y. State.*

Zoology.

American Naturalist.
Record of Zoological Literature.
Class-Book of Zoology. *Jaeger.*
Introduction to Zoology. *Gosse.*
Manual of Zoology. *Nicholson.*
Advanced Text Book of Zoology. *Nicholson.*
Life in its Lower, Intermediate, and Higher Forms. *Gosse.*
Anecdotes of Birds and Fishes. *Clark.*
Wild Men and Wild Beasts. *Cumming.*
Wonders of the Deep. *De Vere.*
Reptiles and Birds. *Figuier.*
Naturalist's Rambles on the Devonshire Coast. *Gosse.*
Beasts and Birds of America, Europe, Asia and Africa. *Hallock.*
Our Poor Relations. *Hamley.*
Our Dumb Companions. *Jackson.*
Seaside Studies. *Lewes.*
Marvels of Pond Life. *Slack.*
Eccentricities of the Animal Creation. *Timbs.*
Population of an Old Pear Tree. *Van Bruyssel.*
Strange Dwellings. *Wood.*
Intelligence of Animals. *Leroy.*
Intelligence of Animals. *Menault.*
Reasoning Power in Animals. *Watson.*
Animal Plagues. *Fleming.*

Darwinism.

Descent of Man. *Darwin.*
Origin of Species. *Darwin.*
Entstehung der Arten. *Darwin.*
Origin of Species. *Huxley.*
Genesis of Species. *Mivart.*
Natural Selection. *Wallace.*
Darwinism Tested. *Schleicher.*
Facts and Arguments for Darwin. *Müller.*
Modes of Origin of Lowest Organisms. *Bastian.*
Anti-Darwinism. *McCann.*
Difficulties of Darwinism *Morris.*
Darwinism Refuted. *Laing.*
Protoplast.
Essays on Darwinism. *Stebbing.*

Quadrupeds.

Mammalia. *Figuier.*
Osteology of Mammalia. *Flower.*
Elements of Mammalogy. *Ruschenberger.*
Cecil's Book of Beasts. *Peabody.*
Dogs and their Doings. *Morris.*

Comparative Anatomy.

Animal Kingdom, and Comparative Anatomy. *Jones.*
Manual of Anatomy of Vertebrated Animals. *Huxley.*

Birds.

Natural History of Birds. *Jones.*
Ornithology. *Ruschenberger.*
History of Birds. *Stanley.*
The Bird. *Michelet.*
British Song Birds. *Nash.*
Curiosities of Ornithology.
Cecil's Book of Birds. *Peabody.*
California Geological Survey. Vol. 1, Ornithology.
Wake Robin. *Burroughs.*

Fishes.

Book of the Roach. *Fennell.*
Herpetology and Ichthyology. *Ruschenberger.*

Insects.

Guide to the Study of Insects. *Packard.*
Elements of Entomology. *Ruschenberger.*
Exotic Entomology. *Drury.*

Insects at Home. *Wood.*
Transformation of Insects. *Duncan.*
Wonders of Insect Life. *Willet.*
Curiosities of Entomology.
Cecil's Book of Insects. *Peabody.*
British Insects. *Staveley.*
Natural History of Ants. *Huber.*
Common Moths of England. *Wood.*
Lepidopterist's Guide. *Knaggs.*
British Butterflies. *Newman.*
Exotic Butterflies. *Hewitson.*
Diurnal Lepidoptera. *Doubleday.*
Synonymic Catalogue of Diurnal Lepidoptera. *Kirby.*
Anatomy of the Blow-Fly. *Lowne.*

Molluscs, etc.

Entozoa. *Cobbold.*
British Sea-Anemones and Corals. *Gosse.*
Otia Conchologica. *Gould.*
Conchologist's First Book. *Poe.*
Conchology. *Ruschenberger.*

Microscopy.

Micrographical Dictionary. *Griffith.*
Microscopical Manipulation. *Suffolk.*
Objects for the Microscope. *Clarke.*
Microscopic Objects.
Microscopic Objects. *Martin*
Objects of the Microscope. *Wood.*
Amateur Microscopist. *Brocklesby.*
Microscope. *Hogg.*
Microscope. *Lardner.*
Microscope. *Ward.*
Medical Microscopy. *Richardson.*

CLASS VII.—BOTANY.

General Treatises.

Journal of Botany.
Natural History of Plants. *Baillon.*
Manual of Botany. *Bentley.*
Familiar Lectures on Botany. *Phelps.*
Elements of Botany. *Ruschenberger.*
Elements of Botany. *Schoedler.*
Domestic Botany. *Smith.*
Trees, Plants and Flowers.
Class-Book of Botany. *Wood.*
Wonders of Vegetation. *Marion.*
La Goutte de Sève. *Grimard.*

Special Plants and Localities.

Hand-Book of British Fungi. *Cooke.*
Popular Names of British Plants. *Prior.*
Compendium of Cybele. Britannica. *Watson.*
Flowers from the Upper Alps. *Walton.*

CLASS VIII.—GEOLOGY.

Generally.

Geological Magazine.
Géologie Populaire. *Boubeé.*
Elements of Geology. *Browne.*
Omphalos; An Attempt to Untie the Geological Knot. *Gosse.*
Subterranean World. *Hartwig.*
Students' Manual of Geology. *Jukes.*
Elements of Geology. *Lyell.*
Principles of Geology. *Lyell.*
Students' Elements of Geology. *Lyell.*
Interior of the Earth. *Malet.*
Earth's Crust; an Outline of Geology. *Page.*

Geology of United States.

Lifted and Subsided Rocks of America. *Catlin.*
Geological Exploration of the 40th Parallel. *U. S.*
California Geological Survey. Vol. 2, Palæontology.
State Geologist's Reports. *New Jersey.*
Green Sand Marl of New Jersey.
New York (State) Geological Survey; Palæontology.
Ohio Geological Survey, by Newberry. Report of Progress in 1870.
Ashley River Phosphates. *Pratt.*
Phosphate Rocks of South Carolina. *Holmes.*
Second Report on Geological Survey of Vermont. *Hitchcock.*

Other Local Geology.

Geology of Oxford and Valley of Thames. *Phillips.*
Gold Field of Nova Scotia. *Heatherington.*
Geology of Brazil. *Hartt.*

Mineralogy; Crystallography.

Ethics of the Dust. *Ruskin.*
Gems. *Castellani.*
Diamonds and Precious Stones. *Emanuel.*
Les Pierres Précieuses. *Rambosson.*

DEPARTMENT OF MEDICAL SCIENCE.

Class I.—General Medicine.

History and General Treatises.

History of Medicine. *Hamilton.*
History of Medicine. *Meryon.*
Reports on the Progress of Medicine. *Dobell.*
University of Albany; History of Medical College.
New Theory and Practice of Medicine. *Inman.*
Institutes of Medicine. *Paine.*
System of Medicine. *Reynolds.*
Medical Works. *Villalobos.*
Method and Medicine. *Foster.*
Medical and Surgical Examination Questions. *Husband.*
Medicine, Disease and Death. *Elam.*
Physician's Problems. *Elam.*
Centenary Address, N. Y. Hospital. *Beekman.*
Remarks on Promotion of Medical Science. *Conkling.*
Addresses, College of Physicians and Surgeons. *Dalton.*
Address, Opening of Medical College. *Elliott.*
Introductory Discourse, Albany Medical College. *Emmons.*
Address to Buffalo Medical Association. *Gay.*
Address, N. Y. Medical College. *Green.*
Medical Systems; a Lecture. *Hun.*
Inaugural Address; with Papers on Infant Asylums. *Jacobi.*
Review of Dr. Ruppaner's Case. *Sayre.*
Reply to Dr. Sayre. *Ruppaner.*
Answer to Dr. Ruppaner. *Sayre.*

Medical Transactions and Journals.

American Eclectic Medical Review.
American Journal of Medical Sciences.
Annales de la Médecine Physiologique *Broussais.*
Braithwaite's Retrospect.
British and Foreign Medico-Chirurgical Review.
Good Health.
Gynaecological Journal.
Half Yearly Abstract of Medical Sciences.
Hall's Journal of Health.
Herald of Health.
Home and Health.
Journal of Psychological Medicine.
London Lancet.
Medical Gazette.
New England Medical Gazette.
New York Medical Journal.
Practitioner.
Quarterly Journal of Psychological Medicine.
Richmond and Louisville Medical Journal.
Scalpel.

Class II.—Anatomy and Physiology.

Anatomy.

Anatomie du Corps Humain. *Blandin.*
Analytic Anatomy, Physiology and Hygiene. *Cutter.*
Anatomy. *Gray.*
Practical Anatomy. *Heath.*
Practical Anatomy. *Keen.*
Description of the Human Body. *Marshall.*
Conversations on Anatomy. *Robertson.*
Anatomy and Physiology of Man. *Todd.*
Sexual and Pelvic Organs. *Dixon.*
Lectures on Dermatology. *Wilson.*
Notes on the Nervous System. *Clymer.*
Deformities of the Human Body. *Broadhurst.*

Physiology.

Human Physiology. *Dalton.*
Human Physiology. *Draper.*
Physiology of Man. *Flint.*
Elements of Physiology and Hygiene. *Huxley and Youmans.*
Physiologie de l'Homme. *Laurence.*
Physiology for Schools. *Lee.*
Essays on Physiological Subjects. *Child.*
Life, its Nature, etc. *Grindon.*
Life as a Physical Phenomenon. *Stevens.*
Physiology of Life. *Lewes.*
Life Theories and Religious Thoughts. *Beale.*
Science of a New Life. *Cowan.*
Mystery of Life. *Beale.*
Physiologische Briefe. *Vogt.*
Human Body and its Connexion with Man. *Wilkinson.*
Physiology and Pathology of Nervous System. *Edes.*

Physiology of the Senses. *Johnson.*
Breath of Life. *Catlin.*
As Regards Protoplasm. *Stirling.*
Cell Doctrine. *Tyson.*
Dynamics of Nerve and Muscle. *Radcliffe.*
Human Hair. *Beigel.*
Wonders of the Human Body. *Le Pileur.*
Transmission of Life. *Napheys.*
Preventive Obstacle. *Bergeret.*
Organic Law of the Sexes. *Dixon.*
Conjugal Sins. *Gardner.*
Sexual Science. *Fowler.*
Man and Woman. *Pedder.*
Parents' Guide. *Pendleton.*
Callipædia. *Quillet.*
Sexual Physiology. *Trall.*
American Womanhood. *Jackson.*
Our Girls. *Lewis.*
Physical Life of Woman. *Napheys.*
La Femme. *Michelet.*
Change of Life, in Health and Disease. *Tilt.*

Class III.—Hygiene.

Hygiene.

Secret of Long Life. *Collins.*
Human Health. *Dunglison.*
Talks to my Patients. *Gleason.*
Fun better than Physic. *Hall.*
Guide-Board to Health. *Hall.*
Health and Disease. *Hall.*
Health by Good Living. *Hall.*
Health Tracts. *Hall.*
Sleep. *Hall.*
Health and its Conditions. *Hinton.*
Thoughts on Health. *Hinton.*
Restoration of Health. *Inman.*
Talks about Health. *Lewis.*
Practical Hygiene. *Parkes.*
Wear and Tear; or, Hints for the Overworked. *Mitchell.*
Dress and Care of the Feet.
Hygiene of the Voice. *Durant.*

Dietetics.

Food Journal.
Digestion made easy.
Eating and Drinking. *Beard.*
Talks about People's Stomachs. *Lewis.*

Physical Training.

Calisthenics. *Laspée.*
Course of Calisthenics.
Manual of Physical Exercises. *Wood.*
Modern Method of Training. *Westhall.*
Pedestrian; a Walk from Boston to Washington. *Weston*
Physiological Effects of Muscular Exercise. *Flint.*
Physical and Vocal Training. *Monroe.*

Alcoholic Liquors.

Stimulants and Narcotics. *Beard.*
Temperance. *Deering.*
Revel of the Rum Fiend. *Dickerson.*
Forty Years' Fight with the Drink Demon. *Jewett.*
Temperance Cause. *Jewett.*
Text-Book of Temperance. *Lees.*
Church and Temperance. *Mears.*
Lectures on Biblical Temperance. *Nott.*
Intemperance and Disease. *Parrish.*
Laws of Fermentation. *Patton.*
Rational Temperance. *Spalding.*
Alcoholic Controversy. *Trall.*
Affidavits for Trustees of *New York* State Inebriate Asylum.

Tobacco, Opium, etc.

Use of Tobacco. *Cowan.*
Tobacco, its History and Associations. *Fairholt.*
Does it Pay to Smoke? *Parton.*
Opium and Opium Appetite. *Calkins.*

Class IV.—Materia Medica.

American Journal of Pharmacy.
Pharmaceutical Journal.
Pharmacopœia of the U. S.
Materia Medica and Therapeutics. *Garrod.*
Elements of Pharmacy. *Lescher.*
Materia Medica. *Milne.*
Pharmacy. *Parrish.*
Materia Medica and Therapeutics. *Riley.*
Materia Medica and Natural History of China. *Smith.*
Druggist's Legal Directory. *Sturges.*
Medical Chemistry. *Rand.*

Class V.—Pathology and Therapeutics.

General Treatises.

Practical Medicine. *Niemeyer.*
Practice of Medicine. *Tanner.*
Present State of Therapeutics. *Rogers.*
Manual of Practical Therapeutics. *Waring.*

Lectures on Physic. *Watson.*
New Theory and Practice of Medicine. *Inman.*
Nosology. *Warwick.*
Student's Guide to Medical Diagnosis. *Fenwick.*
Dissertation on Inflammation. *Stevens.*
Physical Diagnosis of Lungs and Heart. *Sawyer.*
Lectures on Fever. *Hudson.*
Medical Thermometry and Human Temperature. *Wunderlich.*
Auscultation and Percussion. *Gee.*
Percussion and Auscultation. *Hoppe.*
Ophthalmoscope in Diseases of Nervous System and Kidneys. *Allbutt.*
What is Malaria? *Oldham.*
Disease Germs. *Beale.*
Code of Health of School of Salernum.
Emergencies and How to Treat Them. *Howe.*
Family Doctor.
Family Physician. *Gunn.*
First Help in Accidents and Sickness.
Hand-Book for Nurses for the Sick. *Veitch.*
Household Physician. *Warren.*
'Till the Doctor Comes. *Hope.*
Plain Home Talk. *Foote.*
Clinical Medicine. *Tanner.*

Hospitals.

Hospitalism and Zynotic Diseases. *Kennedy.*
Transactions of *Clinical* Society of London.
St. Bartholomew's Hospital, Reports.
New Buildings at Bethlehem Hospital. *Laurie.*
Remarks on the *Child's* Hospital in New York.
British Army and Miss Nightingale. *Shrimpton.*
Brief Plan for an Ambulance System. *Bowditch.*
Hospital Days.

Cholera.

Asiatic Cholera. *MacNamara.*
Epidemic Cholera. *Webster.*

Eye and Ear.

Conservateur de la Vue. *Chevallier.*
Eye in Health and Disease. *Jeffries.*
Diseases, etc., of the Eye. *Lawson.*
Blindness and the Blind. *Levy.*
Treatise on the Eye. *Wallace.*
Aural Catarrh. *Allen.*
Diseases of the Ear. *Troltsch.*

Throat and Lungs.

Young Stethoscopist. *Bowditch.*
Phthisis and Stethoscope. *Cotton.*
Diseases of Respiratory Organs. *Flint.*
Bronchitis and Kindred Diseases. *Hall.*
Coughs and Colds. *Hall.*
Growths in the Larynx *Mackenzie.*
Laryngoscope and Diseases of the Throat. *Mackenzie.*
Diseases of the Larynx. *Marcet.*
Notes on Asthma. *Thorowgood.*
Pulmonary Consumption. *Williams.*

Children's Diseases and Health.

Advice to a Mother. *Chavasse.*
Counsel to a Mother. *Chavasse.*
Physical Training of Children. *Chavasse.*
Woman as a Wife and Mother. *Chavasse.*
Diseases of Children. *Churchill.*
Management of Infancy. *Combe.*
Treatment of Children. *Dewees.*
Diseases of Children. *Ellis.*
Our Children. *Gardner.*
Hand-Book for Mothers. *Parker.*
Paralysis in Infancy. *Roth.*
Eclectic Practice in Diseases of Children. *Scudder.*
Wasting Diseases of Children. *Smith.*
Diseases of Children. *Vogel.*
Nervous Disorders in Childhood. *West.*

Other Special Diseases.

Bright's Disease. *Stewart.*
Cancerous and other Intra-Thoracic Growths. *Bennett.*
Chronic Inflammation of the Uterus. *Byford.*
Clinical Lectures on Women's Diseases. *Atthill.*
Constipated Bowels. *Birch.*
Diseases of the Heart. *Flint.*
Diseases and Infirmities of Advanced Life. *Maclachlan.*
Diseases of the Nervous System. *Hammond.*
Injuries of Nerves. *Mitchell.*
Diseases of Prostate Gland. *Hughes.*
Diseases of the Skin. *Jeffries.*
Diseases of Women. *Taylor.*
Dyspepsia. *Miller.*
Fever in New York, 1805. *Hardie.*
Fistula and other Diseases of the Rectum. *Allingham.*
Gout, Rheumatism and Allied Affections. *Hood.*
Hernial and other Tumours. *Holthouse.*
Horrors of Vaccination. *Schieferdecker.*

Information on Prevention of Small Pox. *Vaccine.*
Kidney. *Dixon.*
Lateral Curvature of the Spine. *Barwell.*
Myalgia. *Inman.*
Parasites of the Human Skin and Hair. *Jeffries.*
Seminal Diseases. *Bostwick.*
Some Abnormal Conditions of Sexual and Pelvic Organs. *Dixon.*
Text-Book of Skin Diseases. *Neumann.*
Syphilitic Diseases. *Parker.*
Exhausted Vitality. *Miller.*
Trichina Spiralis. *Hun.*

Water-Cure; Health Resorts.

How to Treat the Sick without Medicine. *Jackson.*
Water-Cure Manual. *Shew.*
Climate of the South of France. *Williams.*
Climate of Madeira. *Grabham.*
Minnesota; Climates for Invalids. *Bill.*
Winter in Florida. *Bill.*
Minnesota as a Home for Invalids. *Mattocks.*
Season at St. Moritz. *Yeo.*

Homœopathy.

Text-Book for Homœopathy. *Grauvogl.*
Applied Homœopathy. *Bayes.*
Homœopathic Domestic Medicine. *Laurie.*
Annual Record of Homœopathic Literature. *Raue.*
Homœopathy the Science of Therapeutics. *Dunham.*

Other Medical Systems.

Electricity and Practical Medicine. *Meyer.*
Galvano-Therapeutics. *Neftel.*
Illustrated Sketch of the Movement Cure. *Taylor.*
Lifting Cure. *Butler.*
Skim-Milk Treatment of Diabetes and Bright's Disease. *Donkin.*

Sanitary Commissions.

Christian Work on the Battle Field.
Bulletin and Documents. *U. S. Sanitary Com.*

Class VI.—Surgery, Etc.

Surgery.

Surgical Pathology. *Billroth.*
Surgical Diagnosis. *Clark.*
Cooper's Dictionary of Practical Surgery.
Practical Surgery. *Fergusson.*
Science and Practice of Surgery. *Gant.*
System of Surgery. *Holmes.*
Surgical Pathology. *Paget.*
Lectures on Surgery. *Spence.*
Military Surgery. *Hamilton.*
Circulars, *U. S.* Surgeon General's Office.
Surgical Memoirs of the Rebellion. *U. S. Sanit. Com.*
Help for the Sick and Wounded.
Bone Setting. *Hood.*
Silver Sutures in Surgery. *Sims.*
Earth as a Topical Application in Surgery. *Hewson.*
Physiological Action of Nitrous Oxide. *Amory.*
Injuries and Diseases of the Knee Joint. *Swain.*
Deformities of the Mouth. *Coles.*
Failure of Sight from Railway Injuries. *Jones.*
Practical Lithotomy and Lithotrity. *Thompson.*
Annotationes in Colotomiam. *Svitzer.*

Obstetrics.

Lectures on Obstetrics. *Barnes.*
Obstetrics. *Byford.*
Advice to a Wife. *Chavasse.*
Mortality of Childbed and Maternity Hospitals. *Duncan.*
Puerperal Eclampsia. *Gay.*
Parturition without Pain. *Holbrook.*
Midwifery and Diseases of Women. *Milne.*
Signs and Symptoms of Pregnancy. *Montgomery.*
Introductory Notes on Lying-In Institutions. *Nightingale.*
Midwifery and Diseases of Women. *Shew.*
Works. *Simpson.*
Practical Midwifery and Obstetrics. *Tanner.*
Maternity. *Verdi.*

Dentistry.

Family Dentist. *Bostwick.*
Dentistry. *Harris.*
Teeth, and How to Save them. *Meredith.*
Guide to Sound Teeth. *Spooner.*
Taking Impressions of the Mouth. *White.*

Class VII.—Medical Jurisprudence.

Medical Jurisprudence. *Taylor*.
Sphere, Rights and Obligations of Medical Experts. *O'Dea*.
Examination of Medical Witnesses. *Smith*.
Report of Committee of *New York* Medico-Legal Society on Criminal Abortion.
Malpractice and Medical Evidence. *Elwell*.
Trial of Dr. *Crosby* for Malpractice.
Alleged Malpractice Suit of Walsh *vs.* Sayre. *Sayre*.
Comments of the Medical Press on Walsh *vs.* Sayre.

Class VIII.—Mental Diseases.

Behind the Bars.
Insanity and its Treatment. *Blandford*.
Medical Jurisprudence of Insanity. *Browne*.
Mental Disorders. *Davis*.
Plain Talk about Insanity. *Fisher*.
Mental Diseases. *Schroeder*.
Reflex Insanity in Women. *Storer*.
Demoniacks in the New Testament. *Twells*.
Anatomy of Suicide. *Winslow*.
Library of Mesmerism and Psychology.
Macrocosm and Microcosm, by Fishbough. *Library* of Mesmerism.
Fascination; or, Philosophy of Charming, by Newman. *Library* of Mesmerism.
Electrical Psychology, by Dods. *Library* of Mesmerism.
Philosophy of Mesmerism, by Dods. *Library* of Mesmerism.
Psychology, by Haddock. *Library* of Mesmerism.

DEPARTMENT K.—THE ARTS.

Class I.—General Treatises.

Encyclopædias; Dictionaries.

Abrégé du Grand Dictionnaire de Technologie.
Encyclopédie Technologique. *Laboulaye*.
Cyclopædia of Useful Arts. *Tomlinson*.
Dictionary of Arts, Manufactures and Mines. *Ure*.
Repertorium der Technischen Literatur. *Kerl*.
Useful Arts. *Bigelow*.
American Ship-Master's Guide. *Clarke*.
Ship-Master's Assistant. *Steel*.
Manuel de l'Architecte et de l'Ingénieur. *Delaitre*.

Exhibitions.

Paris Exhibition of 1867. *Rimmel*.
Merveilles de l'Exposition de 1867. *Mesnard*.
Reports on Paris Exposition of 1867. *U. S.*
Weltausstellungs Bericht 1867.
Vattemare's Report on the Paris Exhibition. *N. Y.* State.
Premium List 1870, *South Carolina* Institute.

Periodicals.

Building News and Engineering Journal.
Manufacturer and Builder.
Polytechnisches Journal.
Scientific American.

Class II.—Civil Engineering.

General Treatises.

Engineer.
Van Nostrand's Eclectic Engineering Magazine.
Transactions of *Society* of Engineers.
Dictionary of Engineering. *Spon*.
Ingenieur-und Maschinen-Mechanik. *Weisbach*.
Mechanics of Engineering and of the Construction of Machines. *Weisbach*.
Engineers, etc., Pocket Book for 1870.
Workman's Manual of Engineering Drawing. *Maxton*.
Builders' and Contractors' Tables. *Laxton*.

Hand-Book of Specifications. *Donaldson.*
Measuring and Valuing Artificers' Works. *Dobson.*
Report on Tehuantepec Railroad and Ship Canal. *Williams.*
Plans and Drawings. *Sopwith.*

Steam Engine.

Steam Engine for Beginners. *Lardner.*
Steam for the Million. *Ward.*
Practical Treatise on the Condensation of Steam. *Burgh.*
Memorial on Explosion of Steam Boilers. *Guthrie.*
Records of Steam Boiler Explosions. *Marten.*
Engineers' Manual of Marine Examinations. *Ainsley.*
Indicator and Dynamometer *Main and Brown.*
Cornish Pumping Engine. *Poke.*

Railways.

Railroad Gazette.
Useful Information for Railway Men. *Hamilton.*
Manual of the Railroads of the U. S. *Poor.*
Locomotive Engineering and Railways. *Colburn.*
Pacific Eisenbahn. *Schlagintweit.*
Percée des Alpes. *Bignani.*
Mont Cenis Tunnel. *Schanz.*
Survey, on 32d Parallel of *Southern* Pacific Railroad.
Report on R. R. Route from the Hudson. *Sullivan.*

Roads and Bridges.

Art of Constructing Roads. *Law.*
History of Plank Roads. *Kingsford.*
Cast and Wrought Iron Bridge Construction. *Humber.*
Wrought Iron Bridges and Roofs. *Unwin*
Iron Truss Bridges for Railroads. *Merrill.*
Iron Railway Bridge at Quincy, Ill. *Clarke.*
Kansas City Bridge. *Chanute.*
Successful Engineer. *Stuart.*

Surveying and Levelling.

Elements of Surveying and Leveling. *Davies.*
Mensuration, Surveying and Engineering. *Eaton.*
Practical Surveying. *Gibson.*
Levelling Topography and Higher Surveying. *Gillespie.*
Surveying. *Gummere.*
Land and Engineering Surveying. *Merrett.*
Levelling. *Simms.*
Key to Solar Compass. *Burton.*

Canals; Hydraulic Engineering.

Water Power of Maine. *Wells.*
Lowell Hydraulic Experiments. *Francis.*
Waterworks. *Hughes.*
Hydraulic Apparatus. *Farnam.*
Wells and Pumps. *Swindell.*
Filtration of River Waters. *Kirkwood.*
Report on Harbor Encroachments. *N. Y.* Chamber of Commerce.
Embanking Lands from River Floods. *Howson.*
Review of Report on Mississippi River. *Abbot.*
New York State Surveyor and Engineer's Annual Report, 1867 8.
Interoceanic Canals. *Stuckle.*
Is a Ship Canal Practicable? *Abert.*
Interoceanic Ship Canal, via Atrato and Truando. (map.)
Projet d'un Canal de Panama. *Garella.*
Maritime Canal of Suez. *Nourse.*
Suez Canal. *Zenker.*

CLASS III.—ARCHITECTURE; BUILDING.

Generally.

Architectural Magazine.
Architectural Review.
Building News and Engineering Journal.
American Institute of Architects. Proceedings of the 1st, 2d, 3d and 4th Annual Conventions.
Manual of Architecture. *Mitchell.*
Science of Building. *Tarn.*
Wonders of Architecture. *Lefèbre.*
Gothic Architecture in Spain. *Street.*
Ornamentation of Transitional Period of British Architecture. *Sharpe.*
Theory of Strains. *Diedrichs.*
Cast and Wrought Iron for Building. *Fairbairn.*

Churches.

Church of St. Martin-le-Grand. *Kempe.*
Church Design for Congregations. *Cubitt.*

Modern Architecture.

Seven Periods of English Architecture. *Sharpe.*

New Palace at Westminster.
Practical Illustrations of School Architecture. *Barnard.*
Bidrag til Skol-Arkitekturen. *Siljeström.*
Construction of Iron Roofs. *Campin.*

Domestic Architecture.

Country and Suburban Houses. *Atwood.*
Village Builder. *Bicknell.*
Supplement to *Bicknell's* Village Builder.
Model Suburban Architecture. *Croff.*
Model Houses for the Industrial Classes. *Fletcher.*
Stables, Outbuildings and Fences. *Harney.*
The House. *Jacques.*
Gentleman's House. *Kerr.*
House for the Suburbs. *Morris.*
Englishman's House. *Richardson.*
Cottage Architecture. *Thomas.*
Beautifying Country Homes. *Weidenmann.*
Choice of a Dwelling. *Wheeler.*
Homes for the People. *Wheeler.*
English Country Houses. *Wilkinson.*

Masonry ; Carpentry.

Builder's Pocket Manual. *Smeaton.*
Foundations in Compressible Soils. *Delafield.*
Strains in Girders. *Stoney.*
Elementary Carpentry. *Tredgold.*
Elementary Carpentry. Revised by Hurst. *Tredgold.*
British Carpentry; Gothic Roofs. *Morris.*

CLASS IV.—MILITARY AND NAVAL ARTS.

Periodicals; History; Art of War.

Army and Navy Gazette.
Colburn's United Service Magazine.
First Golden Anniversary, *National* Guard.
General Regulations for the Army. *U. S.*
Weapons of War. *Demmin.*
Synoptical Account of European Battles. *Bolus.*
Irish Brigades in France. *O'Callaghan.*
History of 2d Company, 7th N. Y. Regt. *Clark.*
History of the 7th Regiment. *Swinton.*
Military Elements. *Walker.*
American Military Library. *Duane.*
Military Instructions to his Generals. *Frederic* the Great.
Abrégé de l'Art de la Guerre. *Rossel.*
Staff Officer's Manual. *Reide.*
Elémens de Topographie Militaire. *Hayne.*
Act establishing Rules and Articles of War. *U. S.*
New York State Militia Law of 1828.
General Regulations and Orders of the British Army.
Military Resources of Prussia and France. *Chesney.*
Analysis of the Organization of the Prussian Army. *Talbot.*
Rapports Militaires écrits de Berlin. *Stoffel.*
Sketch of Military System of France.
Bases d'un Projet pour le Recrutement. *Ladmirault.*
Projet Motivé de Réorganisation de l'État Militaire. *Chareton.*
England Rendered Impregnable. *Leveson.*
Army Ration. *Horsford.*

Tactics and Strategy.

Modern Tactics. *Smith.*
U. S. Infantry Tactics.
Abstract of Infantry Tactics for Militia of U. S.
Tactics for Non-Military Bodies. *Upton.*
Duties of an Officer in the Field. *Gross.*
Officer's Manual in the Field.
Artillery and Infantry. *Kingsbury.*
Outpost Service. *Mahan.*
Livret de Commandemens de l'Infanterie.
Instructions for Militia. *Cooper.*

Ordnance ; Arms.

Modern Artillery. *Owen.*
Gunnery in 1858. *Greener.*
Instructions for Militia Artillery Exercise. *McKenzie.*
Electro-Ballistic Machines. *Benet.*
Modern Breech Loaders. *Greener.*
Shot Gun and Sporting Rifle. *Walsh.*

Fortification ; Military Engineering.

Elémens de Fortification. *Belair.*
Fortification. *Muller.*
Field Fortification. *Mahan.*
Description des Fortifications de Paris. *Vandevelde.*
Defences of Washington. *U. S.*
Reports of Chief of Engineers 1868–70. *U. S.*

Naval War.

Navy Regulations. *U. S.*
Coast Defense. *Scheliha.*
Harvey's Sea-Torpedo; Instructions for Management.

Torpedo War and Submarine Explosion. *Fulton.*

Navigation; Seamanship; Wrecking.

Nautical Magazine.
Kedge Anchor. *Brady.*
Nautical Surveying. *Jeffers.*
Sailing Directions. *Maury.*
Theory of Navigation. *Read.*
Elements of Navigation. *Robertson.*
Naval Text-Book and Dictionary. *Totten.*
Ocean Steam Navigation. *Forbes.*
Ocean Steam Navigation and the Ocean Post. *Rainey.*
Nautical Astronomy and Navigation. *Jeans.*
New Lunar Tables. *Ward.*
Light-house Illumination. *Stevenson.*
Report on Life-saving Inventions. *Mew.*
Bribery and Piracy; Loss of the Shooting Star. *Hall.*

Shipbuilding.

L'Art Naval à l'Exposition. *Paris.*
Naval Architecture. *Clairbois.*
Ships and Sailors. *Cotterill.*
Construction of Ships for Merchant Service. *Forbes.*
Protection of Ships from Lightning. *Forbes.*
Naval Architecture. *Meade.*
Draughting Vessels. *Pook.*
Naval Architecture. *Russell.*
Steam Power, etc., of U. S. Steam Sloops. *Forbes.*
Our Iron-Clad Ships. *Reed.*
Boilermakers' and Iron Shipbuilders' Companion. *Foden.*

Class V.—Mechanic Arts and Trades.

General Treatises.

Book of Trades. *Wylde.*
Dictionary of Manufactures, Mining, Machinery and Industrial Arts. *Dodd.*
Philosophy of Manufactures. *Ure.*

Periodicals.

American Artizan.
American Horological Journal.
Artizan.
Mechanics' Magazine.
Polytechnisches Journal.
Practical Mechanic's Journal.
Technologist.
Workshop.

Machinery and Inventions.

Patent Specifications and Drawings. *U. S.*
Patent Office Report, 1859; Mechanics. *U. S.*
Patent Reports for 1867, 1868, 1869 and 1870. *U. S.*
Report of F. A. P. Barnard on Machinery at Paris Exposition. (Reports of Commissioners on Paris Exposition. v. 3.) *U. S.*
Welt ausstellungs Bericht. v. 2.
Dictionary of Machines and Mechanics. *Appleton.*
Dictionary of Machines, Mechanics and Engineering.
Imperial Cyclopædia of Machinery. *Johnson.*
Cyclopædia of Machine and Hand-Tools. *Rankine.*
Mechanics' Tool Book. *Harrison.*
Principles and Construction of Machinery. *Campin.*
Mécanique Industrielle. *Christian.*
Elements of Mechanism. *Goodere.*
Elements of Machine Construction and Drawing. *Warren.*
Modern Practice of American Machinists and Engineers. *Watson.*
Principles of Mechanism. *Willis.*
Designing and Construction of Machine Gearing. *Joynson.*
Roll Turning for the Manufacture of Iron. *Tunner.*
Practical American Miller and Millwright. *Craik.*
American Miller. *Hughes.*
Inventions of J. Watt. *Muirhead.*
Young Mechanic.
Perpetuum Mobile. *Dircks.*

Mining; Coal; Oil.

Dictionary of Mining, etc. *Dodd.*
Ore Deposits. *Cotta.*
Mine Engineering. *Greenwell.*
Manual of Mining Tools. *Morgan.*
La Percée des Alpes. *Bignani.*
Der Mont Cenis Tunnel. *Schanz.*
Nitro Glycerine in Hoosac Tunnel. *Mowbray.*
Report on Hoosac Tunnel *Massachusetts.*
Mines and Miners. *Simonin.*
Mineral Resources (Raymond's Report, 1869–70). *U. S.*
Mines of the West. *Raymond.*

Statistics of Mines, West of Rocky Mountains. *Raymond*.
Mines, Mills and Furnaces of Pacific States. *Raymond*.
Quartz Operator's Hand-Book. *Randall*.
La Houille. *Tissandier*.
Gas in Coal Mines. *Atkinson*.
Report of *Clifton* Mining Co.

Metallurgy.

Metallurgy. *Kerl*.
Manuel du Travail des Métaux. *Lardner*.
Metals. *Bloxam*.
Iron and Steel Institute Journal.
Metallurgy of Iron and Steel. *Osborn*.
Iron and Steel. *Styffe*.
Iron and Heat. *Armour*.
Metallurgy of Silver and Lead. *Lamborn*.
Guide to Value of California Gold. *Edelmann*.
Private Book of Useful Alloys, etc. *Collins*.
Guide to Manufacture of Metallic Alloys. *Guettier*.
Useful Metals and their Alloys.
Metallurgy of Lead. *Percy*.
Play-Book of Metals. *Pepper*.
Blast Furnace. *Schinz*.
Concentration of Ores. *Kustel*.
Manufacture of Steel. *Grüner*.
Manufacture of Russian Sheet Iron. *Percy*.
Iron Manufacture of Great Britain. *Truran*.
Metals Used in Construction. *Joynson*.
Strength of Cast Iron Pillars. *Francis*.
Electrotype Manipulation. *Walker*.
Electro-Metallurgy. *Watt*.

Textile Fabrics.

Cotton Manufacture of Great Britain. *Ure*.
Report on Silk and Silk Manufactures, Paris Exposition of 1867. *Cowdin*.
American Jute. *Howson*.

Dyeing.

Chemistry of Calico Printing. *O'Neill*.
Dictionary of Calico Printing. *O'Neill*
Receipts for Calico Printing. *Shepard*.
Traité de l'Impression des Tissus. *Persoz*.
Dyer and Color Maker's Companion.
Family Dyer and Scourer. *Tucker*.

Soaps; Perfumery.

Treatise on Manufacture of Soaps. *Morfit*.
Book of Perfumes. *Rimmel*.

Distilling and Brewing.

Manufacture and Distillation of Alcoholic Liquors. *Duplais*.
Fermented Liquors. *Feuchtwanger*.

Pottery; Porcelain, Etc.

Keramic Gallery. *Chaffers*.
Merveilles de la Céramique. *Jacquemart*.
Chemistry of Pottery. *Shaw*.

Cabinet Making; Upholstery.

Cabinet Maker's and Upholsterer's Companion.
Cabinet-Maker's and Upholsterer's Companion. *Stokes*.

Warming and Ventilation.

Answer to Reply to Defense of Experiments on Fuel. *Bull*.
Our Domestic Fireplaces. *Edwards*.
Heat and Ventilation; General Observations.
Treatise on Ventilation. *Leeds*.

Gas Light.

American Gas Light Journal.
Gas Consumer's Guide.
Report on N. Y. and Phila. Gases. *Torrey*.

Mortars and Cements.

Béton Aggloméré, by Gillmore. *U. S.* Engineers.
Limes, Hydraulic Cements and Mortars, by Gillmore. *U. S.* Engineers.
Treatise on Concrete. *Reid*.

Printing.

History of Printing. *Humphreys*.
Gutenberg and the Art of Printing. *Pearson*.
American Encyclopædia of Printing. *Ringwalt*.
Specimens of Types and Ornaments. *Conner*.

Telegraphy.

History of the Electric Telegraph. *Prescott*.
History of Electric Telegraph. *Sabine*.
Hand-Book of Practical Telegraphy. *Culley*.
Modern Practice of the Electric Telegraph. *Pope*.
Telegraph Manual. *Shaffner*.
Telegraph Code. *Bolton*.
Ocean Telegraphing. *Van Choate*.
Ocean Telegraph to India. *Parkinson*.
Landing of French Atlantic Cable.
C. Colles and the Telegraph. *O'Rielly*.
Annual Report of *Western Union* Telegraph Co.
Mr. Orton's Argument on Postal Telegraph. *Western* Union.

Proposed Union of Telegraph and Postal Systems. *Western* Union.

Photography.

Philadelphia Photographer.
Photographic Art Journal.
Photographic Times.
Hand-Book of Heliography.
Practice of Photography. *Hunt.*
Manual of Photography. *Lea.*
Carbon Process. *Drummond.*
Pictorial Effect in Photography. *Robinson.*

Turning.

Lathes and Turning. *Northcott.*
Specimens of Fancy Turning.
Manual of the Hand Lathe. *Watson.*

Other Mechanic Arts.

Painter's and Colorman's Guide. *Tingry.*
Painter, Gilder and Varnisher's Companion.
Haney's Manual of Sign, Carriage and Decorative Painting.
Art du Peintre, Doreur, Vernisseur et du Fabricant de Couleurs. *Watin.*
How to Keep the Clock Right. *Warner.*
Clock and Watch Making. *Reid.*
American Watchmaker and Jeweler. *Stelle.*
Glass Balance Springs to Chronometers.
Marvels of Glass Making. *Sauzay.*
Wonders of Glass Making. *Sauzay.*
Manuel du Bijoutier, Joaillier, etc. *Fontenelle.*
Art of Cutting. *Ellison.*
Fabrication of Matches. *Dussauce.*
Manufacture of Vinegar. *Dussauce.*

CLASS VI.—AGRICULTURE; DOMESTIC ARTS.

Agriculture, Generally.

Daily Life of Our Farm. *Beever.*
Successful Farming. *Beever.*
Plea for Farming and Farming Corporations. *Child.*
Tim Bunker Papers. *Clift.*
Agriculture; an Address. *Cowdin.*
What I know of Farming. *Greeley.*
Farm Record (blank book). *Hough.*
Five Thousand a Year. *Mitchell.*
Co-operative Agriculture. *Pare.*
Young Farmer's Manual. *Todd.*
Handy-Book of Husbandry. *Waring.*

Agricultural Chemistry.

Agricultural Chemical Analysis. *Caldwell.*
Application of Chemistry to Agriculture. *Johnston.*

Manures.

Treatment and Utilisation of Sewage. *Corfield.*
Leesbock over de Mestmakerij. *Mulder.*
Guano, for Farmers. *Robinson.*
Earth-Closets. *Waring.*
Earth-Closets and Earth Sewage. *Waring.*

Transactions; Periodicals.

Reports of Commissioner of Agriculture. *U. S.*
American Agriculturist.
Cultivator.
Farmer's Magazine.
Florist and Pomologist.
Turf, Field and Farm.
Working Farmer.

Horticulture; Market Gardening.

Gardener's Monthly.
Horticulturist.
Magazine of Horticulture.
Tilton's Journal of Horticulture.
American Flower Garden Directory. *Buist*
Practical Floriculture. *Henderson.*
Amateur's Flower Garden. *Hibberd.*
Gardner's Dictionary. *Johnson.*
Amateur Gardner's Calendar. *Loudon.*
Horticulturist. *Loudon.*
Plain Instructions in Gardening. *Loudon.*
Simple Flower Garden. *Barnard.*
Hand-Book on Indoor Plants, Flowers and Song Birds. *Maling.*
Alpine Flowers. *Robinson.*
Gleanings from French Gardens. *Robinson.*
Hardy Flowers. *Robinson.*
Wild Garden. *Robinson.*
Plain Path to Good Gardening. *Wood.*
Seventy-five Popular Flowers. *Rand.*
Field Flowers. *Hibberd.*
Sub tropical Garden. *Robinson.*
Fern Garden. *Hibberd.*
Window Gardening. *Williams.*
Green House as a Winter Garden. *Field.*
Orchid Grower's Manual. *Williams.*
Book about Roses. *Hole.*
Gardening for Profit. *Henderson.*
Money in the Garden. *Quinn.*
Mushroom Culture. *Robinson.*

Fruit Culture.

Fruit Cultivator's Manual. *Bridgeman.*
Fruits and Fruit Trees. *Downing.*
Fruit Trees. *Du Breuil.*
Apple Culturist. *Todd.*
Peach Culture. *Fulton.*
Pear Culture for Profit. *Quinn.*
Strawberry Garden. *Barnard.*

Grape; Wine.

Champagne, its History and Manufacture. *Tovey.*
Hand-Book of Sulphur Cure for Grapes. *Flagg.*

Sugars.

Practical Sugar Planter. *Wray.*
Beet-Root Sugar. *Crookes.*
Beet-Root Sugar Question. *De Man.*
Sorgo; or the Northern Sugar Plant. *Hedges.*

Forest Trees.

Forester. *Brown.*
Forest Trees for Shelter, Ornament, and Profit. *Bryant.*
Among the Trees. *Lorimer.*

Other Special Plants.

Cranberry Culture. *White.*
Fibre Plants. *Dickson.*
Treatise on Indigo. *Phipps.*
Description of the European Olive. *Hillhouse.*

Domestic Animals.

Pig. *Harris.*
Clever Dogs and Horses. *Hibberd.*

Veterinary Medicine.

Clater's Cattle Doctor, rewritten by Armatage.
Every Man his own Cattle Doctor. *Clater.*
Veterinary Papers. *Dick.*
Diseases of Horses, Cattle and Sheep. *McClure.*
Veterinary Hand-Book. *Pringle.*
Veterinary Pharmacopœia. *Tuson.*

Horse.

Horseowner and Stableman's Companion. *Armatage.*
Horse. *Walsh.*
Horses and Stables. *Fitzwygram.*
Horse Shoes and Horse-Shoeing. *Fleming.*
Horse-Shoeing and Lameness. *Gamgee.*
Gentleman's Stable Guide. *McClure.*
American Trotting Register. *Wallace.*

Cattle.

American Cattle. *Allen.*
Notes on Fields and Cattle. *Beever.*

Dog.

Dog. *Herbert.*
Dog Breaking. *Hutchinson.*
Dog. *Youatt.*

Poultry; Cage Birds.

Brahma Fowl. *Wright*
Canary. *Avis.*
Favorite Song Birds. *Adams.*
Game Fowls. *Cooper.*
Natural History of Cage Birds. *Bechstein.*
People's Practical Poultry Book. *Lewis.*
Pigeons. *Tegetmeier.*
Profitable and Ornamental Poultry. *Piper.*
Poultry Book for the Many.
Practical Poultry Keeper. *Wright.*

Fish Culture.

Book of the Aquarium. *Hibberd.*
Fish Culture. *Norris.*
Trout Culture. *Green.*

Bees.

Honey Bee; its Natural History and Management. *Bevan.*
Bee-Keeper's Text-Book. *King.*
Handy Book of Bees. *Pettigrew.*

Domestic Economy.

American Woman's Home. *Beecher and Stowe.*
Économie Domestique. *Hippeau.*
Family Save-All.
Guide du Domestique.
Helping Hand for Town and Country. *Draper.*
House Servant's Directory. *Roberts.*
How to Live. *Robinson.*
New System of Practical Domestic Economy.
Young Housewife's Counsellor. *Mason.*

Cookery and Food.

Chemistry of Common Life. *Johnston.*
Beeton's Dictionary of Practical Recipes.
Best of Everything.
Neues Kochbuch. *Armster.*
Hand-Book of Practical Cookery. *Blot.*
Market Assistant. *De Voe.*
Cosmopolitan Cookery. *Dubois.*
Family Cyclopædia, or Health in the Household.
Plain Cookery Book. *Francatelli.*
Cuisine Française. *Gogué.*
Book of Preserves. *Gouffe.*
Receipts for the Million. *Hale.*
Adulterations of Food. *Hassall.*
Aus den Mittheilungen eines Gourmands. *Hesekiel.*

New Cook Book. *Hill.*
Lectures on Food. *Letheby.*
Composition of Food. *Marcet.*
Dainty Dishes. *St. Clair.*
Common Sense in the Household. *Terhune.*
Excelsior Cook Book. *Trowbridge.*
Practical Receipts. *Wright.*

Class VII.—Fine Arts.

General Treatises.

Art Journal.
Bulletin de l'Ami des Arts.
Portfolio; an Artistic Periodical.
Hand-Book of Legendary Art. *Clement.*
History of Ancient Art, vol. 3. *Winckelmann.*
Geschichte der Bildenden Künste. *Schnaase.*
History of the Gothic Revival. *Eastlake.*
Early History of the Royal Scottish Academy. *Harvey*
Philosophie de l'Art en Grèce. *Taine.*
Art in Greece. *Taine.*
Philosophie de l'Art dans les Pays Bas. *Taine.*
Art in the Netherlands. *Taine.*
Art in England. *Cook.*
Fine Arts in America; an Address. *Mifflin.*
Academies of Arts; a Discourse. *Morse.*
Meeting, *Metropolitan* Art Museum in N. Y., Nov. 23, 1869.
Geschichte des Italienischen Kunst. *Förster.*
Wonders of Italian Art. *Viardot.*
Wonders of European Art. *Viardot.*
Perspective, Dessin, Peinture et Gravure. *Bulos.*
Manual of the Fine Arts. *Huntington.*
English Artists of the Present Time.
Causeries sur l'Art. *Beulé.*
Contributions to Literature of Fine Arts. *Eastlake.*
Zehn ausgewählte Essays zur Einführung in das Studium der Modernen Kunst. *Grimm.*
Thoughts about Art. *Hamerton.*
Theory of the Arts. *Harris.*
Art Idea. *Jarves.*
Art Thoughts. *Jarves.*
Art, its Laws and the Reasons for them. *Long.*
Identification of Artizan and Artist. *Peabody.*
Lectures on Art. *Ruskin.*
Sermons from the Studio. *Sibree.*
Fine Art. *Wyatt.*

Sculpture.

Merveilles de Sculpture. *Viardot.*
Wonders of Sculpture. *Viardot.*
Thorwaldsen and his Works. *Thiele.*

Painting.

Dictionary of Works of Painters. *Seguier.*
History of Painting in Italy. *Lanzi.*
History of Painting in North Italy. *Crowe and Cavalcaselle.*
Peinture Flamande et Hollandaise. *Michiels.*
Rubens et l'École d'Anvers. *Michiels.*
Anecdotes of Painting. *Walpole.*
Modern Painters. *Ruskin.*
English Painters of the Present Day.
Color. *Cavé.*
Conservation of Pictures. *Holyoke.*
Easy Lessons for Beginners in Landscape.
Field's Chromatography. *Salter.*
Hints on Landscape Painting. *Alston.*
Landscape Painting in Oil Colors. *Tomlinson.*
Laws of Contrast of Color. *Chevreul.*
Harmony and Contrast of Colors. *Chevreul.*
American Painting Book. *Kaufmann.*
Painting in Water Colors. *Warren.*
Theorematical System of Painting. *Finn.*

Drawing.

Appleton's Cyclopædia of Drawing.
How to Draw. *Barry.*
Dessin Linéaire. *Boniface.*
Drawing. *Cavé.*
Second Book of Drawing. *Clark.*
Sketching from Nature. *Delamotte.*
Topographical Drawing. *Eastman.*
Elements of Drawing.
Introduction to Linear Drawing. *Fowle.*
Free Hand Drawing.
Text Book of Geometrical Drawing. *Minifie.*
Graphics. *Peale.*

Perspective.

Elements of Perspective. *De Witt.*
Ombres et Perspective. *Brisson.*

Decorative Art; Lettering.

Grammar of Ornament. *Jones.*
Decorative Art. *Harrison.*
Ornamentation Usuelle de toutes les Époques dans les Arts Industriels et en Architecture. *Pfnor.*
Mural Decoration. *Thomas.*
Sign Writing and Glass Embossing. *Callingham.*
Set of Alphabets. *Copley.*
Alphabet of Monograms. *Lillie.*

Engraving; Books of Prints.

Wonders of Engraving. *Duplessis.*
Merveilles de la Gravure. *Duplessis.*
Catalogue of Works of George Cruikshank. *Reid.*
Falstaff and his Companions. *Konewka.*
Forest Pictures in the Adirondacks. *Hows.*
Poems by Street. Illustrated by *Hows.*
Seize Saintes.
Ups and Downs on Land and Water. *Hoppin.*
West Point Scrap Book. *Wood.*

Landscape Gardening; Parks, etc.

Rustic Adornments. *Hibberd.*
Beautifying Country Homes. *Weidenmann.*
Story of the London Parks. *Larwood.*
Garden Pavilion, Buckingham Palace. *Grüner.*
Parks, Promenades and Gardens of Paris. *Robinson.*
First Annual Report, *N. Y. City* Commissioners of Public Parks.
13th Annual Report on Central Park. *N. Y. City.*
Explanatory Notices of Design No. 30 for Central Park.

Music, Generally.

History of Music. *Ritter.*
Music of the Ancient Nations. *Engel.*
Violins and Violin Makers. *Pearce.*
Musical Dictionary. *Pilkington.*
Musical Cyclopædia. *Porter.*
Méthodes d' Harmonie. *Albrechtsberger.*
Élémens de Musique. *Alembert.*
American and Italian Cantatrici.
Letters on Music. *Ehlert.*
Musical Grammar. *Callcott.*
Musical Composition. *Dawson.*
Musique mise à la Portée de tout le Monde. *Fetis.*
Musical Spelling Book. *Ives.*
Six Lectures on Harmony. *Macfarren.*
Manual of Music. *Manby.*
Manual of Harmony. *Richters.*
Elements of Thorough Bass and Harmony. *Southard.*
Theory of Harmony founded on the Tempered Scale. *Stainer.*
Elements of Musical Composition. *Woodbury.*
Self-Instructor in Musical Composition. *Woodbury.*
Harmony and Modulation. *Zundel.*
Watson's Art Journal.
Letter to a Young Piano-Forte Player.
Juvenile Pianist. *Rodwell.*
Schubert und seine Lieder. *Rissé.*
Musical Development. *Goddard.*
Music and Morals. *Haweis.*
Bible Music. *Jacox.*
Reminiscences of the Opera. *Lumley.*
Musical Anecdotes and Stories.
Neue Bilder aus dem Leben der Musik. *Nohl.*
Il Matrimonio Segreto (words). *Cimarosa.*

Church Music.

Church-Music in America. *Gould.*
Our Church Music. *Willis.*

Vocal Music.

The Voice. *Lee.*
Art of Singing. *Gaertner.*
Method for Orpheon Singing Classes. *Hopkins.*

CLASS VIII.—AMUSEMENTS.

Generally.

American Boys Book of Sports and Games.
American Girl's Book. *Leslie.*
Book of American Pastimes. *Peverelly.*
Conundrums and Puzzles. *Howard.*
Favourite Holiday Book for Boys.
Hand-Book of Games (Bohn's).
Home Book. *Valentine.*
How to Amuse an Evening Party.
Hoyle's Games Improved.
Jeux de Société. *Celnart.*
Magie Blanche Devoilée. *Decremps.*
Mille et Un Amusements. *Blocquel.*
Les Mille Récréations de Société. *Demerson.*
Nouvelle Académie des Jeux.
Parlor Magic.
Sociable.
Secret Out. *Frikell.*

Chess.

Chess Hand-Book, by an Amateur.
Chess Player.
Clipper Chess Problem Tournament. *Hazeltine.*
Key to Chess Openings. *Long.*
Chess Openings. *Longman.*
Chess Player's Hand-Book. *Staunton.*
Chess Brilliants. *Taylor.*
Letters on Chess. *Vogt.*

Athletic Sports.

Wonders of Bodily Strength and Skill. *Depping.*
Hand-Book of Archery.
Cricketers in Council. *Thomsonby*
Modern Art of Fencing. *Rolando.*
Art de Faire les Armes. *Lafaugère.*
Velocipede.

Other Special Amusements.

Billiards. *Roberts.*
Art of Dancing. *Hillgrove.*
Ball-Room Companion. *De Walden.*
Danse des Salons. *Cellarius.*
Drawing-Room Dances. *Cellarius.*
Maitre de Danse. *Conway.*
The Gaming Table. *Steinmetz.*
Sharper Detected and Exposed. *Houdin.*
Theory of the Modern Scientific Game of Whist. *Pole.*
Whist Player's Hand-Book.

Field Sports.

Chace, Turf and Road. *Apperley.*
Moorland and Stream. *Barry.*
Fur, Fin and Feather.
Accessible Field Sports. *Gillmore.*
Wild Sports of the World. *Greenwood.*
Complete Manual for Young Sportsmen. *Herbert.*
American Sportsman. *Lewis.*
Traité de Fauconnerie. *Schlegel.*
Shooting, Boating and Fishing. *Warren.*
Sporting Sketches. *Wheelwright.*

Hunting.

Great Hunts. *Meunier.*
Bear Hunt in the Adirondacks. *Colvin.*
Hints on Shore-Shooting. *Harting.*
A Hunter's Adventures in the Great West. *Gillmore.*
Shooting in Thibet. *Kinloch.*
Trapper's Guide. *Newhouse.*
Glenmâhra. *Roberts.*
Notitia Venatica. *Vyner.*

Angling.

American Angler's Book. *Norris.*
Art of Fishing. *Raymond.*
Modern Practical Angler. *Pennell.*
Notes and Recollections of an Angler. *Cliffe.*
Rod Fishing in Clear Waters. *Wade.*
Salmonia. *Davy.*
Thames and Tweed. *Rooper.*

Rowing and Yachting.

Oxford and Cambridge Boat Races. *Macmichael.*
Notes on Yachts. *Brett.*
Sailing Boat. *Folkard.*
Down Channel. *MacMullen.*
Cruise of the Kate. *Middleton.*
Constitution, etc., of *N. Y. Yacht Club.*
The Yacht Sailor. *Vanderdecken.*
Yachtman's and Amateur Sailor's Primer. *Warren.*

Horsemanship.

Horsemanship. *Lebeaud.*
Seats and Saddles. *Dwyer.*
Young Lady's Equestrian Manual.

Ornamental Works.

Ladies' Complete Guide to Needle-work and Embroidery. *Lambert*
Ladies' Work-Table Book.
Sorrento Wood Carving.
Wax Flower Modelling Made Easy. *Williams.*

NOVELS.

NOVELS, TALES AND ROMANCES,

IN ENGLISH PROSE.

[NOTE.—Instead of the two separated alphabets heretofore used, the names of Authors and of Books are here arranged under a single alphabet.]

A. L. O. E. *See* TUCKER.
ABATI, F. See-Saw.
ABBOTT, J. August and Elvie.
—— Hunter and Tom.
ABBOTT, Rosa. Pinks and Blues.
—— Young Detective.
Abdallah. *Laboulaye.*
Abel Drake's Wife. *Saunders.*
Aben-Hamet. *Chateaubriand.*
ABOUT, E. The Man with the Broken Ear.
—— The Fellah.
Actions Speak Louder than Words. *Neely.*
ADAMS, W. T. All Aboard.
—— Bear and Forbear.
—— Bivouac and Battle.
—— Brake Up.
—— Brave Old Salt.
—— Breaking Away.
—— Cringle and Cross Tree.
—— Down the Rhine.
—— Field and Forest.
—— Fighting Joe.
—— Haste and Waste.
—— Hope and Have.
—— Lightning Express.
—— Little by Little.
—— Northern Lands.
—— On Time.
—— Outward Bound.
—— Plane and Plank.
—— Poor and Proud.
—— Red Cross.
—— Rich and Humble.
—— Seek and Find.
—— Shamrock and Thistle.
—— Soldier Boy.
ADAMS, W. T. Starry Flag.
—— Switch Off.
—— Through by Daylight.
—— Try Again.
—— Up the Baltic.
—— Watch and Wait.
—— Work and Win.
Adela Cathcart. *Macdonald.*
Adrift in a Boat. *Kingston.*
Adrift on the Sea. *Norris.*
Adrift with a Vengeance. *Cornwallis.*
Adventures in the Ice. *Tillotson.*
Adventures of Captain Blake. *Maxwell.*
Adventures of a Man of Family. *Lennox.*
Adventures of a Slaver, *Thomes.*
Ænone. *Kip.*
After Life. *Sewell.*
Afraja. *Mügge.*
Against Tide. *Ross.*
Against Time. *Shand.*
AGUILAR, Grace. Mother's Recompense.
—— Women of Israel.
AÏDÉE, Hamilton. Mysteries and Morals.
AIMARD, G. Chief of the Aucas.
AINSLIE, Herbert. *See* MAITLAND.
AINSWORTH, W. H. Constable de Bourbon.
—— Myddleton Pomfret.
—— Talbot Harland.
—— Tower Hall.
—— Windsor Castle.
Albatross. *Kingston.*
Albert Lunel. *Brougham.*
ALCOTT, Louisa M. Aunt Jane's Scrap-Bag
—— Hospital Sketches.

ALCOTT, Louisa M. Little Men.
—— Little Women. 2d Ser.
—— Morning Glories, and other Stories.
—— Old Fashioned Girl.
ALDRICH, T. B. Story of a Bad Boy.
ALGER, H., Jr. Ben, the Luggage Boy.
—— Charlie Codman's Cruise.
—— Frank's Campaign.
—— Helen Ford.
—— Luck and Pluck.
—— Paul, the Peddler.
—— Paul Prescott's Charge.
—— Phil, the Fiddler.
—— Rough and Ready.
—— Rufus and Rose.
—— Sink or Swim.
—— Strong and Steady.
—— Tattered Tom.
Alice Seymour. *Grey.*
Alice Tracy. *Carrier.*
All Aboard. *Adams.*
All for Greed. *Bury.*
All in the Dark. *Le Fanu.*
Allan Haywood.
Almost Faultless.
Almost a Nun. *Wright.*
Almost a Priest. *Wright.*
American Baron. *De Mille.*
American Cardinal.
American Convent as a School for Protestant Children.
American Family in Paris.
AMES, MRS. M. C. Eirene.
AMES, Nellie. (Eleanor Kirk.) Up Broadway.
Among the Brigands. *De Mille.*
Among the Squirrels. *Dennison.*
Amy Deerbrook.
ANDERSEN, H. G. Fairy Tales.
—— O. T.
—— Shoes of Fortune, and other Tales.
—— Stories and Tales.
—— Two Baronesses.
—— Wonder Stories.
Angela. *Marsh.*
Annals of an Eventful Life. *Dasent.*
Annals of a Quiet Neighborhood. *Macdonald.*
Anne Furness.
Anne Judge. *Robinson.*
Annie Mason. *Averill.*
Anteros. *Lawrence.*
Antonia. *Dudevant.*
Arabella Stewart. *James.*
Arabesques. *Greenough.*
Arabian Days. *Hauff.*
Archie Lovell. *Edwards.*
ARGYLE, Anna. Cecilias.
Ark of Elm Island. *Kellogg.*
Armadale. *Collins.*
ARMSTRONG, F. C. Young Middy.
Around a Spring. *Droz.*
ARTHUR, T. S. Our Neighbors.
—— Pitcher of Cool Water.
—— Three Eras in Woman's Life.
Arthur Brown. *Kellogg.*
Arthur Conway. *Milman.*
Artist's Dream. *Vincent.*
Artist's Married Life. *Schefer.*
Ashcliffe Hall. *Holt.*
Askaros Kassis. *De Leon.*
Asmodeus. *Le Sage.*
Aspendale. *Preston.*
Asphodel.
At the Back of the North Wind. *Macdonald.*
At Home and Abroad.
At Last. *Terhune.*
At the South Pole. *Kingston.*
Athalie. *Dorsey.*
AUER, Adelheid von. It is the Fashion.
AUERBACH, B. Black Forest Village Stories.
—— German Tales.
—— On the Heights.
—— Professor's Lady.
—— Villa Eden.
August and Elvie. *Abbott.*
Aunt Jane's Hero. *Prentiss.*
Aunt Jo's Scrap Bag. *Alcott.*
Aunt Margaret's Trouble.
Aurelia. *Quinton.*
AUSTIN, J. G. Outpost.
Australian Crusoes. *Rowcroft.*
AVERILL, Anna S. Annie Mason.
Avery Glibun. *Newell.*
Away in the Wilderness.
Aylmers of Bally-Aylmer. *Griffin.*
Azilia. *Shaffer.*
B. O. W. C. *De Mille.*
Bach and Beethoven. *Barnard.*
Baffled. *Goddard.*
Baffled Schemes.
BAKER. W. M. The New Timothy.
BALFOUR, F. Perdita.
BALLANTYNE, R. M. Coral Island.
—— Deep Down.
—— Erling the Bold.
—— Floating Light.
—— Freaks on the Fells.
—— Gascoyne.
—— Iron Horse.

BALLANTYNE, R, M. Life-Boat.
—— Sandalwood Trader.
—— Shifting Winds.
—— Young Fur Traders.
Bandit. *Blanche*.
BANIM, J. Works.
—— Ghost Hunter; and Clough Fionn.
—— Last Baron of Crana; and Conformists.
—— Boyne Water.
—— Croppy.
—— Mayor of Wind-Gap; and Canvassing.
—— Father Connell.
—— Peep o' Day; and, Crohoore.
—— Peter of the Castle; and the Fetches.
BANTER, G. R. W. Humor and Pathos.
BARKER, Lady. A Christmas Cake in Four Quarters.
BARNARD, C. The Soprano.
—— Tone Masters; Bach and Beethoven.
—— Tone Masters; Händel and Haydn.
—— Tone Masters; Mozart and Mendelssohn.
BARON Munchausen.
Basil. *Collins*.
BATES, Lizzie. Downward and Upward.
BAWR, Mme. de. Maid of Honor.
BAYER, R. The Sphinx.
BAYLE, Abbe. The Pearl of Antioch.
BEACH, C. Lost Lenore.
—— Now or Never.
Bear and Forbear. *Adams*.
Beatrice Boville. *De la Rame*.
Beauclercs. *Clarke*.
BEAUCLERK, Lady Di. True Love.
Beauseincourt. *Warfield*.
Beautiful Miss Barrington. *Parr*.
Beautiful Widow. *Shelley*.
Beauty and the Beast. *Taylor*.
Beauty and the Beast. *Thackeray*.
BÉCHARD, F. Maurice.
BECKFORD, W. Vathek.
Bede's Charity. *Smith*.
Beechcroft. *Yonge*.
BEECHER, H. W. Norwood.
Beggar on Horseback. *Sauzade*.
Behind the Scenes.
Behind the Veil.
BELL, Catherine D. The Grahams.
—— Home Sunshine.
BELL, Catherine D. Huguenot Family.
—— Margaret Cecil.
—— Rest and Unrest.
—— Rosa's Wish.
—— Sydney Stuart.
Belle Clement's Influence.
Belle of the Family. *Grey*.
Below the Surface. *Elton*.
Ben, the Luggage Boy. *Alger*.
Beneath the Wheels.
BENEDICT, F. L. Miss Van Kortlandt.
—— My Daughter Elinor.
BENNETT, G. The Empress.
BENNETT, Mrs. Pastimes with my Friends.
Benoni Blake, M.D.
BERESFORD, G. de la P. Hoods and Masks.
Berlin and Sans-Souci. *Mundt*.
Bernthal. *Mundt*.
Bertha the Beauty. *Whittlesey*.
Bessy Rane. *Wood*.
Best Fellow in the World. *Wright*.
BETHELL, Hon. Augusta. Millicent and Her Cousins.
Beverly. *Walworth*.
Beyminstre.
Beyond the Breakers. *Owen*.
BIRD, R. M. Nick of the Woods.
Birds of Prey. *Braddon*.
Birth and Education. *Schwartz*.
Bishop's Son. *Cary*.
Bitter Sweets. *Hatton*.
BITZIUS, A. Wealth and Welfare.
Bivouac. *Maxwell*.
Bivouac and Battle. *Adams*.
BJÓRNSON, B. Happy Boy.
—— Love and Life in Norway.
BLACK, Wm. A Daughter of Heth.
—— In Silk Attire.
—— Kilmeny.
—— Love or Marriage?
—— Monarch of Mincing Lane.
Black Band. *Braddon*.
Black Forest Village Stories. *Auerbach*.
Black and Gold. *Saunders*.
Black Moss.
Black Panther. *Wraxall*.
Black Sheep. *Yates*.
Black Tulip. *Dumas*.
Blackgown Papers. *Mariotti*.
BLACKMORE, R. D. Cradock Nowell
BLACKWELL, Antoinette B. Island Neighbors.
Blade O'Grass. *Farjeon*.
BLAKE, Lady. My Stepfather's Home.

BLAKE, Mrs. Lillie D. Zoë.
BLANCHE, A. The Bandit.
Blanche Gilroy. *Hosmer.*
BLAND, T. A. Farming as a Profession.
Blockade of Phalsburg. *Erckmann-Chatrian.*
Bloom and Brier. *Falconer.*
Blue Bell of Red Neap. *Parr.*
Blue Jackets. *Greey.*
BOCCACCIO, G. Decameron.
BÖHL VON FABER, C. Elia.
BORROW, G. Lavengro.
Boston Boy. *Henry.*
Both Sides of the Street. *Walker.*
Bound Down. *Fitch.*
Bound to John Company.
Bound to the Wheel. *Saunders.*
Boy Farmers. *Kellogg.*
Boy in Grey. *Kingsley.*
Boy's Adventures in Australia. *Howitt.*
Boy's Trip across the Plains. *Preston.*
BOYLE, Esmeralda. Thistle Down.
Boyne Water. *Banim.*
Boys at Chequasset.
Boys of Grand Pré School *De Mille.*
BRADDON, M. E. Birds of Prey.
—— Black Band.
—— Charlotte's Inheritance.
—— Diavola.
—— Fenton's Quest.
—— John Marchmont's Legacy.
—— Lady's Mile.
—— Lawyer's Secret.
—— Lovels of Arden.
—— Rupert Godwin.
—— Three Times Dead.
—— What is the Mystery?
BRADLEY, Mrs. A. Wrong Confessed.
BRADLEY, E. Matins and Muttons.
—— The White Wife.
Brake Up. *Adams.*
BRAMSTON, Mary. Cecy's Recollections.
BRANDT, F. F. Frank Marland's Manuscripts.
Brave Lady. *Craik.*
Brave Old Salt. *Adams.*
BRAY, Mrs. Hartland Forest.
Brazen Gates. *Smith.*
Breakers Ahead. *McKeever.*
Breaking Away. *Adams.*
Bred in the Bone. *Sauzade.*
Breezie Langton. *Smart.*
BRÉHAT, A. de. French Robinson Crusoe.
BREMER, Miss F. Life in Dalecarlia.
Brewer's Family. *Ellis.*
BREWSTER, Anne M. H. Compensation.
—— St. Martin's Summer.
Bride of Llewellyn. *Southworth.*
BRIERLEY, B. Irkdale.
BRIGHT, Mrs. Three Bernices.
Brilliant Tales from "London Society."
BROCK, Mrs. Carey. Sunday Echoes in Week-day Hours.
Broken Toys. *Steele.*
BROOKE, H. Fool of Quality.
BROOKS, S. Gordian Knot.
—— Sooner or Later.
BROTHERHEAD, A. P. Himself his Worst Enemy.
Brothers' Bet. *Carlen.*
Brothers and Sisters. *Marshall.*
BROUGHAM, Lord. Albert Lunel.
BROUGHTON, Rhoda. Cometh up as a Flower.
—— Good Bye, Sweetheart!
—— Not Wisely, but too Well.
—— Red as a Rose is She.
Brownies. *Ewing.*
Brownings. *Fuller.*
Brownlows. *Oliphant.*
BRUCE, Mrs. E. M. A Thousand a Year.
BUCKLAND, Anna J. Diary of Nannette Dampier.
Bucklyn Shaig. *Montgomery.*
BUDDINGTON, L. B. Can the Old Love?
BUNBURY, Selina. Florence Manvers.
BUND, L. Puck's Nightly Pranks.
BURNAND, F. C. Out of Town.
BURNEY, Mrs. Camilla.
—— Cecilia.
—— The Wanderer.
BURTON, R. F. Vikram and the Vampire.
BURY, Baroness de. All for Greed.
Bushrangers. *Thomes.*
Butterfly Hunters. *Conant.*
By his Own Might. *Hillern.*
BYR, Robert. (Pseudonym.) *See* BAYER, C. R.
CABALLERO, F. (Pseudonym.) *See* BÖHL VON FABER.
Cabin-Book. *Postel.*
Cabin on the Prairie. *Pearson.*
Cadet Life at West Point. *Strong.*
Caged Lion. *Yonge.*
Caleb Williams. *Godwin.*
Callamura. *Pleasants.*
Called to Account. *Thomas.*
Callirrhoë. *Sand.*

Cameron Hall. *Cruse.*
Cameron Pride. *Holmes.*
Camilla. *Burney.*
CAMPBELL, Lady. Martin Tobin.
Can the Old Love? *Buddington.*
Cancelled Will. *Dupuy.*
Canvassing. *Banim.*
Captain Molly. *Talmon.*
Captain Wolf.
Carl Werner. *Simms.*
CARLEN, E. Brothers' Bet.
—— Guardian.
—— Smugglers of the Swedish Coast; or, Rose of Thistle Island.
Carlino. *Ruffini.*
CARLYLE, T. German Romance.
Carlyon's Year.
Carrie Harrington. *Moos.*
CARRIER, Mrs. S. Alice Tracy.
CARROLL, Lewis. Through the Looking-Glass.
CARY, Alice. Bishop's Son.
—— Pictures of Country Life.
Casper and his Friends. *Lothrop.*
Castaways. *Reid.*
Caste.
CASTLEMON, H. Frank among the Rancheros.
—— Go Ahead.
—— No Moss.
—— Tom Newcombe.
Casual Acquaintance. *Hardy.*
Catherine. *Thackeray.*
CAXTON, Laura. (Pseudonym.) *See* COMINS, Lizzie B.
Cecilia. *Burney.*
Cecilias. *Argyle.*
Cecil's Tryst.
Cecy's Recollections. *Bramston.*
Cent per Cent. *Jerrold.*
Cerise. *Melville.*
CERVANTES, M. Don Quixote.
Cesarine Dietrich. *Dudevant.*
Champion Pig of England.
Changing Base. *Everett.*
CHAPLIN, Mrs. Jane D. Out of the Wilderness.
Charity Hurlbut.
CHARLES, Mrs. Christian Life in England.
—— Draytons and Davenants.
—— Victory of the Vanquished.
CHARLESWORTH, Maria L. Ministering Children.
—— Ministry of Life.
Charlie Bell. *Kellogg.*
Charlie Codman's Cruise. *Alger.*
Charlotte Ackermann. *Müller.*
Charlotte's Inheritance. *Braddon.*
Charlotte and Mary Temple. *Rowson.*
Château Morville or Life in Touraine.
CHATEAUBRIAND, F. A. de. Aben-Hamet.
CHATTERTON, Lady. Gay's Court.
Checkmate. *Le Fanu.*
CHELLIS, Mary D. Father Merrill.
Cherry and Violet. *Manning.*
CHEESEBRO', Caroline. Foe in the Household.
Chief of the Aucas. *Aimard.*
CHILD, Mrs. L. M. Children of Mount Ida.
—— Romance of the Republic.
Child Life in Italy.
Children's Wish. *Raymond.*
Choisy. *Story.*
Chris and Otho. *Smith.*
Christabel Hope. *Mercier.*
Christabel Kingscote. *Marshall.*
Christian's Life in England. *Charles.*
Christie.
Christie. *Robertson.*
Christmas Cake in Four Quarters. *Barker.*
Christmas Guest. *Southworth.*
Christmas Locket, 1871.
Christmas Magazine Annuals, 1870 and 1871.
Christmas Stocking.
Christopher Kenrick. *Hatton.*
Christopher Tadpole. *Smith.*
Christy's Grandson.
Chronicles of St. Mary's.
CHURCH, Mrs. Ross. Gerald Estcourt.
—— For Ever and Ever.
—— Her Lord and Master.
—— Petronel.
—— The Prey of the Gods.
—— Too Good for Him.
—— Véronique.
—— Woman against Woman.
Church and Chapel.
Ciprina. *Reynolds.*
Circe. *White.*
Citizen of Prague.
Citoyenne Jacqueline. *Tytler.*
Clackitts of Inglebrook. *Prosser.*
Clara Vaughan.
CLARE Ada. Only a Woman's Heart.
Clare Savile. *Luard.*
CLARK, C. Tom Crackenthorpe.

CLARK, C. Beauclercs.
—— Which is the Winner?
CLARKE, Mrs. M. C. Portia, and other Stories of the Early Days of Shakespeare's Heroines.
CLARKE, Miss R. S. Dotty Dimple's Flyaway.
—— Little Folks Astray.
—— Prudy Keeping House.
Claude Gueux. *Hugo.*
Claudia. *Douglas.*
Claudia. *Tucker.*
Claverings. *Trollope.*
Clemence d'Orville.
Clergyman's Wife. *Ritchie.*
Clever Jack.
Clifford Castle. *Mackey.*
CLINE, A. J. Henry Courtland.
Clotilde. *Pontmartin.*
Clough Fionn. *Banim.*
Cloven Foot. *Newell.*
CLYDE, Alton. Under Foot.
—— Clyffords of Clyffe.
COBDEN, P. Going on a Mission.
—— Who will Win?
COFFIN, C. C. Winning his Way?
COFFIN, R. B. Out of Town.
COLLINS, C. J. Man in Chains.
COLLINS, M. Marquis and Merchant.
—— Two Plunges for a Pearl.
—— Vivian Romance.
COLLINS, W. Armadale.
—— Basil.
—— Hide and Seek.
—— Mad Monkton, and other Tales.
—— Man and Wife.
—— Moonstone.
—— Poor Miss Finch.
—— Queen's Revenge, and other Stories.
—— Sister Rose.
—— Stolen Mask.
Colloquies of Edward Osborne. *Manning.*
Cometh up as a Flower. *Broughton.*
Comic Tales. *Smith.*
Coming (The) Race; or, The New Utopia.
COMINS, Lizzie B. The Hartwell Farm.
Commander of Malta. *Sue.*
Commonplace. *Rossetti.*
Common Sense.
Compensation. *Brewster.*
CONANT, Mrs. Butterfly Hunters.
Condensed Novels. *Harte.*
Conformists. *Banim*
Congressman's Christmas Dream. *Hall*
CONINGSBY, C. Sheltern.
Constable de Bourbon. *Ainsworth.*
Constance Lyndsay.
Constance Sherwood. *Fullerton.*
Contraband. *Melville.*
COOKE, J E. Fairfax.
—— Hammer and Rapier.
—— Heir of Gaymount.
—— Out of the Foam.
COOLIDGE, Susan. *See* WOOLSEY, Miss.
Copsley Annals.
Coral Island. *Ballantyne.*
CORBERT, R. St. J. Holiday Camp.
CORBIN, Mrs. C. F. Rebecca.
Corinne. *Staël*
CORNWALLIS, K. Adrift with a Vengeance.
COLERIDGE, Christabel R. Lady Betty.
Cost of Gaergwyn. *Howitt.*
Count Mirabeau. *Mundt.*
Count's Niece. *Preston.*
Counterfeit Coin. *Ross.*
Countess of Arnheim. *Reynolds.*
Countess Gisela. *John.*
Countess Kate. *Yonge.*
Countess of Lascelles. *Reynolds.*
Countess of Monte-Cristo.
Countess and Page. *Reynolds.*
County Family.
Courtship and Marriage. *Hentz.*
Cousin from India. *Craik.*
Cousin Mabel's Experiences. *Whately.*
Cousin Maud. *Holmes.*
Cousin Paul. *Glenn.*
Cousin Stella.
COWLES, Miss. Roundhearts.
Crackers for Christmas. *Hugessen.*
Cradock Nowell. *Blackmore.*
CRAIK, Mrs. D. M. A Brave Lady.
—— Domestic Stories.
—— Hannah.
—— Head of the Family.
—— Little Sunshine's Holiday.
—— Romantic Tales.
—— Two Marriages.
—— Unkind Word.
—— Woman's Kingdom.
CRAIK, Georgiana M. The Cousin from India.
—— Esther Hill's Secret.
—— Leslie Tyrrell.
—— Twenty Years Ago.
CRANE, Anne M. *See* MULLER, Mrs.
Cringle and Cross Tree. *Adams.*

Crock of Gold. *Tupper.*
Crohoore. *Banim.*
Croppy. *Banim.*
Cross Purposes. *De Leon.*
CROUCH, Julia. Three Successful Girls.
Crown from the Spear. *Hamilton.*
Crown Jewels. *Moffett.*
Crowned. *Tainsh.*
Cruise of the Casco. *Kellogg.*
Cruise of the Frolic. *Kingston.*
Cruise of the Midge. *Scott.*
CRUSE, Mary A. Cameron Hall.
Crust and Cake. *Garrett.*
Cryptogram. *De Mille.*
Culm Rock. *Gaylord.*
CUPPLES, Mrs. G. Driven to Sea.
Curate and Rector.
Curate of Sadbrooke.
Curate's Discipline. *Eiloart.*
Currer Lyle. *Reeder.*
Cyril Ashley.
Cyril Blount.
DAEMS, S. The Double Sacrifice.
—— Daily Bread, and other Stories.
Daisy. *Warner.*
Daisy's Companions.
Daisy Nichol. *Hardy.*
Daisy Ward's Work. *McLain.*
DALTON, W. Lost among the Wild Men.
—— Wolf Boy of China.
Dame Nature and her Three Daughters. *Saintine.*
Dangerous Guest.
DANIEL, Mrs. M. Elsie's Married Life.
Danvers Papers. *Yonge.*
DARYL, S. With the Tide.
DASENT, G. W. Annals of an Eventful Life.
—— Gisli the Outlaw.
Daughter of Heth. *Black.*
Daughter of an Egyptian King. *Ebers.*
Daughter of an Empress. *Mundt.*
DAVENPORT, R. A. Self-Made.
David Elginbrod. *Macdonald.*
David Garrick. *Robertson.*
David Lloyd's Last Will.
DAVIES, Mrs. C. E. K. Fanny Bright's Blanket.
—— Penny Rust's Christmas.
DAVIS, Mrs. R. H. Margaret Howth.
—— Waiting for the Verdict.
Davy's Motto.
Dawn.
Days of Yore. *Tytler.*
DAYTON, A. C. Theodosia Ernest.
Dead Guest. *Zschokke.*
Dead Letter. *Victor.*
Dead Men's Shoes. *Hadermann.*
Debenham's Vow. *Edwards.*
Decameron. *Boccaccio.*
Deep Down. *Ballantyne.*
Deerings of Medbury. *Townsend.*
DE FOREST, J. W. Kate Beaumont.
—— Miss Ravenel's Conversion.
—— Overland.
DE KRAYFT, Mrs. S. H. Little Jakey.
Delaplaine. *Walworth.*
DE LA RAME, Julia. Beatrice Boville.
—— Folle Farine.
—— A Leaf in the Storm.
—— Puck.
—— Randolph Gordon, etc.
—— Under Two Flags.
Delaware; or the Ruined Family.
DE LEON, E. Askaros Kassis.
—— Cross Purposes.
DE MILLE, J. The American Baron.
—— Among the Brigands.
—— B. O. W. C.
—— Boys of Grand Pré School.
—— The Cryptogram.
—— Fire in the Woods.
—— Lady of the Ice.
—— Lost in the Fog.
Dene Hollow. *Wood.*
DENNISON, Mrs. Among the Squirrels.
De Profundis. *Gilbert.*
De Rohan. *Sue.*
Destiny. *Murphy.*
Detained in France. *Giberne.*
DE WITT, Mme. French Country Family.
—— Motherless.
Dharina. *Paulet.*
Diamonds on the Hearth. *James.*
Diamond Rose. *Tytler.*
Diary of a Milliner. *Otis.*
Diary of Nannette Dampier. *Buckland.*
Diavola. *Braddon.*
DIAZ, Mrs A. M. William Henry and his Friends.
—— William Henry Letters.
DICKENS, C. Lamplighter's Story, etc.
—— Mystery of Edwin Drood.
—— Readings.

DICKEN'S Works (Globe ed.)
DICKINSON, Ellen E. Emanuel, and other Stories.
DICKENGA, J. E., and Ashworth, P. M. Tom Chips.
DISRAELI, B. Lothair.
Distant Cousins.
Dr. Austin's Guests. *Gilbert.*
Doctor Johns. *Mitchell.*
Doctor Kemp.
Dr. Thorne. *Trollope.*
Dr. Wilmer's Love. *Lee.*
DODGE, Mrs. M. E. A Few Friends.
Doings in Maryland. *Douglas.*
Domestic Stories. *Craik.*
Don Quixote. *Cervantes.*
DONBAVAND, B. Wild Ireland.
Dorothy Fox. *Parr.*
DORR, Julia C. R. Lanmere.
—— Sibyl Huntington.
DORSEY, Mrs. Athalie.
—— Lucia Dare.
Dotty Dimple's Flyaway. *Clarke.*
Double Play. *Everett.*
Double Sacrifice. *Daems.*
DOUBNEY, Sarah. Faith Harrowby.
DOUGLAS, Amanda M. Claudia.
—— In Trust.
—— Lucia; her Problems.
—— Stephen Dane.
—— With Fate against Him.
DOUGLAS, Matilda. Doings in Maryland.
Doves in the Eagle's Nest. *Yonge.*
Dower House. *Thomas.*
Down the Rhine. *Adams.*
Downward and Upward. *Bates.*
Draytons and Davenants. *Charles.*
Driven to Sea. *Cupples.*
DROZ, G. Around a Spring.
DRURY, Anna H. Eastbury.
—— The Story of a Shower.
Drummer Boy. *Trowbridge.*
DUDEVANT, Mme. Antonia.
—— Cesarine Dietrich.
—— Handsome Lawrence.
—— Indiana.
—— Jealousy.
—— Mlle. Merquem.
—— Marquis of Villemer.
—— Mauprat.
—— Miller of Angibault.
—— M. Sylvestre.
—— Rolling Stone.
—— Simon.
—— Snow Man.
DUMAS, A. Black Tulip.
—— Felina de Chambure.
—— Palace of Ice.
DUNN, Sara. Heiress of the Mount.
DUNNING, Mrs. A. K. A Story of Four Lives.
DUPUY, Eliza A. Cancelled Will.
—— How he Did it.
—— Michael Randolph.
—— Who shall be Victor?
—— Why did he Marry Her?
Durnton Abbey. *Trollope.*
Eagle Crag.
Earl's Dene. *Francillon.*
East and West.
Eastbury. *Drury.*
EASTMAN, Julia A. Romneys of Ridgmont.
—— Short-Comings and Long-Goings.
EASTWOOD, Frances. Marcella.
EBERS, G. Daughter of an Egyptian King.
—— Egyptian Princess (same original as preceding).
EDGEWORTH, Miss. Harry and Lucy, etc.
Edna Browning. *Holmes.*
Edward's Wife. *Marshall.*
EDWARDS, Amelia B. Debenham's Vow.
EDWARDS, Mrs. Annie. Archie Lovell.
—— Miss Forrester.
—— Ought we to Visit her?
—— Philip Earnscliffe.
—— Steven Laurence.
—— Susan Fielding.
EDWARDS, M. de. Betham Kitty.
—— Sylvestres.
EGAN, P. The Poor Boy.
—— Quintin Matsys.
EGGLESTON, E. Hoosier Schoolmaster.
Egyptian Princess (same as Daughters of an Egyptian King). *Ebers.*
EILOART, Mrs. Curate's Discipline.
—— From Thistles, Grapes?
Eirene. *Ames.*
Elder Sister. *James.*
Eleonore. *Ingersleben.*
Elia. *Böhl von Faber.*
Elizabeth. *Thackeray.*
Elkerton Rectory. *Pycroft.*
ELLIOTT, C. W. Wind and Whirlwind.
ELLIS, Mrs. Brewer's Family.

Ellis, Mrs. Hearts and Homes.
Elms Homestead. *Johnson.*
Elsie's Married Life. *Daniel.*
Elsie Dinsmore. *Finley.*
Elster's Folly. *Wood.*
Emanuel, and other Stories. *Dickinson.*
Emilia Wyndham. *Marsh.*
Emma Parker.
Empress. *Bennett.*
Empress Josephine. *Mundt.*
Empty Heart. *Terhune.*
Enault, L. Pupil of the Legion of Honor.
Enchanted Princess. *Nauman.*
Enchanting and Enchanted. *Hackländer.*
Entrances and Exits. *Winstansley.*
Episodes of Fiction.
Episodes in an Obscure Life.
Erckmann, É., and Chatrian, A. Blockade of Phalsburg.
—— Forest House and Catharine's Lovers.
—— Invasion of France in 1814.
—— Miller's Story of the War or the Plébiscite.
Erling the Bold. *Ballantyne.*
Estelle Russell.
Ester Ried.
Esther Hill's Secret. *Craik.*
Ethel Linton.
Ethelyn's Mistake. *Holmes.*
Eustace Quentin. *Reynolds.*
Evan's, Augusta J. Inez.
—— St. Elmo.
—— Vashti.
Everett, W. Changing Base.
—— Double Play.
Every Day.
Ewing, Juliana H. The Brownies, etc.
Exiles in Babylon. *Tucker.*
Experiences of a French Detective.
Experiences of Richard Taylor, Esq.
Eyster, Nellie. Tom Harding.
Faber, Mrs. Legends of Dundrum Castle.
Fabrics; a Story of To-day.
Fair Harvard.
Fair to See. *Lockhart.*
Fair Gospeller. *Manning.*
Fair Women. *Forrester.*
Fairfax. *Cooke.*
Fairy Alice. *Fitzgerald.*
Fairy Fingers. *Ritchie.*
Fairy Glass.
Fairy Tales. *Andersen.*
Fairy Tales. *Ségur.*
Faith Harrowby. *Doubney.*
Faith White's Letter Book.
Falconer, W. Bloom and Brier.
False Colors. *Thomas.*
Family Fairy Tales. *Pennell.*
Family Doom. *Southworth.*
Fanny Bright's Blanket. *Davis.*
Far above Rubies. *Riddell.*
Farjeon, B. L. Blade O'Grass.
—— Grif.
—— Joshua Marvel.
Farming as a Profession. *Bland.*
Farquharson, Martha. *See* Finley, Mrs.
Farrar, F. W. St. Winifred's.
Fatal Marriage. *Southworth.*
Father's Coming Home.
Father Connell. *Banim.*
Father Merrill. *Chellis.*
Fathers and Sons. *Turgenef.*
Faulkner Lyle. *Lemon.*
Faust. *Reynolds.*
Fay, T. Norman Leslie.
Faye Mar. *Pritchard.*
Felina de Chambure. *Dumas.*
Felix Holt. *Lewes.*
Felix Kent *Hoffman.*
Fell, A. Mrs. Thorne's Guests.
Fellah. *About.*
Female Minister.
Fenton's Quest. *Braddon.*
Fernando de Lemos. *Gayarré.*
Fernyhurst Court.
Ferryman of the Tiber. *La Grange.*
Fetches. *Banim.*
Feuillet, O. Marquis d'Hauterive.
Few Friends. *Dodge.*
Fiddling Freddy. *Forrest.*
Fides. *Wraxall.*
Field and Forest. *Adams.*
Fielding's Works.
Fifteen Days. *Putnam.*
Fifteen Years. *Robinson.*
Fifty Years Ago. *Willard.*
Fighting Joe. *Adams.*
Figure Eight. *Victor.*
Filia. *Graham.*
Finette. *Laboulaye.*
Finley, Mrs. Martha. Elsie Dinsmore.
—— Holidays at Roselands.
—— Lilian.
—— Old Fashioned Boy.
—— Wanted—a Pedigree.
Fire in the Woods. *De Mille.*
Fisher, Miss Frances E. Mabel Lee.

FISHER, Miss Frances E. Morton House.
—— Valerie Aylmer.
FITCH, Anna M. Bound Down.
FITZGERALD, P. Fairy Alice.
—— Never Forgotten.
—— Second Mrs. Tillotson.
Five Days at Wentworth Grange. *Palgrave.*
Five Hundred Majority. *Niles.*
Five Hundred Pounds Reward.
Five Years before the Mast. *Hazen.*
FLAGG, William. A Good Investment.
Floating Light. *Ballantyne.*
Florence Manvers. *Bunbury.*
Florence O'Neill. *Stewart.*
Flower of the Family.
Fly Leaves.
Flying Mail. *Goldschmidt.*
Foe in the Household. *Cheesebro.*
Folle Farine. *De la Rame.*
Fool of Quality. *Brooke.*
For Conscience Sake.
For Ever and Ever. *Marryatt.*
For Lack of Gold. *Gibbon.*
For Richer for Poorer. *Parr.*
For a Woman's Sake. *Phillips*
Fore and Aft. *Phelps.*
Forest House and Catharine's Lovers. *Erckmann-Chatrian.*
Forgiven at Last. *Hadermann.*
Forgotten by the World.
Forlorn Hope. *Yates.*
FORREST, N. Fiddling Freddy.
—— Jack and Rosy.
FORRESTER, Mrs. Fair Women.
Found and Lost.
Foundations. *Porter.*
FOUQUÉ, Baron de la Motte. Thiodolf the Icelander.
Four, and What they Did. *Weeks.*
Four Oaks. *Thorpe.*
Four Sisters.
Foxholme Hall. *Kingston.*
FRANC, Maud J. Vermont Vale.
FRANCILLON, R. E. Earl's Dene.
Frank among the Rancheros. *Castlemon.*
Frank Austin's Diamond.
Frank's Campaign. *Alger.*
Frank Fielding. *Veitch.*
Frank Hilton. *Grant.*
Frank Marland's Manuscripts. *Brandt.*
Freaks on the Fells. *Ballantyne.*
Fred and the Gorillas. *Miller.*
Fred and Maria and Me.
Frederick the Great and his Court. *Mundt.*
Frederick the Great and his Family. *Mundt.*
French Country Family. *De Witt.*
French Robinson Crusoe. *Bréhat.*
Friday Night; Tales of Hebrew Life.
FRIEDRICH, F. The Lost Despatch.
Friendly Hands and Kindly Words.
Friends and Acquaintances.
From Fourteen to Fourscore. *Jewett.*
From an Island. *Thackeray.*
From Thistles, Grapes? *Eiloart.*
FROST, Mrs. L. J. H. Lynda Newton.
FULLER, J. G. Brownings.
FULLER, Lydia. Mistaken.
FULLER, Miss Martha. Righted at Last.
FULLERTON, Lady G. Constance Sherwood.
—— Grantley Manor.
—— Mrs. Gerald's Niece.
—— Stormy Life.
FULLOM, S. W. The Great Highway.
—— Man of the World.
Funny Philosophers. *Yellott.*
Gabled House.
GABORIAU, H. Mystery of Orcival.
Gabrielle André. *Gould.*
GAGE, Mrs. F. D. Steps Upward.
GALLENGA, A. Italy in 1831; Adventures of Castellamonte.
Gambler's Wife. *Grey.*
Gardenhurst. *Steele.*
GARDNER, Mrs. H. C. Rosamond Dayton.
GARIBALDI, G. The Rule of the Monk.
GARRETT, E. Crust and Cake.
—— Occupations of a Retired Life.
GARRETT, E. and R. White as Snow.
GARRETT, Ruth and E. The Quiet Miss Godolphin.
Garstang Grange. *Trollope.*
Gascoyne. *Ballantyne.*
GASKELL, Mrs. North and South.
Gaspar Trenchard. *Hemyng.*
Gavroche Party. *Jerrold.*
Gay's Court. *Chatterton.*
GAYARRÉ, C. Fernando de Lemos.
GAYLORD, G. Culm Rock.
Gayworthys. *Whitney.*
Gem of the Lake. *Wright.*
Gemma. *Trollope.*

George Canterbury's Will. *Wood.*
Gerald Estcourt. *Marryatt.*
Gerard the Lion Slayer, etc.
German Emigrants. *Gerstaecker.*
German Evenings. *Lowdell.*
German Novelists. *Roscoe.*
German Romance. *Carlyle.*
German Tales. *Auerbach.*
GERSTAECKER, F. German Emigrants.
Ghost Hunter. *Banim.*
Ghost Stories.
Giant.
GIBBON, C. For Lack of Gold.
GIBERNE, Agnes. Detained in France.
Gideon's Rock. *Saunders.*
Gil Blas. *Le Sage.*
GILBERT, W. De Profundis.
—— Dr. Austin's Guests.
—— King George's Middy.
—— Struggle in Ferrara.
—— Wizard of the Mountain.
Gilbert Rugge.
Ginx's Baby. *Jenkins.*
Gipsy's Daughter. *Grey.*
Giraffe Hunters. *Reid.*
Girl He Married. *Grant.*
Gisli the Outlaw. *Dasent.*
Gladiators. *Melville.*
GLENN, Jessie. Cousin Paul.
GLYN, H. Uncle Crotty's Relations.
Go Ahead. *Castlemon.*
GODDARD, Julia. Baffled.
—— Wonderful Stories from Northern Lands.
GODWIN, H. B. Madge.
—— Sherbrooke.
GODWIN, W. Caleb Williams.
GOETHE, J. W. von. Wilhelm Meister.
Going & Son.
Going on a Mission. *Cobden.*
Gold Hunters in Australia. *Thomes.*
Gold Hunters in Europe. *Thomes.*
Gold and Name. *Schwartz.*
Gold, Silver, Lead. *Valentine.*
Gold Worshipers.
Golden Hills; a Tale of the Irish Famine.
Golden Ladder. *Wright.*
Golden Lion of Granpere. *Trollope.*
GOLDSCHMIDT, M. Flying Mail.
Good-Bye, Sweetheart. *Broughton*
Good For Nothing. *Melville.*
Good Investment. *Flagg.*
Good Stories.
Gordian Knot. *Brooks.*
GORDON, H. Lovers and Thinkers.
GORE, Mrs. A Life's Lessons.
—— Peers and Parvenus.
GOTTHELF, J. (Pseudonym.) *See* BITZIUS, A.
GOULD, S. B. Gabrielle André.
—— In Exitu Israel.
GOULDING, F. R. Nacoochee.
—— Sal-O-Quah.
—— Sapelo.
—— Young Marooners.
GOURAUD, J. Little Boy's Story.
—— Peter Lipp.
GRAHAM, Agnes. Filia.
GRAHAM, Austyn. Will She have Him?
Grahames. *Whitehead.*
Grahams. *Bell.*
Grandmother's Money. *Robinson.*
Grandpa's House. *Weeks.*
GRANDPRÉ, Pauline de. Prisoners of St. Lazare.
GRANT, J. Frank Hilton.
—— The Girl He Married.
—— Lady Wedderburn's Wish.
—— Rob Roy.
Grantley Manor. *Fullerton.*
Great Highway. *Fullom.*
GREEK Romances: Helidorus, Longus and Achilles Tatius; transl. by Smith.
GREENE, Mrs. The Grey House on the Hill.
—— School-Boy Baronet.
GREENOUGH, Mrs. R. S. Arabesques.
GREENWOOD, J. Reuben Davidger.
—— Little Ragamuffin.
—— Silas the Conjurer.
GREEY, E. Blue Jackets.
GREY, Mrs. Alice Seymour.
—— Belle of the Family
—— Gambler's Wife.
—— Gypsy's Daughter.
—— Hyacinthe.
—— Lena Cameron.
—— Manœuvring Mother.
—— Marriage a Lottery.
—— Marriage in High Life.
—— Old Dower House.
—— Passion and Principle.
—— Young Husband.
Grey-Bay Mare, and other Sketches. *Leland.*
Grey House on the Hill. *Greene.*

Grif. *Farjeon.*
GRIFFIN, G. Aylmers of Bally-Aylmer.
—— Works.
GRIFFITH, C. Uttermost Farthing.
—— Victory Deane.
Griffith Gaunt. *Reade.*
Guardian. *Carlen.*
Guardian Angel. *Holmes.*
Gudrun.
GUERNSEY, Clara F. Merman and Figure-Head.
GUERNSEY, Lucy E. Lady Betty's Governess.
—— Milly.
—— Winifred.
Guild Court. *Macdonald.*
Guilt and Innocence. *Schwartz.*
Guilty or Not Guilty.
Gustave Adolph. *Topelius.*
GUTZKOW, K. Through Night to Light.
Guy Deverell. *Le Fanu.*
Gwendoline's Harvest.
Gypsy Breynton. *Phelps.*
Gypsy at the Golden Crescent. *Phelps.*
Gypsy's Cousin Joy. *Phelps.*
Gypsy's Sowing and Reaping. *Phelps.*
HACK, Maria. Stories and Pictures from Grecian History.
HACKLÄNDER, F. W. Enchanting and Enchanted.
HADERMANN, Jeanette R. Dead Men's Shoes.
—— Forgiven at Last.
HALE, E. E. Sybaris.
—— Ten Times One is Ten.
HALL, A. O. Congressman's Christmas Dream.
HALL, H. More Secrets than One.
HALL, Mrs. S. C. Tales of Woman's Trials.
HAMILTON, Mrs. A Crown from the Spear.
—— Woven of Many Threads.
Hammer and Anvil. *Spielhagen.*
Hammer and Rapier. *Cooke.*
HAMMOND, W. A. Robert Severne.
HANCOCK, S. J. Montanas.
Hands not Hearts. *Wilkinson.*
Handsome Lawrence. *Dudevant.*
Händel and Haydn. *Barnard.*
Hannah. *Craik.*
Hannah. *Moos.*
HANNAY, D. Ned Allen.
HANNAY, D. Singleton Fontenoy.
Happy Boy. *Björnson.*
Hard Scrabble of Elm Island. *Kellogg.*
HARDY, Mrs. D. A Casual Acquaintance.
HARDY, Lady. Daisy Nichol.
HARLAND, Marion. *See* TERHUNE, Mrs. M. V.
HARLEY, Dr. Young Crusoe.
HARRINGTON, G. F. Inside.
HARRIS, A. Martin Beck.
HARRIS, Mrs. S. S. Richard Vandermarck.
Harry Lawley.
Harry and Lucy. *Edgeworth.*
Harry Skipwith. *Kingston.*
HART, G. In the Rapids.
HARTE, F. B. Condensed Novels.
—— Luck of Roaring Camp, etc.
Hartland Forest. *Bray.*
Hartwell Farm. *Comins.*
Haste and Waste. *Adams.*
HATTON, J. Bitter Sweets.
—— Christopher Kenrick.
HAUFF, W. Arabian Days.
Haunted Crust. *Saunders.*
HAVEN, Marion. Joanna.
HAZEN, J. A. Five Years before the Mast.
He Would be a Gentleman. *Lover.*
Head of the Family. *Craik.*
Headless Horseman. *Reid.*
Heart Hungry. *Westmoreland.*
Heart of Mabel Ware.
Hearts and Homes. *Ellis.*
Heavenward Led. *Sommers.*
Hector O'Halloran. *Maxwell.*
Hedged In. *Phelps.*
Heights of Eidelberg. *Tatem.*
Heir Expectant.
Heir of Gaymount. *Cooke.*
Heiress of the Mount. *Dunn.*
Helen's Diary. *Marshall.*
Helen Courtney's Promise. *Jervey.*
Helen Erskine. *Robinson.*
Helen Ethinger. *Whittlesey.*
Helen Felton's Question. *Wylde.*
Helen Ford. *Alger.*
Helen Gardner's Wedding-Day. *Terhune.*
Helena's Household.
HEMYNG, B. Gaspar Trenchard.
Hena. *Hort.*
HENRY, L. The Boston Boy.
Henry and Bessie.
Henry Courtland. *Cline.*
Henry VIII and his Court. *Mundt.*

Henry Powers, Banker.
HENTZ, Mrs. C. L. Courtship and Marriage.
Her Lord and Master. *Church.*
Her Title of Honor. *Parr.*
HERBERT, H. W. Lord of the Manor.
Hereward. *Kingsley.*
Heroines in Obscurity.
Hester's Happy Summer.
Hester Kirton.
Hester Strong's Life-Work. *Southworth.*
Hetty's Resolve.
HEYSE, P. Solitaries.
HEYWOOD, J. C. How will it End?
Hidden Depths.
Hidden Sin.
Hide and Seek. *Collins.*
High Mills. *Saunders.*
Higher Law. *Maitland.*
Hila Dart. *Mumford.*
HILLERN, W. von. By his Own Might.
—— Only a Girl.
Himself his Worst Enemy. *Brotherhead.*
Hirell. *Saunders.*
Hitherto. *Whitney.*
HÖFER, E. The Old Countess.
HOFFMAN, Miss Alice. Felix Kent.
HOFFMANN, Franz. Prince Wolfgang.
Hohensteins. *Spielhagen.*
HOLBEACH, H. Shoemakers' Village.
Holcombes. *Magill.*
Holiday Camp. *Corbert.*
Holidays at Roselands. *Finley.*
Holmby House. *Melville.*
HOLMES, Mrs. M. J. Cameron Pride.
—— Cousin Maud.
—— Edna Browning.
—— Ethelyn's Mistake.
—— Marian Grey.
—— Millbank.
—— Rose Mather.
—— Tempest and Sunshine.
HOLMES, O. W. Guardian Angel.
HOLT, Emily S. Ashcliffe Hall.
—— Isoult Barry of Wynscote.
—— Mistress Margery.
—— Sister Rose.
HOME, C. Lesley's Guardians.
Home at Heatherbrae.
Home in the West. *Thurston.*
Home Life. *Sewell.*
Home made Happy.
Home Sunshine. *Bell.*
Honor Bright.
Honor May.
HOOD, T. Pleasant Tale of Puss and Robin.
Hoods and Masks. *Beresford.*
Hoosier Schoolmaster. *Eggleston.*
Hope and Have. *Adams.*
Hopedale Tavern. *Van Namee.*
HORNE, R. H. Poor Artist.
HORT, Mrs. A. Hena.
HOSMER, Mrs. M. Blanche Gilroy.
—— Two Years of a Life-Time.
Hospital Sketches. *Alcott.*
Hôtel du Petit St. Jean.
Hotspur. *Walworth.*
HOUGH, L. William Bathurst.
House by the Churchyard. *Le Fanu.*
House of Elmore. *Robinson.*
House in Town. *Warner.*
House on Wheels. *Stolz.*
Household Stories from the Land of Hofer.
HOUSEKEEPER, M. R. My Husband's Crime.
How Charlie Roberts became a Man. *Thurston.*
How could he Escape? *Wright.*
How Eva Roberts gained her Education. *Thurston.*
How he Did it. *Dupuy.*
How it All Happened. *Parr.*
How will it End? *Heywood.*
HOWELLS, W. D. Their Wedding Journey.
HOWITT, Mary. Cost of Caergwyn.
HOWITT, W. Boy's Adventures in Australia.
—— Woodburn Grange.
HUGESSEN, E. K. Crackers for Christmas.
HUGO, V. Claude Gueux.
—— Toilers of the Sea.
Huguenot Family. *Bell.*
Huguenot Family. *Tytler.*
Humor and Pathos. *Banter.*
Hunter and Tom. *Abbott.*
Hush Money. *Ross.*
Hyacinthe. *Grey.*
I must Keep the Chimes Going.
I Remember.
Ierne. *Trench.*
In Bonds. *Preston.*
In Duty Bound.
In the Eastern Seas. *Kingston.*
In Exile.
In Exitu Israel. *Gould.*
In Lodgings at Knightsbridge.
In the Rapids. *Hart.*

In Silk Attire. *Black.*
In Trust. *Douglas.*
In the Wilds of Africa. *Kingston*
In the Year '13. *Reuter.*
Ina. *Valerio.*
Incidents of Social Life. *Zschokke.*
Indiana. *Dudevant.*
Inez. *Evans.*
Ingaretha. *Malen.*
INGELOW, Jean. Stories told to a Child.
INGERSLEBEN, Frau von. Eleonore.
Inn of the Guardian Angel. *Ségur.*
Inside. *Warrington.*
Interpreter. *Melville.*
Into the Light.
Invasion of France in 1814. *Erckmann-Chatrian.*
Irene. *Strange.*
Irish Widow's Son. *O'Leary.*
Irkdale. *Brierley.*
Irma. *Vetter du Lys.*
Iron Horse. *Ballantyne.*
Isaac Phelps the Widow's Son.
Island Neighbors. *Blackwell.*
Isoult Barry of Wynscote. *Holt.*
Italian Novelists. *Roscoe.*
Italy in 1831; Adventures of Castellamonte. *Gallenga.*
Jack Hazard and his Fortune. *Trowbridge.*
Jack and Rosy. *Forrest.*
JAMES, G. P. R. Arabella Stewart.
JAMES, Marian. The Diamond on the Hearth.
—— Elder Sister.
James Gordon's Wife.
Janet's Love and Service.
Jasmine Leigh. *Tytler.*
Jealousy. *Dudevant.*
Jeanie's Quiet Life.
JENKINS, E. Ginx's Baby.
—— Lord Bantam.
JENINGS, Mrs. E. Thyra Gascoigne.
JERROLD, W. B. Cent per Cent.
—— Passing the Time.
JERVEY, Mrs. C. H. Helen Courtney's Promise.
Jewess; a Tale.
JEWETT, Mrs. S. W. From Fourteen to Fourscore.
Jilt.
Joanna. *Haven.*
JOHN, Eugenie, Mrs. Countess Gisela.
—— Little Moorland Princess.
—— Magdalena.
—— Old Mamselle's Secret.
John. *Oliphant.*
John Jasper's Secret.
John Marchmont's Legacy. *Braddon.*
John Thompson, Blockhead. *Parr.*
John Ward's Governess. *Macgregor.*
JOHNSON, E. The Judge's Pets.
JOHNSON, A. S. Memoirs of a Nullifier.
JOHNSON, Mrs. M. O. Elms Homestead.
JOHNSON, Virginia W. What the World Made Them.
JONES, J. Virginia Graham.
JONES, M. Stories of the Olden Time.
JONES, S. P. Life of J. S. Batkins.
Joseph and his Friend. *Taylor.*
Joseph II and his Court. *Mundt.*
Joshua Marvel. *Farjeon.*
Journal of Lady Beatrix Graham. *Yonge.*
Journey to the Centre of the Earth. *Verne.*
JOYCE, R. D. Legends of the Wars in Ireland.
JUDD, S. Margaret.
Judge Not. *Sheppard.*
Judge's Pets. *Johnson.*
Kate Beaumont. *De Forest.*
Kate Coventry. *Melville.*
Kate Marston.
Katie; or the Simple Heart. *Richmond.*
KAVANAGH, Julia. Sibyl's Second Love.
—— Silvia.
KEENE, Mrs. S. F. Lyle MacDonald.
Keeping Open House. *McLain.*
KELLOGG, E. Ark of Elm Island.
—— Arthur Brown.
—— Boy Farmers.
—— Charlie Bell.
—— Cruise of the Casco.
—— Hard Scrabble.
—— Lion Ben.
—— Sophomores of Radcliffe.
—— Spark of Genius.
—— Whispering Pine.
—— Young Deliverer.
—— Young Shipbuilders.
Kernwood.
KICKHAM, C. J. Sally Cavanagh.
Kilmeny. *Black.*
KIMBALL, R. B. To-day.
Kind Governess.
KING, Alice. Lady of Winburne.
King George's Middy. *Gilbert.*

KINGSFORD, Jane. *See* BARNARD, Charles.
KINGSLEY, C. Hereward.
—— Madam How and Lady Why.
—— Water Babies.
KINGSLEY, H. The Boy in Grey.
—— Leighton Court.
—— The Lost Child.
—— Mlle. Mathilde.
—— Silcote of Silcotes.
—— Tales of Old Travel.
KINGSTON, W. H. G. Adrift in a Boat.
—— Albatross.
—— At the South Pole.
—— Cruise of the Frolic.
—— Foxholme Hall.
—— Harry Skipwith.
—— In the Eastern Seas.
—— In the Wilds of Africa.
—— Marmaduke Merry.
—— Off to Sea.
—— On the Banks of the Amazon.
—— Pirate's Treasure.
—— Schoolboy Days.
KINZIE, Mrs. Walter Ogilby.
KIP, L. Ænone.
KIRK, Eleanor. *See* AMES, Mrs. Nellie.
Kissing the Rod. *Yates.*
Kitty. *Edwards.*
KNATCHHILL-Hugessen. *See* HUGESSEN.
Knight's Ransom. *Valentine.*
KNOLLYS, W. W. Oswald Hastings.
KÜNST, Herm. Olrig Grange.
KUNTZE, J. Mystic Bell.
LABOULAYE, E. Abdallah.
—— Finette.
Lady Betty. *Coleridge.*
Lady Betty's Governess. *Guernsey.*
Lady Flavia.
Lady of the Ice. *De Mille.*
Lady Judith. *McCarthy.*
Lady's Mile. *Braddon.*
Lady Weddesburn's Wish. *Grant.*
Lady of Winburne. *King.*
LAFITTE, J. P. The Red Doctor.
LA GRANGE, Mme. A. K. de. Ferryman of the Tiber.
—— Last Days of Jerusalem.
LAMB, C., and Mary. Tales from Shakespeare.
Lamplighter's Story. *Dickens.*
LANCEWOOD, L. Sidney de Grey.
Land at Last. *Yates.*
Langleyhaugh.
LANIER, C. Thorn Fruit.
Lanmere. *Dorr.*
LASSELLE, Mrs. M. P. High Life in Washington.
Last Athenian. *Rydberg.*
Last Baron of Crana. *Banim.*
Last Chronicle of Barset. *Trollope.*
Last Days of Jerusalem. *La Grange.*
Laurence Bronson's Victory.
Laurie.
Lavengro. *Borrow.*
LAWRENCE, H. Anteros.
—— Sans Merci.
Lawyer's Secret. *Braddon.*
Leaf in the Storm. *De la Rame.*
Learning to Think.
LEE, H. *See* PARR, Mrs.
LEE, Margaret. Dr. Wilmer's Love.
LEE, M. and C. Rosamond Fane.
LE FANU, J. S. All in the Dark.
—— Checkmate.
—— Guy Deverell.
—— House by the Churchyard.
—— Lost Name.
—— Tenants of Malory.
Left to Herself. *Woodville.*
Legends of Dundrum Castle. *Faber.*
Legends of the Wars in Ireland. *Joyce.*
LE GRANGE, H. M. Salted with Fire.
LEIGHTON, A. Shellburn.
Leighton Court. *Kingsley.*
LELAND, H. P. Grey-Bay Mare, and other Sketches.
LEMON, M. Faulkner Lyle.
—— Leyton Hall.
LENNOX, Lord W. P. Adventures of a Man of Family.
LEONARD, Agnes. Vanquished.
Leonora Casaloni. *Trollope.*
LE SAGE, A. R. Asmodeus.
—— Gil Blas.
Lesley's Guardians. *Home*
LESLIE, Emma. Harry Lawley.
—— Orphan and Foundling.
—— Percy Raydon.
Leslie Tyrrell. *Craik.*
Lessons of Love. *Marshall.*
LEVER, C. Lord Kilgobbin.
—— One of Them.
—— Rent in a Cloud.
—— Sir Brooke Fossbrooke.
—— Tony Butler.
LEWES, G. H. Three Sisters and Three Fortunes.
LEWES, Mrs. Felix Holt.

Leyton Hall. *Lemon*.
Life and Alone.
Life Boat. *Ballantyne*.
Life in Dalecarlia. *Bremer*.
Life and Death.
Life of J. S. Batkins. *Jones*.
Life in a Love. *Wynne*.
Life's Assize. *Riddell*.
Life's Lessons. *Gore*.
Liffith Lank. *Webb*.
Lifting the Veil.
Lightning Express. *Adams*.
Lights and Shadows of Scottish Life. *Wilson*.
Lilian. *Finley*.
Linda Tressel.
LINTON, E. L. Lizzie Lorton.
—— Sowing the Wind.
Lion Ben. *Kellogg*.
LIPPARD, G. The Quaker City.
—— Paul Ardenheim.
Lisa. *Turgenef*.
LISLE, Anna. Quicksands.
—— Self and Self-Sacrifice.
Little Boy's Story. *Gouraud*.
Little Folks Astray. *Clarke*.
Little Grandmother. *Clarke*.
Little Gypsy. *Sauvage*.
Little Jakey. *De Kroyft*.
Little by Little. *Adams*.
Little Lucy's Wonderful Globe. *Yonge*.
Little Maid of Oxbow. *Mannering*.
Little Men. *Alcott*.
Little Moorland Princess. *John*.
Little Nellie, the Clockmaker's Daughter.
Little Pussy Willow. *Stowe*.
Little Ragamuffin. *Greenwood*.
Little Red Riding Hood. *Thackeray*.
Little Savage. *Marryatt*.
Little Sunshine's Holiday. *Craik*.
Little Women. *Alcott*.
Lizzie Lorton. *Linton*.
LOCKER, A. Stephen Scudamore.
LOCKHART, L. W. M. Fair to See.
London Romance. *Ross*.
Long Look Ahead. *Roe*.
Look before you Leap.
Lord Bantam. *Jenkins*.
Lord of the Manor. *Herbert*.
Lords and Ladies.
LORING, F. W. Two College Friends.
Losses and Gains. *Moore*.
Lost among the Wild Men. *Dalton*.
Lost Child. *Kingsley*.
Lost Despatch. *Friedrich*.
Lost Heir of Linlithgow. *Southworth*.
Lost in the Fog. *De Mille*.
Lost Lenore. *Beach*.
Lost Life. *Moore*.
Lost Love. *Owen*.
Lost Name. *Le Fanu*.
Lost Rosary. *O'Leary*.
Lost Sir Massingberd.
Lothair. *Disraeli*.
LOTHROP, Amy. Casper and his Friends.
Lottery of Marriage. *Trollope*.
Louisa of Prussia and her Times. *Mundt*.
Love and Life in Norway. *Björnson*.
Love or Marriage? *Black*.
Love on the Wing. *March*.
Lovels of Arden. *Braddon*.
LOVER, S. He would be a Gentleman.
Lover's Library, vol. 1.
Lovers and Thinkers. *Gordon*.
LOW, C. R. Tales of Old Ocean.
LOWDELL. German Evenings.
LUARD, Julia. Clare Savile.
Lucia Dare. *Dorsey*.
Lucia; her Problem. *Douglas*.
Luck in Everything. *Maxwell*.
Luck of Ladysmede.
Luck and Pluck. *Alger*.
Luck of Roaring Camp. *Harte*.
Lulu. *Walworth*.
LUTTRELL, Hope. Prince Hassan's Carpet.
Lyle MacDonald. *Keene*.
Lynda Newton. *Frost*.
LYNDEN, F. W. Ninety-three.
Lynn of the Crags. *Smith*.
M. or N. *Melville*.
Mabel Lee. *Fisher*.
Mabel's Progress.
McAllisters. *Richmond*.
MCCABE, J. D., Jr. Planting the Wilderness.
MCCARTHY, J. Lady Judith.
—— My Enemy's Daughter.
—— Waterdale Neighbors.
Macdermots of Ballycloran. *Trollope*.
MACDONALD, G. Adela Cathcart.
—— Annals of a Quiet Neighborhood.
—— At the Back of the North Wind.
—— David Elginbrod.
—— Guild Court.
—— Phantastes.

MACDONALD, G. The Portent.
—— Ranald Bannerman's Boyhood.
—— Robert Falconer.
—— Wilfrid Cumbermede.
MACGREGOR, Annie L. John Ward's Governess.
—— The Professor's Wife.
McHENRY, Dr. The Wilderness.
MACKAY, Mrs. Clifford Castle.
McKEEVER, H. B. Breakers Ahead.
—— Maude and Miriam.
—— Silver Threads.
—— Westbrook Parsonage.
MACKENZIE, Mrs. A. S. Married against Reason.
MACKENZIE, E. Roua Pass.
MACKENZIE, W. B. Married Life.
McLAIN, Mary W. Daisy Ward's Work.
—— Keeping Open House.
MACLEOD, Norman. The Starling.
MACQUOID, Katharine S. Hester Kirton.
—— Patty.
—— Rookstone.
Mad Monkton. *Collins.*
Madam How and Lady Why. *Kingsley.*
MADDEN. R. R. The Mussulman.
Madelaine Darth. *Shackelford.*
Mlle. 50 Millions. *St. Mars.*
Mlle. Mathilde. *Kingsley.*
Mlle. Merquem. *Dudevant.*
Madge. *Godwin.*
Madonna Mary. *Oliphant.*
MAFFITT, J. N. Nautilus.
MAGILL, Mary T. Holcombes.
Magdalena. *John.*
Maid of Honor. *Baur.*
Maiden Widow. *Southworth.*
MAITLAND, Edward. The Higher Law.
—— The Pilgrim and the Shrine.
Malbrook.
MALEN, M. E. O. Ingaretha.
Man in Chains. *Collins.*
Man-of-War's Man. *Lee.*
Man of the World. *Fullom.*
Man with the Broken Ear. *About.*
Man and Wife. *Collins.*
Man's Wrong. *Manton.*
MANNERING, May. Little Maid of Oxbow.
MANNING, Miss A. Cherry and Violet.
—— Colloquies of Edward Osborne.
—— Fair Gospeller.
MANNING, Miss A. Selvaggio.
Manœuvring Mother. *Grey.*
Manon Lescaut. *Prévost.*
Manor Farm. *Phillpotts.*
MANTON, Kate. Man's Wrongs.
Manuscript Man. *Walshe.*
Marcella. *Eastwood.*
MARCH, C. Love on the Wing.
Margaret. *Judd.*
Margaret.
Margaret and her Bridesmaids. *Stretton.*
Margaret's Engagement.
Margaret's Old Home.
Margaret Cecil. *Bell.*
Margaret Hamilton. *Newby.*
Margaret Howth. *Davis.*
Margaret Smith's Journal. *Whittier.*
Marguerite Kent. *Wayne.*
Marie Antoinette and her Son. *Mundt.*
Marian Grey. *Holmes.*
Mariola.
Marion Barnard. *Smith.*
Marion Berkley. *Comins.*
MARIOTTI, L. Blackgown Papers.
Mark Rowland. *Martingale.*
MARLITT, E. *See* JOHN, Mrs. E.
Marmaduke Merry. *Kingston.*
Marquis d' Hauterive. *Feuillet.*
Marquis and Merchant. *Collins.*
Marquis of Villemer. *Dudevant.*
Married Beneath Him.
Marriage, a Lottery. *Grey.*
Marriage in High Life. *Grey.*
Married against Reason. *Mackenzie.*
Married for Both Worlds. *Porter.*
Married in Haste. *Stephens.*
Married Life. *Mackenzie.*
MARRYATT, Francis. Little Savage.
—— Masterman Ready.
—— Mr. Midshipman Easy.
—— Privateersman.
Marrying by Lot. *Mortimer.*
MARSH, Mrs. Angela.
—— Emilia Wyndham.
—— Two Old Men's Tales.
MARSHALL, Mrs. Emma. Brothers and Sisters.
—— Christabel Kingscote.
—— Edward's Wife.
—— Helen's Diary.
—— Lessons of Love.
—— Millicent Legh.
—— The Old Gateway.
—— Three Little Sisters.
—— Violet Douglas.
Marston of Dunoran.

Martin Beck. *Harris.*
Martin Tobin. *Campbell.*
MARTINGALE, H. Mark Rowland.
Massingers; or Evils of Mixed Marriages.
Masterman Ready. *Marryatt.*
Matins and Muttons. *Bradley.*
Maud Mohan. *homas.*
Maud Neville.
Maude and Miriam. *MacKeever.*
Mauprat. *Dudevant.*
Maurice. *Béchard.*
Max Kromer. *Smith.*
MAX Meredith's Millennium. *Townsend.*
MAXWELL, W. H. Adventures of Capt. Blake.
—— Bivouac.
—— Hector O'Halloran.
—— Luck is Everything.
—— Stories of Waterloo.
MAY, Sophie. *See* CLARKE.
May Middleton. *Reynolds.*
Mayor of Windgap. *Banim.*
Mea Culpa. *Perrier.*
MELVILLE, G. J. W. Cerise.
—— Contraband.
—— Gladiators.
—— Good for Nothing.
—— Holmby House.
—— Interpreter.
—— Kate Coventry.
—— M. or N.
—— Sarchedon.
—— Tilbury Nogo.
MELVILLE, H. White Jacket.
—— White Rose.
Member for Paris.
Memoirs of a Nullifier. *Johnson.*
Merchant of Berlin. *Mundt.*
MERCIER, Mrs. J. Christabel Hope.
MEREDITH, G. Rhoda Fleming.
Merman and Figure Head. *Guernsey.*
Michael Randolph. *Dupuy.*
MICHEL, T., and Moritz, A. A Will and a Way.
MIDDLEBROOK, Mrs. Grace. One Year of my Life.
Mildred Arkell. *Wood.*
Millbank. *Holmes.*
MILLER, Emily H. Royal Road to Fortune.
MILLER, T. Fred and the Gorillas.
—— My Father's Garden.
Miller of Angibault. *Dudevant.*
Miller's Children.
Miller's Story of the War. *Erckmann-Chartrian.*
Millicent and her Cousins. *Bethell.*
Millicent Legh. *Marshall.*
Mills of Tuxbury. *Townsend.*
Milly. *Guernsey.*
MILMAN, E. H. Arthur Conway.
Milton and his Times. *Ring.*
Minister's Wife. *Oliphant.*
Ministering Children. *Charlesworth.*
Ministry of Life. *Charlesworth.*
Minna Monté. By "Stella."
Miss Forrester. *Edwards.*
Miss Lily's Voyage.
Miss Majoribanks. *Oliphant.*
Miss Ravenel's Conversion. *De Forest.*
Miss Roberts' Fortune. *Winthrop.*
Miss Van Kortlandt. *Benedict.*
Mistaken. *Fuller.*
Mistress Margery. *Holt.*
Misunderstood. *Montgomery.*
MITCHELL, D. G. Doctor Johns.
MITFORD, A. B. Tales of Old Japan.
MOFFETT, Emma L. Crown Jewels.
Monarch of Mincing Lane. *Black.*
M. Sylvestre. *Dudevant.*
Montanas. *Hancock.*
MONTGOMERY, Mrs. A. Bucklyn Shaig.
MONTGOMERY, Florence. Misunderstood.
—— A Very Simple Story.
Moonshine. *Hugessen.*
Moonstone. *Collins.*
MOORE, Emily H. Lost Life.
MOORE, Mrs. J. F. Losses and Gains.
MOORE, W. B. Six Sisters of the Valleys.
MOOS, H. M. Carrie Harrington.
—— Hannah.
Morals and Mysteries. *Aïdé.*
More Secrets than One. *Hall.*
MORFORD, H. Utterly Wrecked.
MORGAN, H. Ned Nevins.
Morning Glories, and other Stories. *Alcott.*
MORTIMER, Charlotte B. Marrying by Lot.
Morton House. *Fisher.*
Moth and Rust.
Mother Goose for Grown Folks.
Mother's Recompense. *Aguilar.*
Motherless. *De Witt.*
Mountain Patriots. *Orme.*
MOWATT, Mrs. *See* RITCHIE, Mrs.

Mozart. *Rau.*
Mozart and Mendelssohn. *Barnard.*
Mr. Midshipman Easy. *Marryatt.*
Mr. Wynyard's Ward. *Parr.*
Mrs. Gerald's Niece. *Fullerton.*
Mrs. Thorne's Guests. *Fell.*
MÜGGE, T. Afraja.
MÜHLBACH, Louise. *See* MUNDT, Clara.
MÜLLER, O. Charlotte Ackermann.
MULOCK. *See* CRAIK, Mrs.
MUMFORD, Mary E. Hila Dart.
MUNDT, Clara. Berlin and Sans-Souci.
—— Bernthal.
—— Daughter of an Empress.
—— Empress Josephine.
—— Frederick the Great and his Court.
—— Frederick the Great and his Family.
—— Henry VIII and his Court.
—— Joseph II and his Court.
—— Louisa of Prussia and her Times.
—— Marie Antoinette and her Son.
—— Merchant of Berlin.
—— Napoleon and Blücher.
—— Napoleon and the Queen of Prussia.
—— Old Fritz and the New Era.
—— Queen Hortense.
MUNDT, T. Count Mirabeau.
MURPHY, Rosalie M. Destiny.
Mussulmann. *Madden.*
Mute Singer. *Ritchie.*
My Confession.
My Daughter Elinor. *Benedict.*
My Enemy's Daughter. *McCarthy.*
My Father's Garden. *Miller.*
My Heroine.
My Husband's Crime. *Housekeeper.*
My Little Lady.
My Son's Wife.
My Stepfather's Home. *Blake.*
My Wife and I. *Stowe.*
Myddleton Pomfret. *Ainsworth.*
Myra Sherwood's Cross.
Myself; a Romance of New England Life.
Mystery of Edwin Drood. *Dickens.*
Mysteries of the People. *Sue.*
Mystery of Orcival. *Gaboriau.*
Mystic Bell. *Kuntze.*
Nacoochee. *Goulding.*
Nanny and I.
Napoleon and Blücher. *Mundt.*
Napoleon and the Queen of Prussia. *Mundt.*
NAUMAN, Mary D. Enchanted Princess.
—— Sydney Elliott.
—— Twisted Threads.
Nautilus. *Maffit.*
NEAL, Alice B. No such Word as Fail.
Ned Allen. *Hannay.*
Ned Nevins. *Morgan.*
NEELY, Kate J. Actions Speak Louder than Words.
—— One Good Turn deserves Another.
Neighbors' Wives. *Trowbridge.*
Never Forgotten. *Fitzgerald.*
New England Legends. *Spofford.*
New Timothy. *Baker.*
New Year's Bargain. *Woolsey.*
NEWBY, Mrs. C. J. Margaret Hamilton.
—— Right and Left.
—— Trodden Down.
—— Wondrous Strange.
NEWELL, R. H. Avery Glibun.
—— The Cloven Foot.
—— Walking Doll.
NICHOLS, G. W. The Sanctuary.
Nick of the Woods. *Bird.*
Nidworth. *Prentiss.*
Nigel Bartram's Ideal. *Wilford.*
NILES, Willys. Five Hundred Majority.
Nimmo's Popular Tales.
Nina Balatka.
Nine Years Old.
Ninety-three. *Lyndon.*
No Church.
No Man's Friend. *Robinson.*
No Moss. *Castlemon.*
No such Word as Fail. *Neal.*
Noble Lord. *Southworth.*
Noble Woman. *Stephens.*
Noblesse Oblige. *Tytler.*
Nobody's Fortune. *Yates.*
Nora and Archibald Lee.
Norman Leslie. *Fay.*
NORRIS, Emilia M. Adrift on the Sea.
North and South. *Gaskell.*
Northern Lands. *Adams.*
Norwood. *Beecher.*
Not Proven.
Not Wisely but Too Well. *Broughton.*
Notice to Quit. *Wills.*
Novelist. *Rothwell.*
Now or Never. *Beach.*
Number Thirty-one.

O. T. *Andersen.*
Oakhurst.
Occupations of a Retired Life. *Garrett.*
Odd Neighbors.
OELSCHLÄGER, H. Strange Folk.
OERTEL, —. Schoolmaster of Abbach.
Off to Sea. *Kingston.*
Old Countess. *Höfer.*
Old Dower House. *Grey.*
Old Fashioned Boy. *Finley.*
Old Fashioned Girl. *Alcott.*
Old Fritz and the New Era. *Mundt.*
Old Gateway. *Marshall.*
Old Mam'selle's Secret. *John.*
Old Neighborhoods and New Settlements. *Southworth.*
Oldtown Fireside Stories. *Stowe.*
O'LEARY, Con. Irish Widow's Son.
—— The Lost Rosary.
OLIPHANT, Mrs. The Brownlows.
—— John.
—— Madonna Mary.
—— Minister's Wife.
—— Miss Marjoribanks.
—— Three Brothers.
—— Zaidee.
Olivia Wyndham.
Olrig Grange. *Künst.*
Omi.
On the Banks of the Amazon. *Kingston.*
On the Edge of the Storm.
On the Heights. *Auerbach.*
On Time. *Adams.*
One against the World. *Saunders.*
One Good Turn Deserves Another. *Neely.*
One of the Family.
One of Them. *Lever.*
One Poor Girl. *Sikes.*
One with Another *Wilberforce.*
One Year.
One Year. *Peard.*
One Year of my Life. *Middlebrook.*
Only a Girl. *Hillern.*
Only Herself. *Thomas.*
Only Three Weeks.
Only a Woman's Heart. *Clare.*
Open Door. *Smith.*
OPIE, Mrs. Simple Tales.
Opportunities. *Warner.*
Opportunity. *Seemuller.*
OPTIC, O. *See* ADAMS, W. T.
ORME, Mrs. Mountain Patriots.
Orphan and Foundling. *Leslie.*
Orville College. *Wood.*
Oswald Hastings. *Knollys.*
OTIS, Bell. Diary of a Milliner.
Ought we to Visit Her? *Edwards*
OUIDA. *See* DE LA RAME.
Our Children's Story.
Our Country Home.
Our Neighbors. *Arthur.*
Out of Charity.
Out of the Depths.
Out of the Foam. *Cooke.*
Out of Town. *Coffin.*
Out of the Wilderness. *Chaplin.*
Outpost. *Austin.*
Outward Bound. *Adams.*
Overland. *De Forest.*
OWEN, A. A Lost Lover.
OWEN, R. D. Beyond the Breakers.
Palace of Ice. *Dumas.*
Palaces and Prisons. *Stephens.*
PALGRAVE, F. T. Five Days at Wentworth Grange.
Palmetto Boys. *Wright.*
PARDON, G. F. Tales from the Operas.
PARR, Harriet. Beautiful Miss Barrington.
—— For Richer for Poorer.
—— Her Title of Honor.
—— Mr. Wynyard's Ward.
—— Poor Match.
PARR, Louisa. Blue Bell of Red Neap.
—— Dorothy Fox.
—— How it All Happened.
—— John Thompson, Blockhead.
Passages from a Wasted Life.
Passing the Time. *Jerrold.*
Passion and Principle. *Grey.*
Pastimes with my Little Friends. *Bennett.*
Patty. *Macquoid.*
Paul Ardenheim. *Lippard.*
Paul, the Peddler. *Alger.*
Paul Prescott's Charge. *Alger.*
PAULET, E. Dharina.
PEARD, Frances M. One Year.
—— Rose Garden.
Pearl of Antioch. *Bayle.*
PEARSON, C. H. Cabin on the Prairie.
PEARSON, Helen C. Roy's Search.
Peasant Life.
Pebbles and Pearls. *Richardson.*
Peep o' Day. *Banim.*
Peers and Parvenus. *Gore.*
Pemberton Family.

Pennell, C. Family Fairy Tales.
Penny Rust's Christmas. *Davis.*
Percy Raydon. *Leslie.*
Percys. *Prentiss.*
Perdita. *Balfour.*
Perrier, A. Mea Culpa.
Peter of the Castle. *Banim.*
Peter Lipp. *Gouraud.*
Peter Wilkins. *Pultock.*
Peterchen and Gretchen.
Petronel. *Church.*
Petticoat Government. *Trollope.*
Phantastes. *MacDonald.*
Phelps, Miss E. S. Gipsy Breynton.
—— Gypsy's Cousin Joy.
—— Gypsy's Sowing and Reaping.
—— Gypsy at the Golden Crescent.
—— Hedged In.
—— Silent Partner.
—— Trotty Book.
Phelps, W. D. Fore and Aft.
Phemie Keller. *Trafford.*
Phemie's Temptation. *Terhune.*
Phil the Fiddler. *Alger.*
Philip Earnscliffe. *Edwards.*
Phillips, W. For a Woman's Sake.
—— Wandering Heiress.
Phillips, W. B. Wooed and Won.
Phillpotts, M. C. Manor Farm.
Picciola. *Saintine.*
Pictures of Cottage Life. *Poole.*
Pictures of Country Life. *Cary.*
Pilgrim and the Shrine. *Maitland.*
Pine, C. Renshawe.
Pioneer Church. *Schuyler.*
Pink and White Tyranny. *Stowe.*
Pinks and Blues. *Abbott.*
Pique.
Piquillo Alliaga. *Scribe.*
Pirate's Treasure. *Kingston.*
Pitcher of Cool Water. *Arthur.*
Plane and Plank. *Adams.*
Planting the Wilderness. *McCabe.*
Played Out. *Thomas.*
Playing for High Stakes. *Thomas.*
Pleasant Tales of Puss and Robin. *Hood.*
Pleasants, Julia. Callamura.
Pontmartin, A. de. Clotilde.
Poole, M. E. Pictures of Cottage Life.
Poor Artist. *Horne.*
Poor Boy. *Egan.*
Poor Humanity. *Robinson.*
Poor Match. *Parr.*
Poor Miss Finch. *Collins.*
Poor and Proud. *Adams.*
Popping the Question. *Smythies.*
Portent. *Macdonald.*
Porter, A. E. Married for Both Worlds.
Porter, Rose. Foundations.
Portia. *Clarke.*
Portrait in my Uncle's Dining Room, and other Tales.
Postel, K. Cabin Book.
—— Rambleton; a Romance.
Potwin, Mrs. H. K. Ruby Duke.
Prairie Crusoe.
Prentiss, E. Aunt Jane's Hero.
—— Nidworth.
—— The Percys.
—— Six little Princesses.
—— Stepping Heavenward.
—— Story Lizzie Told.
Pressensé, Mme. Two Years of School Life.
Preston, H. W. Aspendale.
Preston, L. Boy's Trip across the Plains.
—— In Bonds.
Preston, P. Count's Niece.
Prévost, L. Manon Lescaut.
Prey of the Gods. *Church.*
Priest and Nun. *Wright.*
Prince of Darkness. *Southworth.*
Prince Hassan's Carpet. *Luttrell.*
Prince Wolfgang. *Hoffmann.*
Princess of Brunswick—Wolfenbüttel. *Zschokke.*
Prisoners of St. Lazare. *Grandpré.*
Pritchard, Sarah J. Faye Mar.
Privateersman. *Marryatt.*
Problematic Characters. *Spielhagen.*
Professor's Lady. *Auerbach.*
Professor's Wife. *Macgregor.*
Prosser, Mrs. Clackitts of Inglebrook Hall.
Prudy Keeping House. *Clarke.*
Puck. *De la Rame.*
Puck's Nightly Pranks. *Bund.*
Pultock, R. Peter Wilkins.
Pupil of the Legion of Honor. *Énault.*
Put to the Test.
Put Yourself in His Place. *Reade.*
Putnam, Mrs. M. L. Fifteen Days.
Pycroft, J. Elkerton Rectory.
—— Twenty Years in the Church.
Quaker City. *Lippard.*
Quaker Partisans.
Queen Hortense. *Mundt.*

Queen Joanna; or Mysteries of Court of Naples. *Reynolds.*
Queen's Revenge. *Collins.*
Quicksands. *Lisle.*
Quiet Heart.
Quiet Miss Godolphin; and A Chance Child. *Garrett.*
Quiet Nook. *Ruffini.*
Quintin Matsys. *Egan.*
QUINTON, M. A. Aurelia.
RABELAIS, F. Works.
Race for Wealth. *Riddell.*
Race for a Wife. *Smart.*
Rachel's Secret.
Ralph the Heir. *Trollope.*
Rambleton; a Romance. *Postel.*
Ranald Bannerman's Boyhood. *Macdonald.*
Randolph Gordon. *De la Rame.*
RAU, H. Mozart.
RAYMOND, R. W. The Children's Wish.
Raymond's Heroine.
READE, C. Griffith Gaunt.
—— Put Yourself in His Place.
—— A Terrible Temptation.
Readings. *Dickens.*
Real Folks. *Whitney.*
Rebecca. *Corbin.*
Recollections of Eton.
Recommended to Mercy.
Rector and His Friends.
Rector's Wife.
Red as a Rose is She. *Broughton.*
Red Cross. *Adams.*
Red Doctor. *Lafitte.*
Redwood. *Sedgwick.*
REEDER, Louise. Currer Lyle.
REEVES, M. C. L. Wearithorne.
REGESTER, S. *See* VICTOR, Mrs. O. J.
Reginald Archer. *Seemuller.*
Regular Service.
REID, Christian. *See* FISHER, Miss.
REID, M. Castaways.
—— Headless Horseman.
—— White Gauntlet.
—— Tiger Hunter.
—— Wild Huntress.
—— Wood Rangers.
Renshawe. *Pine.*
Rent in a Cloud. *Lever.*
Resolution. *Roe.*
Rest and Unrest. *Bell.*
Reuben Davidger. *Greenwood.*
REUTER, F. In the Year 13.
REUTER, F. Seed Time and Harvest.
REYNOLDS, G. W. M. Ciprina.
—— Countess of Arnheim.
—— Countess of Lascelles.
—— Countess and Page.
—— Eustace Quentin.
—— Faust.
—— May Middleton.
—— Queen Joanna; or, Mysteries of the Court of Naples.
—— Rye House Plot.
Rhoda Fleming. *Meredith.*
Rich and Humble. *Adams.*
Rich Husband. *Riddell.*
Richard Hunne. *Sargent.*
Richard Vandermarck. *Harris.*
RICHARDSON, Abby S. Stories from Old English Poetry.
RICHMOND, D. Katie; or the Simple Heart.
RICHMOND, Mrs. E. J. The McAllisters.
RIDDELL, Mrs. J. H. Far Above Rubies.
—— Life's Assize.
—— Race for Wealth.
—— Rich Husband.
—— Too Much Alone.
Right and Left. *Newby.*
Right One. *Schwartz.*
Righted at Last. *Fuller.*
RING, Max. Milton and His Times.
RITCHIE, Anna C. Clergyman's Wife, and other Sketches.
—— Fairy Fingers.
—— Mute Singer.
Rob Roy. *Grant.*
Robert Falconer. *MacDonald.*
Robert Greathouse. *Swift.*
Robert Severne. *Hammond.*
ROBERTSON, Margaret M. Christie.
—— Janet's Love and Service.
ROBERTSON, T. W. David Garrick.
ROBINSON, F. W. Anne Judge.
—— Grandmother's Money.
—— House of Elmore.
—— No Man's Friend.
—— Poor Humanity.
—— Stern Necessity.
—— Sweet Nineteen.
—— True to Herself.
—— Under the Spell.
ROBINSON, Mrs. M. H. Helen Erskine.
ROBINSON, Mrs. T. A. L. Fifteen Years.
ROE, A. S. Long Look Ahead.

ROE, A. S. Resolution.
—— True to the Last.
—— Woman Our Angel.
Roebuck.
Roland Yorke. *Wood.*
Rolling Stone. *Dudevant.*
Romance of the Charter Oak. *Seton.*
Romance of the Revolution.
Romantic Tales. *Craik.*
Romneys of Ridgmont. *Eastman.*
Rookstone. *Macquoid.*
Rosa's Wish. *Bell.*
Rosamond Dayton. *Gardner.*
Rosamond Fane. *Lee.*
ROSCOE, T. German Novelists.
—— Italian Novelists.
—— Spanish Novelists.
Rose, Tom and Ned. *Sanford.*
Rose Garden. *Peard.*
Rose Mather. *Holmes.*
Rose of Thistle Island. *Carlen.*
ROSS, C. H. Hush Money.
—— A London Romance.
ROSS, C. H., and A. Clark. Story of a Honeymoon.
ROSS, Miriam. Against Tide.
—— Counterfeit Coin.
ROSSETTI, C. G. Commonplace.
ROTHENFELS, E. von. *See* INGERSLEBEN. Frau von.
ROTHWELL, J. S. S. The Novelist.
Roua Pass. *Mackenzie.*
Rougegorge, and other Stories. *Spofford.*
Rough and Ready. *Alger.*
Roundhearts, etc. *Cowles.*
ROWCROFT, C. Australian Crusoes.
—— Tales of the Colonies.
ROWSON, Susannah. Charlotte and Mary Temple.
Roy's Search. *Pearson.*
Royal Road to Fortune. *Miller.*
Ruby Duke. *Potwin.*
RUFFINI, A. G. Carlino.
—— A Quiet Nook.
Rufus and Rose. *Alger.*
Ruined Cities of Zulu Land. *Walmsley.*
Rule of the Monk. *Garibaldi.*
Runaway Match. *Smythies.*
Running the Gauntlet. *Yates.*
Rupert Godwin. *Braddon.*
RUSSELL, C. True Robinson Crusoes.
RYDBERG, V. Last Athenian.
Rye House Plot. *Reynolds.*
Saint Abe and His Seven Wives.

ST. CLAIR. Somebody and Nobody.
Saint Cecilia: Part 1: Adversity.
St. Elmo. *Evans.*
ST. MARS, Mme. Mlle. 50 Millions.
St. Martin's Eve. *Wood.*
St. Martin's Summer. *Brewster.*
St. Twel'mo. *Webb.*
St. Winifred's. *Farrar.*
SAINTINE, X. B. Dame Nature and Her Three Daughters.
—— Picciola.
Sally Cavanagh. *Kickham.*
Sal-O-Quah. *Goulding.*
Salted with Fire. *Le Grange.*
Sanctuary. *Nichols.*
SAND, G. *See* DUDEVANT, Mme.
SAND, M. Callirrhoé.
Sandalwood Trader. *Ballantyne.*
SANFORD, Mrs. D. P. Rose, Tom and Ned.
Sans Merci. *Lawrence.*
Sapelo. *Goulding.*
Sarchedon. *Melville.*
SARGENT, G. E. Richard Hunne.
SARTORIS, Mrs. Week in a French Country House.
SAUNDERS, J. Abel Drake's Wife.
—— Bound to the Wheel.
—— Hirell.
—— Israel Mort.
—— One against the World.
SAUNDERS, Katherine. Gideon's Rock.
—— Haunted Crust, etc.
—— High Mills.
SAUNDERS, W. H. P. Black and Gold.
SAUVAGE, E. Little Gipsy.
SAUZADE, J. S. Beggar on Horseback.
—— Bred in the Bone.
SAVAGE, M. Woman of Business.
Scapegoat.
SCHEFER, L. Artist's Married Life.
School-Boy Baronet. *Greene.*
Schoolboy Days. *Kingston.*
Schoolmaster of Abbach. *Oertel.*
SCHUYLER, M. Pioneer Church.
SCHWARTZ, Marie S. Birth and Education.
—— Gold and Name.
—— Guilt and Innocence.
—— The Right One.
—— Two Family Mothers.
—— Wife of a Vain Man.
SCOTT, M. Prime of the Midge.

SCOTT, M. Tom Cringle's Log.
SCOTT, W. Tales of a Grandfather.
SCRIBE, E. Piquillo Alliaga.
Sealed Packet. *Trollope.*
SEALSFIED or SEATSFIELD. *See* POSTEL.
Second Mrs. Tillotson. *Fitzgerald.*
SEDGWICK, Mrs. C. M. Redwood.
Seed Time and Harvest. *Reuter.*
Seek and Find. *Adams.*
SEEMULLER, Mrs. Anne M. Opportunity.
—— Reginald Archer.
See-Saw. *Abati.*
SÉGUR, Countess de. Fairy Tales.
—— Inn of the Guardian Angel.
Sejanus, and other Tales.
Self and Self-Sacrifice. *Lisle.*
Self-Made. *Davenport.*
Selvaggio. *Manning.*
Sergeant Atkins; a Tale of Adventure.
SETON, W. Romance of the Charter Oak.
SEWELL, Miss E. M. After-Life.
—— Home Life.
SHACKELFORD, C. Madelaine Darth.
SHAFFER, G. W. Azilia.
Shamrock and Thistle. *Adams.*
SHAND, A. I. Against Time.
Shannondale. *Southworth.*
Shellburn. *Leighton.*
SHELLEY, Mrs. P. B. The Beautiful Widow.
Sheltern. *Coningsby.*
SHEPPARD, Mrs. E. Judge Not.
Sherbrooke. *Godwin.*
SHERWOOD, Mrs. Stories on the Church Catechism.
Shifting Winds. *Ballantyne.*
Shiloh. *Woodruff.*
SHIPTON, Anna. Lost Blessing.
Shoemakers' Village. *Holbeach.*
Shoes of Fortune, and other Tales. *Andersen.*
Short-Comings and Long-Goings. *Eastman.*
Sibyl Huntington. *Dorr.*
Sibyl's Second Love. *Kavanagh.*
Sidney De Grey. *Lancewood.*
Signal Lights.
SIKES, W. W. One Poor Girl.
Silas the Conjurer. *Greenwood.*
Silcote of Silcotes. *Kingsley.*
Silent Partner. *Phelps.*
Silver Threads. *McKeever.*
Silvia. *Kavanagh.*
SIMMS, W. G. Carl Werner.
Simon. *Dudevant.*
Simple Tales. *Opie.*
SINCLAIR, Catherine. Hill and Valley.
Singleton Fontenoy. *Hannay.*
Sink or Swim. *Alger.*
Sir Brooke Fossbrooke. *Lever.*
Sir Harry Hotspur. *Trollope.*
Siren. *Trollope*
Sister Rose. *Collins.*
Sister Rose. *Holt.*
Sisters of Orleans.
Six Cushions. *Yonge.*
Six Little Princesses. *Prentiss.*
Six Months Hence.
Six of One by Half a Dozen of the Others. *Stowe, etc.*
Six Sisters of the Valley. *Moore.*
SMART, H. Breezie Langton.
—— Race for a Wife.
Smiles and Frowns. *Wentz.*
SMITH, A. Christopher Tadpole.
—— Comic Tales.
SMITH, Charlotte. Lynn of the Crags.
SMITH, J. F. Marion Barnard.
SMITH, J. Hyatt. Open Door.
SMITH, Mrs. Julie P. Brazen Gates.
—— Chris and Otho.
—— Widow Goldsmith's Daughter.
—— The Widower.
SMITH, Hannah. Bede's Charity.
—— Max Kromer.
SMOLLETT's Works.
Smoke. *Turgenef.*
Smugglers of the Swedish Coast; or, Rose of Thistle Island. *Carlen.*
SMYTHIES, Mrs. Gordon. Popping the Question.
—— A Runaway Match.
Snow Man. *Dudevant.*
So Runs the World Away. *Steele.*
Soi-Même.
Soldier Boy. *Adams.*
Solitaries. *Heyse.*
Somebody and Nobody. *St. Clair.*
Something to Do.
SOMMERS, Jane R. Heavenward Led.
Sooner or Later. *Brooks.*
Sophomores of Radcliffe. *Kellogg.*
Soprano. *Barnard.*
SOUTHWORTH, Mrs. E. D. E. N. Bride of Llewellyn.
—— Christmas Guest.
—— Family Doom.

SOUTHWORTH, Mrs. E. D. E. N. Fatal Marriage.
—— Hester Strong's Life-Work.
—— Lost Heir of Linlithgow.
—— Maiden Widow.
—— Noble Lord.
—— Old Neighborhoods and New Settlements.
—— Prince of Darkness.
—— Shannondale.
—— Tried for Her Life.
—— Widow's Son.
Sower's Reward.
Sowing the Wind. *Linton.*
Spanish Brothers.
Spanish Novelists. *Roscoe.*
Spark of Genius. *Kellogg.*
SPEIGHT, T. W. Under Lock and Key.
Spencers. *Tyng.*
Sphinx. *Bayer.*
SPIELHAGEN, F. Hammer and Anvil.
—— Hohensteins.
—— Problematic Characters.
—— Through Night to Light.
Splendid Fortune.
SPOFFORD, Harriet P. New England Legends.
—— Thief in the Night.
STAËL, Mme. de. Corinne.
Starling. *Macleod.*
Starry Flag. *Adams.*
Stars in a Stormy Night.
STEELE, Mrs. A. C. Broken Toys.
—— Gardenhurst.
—— So Runs the World Away.
Stephen Dane. *Douglas.*
Stephen Scudamore. *Locker.*
STEPHENS, Mrs. A. S. Married in Haste.
—— A Noble Woman.
—— Palaces and Prisons.
—— Wives and Widows.
Stepping Heavenward. *Prentiss.*
Steps Upward. *Gage.*
Stern Necessity. *Robinson.*
Steven Lawrence. *Edwards.*
STEWART, Agnes M. Florence O'Neill.
STODDARD, Mrs. Temple House.
Stolen Mask. *Collins.*
STOLZ, Mme. de. House on Wheels.
Stonebeach.
Stone Edge.
Storehouse of Stories. *Yonge*
Stories for Darlings.
Stories from my Attic.
Stories, etc., from Grecian History. *Hack.*
Stories from Old English Poetry. *Richardson.*
Stories of the Olden Time. *Jones.*
Stories on the Church Catechism. *Sherwood.*
Stories and Tales. *Andersen.*
Stories Told to a Child. *Ingelow.*
Stories of Waterloo. *Maxwell.*
Stormcliff. *Walworth.*
Stormy Life. *Fullerton.*
Story of a Bad Boy. *Aldrich*
Story of Bethlehem.
Story of a Diamond. *Whately.*
Story of Four Lives. *Dunning.*
Story of a Honeymoon. *Ross and Clark.*
Story of Kennett. *Taylor.*
Story Lizzie Told. *Prentiss.*
STOWE, Mrs. H. B. Little Pussy Willow.
—— My Wife and I.
—— Oldtown Fireside Stories.
—— Pink and White Tyranny.
STOWE, Mrs. H. B., WHITNEY, Mrs. A. D. J., etc. Story of One by Half a Dozen of the other.
STRANGE, H. Irene.
Strange Folk. *Oelschläger.*
STRETTON, Hesba. (Pseudonym.) *See* SMITH, Hannah.
STRETTON, J. Margaret and her Bridesmaids.
Strife. *Wallace.*
STRONG, G. C. Cadet Life at West Point.
Strong and Steady. *Alger.*
Struggle in Ferrara. *Gilbert.*
SUE, E. Commander of Malta.
—— De Rohan.
—— Man-of-War's Man.
—— Mysteries of the People.
Summer in Leslie Goldthwaite's Life. *Whitney.*
Sunday Echoes in Week Day Hours. *Brock.*
Sunny Days.
Sunnybank. *Terhune.*
Susan Fielding. *Edwards.*
Susie Grant.
Sweet Nineteen. *Robinson.*
SWIFT, J. F. Robert Greathouse.
Switch Off. *Adams.*
Sydney Elliott. *Nauman.*
Sydney Stuart. *Bell.*

Sydonie's Dowry.
Sylvestres. *Edwards.*
Talbot Harland. *Ainsworth.*
TAINSH, E. C. Crowned.
Taken upon Trust.
Tales of the Border. *Webber.*
Tales of the Colonies. *Rowcroft.*
Tales of European Life.
Tales from the German.
Tales of a Grandfather. *Scott.*
Tales of Many Lands. *Tytler.*
Tales of Old Japan. *Mitford.*
Tales of Old Ocean. *Low.*
Tales of Old Travel. *Kingsley.*
Tales from the Operas. *Pardon.*
Tales of Other Days.
Tales from Shakspeare. *Lamb.*
Tales of Woman's Trials. *Hall.*
TALMON, T. Captain Molly.
TATEM, M. H. Heights of Eidelberg.
Tattered Tom. *Alger.*
TAYLOR, B. Beauty and the Beast.
—— Joseph and his Friend.
—— Story of Kennett.
Tekel.
Tempest and Sunshine. *Holmes.*
Temple House. *Stoddard.*
Ten Times One is Ten. *Hale.*
Tenants of Malory. *Le Fanu.*
TERHUNE, Mrs. At Last.
—— Empty Heart.
—— Helen Gardner's Wedding Day.
—— Phemie's Temptation.
—— True as Steel.
Terrible Temptation. *Reade.*
THACKERAY, Miss. Beauty and the Beast.
—— Elizabeth, etc.
—— From an Island.
—— Little Red Riding Hood.
—— Village on the Cliff.
THACKERAY, W. M. Catherine.
That Good Old Time. *Vieux Moustache.*
THEED, Marion F. What She Did with her Life.
Their Wedding Journey. *Howells.*
Theodosia Ernest. *Dayton.*
Thief in the Night. *Spofford.*
Thiodolf, the Icelander. *Fouqué.*
Thistle Down. *Boyle.*
THOMAS, Annie. Called to Account.
—— Dower House.
—— False Colors.
—— Maud Mohan.
THOMAS, Annie. Only Herself.
—— Played Out.
—— Playing for High Stakes.
—— Walter Goring.
THOMES, W. H. Adventures of a Slaver.
—— The Bushrangers.
—— Gold Hunters in Australia.
—— Gold Hunters in Europe.
—— Whaleman's Adventures in the Sandwich Islands.
THOMSON, Mrs. White Mask.
Thorn Fruit. *Lanier*
THORPE, K. Four Oaks.
Thousand a Year. *Bruce.*
Three Bernices. *Bright.*
Three Brothers. *Oliphant.*
Three Eras in Woman's Life. *Arthur.*
Three Little Sisters. *Marshall.*
Three Little Spades. *Warner.*
Three Sisters and Three Fortunes. *Lewes.*
Three Successful Girls. *Crouch.*
Three Times Dead. *Braddon.*
Three Weddings.
Through by Daylight. *Adams.*
Through the Looking-Glass and What Alice found There. *Carroll.*
Through Night to Light. *Gutzkow.*
Through Night to Light. *Spielhagen.*
THURSTON, Louisa. Home in the West.
—— How Charley Roberts became a Man.
—— How Eva Roberts gained her Education.
Thyra Gascoigne. *Jenings.*
Tiger Hunter. *Reid.*
Tilbury Nogo. *Melville.*
TILLOTSON, G. Adventures in the Ice.
To-Day. *Kimball.*
Toilers of the Sea. *Hugo.*
Tom Chips. *Diekenga and Ashworth.*
Tom Crackenthorpe. *Clark.*
Tom Cringle's Log. *Scott.*
Tom Harding. *Eyster.*
Tom Newcombe. *Castlemon.*
Tom Pippin's Wedding.
Tone Masters. *Barnard.*
TONNA, Mrs. Siege of Derry.
Tony Butler. *Lever.*
Too Bright to Last.
Too Good for Him. *Church.*
Too much Alone. *Riddell.*
TOPELIUS, Z. Gustave Adolf.
Torch-Bearers.

Tower Hill. *Ainsworth.*
Tower of the Hawk.
TOWNSEND, Virginia F. Deerings of Medbury.
—— Max Meredith's Millennium.
—— Mills of Tuxbury.
TRAFFORD, F. G. Phemie Keller.
TRENCH, W. S. Ierne; a Tale.
Tried for Her Life. *Southworth.*
Trodden Down. *Newby.*
TROLLOPE, A. Claverings.
—— Dr. Thorne.
—— Golden Lion of Granpere.
—— Last Chronicle of Barset.
—— Macdermots of Ballycloran.
—— Sir Harry Hotspur.
—— Ralph the Heir.
—— Vicar of Bullhampton.
TROLLOPE, Mrs. Frances. Lottery of Marriage.
—— Petticoat Government.
TROLLOPE, T. A. Durnton Abbey.
—— Garstang Grange.
—— Gemma.
—— Leonora Casaloni.
—— Sealed Packet.
—— Siren.
Trotty Book. *Phelps.*
TROWBRIDGE, J. T. Drummer Boy.
—— Jack Hazard and his Fortunes.
—— Neighbors' Wives.
True as Steel. *Terhune.*
True Love. *Beauclerk.*
True Robinson Crusoes. *Russell.*
True to Herself. *Robinson.*
True to his Flag.
True to the Last. *Roe.*
Try Again. *Adams.*
TUCKER, Miss Charlotte. Claudia.
—— The Exiles in Babylon.
TUPPER, M. F. Crock of Gold.
TURGENEF, Ivan S. Fathers and Sons.
—— Liza.
—— Smoke.
Turning a New Leaf.
Twenty Years Ago. *Craik.*
Twenty Years in the Church. *Pycroft.*
Twisted Threads. *Nauman.*
Two Anastasias.
Two Baronesses. *Andersen.*
Two College Friends. *Loring.*
Two Family Mothers. *Schwartz.*
Two Lives in One. *Vieux Moustache.*
Two Marriages. *Craik.*
Two Old Men's Tales. *Marsh.*
Two Plunges for a Pearl. *Collins.*
Two Years of a Life-Time. *Hosmer.*
Two Years of School Life. *Pressensé.*
TYNG, S. H. The Spencers.
TYTLER, Christina C. Fr. Jasmine Leigh.
TYTLER, M. F. Tales of Many Lands.
TYTLER, Sarah. Citoyenne Jacqueline.
—— Days of Yore.
—— Diamond Rose.
—— Huguenot Family.
—— Noblesse Oblige.
Unclaimed; a Story of English Life.
Uncle Crotty's Relations. *Glyn.*
Under Foot. *Clyde.*
Under Lock and Key. *Speight.*
Under the Microscope.
Under the Spell. *Robinson.*
Under Two Flags. *De la Rame.*
Unkind Word. *Craik.*
Up the Baltic. *Adams.*
Up Broadway. *Ames.*
Up and Down in the World. *Jerrold.*
Utterly Wrecked. *Morford.*
Uttermost Farthing. *Griffith.*
VALENTINE, Mrs. Gold, Silver, Lead.
—— Knight's Ransom.
Valerie Aylmer. *Fisher.*
VALERIO, Katherine. Ina.
VAN NAMEE, J. W. Hopedale Tavern.
Vanquished. *Leonard.*
Vashti. *Evans.*
Vathek. *Beckford.*
VEITCH, Agnes. Frank Fielding.
Vera.
Vermont Vale. *Franc.*
Veronica; or, The Light-House Keeper.
Veronica
Veronica. *Zschokke.*
Véronique. *Church.*
Very Simple Story. *Montgomery.*
VETTER DU LYS, C. Irma.
Vicar of Bullhampton. *Trollope.*
Victim of Chancery.
VICTOR, Mrs. O. J. Dead Letter.
—— Figure Eight.
Victory Deane. *Griffith.*
Victory of the Vanquished. *Charles.*
VIEUX MOUSTACHE. That Good Old Time.
—— Two Lives in One.
Vikram and the Vampire. *Burton*

Villa Eden. *Auerbach*.
Village on the Cliff. *Thackeray*.
Village Stories
VINCENT, E. Artist's Dream.
Violet Douglas. *Marshall*.
Violetta and I.
Virginia Graham. *Jones*.
Visit to my Discontented Cousin.
Vivia. *Wilford*.
Vivian Romance. *Collins*.
VOLCKHAUSEN, A. Why Did he not Die?
Waiting for the Verdict. *Davis*.
Walking Doll. *Newell*.
WALLACE, Mrs. E. D. Strife.
WALMSLEY, H. M. Ruined Cities of Zulu Land.
WALSHE, Miss E. H. Manuscript Man.
Walter Goring. *Thomas*.
Walter Ogilby. *Kinzie*.
WALWORTH, M. T. Beverly.
—— Delaplaine.
—— Hotspur.
—— Storm Cliff.
—— Warwick.
Wanderer. *Burney*.
Wandering Heiress. *Phillips*.
Wanted—a Pedigree. *Finley*.
WARFIELD, C. Beauseincourt.
WARNER, Anne. Three Little Spades.
WARNER, Susan. Daisy. 2d series.
WARNER, Miss. What She Could.
WARNER, Mrs. The House in Town.
—— Opportunities.
Warwick. *Walworth*.
Was She Engaged?
Watch and Wait. *Adams*.
Water Babies. *Kingsley*.
Waterdale Neighbors. *McCarthy*.
WAYNE, Marion W. Marguerite Kent.
Wayside Pillars.
We Girls. *Whitney*.
Wealth and Welfare. *Bitzius*.
Wearithorne. *Reeves*.
WEBB C. H. Liffith Lank.
—— St. Twel'mo.
WEBBER, C. W. Tales of the Border.
Week in a French Country House. *Sartoris*.
WEEKS, Helen C. Four, and What they Did.
—— Grandpa's House.
—— White and Red.
Westbrook Parsonage. *McKeever*.
WESTMORELAND, Maria J. Heart Hungry.
Whaleman's Adventures in the Sandwich Islands. *Thomes*.
What She Could. *Warner*.
What is the Mystery? *Braddon*.
What she Did with her Life. *Theed*.
What the World made them. *Johnson*.
WHATELEY, Miss E. J. Cousin Mabel's Experiences.
WHATELY, Miss M. L. Story of a Diamond.
When I was a Little Girl.
Where shall He Find Her?
Which is the Heroine?
Which is the Winner? *Clarke*.
Which; The Right or the Left.
Whispering Pine. *Kellogg*.
WHITE, B. Circe.
White and Black.
White Gauntlet. *Reid*.
White Jacket. *Melville*.
White Mask. *Thomson*.
White and Red. *Weeks*
White Rose. *Melville*.
White as Snow. *Garrett*.
White Wife. *Bradley*.
WHITEHEAD, Mrs. T. The Grahames.
WHITNEY, Mrs. Adeline D. T. Gayworthys.
—— Hitherto.
—— A Summer in Leslie Goldthwaite's Life.
—— Real Folks.
—— We Girls.
—— Zerub Throop's Experiment.
WHITTIER, J. G. Margaret Smith's Journal.
WHITTLESEY, Elsie L. Helen Ethinger.
Who is She?
Who shall be Victor? *Dupuy*.
Who will Win? *Cobden*.
Who would Have Thought It?
Why Did He Marry Her? *Dupuy*.
Why Did He not Die? *Volckhausen*.
Widow Goldsmith's Daughter. *Smith*.
Widow's Son. *Southworth*.
Widower. *Smith*.
Wife of a Vain Man. *Schwartz*.
WILBERFORCE, E. One with Another.
Wild Flower.
Wild Huntress. *Reid*.
Wild Ireland. *Donbavand*.
Wild Oats.

Wilderness. *MacHenry.*
WILFORD, Florence. Nigel Bartram's Ideal.
—— Vivia; a Modern Story.
Wilfrid Cumbermede. *Macdonald.*
Wilhelm Meister. *Goethe.*
WILKINSON, Janet. Hands not Hearts.
Will She Have Him? *Graham.*
Will and a Way. *Michel and Moritz.*
WILLARD, Clara A. Fifty Years Ago.
William Bathurst. *Hough.*
William Henry and His Friends. *Diaz.*
William Henry Letters. *Diaz.*
Willis the Pilot. *Wyss.*
WILLS, W. G. Notice to Quit.
WILSON, John. Lights and Shadows of Scottish Life.
Wind and Whirlwind. *Elliott.*
Windsor Castle. *Ainsworth.*
Winifred. *Guernsey.*
Winning His Way. *Coffin.*
WINSTANSLEY, Eliza. Entrances and Exits.
WINTHROP, Lucy. Miss Roberts' Fortune.
With Fate against Him. *Douglas.*
With the Tide. *Daryl.*
Wives and Widows. *Stephens.*
Wizard of the Mountain. *Gilbert.*
Wolf Boy of China. *Dalton.*
Woman against Woman. *Marryatt.*
Woman against the World.
Woman of Business. *Savage.*
Woman our Angel. *Roe.*
Woman's Kingdom. *Craik.*
Woman's Strategy.
Woman's Way.
Women; or Chronicles of the Late War. *Magill.*
Women of Israel. *Aguilar.*
Won, not Wooed.
Wonder Stories. *Andersen.*
Wondrous Strange. *Newby.*
WOOD, Mrs. H. Bessy Rane.
—— Dene Hollow.
—— Elster's Folly.
—— George Canterbury's Will.
—— Mildred Arkell.
—— Orville College.
—— Roland Yorke.
—— St. Martin's Eve.
Wood Rangers. *Reid.*
Woodburn Grange. *Howitt.*
WOODVILLE, Jennie. Left to Herself.
Wooed and Won. *Phillips.*
WOOLSEY, Miss. New Year's Bargain.
WOODRUFF, Miss. Shiloh.
Work and Win. *Adams.*
Work for All.
Works. *Banim.*
Works (Globe ed.) *Dickens.*
Works. *Fielding.*
Works. *Griffin.*
Works. *Rabelais.*
Works. *Smollett.*
Woven of Many Threads. *Hamilton.*
WRAXALL, C. F. L. Black Panther.
WRAXALL, Sir L. Fides.
Wrecked in Port. *Yates.*
WRIGHT, Mrs. Julia M. Almost a Nun.
—— Almost a Priest.
—— Best Fellow in the World.
—— How Could He Escape.
—— Palmetto Boys.
—— Priest and Nun.
WRIGHT, Mrs. Sarah A. Gem of the Lake.
—— Golden Ladder.
Wrong Confessed. *Bradley*
WYLDE, A. Helen Felton's Question.
WYNNE, Mrs. A Life in a Love.
WYSS, D. von. Willis the Pilot.
YATES, E. Black Sheep.
—— Forlorn Hope.
—— Kissing the Rod.
—— Land at Last.
—— Nobody's Fortune.
—— Running the Gauntlet.
—— Wrecked in Port.
Yaxley and its Neighborhood.
YELLOTT, G. The Funny Philosophers.
YELVERTON, Thérèse. Zanita.
YONGE, C. M. Beechcroft.
—— Caged Lion.
—— Countess Kate.
—— Danvers Papers.
—— Doves in the Eagle's Nest.
—— Journal of Lady Beatrix Graham.
—— Little Lucy's Wonderful Globe.
—— Six Cushions.
—— Storehouse of Stories.
Young Crusoe. *Harley.*
Young Deliverers. *Kellogg.*
Young Detective. *Abbott.*

Young Fur Traders. *Ballantyne.*
Young Husband. *Grey.*
Young Marooners. *Goulding.*
Young Middy. *Armstrong.*
Young Recruit.
Young Shipbuilders. *Kellogg.*
Zaidee. *Oliphant.*
Zanita. *Yelverton.*
Zerub Throop's Experiment. *Whitney.*
Zoe. *Blake.*
ZSCHOKKE, H. Dead Guest.
—— Incidents of Social Life.
—— Princess of Brunswick Wolfenbüttel, etc.
—— Veronica.

CONTENTS.

TABLE OF CONTENTS.

[The references are to the pages of the Classification and Novels.]

www.ingramcontent.com/pod-product-compliance
Lightning Source LLC
LaVergne TN
LVHW010213110826
845151LV00004B/1076

* 9 7 8 1 4 2 5 5 2 8 3 3 1 *